Personnel Economics in Practice

Second Edition

Personnel Economics in Practice

Second Edition

Edward P. Lazear
Stanford University

Michael Gibbs
University of Chicago

WILEY

John Wiley & Sons, Inc.

Vice President & Publisher   Don Fowley
Associate Publisher   Judith Joseph
Associate Editor   Jennifer Conklin
Senior Production Editor   Nicole Repasky
Assistant Marketing Manager   Carly DeCandia
Designer   Michael St. Martine
Production Management Services   Katie Boilard/Pine Tree Composition, Inc.
Editorial Assistant   Sarah Vernon
Senior Media Editor   Allie K. Morris
Cover Photo   M.C. Escher, Concave and Convex, © 2007 The M.C. Escher Company-Holland.
All rights reserved, www.mcescher.com.

This book was set in Jansen Text by Laserwords Private Limited, Chennai, India and was printed
and bound by R.R. Donnelley/Crawfordsville. The cover was printed by Phoenix Color.

The book is printed on acid free paper.

To order books or for customer service please, call 1-800-CALL WILEY (225-5945).

Library of Congress Cataloging-in-Publication Data:

Lazear, Edward P.
  Personnel economics in practice / Edward P. Lazear, Michael Gibbs.—2nd ed.
    p. cm.
  Based on: Personnel economics for managers, 1998.
  Includes bibliographical references and index.
  ISBN 978-0-471-67592-1 (cloth : acid free paper)
  1. Managerial economics. 2. Labor economics. 3. Personnel management. 4. Human capital.
I. Gibbs, Michael. II. Title.
  HD30.22.L39 2009
  658.3—dc22   2008008482

1007128222

Printed in the United States of America

10 9 8 7 6 5 4 3 2

In memory of Sherwin Rosen, a great labor economist, teacher, and friend.

ABOUT THE AUTHORS

Edward P. Lazear is the Jack Steele Parker Professor of Human Resources Management and Economics at Stanford University's Graduate School of Business, where he has received several teaching awards. He is also the Morris Arnold Cox Senior Fellow at the Hoover Institution. Lazear is a Research Fellow of the National Bureau of Economic Research, Center for Corporate Performance, the Center for Economic Policy Research, and the Institute for the Study of Labor. He has BA and MA degrees from UCLA, and a PhD in Economics from Harvard. He also taught for many years at the University of Chicago.

Professor Lazear is widely regarded as the founder of the field of personnel economics. He has written over 100 articles and several books. Lazear has written seminal research in many areas, including pensions, discrimination, compensation, careers, incentive pay, human capital, and entrepreneurship. He was the founding editor of the *Journal of Labor Economics*.

Professor Lazear has received many honors, including the IZA Prize in Labor Economics, the Adam Smith Prize from the European Association of Labor Economists, and the Leo Melamed Biennial Prize for Outstanding Research. He is a member of the National Academy of Sciences, the American Academy of Arts and Sciences, and the Econometric Society.

From 2006 through 2009, Professor Lazear was Chairman of the President's Council of Economic Advisers in Washington. He has also served as an economic policy advisor to the governments of the Republic of Georgia, Russia, Ukraine, Romania, and Czechoslovakia.

Michael Gibbs is Clinical Professor of Economics and Human Resources at the University of Chicago's Graduate School of Business. He teaches Executive MBA classes in Chicago, London, and Singapore and has won several teaching awards. Gibbs is a Research Fellow at the Institute for the Study of Labor. He received a BA, MA and PhD in Economics, all from the University of Chicago. Professor Gibbs has taught at Harvard, the University of Michigan, USC, Sciences Po (Paris), and conducted research at the Aarhus School of Business (Denmark).

Professor Gibbs is a leading empirical scholar in personnel economics. His research concerns topics such as careers, performance measurement, incentive plan design, job design, and organizational integration after mergers. He recently was awarded a Notable Contribution to the Management Accounting Literature Award by the American Accounting Association.

PREFACE

WHAT IS THIS BOOK ABOUT?

Organizations and economies are human enterprises. They are the sum result of the motivations, decisions, and actions of many individuals. These individuals and their actions are combined to create innovation, higher economic growth, more job opportunities, and better products. The process by which this occurs is one of the miracles of modern economies and modern firms. It is also the topic of this book.*

One can hardly overestimate the importance of understanding better how firms organize themselves and manage their employees. In large corporations, roughly three-quarters of all costs are human resource related. Similarly, roughly 70 percent of worldwide wealth is in the form of human capital—the skills and knowledge of individuals—rather than in physical or financial capital. Economies grow and change through the creativity and motivation of entrepreneurs and employees. The strategy of many firms today is explicitly human resource driven, emphasizing customization, service, and innovation.

Organization and management are also of fundamental importance to you. The topics discussed in this book take on increasing importance as your career progresses. Those at an early stage tend to focus on specialized areas of knowledge. As careers evolve, however, jobs tend to increasingly depend on supervision and management of others. A broader, general manager perspective becomes essential to coordinate the work of many. As the career evolves further, the ability to set up, structure, and manage the entire organization becomes important. A strategic overview of the organization, and how it relates to the firm's goals and environment, is necessary.

In order for a manager to be effective at these various stages, it helps to have a structured, rigorous framework for analyzing the issues you will face. Gut instinct,

---

*The art on the cover is from the famous lithograph "Concave and Convex" by M.C. Escher (1955). In the picture, human figures move through concave and convex surfaces, and the perspective changes as a viewer continues to look at the work. The field of Microeconomics, of which Personnel Economics is a subfield, often uses concave and convex mathematical functions to model human behavior. Though not intended by Escher, his work is thus a nice metaphor for Microeconomics.

common sense, and wisdom from years of experience can be extremely valuable. However, combined with a deeper understanding of the issues and tradeoffs behind them, you can become even more effective. The purpose of this book is to give you a rigorous framework for understanding organizational design and the management of your employees.

The study of organizations and human resources has not always been rigorous, but that is changing. Economics has proven to be a powerful approach in this area, adding rigor and structure, and clarifying many important issues. This area of economics is often called personnel economics, and much of the founding research in this area was done by Edward Lazear. This second edition is based on Lazear's *Personnel Economics for Managers* (1998).

It may seem odd to apply economics to human resource and general management topics. In fact, it makes perfect sense. Economics is a methodology that has been applied to many areas of human activity, and has had enormous influence on the social sciences. That methodology is quite flexible, and can be applied to many problems of interest involving human behavior. The ability to apply a consistent framework allows us to develop a useful framework for studying organizational design.

❖❖❖❖❖ ## WHAT IS THE ECONOMIC APPROACH?

Economists recognize two elements that drive human behavior. One is pure psychology, or preferences. Understanding such preferences and their formation and evolution is the realm of classical psychology. The second is the environment in which people act to attain their goals. This is the realm of economics. Thus, economics focuses on budgets, prices, constraints, information, and incentives. It also focuses on social interactions, since an employee's colleagues, manager, and customers play important roles in driving behavior.

This distinction between preferences and the environment is recognized in psychology. The subfield of social psychology generally focuses on the impact of the environment on individual behavior—just like economics. The fields of social psychology and personnel economics study many of the same issues, though from somewhat different perspectives. This also means that what we often think of as psychology is not, in the purest sense.

Because economics focuses on the effects of the environment on behavior, it generally starts with only crude assumptions about preferences of individual employees. This is more of a virtue than it might seem. The more abstract and general the model, the wider its applicability. Thus, in economics we may assume that employees attempt to maximize their pay. By pay, we mean not only compensation, but also benefits, job amenities, work environment, and other things offered by the firm that they might value. A theory of pay for performance then has relevance for using any motivational tool, not just cash.

The key part of the economic approach is to focus on how the environmental variables—information, resources, constraints, decisions, and incentives—affect the outcome. Those are the issues that are analyzed in this book. More often than not, the analysis results in a statement of one or more important tradeoffs between benefits and costs that must be balanced.

Two results of this approach are worth noting here. First, the economic tools that we employ are used to analyze a variety of problems. This allows us to provide a more structured approach to the topics covered in this book. By the end of the book, we will be able to develop a framework for thinking about organizational design as a whole.

Second, economics focuses on variables that managers have a great deal of control over. The primary factors analyzed in this book are information, decisions, and incentives. These are exactly the levers that managers tend to have the most ability to pull to better design their organizations. It is much easier to alter the incentives than to change the psychology of your workforce.

It was mentioned earlier that economics and social psychology are different fields analyzing similar topics (organizational sociology could be added to this group as well). There is a great deal of healthy dialogue (competitive and cooperative, as it should be) between economists, social psychologists, and sociologists studying the issues covered in this textbook. The new field of personnel economics has grown out of this dialogue. It started as a small subfield of labor economics (the study of labor markets). It then incorporated new insights from informational economics, to start studying management of employees inside firms. Over time, personnel economics became more refined and more successful, and started to incorporate insights, evidence, and topics from social psychology and organizational sociology. (It can be argued that personnel economics is causing those fields to evolve as well.) Thus, while our approach and emphasis is economics, this book is more properly thought of as the result of an active debate between, and mixing of, different social sciences that study management issues.

Of course, this is not to say that this book is the beginning and end of study in this area. A full understanding of human resource management also requires the study of psychology. This text does not pretend to be the final word on organizational design. Rather, it is a strong complement to more traditional approaches, as well as a fresh approach for most students and managers.

WHO IS THIS BOOK FOR?

This book has several natural audiences. Undergraduates would benefit greatly from studying the book (in most cases, more than they would by taking a traditional labor economics course). Not only will they learn and apply ideas from microeconomics, such as incentive theory, but they will learn principles that will be valuable in their careers.

Though the focus of the book is on personnel policies and organizational design, it is not written for a human resource specialist. Specialist texts focus on detailed examination of how to implement personnel policies, such as design of a pension plan or a performance appraisal form. Nevertheless, the text should be extremely valuable to an HR specialist, since it provides a strategic and analytical overview for human resource policies. It provides the broader perspective that is necessary before focusing on the details.

We both teach MBA students, and naturally write this book from that perspective. It provides a way to think about organizational design overall, as well as specific human resource policies. Since MBAs tend to become consultants, general managers, or run organizations themselves, the issues and approach used here are extremely relevant for MBA students. Executive MBA students should also find the book useful. It should help them take well earned experience and common sense, and make it even more powerful and effective.

● ● ● ● ● OVERVIEW OF THE TEXT

The textbook has three core sections, followed by a shorter section with applications and advanced summary discussions. The first few chapters may seem narrow, but that is intentional. In order to develop a rigorous approach it is necessary to simplify and build each idea carefully. As the book progresses, more elaborate perspectives are developed. The text builds and cumulates tools from chapter to chapter, and from section to section. By the end, a rich model of personnel and organizational design will be built. Here is a brief overview of the contents of each section.

I. Sorting and Investing in Employees

In the first part of the book, employees are thought of somewhat mechanistically: inputs to production that can be rented or managed just like other inputs or assets. In this part of the text, employees have two important characteristics: innate abilities, and skills that they can accumulate in school or on the job. To the extent that employees have skills that are innate, the key issue is to *sort* them into the appropriate firms and jobs. To the extent that they can learn and improve their productivity, the key issue is to *invest* in them.

This part of the textbook focuses on the employee career pipeline—recruiting employees, investing in their skills so that they can advance, and managing employee turnover. The first two chapters consider issues involved in getting employees into the firm. Chapter 1 is a short chapter that considers how firms can think about setting hiring standards—the quality of the workforce that they wish to hire. Chapter 2 continues with the issue of hiring, focusing on the extent to which the firm should invest resources in recruiting, and how the job offer can be structured to improve the effectiveness of recruiting.

Chapter 3 begins to consider what to do with employees once they are inside the organization. It provides a framework for analyzing investment in employee skills through training (by the firm or the employee). This discussion also raises the issue of how to think about the complex economic relationship between the employee and the firm. That issue arises throughout the book, and is picked up again at the end.

Chapter 4 applies the economic tools from the first three chapters. These tools are important in understanding how a firm can manage turnover effectively. This chapter also illustrates how simple economic tools can have wide application.

II. Organizational and Job Design

As the textbook progresses, our model of employees becomes more elaborate. In this section, we consider what the employee actually does on the job. Chapter 5 begins the section by analyzing tradeoffs in decision making. An important idea used here is that an organization has to solve the same problems that an economy does, so the metaphor of a well functioning economy is useful for thinking about organizational design. This chapter uses these ideas to consider decentralization and centralization. Chapter 6 extends this discussion to questions of overall organizational structure.

Chapter 7 brings the discussion to the level of the individual employee's job design. For the first time, employee motivation becomes a key issue. The idea of intrinsic motivation—that the type of work the employee performs has important implications for how, and how hard, they work—is explored. This chapter provides an overview of, and an explanation for, how job design has evolved in recent decades. It also links the psychological idea of intrinsic motivation to the economic idea of decentralization. Finally, Chapter 8 provides an analysis of several advanced job design topics, such as teams, and the effects of information technology on organizational structure.

III. Paying for Performance

The third core section of the text picks up on the theme of motivation from Chapter 7. The focus of this section is on extrinsic motivation—pay for performance. This section adds the perspective of incentive theory from economics to our toolbox. Chapter 9 analyzes how an employee's performance can be evaluated. Chapter 10 considers how such an evaluation can be tied to rewards to motivate better performance, as well as pitfalls and implementation issues that commonly arise.

Chapter 11 provides a bridge between this and the first section of the text, exploring the relationships between an employee's career dynamics (such as promotions) and pay for performance. Finally, Chapter 12 applies the ideas from this section to two important special cases of pay for performance: employee stock options and executive compensation.

IV. Applications

The first three sections of this book constitute the core material. In the last section, the ideas developed in the text are applied to special topics that different readers may find of interest. Chapter 13 analyzes employee benefits. Chapter 14 discusses entrepreneurship and intrapreneurship, or how to promote innovation and value creation in both startup and mature organizations.

Chapter 15 picks up on a topic first raised in Chapter 3—implicit and explicit methods for contracting between a firm and its employees. Good organizational design involves both formal and informal policies (for example, employee evaluation usually includes both numeric metrics and subjective judgments). Here we extend that discussion. Chapter 15 also pulls together several themes that have been developed in the book, providing a broader perspective on the issues, and on how we are trying to help you think about organizational design. Chapter 15 is thus an important part of the overall message of the book, and can be read after the core chapters if there is not enough time to cover Chapters 13 and 14.

◈ ◈ ◈ ◈ ◈ REFERENCES

Lazear, Edward (1998). *Personnel Economics for Managers*. New York: John Wiley & Sons.

◈ ◈ ◈ ◈ ◈ FURTHER READING

Abrahamson, Eric (1996). "Management Fashion." *Academy of Management Review* 21(1): 254–285.

Becker, Gary (1976). *The Economic Approach to Human Behavior*. Chicago: University of Chicago Press.

Brown, Roger (1986). *Social Psychology*. New York: Free Press.

Lazear, Edward (1995). *Personnel Economics*. Cambridge: MIT Press.

ACKNOWLEDGMENTS

*T*his book is based on our research and that of many others. We are indebted to all researchers in this vibrant area of economics. Several colleagues have been especially influential to our thinking over the years. These include Gary Becker, Michael Beer, Richard Hackman, Michael Jensen, Kenneth Judd, Kevin Murphy, Canice Prendergast, Melvin Reder, John Roberts, Sherwin Rosen, and Robert Topel.

Many colleagues tested out drafts of this book with their students, for which we are grateful. Especially detailed feedback was provided by Wally Hendricks and Erik de Regt and their students, as well as Jed DeVaro, Maia Guell, Kathryn Ierulli, and Tim Perri. This book was partially written while Michael Gibbs visited the Aarhus School of Business in Denmark; both of us are grateful to our many colleagues there. Additionally, there are numerous manuscript reviewers who provided invaluable feedback on this second edition. Among them are: Stephen G. Bronars, University of Texas, Austin; Charles H. Fay, Rutgers University; Marie T. Mora, University of Texas, Pan American; and Mark R. Frascatore, Clarkson University.

We received substantial help and inspiration from our students who used various drafts at the University of Chicago, Stanford, and the Fondation Nationale des Sciences Politiques (Sciences-Po).

Finally, we are grateful to our assistants Thomas Chevrier, Kathryn Fitzgerald, Mario Macis, Maxim Mironov, Yi Rong, Yoad Shefi, and Marie Tomarelli, who gave careful and thorough input on every aspect of the text.

BRIEF CONTENTS

CONTENTS

Part One

SORTING AND INVESTING IN EMPLOYEES

*I*n this first section of the text, we take a very simple view of employees. It is one that is quite similar to that taken in much of biology: nature versus nurture. In our context, employees bring to the workplace certain innate abilities, such as to think quickly or creatively, or to work with numbers. They also develop new or more advanced skills over time, through education, experience, and on the job training.

The topics of this section are how to sort employees by their innate or accumulated skills, how to invest further in their skills, and how to manage their exit from the organization, as a function of their talents and skills. One can think of a firm's career policies as a kind of pipeline, bringing employees in, developing and promoting them, and eventually transitioning them out. That is the sequence of this section. In later sections of the book, we broaden our perspective, to consider issues such as the work they perform, their motivation, and the firm's complex relationship to the employees.

In the process of exploring these issues, several important economic concepts are developed: asymmetric information, investment, and different methods of contracting.

Asymmetric information refers to situations where two parties to an economic transaction (in our case, the firm and the employee) have different information that is relevant to the transaction. Problems of asymmetric information are ubiquitous in economies and organizations (e.g., the quality of a new hire; the effort that an employee expends on the job). They also tend to lead to inefficiencies, because incorrect decisions are made, lack of information creates risk, or because one party exploits its informational advantage for personal gain at the expense of overall efficiency.

When we consider recruiting, asymmetric information arises because the employee has more information about suitability for a job than does the firm (the opposite case can also arise sometimes). This presents a challenge for the firm in recruiting. We will see that one way to deal with this is to use the economic principle of *signaling*, which encourages the employee to use their information in a constructive rather than strategic way. The idea of signaling has applications in many areas of business, and we shall mention a few. This is an example of how the tools used in this book have broad application outside of employment.

The second economic tool used is the idea of optimal investment. Employees and their employers can invest in increasing their skills. In studying this issue, we will use the same ideas that play a key role in finance courses.

Finally, we will see three approaches to thinking about economic transactions or contracts. We start with the simplest—a spot market whereby the firm simply pays an employee's market price at each point in time. This is the standard view in introductory microeconomics classes. But in trying to improve recruiting, we will soon see the need for more complex, multiperiod *contracts* between the firm and the employee. These contracts will also be *contingent*, in this case on employee performance. Finally, in some cases we will see that the contract between the firm and the employee involves *implicit* or informal elements, because it is not always possible to write complete formal contracts. This gives us a useful framework for thinking about the overall employment relationship, and even issues such as corporate culture. Those ideas will be picked up again at the end of the text.

Now let us provide a small amount of structure to get started. The firm desires greater employee performance (contribution to profits), and lower labor costs. These must be traded off against each other. For the first six chapters of this book, employee motivation to work harder is *ignored*. Instead, we will simplify the problem by assuming that the employee's performance depends on innate ability, and the degree of their acquired skills (which we will call human capital).

In Chapters 1 and 2, we will be thinking about ways to sort employees on the basis of ability and skills. In Chapter 3, we then analyze how to invest in human capital. Chapter 4 applies the tools from Chapters 1–3 to questions of employee turnover. This not only gives a useful analysis of the turnover issues, but shows how the tools can provide insight into new questions.

SETTING HIRING STANDARDS

> When you're around someone good, your own standards are raised.
> —*Ritchie Blackmore, 1973*

*I*n this chapter our goal is twofold: to introduce the topic of recruitment, and to introduce the economic approach used in the textbook. Let's ease into both by considering an example.

AN EXAMPLE: HIRING RISKY WORKERS

New Hires as Options

Imagine that you are a partner in an investment bank in the City (financial district) in London, and are deciding between two candidates to fill a position as an associate (junior) investment banker. Gupta has the standard background of most of the applicants that you see, including a degree in economics, a few years of experience as a financial analyst, an MBA with a focus in finance, and a summer internship at an investment bank. You feel that his productivity is extremely predictable, and that he can produce £200,000 of value per year. Svensen, however, has a very unusual background compared to other applicants. She has a strong track record and appears quite talented, but does not have much experience related to investment banking. Hence you feel that her success is much less predictable. She may turn out to be a star, in which case she will produce £500,000 per year, but she may also turn out to be a disaster, actually losing £100,000 per year. Suppose that each of these outcomes for Svensen is equally likely (50 percent odds). Then *expected* (average) output from

Svensen in any given year is exactly the same as the output from Gupta:

$$\text{Expected output from Svensen} = 1/2 \cdot £500,000 - 1/2 \cdot £100,000 = £200,000.$$

If the cost (wages, benefits, etc.) of both employees is the same, which is the better hire? The answer might seem counterintuitive, but usually the firm should hire the *riskier* worker.

Suppose that both Svensen and Gupta can be expected to work at your firm for 10 years. Suppose further that it takes one full year to determine whether Svensen is a star or not. The salary is £100,000 a year, and for the moment let us assume that this will be the salary for the foreseeable future.[1] In that case, your firm earns a profit of £100,000 per year from Gupta, for a total value of £1 million over 10 years. The top branch of Figure 1.1 shows this choice.

Alternatively, you can hire Svensen. With probability equal to 1/2, Svensen is a star, producing £500,000 per year, and your firm earns profits of £400,000 from employing her, for 10 years, netting £4 million. With probability equal to 1/2, Svensen loses money for your firm. If this occurs, you can terminate Svensen at the end of the year, so £200,000 is the total loss, including her salary. These two outcomes are the remaining branches in Figure 1.1. Thus, the expected profit from hiring Svensen is:

$$\text{Expected profit from Svensen} = 1/2 \cdot £4,000,000 - 1/2 \cdot £200,000 = £1,900,000.$$

Svensen is therefore almost twice as profitable to hire as Gupta! Even though the two candidates have the same expected value, Svensen is worth much more. The firm can keep her if she turns out to be a good employee, and dismiss her if she turns out to be a bad one. The firm has the option of firing poor workers, and keeping the good ones.

FIGURE 1.1
HIRING A RISKY OR PREDICTABLE WORKER

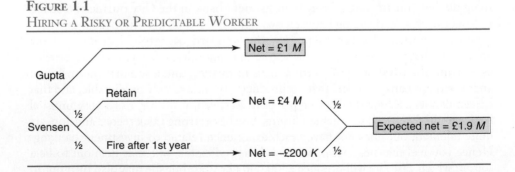

---

[1] In this example, we ignore issues of present value, by assuming that the interest rate is zero to keep things simple. When we do this in examples in this book, it is always the case that the intuition that is developed would be identical if we used discounted present values. Similarly, all examples in this text use inflation-adjusted figures, since inflation does not affect the conclusions.

This is the argument that is sometimes made for hiring workers with potential over conservative, proven ones. With the more proven worker, the firm gets a solid performer. With the risky worker, the firm may find that it made a mistake, but this can be remedied relatively quickly. It may also find that it has a diamond in the rough.

This simple example can be quite surprising to many students, since it seems to contradict the intuition that, if expected values are equal, risk is always a bad thing. However, risk is not a bad thing in the case of real options like hiring employees. It is a nice example because it illustrates how formal economic analysis can lead to better decisions. Our intuition tends to be the opposite of the correct answer in this case.

Analysis

The structure developed here suggests several other factors that are important in deciding whether or not to take a chance on a risky hire.

Downside Risk

The value of taking a chance on a risky candidate can be so large that it is often the better strategy even if the safe worker has a higher expected value per year. Even if Svensen might have been a total disaster, destroying £1,000,000 of value with probability $1/2$, it would have paid to take a chance on her. However, the more the potential there is for an employee to destroy value, the less likely is it to be optimal to take a chance on a risky worker.

Upside Potential

Svensen was valuable because she could generate high profits if she turned out to be a star. The greater those profits, the greater the option value from a risky hire. Thus, in jobs where small increases in talent lead to large increases in value creation, hiring risky candidates will be even more valuable (as long as there is no increased downside risk as well). Think of an entrepreneur assembling a new management team. There is little to lose, but there may well be much to gain. In such a case, it will make more sense to take a chance on a risky candidate.

Termination Costs

The more costly it is to fire a worker, the more costly is a risky candidate. Nevertheless, it may still pay to hire the risky worker, and terminate in the case that the worker does not turn out to be a good fit, even if there are high termination costs. In most countries, firms are prevented from terminating workers at will. Legal or social restrictions can make the option of firing a worker after one year costly. Consider the extreme case where hiring is for life. If the firm is risk neutral (is willing to accept any risks, as long as expected values are equal), as long as Svensen's expected productivity is equal to or greater than Gupta's, it will be a profitable bet to hire Svensen. More generally, the benefits from the case where Svensen turns out to be a star are so high that it would often be worth hiring Svensen even if firing costs were high.

Risk Aversion

If the firm is risk averse, it may still be optimal to hire Svensen. Svensen will now be costly to the firm in a different way, because she is risky. However, the differences in expected productivity are quite large, and should more than compensate for typical levels of risk aversion.

AN IMPLEMENTATION PROBLEM

⬡ ⬡ ⬡ ⬡ ⬡ ⬡ ⬡ ⬡ ⬡

The issue of risk aversion raises an interesting side point. When managers and recruiting specialists are taught this example, their typical response is to reject its conclusions, saying that they would be more conservative in hiring. Why is this the case? Is the theory wrong, or are the managers wrong? Quite possibly, neither. Rather, the analysis is conducted assuming that the firm is relatively risk neutral. However, decision makers are typically risk averse, and this will affect their decisions. For example, they might expect that they will be criticized or receive a poor evaluation if they hire a bad candidate for the job. The more risk averse they are, the more they will make decisions to avoid such an outcome.

To the extent that a manager's risk aversion is different from that of the employer, this is an *incentive problem* or conflict of interest. This is a topic that we will address in Chapters 9–12. In the meantime, if those who make hiring decisions are too conservative, a possible solution to the problem would be to try to avoid punishing them when they make mistakes in hiring. Another would be to appoint less conservative managers to handle recruitment.

Length of Evaluation

The time that it takes to evaluate whether Svensen is a star or a disaster affects the value of hiring a risky candidate. If the evaluation takes 10 years, there is no value to hiring Svensen, in our example. If the evaluation takes only one year, the firm can limit its cost of a disastrous hire to only one year of pay and poor productivity.

Length of Employment

The value of hiring Svensen would have been even greater if the firm could have employed Svensen for more than 10 years. For example, if Svensen was 30 years old when hired, and stayed at your company (for the same salary) until retirement, the profit from hiring Svensen would be £14 million if she turned out to be a star (£400,000 per year × 35 years). This suggests that the value of a risky hire will usually be larger the younger the new hire, and the turnover lower in the company (so that employees tend to stay with the firm longer).

A Counterargument

Our conclusions are only as good as the assumptions behind them. An important element of the economic approach to personnel is careful consideration of when the assumptions do or do not apply, and of what the effect would be of changing key assumptions. In the model above, the conclusion rested primarily on one key assumption: that we can profit when we find a star employee. Let us reconsider this assumption.

If Svensen turns out to be a star, is it safe to assume that we can continue to pay her £100,000? Might she try to bargain for a better salary? Might other employers try to hire her away from us? What would happen to our argument if these considerations applied?

These questions bring up a crucial consideration throughout this textbook: The firm always has to match an employee's outside market value. More precisely, the firm offers a job *package* with many characteristics, including the type of work, extent of effort required to do the work, degree of training, pay and other benefits, possibility for further advancement, and job security. The employee will consider all elements of the package in valuing the job, and compare it to alternative jobs offered by competing employers. Firms must make sure that their job offers match those of competing employers in terms of pay and other characteristics.

For now, let us keep things simple, and focus on pay and productivity. Suppose that other employers can observe how productive Svensen is. Moreover, assume that Svensen's productivity as a star or a disaster would be the same at any other investment bank. These are reasonable starting assumptions for investment banking; the work is often quite public, and is similar at most firms.

When this is the case, if Svensen is revealed to be a star, other investment banks will be willing to pay her more than £100,000 per year. In fact, they should be willing to pay as much as £500,000 per year, since that is her productivity. Labor market competition will tend to drive competing employers toward zero profit from hiring Svensen.

If Svensen is a disaster, no investment bank should be willing to hire her. She is likely to find better employment in a different industry where her productivity is not negative.

What is the benefit to your firm of hiring Svensen in this case? There is none. In order to retain her if she is a star, you have to compete with other firms, and should end up paying about £500,000 per year. In other words, our conclusion that it would pay to hire a risky candidate rested on our ability to earn profit from Svensen if she turned out to be a star.

How can we benefit from Svensen? There are two possibilities.

Asymmetric Information

Competing firms may not figure out Svensen's productivity, at least not immediately. Even though investment banking is often quite public work, some of it is not, and the work is also generally done in teams. Outside firms may find it difficult to estimate Svensen's individual contribution because of these factors. This implies that in industries where productivity is less individualistic, and less public, hiring a risky candidate is more likely to be worthwhile. Furthermore, to the extent that your firm can delay the ability of the labor market to figure out who your stars are, it can profit from the informational advantage. Therefore, your firm may want to avoid public recognition of Svensen's contribution.

The general issue of asymmetric information is one of the key economic ideas used in this book. When one side has important information that the other does not, interesting issues arise. For example, if a firm has trouble distinguishing between the best and worst job candidates, this can lead to ineffective recruitment, and also to a different approach to recruiting (that we will discuss in Chapter 2). Incentive problems are an important example of information asymmetry; they arise when the firm cannot monitor the employee's actions perfectly.

Firm-Specific Productivity

Svensen's productivity may be higher at your firm than at other firms. To the extent that this is true, Svensen may be a star at your firm, but less so or not at all at other firms. Then they will not bid up Svensen's market value as much, and there may be profit to your firm from employing Svensen. In Chapter 3, we will discuss two important reasons why Svensen's productivity may be higher at your firm than elsewhere: firm-specific job matches or human capital. The more important is either, the more likely is it to be profitable to hire a risky candidate.

One last issue here: Even if there is profit from hiring Svensen compared to what she can earn from other employers, there is still a question of how that profit is split between Svensen and the firm. That raises the question of bargaining. We will not focus on that issue in this text. However, we do discuss it briefly in Chapter 3 when we analyze how to share investments in firm-specific human capital.

GOOGLE'S UNUSUAL APPROACH TO RECRUITING
⬡ ⬡ ⬡ ⬡ ⬡ ⬡ ⬡ ⬡ ⬡

Google, a leading Internet search engine, competes with many high-technology companies for talent. It desires talented, creative employees that fit with its geeky and informal culture. To distinguish itself from other recruiters, Google sometimes tries unusual methods.

In one case, it inserted an "aptitude" test in technology magazines. It included questions such as, "How many different ways can you color an icosahedron with one of three colors on each face?" In another case, it placed billboards that read only, "(first 10-digit prime found in consecutive digits of e).com." The correct answer took you to a website seeking resumes of job applicants.[2]

---

[2] An icosahedron has 20 sides, so you can color it with 3 colors as many as 3^{20} ways (allowing for some that use only 1 or 2 colors). That equals 3,486,784,401. The first 10-digit prime number in consecutive digits of e is 7,427,466,391.

Such tactics serve three purposes. One is to provide information to recruits about the type of candidate that fits at Google. Another is to set the tone for future employees, since Google has a distinctive corporate culture. Recruiting is a crucial point at which to start defining the implicit contract, a concept that is discussed in later chapters. Finally, the tactics get Google valuable attention in the press—and in textbooks.

Source: Straits Times (Singapore), Fall 2004

The example of risky hires is a good introduction to the economic approach to studying personnel issues. We used a very simple model to analyze a complex decision. The model was useful in guiding us to important issues to consider in making this kind of hiring decision. Once the structure was set up, we were able to study the problem formally, even expressing some ideas in a few simple equations. The equations can be an effective way to rigorously express certain ideas. We will use these techniques throughout the book.

Simplification of a complex problem makes it easier to solve the problem, and get concrete answers. Of course, too much or inappropriate simplification can lead to incorrect answers, so one must be careful. But when applied intelligently, simple economic modeling can lead to powerful and practical analyses.

When we analyze organizational issues in this textbook, we will see the same set of economic ideas appearing over and over again. By the end of the book, we will have an economic toolbox that can be used to analyze all sorts of personnel problems. You will see examples in Chapter 4, where we use the principles discussed in the first three chapters to analyze some specific personnel policies. Economic concepts that we used in analyzing risky hires include labor market competition (for employees); prices (salary); asymmetric information; and incentives. For those who have studied economics, this will be familiar territory: It is microeconomics applied to how firms are designed and their employees are contracted with.

SETTING HIRING STANDARDS

Let us now step back and think about what hiring standards the firm would like to establish, before it actually begins recruiting employees. We will focus on a very simple case to generate some useful intuition. In the following, keep in mind that the firm's objective is to maximize profit. We assume that there are no constraints on the firm's ability to hire however much labor as it desires. Finally, we also assume that the price at which the firm sells its output, and the price per hour at which it pays employees, are constants.

Balancing Benefits Against Costs

Managers often say that their goal in hiring is to obtain the best quality workers. It sounds like a good idea—but is it? The most productive workers are also likely to be the most expensive. Should the goal instead be to hire the least expensive workers? A simple analysis resolves this question.

Consider the hypothetical productivity data in Table 1.1. These data indicate that college graduates are about 28 percent more productive than high school graduates.

Now consider the data on monthly wages for high school and college graduates in Table 1.2. College graduates cost more than high school graduates.

If the firm has to pay its workers approximately the wages shown in the last row of Table 1.2, then both a high school and college graduate would be profitable to employ. (In a complete analysis we would add in any other costs of employing them, such as fringe benefits, workspace, etc. This example is simplified to focus on the general point.) Moreover, it would be more profitable to employ a single college graduate compared to a single high school graduate:

Monthly profit from hiring HS graduate = \$122,917 − \$2,198 = \$120,719

Monthly profit from hiring college graduate = \$156,944 − \$3,455 = \$153,489.

However, this analysis is misleading. Suppose that your firm wants to hire enough workers to produce \$1 million in monthly sales. This would require 6.4 college graduates, at a cost of \$22,112, or 8.1 high school graduates, at a cost of \$17,804.[3]

TABLE 1.1
PRODUCTIVITY & EDUCATION OF HYPOTHETICAL EMPLOYEES

Worker ID	Monthly sales	Education
A	\$100,000	HS
B	\$108,333	College
C	\$125,000	HS
D	\$125,000	HS
E	\$133,333	College
F	\$141,667	HS
G	\$166,667	College
H	\$175,000	College
I	\$175,000	College
J	\$183,333	College
Average, HS grad = \$122,917		
Average, college grad = \$156,944		

[3]Do not be troubled by the fact that this may require hiring a fraction of a worker. It is possible to hire a fraction of a worker—by hiring someone part time, or allocating them to other tasks part of the time. Moreover, the larger the scale of the firm, the less consequential are such issues of indivisibility.

TABLE 1.2
WAGES FOR HIGH SCHOOL AND COLLEGE GRADUATES, UNITED STATES

| Year | Monthly Wage | | Ratio |
	High School	College	
1990	$2,184	$3,092	1.42
1991	$2,200	$3,050	1.39
1992	$2,157	$2,978	1.38
1993	$2,149	$3,100	1.44
1994	$2,146	$3,110	1.45
1995	$2,169	$3,142	1.45
1996	$2,105	$3,145	1.49
1997	$2,105	$3,024	1.44
1998	$2,191	$3,225	1.47
1999	$2,188	$3,393	1.55
2000	$2,226	$3,310	1.49
2001	$2,221	$3,381	1.52
2002	$2,220	$3,519	1.59
2003	$2,264	$3,610	1.59
2004	$2,260	$3,477	1.54
2005	$2,174	$3,511	1.62
2006	$2,198	$3,455	1.57

Wages are expressed in 2007 dollars.
Source: U.S. Current Population Survey

Employing high school graduates would actually be more profitable, because high school graduates have lower cost per unit of output. Referring to the wage as W, output as Q, and letting subscripts refer to high school or college graduates:

$$\frac{W_H}{Q_H} < \frac{W_C}{Q_C}$$

In this example, high school graduates cost about $18 per $1,000 of monthly sales, while college graduates cost about $22. As long as the expression holds, it is more profitable to hire high school graduates, and vice versa. The most cost-effective employee has the lowest ratio of salary to output. The firm should choose this type, and hire enough of them to reach the desired level of output.

This illustrates two simple but important economic principles. The first is to *always think in terms of tradeoffs between costs and benefits*. In this example, the desire for high quality workers must be balanced against their higher cost. Many questions boil down to assessing the benefits of a given policy against the costs.

The second general principle is to *always compare your approach to your best alternative*. In this case, college graduates are profitable, but less so than high school students. Once we take that into account, college students are not profitable compared to our other choice.

WORKER CHOICE AT DAYS INNS
● ● ● ● ● ● ● ● ● ●

Days Inns of America, a hotel franchiser, traditionally staffed its reservation center with young employees who were willing to work at the minimum wage. The staff answered phone calls from potential guests and booked reservations. However, due to a shortage of low-skilled workers, wages began to rise for this age and experience group. Days Inns decided to re-examine their targeted recruiting group for these positions.

Management realized that the sedentary nature of the job was well suited for elderly workers. In addition, senior citizens were a readily available work force that could be hired for only slightly more than young workers, when training and other costs were included.

What happened? With productivity defined as a combination of average call length and number of reservations booked, older workers talked on the phone longer but made more reservations. The higher proportion of calls that resulted in actual reservations more than offset the additional time used. Elderly workers had a lower salary to productivity ratio, making them the most cost-effective labor. The savings were even higher because the older employees had a significantly lower turnover rate.

Source: McNaught & Barth (1992)

Foreign Competition

This analysis is useful for thinking about globalization of labor markets and the role of foreign competition. It is often argued that countries with low labor costs drive companies in countries with high labor costs out of business. Is that accurate? Table 1.3 shows representative statistics on pay and productivity (GDP, gross domestic product) for several nations. Mexico has the lowest labor costs, while Norway has the highest. However, the real issue is not whether labor is cheaper, but whether it is more cost effective. For example, Japan's labor costs are among the highest, but its productivity is the highest. In fact, Japan has the second lowest labor cost per dollar of productivity. A firm that had a choice between hiring Japanese or Argentinean workers would prefer the more expensive, but also more productive, Japanese workers.

These numbers are meant to be illustrative, rather than definitive.[4] Still, they make clear the point that cheap labor is not necessarily low-cost labor. Similarly,

---

[4]The numbers may contain some aggregation error. Wages are from manufacturing, but productivity is for the economy as a whole.

TABLE 1.3
PRODUCTIVITY AND PAY OF MANUFACTURING WORKERS, SELECTED COUNTRIES

	GDP per worker	Annual salary, manufacturing	Cost per $ of GDP
Mexico	$15,964	$ 5,743	0.360
Japan	$78,065	$33,573	0.430
New Zealand	$40,690	$18,067	0.444
Argentina	$22,399	$ 9,973	0.445
Norway	$85,923	$38,447	0.447
United States	$75,571	$34,682	0.459
Sweden	$55,680	$27,371	0.492
Australia	$45,357	$25,266	0.557
United Kingdom	$54,848	$36,234	0.661
South Africa	$ 7,880	$ 7,828	0.993

Averaged over 2000–2002, in 2005 dollars.

Source: United Nations

high-productivity labor is not necessarily the most profitable labor. You should seek low cost per unit of output, whether that arises from low wages, high productivity, or both.

The Method of Production

So far, we have proceeded as if production was independent across employees. In reality, production is interdependent across employees. We now consider three scenarios representing different approaches to production, to see what effect the method of production has on our analysis. In the first, production is independent across workers. In the second, a worker's production depends on the skills of coworkers. In the third, a worker's production depends on the capital that worker uses on the job.

● ●

1. Productivity is Independent of Coworkers

A manager describes production in his unit as follows:

My team is a sales force. Each salesperson works independently. The organization consists of my salespeople and me. What kind of worker should I hire?

Here each worker's sales depend on his own ability and effort, irrespective of the efforts of other salespeople. This fits closely with the situation described above, so the choice between college and high school graduates is exactly the one that we have focused on so far. The simplicity of this case is best seen by comparing it to the next example.

2. Productivity Depends on Coworkers

A second manager describes her production as follows:

This firm manufactures small appliances. We find it better to have a combination of worker types. High school graduates are cheaper and more cost effective in the short run, but we find that we can't keep their skill levels up without some college graduates around. The high school graduates forget what they knew. The college graduates keep the high school graduates sharp. So we like to have both kinds of workers. The problem is that I'm not sure about the appropriate balance.

Here workers interact with one another. This is much more typical than the first case, since in most workplaces many jobs are interdependent. College graduates affect the output of high school graduates, and vice versa. Since college graduates are not only producing appliances, but also act as part-time teachers, part of their output consists of their effect on high school graduates.

The analysis above still holds, but output must be defined carefully. When measuring the output of college graduates, the number of high school graduates must be specified. Table 1.4 provides an example of the kind of information needed.

It is easy to see that output of a college graduate depends on the number of high school graduates working. For example, if 100 of each type are employed, total output is 63.1 units. If the number of college graduates is increased from 100 to 110, the gain in output is 3.7 units. However, if 150 high school graduates are employed, the gain in total output in going from 100 to 110 college graduates is 4.2. The gain from adding 10 college graduates is larger when there are more high school graduates around. Since college graduates train high school graduates, their services are more valuable when the firm has more potential "students" for them to teach. The larger the number of high school graduates in the workforce, the higher the value of adding college graduates to the workforce.

TABLE 1.4

PRODUCTIVITY (PER WORKER) OF HIGH SCHOOL AND COLLEGE GRADUATES
WORKING TOGETHER

		Number of College Graduates Employed					
		100	110	120	130	140	150
		Output					
	100	63.1	66.8	70.4	73.9	77.2	80.5
Number of	110	64.9	68.8	72.4	76.0	79.5	82.8
High School	120	66.6	70.6	74.4	78.0	81.6	85.0
Graduates	130	68.3	72.3	76.2	79.9	83.5	87.1
Employed	140	69.8	73.9	77.9	81.7	85.4	89.0
	150	71.3	75.5	79.5	83.4	87.2	90.9

Similarly, the more valuable that high school graduates are, the more college graduates are employed. High school graduates are more valuable when the "classroom" in which they learned is less crowded. Thus the firm wants a balance of college and high school graduates. This example reveals the importance of interaction. This can be stated as follows: *When workers interact on the job, a worker's contribution to output includes the effect on coworker output. As a result, it pays to hire better qualified workers when output is interdependent.*

3. Productivity is Independent of Coworkers, but Depends on Capital

A third manager describes the production process as follows:

We are a large clothing company that has our men's dress shirts produced by a factory in Malaysia. Each worker uses a sewing machine, which costs us $7.50 per day to rent. We can use skilled labor, which produces an average of 4 shirts per day, or professional labor, which produces an average of 6 shirts per day. Skilled labor costs $7.50 per hour, and professional labor costs $12 per hour. The sewing machine company says that it will rent us a new machine that doubles output per worker, but the better machine costs $16.50 per day to rent. Should I rent the new machine? What kind of labor should I hire?

The analysis is easy once the relevant data are compiled, as in Table 1.5. First, consider the old machines. Without looking at the table, the manager might be tempted to not rent the new machines, since they double productivity but cost more than double compared to the old machines. But this ignores the fact that producing a shirt involves both machines and labor. Adding a new machine more than doubles the capital cost, but it does not double the total cost. There is no doubt that the firm should use the new machines.

Furthermore, given that the firm is using the new machines, it should hire professional rather than skilled workers. When old machines are used, the cost per shirt is higher with professionals than with skilled labor. But when the new machines are used, the cost per shirt is lower with professionals than with skilled labor. When expensive capital is employed, it may be cost effective to use it intensely.

TABLE 1.5
ANALYSIS OF PRODUCTIVITY USING NEW OR OLD MACHINES

	Output	Labor Cost	Capital Cost	Total Cost	Cost/Output
Old Machines					
Skilled	4	$60.00	$ 7.50	$ 67.50	$16.88
Professional	6	$96.00	$ 7.50	$103.50	$17.25
New Machines					
Skilled	8	$60.00	$16.50	$ 76.50	$ 9.56
Professional	12	$96.00	$16.50	$112.50	$ 9.38

Professionals use the machines more efficiently, which leads us to conclude the following: *A firm should improve the quality of workers that it employs as it increases the amount or quality of its capital stock. More specifically, the optimal level of skill rises as the use of capital relative to labor increases.*

This helps explain why the president of a firm should be very highly skilled. His or her labor is combined with the entire capital stock of the firm, in a sense. It makes no sense to waste the capital by placing it under the stewardship of a low-skilled individual.

We will see later in this book that the labor market has valued highly skilled workers relatively more over time. One explanation for this is that firms have made increasing use of valuable, and very productive, capital in the form of new information technology.

How Many Workers to Hire?

The answer to this question is straightforward. The firm should continue to hire workers so long as the incremental profit from hiring an additional worker is positive.

In our example at the beginning of this section, both college and high school graduates were profitable to employ, but high school graduates were more profitable—they produced more output for the same amount of compensation. We can combine the two decision rules: Hire the type of worker who provides the greatest output per dollar of pay, or least cost per unit of output. (When doing so, take into account the effects of interdependencies with coworkers or capital, of course.) Continue to do so until the point where hiring more of that type of worker is no longer profitable.

This approach implies that there is a limit to the number of workers the firm should hire, because of the principle of *diminishing marginal productivity*. As more and more workers are added to an organization, the value of an additional one falls. Why would marginal productivity fall as you hire more workers? The main reason is that workers are combined with other resources: computers, machines, your time as their manager. The more workers that you hire, holding other resources fixed, the more thinly are those resources spread across each worker. For example, if you have a small office with you, your staff, and three computers, as you hire more workers, each one gets less time on one of the computers, and less supervision by you, which tends to reduce their productivity. This logic holds for *any* resource that is increased while keeping another resource fixed.

Consider Table 1.6. As more workers are hired for the office, the marginal productivity (extra sales) from each additional worker declines. That is a typical pattern in any business. The table also illustrates the principle that you should hire workers up to the point where they are no longer profitable; that is, when marginal productivity is less than or equal to marginal labor cost.

TABLE 1.6
MARGINAL PRODUCTIVITY AND MARGINAL COST OF HIRING AN ADDITIONAL WORKER

Number of employees	Total sales	Marginal productivity of employee	Total labor cost	Marginal cost of employee	Profit
0	$0	$0	$0	$0	$0
1	$100,000	$100,000	$14,404	$14,404	$85,596
2	$141,421	$41,421	$28,808	$14,404	$112,613
3	$173,205	$31,784	$43,212	$14,404	$129,993
4	$200,000	$26,795	$57,616	$14,404	$142,384
5	$223,607	$23,607	$72,020	$14,404	$151,587
6	$244,949	$21,342	$86,424	$14,404	$158,525
7	$264,575	$19,626	$100,828	$14,404	$163,747
8	$282,843	$18,268	$115,232	$14,404	$167,611
9	$300,000	$17,157	$129,636	$14,404	$170,364
10	$316,228	$16,228	$144,040	$14,404	$172,188
11	$331,662	$15,434	$158,444	$14,404	$173,218
12	**$346,410**	**$14,748**	**$172,848**	**$14,404**	**$173,562**
13	**$360,555**	**$14,145**	**$187,252**	**$14,404**	**$173,303**
14	$374,166	$13,611	$201,656	$14,404	$172,510
15	$387,298	$13,132	$216,060	$14,404	$171,238

The next-to-last column shows the marginal cost (compensation and other benefits) from hiring an extra worker. If this is less than the marginal productivity, profit rises from hiring more workers. If marginal productivity is below marginal cost (the lowest rows), profit can be increased by laying off some workers.

The general result is familiar to anyone who has studied economics: Profit is maximized by using any resource, including employees, up to the point where the marginal benefits just equal the marginal costs.

Other Factors

Availability of Workers

In many communities, more high school graduates than college graduates are available. Does this mean that a firm should have a bias toward hiring high school graduates, as they are cheaper to hire? In most cases the answer is no. Most employers, even very large ones, employ a small part of the local labor force, so the total availability of workers is irrelevant. There are two exceptions, both of which arise when the firm employs a sufficiently large part of the relevant labor market that its hiring has some effect on the market price.[5]

The first case is where a firm employs a very large fraction of the local labor force (say, a factory in rural Thailand where there are few other employers). In that

---

[5]This is the economic condition where the firm has *monopsony* power.

case, hiring more of a certain type of worker drives up the wage. The analysis is as before, but the firm needs to take into account the rising wage in analyzing output per dollar labor cost.

The second case is more important. When the type of labor being hired is very specific, the market for it may be thin (there are few buyers for this type of worker). If so, there may be significant search costs to finding a worker with the right skills. The wage must build in these amortized search costs, since it is a cost of employing this type of worker. Once that is done, the analysis is as earlier.

The Firm's Financial Condition

Suppose that the firm is in financial distress. How should this affect its hiring decisions? Similarly, if the firm is having a very successful period, should this affect hiring? Once again, intuition can be misleading. None of the analysis makes mention of the firm's financial condition. Choosing the wrong kind of labor will only make the financial condition worse.

A firm in financial distress may have trouble paying employees because of cash flow problems. However, this is a *financial* problem, not a *labor* problem. The best solution to such a problem would be to arrange financing to cover the short-term cash flow problems, so that the firm can hire workers when it is profitable to do so. In fact, creditors should encourage this, if it increases profits, since it makes it more likely that the debt will eventually be paid off.

♦ ♦ ♦ ♦ ♦   MAKING DECISIONS WITH IMPERFECT INFORMATION

Throughout this chapter, we have conducted our analyses based on data that either exist or were assumed to exist. Unfortunately, the information required is often not immediately available or is expensive to obtain. What can a manager do in such circumstances? There are three possibilities: (1) Make a decision independent of analysis; (2) estimate the relevant information; or (3) conduct an experiment.

Make a Decision Independent of Analysis

A frequent temptation is to conclude that the data are too difficult to obtain. The solution is then to simply guess an answer, using gut instinct, experience, or standard practice. Implicit in the guess are a number of calculations that are not made explicit, but are there nonetheless. This approach is easiest, but least likely to lead to an effective decision. Even a little formal thinking is likely to lead to a better result, and if that thinking is supported by some estimation of the tradeoffs involved, the decision is even more likely to be made effectively. This book is intended to guide you to more structured, and therefore better, decisions about organizational design.

Estimate the Relevant Information

Rather than guessing at the answer, a manager may estimate the key numbers to determine the appropriate course of action. Such an approach is likely to lead to better decision making than will guesswork. Moreover, this book can help with such an approach.

Suppose, for example, that you develop a formal analysis of a personnel issue using the concepts in this book. This analysis will help you uncover the important pieces of information needed to make a good decision. The conclusions depend on certain pieces of information, such as the effect on productivity of high school graduates of working side by side with college graduates. When such information is not available, an estimate—even an informed guess—may be appropriate.

The structured approach also makes it easier for you to consider how robust the conclusion is, by varying estimates up and down. In some cases the correct decision may be the same for a wide range of values for the estimated information. In those cases, the right answer is clear. In other cases it may be that the correct decision depends critically on the specific value of the information. In those cases, it would be worth further expenditures to get a more accurate estimate before making any decision.

This approach may involve educated guesses, but the decision can often be improved further by using available data to estimate the tradeoffs under consideration. This is becoming increasingly viable with the dramatic fall in costs and rise in capabilities of computers. In the old days, firms kept personnel records on computer tapes that were difficult and slow to access. Data entry was costly and cumbersome, and data were rarely used, so firms had little incentive to maintain detailed databases. Now, firms often have detailed personnel records at hand, and database and other software to analyze the data easily. In addition, human resource professional associations and consulting firms can often provide additional data on practices, costs, and effects across a wide sample of firms. It is becoming more and more feasible to provide estimates—sometimes rough ones, and sometimes fairly sophisticated ones—of the impact of organizational policies on desired outcomes such as turnover or profitability.

Experiment

The third option is to experiment. Sometimes this is easy to do and carries little cost. When data on relative productivity of different types of workers is unavailable, the firm might hire some of each type (perhaps even part time, or as temps) and measure their output. Similarly, when trying to figure out the correct commission rate in a sales force incentive plan, the firm might experiment with different rates in different locations, before rolling out a plan for the entire organization.

Sometimes experimenting is difficult and potentially costly. There are five questions that a manager can consider beforehand to determine whether experimenting is a viable option:

1. What are we trying to learn and why do we want to know it?
2. Will obtaining the answer have a large or small effect on profit?
3. What kind of data are necessary to answer the question?
4. How costly is it to obtain these data?
5. Will the data that we are likely to collect provide a reliable answer to the question?

Question 1 must be answered before any experiment can be run. Otherwise the experimenters may get so caught up in running the experiment that it becomes a purpose in and of itself.

In order to justify a major experiment, the answer to Question 2 must be that the potential effects on profits are large compared to the costs of the experiment.

Question 3 must have a well defined answer. If it is difficult to specify in advance the kind of information required, experimentation is likely to result in money spent without useful results. Managers should be able to say in advance that if the results turn out one way, the decision will be made in a certain way. If they turn out the other way, the decision will be different. If this statement cannot be made in advance, it makes no sense to gather the data.

Question 4 must be asked to complement Question 2. If the cost of obtaining the data is large, it may not be cost effective to undertake the experiment, even if the results will have a significant effect on profit.

The data are most valuable if they given an unambiguous answer to the question posed. If the data obtained contain a great deal of error, or if they only roughly approximate the kind of information needed to answer the question, the experience is less valuable.

Of these approaches, the first is almost always the least effective. If the analysis is complex, and information is incomplete or unavailable, you may be tempted to use intuition or gut instinct to make a decision. Your intuition and instincts are usually based on your experience, so they are not worthless. However, we have seen examples in this chapter where the analysis led us to some counterintuitive conclusions. The point of the kind of formal analysis described in this book is to improve your decision making, by making it more rigorous, and clarifying the important (and unimportant) issues. Moreover, more formal thinking can help you realize the situations in which your experience guides you correctly, and incorrectly. Unfortunately, too often in this area managers rely on intuition, because the problems can be very hard to analyze formally and with structure. By the end of this book, you will have tools that will increase the effectiveness of your decisions about personnel and organizational design.

⬥ ⬥ ⬥ ⬥ ⬥ **SUMMARY**

This chapter provided a simple, short introduction to the topic of hiring. We follow this up in the next chapter with consideration of the job offer. The primary purpose of this chapter was to get you started in thinking about organizational issues using economic tools. A little formal thinking can go a long way in clarifying issues, sometimes leading to surprising conclusions.

The chapter raised several issues. We started with a scenario of choosing between two job candidates, one with relatively predictable job performance and one more risky. To the extent that turnover costs can be avoided, this actually may be a good thing for an employer. This is because risky job candidates may have an option value. If one turned out to be a poor choice, the loss is limited, as the firm can terminate the employee. The firm may be able to capture a substantial return if the employee turns out to be a star in some circumstances.

We then considered an employee's output to wage ratio. The best worker is not the cheapest, nor the most productive, but the one with the highest ratio of productivity to cost. We should hire as long as the marginal productivity of the last worker hired is greater than or equal to the cost of the worker.

The chapter introduced some important economic ideas that you should begin to incorporate into your everyday thinking. First, never forget that you are constrained by market competition. In the case of personnel management, the job package that you offer your employees must be adequate to attract and retain the kind of employees that you want—especially if they are known to be stars. Second, always try to think in terms of tradeoffs and alternatives. When you are analyzing a decision, consider not only the benefits but the costs, and balance them against each other. The costs will be determined primarily by labor market pressures, which act as a constraint on optimal personnel policies. The benefits of employees depend on the production process; how they work, whom they work with; and what capital they work with. Some benefits and costs may be subtle or intangible, but they may still be important. One good example is that you should always include your best alternatives when making a decision. A choice may be profitable, but it may be less profitable than other options.

Study Questions

1. You are recruiting to fill a position in your firm. Should you try to "sell" the job to applicants by describing it in the nicest terms that you can? Should you make the job sound as desirable as possible? As a job applicant, should you try as hard as you can to convince the recruiter that you are the perfect candidate for the job? Think about these issues over the next couple of chapters.

2. Potential employees can be unusual in many ways. Can you think of any attributes of job applicants that would make them risky hires, but in a way that might suggest they have high option value as employees? In what ways might candidates be risky that would suggest their option value is not high?

3. Capital (including advanced information technology) can serve as a *substitute* for employees in producing a firm's output. It can also serve as a *complement*, making workers more productive at their tasks. Which effect do you think is likely to be more important in practice? Why? Which kinds of jobs are most

likely to be ones in which computers or machines can *replace* workers? Which are most likely to be ones in which they cannot replace workers, but can help workers perform their jobs better?

4. Many employment issues are complex, and involve interpersonal relationships, psychology, or qualitative considerations. For this reason, they are often difficult to quantify. If you cannot quantify some of the issues that we discuss, are the tools developed in the text irrelevant? Why or why not?

5. Think about this question as you read the rest of the book: Why might a firm delegate design of most human resource policies to an HR department? What costs and benefits do you see from such a practice? What is a feasible alternative approach?

6. After reading the introduction and this chapter, how would you characterize the approach of personnel economics? What distinguishes it from other approaches to studying organizational design that you are familiar with?

References

Blackmore, Ritchie (1973). Interviewed in *Guitar Player*, July–August.

McNaught, William & Michael Barth (1992). "Are Older Workers Good Buys? A Case Study of Days Inns of America." *Sloan Management Review*, Spring.

United Nations (various years). *Common Database & World Development Indicators*.

U.S. Department of Labor (various years). *Current Population Survey*.

Further Reading

Lazear, Edward (1995). "Hiring Risky Workers." In *Internal Labour Markets, Incentives, and Employment*, ed. Isao Ohashi & Toshiaki Tachibanaki. New York: St. Martins Press, 1998.

Appendix

The formal theory behind the conclusions in the second section of this chapter is the standard economic theory of production. Assume that firm output Q is a function of high school graduate labor H, college graduate labor C, and capital K:

$$Q = f(H, C; K)$$

The firm minimizes costs by deciding how much of each type of employee to hire. For a given amount of output, the firm would choose between H and C to minimize costs:

$$\min_{H,C} W_H \cdot H + W_C \cdot C + \lambda[Q - f(H, C; K)],$$

where W represents wage rates, and λ is a Lagrange multiplier. The first-order conditions with respect to H and C are:

$$W_H - \lambda \frac{\partial f}{\partial H} = 0$$

$$W_C - \lambda \frac{\partial f}{\partial C} = 0.$$

These may be rewritten usefully as:

$$\frac{W_H}{W_C} = \frac{\partial f / \partial H}{\partial f / \partial C}$$

or:

$$\frac{W_H}{\partial f / \partial H} = \frac{W_C}{\partial f / \partial C}.$$

The multiplier λ reflects the marginal cost of output for a given Q. Once λ has been determined, the firm sets marginal cost equal to marginal revenue to determine the amount it wants to sell, which determines the optimal output Q. We now model the three scenarios described in the chapter.

⬡⬡⬡

1. Productivity is Independent of Coworkers

The independence is easily modeled by an additive production function:

$$f(H, C; K) = [aH + bC]^z,$$

where we assume that $0 < z < 1$; $0 < a < 1$; and $0 < b < 1$. In this case,

$$\frac{\partial f}{\partial H} = az[aH + bC]^{z-1}$$

$$\frac{\partial f}{\partial C} = bz[aH + bC]^{z-1}.$$

Collecting results we have that:

$$\frac{a}{b} = \frac{W_H}{W_C}.$$

All four of these terms are exogenous parameters (unless the firm is a monopsonist, in which case the W's are endogenous). This means that the first-order conditions cannot be met except by coincidence, so that a corner solution is the optimum. Either $H > 0$ and $C = 0$, or $H = 0$ and $C > 0$. If the left-hand side of the last expression is larger than the right-hand side, high school graduates should be employed, and vice versa.

2. Productivity Depends on Coworkers

A good way to model this case is:

$$f(H, C; K) = zH^a C^b.$$

Analysis similar to the previous case yields the condition:

$$\frac{H}{C} = \frac{aW_C}{bW_H}.$$

Here we can have an interior solution, and the optimal amounts of H and C depend on each other.

3. Productivity is Independent of Coworkers, but Depends on Capital

This case could be modeled similarly to Case 1, but with the marginal productivities of H and C depending positively on K. In this case, a corner solution would again apply, but the optimal amounts of H and C would be positively related to the level of K. A similar approach could be applied to Case 2, of course.

2

RECRUITMENT

> I sent the club a wire stating, 'Please accept my resignation. I don't want to belong to any club that will accept me as a member.'
>
> —*Groucho Marx, 1959*

INTRODUCTION

In this section of the book we are interested in how firms bring employees into the organization, and the patterns of careers they have once they are there. Table 2.1 presents some data on these questions. The data are from confidential personnel records for all management employees in a U.S. firm, over a 20-year period.[1] Since the data are confidential, we will refer to the firm as Acme Incorporated. We will present data from Acme in several chapters to help illustrate concepts.

Acme is in a service industry. Its management ranks have eight hierarchical levels, from entry (Level 1) to CEO (Level 8). Most management employees are in the first four levels. Level 1 is what is often called a *port of entry*; virtually all who work in jobs at this level were hired into Acme at this level. Since it is at the bottom of the management job ladder, this should not be surprising, as demotions are very rare in most companies. At Levels 2–8, most employees were not hired from the outside, but were promoted from within.

Because of promotion from within, managers in upper levels have substantial experience at Acme on average. For example, Level 4 managers have almost 8 years of experience in the company. It also appears that movement between levels (promotion) is more rapid at lower levels, since the average number of years in the current job is longer in upper levels.

The last four columns give some sense of turnover and career length for Acme's managers. There are two patterns. First, many leave Acme very quickly after being hired. For example, about 11% of those who are hired at Level 1 leave within the

---

[1]The Acme tables are based on Baker, Gibbs, & Holmstrom (1994a,b). The Acme data are from a single firm, but the patterns that we illustrate with the Acme data in this book appear to be fairly representative of the policies in many firms, in different countries. See the papers cited in Gibbs & Hendricks (2004).

TABLE 2.1
CAREER PATTERNS AT ACME INCORPORATED

Hierarchical Level	Percent of total employees	Percent hired at this level	Number of years in		Percent who stay at Acme			
			Current position	Acme	Only 1 year	Only 2 years	5–10 years	More than 10 years
1	25.4	99.0	2.3	2.4	10.7	10.4	25.5	39.8
2	26.2	31.0	2.5	4.5	15.2	10.2	19.7	38.5
3	25.4	31.0	3.0	6.0	10.7	10.1	25.5	35.6
4	20.5	27.0	4.1	7.9	15.3	7.9	24.9	30.7
5–8	2.5	19.0	4.0	9.7	7.1	14.3	42.9	28.6

first year, while another 10% leave the next year. Conversely, if a manager stays at Acme beyond the first year or so, he or she has a good chance of staying for many years. For example, about a quarter will stay for between 5 and 10 years, while about a third will stay for more than 10 years.

Thus, there seems to be evidence of *sorting* in the first few years on the job. Almost a quarter of new hires will leave within two years, either because Acme decided it did not want to keep them, or because new employees decided they did not want to stay. Second, if employees survive the sort, they often enjoy careers at the company that last for many years. This suggests there is some value to having employees remain with the firm. These are issues we explore in this and the next three chapters.

With this introduction, let us now return to the issues we raised in Chapter 1. Once your firm has decided which types of workers it would like to hire, it must recruit for those types. There are two general issues. First, how can it weed out undesirable applicants? In some jobs, hiring the wrong type of employees can cause major problems, disrupting output and costing the firm not only wages but lost profits. Second, how can the firm attract the right types of applicants? Attracting the right type will reduce workforce problems, as well as recruitment and turnover costs. Put another way, your firm must sort new hires, just as Acme apparently does. How can you think about sorting for the most effective workforce?

⬡ ⬡ ⬡ ⬡ ⬡ SCREENING JOB APPLICANTS

One strategy for attracting good quality job applicants is to offer a high level of pay or benefits. This will generate a large pool of applicants, and higher quality applicants will be more likely to apply for the job than if pay was lower. Unfortunately, so will low quality applicants. The personnel office will be flooded with resumes, and only a small portion may be qualified. Some undesirable workers will slip through the hiring process and become employees, while some desirable workers will get lost in the shuffle and never hired. This is not a very useful approach just by itself.

The problem of the wrong type of applicant applying to the firm is called *adverse selection*.[2] This is a general problem in economics, not just in employment. The problem arises because of asymmetric information. One party knows what type they are (in this case, a high or low quality job candidate), and the other does not. The one that knows uses this information strategically to personal advantage. A classic example involves used car sales. Owners know the quality of their used car. Those with good quality used cars are more likely to keep them, while those with low quality used cars are more likely to sell them. This implies that the quality of used cars is lower than it would otherwise be. It also implies that owners of high quality used cars may find it difficult to get a good price for their car, since buyers worry that it is a low quality car.

Adverse selection arises in our case when the wrong kinds of workers are attracted to the firm. A number of approaches can be used to mitigate the problem of adverse selection in recruiting. Let us begin with a simple case first, the use of credentials.

Credentials

An obvious approach to weeding through resumes of job applicants is to look for credentials that distinguish some applicants from others. The most important ones are generally the type of experience (job and promotion history) the applicant has, the type of training (e.g., college major or MBA), and the quality of school the applicant attended. Indeed, these are almost always the most important lines on anyone's resume. What makes a credential useful for hiring? Here are some considerations:

Informativeness of the Credential

Ability to perform well on the job must be positively correlated with ability to obtain the credential. For example, a university degree is a useful credential only if university graduates tend to be more productive at the job in question. A credential can be informative in two ways. First, it may mean that the holder of the credential has knowledge or skills that apply directly to a job. This might be the case with a CPA or an MBA. Second, it may mean that the holder of the credential has innate abilities that tend to make one more productive on the job. An example might be a high score on an aptitude test, or winning a scholarship.

Cost of Obtaining the Credential

A valuable property of the credential is that it is relatively easy for well qualified workers to obtain, compared to poorly qualified workers. When this is true, the

---

[2]In 2001, George Akerlof (1970) was awarded the Nobel Prize in Economics for analyzing the problem of adverse selection. He shared it with Michael Spence (1973), who was awarded the prize for analyzing the problem of signaling that we discuss later in this chapter. Joseph Stiglitz also shared the prize that year, for analyzing problems of asymmetric information.

credential is very likely to signal differences in ability. For example, it is not very difficult for a qualified accountant to pass the CPA (Certified Public Accountant) exam, but it is virtually impossible for someone with no training in accounting to pass. Thus, using the CPA as a screen effectively sorts qualified and unqualified accountants.

On the other hand, a credential that is extremely expensive for all workers to obtain will not do well in sorting them. If a credential is very difficult to obtain, few applicants will have it. For a credential to be effective, it must be that most qualified applicants possess the credential while most unqualified ones do not. If a very small subset of qualified applicants has the credential, or a large subset of unqualified ones does, the credential is not helpful.

Return on investment in the credential

If the difference in wages between those who have credentials and those who do not is not very great, small differences in credentials will signal large differences in ability. For example, if the credential is education, and the increase in earnings from obtaining a college degree is small, only the most talented will get the degree. This is because they are the ones for which obtaining the degree is cheapest. When the rewards for obtaining a degree are large, even not-so-able people can be induced to get the degree.

Signaling is one way of resolving adverse selection problems. In many cases, a high quality type can incur some costs to *signal* to others that they are high quality. If low quality types do not also invest in the signal, then it can serve to distinguish the high quality types from the low quality types: For example, an owner of a high quality used car can offer a warranty. It may also be possible for a high quality job applicant to signal this to potential employers. Before we discuss this idea, it is useful to consider simpler sorting issues.

Learning a Worker's Productivity

Suppose that you advertised an investment banker job, as in Chapter 1. In response you received a set of resumes from job applicants. You looked through them, and selected a subset with appropriate credentials. In a job like investment banking, small differences in ability, personality, or other employee characteristics may lead to large differences in effectiveness on the job. Unfortunately, the self-selection of applicants to the job, and further winnowing by sifting through their resumes, makes the pool of remaining applicants look more and more alike. In general, the more that a set of applicants has already been sorted, the lower the variance between the remaining candidates. What should you do next?

You could hire one at random, and take a chance. However, given the stakes it is likely to make sense to expend some resources to screen them further.

There is a variety of methods that firms use to screen applicants. Some give job applicants tests, to see how they perform on specific tasks. This approach is more likely to work well for jobs with fixed, measurable tasks; it is not likely to work well for an investment banker. Many firms use psychological profiling.

Unfortunately, this technique does not tend to work well in practice. One reason for this is that psychology is a highly inexact science. Another is that job applicants have an incentive to game the test, trying to sound like better employees than they are. For example, one study found that 90% of job applicants who took one popular psychological test were able to inflate their "conscientious" score.[3] Finally, virtually all firms conduct personal interviews of job applicants. Such interviews can vary from simple to elaborate. In the case of investment banking, applicants may be put through several rounds of interviews, eventually being flown to the company's headquarters to meet with high-level partners over several days. Such a process can be extremely expensive.

All of these examples involve some costs (except when the firm hires applicants without any screening whatsoever). Consider the following example, and think about the extent to which your firm should invest resources in screening applicants carefully.

Screening Bankers

Table 2.2 shows productivity levels for five hypothetical types of job applicants (A through E) in two different firms, an investment bank and a commercial bank. Assume that the remaining applicants (after earlier rounds of weeding out) are paid about £100,000, so each bank expects to pay about the same salary to anyone it hires.

Finding out what type a job applicant is has obvious value to each firm. The investment bank would want to avoid A and B types, because productivity would be lower than pay, while the commercial bank would want to avoid A types.[4] Suppose that applicants can be put through a series of tests that cost £2,000 per person, and give definitive information on which type the applicant is. How valuable is such information? In other words, how much would each be willing to pay to screen workers before hiring? Table 2.3 provides figures to help us answer this (all numbers are expected values rounded to the nearest £100).

TABLE 2.2
SCREENING INVESTMENT BANKING JOB APPLICANTS

		Type				
		A	B	C	D	E
Percent of Job Applicants		10%	20%	40%	20%	10%
Productivity	Investment Bank	−£250	0	125	200	450
(£ thousands)	Commercial Bank	£95	100	110	120	125

---

[3] See Paul (2004).

[4] You should remember from Chapter 1 that each bank would want to hire those with the highest productivity per £ of compensation cost. That is true; the firm will also want to keep hiring as long as expected productivity is greater than expected employee costs (profit from the hire is positive).

TABLE 2.3

PROFITABILITY OF SCREENING AT AN INVESTMENT BANK AND A COMMERCIAL BANK

	Screen?	Productivity	Salary	Screening Cost	Profit
Investment Bank	No	£110	£100	£0.0	£10.0
	Yes	193	100	2.9	90.1
Commercial Bank	No	110	100	0.0	10.0
	Yes	112	100	2.2	9.8

With no screening, both banks would have £110,000 average productivity from each new hire, or an average profit of £10,000.

With screening, the investment bank would reject types *A* and *B*, and accept only 70% of all applicants. The average productivity of the *C*, *D*, and *E* types hired would be about £193,000, substantially higher than without screening. The screening cost per worker actually hired would be £2,000 × 10/7 (since the bank would hire an average of 7 out of every 10 applicants), or £2,857 per hire. Average profit from each new hire would rise with screening to about £90,100. The investment bank would profit greatly from screening applicants.

If the commercial bank screened applicants, it would reject those of type *A*, hiring 90% of all applicants. Average productivity would rise only slightly to about £112,000, but at a screening cost of £2,000 × 10/9, approximately £2,222, per new hire. Profit per new hire, net of screening costs, would fall to about £9,800. The commercial bank would not benefit from screening.

Why the difference? There are two reasons. First, the investment bank wanted to screen out three times as many workers as the commercial bank. The point of screening is to avoid hiring the applicants who would not be profitable. Second, the downside from hiring poor candidates was worse at the investment bank; some applicants would have produced nothing, and others would have destroyed value. The investment bank was more at risk from hiring the wrong type of worker.

This example motivates issues to consider when screening (see the Appendix for a formal treatment):

Screening is more profitable when the test is more effective. A test can be more effective in several ways. First, it can be cheaper to administer. Second, it can be more accurate. That is, it can correctly distinguish between desirable and undesirable job applicants a higher percentage of the time. No test is 100% accurate. Moreover, as noted earlier, job applicants often try to game such tests so as to appear to be better candidates than they really are. Finally, an effective test is more discriminating; it weeds out a higher fraction of candidates, recommending a smaller fraction for hiring. In the example, the commercial bank's screen was not very valuable because only 10% of candidates were rejected.

Screening is more profitable when the stakes are higher. The purpose of screening is to avoid the unprofitable candidates. Therefore, the greater the downside risk from hiring the wrong person, the more value there is to screening. Similarly, the longer that a new candidate can be expected to stay with the employer, the more valuable the screen. Firms that intend to hire employees for the long term thus tend to invest more in careful screening before committing to a new hire.

Is Screening Profitable? For Whom?

If the investment bank screens workers, productivity is much higher for its employees than for random job applicants. Now the same issue arises that we faced with our risky hire in the previous chapter, Svensen, when she turned out to be a star. The labor market will value our screened employees more highly, simply because we decided to hire them (they passed our screen). Therefore, it is not realistic to assume that we can continue to pay £100,000 at the investment bank, if productivity is almost double that. Other investment banks would bid away our workers, once they realized that we screen our employees carefully.

What will we end up having to pay our employees? It is hard to tell without additional information. It is even conceivable that we would have to pay as much as their productivity, £193,000, if the labor market is very competitive. Screening may not always be profitable to the employer; indeed, some firms screen extensively, while others hardly screen at all.

What about job applicants? Why would they apply to a firm if they knew they would be screened? It must be that the potential higher pay, if they pass the screen, compensates for the trouble and risk involved in the screening. If the application process is not too difficult, then the extra compensation need not be too high to make it worthwhile for applicants to try. If the screen is extensive, such as probation (described below), however, job applicants may have to be compensated significantly in order to be willing to undergo the screening process.

When the firm cannot benefit much from the screen because labor markets are competitive, job applicants will have to pay for much or all of the screening. Of course, this happens already in the case of pre–job market screening such as education or professional certification. But it may also happen with on the job screening. Workers can pay for the screening implicitly, by their willingness to accept lower pay during the screening period then they would otherwise earn.

In any case, it is likely that both the employer and the employees will share the benefits (and costs) of screening. Firms that screen more extensively will tend to pay more, both because their employees are more productive, and because applicants will require some compensation for the costs and risks of trying to successfully earn long-term employment at the firm.

A further consideration arises when employees have some idea about whether they are of high or low ability. Those who are of high ability have a better chance of passing the screen, so they have more to gain from the screening. Thus, they should be more willing to undergo and pay for the screening. We discuss this later under the topic of signaling.

Probation

The screening methods described may be useful, but are imperfect. An important concern is that they are only proxies for what the firm really cares about—how the person actually performs the job. In many cases, the only way to truly tell if a job applicant is a good fit for the job is to have them *perform* the job itself. Thus, a final approach to screening is to have the job applicant do the job for some period, either very briefly during interviews, or more extensively during some testing period. The most elaborate form of this is to hire a worker for a probationary period, and only hire them long-term if their performance during probation is adequate.

Of course, a problem with probation is that costs of terminating employees can be substantial. In Italy, if the firm is found to have fired an employee who has worked for the firm long enough without legal cause, the firm must rehire the worker, pay lost wages and social insurance contributions, and pay a penalty to the government. In Indonesia, firms must pay workers severance of more than 1 month of salary for each year that the employee worked for the firm—up to 9 months of severance—plus 15% of salary as "worker's rights replacement money." By contrast, turnover costs are usually very small in Denmark. The general trend has been toward increased turnover costs, due to greater employment regulation and litigation over wrongful termination.

Where firing costs are high, employers can often still use probation, under a different form. For example, employees might be hired on a temporary basis through a temporary employment agency. Those who perform well could then be offered regular employment. Those who do not perform well do not need to be fired; they are just not hired from the temporary agency. Indeed, some temp agencies have an explicit strategy of serving as a screening agency of this kind for employers.

A similar approach that firms can sometimes use is to hire applicants on temporary (fixed term) contracts. When the contract term is over, the firm can elect to hire the worker more permanently, offer a new fixed term contract, or not rehire the worker at all. Such contracts are not just used for low skilled jobs; many firms hire high level consultants in a similar fashion.

Evidence suggests that increasing regulation of employment is one factor behind the recent growth in temp agencies worldwide. For example, in the United States some employment regulations vary from state to state. Those states that regulate termination more strongly tend to be the ones where firms are more likely to use temporary workers. In Europe, the employment relationship is more highly regulated than in most other parts of the world, and hiring of temps is quite common. According to one study, 13% of all wage earners in the European Union were employed on temporary contracts. In Spain, the corresponding figure was 31%, and roughly half of workers under the age of 30 were employed on temporary contracts.

REDUCING FIRING COSTS IN FRANCE

● ● ● ● ● ● ● ● ● ●

In September 2005, the French government passed a new law designed to make it easier for companies with 20 or fewer employees to hire and fire workers. It specified a "New Recruit Contract" allowing such companies to lay off workers anytime in their first 2 years on the job, for any reason. Those laid off were to be given at least 2 weeks' notice, and would be entitled to unemployment benefits, but would not have to be given the level of severance pay that is standard for other French workers.

Labor unions and opposition party leaders criticized the law, which was initially passed by decree under a new "emergency procedure" that allows the French government to enact employment legislation without consulting lawmakers. In April 2006, students, union members, and others marched in protest in the streets of Paris. In response the law was cancelled by President Jacques Chirac.

Source: Associated Press (2005–2006)

Implications of Probationary Screening

If the firm uses probation to screen workers, and retains those who are good performers, there are several interesting implications. First, the firm is likely to promote those who survive the screening. They have been revealed to be more productive than average job applicants. Once this is evident, the firm is likely to give them greater responsibility.

Second, the system will generally be up-or-out, since those not promoted will typically not be rehired. This is much like the lower levels of promotion ladders that are seen in most professional service firms.

Third, a large raise in compensation will usually accompany the promotion. The firm promotes those it finds most productive, so a promotion implies that you are more talented than the average new hire, which raises your market value. For this reason, firms typically have to offer raises on promotion, or risk losing those promoted. Moreover, since promotion is based on performance, and performance depends in part on an employee's effort on the job, the promotion will become a form of incentive pay. We return to these issues in Chapter 11.

SIGNALING

● ● ● ● ●

Most people have a good idea about their skills, work ethic, and ambition—the things that make them good employees. Let us now assume that workers know what type of employee they will be. If workers know what type they are, and share this information honestly with employers, a firm could recruit employees of a certain type by simply putting up a notice that it is looking for workers of that type. Unfortunately, this is not likely to be an effective approach. Recall our discussion earlier in this chapter about offering high wages to high skilled workers. A firm that tried this would find itself facing adverse selection, since job applicants who were not highly skilled would be tempted to apply anyway. This is why we decided that some kind of screening would be necessary.

When workers know more about their employability than employers do, screening can be used to solve this adverse selection problem. After all, screening works by sorting workers, and keeping those who fit well and are most productive with the firm. It then pays higher wages to those who are screened out. Shouldn't this attract those who are good candidates to apply in the first place, and deter those who are not good candidates? Let us consider an example to see how this might work.

Consider a simplified example of recruiting for an investment bank. Suppose that simple interviewing allows the bank to weed out Types A through C easily, but that it is much harder to distinguish between Types D and E without further screening. The bank would like to hire E types because they are the most profitable. Instead of screening, can it construct a job offer involving probation, up-or-out promotion, and a raise on promotion that is attractive to the E types, but not to the D types?

To model this situation, we need a little more information. First, let us assume that the bank can figure out what type an employee is after observing them on the job for one year. However, the accuracy of this judgment is not perfect: Ten Percent of the time, the wrong decision is made. Thus, 10% of D types are promoted when they should not be (does this remind you of your boss?), and 10% of E types are not.

We also need to know what each type could earn elsewhere, since we have to offer a more desirable package to E types, but a less desirable package to D types. Assume that D types can earn £175,000 in other jobs, while E types can earn £200,000 in other jobs. Thus, their alternatives working elsewhere for two periods are twice these salaries—£350,000 for D types, and £400,000 for E types.

Finally, we need to know how long those promoted will work for us. To keep things simple, assume that they will work for one year after promotion. Table 2.4 provides these figures (rounded to the nearest £1,000), and calculates the expected value of the job offer to each type, for different salaries in the two years W_1 and W_2.

The first offer considered equals what E type applicants could earn elsewhere, £200,000 per year. This obviously attracts D types, but is no lure to E types. The second offer lowers pay during the probation period (W_1), and raises pay after promotion (W_2). Each row below further lowers W_1 and increases W_2. Because the promotion is not guaranteed, the firm must offer more than £400,000 in total pay $W_1 + W_2$ in order to attract E type applicants. For this reason, and reflecting the risk involved in accepting lower initial pay compared to what E types could earn elsewhere, each subsequent row involves higher total pay for those who win promotion.

To calculate the actual values to D and E if they apply, note that each earns W_1 in Period 1. In Period 2, D types earn W_2 with 10% odds, and their alternative

TABLE 2.4
MOTIVATING SELF-SELECTION OF JOB APPLICANTS

W_1	W_2	Type					
		D			E		
		Expected pay		Apply	Expected pay		Apply
		Alternative	Apply		Alternative	Apply	
£200	£200	£350	£378	yes	£400	£400	no
180	225	350	360	yes	400	403	yes
160	250	350	343	no	400	405	yes
140	275	350	325	no	400	408	yes
120	300	350	308	no	400	410	yes
100	325	350	290	no	400	413	yes

wage with 90% odds. Similarly, in Period 2, E types earn W_2 with 90% odds, and their alternative wage with 10% odds:

$$\text{Value of applying for } D = W_1 + 0.9 \cdot \£175{,}000 + 0.1 \cdot W_2$$

$$\text{Value of applying for } E = W_1 + 0.1 \cdot \£200{,}000 + 0.9 \cdot W_2.$$

The first two offers are attractive to D types. This is because pay is higher at the investment bank than they could get elsewhere, even during probation. Our first lesson is that in order to deter some applicants from applying, we must pay less than those applicants can get elsewhere before probation.

Similarly, the last few offers are attractive to E types, because the high pay after promotion is enough to compensate for the low initial pay, given the high probability that E types will be promoted. Our second lesson is that in order to attract some applicants, we must offer more than they could earn elsewhere after probation.

Thus, probation can generate good self-selection of job applicants, thereby solving the adverse selection problem, if we pay a sufficiently low amount during probation, and a sufficiently high amount after probation. One way to understand this is to note that in effect the firm is demanding that each applicant *post a bond*—by accepting less than they could earn elsewhere—during probation. In return, if they perform well and are promoted, the firm will *give them a reward*—by paying them more than they could earn elsewhere. Figure 2.1 shows the type of contract that we are considering.

Note in Figure 2.1 that the higher ability employees of type E receive a *smaller* reward on promotion, and pay a *larger* cost during probation, than do lower ability employees of type D. The up-front bond $W - W_1$ is larger for E types, since their outside alternative is larger. Similarly, the deferred reward $W_2 - W$ is smaller for E types for the same reason. If the D types would pay a smaller bond, and earn a larger reward if promoted, than how can this type of job offer deter them from

FIGURE 2.1
DEFERRED PAY AS A SCREENING MECHANISM

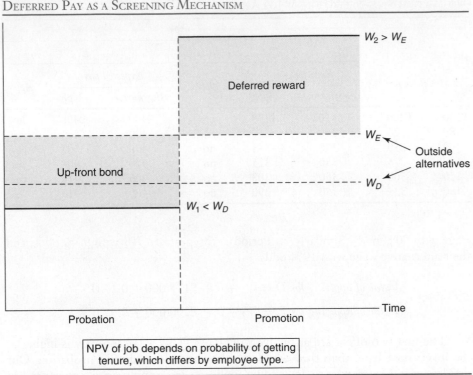

NPV of job depends on probability of getting tenure, which differs by employee type.

applying, while motivating E types to apply? The answer is that the firm must put the employees through a rigorous performance evaluation before awarding promotion. The evaluation must result in sufficiently high probability that E types will be promoted, and sufficiently low probability that D types must be promoted. The low success rate for D types reduces the expected value of the job for them compared to E types.

This discussion illustrates the general economic idea of *signaling*. Signaling is a method that can sometimes be used to solve adverse selection problems. The high quality type signals his or her type to the market by *incurring a cost*. If low quality types are not willing to incur this same cost, then the signaling is effective: The fact that someone incurs the cost proves that they are the high quality type.

Who Pays, and Who Benefits?

Signaling only works if the incentives of job applicants are addressed: Type Ds must be deterred, but Type Es must be motivated to apply. Thus, it is the employee who will pay for most or all of the cost of signaling, and enjoy most or all of the benefit of the signal. In Figure 2.1, we see that employees pay for the signal by accepting wages below what they could get elsewhere initially. They also pay in the sense that they incur some risk that they will not get promoted, even if they are high ability (if the screening is imperfect). They are rewarded later by earning more than they could earn elsewhere after promotion.

The employer may also pay for part of the probation, and get some of the benefits. Whether this happens depends on what average wages end up being compared to productivity. The firm benefits during the probation period from pay that is below productivity, but incurs costs when it pays more than productivity to those that are promoted.

Examples

An example of signaling is the seller of a used car who offers a warranty. The warranty is costly to the seller, and is the signal. The fact that the seller is willing to offer the warranty, while some other sellers are not, may signal that the car is of higher than average quality. In our employment example, Type Es can signal their type (and confidence in their ability to perform well and earn promotion) by their willingness to accept low pay in the first period. This only works if the D types are not also willing to accept the same contract.

There are many applications of signaling in the business world. For example, venture capitalists typically demand that entrepreneurs invest all of their family's personal funds in a new business venture. They may even demand that the entrepreneur mortgage his or her home, and invest the proceeds in the startup. At first glance this may seem odd—isn't the venture capitalist supposed to provide the funds? Demanding that the entrepreneur put some "skin in the game" is important, however, as it helps the venture capitalist separate the most confident and serious candidates from the least.

Another example involves joint ventures between two firms. In such cases, it is common for both firms to invest some funds. One reason for this may be so that each firm can signal to the other the seriousness of their intentions to make the joint venture profitable.

As discussed, probation is a form of pay for performance. It can serve as a signal if high ability job applicants are willing to accept a job offer with a risky but potentially lucrative promotion ladder. The same idea applies to any form of pay for performance. If a new hire is willing to accept more risky pay for performance, this may signal that they are higher ability, and believe themselves to be a good fit for the job. The opposite is true if they try to renegotiate to reduce the pay for performance. Thus, pay for performance helps sort employees in addition to motivating them.

Education as a Signal

Education is an important potential example of signaling. Assume for the sake of argument that students learn nothing useful in school. However, suppose that more talented students find it easier to learn the material quickly. If so, then they might be able to signal their talents to the labor market by investing in more education than less talented students. In this view of education, instructors require students to pass through increasingly difficult screens. At each stage, some find the cost of passing the next screen to be too high, so they do not get that level of education. Those who find the screen relatively cheap do enroll for that level of schooling. The labor market recognizes this, paying more to those who have obtained more schooling.

Indeed, as Table 1.3 in the last chapter showed, those with more schooling do earn more. Is this due to signaling? It is possible, but it seems extremely implausible that this is the only explanation. If the only purpose of education is to screen, we could probably find more efficient ways to do so than to have students go to college for 4 years: For example, we could give them a large test at the end of high school. In Chapter 3, we consider investments in new skills. Education clearly plays an important role in doing this.

That said, there is evidence that education does have some role in screening workers. For example, those who almost complete 4 years of college earn a little less than those who go a little bit farther and complete their degree—there is a discrete jump in earnings associated with earning the formal credential. This is hard to explain by training alone.

Signaling More Formally: Separating and Pooling Equilibria

Let us consider a formal example of signaling so that we can see how it works. Suppose that junior accountants can invest in some education or on the job training. If they complete the training, they become CPAs. Assume that there are only two types of accountants, "quicks" and "slows," depending on their ability as accountants: Quicks are more productive, and also find it easier to obtain the training necessary to pass the CPA exam.

To formalize these ideas, denote the present value of the employee's productivity as Q, and the cost of obtaining the CPA credential as C. Subscripts refer to the two different types of accountants.

Assume that the labor market pays accountants a salary that exactly equals their expected productivity. The fraction of accountants who are quicks is α, so the fraction who are slows is $1 - \alpha$. Thus, if the labor market cannot tell the two types of accountants apart (if there is no signaling), pay equals:

$$Average\ productivity = \overline{Q} = \alpha \cdot Q_q + (1 - \alpha) \cdot Q_s.$$

On the other hand, if the quicks *do* succeed in distinguishing themselves, they will be paid their productivity Q_q. Those who do not signal will then be assumed to be slows, so anyone who does not signal is paid Q_s.

The quicks would like to distinguish themselves from the slows, so that they can be paid more. At the same time, the slows would like to be confused with the quicks, so that they can avoid being paid less. This is a general property of adverse selection models: The lower quality types generally attempt to associate themselves with the higher quality types, who conversely attempt to set themselves apart from the lower quality types. Will the quicks be able to signal their ability by obtaining a CPA?

In order for signaling to work, three conditions are necessary. First, if all other quicks are signaling, and slows are not, an individual quick must be better off with signaling too. This requires that pay net of the quick's cost of the CPA is higher than pay if she decided to join the slows by not getting a CPA:

$$Q_q - C_q > Q_s.$$

Second, if all other slows skip the CPA and quicks invest in the CPA, an individual slow must be better off not getting the CPA as well. If a slow decided to infiltrate the quicks, he would be paid Q_q, but it would cost C_s. If he did not, he would earn Q_s. Thus, for slows to skip the credential, it must be true that:

$$Q_q - C_s < Q_s.$$

These two together imply that:

$$C_q < Q_q - Q_s < C_s.$$

Intuitively, the gain from signaling must be higher than the cost for high ability types, but not so high that low ability types are also motivated to signal.

Third, for *all* of the quicks to be *willing* to signal, their profit from doing so must be higher than what they would get if none of them signaled at all. If none signal, everyone is paid average productivity, so this requires that:

$$Q_q - C_q > \overline{Q}.$$

This condition is even stronger than the other condition for quicks described above, since $\overline{Q} > Q_s$. Very large α implies that $\overline{Q}$ is very close to Q_q, making it more likely that this last condition cannot be met.

Intuitively, signaling to distinguish themselves from the crowd is more likely to be profitable for quicks the rarer that they are. If there are many high quality types, it is relatively easy for low quality types to hide themselves among the high quality group.

If these conditions are *not* met, neither has an incentive to obtain the credential, and quicks do not distinguish themselves from slows. In this case there is no signaling. Such a case is called a *pooling equilibrium*. This illustrates that signaling is not always possible.

If the conditions are met, quicks signal and slows do not. This is called a *separating equilibrium*, since quicks are able to separate themselves out from slows by investing in the credential.

These points provide a formal illustration of arguments we provided about screening earlier. Signaling involves screening, but adds an important new ingredient: workers know their type, and firms try to structure job offers so that those who are a better match for their firm reveal this by their willingness to accept the offer, while those who are a poor fit reveal this by refusing to accept the offer.

Which Type of Firm is More Likely to use Signaling?

Signaling is helpful when employers do not have enough information about job applicants to assess their potential accurately enough. It is useful when differences in talent among potential employees matter a lot to productivity. When differences in talent do not make much difference to productivity, signaling will not be very useful. These ideas suggest when we should expect to see employment practices consistent with signaling.

First, signaling should be more important in jobs where skills are most important. Such jobs tend to be those that are at high levels of the hierarchy, in research and development, and in knowledge work. They also correspond well to professional service firms, such as consulting, accounting, law firms, and investment banks. In such professions, even small differences in talent can lead to large differences in effectiveness on the job, so sorting for talent is very important. For this reason, such firms tend to screen very carefully at recruiting, and usually have promotion systems that correspond well to our probation story above, at least in the first few years on the job.

Signaling is also more likely to be used where there is not much information already available about job applicants. Workers who are new to the labor market (say, having just graduated from college or an MBA program) are more likely to see such policies. New hires with many years of experience, and an extensive resume of past accomplishments, should expect to see less use of signaling policies in the job offers that they receive. Nevertheless, firms can use these techniques even for hiring experienced talent at very high levels, when appropriate. For example, a new CEO is often hired for a fixed period contract, with extensive pay for performance. To the extent that the CEO's ability to implement the strategy is hard to determine, and the CEO knows more about this than the board's hiring committee, such practices can improve CEO recruiting.

◆ ◆ ◆ ◆ ◆   ## SUMMARY

An important objective of personnel policies is to sort talent to appropriate employers and positions in order to increase organizational effectiveness. Since there is incomplete and often asymmetric information during recruiting, firms must screen job applicants. When a high salary is offered, unqualified workers may apply for the job if there is a significant chance that they can survive. This is the economic problem of adverse selection.

There is a number of ways that a firm can cut down the number of undesirable applicants. One way is to look for credentials that are good predictors of on the job performance. This works well when the credential is easy to obtain for qualified people but difficult to obtain for unqualified ones.

Beyond credentials, firms can invest in more or less extensive screening when hiring. This can include formal testing, psychological profiling, lengthy and multiround interviews, and trying workers out on the job briefly. All of these can be helpful, though it is likely that they will be far from perfect predictors of job performance.

The most accurate screen is to employ workers for some probationary period on the job. Of course, it may also be the most expensive. The worker must be paid during this period, and costs can be especially severe in jobs where there is a large downside risk in the worker's job (ability to destroy value). Many firms use some form of probation, either formally or informally, in their hiring practices.

In our analysis workers were offered a contingent contract. In the case of probation, workers receive sufficiently low pay during probation so that only those who believe that they will be successful are willing to apply for the job. A well crafted probation and postprobation salary schedule can keep undesirable applicants from applying, while attracting desirable ones. This is easier to achieve when it is difficult for unqualified workers to sneak past the probationary period and when qualified and unqualified workers have similar outside opportunities.

Screening and probation introduced the economic idea of signaling. Signaling is a method that sometimes can solve adverse selection problems. If workers know their ability, qualified workers would try to make this known to employers by signaling, and unqualified workers would try to hide the fact that they are unqualified. Therefore, firms should design recruiting policies to encourage qualified workers to apply, while making it difficult for unqualified workers to get through probation.

Another possible way to induce good self-selection among job applicants is to use strong pay for performance. In fact, probation does this, since the postprobation promotion and raise in pay is contingent on good performance. More generally, incentive pay of any kind tends to improve recruiting, since better fitting employees are more likely to accept strong incentive pay.

Firms can use contingent rewards after probation to attract higher quality workers. However, this is not free; it comes at the cost of higher wages. These policies are most likely to be useful in companies where small differences in talent can lead to large differences in productivity of employees. This is most likely at high levels of the organization, and in firms where intellectual work is emphasized. Professional service firms, especially leaders in their respective industries, often employ policies of this type. These include careful recruiting, extensive performance evaluation during the first few years of employment, and up-or-out promotion systems with large rewards to those who are retained. They may also include strong individual pay for performance.

In the classic view of economics, goods are bought and sold on spot markets, with the terms of the transaction consisting of quantity, quality, and price. Our analysis in this chapter has opened up a different view: When firms use probation or contingent pay to screen workers, they offer a *multiperiod* contract. This contract is *contingent* on the employee's performance: How they are treated depends on how they perform. Finally, it also involves a *promise* by the firm—to reward those who perform well with higher pay later. These complications arise because the quality of the good—ability of the worker—is not readily available information. Thus, the economic relationship between the employer and the employee becomes complex. This idea is developed further in the next chapter, and even further still in Chapter 15.

●●●●● STUDY QUESTIONS

1. If workers might also be screened by universities, can a firm earn profit from screening them? Under what circumstances is screening more likely to take place on the job rather than before workers enter the labor market?

2. For what types of workers is screening more important?

3. What kinds of firms are most likely to sort aggressively through workers and use up-or-out career systems? Why?

4. How might a firm signal to potential employees about important characteristics of the job it is offering? Can you give any examples?

5. Can you give any examples of signaling in other business contexts? That you have seen in your own life? In each case, what is the cost of the signal? In what way do those who signal differ from those who do not? Does the signal meet our criteria for a separating equilibrium?

6. Think about the French law allowing small firms to lay off workers at lower costs in the first 2 years on the job. Who would benefit from passing such a law? Would any workers (or potential workers) benefit? Were the students protesting at the Sorbonne in Paris (one of the most prestigious universities in France) likely to be affected by the law? How? What about unions?

●●●●● REFERENCES

Akerlof, George (1970). "The Market for 'Lemons': Quality Uncertainty and the Market Mechanism." *Quarterly Journal of Economics* 84(3): 488–500.

Baker, George, Michael Gibbs, & Bengt Holmstrom (1994a). "The Internal Economics of the Firm: Evidence from Personnel Data." *Quarterly Journal of Economics* 109: 881–919.

Baker, George, Michael Gibbs, & Bengt Holmstrom (1994b). "The Wage Policy of a Firm." *Quarterly Journal of Economics* 109: 921–955.

Gibbs, Michael, & Wallace Hendricks (2004). "Do Formal Salary Systems Really Matter?" *Industrial & Labor Relations Review* 58(1): 71–93.

Marx, Groucho (1959). *Groucho and Me*. Free New York: Bernard Geis Associates.

Spence, Michael (1973). "Job Market Signaling." *Quarterly Journal of Economics* 87: 355–374.

FURTHER READING

Lazear, Edward (1992). "The Job as a Concept." In *Performance Measurement, Evaluation, and Incentives*, William Bruns, ed. Boston: Harvard Business School Press.

O'Flaherty, Brendan, & Aloysius Siow (1996). "Up-or-Out Rules in the Market for Lawyers." *Journal of Labor Economics* 13: 709–735.

Paul, Annie Murphy (2004). *"You Are What You Score."* Free Press.

APPENDIX

Screening

Here we provide a formal example of the principles of screening discussed in the chapter. Assume that there are two types of job applicants, E and D. Productivity is Q; E types are more productive than D types, so that $Q_E > Q_D$. The probability that a random job applicant is type E equals p; the probability the applicant is type D equals $1 - p$. The firm pays wage W to those it hires; $Q_E > W > Q_D$. Thus, the firm makes profit from E types, but a loss from D types.

$$\textit{Expected profit from random new hire} = p(Q_E - W) + (1 - p)(Q_D - W).$$

The firm has a screen available that costs s, with accuracy q. That is, q equals the probability that the correct decision is made, while $1 - q$ equals the probability of a mistake.

$$\textit{Expected profit with screening} = p \cdot q(Q_E - W) + (1 - p)(1 - q)(Q_D - W) - s,$$

since a fraction $(1 - q)$ of E types are mistakenly rejected, and the same fraction of D types are mistakenly hired.

The change in profits from screening compared to not screening equals:

$$\Delta profit = -p(1 - q)(Q_E - W) - (1 - p)q(Q_D - W) - s.$$

The first term is negative. It is the loss from mistakenly rejecting candidates of type E. The second term is positive, since $Q_D < W$. It is the gain from appropriately rejecting D types. Of course, the third term is also negative.

That the test is more effective when it is more accurate, cheaper, or more discriminating follows immediately:

$$\frac{\partial \Delta profit}{\partial q} > 0; \quad \frac{\partial \Delta profit}{\partial s} < 0; \quad \frac{\partial \Delta profit}{\partial p} < 0.$$

The more negative the loss $Q_D - W$ from hiring the wrong type, the greater the gain from screening. Therefore, the test is more effective when the stakes are higher. The longer the wrong type remains employed at the firm, the larger this expression.

Signaling

We now incorporate signaling into the probation model described above. We show how the wage must be structured each period to ensure signaling. There are types E and D, as defined before. The firm offers W_1 and W_2 in two periods. In Period 1, workers are observed on the job. Those deemed to be good fits are promoted and paid W_2, while the rest are fired and earn their outside pay. The promotion decision is made with accuracy q as above.

The outside alternatives for each type are $W_E > W_D$. In assuming that there are different outside alternatives, we are taking a different tack than in the formal treatment of signaling in the chapter. In effect, we are assuming that while this firm may be able to induce self-selection of E types, we are begging the question about whether or not E types signal in other firms as well. This may not be the case. However, it seems reasonable to assume that E types can expect to have higher average earnings over their careers than D types through some means or another, since they have higher ability.

In order to deter D types, but attract E types, we must meet both of these conditions:

$$W_1 + (1 - q)W_2 + q \cdot W_D < 2 \cdot W_D$$
$$W_1 + q \cdot W_2 + (1 - q)W_E > 2 \cdot W_E$$

The first expression says that D types expect to do worse at this firm. The second says that E types expect to do better. A little algebra shows that this scheme can induce self-selection if:

$$W_1 < W_D + (1 - q)(W_D - W_2) < W_D$$
$$W_2 > W_E + (W_E - W_1)/q > W_E.$$

In fact, the optimal wages (that minimize compensation cost) are:[5]

$$W_1 = W_D - \left(\frac{1 - q^2}{2q - 1}\right)(W_E - W_D)$$

$$W_2 = W_E + \left(\frac{2 - q}{2q - 1}\right)(W_E - W_D).$$

---

[5]Technically, there are infinite optimal wage pairs. For example, the firm could subtract £1 from W_1 and add £1/(1 − q) to W_2. The wages provided here minimize the employee's spread in wages from W_1 to W_2 among the set of wage pairs that minimize the firm's compensation costs.

These imply that $W_1 < W_D < W_E < W_2$, of course, so the scheme involves *deferred pay*. By inspection of either of the last two sets of expressions, it is easy to see that:

- The more accurate the test (larger q), the larger W_1, and thus the smaller the bond posted by E types. Similarly, W_2, and thus the reward on promotion, is smaller the more accurate the test. Intuitively, a more accurate test makes E types more willing to accept a smaller reward for accepting the risk of signaling, since there is less chance of a mistake.
- The smaller W_D, the smaller W_1. The larger W_E, the larger W_2. Thus, the larger the differences in productivity between the two (reflected in their outside market values), the larger the reward on promotion.

3

INVESTMENT IN SKILLS

An investment in knowledge pays the best interest.
                                    —*Attributed to Benjamin Franklin*

INTRODUCTION

This chapter is about what you are doing *right now*: investing in skills and knowledge. Is Ben Franklin correct that this is a good investment for you? How can you tell? Should your employer pay for your education? Offer on the job training?

When asked about turnover, most firms express concern that they will lose their investments in employee skills. This suggests that they do offer some training, and would like to avoid turnover when they make such investments.

The data in Table 2.1 showed that turnover is high among Acme's new hires, but that many others stay for a relatively long time. One interpretation is that Acme sorts new hires through probation. Those who do not fit leave quickly, and those who do fit stay for a long time. But could long careers for some employees be a result of on the job training as well?

Another interesting finding was that Acme tends to promote from within. This too might be explained by sorting: Upper level positions are filled with current employees who have already passed the screen. In other words, new hires are more uncertain than internal candidates. Once again, though, could on the job training have anything to do with promotion from within?

Table 3.1 tests the idea that promotion from within is solely due to sorting. It compares the future performance of new hires and internal candidates that Acme uses to fill positions in Level 2. If internal candidates have already been sorted, we would expect less variation in their career performance after entering Level 2, compared to outside hires.

The data are consistent with our hypothesis (patterns are also similar in higher levels of Acme's hierarchy). For example, outside hires leave Acme with higher probability than do internal candidates. This is strong evidence that new hires still need to be sorted. Of those who stay, new hires are more likely to be demoted, and less likely to be promoted. However, when they are promoted, they advance further

TABLE 3.1

PERFORMANCE OF NEW HIRES AND PROMOTED EMPLOYEES AT ACME

			No. of years after entering Level 2				
			2	3	4	5	10
New hire into Level 2	Percent who left Acme		15.4	25.6	33.5	42.0	61.7
	Of those remaining at Acme . . .	Percent demoted	1.4	1.6	1.8	2.1	1.0
		Percent still at Level 2	79.4	51.5	39.7	33.3	22.0
		Percent promoted	19.2	46.9	58.5	64.6	77.0
		Average no. of levels promoted	1.0	1.0	1.7	1.4	1.8
Promoted to Level 2	Percent who left Acme		11.3	21.1	28.4	33.6	59.1
	Of those remaining at Acme . . .	Percent demoted	0.0	0.0	0.0	0.1	0.0
		Percent still at Level 2	84.2	49.7	32.1	23.7	8.6
		Percent promoted	15.8	50.3	67.9	76.2	91.4
		Average no. of levels promoted	1.0	1.0	1.1	1.3	1.6

on average than do internal candidates who are promoted. In other words, new hires are more likely to have extreme outcomes: demotion, exit, or rapid promotion. They are more variable in their value to Acme compared to those Acme hired at Level 1 and promoted to Level 2.

New hires may be valuable to Acme because they are risky and have an option value, as described in Chapter 1. But do they differ from Acme's internal candidates in other ways as well? Table 3.2 provides some evidence on this question, for outside and internal candidates in Levels 2–4. Acme's new hires tend to have about a half to one more year of education, and several more years of work experience, than those who are promoted to similar jobs from within Acme. In other words, their average education and experience is higher.

What can explain this observation? One possibility is that Acme is risk averse. In order to be willing to hire a risky candidate from the outside, Acme might require that their credentials be superior to those of internal candidates. However,

TABLE 3.2

HUMAN CAPITAL OF NEW HIRES AND PROMOTED EMPLOYEES AT ACME

		Level		
	Average years of . . .	2	3	4
New hire into level	Schooling	16.4	16.5	17.0
Promoted to level		15.7	16.1	16.5
New hire into level	Work experience	12.9	15.8	20.5
Promoted to level		12.3	14.0	16.2

even risk averse employers might well be willing to hire risky candidates because of their option value.

An alternative explanation is that employees who have been at Acme for a few years have a different advantage: They have been trained by Acme in ways that increase their productivity. If the training is specialized to Acme's business, outside hires would not have this knowledge. This would give internal candidates an advantage in filling job slots. If so, new hires would have to be better along other dimensions, like general work experience, in order to be considered for the job. Thus, some of the patterns that we are seeing may well be due to training.

Until this point we have assumed that workers have fixed talents, in order to analyze implications of sorting the workforce. We now add a new and important consideration: Workers learn over time, both through formal education and on the job. Moreover, the Acme data suggest that such training might improve a worker's productivity at the current employer more than at other firms, at least in some cases. Here we develop a framework for thinking about training overall, and how training might have different effects on productivity in one firm compared with others.

MATCHING

Before we consider investments in skills, there is another explanation for the career patterns we have seen that only involves sorting: *matching*. Suppose that, because every firm is different in its business, organization, and corporate culture, employees with similar abilities will not fit equally well at the same employer. If so, employees and firms need to seek out good matches with each other. Two employees of similar ability may be more productive in two different firms. Perhaps one firm has an aggressive culture that expects employees to work long hours and on weekends, and one worker is well suited to that environment while the other is not.

If such matching is important, workers must be sorted, just as when they differ in ability. However, the sorting would be based on whether or not a worker's attributes other than skills match well with a firm's (or job's, within a firm) attributes.[1] This would include factors such as the worker's portfolio of different skills, personality (and how it fits the company or workgroup's culture), or locational preference. These factors are much of what is meant when people talk about their fit with an organization.

Matching would imply high turnover early in the career, as workers and firms test the relationship to see if there is a good fit, and low turnover later. It might also imply that workers experience increases in pay once they are found to be a good fit, if pay rises after probation.

---

[1]Given this description, it should not be surprising that the metaphor of dating and marriage is often used by economists when analyzing the topics that we discuss in this chapter. In fact, similar principles have been employed by economists to study marriage and related topics.

Furthermore, this is just another form of sorting, so outside hires would have greater variance in employment outcomes than internal candidates. Finally, internally promoted candidates would, on average, have a better match with the firm than would outside hires, since internal candidates have already survived screening. This would put them at an advantage, which external candidates could overcome only if they had stronger credentials in other dimensions, such as more work experience or education.

The sorting story and its more subtle counterpart, matching, are based on the assumption that the employee's productivity does not change on the job. Nevertheless, people do acquire new skills through education and on the job training, so trying to explain career patterns without such considerations is unrealistic.

❖❖❖❖❖ INVESTMENTS IN EDUCATION

Economics, and increasingly the business world, view education and training as investments which can be modeled just like any other kind of investment. The analysis of investments of this kind is called *human capital* theory. It is such an important part of modern economics that two Nobel Prizes in economics were awarded, at least in part, in recognition of this theory.[2]

One argument stated earlier is that education does not provide any actual learning, but only signals about student's abilities. That view is farfetched. The human capital analysis of education provides a much more realistic way to think about education.

Human capital can be acquired in many ways. Examples include investments in exercise and healthcare. The two most important for our purposes are education or other pre-labor market training, and on the job training. Here we analyze education; in the next section we analyze on the job training.

In capital theory, investments are made if the *present value* of the cash flow or other benefits generated by the investment exceeds the present value of the costs of the investment.[3] Let us formalize our thinking. Suppose that an individual is choosing whether to drop out or finish college this year, which we will call Period 0. Future years will be denoted years $1 \ldots T$, where T is the last year of her career.

If the student drops out now, her earnings in future years will be H_t, where the subscript t refers to future periods. If she continues on in school, earnings in future years will be K_t. Given this, the increased earnings from finishing school are $K_t - H_t$ each year.

Education provides many benefits beyond increased earnings. One is the pure joy of learning. Education may also make you more effective at home or leisure

---

[2] Theodore Schultz (1979) and Gary Becker (1992).

[3] For those who are not familiar with the term, present value refers to the value, from today's point of view, of costs or revenues that accrue later. Income earned next year is worth less now, because you are not able to use the funds for a full year. Interest rates are the way that economies price cash flows in future periods. For example, if you invest $100 dollars today in a CD (certificate of deposit) earning 5% interest, it is equivalent to $105 next year. Put another way, the present value of $105 next year is $100.

activities, or increase your enjoyment of travel or literature. We focus on earnings because this is the most important benefit in the labor market. However, the arguments easily incorporate any nonpecuniary benefits from learning. If there are nonpecuniary benefits, their value should be included in K_t. They would simply increase the return on the investment, and should be included in any investment decision.

Suppose that the interest rate is r per year. This means that an investment of $1 made today would be worth $(1 + r)$ next year, $(1 + r)^2$ after two years, and so on. Similarly, $1 received next year is worth $1/(1+r)$ this year.

With these assumptions, the present value of the return on the education investment (again, focusing only on financial gains from education) is:

$$Return\ on\ education\ (present\ value) = \sum_{t=1}^{T} \frac{K_t - H_t}{(1 + r)^t}.$$

There are two costs of investments in education. The first is the direct cost of tuition, this textbook, supplies, etc. Denote this by C_0. The zero subscript calls attention to the fact that direct costs for training investments are generally borne up front and do not need to be discounted.

The second cost is the opportunity cost of the time spent on education. For example, typical (full time) MBA students quit relatively high-paying jobs to go back to school for 18 months. When they do, they give up salaries that in many cases are greater than the direct cost of tuition. Even part-time students can incur important opportunity costs: They give up evenings and weekends to study and attend classes, and have less leisure and vacation time than they would otherwise. If the student could work at home, on the farm, or in the family business, there would still be opportunity cost even if there is no salary. This is because the work has value to the family, and the family may need to pay to get someone else to do the work. Any proper analysis of an investment, including in training, should include opportunity costs in addition to direct costs.

Therefore we need to include the (additional) earnings that a student would receive if she were to drop out before completing college. If she stays in college, she will not receive those earnings. Let us call that F_0. The total cost of the remaining investment in college equals $C_0 + F_0$.

The decision rule for any investment is that it should be made as long as the present value of the return on the investment exceeds the present value of the cost of the investment. This *net present value* equals:

$$Net\ present\ value\ of\ investment\ in\ education = \sum_{t=1}^{T} \frac{K_t - H_t}{(1 + r)^t} - (C_0 + F_0) \qquad (3.1)$$

When the expression in Equation 3.1 is positive, finishing college is a good investment. When the expression is negative, college is not a good investment. Put another way, if the costs are larger than the increased income, she would be better off by dropping out of school, going to work, and investing the tuition cost C_0 and extra earnings F_0. The interest earned would exceed the increase in earnings by finishing school, in present value.

For early years of schooling, the returns to schooling exceed the costs. There are two reasons for this. First, there is much to be learned when an individual knows very little. A little bit of school can affect productivity dramatically, but gradually diminishing returns usually set in.

Second, the costs of going to school are very low during the early years of schooling. With public subsidies to education, direct costs C_0 are virtually zero up through high school or college in most societies. Furthermore, foregone earnings during the early years of schooling F_0 are very low (though they are not zero, because even children could work in a family business or in household production).

Eventually, however, the reverse must be true. Costs of schooling could exceed the (financial) returns. Consider an actual former executive MBA student of one of the authors. He had a college degree. He was both a doctor and a lawyer, each of which requires its own advanced degree. After earning his MBA, he decided to enroll in a PhD program. The extra degree was unlikely to improve his earnings, and would never allow him to recoup the direct and opportunity costs of the PhD. At that point, the educational benefits were purely consumption. In his case, the nonpecuniary benefits of education were very high.

This logic implies that it pays for almost everyone to invest in some formal education, but that there is also an optimal stopping point for each individual. The stopping point is the year when the net present value of investment in education calculated in Equation 3.1 switches from positive to negative.

Effects of Costs and Benefits

Equation 3.1 has several other implications that are borne out in practice.

Costs

Increases in tuition or other costs reduce enrollment. The reason for this is that any students who were close to the margin (net present value of education close to zero) will now find that the costs exceed the benefits.

A related point is that those who already have high-paying jobs will be reluctant to go back to school, all else equal. For this reason, universities and MBA programs generally have rising application rates when an economy is in recession, and falling application rates when the economy is doing well. Education is a better investment when your labor market opportunities are weaker, and vice versa, because this is the opportunity cost of schooling.

Interest Rates

Increases in interest rates mean lower optimal levels of schooling, just as with any investment in which the returns are realized in the future. The higher the interest rate, the more that future earnings are discounted from today's point of view.

That said, interest rates do not have dramatic effects on schooling decisions, for two reasons. One is that schooling is an investment with a long payout period, so long-term interest rates are more relevant than short-term rates, and they are generally less volatile. Moreover, the rate that is often important for schooling decisions is the implicit borrowing rate that parents charge their children to finance schooling. What parents extract in kind or through direct transfer from their children later (if anything) may not be closely tied to the interest rates that were in effect when the child was in school.

Career Length

An additional set of implications of Equation 3.1 involves the term T. The longer the work life, the larger the optimal investment in schooling. Thus, people are more likely to invest in schooling when they are young, because they expect to be able to enjoy the return on their investment for longer.

The same logic predicts that women will tend to invest less in schooling than men, even though women tend to have longer life expectancies than men: The average woman spends less time in the labor market than the average man, which reduces the return on investment in education.[4] This point can be extended. The primary reason that women tend to spend less of their career in the labor market is fertility. This often leads to careers that are interrupted for a few years, and then continued. Thus, women have some incentive to focus their education relatively more on occupations in which their skills depreciate less quickly over time.

Specialization of Human Capital

Most students eventually specialize their education, for example by focusing on a major area of study in college. Further education beyond college is usually even more specialized, with almost all classes focused on one field. Why is that the case? Education, like most investments, tends to have diminishing returns. That is, one more year of study in a particular field tends to have less impact on mastery of the field than did the previous year. This would seem to indicate that people should invest in a portfolio of skills rather than focus, to avoid the problem of diminishing returns. Indeed, we do, at lower levels of education. Almost all education systems require every student to develop a general education with a little knowledge of many different subjects. It is only at relatively advanced stages of knowledge, in education and on the job training, that specialization becomes important.

People generally specialize in advanced education because of one of the most important factors in an economy: *comparative advantage* and *gains from trade*. We already mentioned this idea in Chapter 1. If individuals focus on one area and become relatively expert, they can trade their output with those who specialize in other areas of expertise. We all benefit from the fact that advanced chemists develop

[4]Women reading this book are not likely to be very different from the men reading it, in terms of labor force behavior. Women who specialize in advanced fields have already made clear by their investment behavior that they plan to participate actively in the labor market. Furthermore, their high wages will help fuse them even more to the labor market.

new products and pharmaceuticals. They benefit from the fact that we specialize in other areas of work. Neither group has to learn about all topics.

In other words, it is usually true that the effective learning in one field gradually falls as more time is devoted to studying that field. However, the economy tends to reward relatively highly incremental advanced knowledge in many fields. Thus, it usually pays to specialize one's advanced education.

Specialization is an important issue inside firms, with implications for both organizational structure and job design. We will return to this topic in Chapters 6–7.

Effectiveness of Learning

The final set of implications revolves around differences in K. $K - H$ is the difference in earnings due to education. It depends on how much is learned, and how much those extra skills are valued by the labor market. When $K - H$ increases, the net present value of education rises and schooling should rise.

It seems plausible that those with more innate ability tend to learn more efficiently in school, leading to higher K. If so, the benefits of schooling are higher for those who are already highly talented, and smarter students should invest in more schooling.[5] Of course, this increases inequality in skills, and earnings, in the economy.

Improvements in school quality should have a positive effect on K, and vice versa. Technological innovation in education can be expected to increase investments in education by citizens. Similarly, changes in the effectiveness of teaching methods or quality of teachers (which could be positive or negative) change the returns to education investments.

An important factor is the level of technology associated with the average job. Although college education may be valuable to farmers, it is not likely to have as much value to a farmer as to an accountant. Education is complementary with a technologically advanced society. Being uneducated, unable to read, or unable to do simple mathematics is more of a hindrance in a society that has a majority of white-collar jobs than in a society of farmers. Thus, K and overall levels of education are higher in advanced societies than they were in 1900. This logic can also help explain current patterns of education across different societies, and trends in returns to education over the last several decades, which we describe now.

Was Benjamin Franklin Correct?

The quote at the beginning of this chapter suggests that education is a good investment. Generally, it is. Economists have estimated the *internal rate of return* (implied interest rate on the investment) from education in a variety of countries, and it is generally quite high. For example, most students reading this textbook are investing in college or an advanced degree. In the United States, Asia, or Europe, the rate of return on higher education is usually estimated to be about 11% per year

---

[5] This is one reason why education is a good credential.

FIGURE 3.1

RETURNS TO SKILLS, U.S.

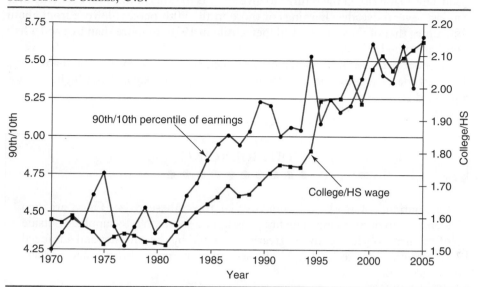

Source: Current Population Survey, Bureau of Labor Statistics.

or more. This tends to be better than the stock market, once we adjust for relative risk.

Not only is education a good investment, but it has become an even better one in recent decades. The labor market has valued skills more and more in recent years. Figure 3.1 illustrates this for the U.S. labor market. The series marked with circles (which uses the scale on the right) plots the ratio of average hourly wages for workers with a college degree, divided by average hourly wages for those with a high school education, over time. It shows a strong trend over the last three decades toward relatively higher earnings for those with a college degree. In 1970, college graduates earned about 50% more than high school graduates. By 2006, they earned more than twice as much. Similar patterns exist for more advanced degrees, such as an MBA or MD.

The series marked by diamonds (the left scale) shows a different measure of the value the labor market places on high skills. It was created by calculating the 10th and 90th percentiles of the distribution of hourly wages among U.S. workers each year. The 10th percentile is the wage level that 10% of U.S. workers earn less than; it is a measure of what relatively low-skilled workers are paid. The 90th percentile is the wage level that 90% of U.S. workers earn less than; it is a measure of what relatively high-skilled workers are paid. Comparing these two each year gives us an idea of how the distribution of overall pay has evolved over time. The figure plots the ratio, which shows how pay of relatively high skilled workers evolved compared to pay of relatively low skilled workers.

The pattern is quite similar to the college/high school comparison—there has been a dramatic rise in the returns to investments in skills in the U.S. economy over the last several decades. Earnings of those in the 90th percentile rose from about four times that of those in the 10th percentile in 1970, to more than five and a half times as much by 2006.

Similar patterns show up in most advanced economies world wide. If anything, some estimates suggest that returns to advanced skills may be even higher in less advanced economies.

OUTSOURCING

❖ ❖ ❖ ❖ ❖ ❖ ❖ ❖ ❖

Outsourcing of work is a controversial topic these days. There are two elements to outsourcing. The first is assigning some tasks to suppliers outside of the firm (obviously, this is greatly facilitated by the Internet and advanced communications technology). The second is the use of lower wage workers overseas.

In advanced economies, outsourcing has traditionally been focused on the lowest skilled jobs, such as manufacturing. In recent years, however, outsourcing of middle and even some highly skilled jobs has risen substantially. Many customer service centers now outsource work to call centers quite far away. Perhaps more interestingly, software engineering is now being outsourced in many cases, to places like India and Russia. In the 1980s, software engineering was a very prestigious and highly compensated occupation.

There are two reasons why outsourcing has crept into higher skilled jobs. One is that some of what used to be high skilled is actually not that highly skilled now. Modern software engineering techniques such as object-oriented software enable relatively low skilled programmers to develop more advanced applications than would have been possible 10 or 20 years ago.

The second reason is the high returns to skills. As any resource becomes expensive, buyers try to find other sources for the resource. Thus globalized labor markets, through outsourcing, temper the rising returns to skills in occupations for which outsourcing works well.

Figure 3.2 presents similar evidence for a more specific sample. It plots average earnings for U.S. engineers by level of responsibility. Level of responsibility was determined for a random sample of engineering jobs by professional analysts; think of it loosely as corresponding to how senior the engineer is in his or her firm. Thus,

FIGURE 3.2
SALARY OF ENGINEERS BY LEVEL OF RESPONSIBILITY

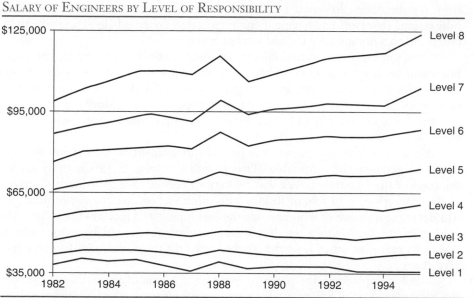

Source: Bureau of Labor Statistics

a Level 6 engineer has greater engineering or other valuable skills than a Level 5 engineer, and so on.

As can be seen, inflation-adjusted salaries have not changed much for lower level engineers in the last two decades. However, the relative pay of engineers at higher levels has increased markedly over the same period. Once again we see that more highly skilled workers are paid relatively more now than they were before.

Why has the labor market valued high skilled workers so much more than low skilled workers in the last few decades? Several explanations have been examined by researchers. The most important seems to be the increasing use of advanced technology, including computers, in the workplace. (We return to this issue in Section III.) As discussed in Chapter 1, capital tends to be complementary in production with a skilled workforce. Greater use of technology, and more effective technology, increases the value of having highly skilled workers. This increases the demand for skilled workers, which increases their labor market value.

INVESTMENTS IN ON THE JOB TRAINING

Let us now turn to on the job training. This investment is like education in many ways. It increases worker skills and raises productivity. This benefits both the employer and the worker. There may be direct costs (books or other resources, compensation for trainers, etc.). There may also be indirect costs, of two kinds.

First, formal on the job training may take the worker's time and attention away from regular duties, lowering productivity. Second, putting a worker who is not fully trained into a job, and having them learn as they do the job, lowers productivity compared to putting a fully trained worker in the job.[6]

Thus, the implications are similar to our discussion of investments in education. For example, firms and workers have an incentive to invest more in on the job training for younger workers, and younger workers will tend to be more interested in applying for jobs that offer extensive training opportunities. Since the investment is being made on the job, additional interesting implications arise, which are derived now.

We start by considering when a possible investment in on the job training would be economically profitable. That is, will the gains in productivity exceed the costs of the investment? We will distinguish between the gains in productivity in the worker's current job, or in jobs with other employers. For the moment we will defer the question of who pays for the investment and receives the return (the worker or the firm). Once we decide what investment should be made, we can return to the question of how the worker and firm might contract to make that investment.[7]

A real example from the personal experience of one of the authors illustrates the basic idea. A small Silicon Valley startup provides enterprise software that does tax optimization. A typical employee in this company must know something about tax laws, as well as programming in Java. This is an unusual combination of skills. There are many firms that value both skills independently. However, few other employers would value an employee with the same combination of expertise in tax law and Java as this firm.

Therefore, an employee who leaves the startup will have a difficult time finding a firm that can make use of all of the skills that he acquired in the first firm. The second job will value one of the skills, and perhaps even both, but not to the same extent or in the same proportion.

A similar question faces you in your job. To what extent should you invest in skills and knowledge that help you in this job and a career in this firm? To what extent should you instead invest in training that would improve your job prospects in the outside labor market?

Consider an employee at the startup whose current productivity (in Period 0) equals $10,000 per month. Imagine three options for on the job training, outlined in Table 3.3. One focuses completely on Java, another completely on tax, and a third splits the training time between the two in proportion to how the employer values those skills in this job. (These are meant to illustrate the general points. Of course, there are many possible ways to mix the training.) Assume that the

---

[6]However, this ignores the potential effects on intrinsic motivation and continuous improvement that we discuss in Chapter 7.

[7]For students of economics, this is an application of coase theorem logic. We first focus on how economic value can be created. Only after that do we consider how this value is split between the worker and the firm. Of course, this approach will not work if there are bargaining costs, as we will see.

TABLE 3.3
RETURNS ON INVESTMENTS IN JAVA AND TAX SKILLS

	Task	Potential increase in productivity	Stay		Leave	
			Weight (%)	Value of training	Weight (%)	Value of training
100% Java	Java	8	40	3.2	80	6.4
	Tax	0	60	0	20	0
				3.2		**6.4**
40% Java,	Java	4	40	1.6	80	3.2
60% Tax	Tax	6	60	3.6	20	1.2
				5.2		4.4
100% Tax	Java	0	40	0	80	0
	Tax	8	60	4.8	20	1.6
				4.8		1.6

total costs of training (both direct costs and indirect through lost productivity while training) are the same for all three choices, $5,000; only the fraction of training time spent on Java or tax varies. Ignore discounting, just to keep things simple.

For example, consider the first option, which raises the employee's proficiency in Java. If he worked only on Java projects, productivity would rise by $8,000 per month. However, in this firm he does not spend all of his time on Java. Instead, his job involves spending about 40% of his time on Java, so productivity would rise by only $3,200. His productivity on tax-related tasks would not change, since he receives no tax training.

How would the training affect his productivity if he were to find a job at a new firm? That depends on the kind of job that he can find elsewhere. Since the combination of Java skills and knowledge of tax law is quite unusual, and Java skills are more highly sought after in Silicon Valley than tax skills, it is more likely that the best job he could find elsewhere would also emphasize Java. However, even if a new job is 100% Java programming, it probably involves a focus on somewhat different Java techniques than the ones he emphasized in the training offered by the tax software startup. After all, the on the job training will probably focus on how he can program the tax software more effectively.

Therefore, it is unlikely that he can get the full benefit of the Java training in some other job, though he may be able to come close. Assume that the Java training would have about 80% as much effect in a new job as it would in his current job, so that his productivity in an alternative job would rise by $6,400 on average.

Now consider the opposite type of training, which emphasizes only tax. This would raise his productivity at tax-related tasks by $8,000 per month. However, in his current job, he spends about 60% of his time on such work, so productivity would rise by $4,800. If another job that he might find is likely to emphasize tax work only about 20% of the time, the training would raise his productivity at other jobs by about $1,600 per month on average.

The third alternative is to spend some of his time on each form of training. In this example, we assume that the training is more effective if he does a little bit of both kinds, so that the total increase in productivity would be $5,000 for each skill, or $10,000 total per month. The reason for this is the familiar idea of diminishing marginal productivity: the more that you focus your study on one topic, the less you learn with each new hour of study. However, this assumption is not important for the conclusions.

If he obtains mixed training, productivity rises in both tasks. Total productivity rises by $5,200, more with his current firm than in the outside market. That is because the training is designed to match his current job's skill mix, *not* the average skill mix required by the labor market.

Our question to answer: What is the best on the job training for this employee? The answer depends on where he is most likely to be employed after the training, because the jobs emphasize the two skills differently. The optimal investment maximizes expected productivity. If he expects to stay at the current firm, he should train in both tax law and Java programming. If he expects to quit this firm, he should focus only on Java. The answer depends on the likelihood that he will switch firms.

Suppose that he believes that there is some chance that he will stay with the current firm, but also some chance that he will leave (or his firm will go bankrupt, etc.). What is the best kind of training then? If the odds that he will stay with this firm are high, it is a mix of tax and Java programming. If the odds that he will leave are high, it is 100% Java programming.

This illustrates a very natural way to think about investments in skills on the job. The optimal skills for you to invest in will be quite different if you expect to stay with your current firm for a long time, or if you expect to leave. If you expect to stay at the current firm, your best strategy will be one that focuses training on the skills that your employer values the most. If you expect to leave, your best strategy is to invest in skills that the *labor market* values the most.

General vs. Firm-Specific Human Capital

In our discussion of the programmer, Java and tax skills had value with both the current employer and other employers. However, the value of the skills learned on the job was more valuable with the current employer than elsewhere. There are two extreme possibilities: The training is equally valuable inside and outside the firm, or it has no value at all outside the firm. These two cases are often called *general human capital* (GHC) and *firm-specific human capital*. Most training falls somewhere in between, as in the example.

General human capital is skills or knowledge that a worker can acquire that raise productivity *equally* at both the current employer, and with many other employers. In other words, there is a thick labor market for the skills. Most skills are closer to this type. An MBA is GHC because the ability to be a good manager has value to thousands of possible employers. Knowledge of a foreign language such as Mandarin would be another example. A good rule of thumb is that most skills that you can acquire outside of the workplace, such as at a university, are general human capital.

Firm-specific human capital (FHC) is the opposite of general human capital: It raises productivity at your current employer, but does *not* raise your value to other firms at all. It is more difficult to come up with examples of purely firm-specific human capital. Most knowledge that improves your productivity at one firm is very likely to help you in at least *some* other jobs at *some* other employers. Nevertheless, there are some examples of training that is largely firm specific in value. If your firm has an unusual machine that they have designed for their own use, knowledge of how to operate the machine raises your productivity in this job, but would be of no value if you switched employers. Any idiosyncratic process or method might be firm-specific human capital.

Many examples of training that is more firm specific involve intangible knowledge. If your firm has a strong and unusual corporate culture, knowledge of the culture helps you in this job, but is probably useless elsewhere. An understanding of informal networks and power relationships inside your firm is quite similar. Finally, if you have developed close working relationships with clients, and deep knowledge of their particular organizations, that may be primarily firm-specific human capital—unless you can get a job with your client, or take your clients with you to a new job.

As our discussion of the Java programmer illustrates, however, the concepts of general and firm-specific human capital are usually not clearcut in practice. Many skills have a value both inside and outside the firm, though the values may be different. For example, knowledge of Java raises productivity somewhat more in the current job compared to alternative jobs. To the extent that it raises productivity equally inside and outside the firm, it is more like general human capital. To the extent that it raises productivity more inside the firm, it is more like firm-specific human capital.

A better way to think about this distinction is to ask whether the value that the employer places on the employee's training is relatively idiosyncratic or not. To the extent that the firm values the worker's particular portfolio of skills similarly to other firms, that set of skills is largely general human capital. By contrast, to the extent that the employer values a set of skills idiosyncratically, the skills are largely firm-specific human capital. The startup's desired skill mix of Java and tax knowledge is quite unusual. Therefore, on the job training at that firm is more specific to that firm and less general. This distinction will be useful shortly when we consider who pays for the training.

Special Case: Intellectual Property

Suppose that you are a research chemist. Your firm provides you with a very expensive lab, supplies and equipment, and lab staff. These resources are superior to those that you could use in other jobs that are available to you. They require that you do research in a particular, obscure type of polymers that few other labs are studying, because they already have special expertise in manufacturing products that use this type of polymer. Is your investment in learning about this obscure type of polymer more like general human capital, or more like firm-specific human capital?

At first glance it would appear that this investment is largely firm specific, because you and your employer probably shared the costs of investing in the intellectual property. Your relatively obscure skills may be less valuable in any other job that you can get. Moreover, your employer may have required that you agree to grant all patent rights to the firm, so that you cannot take any of your patents with you if you leave.

However, in some ways the investment is more like general human capital, because you may be able to take some of the benefits with you to a new employer. In general it is very difficult to fully assign the intellectual property rights to the employer. Even if you cannot take any patents with you, you may be able to take many of the insights and ideas, and they may be valuable to competing firms.

In other words, intellectual property has elements of both general and firm-specific investing. Like firm-specific human capital, it is typically a shared investment, with the hope of a shared benefit. The intellectual property often has a higher value if the employee stays at the current firm, since the skills and knowledge were designed to match with that firm's strategy. Therefore both have an incentive to try to maintain the working relationship. But like general human capital, the worker may be able to capture some of the benefits by quitting and going to a competing firm.

NONCOMPETE AGREEMENTS
⬢ ⬢ ⬢ ⬢ ⬢ ⬢ ⬢ ⬢ ⬢

Firm-specific investments, particularly intellectual property, sometimes cause firms to include employee noncompete agreements in employment contracts. These agreements attempt to prevent an employee from taking intellectual property with them if they quit the firm. Such agreements try to restrict the employee's next job in some way, typically for one year after quitting. Examples are clauses that state that the employee cannot work in a very similar job with a competitor, or cannot take clients to the new employer for one year.

Noncompete agreements are often quite difficult to enforce in court. Most courts frown on them, because of the longstanding principle (since the abandonment of practices like indentured servitude or slavery) that people should be free to work for whomever they wish. In order to make a noncompete agreement more likely to be enforced, the firm should make sure that the restrictive clauses are not too onerous, and do not last for too long a period.

Some courts have also imposed a requirement that employees be compensated in some way for signing a noncompete agreement. In fact, this may be necessary and appropriate, if an agreement is added to the employment contract of an existing employee after hiring, because the agreement reduces the value of the job to the employee.

Possible clauses.   Some clauses that courts are more likely to approve:

- Require that the employee give adequate notice and describe their new job duties before leaving, so that the firm has time to react
- Require that the employee train his or her successor and introduce them to important clients before they leave
- Prohibit the employee from recruiting colleagues to leave with him
- Require that some benefits vest gradually after the employee quits, contingent on the former employee acting in accordance with the noncompete agreement

Alternative approaches.   To the extent that noncompete agreements and legal property rights do not fully protect against an employee quitting and taking intellectual property with them, the firm has several options to improve matters. First, pay for performance, especially if tied to the value of the intellectual property that the employee is developing, can better align incentives. It not only motivates the employee to stay, but to increase the intellectual property's value. Second, the firm might offer deferred pay, rewarding the employee for remaining with the firm. Conceivably, the firm might even offer to pay bonuses to employees a year or two after they have left the firm, as a reward for not competing with the firm in their new job. However, such an approach would seem to have practical limitations.

Who Should Pay for Training?

Who will pay for, and benefit from, training investments? We will consider two cases: education, and on the job training. Education is general human capital, while on the job training can be either general or firm-specific human capital. The conclusion is straightforward in the case of general human capital: The worker should pay for these investments. The case of specific human capital is more complex.

Education

Some part-time students have employers who pay for their schooling. Is this a good investment for the employer? In general the answer has to be no: Most academic training has wide applicability at many different employers. This makes it general human capital. Imagine, for example, that a firm pays for our student considering finishing her college degree. Once she earns the credential, her market value will rise. In order to keep this employee, the firm will have to raise her salary. In other words, the employer is highly unlikely to capture most of the benefits from the schooling investment. By contrast, the employee almost certainly will enjoy most of the benefits from the schooling. For the rest of her career, her earnings will tend to be higher.

For this reason, it almost never makes sense for an employer to pay for schooling. Instead, the typical solution is for individuals (or their families) to pay for schooling, and to invest in it before entering the labor market if possible. The vast majority of students do not have their tuition paid for by an employer.

That said, some students do have part or all of their tuition paid for by their employer. These are the exceptions that prove the rule. However, it is worth briefly trying to explain these exceptions as well. There are several reasons why a firm might pay some of the tuition costs of some employees.

Implicit cost to employee and benefit to employer. It is possible that the employee is, in fact, paying for the tuition, by accepting lower salary at the job in order to get access to the tuition benefits. In fact, it is not unusual to see employers impose a contractual obligation on employees to pay back the tuition if they quit the firm within a few years of graduation. This cost of quitting makes it possible for the firm to capture some of the benefits of the investment, by paying the employee less than market value for a few years once they are educated.

Matching. If the firm offers the tuition benefit only to a few select employees, an explanation might be that these employees are a strong match for this employer. The firm expects that these employees will stay at the firm for many years, and may wish to groom them for key positions. In such a case, the firm can expect to recoup some of the benefits of the schooling if the worker has some incentive to stay with the firm. Essentially, the firm and the employee split the profits from the investment in education. This is similar to our conclusion for firm-specific human capital later. However, the specificity is not in skills, but in the match.

Recruiting. We discuss benefits in Chapter 13. Briefly, offering a certain benefit may generate useful self-selection in recruiting. UPS, for example, offers tuition reimbursement to its employees. Most of them do not attend expensive universities, so the program may not be very costly. A benefit may be that UPS attracts a harder working, more ambitious workforce. Another benefit is that the workforce will tend to be young, and UPS needs employees that can haul heavy packages as part of the job.

Arbitrage. If there are tax benefits to paying for education or training, the firm might have a cost advantage in paying for schooling compared to the employee.

Other than these kinds of unusual cases, in general firms do not, and should not, pay for investments in education of their workforce. Note that this is the same logic that we used in the previous two chapters, when thinking about risky hires, screening, and signaling. The firm always faces pressure to match an employee's outside market value. Anything that raises the outside value will tend to force the firm to raise compensation. Education and general human capital are two important examples.

This is why firms generally do not run extensive formal education programs; rather, schools are organized as independent institutions. The Control Data Institute example illustrates this nicely. Wipro Technologies provides a contrasting approach that is not likely to work in most countries.

CONTROL DATA INSTITUTE

Control Data Corporation was one of the first builders of supercomputers. In the 1960s, their computers were some of the fastest in the world. In 1965, they established a division called the Control Data Institute to train operators for their computers. CDI provided some of the best training in the industry, which is not surprising since CDC built the computers the training was for.

CDC found that a substantial fraction of employees who had trained at CDI quit to work for competitors or clients. That is because the training was largely general human capital, since it had wide applicability in the labor market. In 1989, Control Data decided to spin off the Control Data Institute as an independent training company.

WIPRO TECHNOLOGIES

Due to explosive growth in technology companies and extensive on the job training in software design, which is largely general human capital, Indian software companies find it very difficult to retain employees. Most require new hires to sign contracts pledging that they will stay with the company for a specified period of time. Wipro Technologies in Bangalore takes that a step further.

Wipro requires that new hires provide a deposit of Rs 75,000 (Indian rupees; Rs 75,000 equals about $1,400) before they can receive their employment letters. The money is deposited in a bank. Employees who are unable to place the deposit may borrow it from the bank.

The deposit, with any interest earned, is refundable to engineering employees who work for Wipro for at least 12 months after completing Wipro's 3-month training program. Employees with science degrees are given 6 months of training, and are required to work for Wipro for 18 months before their deposit is returned.

Wipro reports that this program has not adversely affected its ability to recruit on college campuses.

Source: rediff.com, January 22, 2005

On the Job Training

General human capital. Now think about who pays for on the job training. Consider first the extreme case where the skills are pure general human capital. That is, the new training is valued equally by both *other employers* and the current employer. In this case, the logic is the same as for education investments. When the worker gets the training, his or her market value rises. The firm will thus have to pay the worker a higher salary once the training is completed, or risk having the worker quit. For this reason, the general rule is that *if skills are completely general human capital, the worker should pay for 100% of the investment, and receive 100% of the benefits.*

Human capital that is partly or fully firm specific. The more realistic case is where on the job training is valued differently (and more) by the present employer than by the labor market. Our programmer investing in Java or tax skills is one such example. In that case, the worker's outside value is lower than his inside value after the training, even though the labor market does value the training. Most on the job training has this flavor; it tends to be at least somewhat focused toward the current job's skill requirements. What happens in this case?

To think about this, consider the investment for our software programmer as graphed in Figure 3.3. Assume that the probability that he will stay at the current firm is high enough that the best investment choice is the middle option, which provides training in both Java and tax laws. There are two periods, training and post training, and we have kept things simple by ignoring discounting. If the worker gets no training, productivity is $H = \$10,000$ per month, the dashed line, in both periods.

If he receives the training, it costs $\$5,000$ in direct and indirect costs $(C + F)$ during the first period. Thus, his net productivity will be $H - C - F = \$5,000$. This is represented by the solid line during the training period. The cost of the training is represented by the shaded area between the dashed line and the solid line during that period.

After the training is received, the worker's productivity rises to $\$15,200$ at his current firm: it rises to $\$14,400$ in the labor market as a whole. These figures are calculated as the initial productivity, $\$10,000$, plus the increase due to training. In Figure 3.3, these two productivities are the solid lines above the dashed line in the

FIGURE 3.3

INVESTING IN GENERAL HUMAN CAPITAL

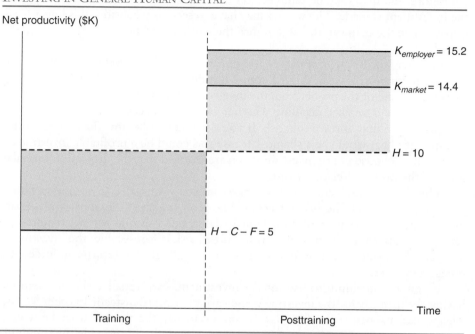

post-training period. The return on the investment if the worker *leaves* the firm is represented by the lighter shaded area between the solid line at $14,400 and the dashed line at $10,000. The return on the investment if the worker *stays* at the firm is represented by that area *plus* the darker shaded area above it: It is the total area between the solid line at $15,200 and the dashed line. Because the return on the education investment is larger if he stays, this investment is somewhat specific to this firm.

This is a profitable investment for the firm only if there is strong reason to believe that he will stay at this firm. There is an incentive for the worker and the firm to figure out a way to make this investment, and have the worker stay at this firm in the second period.

Suppose that, like education and purely general human capital, the worker pays for the investment, expecting to earn the returns in the second period. In other words, assume that the firm agrees to pay the worker a salary equal to his productivity in both periods. Under that contract, the firm earns no profit or loss in either period. In the first period, the worker suffers a loss (pay is $5,000 less than he could earn elsewhere). However, in the second period he earns a profit (pay is $5,200 more than he could earn elsewhere).

Consider the situation *after* the investment is made (so that it is now a sunk cost). What might the firm do now? If it pays $15,200, it pays more than it has to, to keep the employee. The employee can only earn about $14,400 elsewhere. Therefore, the firm may be tempted to only pay a little more than $14,400 after the investment is made. The worker may have to seriously consider this lower level of pay, since the firm can threaten to fire the worker, and he can only get $14,400 elsewhere.

In other words, *the firm may be tempted to renege on its promise, and renegotiate after the investment is made.* Why? Because if it does pay less than $15,200 it is able to capture some of the profits from the investment that the worker made!

If you are a worker deciding whether or not to accept the contract in the first place, you may foresee this risk. If you do, you will be unwilling to make the investment. That would be a shame, because this could be a profitable investment. Yet you may choose not to invest since you are worried that the firm will try to take some of the profits after you invest.

This is a general concern that arises in many investment contexts, which economists often call the *holdup problem.* The problem arises if one party makes an investment and expects to earn the benefits later, but a second party is tempted to renegotiate after the investment is made. If this risk is foreseeable, the investment may not be made, for fear of losing some or all of the returns if forced to renegotiate later.

If you are unwilling to pay for the investment, can we solve the problem by having the firm pay for the investment and earn the reward instead? In other words, what would happen if the firm agreed simply to pay the worker what he would get if there were no investment ($10,000 in each period), but provide the training? Then the firm would pay the cost, since productivity would be less than pay during training. The firm would also capture the benefits, since productivity would be higher than pay after training.

You can already answer this for yourself: It runs the same risk of renegotiation. Once the investment is made, the employee may be tempted to try to renegotiate pay that is higher than $10,000. After all, his market value has risen to $14,400, so there he can credibly threaten to quit. Moreover, his value to this employer is $15,200, so he might even ask for pay that is close to that amount. The firm will be tempted to negotiate with him, since they would lose $5,200 in profits if he left. But if they do, the employee will get some of the profits from the firm's investment!

No matter who makes the investment and hopes for the return, the other side has an incentive to break its promise and try to renegotiate after the training has been paid for. The investor may be forced to renegotiate, because if the relationship is severed, the investor has more to lose. Unfortunately, this *renegotiation risk* will lower the expected returns on the investment, possibly to the point where neither is willing to make the investment.

How can we solve this problem? There are two possibilities. One is to rely on the trustworthiness of one or both parties; we discuss that below and in Chapter 15. A second is to *split the cost and the return* on the investment. An example of how to do so is shown in Figure 3.4. In this case, the costs are split by paying a wage W_1 during training that is somewhere between actual net productivity and what the worker could get elsewhere (if the split is 50–50, $W_1 = 7.5$). Splitting the costs

FIGURE 3.4

INVESTING IN FIRM-SPECIFIC HUMAN CAPITAL

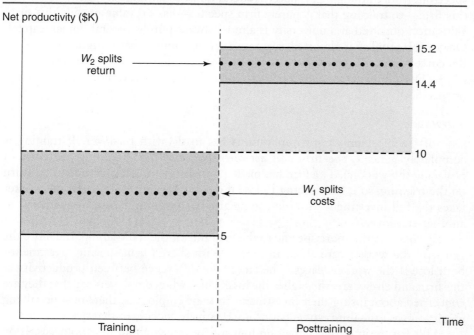

reduces the risk of the investment in the first period, since there is less to lose. The benefits would then be split by setting W_2 after training somewhere between what the worker could earn elsewhere, and actual productivity (if 50–50, $W_2 = 14.8$). Splitting the benefits reduces (though it does not eliminate) the temptation to renegotiate. Moreover, since both would have something to lose if the relationship were broken, both have some incentive to avoid renegotiation.

Therefore, investments in on the job training that are specific to the firm are likely to be made differently than investments that are purely general human capital, or education: they are likely to be split by the worker and the firm. This means that pay would be less than the worker could earn elsewhere, but greater than net productivity, during the investment period. Pay would then be greater than the worker could earn elsewhere, but less than productivity, after the training was complete.

Implications of On the Job Training

On the job training has a number of important implications for the employment relationship. Now that we have analyzed the investment, and considered who pays for it and receives the return, we develop these implications.

Before we delve into these, remember that on the job training will vary along a spectrum from training that is purely general—has equal value at other jobs outside this firm—to training that is purely firm specific—has no value outside this firm. Education obtained at a university is almost always purely general human capital. On the job training is almost always a mix. Even training that is highly focused on the current job will tend to benefit the employee if they leave the firm, just not as much. Therefore, we will talk about training as being relatively more or less general or specific.

Turnover

One of the most important implications has to do with turnover. If training is completely general, the firm *does not care about turnover* (ignoring the costs of replacing the worker). The firm has made no investment, and is earning no return on the training, so it has nothing to lose if the worker quits. Similarly, the worker takes the full investment with him, so he also has nothing to lose by switching to another employer.

By contrast, the more specific to the firm the on the job training, the more the firm and the worker care about turnover. With shared firm-specific investments, both lose if the worker leaves. The larger the difference between productivity at this firm and elsewhere, the higher the loss. Thus, when employers say that they are concerned about losing their investments in their employees, they must be talking about human capital investments that are relatively specific to that firm.

This has an important effect on how a firm thinks about its employees. If on the job training is general or not important in the firm, then, excepting sorting considerations, employees are largely hired through spot-market type transactions. However, once specific investments play a role, a *relationship* arises between the worker and the firm. Both have some incentive to invest in and maintain the relationship. The term that is often used for this is that such firms emphasize *internal labor markets*. The more idiosyncratic the skill mix that a particular firm requires of its workforce, the more this view of employment becomes important. These ideas are discussed further in Chapter 15.

Investment

The lower the turnover in a firm, the more workers tend to invest in a mix of skills that is a strong fit for the current job and employer. The higher the turnover, the more workers tend to invest in skills that can be easily applied at other firms. Thus, firms that desire an unusual mix of skills will generally adopt policies to try to reduce turnover.

Investment patterns should change with tenure. The longer an employee has been with the firm, the more likely she is to have already invested in skills that are closely matched to that firm. This increases incentive to stay with this employer. That reinforces the tendency to invest even more in firm-specific skills. Thus, as job tenure rises, workers tend to become even more invested in their current employer.

Compensation

These ideas have implications for compensation patterns. First, pay will tend to rise with one's labor market experience, because most jobs provide some on the job training. Second, beyond this effect of total experience on earnings, those who have higher tenure in a firm will tend to have higher pay than those who do not, because their skills will tend to be more heavily oriented toward the mix that is appropriate for that firm, and because they will be earning some returns on their prior investments in firm-specific skills.

Third, the more firm-specific the employee skills, the more pay they tend to lose if they switch jobs, because the skills will be more tuned to the current job instead of a potential new job. The higher the expected loss in compensation from leaving the firm, the lower the likelihood that the employee will leave the firm. This is because workers tend to invest more in skills that are specific to their current employer, the more that they expect to stay in that job.

Labor Market Thickness

Labor markets are sometimes characterized as thick or thin. A thick market is one in which the worker finds it relatively easy to get a new job that values his or her skills well. A thin market is the opposite. To some extent, the thickness of the labor market depends on the occupation of the worker. There are many more jobs for lawyers than for academic economists in most cities. Thickness also depends on the business cycle. If an economy is in recession, few firms are hiring, so it is more difficult to obtain a job offer with pay similar to one's current job. The opposite tends to be true when the economy is improving, especially at the beginning of an upturn. Thickness is affected by the size of the local economy, if there are costs to the worker of moving elsewhere for employment.

Finally, thickness also depends on the employee's skill mix; the more idiosyncratic the skill mix, the thinner the labor market for that particular employee. This logic illustrates that the concept of general vs. firm-specific human capital is endogenous: It depends on how thick the labor market is. In markets that are thicker, all else equal, a worker's skills tend to be less firm specific.

Firm Size

Workers in larger firms will tend to invest more heavily in a mix of skills that is specific to their employer, for two reasons. First, empirically larger firms tend to have lower turnover than smaller firms. Second, larger firms are more likely to be able to find alternative work for their employees who wish to change jobs. In fact, very large firms sometimes have relatively formal internal labor markets, in which the human resources department actively posts jobs and searches for internal candidates to fill open positions. To the extent that the skill mix is similar across jobs in the same firm, this in effect thickens the market for an employee's skills when they work for a larger firm.

●●●●● ## RENT SHARING AND COMPENSATION

The concepts of education investments and signaling allow us now to briefly discuss the overall level of compensation. By compensation, we mean cash and other benefits paid to the employee. Benefits have value to the employee, so an employee will be willing to accept some amount of lower salary in exchange for a given benefit.

How is the overall level of compensation determined? Abstractly, perfect competition between firms should imply that firms earn zero profits on their employees. This does not mean that they do not earn accounting profits, shareholder returns, and so on. It only means that the level of accounting profit that they earn from hiring employees is about the same as that earned by other employers.

Similarly, perfect competition between employees should imply that employees earn about the same at any firm.

When these two conditions hold, an employee and a firm would be largely indifferent about who they work for, who they hire, and turnover. This is analogous to the case of pure general human capital investments. The level of compensation would be the same at firms that have similar jobs, and would just equal the marginal value of the worker's output to the firm.

Obviously, this is not realistic, but it is a useful theoretical base case. In reality, of course, workers do tend to lose earnings if they switch employers. And employers usually do not want to lose most of their employees. These observations suggest that both are earning some profits (in formal economics lingo, *rent*) from working with each other, compared with working with another employee or employer. This raises two questions. First, what are the sources of these rents? Second, do they imply that labor markets are not perfectly competitive?

In this chapter we have seen two reasons why a worker and firm might earn some extra profit if the worker stays at this firm. The first was matching: If a worker is, for any reason, a particularly good fit for one employer, then there is some benefit to the employee staying at that firm. That is, in effect, a violation of perfect competition, because it implies that either the worker or the firm cannot find a perfect substitute for their employer or employee. In that case, some monopoly profits would be accruing.

Firm-specific human capital is the second condition in which a worker and firm generate extra profits if they stay together. However, in this case labor markets can still be perfectly competitive for both workers and firms. The bidding would occur at the time the initial job offer is negotiated. For example, firms might compete with each other over the training opportunities that are offered to job applicants. Job applicants might compete with each other over the salaries or other job aspects that they are willing to accept from a given employer. Once the firm-specific investment is made, there is some profit from working together. However, there can be competition over the terms of the total investment.

There are other reasons why a worker and/or a firm might enjoy some rent for working with each other. For example, either party may have expended resources searching for a job or a new employee. Finding a new job or replacing the existing worker would be costly. Therefore, there is something to lose from ending this employment relationship, for both. This is quite analogous to matching and firm-specific human capital. Again, the profits from search and recruiting might be driven to zero by competition. These are another investment, similar to signaling and training. Once the costs are incurred and the job match is found, the return on the investment is earned. If search or recruitment costs are high, this would be another reason that there is some surplus for the worker and the firm to share, once they have agreed to work together.

The important word here is *sharing*. In cases where there are some rents or joint surplus to be earned from working together, there arises a question of how those rents will be shared between the worker and the firm. As we have seen, these rents are largely split *at the time of hiring*, when the explicit and implicit contractual terms are determined. How the rents are split depends on the outcome of this negotiation. That will depend to some extent on the bargaining sophistication of the worker and the firm. It will also depend on some economic factors that we have already seen.

One consideration for how the costs and benefits are shared is to improve incentives for either side to take the right action. Workers generally pay for signals, to motivate their efficient self-selection in applying for jobs. By contrast, both share specific investments, to reduce incentives to renegotiate later.

Another consideration is the bargaining power of each side. If there is a lot of competition between firms, employees will tend to capture a larger share of any potential profits. If there are many workers who are very similar, employers may be able to capture a larger share of any profits, because the workers will compete with each other.

A third consideration is the reputation of each party; we discuss this briefly below, and more extensively in Chapter 15.

The main point of this section is that there are several reasons why, once employees and firms decide to work together, they may want to keep working together. These are sometimes referred to by terms such as rents, quasi-rents, or surplus. They affect incentives for turnover and complex employment contracting. They also mean that the overall level of compensation will often be somewhat indeterminate, since it will depend on a complicated bargain struck between the worker and the firm.

In some cases in later chapters, we will assume that labor markets are perfectly competitive to illustrate the arguments. In no case does this assumption really matter. It is merely a simplification to make the arguments more straightforward. When you see those cases, you can imagine that there may be other sources of surplus for the worker and the firm, and if so there may be some kind of bargain that splits the surplus between them.

●●●●● ## Implicit Contracting

On the job training investments that are relatively specific to one's current employer, and intellectual property, are special cases of a more general phenomenon. Any time that two parties can make an investment that creates profits *only* if the parties continue to work together, we have a *relationship-specific investment*. This issue arises in many contexts in the business world. Consider two firms that have a joint venture with each other. If they discontinue the relationship, profits from the joint venture are lost. Similarly, two partners who start a firm together also engage in a relationship-specific investment as they build the firm (if the firm has more value as long as they stay together).

Our analysis of training that is more firm specific concluded that the firm and employee will share the investment. Splitting the benefits reduces the risk of the holdup problem, which may happen after one party makes an investment hoping to earn benefits later, but the second party tries to renegotiate after the investment is made. Unfortunately, this problem cannot be completely eliminated by splitting the benefits.

We saw a similar issue in Chapter 2 caused by lack of trust. Probation periods involve a promise by the firm to give the job applicant pay higher than productivity after probation, as a way to motivate self-selection. This means that the firm might suffer a loss on the employee after probation.[8] What we did not discuss then is the concern that the firm might be tempted to renege on its promise to employees once they have been sorted. If there is a nontrivial chance that this might occur, high ability workers would be unwilling to apply for the job in the first place.

Thus, we have another situation where holdup concerns might prevent our solution from working properly. This concern can arise in any situation where there is a relationship-specific investment. Is there anything that we can do to reduce holdup problems?

In the case of a joint venture, there is a direct solution: The two firms can merge. Once they merge, they have no conflict of interest, and the investment will be made.[9] Obviously, merger is not possible in the case of employment, so this is of little help for on the job training.

An alternative is to write a formal contract specifying what the firm and employee pay or receive under all circumstances (e.g., severance pay, or noncompete agreements). This could be used to give both incentives to not break their promises.

---

[8]Not necessarily an accounting loss, but an economic loss. They would be paying the employee more than would be paid to employees of similar productivity at other firms that did not use such a probation system.

[9]The example of Fisher Body Works is a staple of MBA strategy courses. The story is that General Motors wanted FBW to build a factory specialized to work with GM–a relationship-specific investment. In order to solve the holdup problem, GM eventually bought FBW. Apparently most of these facts are incorrect, and the overall story is a fable (Casadesus-Masanell & Spulber, 2000). Nevertheless it does illustrate how a merger can solve the problem.

A related approach is to rely on government regulations or common law. In most economies, employment is highly regulated. Some of these regulations may protect either the firm or (more likely) the employee from attempts at renegotiation. For example, in most societies firms do not have complete control over the management of employee pension funds. This reduces the risk to employees that earnings they are promised now will be taken away later.

Unfortunately, the employment relationship is so complex and unpredictable that it is usually impossible to write a contract, design a law, or make a judicial ruling that can cover all possible contingencies. What else can be done?

An important way to reduce holdup problems is to rely on *implicit contracting*. In our examples, the firm in effect promises employees that they will be rewarded later if they perform well or invest in skills that are idiosyncratic to this firm. If the employee has enough reason to trust that the firm will keep its promises, he may be willing to do so.

This approach is called implicit contracting because it is distinctly different from formal contracting or regulation—it is the part of the employment relationship that is difficult or impossible to enforce through the legal system.[10] When the legal system is not available, parties to a relationship-specific investment must rely on trust, reputation, and similar mechanisms to impose some reliability on the relationship.

We will see this issue arise several times. For example, most incentive systems require some element of subjective evaluation. Since subjective evaluations cannot easily be independently verified, implicit contracting becomes an important part of managing incentives. The topic is discussed more extensively and formally in Chapter 15; this has been only a brief introduction.

SUMMARY

In this chapter we have analyzed investing in worker skills. Education and on the job training are some of the most important investments that can be made in an economy. Historically, and especially so in recent years, these investments have paid high interest. We discussed what factors affect decisions about investments in education.

Education increases human capital. There are types of human capital, general and specific. The former is skills or knowledge valued equally by many employers (having a thick market). The latter is skills or knowledge that have unusual value at a particular employer. Training can involve some learning that is more like general human capital, and some that is more like firm-specific human capital.

We then discussed the question of who should pay for the training. We argued that a worker should pay for training that is general, accepting lower compensation than could be earned elsewhere during the training period. The worker will then enjoy the return on the investment through raises and promotions received later.

---

[10]Other terms that are sometimes used are *relational contracting* and *psychological contracting*.

To the extent that this is true, the firm is in effect *selling a service*—training—to the worker. We saw similar intuition earlier, when the firm sometimes provides a service to the worker by being particularly effective at sorting through and identifying the most talented workers. This intuition is interesting, because it flips the employment relationship around. It is not just the worker that sells a service to the firm, but often the firm sells something of value to the worker as well. We will see this again in the contexts of job design and pay for performance. This illustrates the fundamental point that a healthy contract between the worker and the firm is one that maximizes the total benefits, to both the worker and the employees. This should be the first consideration, with analysis of how to split those benefits only analyzed second (and depending on issues like incentives, competitive pressures on the firm, and labor market constraints).

Having the worker implicitly pay for on the job investments in general human capital means that not every firm should invest in its workforce's skills. To the extent that there is a thick market for its employees, workers should invest in those skills instead, and the firm should care little about turnover.

When human capital is firm specific, the question of who pays for the training is complex. If the employee does, she runs the risk that the firm will attempt to renegotiate or renege on promises of higher pay after the training period. If the firm pays for the training, it runs a similar risk from the employee. This is an example of the holdup problem, which may occur when one party tries to renegotiate terms after a relationship-specific investment has been made.

However, employees are more productive if their skill mix closely matches the demands of the job. Since most jobs are somewhat idiosyncratic, this means that optimal on the job training usually is somewhat firm specific. When that is so, a host of new considerations arise. Workers and firms will tend to split the costs and benefits of the investment, in order to mitigate holdup problems. Turnover therefore becomes costly for each; they have an incentive to maintain a long-term relationship. The longer they have worked together, the more they will tend to have invested in each other, only reinforcing such effects.

Investments in skills vary in the extent to which there is a thick market of firms that value them. When the market is thick, the skills are toward the general human capital end of the spectrum. Most skills of this kind are provided by specialized organizations like universities, rather than on the job. Such investments are almost always paid for, and the returns enjoyed by, the worker. (Societies often subsidize these investments.) However, some skills are most effectively learned on the job, by actually doing the work. When that is the case, the firm may provide that training to the worker.

Since contracting over complex employment relationships is typically incomplete, when there are relationship-specific investments, reputation and trust become an important way in which firms and employees can improve the value of their economic relationship. Thus, where skill investments should be more idiosyncratic and matched to a given employer, the employer will adopt policies that foster an internal labor where employees are hired at the bottom and spend long careers working their way up the corporate ladder in that firm. Where skill investments are more typical of those needed by other employers, by contrast, a firm may adopt more of an aggressive weeding out approach, since turnover will not be costly. In short, different contexts require different approaches to managing the employee–employer relationship.

In the first three chapters of this book, we have seen a sequence, from a simpler to a more complex economic relationship between the worker and the firm. We started by imagining that workers are paid on a spot market, with wages roughly corresponding to productivity. The analysis almost immediately led to thinking about multiperiod contracts, to exploit the option value of risky hires, and to sort employees. The next step was to make investments, often jointly, in worker skills. Finally, we add the notion of implicit contracting over the employment relationship.

The concept of implicit contracting gives us an important piece of the puzzle for modeling organizational design. Much of what is sometimes thought of as the soft side of personnel management falls into this category. While it is difficult to develop a comprehensive formal model of all of the issues that arise, in Chapter 15 we will be able to provide an economic framework that improves your thinking about issues such as reputation, trust, and corporate culture.

STUDY QUESTIONS

1. Why is it a good rule of thumb that skills typically taught at universities are general human capital?
2. Think of jobs that you have worked in. Was the skill mix more firm specific or general? Why?
3. If a firm requires that its employees invest in a mix of skills that is very specific to that firm, will there be any cost to the firm? Should a firm ever try to design jobs so that employees develop readily marketable skills? Explain.
4. Some firms hire employees at lower levels, train them extensively, and nurture long-term relationships with them. Others aggressively weed out employees. What characteristics of firms would push them toward one of these extremes or the other? Why? Try to list as many characteristics as you can think of.
5. Some firms hire employees at lower levels, train them extensively, and then aggressively weed out many of them through up-or-out promotion. How can such a policy be profitable for a firm?
6. What is the holdup problem? Why does it happen? Can you give specific examples (say, from the sports or entertainment industries)? What are possible ways to avoid such problems?

●●●●● REFERENCES

Casadesus-Masanell, Ramon & Daniel Spulber (2000). "The Fable of Fisher Body." *Journal of Law & Economics* 43(1): 67–104.

Lazear, Edward (2006). "Firm-Specific Human Capital: A Skill-Weights Approach." Working paper, National Bureau of Economic Research.

U.S. Department of Labor, Bureau of Labor Statistics (various years). *Current Population Survey.*

●●●●● FURTHER READING

Becker, Gary (1975). *Human Capital: A Theoretical and Empirical Analysis, with Special Reference to Education.* New York: Columbia University Press for the National Bureau of Economic Research.

Mincer, Jacob (1974). *Schooling, Experience & Earnings.* New York: Columbia University Press for the National Bureau of Economic Research.

Murphy, Kevin (1986). "Specialization and Human Capital." PhD thesis, Department of Economics, University of Chicago.

Murphy, Kevin & Finis Welch (1991). "The Structure of Wages." *Quarterly Journal of Economics* 107: 285–326.

●●●●● APPENDIX

In this appendix we present a simple model that illustrates some of the points about investments in on the job training. For details, see Lazear (2006).

We abstract from bargaining over the investment. Assume for simplicity that the firm and the worker share the costs and benefits of the investment. Furthermore, since we abstract from bargaining, we will treat the investment decision as being made by the employee. Of course, if there is efficient bargaining, the optimal investment decision will arise through the bargaining between the firm and the employee.

A worker invests in skills J (Java) and T (tax), at cost $\frac{1}{2}(J^2 + T^2)$. Different employers have different relative values for the skills. Let λ be the weight that the firm gives to skill J, and $1 - \lambda$ the weight given to skill T. Thus, the potential earnings that a worker can earn at the current firm equal:

$$W = \lambda J + (1 - \lambda)T.$$

Wages will be determined similarly at other firms, but the weights λ will vary from firm to firm. There are two periods. In the first, the worker invests in on the job training. In the second he may or may not switch employers, and works with no further investment. The probability that the worker stays at the current firm next period equals p. Thus, the worker chooses $\mathcal{J}$ and T to maximize net earnings:

$$\max_{\mathcal{J},T} p[\lambda\mathcal{J} + (1-\lambda)T] + (1-p)[\bar{\lambda}\mathcal{J} + (1-\bar{\lambda})T] - \tfrac{1}{2}(\mathcal{J}^2 + T^2),$$

where $\bar{\lambda}$ is the expected weight put on Java skills at potential other employers. The first-order conditions are:

$$p \times \lambda + (1-p) \cdot \bar{\lambda} - \mathcal{J} = 0,$$
$$p(1-\lambda) + (1-p)(1-\bar{\lambda}) - T = 0.$$

Investment is a weighted average of the relevant skill-values inside the firm and outside, where the weights depend on the probability of *separation*. The intuition should be clear. If $p = 1$ so that continuation in the firm is certain, the only skill value that matters is λ, the current employer's relative valuation of skill $\mathcal{J}$. If $p = 0$ so that separation is certain, the current firm's valuation does not matter. In that case only $\bar{\lambda}$ matters.

Define the optimal values of skills invested in as $\mathcal{J}^*$ and T^*. Now consider what happens to a worker who switches to another firm after investment. We denote the wage in the second firm by W', and the weight given to skill $\mathcal{J}$ in the second firm by λ'. The change in earnings is:

$$W' - W = (\lambda' - \lambda)(\mathcal{J}^* - T^*).$$

The sign for this equation is uncertain. The typical case would be where the probability of separation is relatively low, and the worker invests with an emphasis on the skills that the current employer values. However, if the probability of separation is very high, or the current firm's relative valuation of skills is not too unusual, the worker's investment will tend more toward $\bar{\lambda}$. If so, leaving the firm might lead to an increase in earnings. In any case, it can be shown that the change in earnings from switching employers decreases with the probability that the worker will leave the firm next period (Lazear 2006).

It is straightforward to show that an increase in market thickness leads the worker to invest in a way that is more consistent with the current firm's relative valuation of skills. The reason is that when the market is thick, the worker in effect gets additional random draws of λ's from other firms. The worker is therefore more likely to find an alternative job that is similar to the current job, which reduces the extent to which the original employer's valuation of skills is idiosyncratic. In other words, the firm-specificity of human capital is endogenous with respect to market thickness.

Finally, we could extend the model to three or more periods. Consider a worker who is two or more periods away from retirement. They have relatively less incentive to invest in skills that emphasize the current employer's valuation. This is because, with more than one period remaining, the probability that the worker will move to another employer is higher. This has an interesting implication: A worker's on the job training should become increasingly firm specific as tenure at the firm lengthens: Investments become more idiosyncratic, and less generally applicable in the labor market.

Managing Turnover

You are the weakest link. Goodbye.
  —*Slogan of the popular, ruthless British TV game show The Weakest Link*

Introduction

One theme of this text is that there is no single best approach that works for all firms. In the previous three chapters we developed an economic analysis of recruiting, structuring the job offer (pay, probation, and eventual screening for promotion), and investment in skills. Firms differ quite a bit in their overall strategy for these policies. In some firms, turnover is viewed as healthy, as it brings in new blood and facilitates sorting to find the most talented. In others, turnover is costly, because of investment in employee skills that match the idiosyncratic needs of the firm's business.

In the process, we developed several economic tools that have many applications inside and outside employment. These included adverse selection, signaling, and relationship-specific investments.

In this chapter, we finish this first section of the text by using these tools to analyze some related issues in the management of employee careers. The theme in the first two chapters was bringing employees into the organization. The theme of Chapter 3 was developing their talents so that they could be more productive and advance in their careers. The theme here is turnover—under what circumstances is it desirable, and how can it be effectively managed? While we return briefly to the subject of recruiting when we think about trying to hire employers from a competitor, most of the analysis focuses on turnover.

Is Turnover Good or Bad?

There are two different circumstances for thinking about employee turnover. One is the dramatic, hopefully rare need to lay off workers due to downsizing. The other is the general need to manage regular workforce flows in and out of the firm. We will talk about layoffs below. In this section, we consider the factors that affect a firm's optimal turnover when business conditions are normal. Every firm should have some employee turnover as part of its business; the question is how much, and of what kind.

In thinking about turnover, there is often a question about the appropriate level of analysis.[1] Should we think about turnover at the firm level overall, or differently for different jobs? For example, should we think about the right level of turnover at the organizational level, or should it vary from one job to the next? In general, the answer is the latter. Different jobs have different characteristics. Some jobs may require substantial turnover, while for others the firm may want to keep turnover to a minimum. There may be patterns across the entire organization, if some of the issues discussed apply to many jobs in the firm, but that does not need to be the case. In fact, most firms have quite different turnover rates for different types of jobs, by occupation, hierarchical level, location, and so on.

Importance of Sorting

One of the most important reasons to encourage some turnover is sorting. Sorting allows the firm to increase workforce quality, by screening more candidates per period of time. The more chances the firm gets to consider new job candidates, the greater the odds more talented workers will be discovered. The concept of matching from Chapter 3 also applies, since additional sorting increases the odds that a position can be filled by an employee who is a better match for the firm.

Of course, sorting is valuable only to the extent that differences in ability (or matching) are valuable. One such situation is when there is more to be learned about workers: Abilities are more variable, and less is known about them. For example, turnover is especially likely to be useful for new hires that are young and have a short track record. Turnover is also desirable, to some extent, for employees who have been promoted to new positions, since there is uncertainty about whether they will fit with the new job. These are ideas that we saw in Chapters 1–2.

Sorting is also valuable when small differences in talent or matching lead to large differences in productivity or costs. Thus, jobs where talent is particularly important are good candidates for higher turnover, to sift candidates continuously to find the best ones.

Putting these ideas together, it becomes clear why turnover is so important, especially early in the career, in professional service firms, and in academia. These firms are filled with knowledge workers. Ideas and creativity matter, and small differences in ability can be leveraged effectively. These kinds of firms often have fairly aggressive probation and up-or-out systems so that they can sort continually for the most skilled employees available.

---

[1] In fact, this issue is in the background in much of the analysis in this text: Should we think about a "one-size fits all" set of personnel policies, or tailor them to different jobs, groups of workers, etc.? This is really a question about centralization versus decentralization, which is a topic of the next two chapters.

Technical Change

An important benefit of turnover is that it brings new blood into the organization. New employees are more likely to have new insights, bring different perspectives, and understand the latest ideas, technology, or other developments.

Thus, turnover should be higher in industries where technology advances more rapidly. Computers and telecommunications are two obvious candidates. Some of the turnover can be the hiring of workers from other firms. This benefits your firm because you can obtain some of the new ideas and innovations from competitors (because of imperfect employee noncompete agreements). There is also likely to be a benefit from hiring *younger* workers in these settings. Younger workers learned the latest techniques in college or graduate school. Thus, we would expect that wages would not grow as rapidly with tenure in industries where much of the innovation occurs through university research.

There may also be an optimal mixing of younger and older workers. While younger workers bring fresh ideas and technology, older workers have a deeper understanding of the business, and are likely to have invested in knowledge that is specific to the firm. They have more ability to profitably apply the new ideas that younger workers bring. In a sense, there is an opportunity for the two groups to cross-train or collaborate with each other. To the extent that skill requirements are specific and cannot be learned at school (say, because the business is somewhat unusual), there will be greater benefit to matching younger workers with older workers to provide this training.

Organizational Change

Organizational change also generally benefits from turnover to bring in new ideas. Current employees are experts at the firm's current way of doing business. Unfortunately, if the firm needs to change methods, they are almost certainly no longer the best fit. This is particularly true for senior management.

We can flip this argument around as well. As we will see in Chapters 7–8, sometimes firms can become highly optimized to a certain way of conducting their business. When this is the case, they are more likely to hire employees at the bottom and promote from within, to develop specific human capital. However, such firms may face a substantial problem if the industry changes dramatically, because their management is inbred and has little experience with alternative methods. They may not even realize that they face this problem, because they have been successful in the past and have little exposure outside their current firm. To avoid this inward focus, it can be helpful to bring in at least a few employees—at all levels—with outside experience on an ongoing basis.[2] Firms that continuously bring in outsiders are more likely to recognize when times change, and adapt effectively.

---

[2] A good example is a company that tries to expand its operations to a different country for the first time. Its management is unlikely to have a sophisticated understanding of the many issues that arise in a business that operates across borders, unless it hires some employees who have that kind of experience.

Hierarchical Structure

Higher turnover may be necessary when the organizational structure dictates that the hierarchy narrow rapidly at some level. Take a quick look back at Table 2.1 at the beginning of Chapter 2. The second column shows the percentage of Acme's workers at different levels. The hierarchy narrows dramatically between Levels 4 and 5 (roughly speaking, where middle management becomes top management). Some turnover is inevitable here, because there will be very few promotion opportunities for Level 4 managers. Some managers may become frustrated and quit to pursue other opportunities.

In fact, Acme may want to encourage this. Otherwise, as Level 4 becomes clogged with managers who cannot be promoted further, promotion slots decline for Level 3 managers; this effect will eventually trickle down the hierarchy to Levels 2 and 1. This will reduce incentives, because promotions are an important form of pay for performance. Moreover, Acme's best workers are most likely to be lost if promotions are not available. A promotion system is like a pipe in which a continuous flow both in and out is the goal.

Specific Human Capital

As we saw in Chapter 3, on the job training does not generate turnover costs if the training is purely general. By contrast, the more specific to the firm the training, the higher the turnover costs. Typically, these costs will be borne by both the worker and the firm, because of sharing of the investment. Therefore, firms with more idiosyncratic businesses, methods, or cultures are more likely to want to have low turnover. Similarly, in jobs where valuable intellectual property is developed, it is important to try to reduce turnover. Finally, in positions where workers develop strong client relationships, turnover can be quite costly.

◆ ◆ ◆ ◆ ◆ RETENTION STRATEGIES

A variety of tools can be used to reduce turnover. The most obvious is to increase compensation. Of course, that is simple but expensive. But for key employees, in some cases you may have to respond if they receive outside job offers (see the next section).

For your key employees, consider treating them as partners. These are the small number of employees who create the most value or innovation for your organization. They are the most likely to possess valuable intellectual property or customer relationships that they might take with them if they leave. Losing such employees can be very damaging—especially since they may go to your competitors and compete directly against you.

To avoid such problems, you might offer them stock, options, or other pay for performance directed at their particular area of business. In the extreme, such key employees might be made partners. After all, in some cases those employees *are* the business, and can take it with them. It is this consideration that explains why so many professional service firms are organized into some form of partnership. The bottom line is that *you must pay key employees their market value or you will probably lose them*.

FRANK QUATTRONE'S INVESTMENT BANKING TEAM

❀ ❀ ❀ ❀ ❀ ❀ ❀ ❀ ❀

Frank Quattrone was one of the earliest, and most successful, investment bankers in Silicon Valley history. His career began at Morgan Stanley's San Francisco office in 1981. Quattrone had a fascination for the technology companies of Silicon Valley, and developed close ties to those firms and their executives. He moved his family there, and eventually opened the first investment banking office in the Valley, for Morgan Stanley. With his close ties to the industry, he was able to obtain some of the most famous and lucrative initial public offerings (IPOs) for Morgan Stanley, including Silicon Graphics, Cisco, and Netscape. At the time, Netscape's IPO was the most successful in history, with a 150% rise in price the first day.

Because his Morgan Stanley office was so dominant in Silicon Valley investment banking, Quattrone became more powerful within his firm. He gradually pushed for greater control of operations at the office. In 1996, when Morgan Stanley refused some of his requests, Quattrone and his entire technology investment banking team quit and set up an office for Deutsche Bank Securities, Inc. By 1998, the team had moved to Credit Suisse First Boston (CSFB).

CSFB offered Quattrone's team a very generous incentive plan: 33% of the revenues their group generated above $150 million. The result was that from 1998 to 2000, the team was responsible for almost as many IPOs as the next two largest competitors—one of which was Morgan Stanley. Quattrone's group was the single most important source of growth at CSFB in the late 1990s.

(Quattrone was eventually indicted for securities fraud, leading to the shutting down of his group and substantial business problems for CSFB.)

Source: Himelstein, Hamm & Burrows (2003)

What other retention strategies can you employ? You may be able to retain a specific employee by tailoring some benefits or characteristics of the work to that worker's tastes. For example, flexible working hours would allow an employee to pursue outside interests or meet family obligations more easily. If such flexibility is difficult for them to find elsewhere, they may be inclined to stay at your firm. Depending on how costly such flexibility is to you, it may be profitable for you as well.

Offering new opportunities to an employee with talent or a good match for your firm can reduce the likelihood that she will seek a new job. This might involve new training, job enrichment (Chapter 7), or early promotion. There are several reasons why this can help. First, new tasks or responsibilities make the job more interesting. Second, training increases the long-term value of the job. To the extent that the training is specific to the firm, it increases the incentive to stay with your firm (as in the last chapter). Third, an early promotion can signal to the employee the value that you place on their long-term employment at your firm.

One of the reasons employees leave jobs is because they feel that they have not been treated well. This can occur if they believe that their manager did not evaluate them correctly. It might be because they believe that certain promises (for training, promotion, or etc.) were not fulfilled. A healthy firm has a healthy working environment in which these kinds of issues do not arise often, and are addressed effectively when they do. This does not mean that there will not be some complaints and some disappointed employees. However, reducing the extent to which employees are treated arbitrarily can reduce turnover problems.

A simple example will illustrate some issues here. When recruiting it is tempting to overstate the value of the job; doing so makes the employee more likely to accept the offer. However, overstating the value means that the employee will inevitably end up disappointed. Moreover, the employee may infer that the employer is untrustworthy. This effect can be corrosive to the work environment and raise turnover. Therefore, paying attention to implicit contracting issues, as described in Chapter 15, can be an effective way to reduce turnover of all employees.

AN UNUSUAL RECRUITING VIDEO

Cummins Engine is one of the world's largest manufacturers of diesel engines. In the early 1970s, Cummins adopted what was at the time a relatively new approach to organizing its Jamestown, NY plant. Workers were put in teams, and given substantially more tasks and responsibilities than traditional assembly line workers. (We will discuss this general approach in Chapter 7). The teams were expected to become relatively self-managed, even playing an important role in the hiring (and potential firing) of their members.

Because the work design was so different from other factories in the area, many recruits found their new jobs to be highly stressful. In some cases, the workers did not fit well with the new system. In one case, a team ended up firing one member because of such concerns.

The remaining team members found this incident to be so painful that, on their own initiative, they developed a recruiting video for Cummins to show to job applicants. The first screen on the video showed, in very large letters, the word *Stress*. The first few minutes of the video consisted of interviews with workers discussing how hard they found the job when they first started, and the personal problems (in and out of work) that arose because of this.

Why would they design such a recruitment video? The point was to set accurate expectations for job applicants, to avoid painful turnover costs in the future. This was particularly important because of the unusual organization of the Cummins plant—new recruits had never seen anything like it elsewhere.

The second part of the video showed workers describing how they eventually got past the initial adjustment to the job, and found the work to be challenging and motivating (this is useful to remember when reading Chapter 7). But the primary point was to serve as an honest warning to job applicants that they would be better off not applying if they did not fit with this particular job. It was a very powerful recruiting video.

Source: Author's personal knowledge of unpublished video

Reducing Costs of Losing Key Employees

Some turnover is inevitable, but firms can employ a few strategies to make turnover less costly. In the last chapter we discussed noncompete agreements. They generally have limited effectiveness, because of the reluctance of courts to enforce strong clauses in them, and because it is impossible to control some information and ideas that an employee carries to a new firm. However, there are a few alternative approaches that can help.

First, turnover is most costly when the worker has complex, detailed knowledge that other employees do not share. Going back to our Silicon Valley software company that sells tax management software, if the primary routines in the program were written by one employee, the firm would be in serious trouble if that employee left. Software code can be extremely complex and hard to understand if you did not write it yourself.

This suggests some policies that can help avoid such a problem. First, have workers collaborate on key tasks so that key knowledge is not monopolized by one employee. Second, cross-train to reduce the risks even further. By having each worker train colleagues in what they do, and perhaps switch tasks periodically, each develops a broader knowledge of the product or process. If one person leaves, it is easier for others to fill in, and they will already be somewhat up to speed on the work.

Job design can also affect turnover costs. The more standardized the jobs, the less costly to the firm is losing one employee, because others can step into the void. Of course, not all jobs can be standardized, especially in smaller organizations.

Finally, a firm could have a general *knowledge management* strategy: Some attention can be given to procedures by which the knowledge that is created as part of conducting the work can be documented for reuse. As an example, some consulting firms set up databases to document new methods that their consultants have devised on projects. At the end of a new project each consultant is expected to write a description of new ideas and products that they have created on the project, and submit them to a manager who is responsible for knowledge management. That manager enters the description into the database, along with a set of keywords. Later, this knowledge can be accessed by others who search appropriate keywords. Then they can apply the ideas to new applications without having to figure out new solutions from scratch. To the extent that this system works, it saves the firm from having to reinvent approaches, and instead allows them to leverage what they have already created. And, it allows the firm to capture at least some of the knowledge of employees if they quit—as long as they documented what they learned.

Embracing Turnover

As we have noted before, turnover is not always a bad thing for an organization. In fact, some organizations *embrace* turnover. Here are two examples to illustrate why this might be beneficial, and how a firm might usefully encourage turnover through its personnel policies.

The first case is professional service firms that have up-or-out systems. An up-or-out system, like our probation analysis in Chapter 2, is one in which employees who are not promoted must leave the firm and seek a new job. Such systems are quite common in professional service firms (consulting, law, and accounting) as well as universities (professors). In a professional service firm, because employees work closely with clients, it is quite common for an employee who leaves to go to work for their client. This reinforces the working relationship between the firm and its client, benefitting both.

Next consider Hewlett-Packard. They are one of the original technology companies in Silicon Valley. As the Valley developed, many more technology companies entered the area, competing for H-P's employees. In addition, many H-P employees quit to start their own companies, often competing with H-P.

For many years, H-P's response when an employee quit was to encourage them in their new venture, but also encourage them to apply to return to H-P in the future if their new venture was not successful.

Such a scheme would seem to motivate H-P employees to use company resources to develop new product ideas, and then quit to profit from those ideas on their own. This was less of a risk at H-P than at other firms, because during this period H-P had strong internal policies to motivate employees to develop new products from within H-P (see Chapter 14). Why might H-P have such an approach?

First, such employees may well be some of the best in H-P's workforce—that is why they have such good outside opportunities. H-P's policy can increase the quality of its workforce because some may return later. Second, like the professional service firm, those employees who leave may bring future business to H-P. Third, employees who leave H-P and then return may be valuable because they have a mix of inside and outside experience. That is particularly important in an industry that is dynamic and constantly changing.

There is an additional benefit that may accrue to H-P from this approach. It is essentially taking the point of view that when its employees do well, it will also do well. By encouraging them to pursue successful careers, H-P is probably able to recruit employees that are more talented and ambitious. It is also able to develop a reputation as an employer who cares about the interests of its employees, which is likely to increase motivation and reduce conflict in the workplace. This is a broad theme that we are seeing in this text: The interests of the firm and its employees are not in conflict, when thought about properly. We return to this at the end of the book.

BIDDING FOR EMPLOYEES

How to respond when an employee receives an outside offer and threatens to quit? We discuss those issues now. First, however, we consider the related question of whether or not you should try to raid employees from competing firms. Both illustrate that firms are engaged in an active auction market, bidding against each other for employees, especially for the most talented ones.

Raiding Other Firms: Benefits and Pitfalls

Sometimes an individual who is working at another firm is a particularly attractive hire. This is generally the case when the individual has some idiosyncratic set of skills. It is the unusual nature of the skills that make raiding another firm, rather than hiring from the pool of self-announced applicants, attractive.

If an individual has skills that are commonly found throughout a large fraction of the workforce, the disadvantages of hiring from another firm may outweigh the advantages of hiring from the pool of applicants. The major disadvantage of hiring from another firm is that the worker's current employer usually knows more about a worker than does an outsider. Outsiders are usually in a weaker position to judge the quality of a worker.

This is sometimes called the *winner's curse* problem. More often than not, the workers who are easy to steal are the ones not worth stealing. After all, a worker's current firm always has the option of raising the worker's salary to keep the employee. If the outside firm can outbid the worker's current employer, then maybe the outsider is bidding too much. This is much like the Groucho Mark quotation at the beginning of Chapter 2. It is also another example of the idea of adverse selection: your firm bids against employers who have better information about the quality of one of their employees. Your firm is less likely to be able to hire a high quality applicant in such circumstances, because the other firm will use its information to its own advantage in deciding how to bid against you.

When a worker's skills are sufficiently rare, and when those skills are a particularly good match with an employer other than the current one, it may pay for an outside firm to launch a raid. Figure 4.1 illustrates all the decision possibilities related to raiding an employee by an outside firm. First, the firm decides whether to raid a competitor for a potential hire. If it does, it incurs the costs of time and other resources involved in the bidding war. If it does not, it incurs no direct costs.

The outcome then depends on whether the employee is more valuable to his current employer, or to the raiding firm. The firm that values him more will eventually outbid the other, and have the employee in the future. These cases are illustrated as the two branches coming off of the raid decision in Figure 4.1. This leads to four possible outcomes if the outside firm decides to raid, and two if it does not.

FIGURE 4.1
TO RAID OR NOT TO RAID

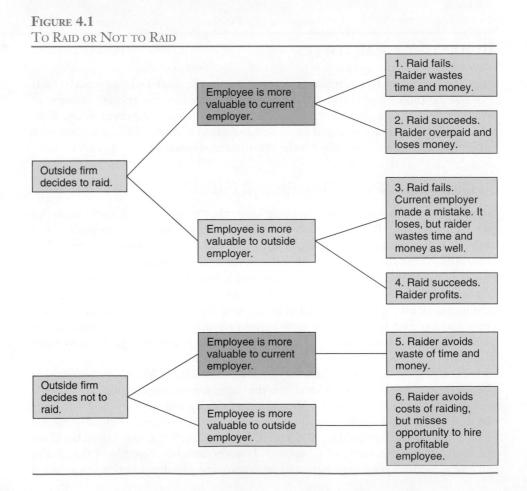

Workers generally have specific skills that make them more valuable to the current employer than to an outsider. But such is not always the case. There are situations in which a worker has skills that are so special and so well suited to another firm's current situation that the outsider is willing to pay more for the worker than is the current employer.

Consider, for example, the case of Lee Iacocca, who was hired away from Ford by Chrysler. Chrysler was on the verge of closing, and Iacocca was judged by Chrysler's board as one of the few people with the skills to steer the company back to prosperity. As such, he was worth more to Chrysler than he was to Ford. Ford either underestimated his talents or believed that he was not as valuable to Ford because of Ford's stronger economic position.

The Iacocca situation is illustrated by Box 4 in Figure 4.1. In this case, Chrysler elected to make Iacocca an offer, and Iacocca is more valuable to Chrysler than to Ford. In the end, Chrysler succeeded.

The problem with raiding another firm is in Box 2. Because of matching and investments in firm-specific human capital, a worker is more likely to be worth more to the current employer than to the outsider. Under such circumstances, the outsider should not raid. However, the outsider has less information about the quality of the worker than the current employer does, and sometimes overestimates the worker's potential productivity. If it does, it might win the bidding war and hire the new employee. This would be a mistake. Given the current employer's natural information advantage, this is often likely to be the case.

When should a firm raid another firm for an employee? The first criterion is that the raider must be very certain that the target worker's value is greater to the raider than to the worker's current firm. The second criterion is that the worker's current firm not overvalue and therefore overpay the worker.

If the worker is more valuable to the current firm than to the raider, then either the raider acquires the worker but pays too much, or more likely, the raider simply fails to attract the worker away and wastes time and money in the process.

Raiding is most likely to yield profitable outcomes when the target worker is worth more to the raider than to the current firm and when the current firm is aware of that fact. If the worker is worth more to the raider than to the current firm, the raider will succeed in outbidding the current employer unless the current firm overvalues the target worker as well.

In which situations are the conditions for a profitable raid most likely to be met? The main condition, that a worker is worth more to another firm than to the current firm, is most likely to hold when recent changes have occurred, either with respect to the worker's skills or in the industry in question. Some examples come to mind.

First, workers who have recently completed a schooling program are ripe for the picking. Chances are that a new degree recipient can be more productive in a job other than the one they currently hold. The current firm may be able to offer the better job, but it is quite likely that the current firm does not have an opening in an appropriate higher level position. A raiding firm will probably succeed in attracting the new graduate from the current firm. Indeed, the statistics on this are impressive.

Schools that have part-time MBA programs report that the vast majority of their graduates leave the firm that they were with during graduate school within a short time of graduation.

Second, workers who are employed by firms in rapidly changing industries, especially those that are declining, are good targets for raiding. Since the firm in which the worker is currently employed is changing, the expectations that brought the worker to the firm in the first place are probably not being met. As a result, the worker's value at the current firm is probably lower than it could be elsewhere. This is exactly the situation in which the worker is more valuable elsewhere than at the current firm.

Third, workers who are employed in industries undergoing rapid technical change are likely to be good targets. When change is rapid, it is not neutral, so that some firms experience significantly more rapid increases than others. Workers who are capable, but are located in a firm that is behind the leader, are good candidates for a raid. This explains why there is so much turnover among software and hardware companies. A worker who starts out with an innovative firm may find that firm to be trailing the industry within a period of 6 months. The worker is probably worth more elsewhere, and will seek out a new job or will be pirated away by a leading firm.

Is it always better to be a raider? If that were the case, all firms would raid the best employees from each other and nobody would hire unproven talent. Firms that hire directly from the pool of applicants get a random sample of the population. Some of the workers are very able, and some are less able. As long as the firm does not pay more than commensurate with the average quality of a worker, it can survive quite well. But firms must recognize that the average quality of the workers employed by the firm that hires all applicants is not as high as the average for the population as a whole. Raiders are going to steal away a nonrandom sample of the population; specifically, raiders tend to steal away the most able. Thus, the wage that a primary employer pays to its workers must be low enough so that it can avoid losses even after the secondary raiding firms have picked off some of the better employees. So, for example, if the average worker is worth $30 per hour, a wage of $30 per hour will cause a firm to lose money. Since the better workers tend to be picked off, those who are left do not provide an average productivity of $30 per hour.

LAYOFFS AND LEMONS

Firms have discretion over which employees to terminate, which implies that the idea of adverse selection can be applied to workers who have lost their jobs. From the perspective of the labor market, such employees are like used cars. A potential employer will worry that the worker is not of high quality (a "lemon"), because their prior employer let them go. This (and lack of specific human capital) can make it quite difficult for someone who is laid off to find a new job quickly, and may also imply that the new job is at much lower pay than the old job.

Studies have found that used cars that come onto the market because they were leased, but the lease contract expired, are much less subject to the lemon problem. The reason for this is that almost *all* cars that come off a lease contract will be sold as used cars, regardless of quality. There is little self-selection, so they tend to be of average quality.

A similar result applies in the labor market. One study found that workers who are laid off when *all* workers lost their jobs—due to a plant closing, for example—were able to find jobs more quickly, and generally earned higher pay in their new jobs, than workers who were laid off in other situations. The workers who suffered from a plant closing were able to explain their job loss in such a way that it did not stigmatize them.

Source: Gibbons & Katz (1991)

Offer Matching

We now realize that bidding for a worker is a common part of labor market competition. But sometimes, current employers refuse to match offers of outsiders. An announced policy of "no offer matching" is thought to discourage disloyal attempts by employees to raise their salaries by obtaining outside offers at higher wages.

When is it reasonable to match outside offers and when not? First, it is important to determine what affects worker search behavior. Let's take a stylized example. Suppose that a worker is currently earning $20 per hour. Suppose further that there is one (and only one) job in his labor market that will pay him more than this; it will pay $20.50 per hour. There are 50 firms other than his own where he believes that he has some prospect of finding the high paying job. The problem is that he doesn't know which firm of the 50 is the high payer.

The worker can take time to fill out applications for some of the 50 firms. Each application takes time and effort, which the worker values at some amount, say X. The question is, When does it pay to search?

Suppose that the worker's current firm agrees to match any outside offer. Then he will search whenever the expected present value of the increased earnings exceeds the costs. The expected present value of searching at the first firm is:

$$\frac{1}{50} \sum_{t=0}^{T} \frac{(2000)(0.50)}{(1 + r)^t}.$$

This is like a formula for the return on a human capital investment, because searching for a job is like investing in human capital. The 1/50 comes from the fact that the worker has a 1/50 change of finding the high paying job. If he does, because his firm matches the offer, he gets to enjoy an increase in hourly wage for 2,000 hours per year for every year that he works from time zero to T. If this expression is greater than the cost X, he searches. Low values of X and long work lives tend to lead to higher return to searching for a better job offer.[3]

The firm is unhappy that the worker is searching for a high paying job. Under offer matching, the search may result in the firm having to pay higher wages for any given worker. How will a policy of "no offer matching" affect the worker's behavior?

This depends on whether the worker will actually leave to take another job. If he is willing to leave for the new job, then there is no effect on search behavior of announcing no offer matching. The returns to the worker from search are the same. The only difference is that in order to reap the returns, it is necessary that the worker actually take the job offer at the new firm. With offer matching, the worker need only threaten to leave.

Which situation does the firm prefer? With no offer matching the worker leaves. With offer matching, the worker stays. Although the firm might not always want to match offers, one would think that the firm would always prefer having the option to match offers. If the wage that the firm must pay exceeds the worker's worth, then the firm can always let the worker go.

Since the policy of "no offer matching" does not seem to discourage search, why announce it? The answer is that it might discourage certain kinds of search under special circumstances.

Suppose, for example, that the worker has a strong preference for his current firm, perhaps because he likes his coworkers, the plant's location, or its general work environment. The worker might be unwilling to move to another firm, even at a wage of $20.50 per hour. If the firm matches alternative offers that are below the worker's value to the firm, it will raise wages to $20.50. This provides the worker with an incentive to search for an offer that he has no intention of accepting. If the firm had a policy of "no offer matching," the worker would not search, because he would actually have to accept the job in order to reap the benefits of his search. Since the worker is unwilling to accept the job at the higher wage, the policy of no offer matching discourages search and saves the firm money.

Now, were the firm to know that the worker was unwilling to accept the $20.50 to work for a competitor, it could simply refuse to match that offer. In essence, the firm could declare that the offer was not a genuine threat, because the worker had no intention of accepting it. The problem is that it is sometimes difficult for a firm to distinguish between genuine threats and offers that the worker

---

[3]If the worker applies to the first firm and fails, he will surely apply to a second. The returns to applying to the second are greater than applying to the first, because the odds of finding the high paying firm have risen to 1/49. Of course, in practice a worker will first apply to the firm where he believes the odds of success are highest, which works in the other direction.

would decline. When this is the case, firms can benefit from a policy of no offer matching.

This situation is most likely to arise when the following conditions apply:

1. There is a large nonpecuniary component to compensation.
2. The worker is being paid less than he or she is worth to the firm.

Compensation with a Nonpecuniary Component

Wages can be compared easily, but compensation packages that include a nonpecuniary component may be difficult to compare. If jobs were identical, except for their monetary compensation, the firm could quickly determine whether a worker was likely to accept an outside offer. If the dollar wage offered by the competitor exceeded that being paid by the current employer, the worker would accept the offer and leave. Under these conditions, the outside offer is a credible threat to the current employer.

Unfortunately, evaluating offers is not so easy. Much of what a worker receives on the job is psychic. Working conditions, status, flexibility, or the ability to work in a particular location may be quite important, but may have different values to different individuals. When the nonpecuniary aspects of a job are important, it will be difficult for an employer to evaluate the significance of an outside offer. Workers are then more likely to search for outside offers that have high monetary rewards that compensate for psychic disadvantages unobservable by the current employer.

As such, the gains to a worker from engaging in a strategic search for offers that are high, but which the worker has no intention of accepting, are largest when the nonpecuniary component of compensation is significant. Under the circumstances, an employer benefits from discouraging search for frivolous offers by announcing a policy of no offer matching.

When workers are in the job "for the money," the nonpecuniary components of the job are less important. This is a situation where little is gained by announcing a policy of no offer matching. Workers will simply move if the firm does not match, and the firm cannot discourage needless search by refusing to match. Investment banks rarely adopt "no offer matching" policies, because money is the driving factor in these industries. At government agencies, nonpecuniary components of the job, including job security, short hours, and perhaps easier workdays, are of significant concern to workers. At these firms, it is more difficult for management to know whether an outside offer at a slightly higher wage is indeed a credible threat. To prevent workers from searching for such offers merely to raise their salaries, public utilities can refuse to match outside offers.

Undervalued Workers

A firm that matches offers is most susceptible to disingenuous search by workers when the firm has much to gain from keeping the worker. If the firm were paying the worker exactly what she was worth, then an offer from an outsider that exceeds her current wage—credible or not—would elicit no response from the current employer. It would be better to lose the worker than to increase the wage.

The worker is most likely to succeed in getting her wage raised by an outside offer when the firm makes a large profit on her. This happens when the worker is paid less than she is worth. If there is a surplus to be had, the worker can capture some of that surplus by threatening the employer with a departure. It is under these circumstances that a policy of no offer matching is most likely to be profitable.

To summarize, retaining flexibility is generally better than being locked into a rigid policy. As such, a policy that prevents a firm from matching offers is usually a bad idea. To every rule, however, there is an exception. When a worker's current employer is uninformed about a worker's willingness to accept outside offers, a policy of not matching offers may be a good idea. This is particularly relevant when the firm is paying its workers less than the value of their output.

●●●●● Layoffs and Buyouts

Unfortunately, sometimes firms must downsize by laying off large groups of employees. If you had to lay off part of your workforce, how would you think through the issues? For example, should you target the most highly paid workers first? If you decide to offer buyout packages to motivate workers to leave on their own, how can you do so most effectively?

Who to Target for Layoffs

Should you lay off your most expensive employees? Those with the worst performance? The answer is not necessarily, but these are good places to start looking for candidates.

As we saw in Chapter 1, pay must be balanced against productivity. One must be careful about laying off the most highly paid employees, because they are often the most productive as well. A better approach is to target those employees from which the firm is losing money relative to other employees. These could be high or low paid workers. That said, some highly paid employees have high compensation because outside offers were met, they are tough bargainers, or for other reasons. Therefore, highly paid but relatively unproductive workers are good candidates for layoffs.

A similar argument applies to employee performance. Again, employees with low performance ratings may have high productivity relative to their compensation, so one must be careful. However, low performance ratings usually imply that the worker is performing poorly compared with others with similar skills and jobs. If that is the case, odds are very good that the ones with low performance ratings are being paid too much relative to more productive colleagues, and thus should be targeted for layoffs.

Specific Human Capital

An important factor in deciding who to target is the degree of firm-specific human capital. As we saw in the last chapter, to the extent that workers have human capital that is specific to the employer, both the worker and the firm are likely to be sharing the costs and benefits of training investments. This has an important implication for thinking about who to target for layoffs.

It is quite straightforward to state the result, but the analysis will be somewhat lengthy: When firm-specific human capital is important, the firm maximizes its profits by laying off from both ends of the age distribution first. These are the workers who have recently started with the firm, and those who are nearing retirement.

The intuition behind this result is presented in Figure 4.2. The top panel shows profiles of a hypothetical worker's earnings and productivity over the career, with an investment in firm-specific human capital. Productivity at the firm is labeled K_t. The wage is labeled W_t.

The value of the worker's best alternative outside of the firm is labeled A_t. This depends on two factors. The first is the earnings that the worker could receive in another job. That is the most important factor for younger workers. The second is the value that the worker places on leisure. The older the worker, the more

FIGURE 4.2
EARNINGS & PRODUCTIVITY OVER THE CAREER

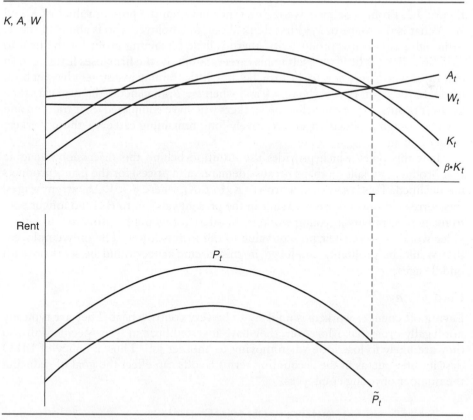

he will tend to value leisure. At some point, a worker's best outside alternative is retirement. Furthermore, eventually all workers would be better off by retiring; that is represented by a rising profile A_t. If the older worker's outside earnings are less than what could be earned at this firm, then the optimal point of retirement is at $t = T$, where A_t rises above K_t.

In competitive labor markets, the present value of the W_t profile must approximately equal the present value of the K_t profile.[4] If $PV(W) > PV(K)$, the firm would lose money over the worker's career. If $PV(W) < PV(K)$, the firm would have difficulty recruiting workers. The present value of both should generally exceed the present value of the A_t profile, or the worker is employed at the wrong firm.

Though the present values of wages and productivity are equal at the time when the worker is hired, they are not thereafter. Since the worker's training is partly firm specific, the worker and the firm will share the costs and benefits of the training. Thus both bear losses initially. Once the training is complete, both earn a return on their investment. At the beginning, $W_0 > K_0$ as the training begins. Therefore, at any point *after* $t = 0$, the present value of the productivity profile K_t is higher than the present value of the wage profile W_t. The difference represents the part of the return that is earned by the firm.

The amount of profit P_t going to the firm is plotted in the bottom panel of Figure 4.2. Profit is defined as the difference between the present values of K and W. What is the shape of P_t? First think about an employee who is about to retire. Although pay is below productivity, there is little remaining profit for the firm to earn since there is little time left in his career. Similarly, the firm loses little from an employee who is very new to the firm, because little training investment has yet been made. In the limit, $P_t = 0$ when $t = 0$ and when $t = T$. In general, the firm earns the greatest profits (in present value) on workers who have completed their training and have both high productivity and relatively long remaining careers—those workers of medium age.

It is this point which provides the intuition behind this discussion. Imagine that productivity falls, perhaps because demand (and prices) for the firm's products has declined. This is shown as a drop in K_t to $\beta \cdot K_t$, where $\beta < 1$. At current wages, this corresponds to a downward shift in the present value P_t to $\tilde{P}_t$. It no longer pays to make investments in young workers. Similarly, it would be profitable to lay off older workers, since their present value to the firm is lower. The only employees that would be profitably employed in this circumstance would be workers with middle ages.

Costs of Layoffs

Laying off younger workers is unlikely to be very controversial. They are typically not legally protected. Moreover, they have invested little in firm-specific skills, so they are likely to lose little when moving to another job. Thus, a policy of LIFO (last in, first out, as in the accounting term) layoffs can effect the goal of reducing the number of young employees.

---

[4]See the discussion of rent sharing near the end of Chapter 3.

Laying off older workers is quite likely to be controversial, and may also be illegal. Older workers are protected by antidiscrimination regulations in most countries. Technically, the firm's lawyers might argue that the layoffs are based on net present values for each employee, but they are not likely to win that case. Thus, the firm may be subject to prosecution by the government, and discrimination lawsuits by older employees.

Moreover, older workers have invested in firm-specific skills, and are now enjoying the returns on their investments that were promised to them (usually implicitly) by the firm. Laying off such workers may be perceived as a breach of trust by the employer, though this may be alleviated to the extent that the firm honors its pension commitments.

Is it truly a breach of trust? That is not so obvious. Any sensible implicit contract would surely provide for the right of the firm to lay off workers when business conditions become severe enough. This might be one of those times. While that may be true, it is still likely that the firm will face criticism (perhaps opportunistic) about breach of trust. Therefore, to the extent that the firm cares about its reputation as a fair employer, it should think carefully before implementing layoffs, either for older workers or more generally.

For example, suppose that the firm has a strong reputation in the labor market, and the current downturn is believed to be only temporary. In that case, the firm will care very much about its reputation, and implement layoffs in such a way that its reputation is damaged least. On the other hand, if the industry is declining dramatically, or if the firm needs to signal about the seriousness of its intentions (say, as a negotiating stance with unions), then dramatic action may be necessary.

Finally, a serious cost of layoffs is the litigation that may ensue. Because many economies provide protection for workers against wrongful termination, employees may sue if they are fired. Such litigation is costly is its own right, as would be any settlement to avoid legal costs. Moreover, if the firm loses the lawsuit, it will have to pay damages.

Buyouts

Because of the costs of layoffs, many firms opt to offer employees buyouts instead. A buyout is a contract between a worker and a firm. In exchange for some compensation, an employee agrees to end employment with the firm. Buyout agreements may include other clauses; e.g., the employee agrees to not sue the company for wrongful termination, and to not criticize the company in public forums.

AMAZON'S NONDISPARAGEMENT CLAUSE

❋ ❋ ❋ ❋ ❋ ❋ ❋ ❋ ❋

In early 2001 Amazon.com laid off 1,300 workers, offering severance pay of 6 to 8 weeks of salary. Employees were required to sign a clause that prohibited them from making derogatory comments about the company, or their severance would be limited to 2 weeks of pay. After public criticism of this clause, Amazon removed the requirement from the buyout package.

The buyout package had another feature that is very unusual. Amazon set up a trust fund of $2.5 million worth of company stock, to be sold 2 years later and distributed to laid off employees. In effect, those laid off were given some options.

Why might Amazon have done this? One answer is that this was right before the tech market crash, so there was still great enthusiasm for options (and they were often used without much thought as a compensation tool; see Chapter 12). Another is public relations. A third is that Amazon wanted to tie the interests of those who were laid off to Amazon, both to discourage public disparagement, and perhaps because they hoped the layoffs to be temporary, and wanted to hire some back later.

Sources: Wolverton (2001)

If a firm does opt to award severance pay, should all employees be eligible? It depends on who is most likely to accept the buyout offer.

One concern is adverse selection. At any wage category some employees are more productive than others. In other words, some are relatively overpaid, and some (the better performers) are relatively underpaid. The more productive are also likely also to have better alternative employment elsewhere. If this is the case, then they lose the least in accepting the buyout, and are thus more likely to accept it.

Consider the 1990s attempt by Stanford University to offer early retirement buyouts to professors older than 55. A number of professors accepted the offer. Unfortunately, in many cases the professors who departed were the most productive—because they found it easier to obtain good jobs at other universities than did less productive professors. This suggests that buyout packages should be carefully designed so that they target and motivate the desired groups to leave or stay, respectively. For example, the best performing employees might not be offered buyouts, or might be offered buyouts that are less lucrative, if possible.

Similar considerations apply to how buyout packages might vary with the employee's age. As described, the main concern will generally be the most senior workers. Of that group, those close to retirement have little to lose from leaving the firm, since they have already earned most of the return on their investment in skills. They require only small buyout packages. Those farther from retirement usually require larger buyouts. To illustrate this, Table 4.1 presents a hypothetical situation similar to Figure 4.2.

In this table all values are expressed in $1,000s. The table shows the wage (assumed for simplicity to be a constant $30,000), the value of the worker's best

TABLE 4.1
ANALYSIS OF WHICH WORKERS TO LAY OFF

Age	W	A	K	PV(W)	PV(A)	PV(K)	βK	PV(βK)
25	$30	$20.0	$20.0	$145.5	$ 99.3	$145.5	$14.0	$101.8
26	30	20.1	23.2	145.5	99.9	158.1	16.2	110.6
27	30	20.3	26.2	145.5	100.5	169.9	18.3	118.9
28	30	20.4	29.1	145.5	101.1	181.1	20.4	126.7
29	30	20.5	31.8	145.5	101.7	191.5	22.3	134.0
30	30	20.6	34.4	145.4	102.3	201.2	24.1	140.8
35	30	21.3	45.0	145.4	105.3	238.6	31.5	167.1
45	30	22.5	55.0	144.3	110.5	258.7	38.5	181.1
55	30	23.8	50.0	134.0	109.1	211.3	35.0	147.9
56	30	23.9	48.7	131.0	105.8	191.2	34.1	141.3
57	30	24.0	47.2	127.3	103.2	179.6	33.0	125.7
58	30	24.1	45.6	122.5	99.7	166.8	31.9	116.7
59	30	24.3	43.8	116.6	95.3	152.7	30.7	106.9
60	30	24.4	41.9	109.1	89.5	137.2	29.3	96.0
61	30	24.5	39.8	99.6	82.0	120.1	27.9	84.0
62	30	24.6	37.6	87.7	72.4	101.1	26.3	70.8
63	30	24.8	35.2	72.7	60.2	80.0	24.6	56.0
64	30	24.9	32.7	53.8	44.7	56.5	22.9	39.5
65	30	25.0	30.0	30.0	25.0	30.0	21.0	21.0

alternative A_t, and productivity K_t. The table also calculates the present values of each.[5] Notice that, as in Figure 4.2, the present values of K and W are equal for new and retiring workers. As described, competition forces this result, all else equal. Finally, the last two columns imagine that the value of the worker's productivity falls by 30% ($\beta = 0.7$) because of a decline in demand for the firm's products.

In deciding whether or not to accept a buyout of amount B, the worker will compare what he can earn if he stays in the firm, $PV(W)$, to what he can earn if he takes the buyout, $B + PV(A)$. This means that the buyout will be accepted only if it is higher than the profit that the worker earns from staying:

Profit to the worker from staying (rejecting a buyout) $= PV(W) - PV(A)$.

In the table, the present value of wages is higher than the present value of the best alternative for all workers. All workers would have to be offered a buyout to be willing to leave.

The profit to the firm if the worker leaves is the difference between the present values of compensation and productivity:

Profit or loss to the firm from having the worker leave $= PV(W) - PV(K)$.

---

[5]The interest rate is about 25%. The principles illustrated are valid regardless of the interest rate.

[After production falls, this expression changes to $PV(W) - PV(\beta \cdot K)$ in our example.] If this is positive, the firm would like the worker to leave. In that case, the expression equals the *maximum* profitable buyout B that the firm can offer. If it is negative, the firm would prefer to keep the worker. In the table, all workers were profitable to the firm before the value of productivity fell. After productivity fell, workers aged 57 and higher or 30 and lower are no longer profitable for the firm. These are the ones that the firm would like to target.

We are now in a position to give the rule for optimal buyouts. As long as the gains to the firm from losing the worker exceed the losses to the worker from leaving, there is room for a deal to be made. The firm can offer a buyout that increases its profits, and also makes the workers better off when they leave. Putting these together, we can make a deal as long as:

$$PV(W) - PV(K) > PV(W) - PV(A),$$

or

$$PV(A) > PV(K).$$

Our result: *A buyout is possible if the present value of the worker's alternative exceeds the present value of the worker's productivity at the firm.* Indeed, this should make intuitive sense to you. Thus, low output and good alternatives make buyouts feasible.

It is important to recognize that the individuals that the firm would like to lay off are not necessarily the ones for whom a buyout offer is possible. While the firm would like to lay off those aged 57 and older or 30 and younger (after productivity falls), a deal cannot be struck with all of them. Only workers 62 and older have alternatives sufficiently attractive to make an offer feasible. The firm loses money on those between ages 57 and 61, but not enough that a buyout would be a better option, given the amount of buyout that they would require. Similar logic applies to those aged 30 and younger.

Implementation of Buyouts

Window plans.   Often, announcements of buyout offers are a surprise, and workers are given only a limited time to accept the offer. Such plans are often called *window plans* because there is a small period or "window" during which the buyout is available.

There is a very good reason for such practices. Recall that the buyout that the firm is willing to offer the worker depends on the difference between the wage and productivity. The lower his productivity, the more anxious is the firm to be rid of him, and the higher the buyout offer the firm is willing to make. If a buyout is anticipated, a worker has incentives to reduce productivity. A short fuse prevents the worker from strategically reducing productivity for any significant time period to gain a higher buyout price. It also reduces the chance that the worker can find a suitable outside offer, since there is less time to search.

Threat of layoff.   Another way to increase acceptance rates for buyout offers is to credibly threaten to lay off some fraction of those who do not accept the offer. Suppose that the firm were to announce that it would lay off 50% of all workers who did not accept the buyout offer, chosen at random. If you were faced with this offer, how would it affect your incentives? It would make you more likely to accept the offer.

Think about it this way: Suppose that if a worker loses his job, he expects that the next job will give him about $10,000 less in present value. Under the analysis given, this is the minimum buyout that he will accept. However, if the firm threatens to fire half of those who reject the buyout, there is a 50% chance that he will lose $10,000 with *no buyout*. He is then willing to accept a buyout of only $5,000 (or even less, if he is risk averse). In general, greater odds of being laid off lower the buyout that a worker requires. The Appendix proves this result formally.

Of course, there are costs to the firm of such a strategy—it will have to lay off some workers. We have already discussed these costs. The firm needs to balance the benefits of lower buyouts against the costs of implementing some layoffs after the buyout window ends. However, threatening to lay off those who reject buyouts has two advantages for a firm: It increases the probability that a worker will accept a given buyout amount, and it reduces the buyout that is required to motivate an employee to quit.

Speed and extent of downsizing.   An additional benefit from implementing layoffs quickly and by surprise is that it reduces the amount of organizational trauma that is experienced. Downsizing can be highly emotional, and organizations that go through the process tend to find that workers are extremely unproductive while it is ongoing. One of the reasons for this is that workers focus, quite naturally, on who will be laid off, when, and under what terms. This can be quite a distraction from ordinary business. Thus, it often pays to get the pain over with quickly, and unexpectedly.

For similar reasons, a firm should consider laying off more workers than seems apparent at first glance. If it can do so, it minimizes the odds that it will have to do so again soon (many downsizing firms go through several waves of layoffs before they are finished). An additional advantage is that it makes it possible to clean house thoroughly in areas of the organization that need radical restructuring, because the costs of firing a worker tend to be lower when implemented in the context of a larger set of layoffs.

Retirement bridges.   The minimum buyout price necessary for a worker who is close to voluntary retirement is relatively small. However, a buyout formula that offers less to 64-year-olds than to 56-year-olds might run into legal difficulties. A provision that is less likely to encounter legal challenges, but has a similar effect, is a *retirement bridge*. A bridge gives a worker seniority credit for the purpose of pension calculations as if he had stayed on until the normal retirement date. For example, if the normal retirement age is 65 and a worker leaves at 55 with 18 years of service, he is treated as if he had 28 years of service for the purpose of calculating retirement benefits. Since the number of years awarded by the bridge declines with age, older workers are in effect given a smaller buyout award than their juniors.

Job placement services. Firms sometimes set up job placement services for workers they lay off or offer buyouts to. Is this rational, or does it merely reflect the employer's guilt about layoffs, or perhaps an attempt at improving public relations?

The practice may not only be good for public relations, but may also result in cost savings. Improving the odds that workers can find outside work lowers the buyout price that they will require. To the extent that the firm can help severed workers find new jobs, their alternatives are better and the firm may be able to offer lower buyout prices.

Whether this logic holds, however, depends on the firm's efficiency in securing new employment for its workers. The service should be offered only if the firm can provide it (or contract with an outplacement agency) more cheaply than the worker can buy a similar service himself. Otherwise, it would be cheaper for the firm simply to pay for outside services that a worker purchases (e.g., through some kind of voucher system). In most cases, that is probably the best route. Placement agencies specialize in relocating workers, and the firm is unlikely to do a better job (especially when distracted by the downsizing).

In either case, however, the point remains. Offering outplacement services in kind or by reimbursement may lower the costs of implementing buyouts.

● ● ● ● ● # SUMMARY

There is a fundamental tension in the operation of any company's internal labor market, between the desire to sift through employees to find the best fits, and the desire to build employee loyalty. Sifting improves overall quality. Loyalty improves motivation, reduces turnover costs, and encourages firm-specific skill investments. A healthy firm balances these two desires to achieve some of both goals. The right balance varies from company to company, depending on the relative importance of each of these factors.

In this chapter we analyzed this tradeoff using the tools developed in Chapters 1–3. We saw that recruiting and turnover are intimately related. Understanding optimal turnover, and how to motivate it, requires use of several economic concepts. These include adverse selection, investment, and incentives.

Turnover has many benefits. It allows the organization to update its talent continuously. Not only does this increase quality; it also keeps the firm's skills from depreciating. In changing environments with technological advancement, this can be quite important. Turnover also makes it less likely for a company to fall into the trap of becoming too inwardly focused. A company may be very good at what it does, but unaware of how the industry is changing, and thus may find it difficult to adapt. Employees with diverse outside experiences make this less likely to happen. A final benefit of turnover is that it frees up promotion slots, allowing the company to advance and motivate its best employees.

Turnover also has many costs. A prosaic one is the costs of recruitment for the firm, and job search for the worker. A less prosaic one is that both will lose the value of any specific skill investments they have made. A more subtle effect is that, if turnover is higher, both will be less willing to make such investments in the first place.

This chapter completes the first section of the textbook. After analyzing the employee career pipeline of recruitment, investment, and turnover, we now consider what the firm will do with the employee. We turn to issues of job and organizational design in Section II.

STUDY QUESTIONS

1. Google recently held an IPO (initial public offering). Because of this and the extensive use of employee stock options, many Google employees are now multimillionaires. What retention problems do you foresee for the company? What, if anything, might Google do?

2. You and a friend from school are starting a consulting firm together. You want to organize it as a partnership. Realizing that things don't always work out as intended, how might you structure the partnership agreement to protect you and your friend from future conflict? How will that affect that ways that you each conduct business in the new firm?

3. If you receive a job offer, should you always tell your employer?

4. You are the CEO of Morgan Stanley at the time that Frank Quattrone and his team quit to work for a major competitor. Is this a threat? How can you tell? How would you react? Once the threat has passed, what might you do to avoid such events in the future?

5. You are negotiating with a potential new employer. One issue is whether the firm will pay your tuition in an evening MBA program. What arguments would you make to convince your employer? If you were the employer, what counterarguments would you make?

6. What kinds of skills are likely to be most effectively trained for on the job? What kinds would be best learned in a classroom?

REFERENCES

Gibbons, Robert & Lawrence Katz (1991). "Layoffs and Lemons." *Journal of Labor Economics* 8: 351–380.

Himelstein, Linda, Steve Hamm & Peter Burrows (2003). "Inside Frank Quattrone's Money Machine." *Business Week*, October 13.

Wolverton, Troy (2001). "Amazon Gives Cut Workers More Time to Sign." *Cnet News*, February 21.

●●●●● **FURTHER READING**

Barron, John, Mark Berger, & Dan Black (2006). "Selective Counteroffers." *Journal of Labor Economics* 24(3): 385–409.

Lazear, Edward (1986). "Raids and Offer Matching." *Research in Labor Economics* 8: 141–165.

Lazear, Edward & Richard Freeman (1997). "Relational Investing: The Worker's Perspective." In *Meaningful Relationships: Institutional Investors, Relational Investing and the Future of Corporate Governance*, Ronald Gilson, John Coffee and Louis Lowenstein, eds. New York: Oxford University Press.

Pfann, Gerard & Ben Kriechel (2003). "Heterogeneity Among Displaced Workers." *Royal Economic Society Annual Conference*, 164.

Wilson, Robert (1969). "Competitive Bidding with Disparate Information." *Management Science* 15: 446–518.

●●●●● **APPENDIX**

Here we prove that if the firm threatens to lay off a fraction p of workers who do not accept a buyout offer, it can offer lower severance payments.

Recall that the profit to the worker from staying (rejecting a buyout) is:

$$PV(W) - PV(A) > 0.$$

That expression is positive, or she would quit on her own. Now consider the worker's decision (assume risk neutrality). If she accepts a buyout, she receives B plus her alternative value $PV(A)$. If she rejects a buyout, she continues in her employment with probability $1 - p$, earning $PV(W)$. However, with probability p she is laid off, and earns $PV(A)$. Therefore, she will accept the buyout if:

$$B + PV(A) \geq (1 - p)PV(W) + p \cdot PV(A).$$

Therefore, the minimum buyout that she will accept is:

$$B^* = (1 - p)[PV(W) - PV(A)].$$

This expression is largest when $p = 0$, and $dB^*/dp < 0$. A greater threat of being laid off makes the worker more likely to accept a given buyout offer, and reduces the amount of buyout that she is willing to accept.

Part Two
ORGANIZATIONAL AND JOB DESIGN

*P*art One I viewed the firm as a pipeline of skills flowing in, being augmented, and eventually leaving the firm. While this is a useful view, it does not say much about what to do with employees once you have them. That is the topic of this section; here we consider job design. In doing so, we also analyze overall organizational design, as similar principles apply to both. Chapters 5–6 discuss decision making and organizational structure, while Chapters 7–8 discuss design of an individual employee's job.

In Chapter 5, we start by stepping back briefly and thinking about important principles for the design of an effective *economy*. By understanding key problems and tradeoffs that well designed economies address, we develop important ideas that we can use to think about the design of smaller economic units: firms, business units, or individual jobs. In other words, we will develop and then apply a *market metaphor* to modeling organization inside of firms.

Our discussion of markets brings out several important ideas. First, markets are powerful information processing mechanisms. They provide *collective intelligence* difficult to achieve in any other way. Second, markets provide *coordination* between different economic agents (though not always perfectly). We will see that firms often face tradeoffs between the goals of effectively using information, and coordinating among employees or business units. This tension is the basis for our discussion of decentralization and centralization in Chapter 5.

Chapter 6 analyzes overall organizational structure. This is the point in the text where we take the most macro view of the firm; in most other parts of the book, we focus on management of individual employees. Here we consider issues such as how a firm might break its structure into separate divisions, and how it might coordinate activity across business units.

Chapter 7 moves us back to the micro level of analysis: We now consider how to design an individual employee's job. In fact we will do so implicitly in Chapter 5, since the decision rights given to an employee (or not) are an important part of job design. In Chapter 7 we extend that argument to analyze how many and which tasks to bundle into the same job. Once more, classical economics plays a role. Also playing a role is the psychology of *intrinsic motivation*: how job design might affect a worker's motivation in performing the job. We will see that there is a nice complementarity between the economic and psychological views of job design. This chapter is one of the places in the text where the interplay between organizational psychology and personnel economics is most evident.

Chapter 8 extends the analysis from Chapter 7 to consider more advanced topics in job design. An important topic is the use and structuring of teams. We also consider what are sometimes called *high reliability organizations*. These are organizations, such as aircraft carriers, in which the organizational and job design tradeoffs are much harder to strike than in more typical firms, because the stakes (e.g., cost of failure) are so high. Thinking about how such organizations solve their design problems can provide useful insights into how your firm can solve less dramatic, but similar, issues.

The third topic in Chapter 8 is highly relevant today: the effects of information technology on job design and structure. Our discussion in Chapter 5 highlights the importance to firm structure of using information, and of the costs of communicating information. Information technology sometimes dramatically changes the costs of communicating information, which has implications for patterns of decision making in the firm, the use of hierarchies, and individual job design.

In Part Two, we will develop a point of view about firm design. As mentioned, part of the idea is that firms can usefully be viewed as large-scale information systems. In this role they do not just process knowledge, but *create* knowledge. Thus, a theme that arises in this part of the text is that a firm can design overall structure and individual jobs to optimize at a point in time, or innovate and adapt. You will see this playing some role in every chapter in this section.

These ideas also tie into Part One. The importance of knowledge creation and exploitation by the firm helps you understand why skills may be so valuable in firms. It should also help you (especially after reading Chapters 7–8) understand what kinds of skills are particularly valuable in many jobs in today's economy. And, it will help you see why skills have become even more valuable in recent decades, as discussed in Chapter 3.

Finally, markets provide important incentives to create value. Ownership of assets, and the ability to sell those assets in a competitive market, generates incentives for individuals to use those assets effectively. Prices for different goods and assets become, in this sense, a performance evaluation system. Like markets, firms also need to motivate effort and effective decisions by employees. That is why intrinsic motivation is discussed in Chapter 7. The importance of motivation in our market metaphor also provides an introduction to Part Three, which will focus on performance evaluation and pay for performance. As we will see there, it helps to discuss job design before thinking about evaluation and incentives.

5

DECISION MAKING

> Let no one say that taking action is hard. Action is aided by courage, by the moment, by impulse, and the hardest thing in the world is making a decision.
> —*Franz Grillparzer, 1844*

INTRODUCTION

You have just founded a new startup company. In addition to recruiting talent, a basic question that you face is how to structure your firm. Part of that is allocating decision making. Decisions will need to be made on myriad questions. Who should decide what? As the leader of the organization, should you make most of the decisions yourself, for consistency and control? Or, would that overwhelm you?

You have probably read in the business press that there has been a trend toward empowering workers in recent years. Should you do the same? If you push decision making downward, what problems might develop? And what exactly does it mean to empower an employee?

More fundamentally, what does it mean to make a decision? Are there different approaches to decision making? What structures are more likely to lead to correct or incorrect decisions? Which inhibit creativity and innovation? In this chapter, we will analyze these questions.

THE ORGANIZATION OF AN ECONOMY

Before we turn to those topics, let us briefly consider the design of the largest organization: the economy itself. The optimal organization of an economy was one of the most debated issues in the 20th century. On one side were advocates of centralized economies that were largely run by the government; on the other side were advocates of decentralized economies with much less of a role for government. The ideas raised in this debate are useful for thinking about the topics covered in Chapters 5–8.

By the end of the 20th century, it was apparent that more decentralized market-oriented economies are much more efficient—they are better at creating economic growth, jobs, and overall prosperity. They are also much more creative and adaptable than economies that are more centrally planned. Why is this the case?

An excellent starting point in answering this question is one of the most famous passages in all of economics: Adam Smith's *invisible hand* metaphor for decentralized economies:

> ... he intends only his own gain, and is ... led by an invisible hand to promote an end which was no part of his intention ... By pursuing his own interest he frequently promotes that of society more effectually than when he really intends to promote it.
> —*Adam Smith, The Wealth of Nations, 1776*

Smith was remarking on the amazing power of market economies to create economic value without the government playing a major role in their functioning, despite the fact that individual agents are acting in their own selfish interests. Decentralized economies are efficient. They are *self-organizing systems*; they arise and evolve largely spontaneously, and arrive at equilibrium prices and quantities on their own, without any central planner directing the market.

Consider the case of a small, ordinary neighborhood grocery store near the University of Chicago. The products on its shelves come from all parts of the world. The store sells a dozen varieties of coffee beans, from Colombia, Kenya, and elsewhere. It sells tea from Sri Lanka, China, and Japan. At this little local store, you can buy butter from Normandy, smoked salmon from Norway, and prosciutto from Italy. Milk sold there comes from Wisconsin. The breads use wheat grown in Kansas or Alberta, Canada. There are vegetables that were grown on nearby farms, and fruit from California, Mexico, and South America. Finally, you can purchase chocolate bars produced by a small manufacturer in Barcelona.

Somehow, goods from all over the planet were produced, used as inputs into other goods, shipped to Chicago, and placed on these store shelves. Somehow, the supply is regular enough that the store's goods are rarely out of stock, and are reasonably fresh. It is an amazing outcome, given that no one is directing this complex process. If you were designing the internal organization of a firm, a logical approach would seem to be to hire the most talented individuals that you could find, and have them set up and run your organization. It would seem logical that a skilled central planner could allocate resources and run an economy more efficiently than a chaotic, undirected market of individual, selfish decision makers. Yet the opposite tends to be true. Why is that?

Markets as Information Systems

Friedrich von Hayek elaborated on Adam Smith's *invisible hand* argument to provide an answer.[1] His main point was that markets are a form of *collective*

---

[1] In 1974 Von Hayek received a Nobel Prize for his writings on this topic, as did Wassily Leontief in 1973.

intelligence—a powerful *information system* that cannot be replicated by a central planner:

> How can . . . fragments of knowledge existing in different minds bring about results which, if they were to be brought about deliberately, would require a knowledge on the part of the directing mind which no single person can possess?
>
> —*von Hayek, 1945*

To understand his argument, imagine that you are a central planner running an economy. One of your many jobs is to allocate resources to produce coffee, and then to allocate the coffee to various consumers. What information do you need in order to allocate these resources efficiently?[2]

First, you need to know the value that different citizens place on coffee. How much do they prefer coffee to tea? To orange juice? How much would they be willing to give up in other resources to get coffee of higher quality? How much coffee will various workplaces wish to have? Hotels and restaurants?

Second, you need to know how to grow coffee. Thus you need knowledge of the technology of farming: fertilizer, weather and soil conditions, and so on. Similarly, as the central planner you need the same information about other industries, because you need to know about potential other uses for the resources devoted to producing coffee. To make coffee, you need land, water, labor, fertilizer, logistics. These could all be used to produce other goods, and you will have to make appropriate tradeoffs in the use of those resources. In economic terms, you need to know the opportunity costs of the resources used to make coffee.

These kinds of information require experience and technical expertise, but are largely predictable, systematic and foreseeable. A third kind of information that you need to know is information that is unsystematic and unpredictable. For example, to run the coffee industry effectively you need to know the optimal time to plant the coffee beans, when to provide water or fertilizer, and when to harvest the beans. These may vary from one field to the next. Such information is local and idiosyncratic. By its nature, it is going to be very difficult to communicate all of this knowledge to the central planner. Quoting von Hayek again:

> If we . . . agree that the economic problem of society is mainly one of rapid adaptation to changes in the particular circumstances of time and place . . . decisions must be left to the people who are familiar with these circumstances, who know directly of the relevant changes and of the resources immediately available to meet them. We cannot expect that this problem will be solved by first communicating all this knowledge to a central board which, after integrating all knowledge, issues its orders. We must solve it by some form of decentralization. (*Ibid*).

Thus, von Hayek points to the importance of *decentralization* to make use of information of "particular circumstances of time and place." Decentralized markets allow individual coffee farmers to optimize their activities by making decisions

---

[2]In the language of economists, you need to know demand curves and production functions for coffee, and for all other goods and services as well.

using the idiosyncratic knowledge they possess from doing their day-to-day jobs. It would be virtually impossible (too costly) to provide all of that information to a central planner, and this is why the central planner's decisions tend to be less effective.

At the same time, markets also make use of the more systematic types of knowledge described above. An individual farmer incorporates the value of coffee to consumers, because his decisions are based on the market price for coffee. He incorporates the value of alternative uses for the resources he employs, because his use of labor, land, and other inputs is based on the market prices for those inputs. He does not need to know how inputs could be used in other ways. Nor does he need to know that some of his coffee might be consumed in Chicago, and by whom. All he needs to know is the market prices for his inputs, and for his products. When he uses those prices in his decision making, he takes into account all of these types of information implicitly without having to possess any of that information except for prices.

In other words, prices provide a great deal of information needed to coordinate resource allocation across industries and even countries, without having to provide all of the detailed underlying information that a central planner would require. Prices are an economical information system.

Markets as Incentive Systems

Markets provide another powerful benefit in addition to effective use of dispersed knowledge. Consider our farmer again. Because he owns the farm, he has an incentive to run the farm profitably. In a centrally planned economy, he would be more like a bureaucrat, and would not have strong incentives to use the assets efficiently.

Moreover, the incentives that a market economy provides imply that resources tend to be placed in the hands of those with the information or skills that are most valuable when combined with those resources. Suppose that our farmer is not a good coffee farmer. In a decentralized economy, he has three options: He can invest in coffee farming human capital; hire help/rent out the land; or sell the land. If he chooses to hire someone, he has the incentive to hire someone who knows how to use the assets effectively. If he rents or sells the land, who will be willing to pay him the most? Someone who has the skills or information that can most profitably be combined with that land.

Markets and Innovation

A final important benefit of market economies is that they are great sources of innovation and adaptation. This arises from the two general principles discussed. Incentives mean that asset owners are motivated to respond to problems and opportunities quickly and effectively. It also means that they have incentives to invest, and to create new products or services that might be profitable.

Decentralization also helps innovation and adaptation in most cases. It allows the economy to make use of the creativity and ideas of all individuals dispersed throughout society. In a more centrally planned structure, the ideas of those who are far from the central planner are not likely to be considered. Similarly, the ability to respond flexibly to local circumstances allows a market economy to adapt to new situations efficiently and quickly.

Benefits of Central Planning

There are cases in which markets may not generate perfect efficiency, and they are relevant when we discuss centralization later. One case is natural monopoly, caused by *economies of scale*. A firm has economies of scale when its average total costs—costs per unit of output—decline as the firm gets larger. If production of a good is subject to economies of scale for high levels of output, then a larger firm has lower per-unit costs than a smaller firm, and can drive it out of business. Such a situation can lead to monopoly, or near-monopoly, in an industry. Economies of scale are usually driven by large *fixed costs*—the costs the firm must incur to be in business, but that do not vary with the level of output. Large fixed costs must be incurred by both small and large firms, but they can be amortized over more units of output by larger firms, putting them at an advantage. Monopolies are usually regulated by the government to reduce the firm's ability to exploit its monopoly power inefficiently.

In some cases, a government goes so far as to provide a good itself. This is often caused by a *public good* problem. A public good is a good that will not be provided by profit-seeking firms because they are unable to charge enough for the good to cover their costs. One reason for this is that for some goods, consumption cannot be prevented. For example, consider radio. Radio waves can be picked up by any consumer who owns a receiver. For this reason, it is impossible for a radio station to charge listeners to hear their programming. If they were unable to generate revenues from advertisers, there would be no private radio companies, and the government might have to provide such a good.

Another cause of market inefficiency is positive or negative *externalities*. Externalities result when a transaction between a buyer and seller imposes costs on, or provides benefits to, a third party who is not part of the transaction. The classic example of a negative externality is pollution. Because buyers and sellers of steel are not charged for the pollution that they create, a market economy ends up with too much pollution. The government may be able to improve the situation by imposing limits on pollution, taxes on steel, or other policies.

An example of a positive externality is *technology spillovers*. In many cases firms can copy the ideas of others, without compensation, because patents and copyright protection are imperfect. This reduces the incentives for an individual firm to innovate. For example, if a pharmaceutical company believes that some of the benefits of its research will be copied by a competitor, it has less incentive to invest in R&D. In this case market economies may invest insufficiently in innovation, and the government can improve efficiency by subsidizing R&D.

A related problem may arise in cases where a *standard* is valuable. A standard is important when there is value to having more consumers use the same product. This phenomenon is called *positive network externalities*. A good example is fax machine protocols. If fax machines use different protocols, then the fax machines are less valuable, since there is no guarantee that you can send or receive faxes with someone else. Decentralized economies often lead to competition among firms to establish standards. Sometimes this process works well, but not always (consider the different cellular phone standards in Europe and the United States). A central planner could choose a standard for everyone, reducing this wasteful competition.

This last example is not quite so simple, of course. Competition for setting the standard increases innovation, widens the number of possible choices, and may improve the technology. This would not happen if the government set the standard. Thus there is a tradeoff between having the standard set by the central government, or set through competition among decentralized firms. However, it is clearly the case that there can be too much competition to set the standard, so that there may be some role for the government to help coordinate in such cases.

The Market as Metaphor for Organizational Design

A firm's organization must provide the same important functions as a market. First, markets use knowledge dispersed throughout the economy. A great deal of information is summarized in prices, and in that way communicated cheaply throughout the system. Second, in cases where knowledge is costly to communicate, markets are effective at moving talent and decision making to the location of the knowledge. Third, coordination is achieved despite decentralized decision makers, through the price system. Fourth, markets provide strong incentives for effective decision making, investment, and creativity.

These are the concepts that we cover in the next eight chapters. A key question in Chapters 5–8 is how organizations can develop and use knowledge. We distinguish between information that is cheap or costly to communicate. A key idea is decentralization to make use of local knowledge. However, we also recognize the importance of coordination, either through incentives or other mechanisms, which sometimes leads to centralization. Finally, incentive systems are how firms approximate the role of ownership in an economy.

Therefore, our task is to develop a model of organizational design so that the firm can:

- Use both central and local knowledge effectively
- Coordinate decisions as necessary
- Provide strong incentives to make good, coordinated decisions
- Innovate and adapt

COLLECTIVE INTELLIGENCE AND DECISION MAKING AT HEWLETT-PACKARD

One of the ways in which markets serve as collective intelligence is prediction and risk assessment. Insurance and securities markets are very effective at pricing risks, based on the private information and assessments of those risks that individuals possess. For example, the discounted present value of a firm's future cash flows (net of debt obligations) is summarized in the stock price of the firm. The stock price is determined by thousands of individual investors and mutual fund managers, and incorporates their knowledge and assessment of the firm's prospects.

A similar example arises in gambling industries. The equilibrium odds of one team winning a sports event, for example, are the outcome of bets placed by many individuals, and are in effect the price for that risk.

In these two examples, markets are good at risk assessment not only because prices incorporate and summarize dispersed knowledge of informed individuals, but also because investors and gamblers have incentives to place intelligent bets.

Some firms are trying to replicate this collective intelligence effect inside their organizations. In an effort to improve monthly sales forecasting, Hewlett-Packard hired economist Charles Plott to set up a trading system for its employees. A few dozen employees with relevant knowledge were given trading accounts with small budgets (about $50). They used their budgets to place bets on computer sales for the month—in effect, buying or selling futures contracts. Traders kept their profits, and won additional rewards for placing correct bets. H-P found that market estimates (that is, the most likely outcomes implied by the trading between their employees) beat the estimates generated by their marketing staff 75% of the time. The company has incorporated the system into its forecasting, and is now experimenting with other applications.

Source: Kiviat (2005)

Our first step is to consider whether a decision should be centralized or decentralized. The basic idea is simple. The more valuable is lower level knowledge that is difficult to communicate to top management, the more should we expect to see decentralization. That is what von Hayek emphasized as knowledge of "particular circumstances of time and place." On the other hand, the more important coordination and control problems, the more should we expect to see centralization.

Suppose, then, that a decision has to be made, and it requires some information in order to be made effectively. The firm can move the information to the decision maker, or it can move the decision to the information.

If the information is not costly to communicate, there is no reason to decentralize the decision. Instead the firm can have the decision made at a high level in the hierarchy, and pass the information to the decision maker. This allows it to use the information, but also to coordinate well (since the most straightforward coordination mechanism is to have decisions made by top management).

If the information is costly to communicate, the firm faces a tradeoff. The more valuable the information, the more likely is decentralization the right answer. However, the greater the benefits of coordination, the more likely that centralization is the right answer.

In principle, the firm can mimic the market by using incentives to provide coordination, and then decentralize the decision. However, inside firms incentive systems are nearly always imperfect, so this is not always the best approach. When we think about centralizing decisions, remember that we think of (perfectly typical) cases where coordination cannot be achieved adequately solely through pay for performance. This is the key reason why the market metaphor is an imperfect one for firm design: Market prices are better measures of value than the performance measures that firms usually have available.[3]

Instead of centralizing or decentralizing a decision, the firm can also take an intermediate approach. It can put the decision somewhere in between in the hierarchy, say with a middle manager. An employee in the middle of the organization is likely to possess some of the knowledge that the firm is trying to make use of, or the information can be communicated part of the way up the hierarchy at lower cost than communicating it all the way to the top. At the same time, a middle level manager is generally more likely to take into account coordination issues than is a lower level employee. If so, the firm might get a better balance of use of lower level knowledge against the need for coordination by having the decision made somewhere between the lower and higher level of the firm.

For the rest of this chapter, we analyze where and how a *single decision* should be made in an organization. Imagine a firm that is organized along traditional hierarchical lines. A completely centralized decision would be made by the CEO. A completely decentralized decision would be made by a line worker. Some decisions could be made at middle levels as well. The right to make each decision can, in principle, be given to any employee at any level. Most of this chapter will focus on decentralization. First, however, let us consider the benefits of centralizing a decision.

---

[3] If we could measure performance perfectly, taking into account all short-and long-term factors correctly, then we could outsource the employee and write a contract with them. Firms exist in part because it is difficult to price all labor transactions on a spot market. We saw some of the reasons for this in earlier chapters. We will see others in Chapter 9.

BENEFITS OF CENTRALIZATION

CENTRALIZATION AT GENERAL MOTORS

General Motors has been famous for its decentralized structure since the 1920s. GM has been organized into relatively autonomous product divisions and regional subdivisions. It recently changed its structure to use more centralization for many key decisions.

In particular, it now requires that cars made by different divisions share basic parts, and collaborate on product design. It is doing so to reduce duplication of effort, and gain economies of scale in production and purchasing. GM is also hoping that this will speed up development, presumably since less time and effort will have to be spent communicating up and down the hierarchy and coordinating across independent units.

Source: Hawkins (2004)

Economies of Scale or Public Goods

Different units of the firm may share common assets. These may imply economies of scale or public good effects for the whole organization. For example, different departments may share space in the same corporate headquarters. Divisions may share a common product design group. All departments can share in the costs of designing and implementing an accounting system. Shared assets may also be intangible, such as a valuable brand name, corporate culture, or particularly effective leadership.

Conceivably assets can be shared with decentralized decision making through some kind of incentive system. Most firms do try to allocate overhead expenses through their accounting systems, for example. However, it can be quite difficult to determine how much of the cost of using an asset, or how much of the credit for generating the asset, should be attributed to each unit. When shared assets are intangible, such measurement problems are even worse. In such cases decentralization may lead to distorted incentives and ineffective use of the asset. Departments that are undercharged will use too much of the asset, while those who are overcharged will use too little. Those who are not given enough credit for investing in an asset will invest less than is optimal.

An alternative is to centralize some of the responsibility for the creation, allocation, and maintenance of shared assets. For example, a firm with a strong brand name is more likely to centralize decisions about product lines than is a firm with a group of unrelated products. A firm with a strong reputation as an employer is more likely to centralize human resource policies.

Better Use of Central Knowledge

von Hayek emphasized the importance of knowledge that is dispersed throughout the system. However, in some cases the most important knowledge resides at the top of the firm. Consider a firm that has operations in many regions. As information from different divisions flows to the central office, that office may see patterns and trends that are not apparent at the local level. Such a big picture view based on the combined experience of the entire firm means that some decisions should be centralized. In many cases, these decisions involve overall strategy.

Similarly, centralization can improve the use of knowledge because it improves the transfer knowledge across units. Unless units communicate directly with each other, they cannot learn from each other's experience, unless central management passes on the lessons.

Coordination

The most important benefit of centralization is to improve coordination. When coordination is more valuable, the firm will centralize more decisions. What are examples of coordination problems?

Coordination can be necessary because output from different units of the firm must be combined in some way. An assembly line is a classic example. An example at the macro level is when one division's product is used by a different division as part of the creation of their product. Of course, whether output of different divisions of a firm must be combined to create the product is endogenous: The firm chooses its divisional structure. It may well do so to *avoid* such coordination problems. However, these problems do arise in many circumstances.

Coordination problems may arise when different units need to synchronize. Consider the military in wartime. If the infantry goes in before the artillery softens up the battlefield, disaster will ensue. In the case of war it is essential that the units act in a certain sequence. In order to ensure that, decisions about when to act might be centralized. (An alternative would be to let them communicate with each other, an example of what we will call a lateral mechanism for coordination.)

Strategic decisions are often centralized. That is because strategy, by definition, usually involves consideration of most or all business units. However, it is not quite obvious that strategic decisions should always be centralized. In some businesses, the firm's strategy is, essentially, decentralization. This is the case for firms where innovation is important, but where individual products do not need to work with each other (the different departments of a university is a good example). However, to the extent that the firm's products do need to be compatible or consistent with each other, strategy must be centralized. This is similar to having the government determine a standard for technology.

STRATEGIC PLANNING AT DISNEY

❖ ❖ ❖ ❖ ❖ ❖ ❖ ❖ ❖ ❖

In early 2005, Robert Iger took the reins as the new CEO of Walt Disney Co., replacing the famed Michael Eisner.

Disney is a very large, multidivisional firm. For years, Disney's strategy had largely been in the hands of its strategic planning group at the head office. In the past, divisions could initiate new products, joint ventures, or acquisitions, but all major strategic decisions had to be approved by the strategic planning unit.

Less than 2 weeks after taking over, Iger shut down the strategic planning office. The powers that it once had were almost completely decentralized to the divisions. Larry Murphy, who had originally run strategic planning when it was set up by Eisner, stated that, "The disbanding of strategic planning is the natural evolution from a centralized system to a more decentralized control."

This change probably makes sense for several reasons. First, centralization fit better when Eisner was CEO, because Eisner had long experience at Disney and knew its operations intimately—he built up much of the company personally. While Iger worked at Disney for many years, he could not have the deep knowledge of all aspects of the business that Eisner had. Thus many decisions would be made more effectively by the divisional managers. Second, Disney had emphasized centralized strategy for a long time, so most of the benefits of coordination across product lines (e.g., films, video distribution, and television) had already been realized. Third, the divisions had chafed at the strong centralization of strategy, which limited their creativity.

Source: Marr (2005)

More abstractly, coordination problems can arise when there are *externalities* between different organizational units if they are decentralized. For example, suppose that one division's R&D investments benefit the products of a different division of the firm. In that case, there is a positive externality. If decisions about R&D are completely decentralized, the first division is likely to ignore the effects of its research on other products. Or suppose that one division launches a new product that competes directly with an existing product in a different division. That is an example of a negative externality. If product line decisions are completely decentralized, such problems are more likely to arise.

♦ ♦ ♦ ♦ ♦ ## BENEFITS OF DECENTRALIZATION

We now consider benefits of decentralizing a decision. The most important consideration here derives directly from von Hayek's analysis: whether there is valuable information at lower levels that is costly to communicate. If there is, the firm should seriously consider decentralizing some decisions to make use of that knowledge. We first focus on factors that determine how costly information is to communicate, and then list a few other benefits of decentralization.

Specific vs. General Knowledge

Information or knowledge falls along a spectrum from cheap to communicate, to costly to communicate. For example, the price of a pound of coffee is very cheap to communicate. It is a single number, and can be transmitted via information technology instantly. By contrast, the field of personnel economics is costly to communicate. It is complex, and much of it cannot be quantified easily. Even putting it in the words of a text does not completely explain the concepts. Students require the professor to explain and develop ideas more fully. Understanding is also helped by the use of examples, such as case studies, and by the student's personal work experience.

In economics, information that is cheap to communicate is usually called *general knowledge*. Information that is costly to communicate is usually called *specific knowledge*. When we say costly to communicate, we mean either costly to transmit, or costly to understand once received. Information may be passed from one person to another, but if the receiving person does not understand the information, it has not been communicated. Figure 5.1 shows our spectrum on which to analyze knowledge. (Let us take a moment to clarify terms, since this terminology that economists use can, unfortunately, be confusing. Specific and general knowledge sound like specific and general human capital, and also sound similar to specialization. However, those are different ideas. To refresh your memory, the concepts of specific and general human capital refer to skills that are

FIGURE 5.1
SPECIFIC VS GENERAL KNOWLEDGE

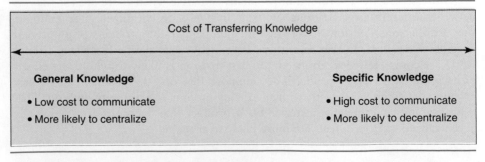

relatively more valuable at one employer, or valuable at many employers. Think of human capital as training, while what we are talking about in this section is the information that arises as you perform your day to day job. Finally, specialization refers to the extent to which a worker's skills [and, in Chapter 7, tasks on the job] are narrow or broad. Choosing a college major means specialization in this sense. An MBA, by contrast, is relatively unspecialized, since it involves studying a little bit about many different fields.)

Specific knowledge is the key idea here, since it will favor decentralization. Below are several attributes of information that make it more specific. These are the kinds of information that von Hayek had in mind in his famous phrase about "the particular circumstances of time and place."

Information That is Perishable

Information may be costly to communicate simply because it must be acted on quickly or it loses its value. A trader on a stock exchange must respond to market movements immediately or lose the ability to exploit new information and buy or sell orders as they appear. For this reason, traders are carefully screened, trained as needed, and then largely given the right to make trading decisions themselves. Similarly, suppose that a firm's sales force sometimes receives large rush orders from key customers. If the customers will turn to alternative suppliers when they cannot receive a quick confirmation on the order, the firm is likely to give the salesperson some direction (possibly within limited parameters) and allow him to negotiate terms and decide whether to accept the order.

This is an example of an idea you will see again later. Centralization and hierarchy take time. Firms that employ those methods are more deliberative, but also slower to react and adapt.

Information That is Complex

One of the main reasons why information can be costly to communicate is *complexity*. Complexity can mean that there are many variables (as opposed to just the price of a pound of coffee). More important, however, is complexity in the sense of interdependence between different pieces of information. Consider the difference between a spreadsheet with a simple list of prices, one with many numbers and formulas, and one with many cross-references between cells. The latter is much more costly to communicate, since the recipient of the spreadsheet must understand the formulas and reasoning behind them.

We will use the same sense of complexity when talking about job design in Chapter 7. Interdependence between tasks makes it more difficult to separate tasks into different jobs. It also makes it more likely that the worker who performs those tasks has some specific knowledge about the work, because the work is complex in the sense we describe here.

Information That Requires Technical Skills

An important special case is when information being transmitted requires advanced human capital in order to be completely understood. This is the case with most scientific or *technical* knowledge. For example, many decisions about R&D must be made by the firm's engineers, often with little oversight by management, simply because the decisions require technical knowledge that only the engineers possess.

Information That is Unforeseeable/Idiosyncratic

Information can be costly to communicate simply because frequent communication is necessary, which multiplies the costs of communication proportionally. This is the case when the environment is more dynamic and random. However, random environments do not necessarily imply that there is specific knowledge. Suppose that the job circumstances change constantly, but only vary in predictable ways. Perhaps a customer service representative handles 12 different types of customer complaints, but the same types of complaints arise over and over again. This does not require much decentralization. Instead, the firm can set up standard operating procedures that dictate what the employee must do in each of the 12 circumstances. Thus, to the extent that the environment is unforeseeable or *idiosyncratic*, the employee is more likely to possess specific knowledge on the job.

Information That is Subjective/Experiential

There is a famous Supreme Court case in the United States in which a judge ruled that he could not define a concept, but knew it when he saw it. That is an example of information that is *subjective* or *experiential*. Such information is usually costly to communicate by its nature. It is called subjective or qualitative because it is impossible to quantify, and difficult to rigorously describe in an economical way. Communicating subjective information usually requires sitting down and talking about the situation, explaining it verbally, and allowing the recipient to ask clarifying questions. In some cases the level of subjectivity is so high that the information is called experiential—in order to really understand the information, you have to experience it for yourself.

In order to use subjective or experiential information effectively, it is almost inevitable that some decentralization will be required. For example, performance evaluations in white collar jobs are usually quite subjective. For this reason firms usually allow supervisors to conduct such evaluations, even though this subjects the firm to the risk of inconsistency and legal liability from discrimination.

Other Benefits of Decentralization

Saves Management Time

Decentralization of some decisions is necessary to prevent overwhelming central management. Less important decisions, and those that require less coordination, tend to be pushed to lower level management simply so that top management can focus resources on the most important decisions. The same applies at all levels of the hierarchy, so that less important and less coordination-dependent decisions tend to get pushed farther down in the firm.

Develops Management Skills

Analysis and decision-making skills are forms of human capital that, to a good extent, must be learned on the job. In order to develop good future managers, the firm must give lower level managers some room to make decisions. As a first step, a new manager will be given discretion over less important issues, and may be constrained (e.g., by limiting expenditures via a budget) to prevent too much damage from mistakes. As the manager's talent grows, he is given greater discretion, and over decisions with higher stakes. This is an excellent way for the firm to train managers who can then be promoted into higher positions.

Note that this is one reason why it is common for subordinates to be promoted into positions similar to those of their supervisor. As a subordinate gains more experience in the job, the supervisor passes on more tasks and decisions to the subordinate, in effect training the employee in how to do the supervisor's job.

Intrinsic Motivation

Decentralization is one part of what is often called *job enrichment*, which we discuss in Chapter 7. The other part of job enrichment is assigning more tasks to the worker. One benefit of both is that the job may be more challenging and interesting to the worker. Therefore, the worker may be more intrinsically motivated to perform the work diligently.

AUTHORITY AND RESPONSIBILITY

In the Army, the lowest position is denoted private. Corporals and then sergeants have authority over these lowest level soldiers. Sergeants report to lieutenants, who in turn report to captains. Captains are below majors, who are themselves below lieutenant colonels and colonels. Generals are at the top of this hierarchy, and the number of stars that a general wears determines rank among generals.

There is a number of reasons for having a strict hierarchy in the military. The most obvious is that in combat situations decisions must be made quickly. Collective decision making is slow and highly impractical during battle. Thus, a clear hierarchy is set up in which orders to subordinates are obeyed without question or delay.

Very few firms are engaged in the kind of production that requires split-second decisions with absolute deference to higher authority. But there are some business situations that do fit into this category. Even when a team may be involved in the negotiations to discuss a deal with another firm or client, one member must speak for the team and must have the authority to make the decision.

When jobs are designed, it is generally important to determine the level of authority associated with the job and how much responsibility is assigned to any given job. More often than not, the degree of authority and responsibility associated with a given job depends on the job holder. Some vice presidents have more authority than others, the difference presumably determined by ability differences.

An important consideration discussed is the extent to which the job holder has specific knowledge that is costly to communicate to colleagues, but that is valuable for the firm. Another important consideration is the extent to which the job holder's work must be coordinated with colleagues. We used these ideas to characterize a decision as being relatively centralized or decentralized. While useful, this is a simplification. In this section, we go beyond this basic tradeoff of use of specific knowledge vs. coordination, and think about decision making a little more carefully.

Decision Making as a Multistage Process

A decision is not just a binary answer to a question; it is a deliberative process. It can be helpful to think of a decision as having several stages. One way to do so that fits many types of decisions is to characterize the decision as having four stages:[4]

1. *Initiatives*
2. *Ratification*
3. *Implementation*
4. *Monitoring*

The first stage, initiatives, is the process of coming up with a set of options. This is perhaps the most crucial stage for creativity and innovation. We sometimes think of this stage as brainstorming—what are our possibilities?

Once the possibilities are identified, one of the options must be chosen. This is the second stage, ratification. This stage corresponds to the term strategy in common usage. It is when the basic direction of future actions is decided.

Once the strategy is chosen, there may be many possible ways in which the strategy can be pursued. This is the third stage, implementation. Another common term for this stage is tactics. Once more, there can be quite a bit of creativity, though of a more applied sort, at this stage. As is often said, the devil is in the details.

Finally, it is important that implementation conforms to the strategy chosen at the second stage. Thus, the fourth stage is monitoring of the implementation.

Almost any decision-making process fits this description to a good degree. Suppose that you are a plant manager and have been told to cut costs by 10% in the next year. How would you do so? First, you need to figure out what basic approaches you might take. These would include things like cutting salary; layoffs; obtaining better terms with suppliers; or programs to increase efficiency on the plant floor. Then you need to choose between these ideas (though you can choose more than one option, in this example). Once you have chosen some options, you need to figure out how to implement them. And, finally, you will want to monitor your progress (and certainly the central office will do so) as the year progresses.

It is useful to break decision making into different steps because different steps can be given to different people. In particular, Stages 1 and 3, initiatives

---

[4]See Fama & Jensen (1983).

and implementation, are more likely to be decentralized, while Stages 2 and 4, ratification and monitoring, are more likely to be centralized, for two reasons.

The first reason to decentralize Stages 1 and 3, and centralize Stages 2 and 4, is to balance the goals of using specific knowledge at lower levels against the need for coordination. Often, much of the information needed to figure out what options are available resides with lower level employees. The same is even truer for the implementation stage. Consider again the example of the plant manager who needs to cut costs by 10%. He is likely to ask his staff for suggestions about ways to do so. They, in turn, are likely to turn to their staffs for advice. That is decentralization of Stage 1, initiatives. At the implementation stage, the manager will again ask his staff to devise ways to implement the cost cutting, since lower level employees will know many details that he will not.

However, the choice of the overall cost cutting strategy is likely to be made by the plant manager, in order to make sure that it is consistent with firm goals. The same is true with monitoring of implementation, to make sure that cost cutting programs do not conflict with each other or with the firm's strategy (say, by harming product quality too much). Thus, relative centralization of Stages 2 and 4 provides better coordination.

The second reason to centralize Stages 2 and 4 compared to Stages 1 and 3 is that employees tend to have imperfect incentives, so their interests are not always aligned with the firm's. When that is the case, the firm must safeguard against empowered employees who make decisions that favor their goals over the firm's. An important way to do so is to limit their discretion, by retaining the right to ratify their decisions, and by monitoring how the decisions are implemented. In other words, when decision makers have imperfect incentives, some system of checks and balances is necessary.

This idea applies not only at lower levels, but all the way to the top of the organization. One of the key roles of a board of directors is to provide oversight for a CEO with imperfect incentives. Note that privately owned companies do not generally need to worry about such *governance* structures, because their managers are owners, and thus have no incentive problem.

As can be seen, the stark distinction between centralizing and decentralizing a decision that we started with above is too simplistic. In practice, decisions are made over several stages, and a typical pattern is for decentralization of early stages, followed by centralization, and then decentralization for additional initiatives or implementation, followed by centralization for more ratification or monitoring. This allows the firm to get many of the benefits of *both* use of lower level specific knowledge and coordination simultaneously.

The first and third stages are often referred to as *decision management*, while the second and fourth are often referred to as *decision control*. Our basic point is that decision management tends to be more decentralized, while decision control tends to be more centralized.

This characterization is a simple but useful framework for thinking about making many different kinds of decisions. For example, it gives guidance to your thinking about how a company can implement a change program. Furthermore, it clarifies what it means to empower your workers. Empowerment usually means giving decision management rights to employees, but reserving at least some decision control rights (especially the final stage, monitoring) for yourself.

Finally, the distinction between decision management and decision control provides a way to think about what managers and their subordinates do. It is often said that a hierarchy involves the passing of information and decisions up and down. Much of middle management work involves two things. The first is ratifying and monitoring the work of subordinates, and passing them relevant general knowledge as needed. The second is taking their output, processing it in some way, and making suggestions about initiatives and implementation to a higher level manager. Thus, decision control is what we mean by the term *hierarchy*.

We now present a further refined way of thinking about decision management and decision control. A firm can emphasize the creative stages, decision management. Or, it can emphasize the control stages, decision control. The relative emphasis has important implications for the type of firm that it is—how innovative, how risky, the culture it develops, and so on.

Flat vs. Hierarchical Structures

A firm has a great deal of leeway with respect to the ways in which it sets up authoritarian relations. For example, it is possible to have a flatter organization in which each individual has more authority over which projects are approved or rejected. Alternatively, a firm can be set up with a very steep authoritarian pyramid, where each level has the ability to veto decisions made by lower levels. In the language we just defined, a flat structure places more emphasis on decision management, while a steeper structure places more emphasis on decision control.

A Tradeoff Between Two Types of Errors

Whether jobs should be designed with flat or steep authority structures depends on the costs of accepting poor projects relative to the costs of rejecting good ones. In statistical parlance, the issue is the trading off false positives (Type I errors) versus false negatives (Type II errors).

To make this more concrete, consider an example provided by a former Stanford student in the women's apparel business. Hong Kong natives Gladys and Willie run a New York-based firm that imports women's lingerie and sleepwear. They describe themselves as having a "young and funky" image. Gladys needed to decide whether to branch out into more romantic lingerie. Doing so required some up-front investment in marketing, distribution and, most significantly, in setting up the production line. Major losses would occur if the line did not sell as hoped. She had to decide between going into the romantic lingerie line and forgoing the opportunity. There are two types of errors that she could have made. She might have invested in the line when doing so turned out to be unprofitable, or she could have decided not to produce the line when doing so was profitable. Table 5.1 lists the possibilities.

TABLE 5.1
POSSIBLE TYPES OF CORRECT OR INCORRECT DECISIONS

	Produces	*Does not produce*
Line is profitable	Good decision	False negative error
Line is unprofitable	False positive error	Good decision

If she produces lingerie and it turns out to be unprofitable, then she has committed a *false positive* error. False positive error is defined as accepting an unprofitable project. If she chooses not to produce lingerie and the line would have been profitable, then she has made a *false negative* error. False negative error is defined as rejecting a profitable project.

There is a tradeoff between false positive and false negative errors. If Gladys adopts a very aggressive policy and accepts every new project that comes along, she will never commit a false negative error. Because she always produces, she is certain to make false positive errors whenever a project is unprofitable. The more aggressive her posture, the higher the likelihood of a false positive error, and the lower the likelihood of a false negative error.

Alternatively, she can adopt an extremely conservative posture, rejecting every new project that comes along. Because she never produces a new line, she can never find herself in the box where she produces, but shouldn't have. She never commits a false positive error, but now some false negative errors are certain to occur. Whenever a new product would have been profitable, she commits a false negative error because she never accepts it. The more conservative her posture, the lower the likelihood of a false positive error and the higher the likelihood of a false negative error.

Figure 5.2 shows the tradeoff. On the horizontal axis is the probability of making a false positive error—that is, going ahead with the project when it is unprofitable. On the vertical axis is the probability of making a false negative error—that is, rejecting the project when it is profitable. At point D all projects are accepted, so the probability of accepting a project given that it is unprofitable is 1, and bad projects are accepted with certainty. At point C all projects are rejected, so the probability of rejecting a project given that it is profitable is 1 and good projects are rejected with certainty. The tradeoff is shown by the solid line between C and D. If some projects are accepted and some are rejected, then the firm ends up at an interior point, like A. At A, some but not all good projects are rejected, and some but not all bad projects are accepted.

How does the firm decide how aggressive it should be when accepting new projects? If it is very costly to accept bad projects, the firm wants a more stringent rule, which moves it toward C. If it is very costly to pass up a good project, then the firm wants a more lenient rule, pushing it toward D.

The goal is to enhance the information set so as to allow for fewer errors of each type. If decisions were better informed, then the tradeoff would be along the dotted curve rather than the solid one. Note that on the dotted curve, the firm can

FIGURE 5.2
ERROR TRADEOFFS AND AUTHORITY STRUCTURE

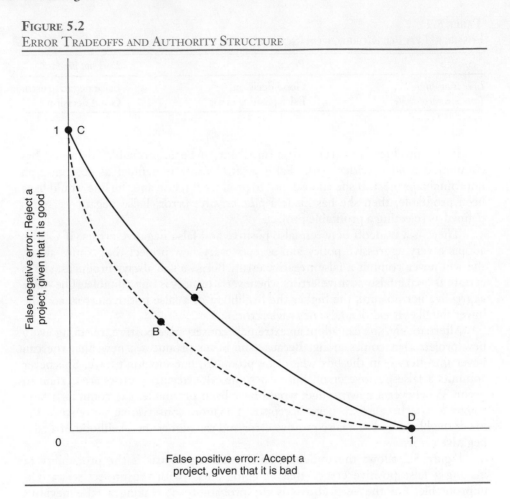

make less of each type of error. Point *B* implies less false positive error and less false negative error than point *A*. The firm would always prefer the dotted curve to the solid curve. However, keep in mind that information is costly. Decisions are better along the dotted curve, but the cost of obtaining the dotted curve might be more delay or higher consulting fees.

Three Examples of Authority Patterns

We now return to job design and authority patterns. By structuring the authority relations in different ways, different kinds of errors are made more or less likely. Consider two different decision making structures for Gladys and Willie, shown in Figure 5.3.

A hierarchical structure places Gladys above Willie in decision making. Willie comes up with new ideas, and is allowed to reject any project, but does not have authority to accept any project on his own. All he can do is render a

FIGURE 5.3
TWO POSSIBLE AUTHORITY STRUCTURES

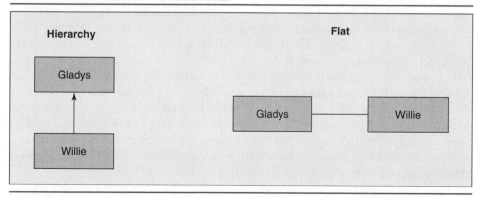

recommendation to accept. This is what we previously called decision management; he is recommending either new ideas, or how to implement ideas that were already chosen. Gladys then has the authority to make the final call. This is decision control: either ratifying new ideas, or monitoring implementation. Such a structure works in the direction of reducing false positive error and increasing false negative error.

The second structure, called a *flat authority structure*, tends to have fewer false negative errors and more false positive errors. In this case the firm is set up such that both Gladys and Willie evaluate projects and choose whether to accept or to reject individually. Both spend their time coming up with and evaluating new projects, but do not check each other. There is relatively more emphasis on decision management, and less on decision control, compared to the hierarchy.

Which structure is better? It is easy to show that a hierarchical structure will approve fewer projects than a flat decision structure (see the Appendix for formal derivations of ideas discussed in this section). The hierarchical structure makes fewer false positive errors, but more false negative errors. Fewer bad projects are accepted, but more good projects are rejected. There are two reasons for this. First, since the hierarchical structure requires two approvals rather than one, the test that a project must pass is more stringent. Second, since two people are required for an evaluation rather than one, fewer decisions are made. Gladys and Willie, working in parallel, can evaluate more projects than each can alone.

If each project must be evaluated by Willie before it goes to Gladys, then half as many projects get an initial screening. Thus, fewer projects are approved. Failure to review a project is an implicit rejection. The bottom line is that a hierarchical decision structure, where low level jobs are denied the authority to make the final decision on a project, results in a more stringent criterion and fewer project approvals than does a flat, egalitarian authority structure.

There is a third possibility. The structure can be made flat with second opinions required. Rather than putting Gladys above Willie, the firm can simply require that every project reviewed by Willie is also reviewed by Gladys, and vice versa. If both agree, the decision is obvious. If they disagree, then some other rule must be used to reconcile the differences. There is a number of possibilities, but for our purposes the details of reconciliation are irrelevant. It is always true, irrespective of the reconciliation rule used, that a second opinion structure is less stringent than a hierarchical structure, but more stringent than a single opinion flat structure.

Think about it this way. Under the hierarchical structure, when Willie rejects a project, Gladys never even sees it. She only sees those projects that he passes up to her. In the case of a second opinion structure, Gladys sees even those projects that Willie rejects. If Gladys likes the project, then the two opinions must be reconciled. As long as some of these reconciliations result in positive outcomes, projects that would not have been accepted by the hierarchical structure will be accepted by the second opinion structure. Therefore, although both structures review the same number of projects, the second opinion structure is less stringent and approves more projects than the hierarchical structure.

On the other hand, the second opinion structure is more stringent than a flat, single decision maker structure. This is somewhat less obvious than it seems. It is true that a second opinion can sometimes reverse an initial decision to reject, but it is also true that a second opinion can reverse an initial decision to accept. The main reason that a second opinion structure is more stringent is that when second opinions are required, fewer projects are considered at all. If it takes, say, a week for one person to review a project, then the flat structure with a single decision maker produces two decisions per week: one by each. In contrast, the second opinion structure produces only one decision per week, since both must review every proposal.

Figure 5.4 augments Figure 5.2 by showing the locations of the different job authority structures with respect to false positive and false negative errors. Which structure should a firm choose? Since there is an implicit tradeoff in the choice, the answer depends on the payoffs associated with each outcome. Now that three structures are identified, let us consider three types of payoff regimes, shown in Figures 5.5–5.7.

Small upside, large downside. Figure 5.5 shows a payoff structure that might be appropriate for the *Exxon Valdez*, a large oil tanker. As you may recall, a few years ago the *Valdez* was involved in an accident that caused a major oil spill for which Exxon was financially responsible. The losses associated with the oil spill ran into the billions of dollars in cleanup, litigation, and settlement costs. The captain of the ship was blamed for the accident, and there was evidence that alcohol was in part to blame.

The *Valdez* situation is typical of one variety of payoff structure. Doing the job extremely well results in small gains relative to the expected amount, but making a mistake can be disastrous. The upside of payoffs is limited, but the downside implies losses in the billions.

The *Valdez's* captain makes more profit for the company by bringing the oil shipment in somewhat early, but it is not worth the risk of trying to guide the ship while under the influence of alcohol. A mistake is just too costly. When the payoff structure looks as it does in Figure 5.5, the firm wants to minimize false positive

FIGURE 5.4
AUTHORITY STRUCTURE AND ERRORS

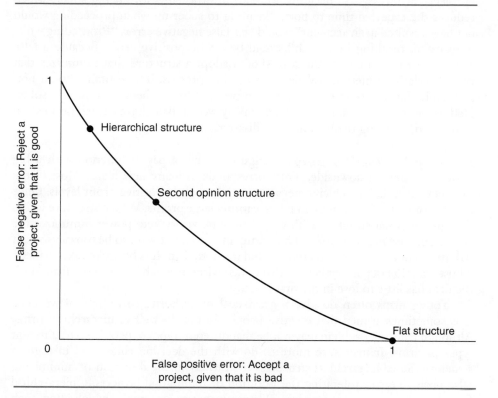

FIGURE 5.5
SMALL UPSIDE, LARGE DOWNSIDE

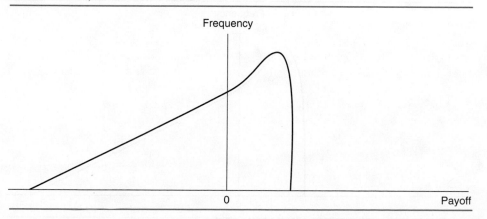

error and is willing to accept higher levels of false negative error. Think of the "project" in this case as deciding whether to proceed before being sober, which reduces the expected time to port. "Waiting to sober up when proceeding would not have resulted in an accident" would be a false negative error. "Proceeding while intoxicated, resulting in a crash" would be a false positive error. Because a false positive error is so costly, the firm should adopt a structure that minimizes that risk—a relatively hierarchical decision making process. The captain should not, and likely did not, have the authority to proceed before being completely sober. Had he radioed in for approval, the company would likely have denied permission to proceed, reducing the likelihood of disaster.

Large upside, small downside. Figure 5.6 has a payoff function with a big upside and limited downside. This corresponds to many new firms. Most of the time new firms fail, producing negative or only slightly positive profit levels. Once every so often the innovators hit it big, earning large profits. Which structure favors the upside? A flat structure with very little supervisory veto power minimizes the amount of false negative error. The startup firm does not want to be too cautious. It has little reputation or capital to lose, and much to gain. It is better to take chances. Those that do not pan out can be abandoned without much harm to the firm, since the firm has little to lose in the first place.

Young firms often do give a great deal of authority to individual workers. It is sometimes argued that creative people do not do well in hierarchical firms. Although true, the problem may not be that different types of people go to different types of firms. It may have more to do with the decision rules used in a given structure. Since hierarchical structures tend to err in the direction of minimizing false positive error, tolerating the rejection of some good projects, a hierarchical firm does not encourage creativity. Flatter authority structures, which allow each

FIGURE 5.6
LARGE UPSIDE, SMALL DOWNSIDE

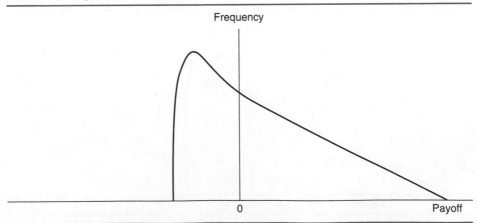

FIGURE 5.7
SYMMETRIC PAYOFFS

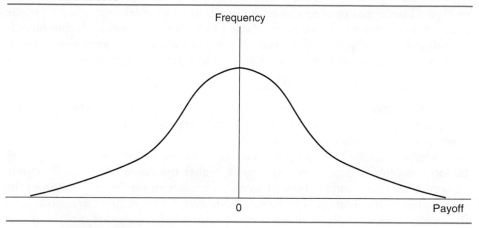

worker more choice, also allow creativity to flourish. Risky, wild ideas that would be rejected in a hierarchical structure may be allowed to proceed in the flat, single decision maker structure.

This discussion is another way to see the idea that we discussed earlier—decentralized structures tend to foster creativity, while centralized structures are better at maintaining control and avoiding large mistakes.

Symmetric payoffs. Most firms are in neither the *Exxon Valdez* nor startup category. Payoffs are more symmetric in most businesses, especially established ones. Figure 5.7 shows a payoff function for a local store. Great performance and innovative work are unlikely to generate the large upside that a startup might experience. Poor performance and shoddy work may cost the firm some money, but not the disastrous losses incurred by Exxon when the oil spill occurred. In this case, the firm prefers tolerable levels of false positive error and false negative error, minimizing neither at the expense of the other.

Investing in Better Quality Decision Making

In Figure 5.2 two curves were drawn. The dotted curve lies inside the solid curve. Other things equal, it is better to face the constraint of the dotted curve than that of the solid curve because for any given level of false positive error, the dotted curve implies less false negative error than does the solid curve (except at the endpoints). In other words, fewer errors of either type are made along the dotted curve than on the solid curve.

How does the firm move to the dotted curve? Unfortunately this cannot be done without cost. Fewer errors of either type are made along the dotted curve than on the solid curve. To get to the dotted curve, it is necessary to improve the decision process. There is a number of ways to do so, all of which are costly. The firm can attempt to hire better evaluators by going for more able, higher priced workers. The firm can give an evaluator more time to consider each project. Or, the firm can make more information available to the evaluator, say by hiring outside consultants or buying other data. Whether any of these steps is profitable depends on how much is gained relative to the amount lost by making poor decisions.

An Application: Air Traffic Routes

Consider an example of an airline pilot trying to decide whether to take a quicker route through thunderstorms or a safer but lengthier route around the storms. Some hypothetical information is given in Table 5.2.

What should the firm do? If a plane crash occurs, the firm incurs a cost of $1 billion from loss of capital and reputation, higher insurance rates, and litigation. However, fuel costs and the odds of a crash are different on the two routes, so the expected costs are different. The better choice here is for the airplane to go around the storm. This example, with some upside and a large downside, fits the payoff structure in Figure 5.5. Thus firm could set up a hierarchy, but here the situation is somewhat different because there is an incentive problem. The pilot is more likely to care about her own life than about firm profitability. To offset the tendency to be too conservative, the airline might make a rule that pilots take the shortest route unless they receive approval from the company to deviate. Then, when faced with thunderstorms, the pilot radios in to request the longer, more costly route. The company can approve or deny the request.

Given the probability and payoff structure in the table, the airline would always approve the pilot's request to take the longer route. If the pilot flies through the storm, the expected cost is:

Expected cost of going through the storm $= (10^{-5})(\$1B) + \$17,000 = \$27,000.$

The first term reflects the probability of a crash, given that the pilot flies through the storm, times the loss to the company from a crash. The $17,000 is the fuel cost. If the pilot takes the longer route, the expected cost is:

Expected cost of going around $= (10^{-9})(\$1B) + \$20,000 = \$20,001.$

The first term reflects the probability of a crash, given that the longer route is chosen, times the cost to the company of a crash. The $20,000 reflects the higher fuel cost. The expected cost is lower than that of flying through the storm.

TABLE 5.2
THUNDERSTORMS AND AIRPLANE TRAVEL

	Probability of crash	Cost of crash	Expected cost of crash	Expected fuel cost
Go through storm	10^{-5}	$1 billion	$10,000	$17,000
Go around storm	10^{-9}	$1 billion	$1	$20,000

Since the company will always grant permission when asked, there is no sense in having pilots call in for approval in this case. Under these circumstances, the pilot is given full authority to select a longer route when there are thunderstorms along the shorter route. In other words, a flat structure is preferred.

Note that the probability of committing a false positive error is zero. Since the shorter route is never taken, there is no chance that the short route would be taken when it would have resulted in a crash. Conversely, the probability of committing a false negative error is 1. It is certain that the shorter route through thunderstorms will be rejected even when going through a storm would not have resulted in a crash, because the shorter route is always rejected.

Now suppose that the company can buy some additional information. A new device, the Forecaster, can more accurately forecast lightning strikes. By doing this, it can offer a recommendation on when it is safe to fly through the storm and when it is not. Table 5.3 provides statistics on the accuracy of the Forecaster.

The Forecaster recommends that the route through the storm be taken 9,999/10,000 times. The probability of a crash, given a positive recommendation, is only 1 in 100 million. However, when the Forecaster recommends that the storm be avoided, going against the advice will result in a crash in 1 in 10 times. The Forecaster provides very accurate information that allows much better decisions to be made.

If the device is used, the optimal decision from the company's point of view changes. Whereas before, the company always preferred that storms be avoided, now the company would prefer that the shorter route be taken whenever the Forecaster recommends so. Under a positive recommendation, the expected cost of a trip is:

Expected cost of going through the storm $= (10^{-8})(\$1B) + \$17,000 = \$17,010.$

while the expected cost from taking the route around the storm is still $20,001. Thus, the company would prefer the shorter route to be taken whenever the Forecaster makes a positive recommendation, but the longer route to be taken whenever it makes a negative recommendation.

Two questions arise. First, should the firm purchase the Forecaster? The answer depends on the cost of the Forecaster and on its frequency of usage. Second, and more important, what kind of authority structure should be used if it is purchased?

TABLE 5.3
ACCURACY OF THE FORECASTER

| | | | Probability of crash when going | |
			Through	Around
Probability of	Go through	0.9999	10^{-8}	10^{-9}
recommendation	Go around	10^{-4}	10^{-1}	10^{-9}

Without the Forecaster, each pilot could be left to choose the route. Because the pilot's incentives were aligned with the firm's interests, there was no incentive problem from such decentralization. With the Forecaster, the situation is different. The airline prefers that the shorter route through the storm be taken 99.99% of the time. The pilot may have a different view. First, the likelihood of a crash when the Forecaster recommends the shorter route is 1 in 100 million. If the longer route is taken, the likelihood of a crash is 1 in 1 billion. Both numbers are small, but the former is still 10 times greater than the latter. Other things equal, the pilot prefers the lower odds of a crash and chooses the longer route, even though the shorter route is more cost effective. Second, crashes aside, it may be more difficult to fly through thunderstorms than to divert. Both of these considerations suggest that the pilot might not make the same decision that the company would make.

In this case, the authority structure should change if the Forecaster is purchased. The firm now prefers a hierarchical structure, in which the pilot must request permission to divert around the storm and in which the airline has the right to refuse permission.

This example illustrates the interplay between available information, decision making structures, and employee incentives. When central information is available (the Forecaster), centralization through greater use of hierarchy is more likely to make sense. When it is not, decentralization makes sense. However, decentralization works well only when the interests of the decision maker correspond reasonably well with the interests of the organization.

●●●●● ## SUMMARY

Organizations are more than just a collection of workers performing physical tasks. A more valuable view, especially in modern economies, is that it is a generator and processor of knowledge. Much of an organization's structure, and (as we will soon see) its job design, has the goal of making use of information to improve efficiency, adapt, and innovate.

Economies themselves face the same issues. The most effective organization of an economy is a market-oriented one. This provides decentralization so that specific knowledge of time and place can be exploited. Using knowledge dispersed through the economy makes production more efficient. It also makes the economy more adaptable, since adaptation usually requires continuous reaction to local events. Finally, it makes the economy more creative, since it encourages all individuals to invest in and make use of their ideas.

Market economies are self-organizing systems—there is little central direction of the system. Yet they are able to achieve a great amount of coordination despite this. The way this is achieved is through prices, which serve as signals of the value of different goods and services. Decentralized decision makers use this information to guide their decisions, without having to know the details of other possible uses of the goods and services, or of who their customers might be and how they will use the product. Thus, prices are an efficient way to transmit general knowledge and coordinate across the economy.

Finally, markets work well because they provide strong incentives through ownership of assets. Because individuals can own, buy, and sell assets, they are motivated to maximize the use of those assets. This also improves the matching of information and decisions, since there is an incentive to move information to decision rights, and vice versa, to maximize the value of both. The strong incentives in a market economy are also important reasons why decentralized economies are so innovative and dynamic.

The market metaphor is very useful in thinking about organizational design. While no firm will be able perfectly to mimic a market structure, the basic goal of its organization should be to replicate, as well as possible, the way markets work. Thus, organizational structure should be designed to achieve several key goals: use information, especially specific knowledge dispersed throughout the firm and its customers or suppliers; coordinate as needed across the firm; and provide appropriate incentives to maximize firm value.

A good starting place for thinking about organization design is to identify the most valuable specific knowledge. One way to do so is to ask who/what/where/when/why about specific knowledge. Who in or outside of the firm has knowledge that is valuable to the business, but difficult to communicate to central management? What kind of knowledge is it? Is it tied to a location, or is it perishable? When and why is it valuable to the business? Answering these questions will give strong guidance about situations where decentralization of some decision rights is likely to be important.

The next step would be to think about coordination problems that might arise if decisions were decentralized in the ways suggested in that analysis. To the extent that coordination problems arise, three steps could be taken. One would be to try to improve incentives for coordination; this often does not work adequately, however. Another would be to tip the balance toward greater centralization of some decisions. A third would be to implement some other coordination mechanisms (discussed in the next chapter).

At this stage, it would be appropriate to think about decision making processes. Separating out different stages of decision making and giving them to different individuals or units can further improve the use of specific knowledge and coordination. In addition, a firm can choose different structures that emphasize decision management or decision control more. This allows the firm to choose how it approaches the fundamental tradeoff that any decision making system has between creativity and control.

Most of our discussion in this chapter has looked at allocation of decision making from the point of view of the entire organization. However, the extent of discretion given to an employee is a major part of the job design. Thus this chapter also serves as an introduction to the topic of job design. After discussing additional issues in overall organizational structure in Chapter 6, in Chapter 7 we take up the topic of job design.

● ● ● ● ● Study Questions

1. Define the concepts of specific and general knowledge carefully. Go back and review the concepts of specialization of human capital investments, and of general versus firm-specific human capital. These terms all sound similar, but mean different things, so make sure that you understand the differences.

2. Provide examples of specific knowledge of particular circumstances in a job you held. In other words, give examples of knowledge or information that was important to your work, but would be costly for you to communicate clearly to your boss. Did your employer allow you to make decisions that required that information? Why or why not?

3. Information technology lowers the costs of communicating many forms of information. What effect do you predict that this will have on organizational structures?

4. Your job is to oversee R&D for a large pharmaceutical company. A new blockbuster drug can mean enormous profits for your firm, partly because of many years of patent protection. New drug development is an extremely large financial investment. Mistakes can be very costly, because new drugs might harm customers, and damage the firm's brand name. Finally, the government's Food and Drug Administration imposes its own very stringent oversight (decision control) of your drugs at the last stage, before they are approved as new products. Describe the decision making process that you would recommend. Would it vary with different stages of new product development (e.g., basic exploratory research compared to final drug development)?

5. Do you think that a firm's decision making methods will evolve as it grows from a small startup into a mature company? If so, how and why? What effect is that likely to have on the company's workforce? Its corporate culture? Is it likely to alter its effectiveness at product design? How might its emphasis change as the company matures?

6. Your boss is frustrated with the decision making process used at your firm. He asks you to prepare a memo detailing the costs of this process. How would you measure the costs of a given decision making process? What are the dimensions of costs and benefits to a firm from a specific process?

● ● ● ● ● REFERENCES

Fama, Eugene & Michael Jensen (1983). "Separation of Ownership and Control." *Journal of Law & Economics* 26.

Grillparzer, Frank (1844). *Libussa* (opera).

Hawkins, Lee, Jr. (2004). "Reversing 80 Years of History, GM is Reining Global Fiefs." *Wall Street Journal*, October 6.

Kiviat, Barbara (2004). "The End of Management?" *Time*, July 6.

Marr, Merissa (2005). "Disney Cuts Strategic-Planning Unit." *Wall Street Journal*, March 28.

Smith, Adam (1776). *The Wealth of Nations*. Modern Library Classics, 2000.

von Hayek, Friedrich (1945). "The Use of Knowledge in Society." *American Economic Review* 35(4).

FURTHER READING

Aghion, Philippe & Jean Tirole (1997). "Formal and Real Authority in Organizations." *Journal of Political Economy* 105(1): 1–29.

Jensen, Michael & William Meckling (1992). "Specific and General Knowledge and Organizational Structure." In *Contract Economics*, Lars Werin & Hans Wijkander, eds. Oxford: Blackwell.

Sah, Raaj Kumar & Joseph Stiglitz (1986). "The Architecture of Economic Systems: Hierarchies and Polyarchies." *American Economic Review* 76: 716–727.

APPENDIX

Hierarchical, Flat, and Second Opinion Structures

Here we formally compare hierarchical, flat, and second opinion decision making structures, using our example of Willie and Gladys' firm. In a hierarchy, Willie evaluates new projects, rejects some, and recommends the rest to Gladys. Gladys evaluates the projects that Willie recommends, rejects some, and implements the others. In a flat structure, each evaluates different new projects. Those that are accepted by one or both are implemented. In a second opinion structure, both evaluate all projects. If there is disagreement, the firm uses some resolution procedure that results in a fraction $\lambda < 1$ being accepted and implemented. We will simplify by assuming that they flip a coin, so that $\lambda = 1/2$, but it is easy to show that the same results hold for any λ between 0 and 1.

Each person reviews N new or recommended projects per period. Thus, in a hierarchy the bottleneck is Willie, and N projects are evaluated per period. In a flat organization, $2N$ projects are evaluated. In a second opinion structure, N are evaluated, and each spends half of their time on new projects and half on those already checked by their colleague. Projects have binary outcomes: They can be good (profitable) or bad (unprofitable).

The probability that a correct decision is made when a project is first evaluated $= p > 1/2$. If it were not greater than $1/2$, then the firm would be better off flipping a coin to make decisions. The probability that a mistake is made when a project is first evaluated $= 1 - p$.

If a project is evaluated a second time, the decision is more accurate. This is because a project that was already recommended at the first stage is more likely to

FIGURE 5A.1
HIERARCHICAL STRUCTURE

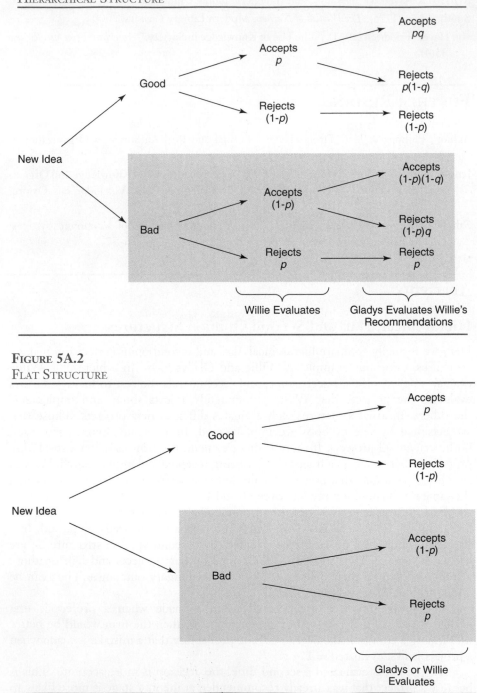

FIGURE 5A.2
FLAT STRUCTURE

FIGURE 5A.3
SECOND OPINION STRUCTURE

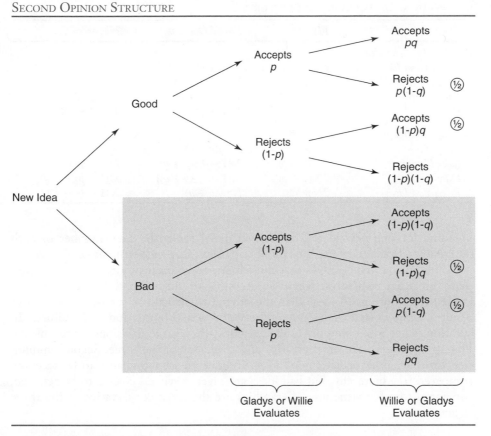

be a good project than if it was not yet evaluated. Therefore, the probability that a correct decision is made if a project is evaluated a second time $= q > p$; thus the probability that a mistake is made $= 1 - q < 1 - p$. Of course, this only applies to the hierarchy and the second opinion model.

Figures 5A.1–3 show flow charts for a random new idea under each structure. In Figure 5A.3, the $1/2$s note where a coin toss is necessary; half of those projects are accepted and half rejected (more generally it would be a fraction λ accepted).

Table 5A.1 collects from these the probabilities of the four ultimate decisions (correct acceptances and rejections, and errors of both types), and shows the results after some algebra to simplify. In the top panel, probabilities are calculated for a single random idea. In the bottom panel, the total number of ideas resulting per period is calculated for each category, by adjusting for the fact that a flat structure evaluates twice as many ideas per period.

Table 5A.2 then summarizes these results in a more convenient form, ranking the three structures against each other. The top panel ranks the likelihood of each

TABLE 5A.1
COMPARISONS OF AUTHORITY STRUCTURES

	Flat	*Second Opinion*	*Hierarchy*
Rate for One New Idea			
Accept Good Idea	p	$\frac{1}{2}(p + q)$	$p\,q$
False Negative	$1 - p$	$1 - \frac{1}{2}(p + q)$	$1 - pq$
False Positive	$1 - p$	$1 - \frac{1}{2}(p + q)$	$(1 - p)(1 - q)$
Reject Bad Idea	p	$\frac{1}{2}(p + q)$	$1 - (1 - p)(1 - q)$
Overall Throughput			
Accept Good Ideas	$2N\,p$	$N\frac{1}{2}(p + q)$	Npq
False Negatives	$2N(1 - p)$	$N[1 - \frac{1}{2}(p + q)]$	$N(1 - pq)$
False Positives	$2N(1 - p)$	$N[1 - \frac{1}{2}(p + q)]$	$N(1 - p)(1 - q)$
Reject Bad Ideas	$2N\,p$	$N\frac{1}{2}(p + q)$	$N[1 - (1 - p)(1 - q)]$

outcome for one new idea. The bottom panel ranks the total number of each outcome realized, given the total number of ideas that each structure evaluates.

The bottom panel shows that the flat structure means more mistakes overall than the other structures, when we account for throughput. However, it also implements more good ideas than the other two structures. Thus, flat structures result in more overall change, more successful new projects, and more failures. In addition, since ideas are only evaluated once, they make decisions more quickly. Flat structures are the most creative and turbulent of the three. Second opinion structures are intermediate; good ideas are given a second chance to be accepted compared to a hierarchy, but bad ideas are given a second chance to be rejected, compared to a flat structure. Hierarchies are the most conservative of the three structures.

TABLE 5A.2
SUMMARY OF RESULTS

	Most		*Middle*		*Least*
Rate For One New Idea					
Accept Good Idea	Second opinion	>	Flat	>	Hierarchy
False Negative	Hierarchy	>	Flat	>	Second opinion
False Positive	Flat	>	Second opinion	>	Hierarchy
Reject Bad Idea	Hierarchy	>	Second opinion	>	Flat
Overall Throughput					
Accept Good Ideas	Flat	>	Second opinion	>	Hierarchy
False Negatives	Flat	>	Hierarchy	>	Second opinion
False Positives	Flat	>	Second opinion	>	Hierarchy
Reject Bad Ideas	Flat	>	Hierarchy	>	Second opinion

6

ORGANIZATIONAL STRUCTURE

Chaos was the law of nature; Order was the dream of man.
                                                    —*Henry Adams, 1983*

INTRODUCTION

In the last chapter, we focused on allocation of individual decisions. We now concentrate on a closely related, macro-level question: the structure of the overall organization. This is an enormous topic that could easily be the subject of an entire course in its own right. Here we concentrate on just a few key questions.

Imagine that you are part of the management team for the new CEO of a large aerospace firm. The firm has had mixed success in the past decade. Some very sophisticated new products have been launched with great success, but others have failed. Your firm faces increasing competition from more aggressive, fast moving competitors. A competitor has been plagued with quality problems, and the CEO wants to avoid similar troubles here. Finally, there have been serious conflicts between several divisions, over both product design and marketing. Your CEO asks you to think about the best way to structure your firm to continue past successes and address the concerns. Where do you start?

Clearly, you are going to have to think about how to break the firm up into smaller subunits. Large firms are almost always too complex for a single management team to oversee. One issue that we discuss here is how a firm can break its organization into divisions or other business units.

A second question that you will have to consider is how to set up broad patterns of authority. Your boss is concerned that the competition is fast moving, suggesting that your firm's decision making is too slow. At the same time, your firm has had some success at innovation, and there are pressures to maintain high quality. The issues discussed in the last chapter are relevant, and they will be useful in this chapter too. For example, you should know from Chapter 5 that you generally face a tradeoff between speed of decision making and likelihood of errors in decision making, which could cause quality problems.

Organizational structures can have an important effect on career patterns for employees. Traditional functional hierarchies imply that most employees spend their careers investing in more in-depth knowledge within their functional area. Other structures may weaken the link between structure and job ladders, potentially weakening skill development. In addition, the choice of structure can have an impact on the effectiveness of performance evaluations. We will mention this at several points in this chapter (Chapter 9 focuses on evaluation in more depth). An aerospace firm must maintain a cutting edge engineering staff, so these could be serious concerns.

Finally, the conflicts between different divisions suggest that coordination should be improved within your organization. What implications do the various structures have for the severity and types of coordination problems that tend to arise in a firm? What methods are available for coordinating? These are the types of questions covered in this chapter.

TRENDS IN ORGANIZATIONAL STRUCTURE

It is common for the popular business press to say that organizational structures have flattened in the last two decades, but what does this mean?

One study analyzed the structure of the top management hierarchy in over 300 large U.S. firms from 1986 through 1999. They found that the number of hierarchical levels between the CEO and the lowest level managers had decreased by over 25% during that time. At the same time, the number of managers reporting directly to the CEO increased dramatically. Firms are indeed flattening their structures.

The authors found several other interesting patterns. The evidence suggests that firms have decentralized decision making as they flattened. An explanation for this is that a manager who oversees more subordinates has less time to make decisions, and must delegate more. In addition, firms with flatter hierarchies tended to make greater use of incentive compensation based on broader performance measures (a term that we define more carefully in Chapter 9), such as long-term financial performance or stock ownership.

Source: Rajan & Wulf (2006)

Types of Organizational Structures

In this section we describe four general types of structures that firms tend to use. In the following section, we discuss the factors that favor use of each structure. If you are already familiar with the basic organizational structures, this section may be skipped or skimmed quickly.

Actual firm structures can be exceedingly complex. They are often a combination of the structures outlined here. For example, a firm may have many divisions, with some using a matrix structure, others using traditional functional hierarchies, and still others using more informal network structures. Even a given unit can combine approaches. A business unit might be organized along functional hierarchical lines, but make extensive use of informal communication and collaboration—a network approach—at the same time. Finally, a unit might organize some decisions and employees in one way, but other decisions in another. Thus, think of these four structures as basic building blocks. The larger and more complex the firm, the more likely that its structure will combine elements and be too complicated to describe adequately in an organizational chart.

Before we describe the four general types of structures, we first note that all but one of these structures make extensive use of an important principle that we introduced in the last chapter: hierarchy.

Hierarchy

Figure 6.1 shows the classic organization structure that has played the most important historical role: functional hierarchy. A functional hierarchy has two important elements: functional structure and hierarchy.

Hierarchy means that most communication, supervision, and decision making occurs in clear linear paths between the bottom of the organization and the top. In Figure 6.1, each functional area has a head [such as the Executive Vice President (EVP) of Sales]. The Vice President (VP) reports to the EVP, the Manager to the VP, and the Assistant to the Manager. Each employee is expected to generally work directly with the next levels (above and below) in the chain of command, and not communicate much (if at all) with employees at two or more levels above or below. In this structure, there is no ambiguity about who reports to whom. This structure is exactly what we analyzed in Chapter 5.

In a hierarchy, ultimate authority resides with the CEO. However, many decisions are made at lower levels, for the reasons described in the last chapter. Decentralization is often necessary to make use of lower level specific knowledge, and to economize on the time of top management. Decentralization then leads to some separation of decision management and control, to provide oversight and better coordination.

Virtually all structures have hierarchy in this sense, because of the benefits of having a *single decision maker*, as mentioned briefly in Chapter 5. If it is not clear who an employee should report to, and who is the ultimate decision maker, the

Figure 6.1

Functional Hierarchy

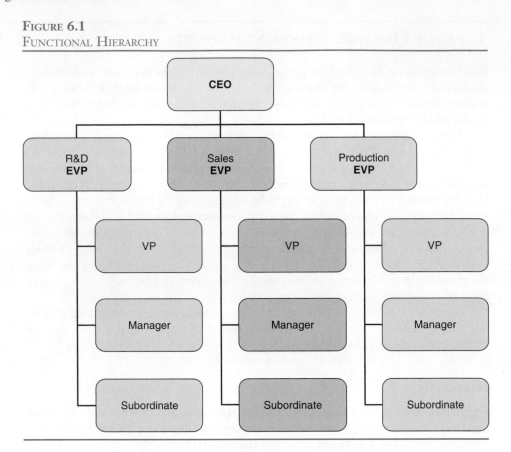

organization will incur several costs. Decision making is likely to be slower as the group tries to achieve consensus. There will be more confusion, as employees are not certain who they should go to with questions. Finally, group decision making increases the importance of politics in how things get done in the organization. For these reasons, virtually all structures make extensive use of hierarchy in making decisions.

Hierarchy can become costly in larger organizations. To see why, recall the childhood game of Telephone. In Telephone, the players sit in a circle. The first player whispers a phrase in the ear of the person next to him. The second person whispers what he heard in the ear of the next person, and so on. Once the circle of whispering is complete, the last participant says out loud what he heard. Typically, the result is nothing like the original phrase—it has become garbled in the process.

The same may occur in hierarchies, especially ones with many levels. Imagine that a lower level employee has information that the CEO needs in order to coordinate the function with other functions in the firm. The employee communicates the information to his boss, who communicates it to her boss, and so on until the information reaches the top. Unless the information is easily quantifiable, it is likely to be somewhat garbled on retelling. This becomes even more likely if, as is often the case, at each level the information is processed in some way before being passed on further. A similar garbling effect can occur in the opposite direction with respect to implementation of decisions. If the CEO makes a decision that affects the lower level worker, this must be communicated downward.

The first formal organizations developed in the first large institutions: governments, armies, and religious bodies. Hierarchy was an important element in all of these early structures, and remains so to this day.

Functional Structure

The second element of classical structure is use of functional organization units. Once a firm grows to a certain size, the overall structure must be broken up into more manageable subunits, or top management will be overwhelmed. One logical way to do so is to group employees who are similar in some way together in the same unit. A very common way to do so is to divide the organization into units based on related skills and tasks.

In Figure 6.1, the firm is organized into three functions (realistically, there would be more). One group of employees focuses on research and development (R&D). Another focuses on production of the product, while a third focuses on sales.

In this structure, an employee's career tends to be solely within the function. An entry level production employee would gradually earn promotions, but stay within the production function. A sales employee would similarly be promoted to positions of greater responsibility within sales.

Functional structures are driven by the substantial benefits of *specialization*. In a *functional structure*, an employee works almost entirely with colleagues in the same function. Communication between the functions tends to occur at higher levels (in the extreme case, at the level of the CEO and top management). To perform his tasks, a functional employee only needs to have knowledge of the concepts and skills related to his functional area: An accountant would need to have expertise in accounting, but little or none in production or marketing. This creates enormous economies in skill investments, as stated in Chapter 3.

A second benefit of specialization is an important element in the next chapter: Jobs can be specialized, so that workers do a limited set of tasks that are closely related in the knowledge and skills needed to do them. A functional hierarchy makes it easier to design what we will call *narrow* jobs with a limited number of tasks. And, of course, narrowly designed jobs tend to be quite compatible with narrowly focused human capital.

A functional structure has additional benefits in that the hierarchy will tend to work more smoothly. Because employees usually start at the bottom of the hierarchy and are promoted upward, a boss in a functional structure usually supervises a job very much like one she once worked in. This means that she will be a much more effective manager. She will be better able to process information provided by, and give direction to, her subordinates. (In other words, both decision management and decision control are likely to be more effective.) Communication will be easier because she has the same skills as her staff. Performance evaluation will be more accurate, because she understands the context of the job and how to determine the extent to which performance is due to the employee's efforts or other factors.

As can be seen, there are tremendous advantages to a functional structure, in terms of training, job design, decision making, and communication. However, there can also be an important disadvantage. Specialization implies that workers usually have little understanding of how their work affects employees in other parts of the organization, so their work may end up poorly coordinated with that of other functions.

There are two sources of this problem. The first is that specialization in skills and tasks makes it unlikely that employees will take into account the perspectives of colleagues in other functions. This is partly due to ignorance of other functions, and partly to distorted incentives (in a functional structure, performance evaluation tends to focus on functional expertise at the expense of coordination with other functions; Chapter 8 should give you some tools to understand why). The second is the kind of garbling of communication and decisions that can occur in a hierarchy, as described. In a functional structure, most communication is up and down within the function, rather than across functions.

Divisional Structure

The larger the firm, the more the CEO will need to break the structure into manageable subunits. Authority for most major decisions within each unit is then delegated to the unit manager. One way to break up the organization is into functions. This takes advantage of the compelling economic advantages of specialization. However, a simple functional hierarchy is usually inadequate for larger organizations, because the functional units may be too large to be managed effectively (for example, the garbling phenomenon described above can become too severe).

Moreover, larger firms tend to be more complex firms. Their product lines expand. They sell in more regions. They begin to use a greater variety of techniques and technologies. All of these imply that coordination problems across functions are likely to become even more severe. For these reasons, most midsized to large firms also break their structures into some form of divisions. An example of a *divisional structure* is shown in Figure 6.2.

In this example, the firm is divided into three divisions. Within each division, the firm uses functional hierarchy. This illustrates that firms can and do combine elements of all of the structures described in this chapter.

In addition to ameliorating problems that arise from a too-large functional structure, a divisional structure allows each division to focus on a narrow part of the overall company business. This is, in effect, a large-scale version of the gains from specialization.

FIGURE 6.2
DIVISIONAL STRUCTURE

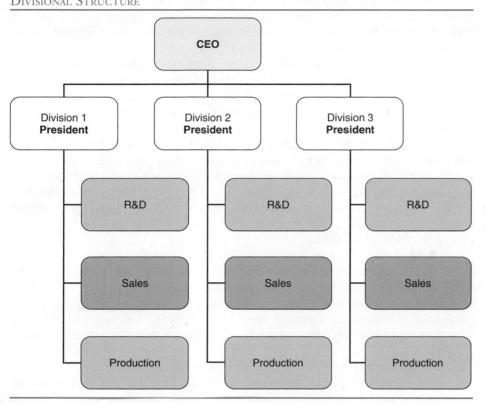

For example, consider a firm that designs and sells high end computers. It sells desktop, laptop, and handheld computers to educational customers (schools and universities) and corporate customers. Some computers use the latest technology and are very powerful, while others use commodity parts, perform only basic tasks, and are intended to be inexpensive.

This firm has a somewhat complex business, with important variation in customers, product type, and technology. If there is one large unit to oversee all of these activities, top managers will continuously have to make difficult tradeoffs between how they focus their efforts and resources.

Instead, the firm might consider splitting the firm into different divisions. Each division would be assigned to a particular area of focus. This would simplify the mission and operation of each division.

Suppose, for example, that the firm decided to organize into product divisions. The three divisions in Figure 6.2 would be for desktop, laptop, and handheld products. An employee working in the laptop products division would focus his efforts on how he can best improve the design, manufacture, or sale of laptop computers. His work is greatly simplified, since he does not have to take into consideration how his work affects desktop or handheld computers. The same is true throughout the laptop products hierarchy, all the way up to the president of laptop products.

In other words, specialization can occur along many lines. The ones usually emphasized in economics (and this text) involve investments in human capital, and narrow job design. At the level of organizational structure, however, the same principle comes into play, and the specialization could be along many different dimensions.

For example, our computer company could just as easily organize into divisions based on customer types. In that case, there might be two divisions, for education and for corporate products. Employees in each division would structure their work to emphasize success of the product line that their division was responsible for. Notice that their focus would be slightly different. Now an employee might work on desktop, laptop, and handheld computers, but emphasize how they can be designed or sold to education customers.

A third possible divisional structure would be to organize along technological lines. Our computer firm might then have divisions for high end, advanced technology computers, and a different one for low end commodity products. This type of divisional structure is less common than the others, but certainly occurs frequently. A final common example would be to organize into regional divisions. The firm might have one division for the Americas, a second for Europe, and a third for Asia.

Any time workers are specialized, there is the potential for coordination costs to arise between workers with different specializations. This also applies to divisional structures. Organizing a firm into divisions means that, to some extent, the firm becomes a set of autonomous minifirms. Typically, the president of a division is evaluated and rewarded largely for her division's performance. Specialization of incentives, strategy, skills, and job design within each division may mean that the divisions do not adequately consider the effects of their work on the other divisions.

Using our market metaphor for organizational design from Chapter 5, coordination problems arise because different organizational units impose positive or negative externalities on each other. In the case of positive externalities, there is inadequate cooperation. In the case of negative externalities, there is too much competition.

Consider our computer company once more. If we organize the firm into product divisions, the laptop and desktop products divisions will compete with each other for sales. This competition may reduce overall profits, since each division has inadequate incentives to consider the negative externality it imposes on the other. Thus, much of the CEO and top management's job in a divisional firm is to oversee the activities of each division to improve coordination between them. This can involve retaining some decision rights over strategy of divisions, establishing incentive schemes that reward cooperation, and settling any disputes that arise.

How Should a Firm Define Divisions?

How does a firm decide which divisional structure to use? That is difficult to say without knowledge of the specific business. The question largely boils down to deciding along which dimension the firm needs to differentiate its activities more. For example, suppose that in this firm similar technology is needed for each of the three products. If so, then breaking the firm into technology based divisions would be a mistake. Each division would attempt to focus R&D on its particular product type. This would lead to duplication and incompatibility of R&D across the divisions. If, on the other hand, very different technology is required for each type of product, little would be lost by dividing R&D into three different product areas.

It often makes sense to organize sales and marketing into geographical, product, or customer divisions. A geographical structure may make sense if the same sales team can effectively sell to all types of customers, in which case they can be assigned to all customers in a specific area. In addition, geographical divisions make it easier for the firm to vary marketing, product information, and selling techniques across regions with different languages or cultures.

Organizing sales by product or customer may make sense if different types of products or customers require different sales and marketing techniques. For example, corporate or high end customers may be less price sensitive, but demand more sophisticated and specialized products and service.

One important principle for organizing work at any level of the firm is *modularity*. A system is *modular* to the extent that it can be broken up into largely distinct, functionally separate parts. The principle of modularity has applications in many areas, from software design to evolutionary biology to sociology. It also can be applied to organizational structure and job design.

Breaking work up into different jobs, or work groups, or business units, or divisions creates coordination costs across those units. To the extent that the work lends itself to modularity, coordination costs tend to be lower. Therefore, a helpful rule of thumb when thinking about how to define divisions is to look for modularity. How can your business be broken into largely self-managing groups? Earlier we discussed a case where it made little sense to break up R&D—this function is not easily modularized in the computer firm. By contrast, it is often relatively simple to modularize a sales organization by region or product.

Modularity is possible to the extent that externalities or coordination costs are not too large across units. In software design, this principle is sometimes called *low coupling* and *high cohesion*. When tasks require high cohesion, it is important to put them together in the same organizational unit, or develop strong coordination mechanisms (see box). Tasks that require only loose coupling are good candidates for being assigned to different modules (jobs, units, or divisions). We will use the principle of modularity again in the next chapter.

SOFTWARE DESIGN AT MICROSOFT

In early 2007, Microsoft released the much anticipated Vista upgrade to the Windows operating system—over a year later than announced initially. The reason was apparently inadequate modularity in design of Windows—a very complex, large software program (technically, a set of interconnecting programs).

Individual programmers were tasked to produce their own parts of the overall code. These parts were then pieced together into the overall program. However, Microsoft has found that the development process gave inadequate attention to the principle of modularity. There were over 4,000 engineers working on Windows, and they were all managed together as one seamless project.

Microsoft altered the development process in two ways. First, it broke the project up into more subprojects, much like divisions in a firm's structure. When managers drew up a chart of the overall Windows project, it was "8 feet tall and 11 feet wide and looked like a haphazard train map with hundreds of tracks crisscrossing each other." The leaders of the project redesigned the project into subprojects which could be added or removed without compromising the whole operating system.

Second, managers pushed for better modularity by requiring higher quality in the code of individual parts before they were added to the larger project. Engineers were expected to more completely debug their projects, and design them to be more like independent Lego blocks responsible for single functions.

Source: Guth (2005)

As a final note on divisional structure, in principle a firm can organize different sets of tasks into different structures. For example, R&D might be centralized into one group for the entire firm. This would maximize the benefits from economies of scale and standardization of parts and products across the company. The same firm might then break marketing and sales into customer divisions, to maximize flexibility in selling techniques. Production might be organized by region, to minimize distribution costs. However, when different areas of the firm are organized along completely different lines, complexity escalates rapidly. Production will be focused on regional variation in its methods, and not coordinate well with sales or R&D. R&D may focus on developing cutting edge LCD screen technology, but not on how to vary its designs for different types of customers. The job of the CEO and top management in coordinating these groups that are given different focuses only becomes harder. For this reason, there are benefits from keeping the structure simple, and grouping employees into divisions that are relatively consistent with each other.

Matrix or Project Structure

One drawback of a divisional structure is that the firm loses some of the gains from specialization and economies of scale that a simple functional structure would provide. If different divisions have their own sales staffs, for example, efficiencies may be lost as each sales group provides some services separately. Similarly, if each division has its own accounting department, the firm may end up with multiple, incompatible, and relatively expensive accounting systems.

This problem can be especially severe in functions like R&D that require very advanced technical knowledge. If there are multiple functional groups in separate divisions, each has to develop this technical knowledge on its own (or use some form of knowledge management system; see below). That tends to be wasteful and can lead to less effective R&D compared to combining all research efforts in one organizational unit.

The third structure, matrix or project, can be used to balance the desire for economies of scale in specialized functional areas against the desire for a divisional structure. Figure 6.3 shows an example. In this case, the firm is organized into *both*

FIGURE 6.3
MATRIX OR PROJECT STRUCTURE

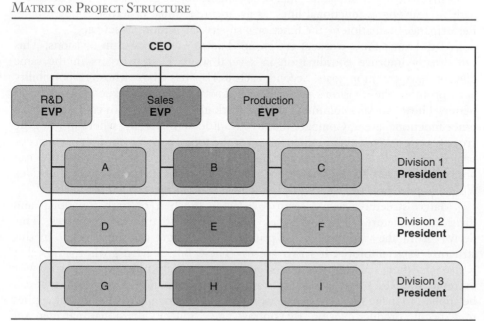

functional and divisional groupings. Each employee is assigned to two groups: a functional area and a divisional area. For example, an engineer might be assigned to software design, and to laptop computers. Notably, each employee has *two* bosses—one in his function, and one in his division.

A relatively permanent, formal structure of the type shown in Figure 6.3 is called a *matrix structure*. The term matrix refers to the two-dimensional design where each employee has two organizational assignments. In fact, the organizational chart in Figure 6.3 looks like a 2×2 matrix.

Many firms assign functional workers to projects that span functions. Such projects are more temporary in nature than the formal divisions illustrated in Figure 6.3. Project structure refers to such relatively temporary matrix-type structures. Both use the same techniques; the difference is one of relative permanence and formality. Finally, ad hoc, short-lived cross-functional teams use the same general principles, but are even more temporary than a project structure.

It is worth noting that in a divisional structure an employee also has, in a sense, two organizational affiliations: division, and function within the division. However, this is different from the matrix approach. In the divisional approach, there are different functions (e.g., different sales groups) for each division. In the matrix approach, there is a single functional organization that spans divisions. In other words, in a divisional structure functions are nested within divisions, while in a matrix structure functions are overlaid across divisions.

The matrix or project structure allows for many of the benefits of both functional and divisional structures. By having one side of the matrix organized by function, many of the benefits of functional structure are achieved. An employee can focus investments in human capital, becoming a subject-matter expert. The career path is clear (along functional lines, as greater functional expertise is developed). Performance evaluation by the functional supervisor is more effective.

At the same time, workers are grouped *across functions* within divisions. This can greatly improve coordination in several ways. First, workers in the same division have common goals. Second, each worker has a boss whose responsibility is to promote the division's performance. This motivates workers to coordinate better. Third, workers communicate and work more directly with colleagues from other functional areas. Compare that to a traditional hierarchy, where most of the cross-functional coordination is achieved at the top of each function. In a matrix or project approach, an important advantage is that a great deal of coordination can occur at lower levels, closer to where most of the work is actually done. This idea will be important when we introduce the idea of an *integration problem* below.

Matrix structures would seem to provide the best of both functional and divisional structures. However, they also have substantial disadvantages. This derives from the violation of the principle of a single decision maker. In this structure each employee has two bosses. These bosses have goals that conflict with each other. The functional boss' goal is to maximize functional expertise. For example, the R&D boss is likely to want to emphasize more basic R&D that can be applied to many different products, rather than more applied R&D that applies to a specific product division. By contrast, the engineer's divisional manager will pressure the engineer to focus efforts on the specific product.

In most cases, a worker's primary loyalty is likely to be to his functional boss, since his career will be within the functional job ladder. Therefore, matrix structures may end up with relatively more emphasis on functional expertise (rather than divisional performance) than a pure divisional structure (but less than a functional structure).

This is a very difficult situation for the engineer to be in. He will constantly be pressured by both managers to focus his work in different areas. The bosses will disagree with each other about how his performance should be evaluated and rewarded. Thus, matrix structures tend to lead to more office politics, greater conflict, slower decision making, and more bureaucracy (for example, more time spent in meetings to resolve conflicts). Of course, to some extent that is the point: The conflict is a coordination mechanism that reveals and resolves coordination problems. The problem is that it is a complex, costly mechanism, so it should only be used if the advantages of a matrix type structure are high enough.

Network Structure

A final structure that has received increasing attention in the last two decades is the *network structure*, illustrated in Figure 6.4 (the circle represents the boundary of the firm). A network structure is difficult to define rigorously. It is a structure that gives more emphasis to informal relationships between individual workers and managers inside and outside the organization. In all organizations, there is an informal structure that runs parallel to the formal structure. This informal structure is each manager's *network* or set of relationships with colleagues. When an employee needs to get something done, he does not always follow the formal chain of decision making implied by the organization chart. Instead, sometimes he directly contacts a colleague somewhere else in the organization. The benefit of doing so is that decision making can be done more quickly, with less garbling and better coordination. The cost is that it can undermine the formal chain of command.

Similarly, most firms make at least some use of ad hoc crossfunctional teams as described in the previous subsection. These provide some balancing of functional expertise and divisional focus, but more flexibility than a rigid matrix. Some firms place particularly great emphasis on these kinds of ad hoc work groups, and on encouraging managers to use their network of relationships to directly communicate and coordinate. Such organizations are sometimes called network structures.

In Figure 6.4, the firm is organized into three different teams. These teams might be responsible for designing specific new products, or for working with specific clients. The firm also has two other organizational units of the more traditional functional form, R&D and production. These are presumably organized this way to maximize gains from specialization and economies of scale. Finally, in this case there are three outside groups that one or more of the inside groups works with regularly, a major customer, an industry consortium, and a key supplier.

In this structure, employees in the teams collaborate with each other to promote the team goals. In this sense, one could easily have written the organization chart in Figure 6.4 as having two functional divisions, and three other divisions (the teams).

FIGURE 6.4
NETWORK STRUCTURE

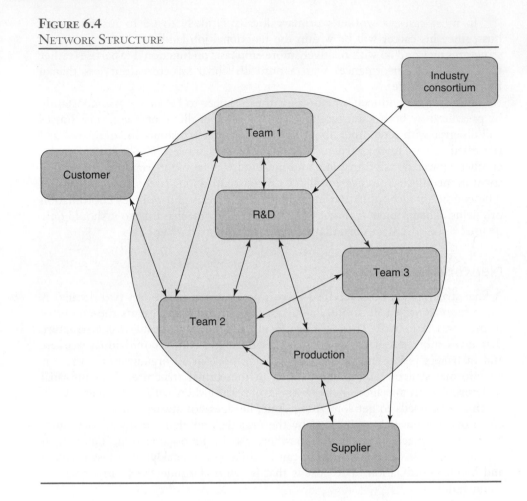

The idea that a network structure is meant to emphasize is that not all work is organized into traditional hierarchies. In this example, a manager in Team 2 may need to develop good working relationships with managers in the other two teams, with R&D and production, and also with the major customer.

One way to think of network structures is that they are a form of internal market mechanism for getting work done, but the asset that is used in this market is not a tangible financial one. Instead, it is a manager's intangible personal relationships with others, often called *social capital*. Network analysts have found that managers who fill *structural holes*—gaps between two larger networks—have particular value in a network structure. This is because they complete the network structure, better matching supply with demand and making the influence market work more effectively. However, the use of intangible social capital means that the influence market does not have readily observable prices. For this reason, the transactions involve more negotiation and are more political in nature. Thus, while network structures approximate a market design in quite interesting ways, they are an imperfect substitute.

Putting this all together, some firms use techniques associated with functional, divisional, or matrix structures, but in relatively impermanent and fluid ways. To the extent that they do, decision making and coordination are based more on informal relationships than on formal chains of command. In practice, most firms use elements of all four approaches to structure; it is a question of degree.

WHICH STRUCTURE SHOULD A FIRM USE?

Which structure should your firm use? The first point is that it should not use a single structure for the entire firm. Firms use a blend of structures for different parts of their organization. Moreover, even for the same set of employees, techniques from several different structures are often blended (say, for different sets of decisions). Thus, the question is better framed as, Which structure should your firm emphasize in each area?

Regardless of approach, there are two important forces that should always be remembered: the principle of a single decision maker, and the value of specialization. Consider the first of these two. Network-style structures can be costly because they are confusing. When the ultimate decision maker has not been clarified, it is more likely that employees can work at cross purposes. Therefore, even in a network structure it is usually important to clearly specify leaders and goals of teams and other organizational units. For the same reason network organizations usually still make extensive use of hierarchical decision making. A network approach can be quite effective for decision management—brainstorming and creative activities—but decision control is still necessary.

A second important force is specialization. Virtually all firms make extensive use of functional structures. This allows employees to focus their skills, tasks, and careers. Therefore, functional hierarchy is generally an important part of almost every organization, and should be the starting point for most discussions of structure.

Beyond the importance of specialization and a single point of authority, other factors matter. A third factor affecting optimal structure is complexity of the business. Complexity implies that there are more areas that the firm has to master. The desire for gains from specialization therefore tends to lead to greater *differentiation* into smaller organization units. This drives not just functional organization, but also divisions and subdivisions. Therefore, the more complex the business, the more elaborate the structure (divisional, matrix, or network).

As we will argue in the next chapter, complexity also tends to imply that there is more specific knowledge at lower levels in the organization. For this reason, greater complexity generally means that a firm should make greater use of decentralization. Thus, there is a positive relationship between more complex structures like divisional, and use of decentralization, both to and within the division. Similarly, simple functional organizations are more likely to use relatively centralized, hierarchical decision making.

Decentralization, and differentiation of the organization into subunits, generates a greater need for coordination. Therefore, firms that use these approaches to structure have to make greater use of coordination mechanisms. We describe various coordination mechanisms below.

A fourth factor affecting optimal structure is stability of the firm's business environment. The more stable the environment, the less important specific knowledge at lower levels, and the more will the firm be able to centralize decisions. In addition, stability implies that the firm is more likely to have mastered its business processes, so that formal procedures can be established. When this is the case, there is less value to differentiating the firm into subunits that focus on making related sets of decisions—because there are fewer important decisions to be made.

We saw in Chapter 5 that more hierarchical structures provide greater control, but at the cost of both slower decision making, and less creativity. Therefore, firms that need to act more quickly, have a stronger strategic need for creativity, and have less *downside risk* should decentralize more and make less use of hierarchy.

A fifth factor in determining the optimal structure is the nature of the coordination problem. In the next section we define two types of coordination problems. The latter, integration problems, favor matrix or network approaches. The former are amenable to simpler divisional approaches.

● ● ● ● ● COORDINATION

Two Types of Coordination Problems

Coordination is needed when the work of two or more subunits of the organization must be combined in some way to create greater firm value. A very simple example is an assembly line, where the output of one worker is given to the next, who adds some work to it, and passes it down the line. These workers need to coordinate the quantity and timing of their output with each other. They also may need to coordinate in more subtle ways so that their parts work well together and do not create quality problems.

Let us distinguish between two general types of coordination problems. One is coordination problems that do not require units to communicate with each other in order to coordinate. Call this a *synchronization problem*. The output of workers must be synchronized in some way, but they do not need to speak to each other to do so. The quantity and timing of assembly line work is an example in most cases.

Another example would be a multiproduct firm that has a strong brand name. In that case, products must be designed so that they are all consistent with the overall product image, quality, and look-and-feel that the firm is trying to establish. However, individual product line managers do not need to communicate with each other on a daily basis. A final example is a firm whose strategy is to provide uniform service at all of its retail locations. The stores do not need to communicate with each other, but they do need to be coordinated so that they all provide roughly the same type of service to their customers.

A second type of coordination problem is an *integration problem*. Consider our laptop computer product design problem. In the last chapter, we argued that a firm should ask "who/what/where/when/why" to determine the specific knowledge in the organization that must be used to create firm value. We then argued that the firm should decentralize decisions to the employee who possess that specific knowledge. Let us think about laptop computer design. What specific knowledge is necessary in order to design a profitable laptop computer?

Clearly, engineering knowledge is crucial. Electrical engineering expertise is needed to design the motherboard and other electronic parts. Software engineering expertise is needed to design the operating system and applications. Materials engineering expertise is needed to design the case and parts. All of these are specific rather than general knowledge, because they are costly to communicate to someone else. Therefore, according to our previous arguments we should decentralize most decisions about the laptop's design to our R&D staff.

However, there is other specific knowledge that is important to laptop computer design. One example is knowledge of customer's demand for computers. There are thousands of possible laptop computer designs. Each trades off some features against other features (e.g., computing power, battery life, weight, and price). In order to design a profitable laptop, the firm needs to decide which combination of features to produce and sell. The knowledge required to estimate which types of designs will sell best resides with the firm's sales and marketing staff (and its customers). This knowledge is also at least partly specific rather than general, because it is somewhat complex, and because much of the knowledge is likely to be qualitative. Therefore, to make best use of this specific knowledge, the laptop computer design should be decentralized to sales and marketing.

Other kinds of specific knowledge are also important for designing the laptop computer, including product costing, production, and distribution. Putting all of this together, we have a problem: there are *multiple pieces of specific knowledge that must be combined* to decide how to design the laptop computer. The firm cannot decentralize the decision to one of the groups, or the decision will emphasize that group's specific knowledge but ignore the knowledge from the other groups. This is what we call an *integration problem*.

There are two possible ways to solve an integration problem. One is to coordinate all of these groups at a high level. For example, the CEO could oversee product design. However, this is likely to fail, because each piece of information is very costly to communicate to the CEO, and there are multiple pieces.

The best way to solve this problem is usually to use a lateral coordination mechanism at lower levels, so that those who possess the disparate pieces of specific knowledge needed to make the decision work together. This is exactly what a matrix or project structure is designed to do. Thus, matrix-type structures are best used when there are multiple pieces of specific knowledge that must be *combined* to make an important decision. Not surprisingly, matrix-type structures (including crossfunctional teams and network structures) are most common for new product development.

Coordination Mechanisms

So far we have seen two coordination mechanisms. One is centralization. This works best when knowledge is easy to communicate. The second is a lateral coordination mechanism such as a crossfunctional team or matrix structure, or an informal version like a network structure. These structures suffer from the fact that they are typically complex, confusing, and costly to manage. However, they are generally necessary evils when a firm faces an integration problem.

Synchronization problems can be coordinated much more easily, because they require little or no ongoing communication between units, through a variety of mechanisms. Here we briefly describe a few.

Central Budgeting and Planning

Firms often have formal annual budgeting and planning processes. Organizational units propose plans and budgets for the next fiscal year. These are combined at the next level, and ultimately at the level of each division. The central corporate office then considers these proposals from each division, compares likely returns on investment, and allocates resources to each division. Each division then takes this budget and allocates it to the levels below, and the process continues to the bottom of the organization.

It is striking how similar this approach is to the central planning in nonmarket economies. These techniques are more important in companies where the benefits of centralization, described above and in Chapter 5, are greater.

This process achieves coordination in several ways. First, it provides some control, since it limits discretion over spending by each unit. Second, the bottom-up process generates a great deal of information that is processed and accumulated at the top of the firm. This enables central decision makers to make better investment and strategic decisions through a form of decision management (to the extent that the information is not distorted). Third, the process of pushing budgets and annual plans down to lower levels provides broad coordination that divisional activities over the next fiscal year will be largely consistent with each other.

Training and Standard Operating Procedures

An excellent way to achieve consistency across employees and organizational units is to standardize practices. Thus, firms that desire a uniform customer experience in every store may require that employees wear identical uniforms. They also tend to invest more in extensive training in how to perform the job. The greater is the use of standard procedures, and the greater is the investment in uniform training across the organization, the more predictable will be behavior of employees. Predictability then provides coordination (synchronization) with no need for communication.

Corporate Culture

One benefit of a strong, consistent corporate culture is that employees tend to act in similar ways. This is quite similar to the effect of standard operating procedures and extensive training mentioned above. For example, a corporate culture in which all employees understand that cooperation is valued will foster greater coordination across units. However, a strong corporate culture does not necessarily improve coordination. Apple Computer for many years was famous for a strong culture of *individualism*. Because of this, employees often worked at crosspurposes and there was great conflict and poor coordination in the organization.

Communication

Another way to improve coordination is to develop communication systems that span the organization. These can include company newsletters, annual meetings, memos from central management, as well as many other examples. These improve coordination by increasing the extent to which dispersed business units have the same understanding of the goals and methods of the organization at a given point in time.

General Managers, Liaisons, and Job Rotation

Much coordination happens because some managers provide an interface between specialists. In Figure 6.1, the CEO provides the coordination. The CEO will be better able to coordinate across R&D, production, and sales if he or she has a better understanding of each of these areas of the firm. Therefore, a manager who has a *less specialized* experience may be a better coordinator than one who is a specialist. For this reason, there can be great value to a firm from having a small set of managers who are generalists rather than specialists.[1] Most employees are specialists, so the firm enjoys all of the economic benefits from specialization that are described in this book. A smaller set then coordinates across the specialists, by developing relatively shallow knowledge, but over a broad set of functions.

One way to develop generalists is through job rotation. Firms often identify a small number of very promising junior managers and put them in formal job rotation programs. These managers move from one part of the firm to another over time, violating the principle of specialization. In the process, they develop some knowledge about different functions, but not a deep knowledge of any single function. They also gain a better big picture perspective of the firm than do specialists. Finally, they gain a network of contacts throughout the organization, which they can draw on later to improve coordination.

This coordination role is also one of the most important roles for MBAs. An MBA curriculum by definition is a general management curriculum that provides some working knowledge of the most common functional areas of a typical firm. It does not usually provide in-depth knowledge of each area. MBAs are more likely

---

[1]In a small firm, generalist managers are more important, as there may not be enough staff to specialize on some tasks. We elaborate on this point in the discussion on entrepreneurship in Chapter 14.

to be hired or promoted into positions where coordination is important than are specialists, all else equal.

Personality

In any position where coordination is needed, the personality of the manager matters. Coordination requires the ability to talk to, understand, and work with a diverse set of colleagues. It requires the ability to forge compromises and work within a more relationship- or politics-oriented setting. For this reason, MBAs, liaisons, and those who work in matrix or network structures need a somewhat different set of interpersonal skills than do those who work solely in a specialized area. The firm should keep this in mind both in recruiting and training specialists and generalists.

Networks

As the examples of corporate culture and personality illustrate, coordination often comes through informal mechanisms as well as formal ones. One benefit of a network organization is that whenever coordination is needed between two units, the relevant managers can simply communicate with each other without having to worry about formal reporting relationships. More generally, organizational sociologists emphasize the value to a manager of developing a strong network of contacts inside and outside the organization. A person with strong contacts to groups that otherwise would not be closely linked can be quite influential in an organization, filling in *structural holes* in the network.[2] An effective manager is often one who is entrepreneurial about developing strong contacts, and recognizing opportunities to effect better coordination between groups.

Performance Evaluation and Incentives

We have left a very important formal coordination mechanism for last: performance evaluation and incentives. Pay for performance inside an organization is analogous to the price system in market economies. As von Hayek argued, prices generate an enormous amount of coordination (more along the lines of what we termed synchronization problems above, rather than integration problems), because prices are sufficient statistics for a great deal of information about marginal costs and benefits of resources. Decisions made on the basis of market prices mean that decision makers are taking into account the value of resources in their alternative uses—coordinating—without needing to know what those alternative uses are.

If structured properly, a good incentive system can provide exactly this kind of coordination inside a firm. It does so by evaluating performance in a way that includes the effects of one employee's actions on those of colleagues. That is, a good performance evaluation must measure and include the effects of any positive or negative externalities of the employee on the rest of the firm. We leave this topic for last, even though it is extremely important, because it is the subject of the entire third section of the textbook, Chapters 9–12. When performance evaluation

---

[2] See Burt (1995).

is imperfect (and as we will see, it usually is), the firm may want to use some of the additional mechanisms described above to further improve coordination.

We now turn to some additional issues in the design and implementation of organizational structure.

IMPLEMENTATION

Span of Control and Number of Levels in a Hierarchy

As we have seen, virtually all firms make use of hierarchy to some extent. In Chapter 5 we discussed how more levels of decision control in a hierarchy increases the organization's control, but at the expense of innovation. We now extend that discussion to other factors affecting the number of levels in the hierarchy.

Firms face a tradeoff in how to structure a hierarchy, illustrated in Figure 6.5. A greater number of levels increases costs in several ways, in addition to less innovation. Information has to be passed between more managers, increasing the extent of garbling described above. Information processing and decision making takes longer, as each step of communication takes a certain amount of time.

If the firm wishes to reduce the number of levels, it must expand the number of managers within each level in order to perform the same amount of work. That would be a flatter structure. A flatter structure has a greater *span of control*, or number of employees reporting to each manager. A steeper structure has a lesser span of control.

A flatter span of control reduces the costs implied by adding layers to the hierarchy, but creates its own costs. Each manager must now supervise and direct more subordinates. This takes more of the manager's time, reducing the time that can be spent on other tasks. In addition, it will generally reduce the effectiveness of supervision, since attention is spread more thinly. For example, the ability to monitor the work of subordinates will be weaker, so they are more likely to shirk

FIGURE 6.5
SPAN OF CONTROL V. NUMBER OF LEVELS

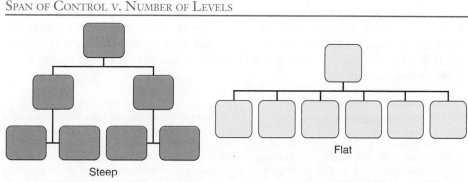

Steep

Flat

their duties. The ability to communicate effectively with each one, direct their activities, train them, and so on, will be reduced.

Thus, a hierarchy trades off span of control versus the number of levels. There are many factors that affect the optimal span of control and number of levels in a hierarchy. Anything that lowers the cost of supervising a subordinate generally will imply a larger optimal span of control, since the marginal cost of increasing the span of control by another subordinate is lower. Similarly, anything that lowers the cost of acquiring or passing on information will generally increase the optimal number of layers in the hierarchy, since it lowers the marginal cost of adding a new layer.

Type of Tasks to be Performed

The type of work to be performed affects the optimal structure of the hierarchy. The more that the work is routine, the easier is it for the manager to supervise each employee. The manager has to spend less time training the subordinate, and deciding (or helping the subordinate decide) what to do in nonstandard situations. Most of the activity of supervision involves simply giving directions about general policies, and passing along information about the current situation. Therefore, more routine work implies that the span of control will tend to be larger, and the number of hierarchical layers smaller.

By contrast, work that is complex and varied requires more input from the supervisor. The subordinate is more likely to need the experience and skills of the supervisor in order to analyze the situation and decide what to do. Less of the lower level work can be specified in advance through a set of standard operating procedures. More monitoring is also necessary, since how the worker chooses to spend his time is more variable and the choice is more important. Therefore, more complex and varied work implies a lesser optimal span of control, and a greater number of levels in the hierarchy.[3]

Skills of Managers and Subordinates

Higher skills of both managers and subordinates will tend to increase the optimal span of control, and reduce the number of layers of a hierarchy. Each manager and subordinate can process more information and solve more difficult problems. More talented managers will generally be more effective at supervision and direction. More talented subordinates will generally be more effective at implementing the directions of their boss. Since almost all firms put more talented managers in higher levels (see below), this effect increases the optimal span of control at higher levels compared to lower levels.

---

[3]A countervailing effect is that more complex environments may also be ones where firms need to make decisions more quickly, and where innovation is more important. These issues are discussed throughout Section II. These effects would favor a hierarchy with fewer levels. In order to reduce the span of control, the firm might have to break the hierarchy into smaller units. It might also find that diseconomies of scale are particularly large in such circumstances. Innovation and fast decision making tend to favor smaller firms.

Incentive Problems

Hierarchy implies delegation of some decisions. Delegation, in turn, means that the firm must ensure that employees have reasonable incentives to perform their tasks in the interests of firm objectives rather than personal objectives. There are two broad ways to do this. One is to develop performance evaluation and incentive systems; this is the topic of Part Three. The other is to monitor subordinates more closely to detect shirking. If performance evaluation is more effective, less monitoring is necessary, freeing up some of the supervisor's time. Thus, where firms have access to better incentive plans, the span of control can be greater. Roughly speaking, performance evaluation tends to be better the closer the manager is to the top of the hierarchy. This is because the manager's actions have a more direct effect on firm value, and are better reflected in available performance measures (especially accounting numbers). This effect tends to increase span of control at higher levels of the hierarchy.

Costs of Acquiring and Communicating Knowledge

An important determinant of optimal hierarchical structure is the cost of acquiring and communicating knowledge. Lowering the costs of acquiring knowledge increases the productivity of knowledge workers in a hierarchy. This, in turn, means that a manager can increase the span of control. For example, access to inexpensive analysis tools such as spreadsheets and statistical analysis programs increases the ability of a manager to analyze information collected from subordinates, so the manager will be able to analyze inputs from more subordinates. Similarly, subordinates will be able to solve more complex problems assigned by the supervisor. This has an effect similar to that of increasing the skills of the subordinate as described above.

Put another way, modern information technology tends to be a complement to the work of managers in a hierarchy, rather than a substitute. This raises the productivity of managers, and especially those who are highly skilled and at higher levels. This, in turn, affects wages as discussed below.

Lowering the costs of communication has very similar effects. Managers and subordinates are able to communicate with each other more effectively (with less garbling), cheaply, and quickly. This allows the manager to oversee more subordinates. Thus, the effects of advances in information technology are generally to increase the span of control, leading to flatter organizations. This is exactly what was found in the study by Rajan & Wulf described at the beginning of this chapter.

Advances in information technology may have ambiguous effects on the number of layers in the hierarchy, however. Lower cost of communication tends to increase the optimal number of layers, as communication is faster and there is less garbling at each stage. On the other hand, the greater productivity of knowledge workers, combined with higher spans of control, implies that more can be accomplished by each layer of the hierarchy, implying that fewer layers are needed for a given level of output.

Skills, Pay, and Structure

Firms almost universally assign new employees to lower levels of the hierarchy, and promote the best performers *upward* to higher levels as they advance in their careers. This sorting, and the fact that managers increase their human capital as they gain experience, implies that firms assign their most talented managers to the highest hierarchical levels.

This pattern makes sense. Consider once more the Steep hierarchy depicted in Figure 6.5. Each manager communicates directly with his boss, and with each of his subordinates. To the extent that he makes his subordinates more effective in doing their work, this effect also increases the productivity of their subordinates, who are two levels below the original manager. There is a cascading effect, as the productivity of a high level manager improves productivity of all employees below.

The same effect does not tend to work in reverse for several reasons. First, a lower level manager works directly with only a single higher level manager—most of the direct communications are downward. Second, by design a manager has a greater impact on the subordinate's productivity than the opposite. The manager monitors the subordinate to prevent shirking and evaluate performance. The manager provides direction and training. While the subordinate's work is often used as an input by the supervisor, it is combined with that of other colleagues at the same hierarchical level.

For these reasons, the effect of ability (and effort) rises with hierarchical level. This has several very important implications. The first, as we have already highlighted, is that the firm should sort employees so that the most talented rise to the top of the organization. This then implies hiring at the bottom, and an *internal labor market* of upward promotion over the employee's career. (This system is especially well suited to functional hierarchies, of course.)

The effect also means that compensation should rise with hierarchical level. This happens because more talented managers are placed at higher levels; they must be paid more because they are more productive and have better market values. However, the effect on pay is reinforced by the fact that productivity rises more rapidly than does ability in a hierarchy. Why? For all of the reasons we have discussed in this subsection. Therefore, in most firms not only does pay rise with hierarchical level, but it rises more rapidly at each new level, up to the very top of the organization. For an example of this, see Figure 11.1 in Chapter 11.

This and the previous section reinforce the discussion of the rising returns to skills that is threaded through the text, starting in Chapter 3. Decreases in the costs of acquiring and communicating knowledge increase the productivity of managers. In a hierarchy, these effects are generally even stronger at higher levels. That only strengthens the impact of advances in information technology on the widening of pay across different skill levels. We return to these issues in Chapter 8.

Evolution of a Firm's Structure

The optimal structure of a firm is likely to evolve over time in several ways. First, consider the lessons of this and the previous chapter. Younger firms are more likely to emphasize decision management. That is, they will tend to make less use of hierarchy. It is important for such firms to innovate and take risks. The downside risk from mistakes is very low, and the upside potential from successful new projects is relatively high.

In addition, young firms tend to be small firms. The smaller the firm, the more likely is a network structure to be feasible. Most employees will know each other, so it is easy to develop a system in which employees communicate with each other directly as necessary.

As the firm matures and grows, however, it is very likely to develop more formal structure (of a divisional or matrix form) because the larger number of employees makes an informal network structure less efficient. It is also more likely to adopt a more formal hierarchy, because the firm now has an established product line and brand name, so it should naturally become more conservative in decision making. A key issue facing growing companies is the ability to introduce gradually more formal structures in such a way as not to damage the existing organizational culture.

As a firm matures, it is usually possible to standardize procedures more. The firm has had time to learn effective methods. Similarly, the fact that the firm has survived tends to mean that its industry is relatively stable compared to those of new firms that failed to survive. Both effects mean that the firm can now institutionalize the knowledge that has accumulated. Standardizing procedures is a form of centralization, since it removes some discretion from lower level employees. Thus, in this way as well, older, more mature organizations tend to become more formal, conservative, and hierarchical.

An interesting phenomenon is *churning* of organizational structure. It is common to observe firms change some elements of their structure quite often. In one extreme case, Apple Computer reorganized parts of its structure 14 times in 4 years. Why might this be the case?

A plausible explanation is that no structure is perfect. Any given structure is relatively good at achieving some objectives for the firm, but trades that off with less effectiveness for other objectives. For example, Apple's structure long favored engineering (the advanced technology group), but was poor at developing products that reflected knowledge of customer preferences. Reorganizing to give greater input to sales & marketing alleviated these problems. Another firm might find that organization by region made the company effective at differentiating its product and marketing across regions, aiding implementation of a globalization strategy. However, this might come at the expense of some economies of scale in some areas. Once the firm has learned what to differentiate by region, and how, it might reorganize to give greater importance to economies of scale to reduce costs. Later, it might reorganize yet again, to give more emphasis to some other objective, such as developing stronger advanced technological expertise.

●●●●● ## SUMMARY

Organizational structures in large firms can get extremely complex. As a result, firms take on a certain degree of bureaucracy. Such firms become slower at decision making, and less innovative and dynamic than smaller, younger firms. These patterns are often criticized, but this is often misguided. Directing a large complex enterprise in a coordinated fashion is a quite difficult problem. The market metaphor only gets us so far in designing the internal organization of the firm. After all, if a market organization would work, one should question why the firm exists as a large organization at all.

In microeconomics, the equilibrium size of a firm in a competitive market is determined by the extent of economies of scale (the range of output over which the firm's per unit costs fall). A firm's product line is determined by the extent of economies of scope (whether increasing output of one product decreases per unit costs of producing a different product).

These bureaucratic costs of organizational structure are almost certainly one of the most important sources of diseconomies of both scale and scope. Consider first diseconomies of scale. As the firm gets larger, more employees are required. These require supervision and direction, which requires management. As the firm grows, more layers of hierarchy and more divisions or other subunits are likely to be added. These slow down decision making, and create a more conservative firm. Lower level employees and top management are farther from each other, increasing the extent to which information and decisions are garbled in communication. More talented, and expensive, managers are required to oversee operations.

Now consider diseconomies of scope. The more complex the firm's business, the more differentiation into divisions and other subunits will be necessary. Even if the firm is able to exploit modularity effectively, there are more connections between the modules (divisions) to manage. Coordination becomes a larger scale problem, since a great spectrum of specializations need to be overseen. Coordination costs will generally be larger in more complex organizations, holding size of the hierarchy constant. Once more, more talented and expensive managers are needed. All of these effects are likely to be more severe, the more that a firm's product lines are dissimilar. In fact, the argument that firms should focus on their *core competence* recognizes that diversifying the firm's operations increases organizational costs.

Every firm makes extensive use of functional hierarchy, even when more modern innovations like network structures are implemented. This is because of two important factors. The first is that it is almost always more efficient to have a single decision maker in an organization—firms are almost never organized as democracies or anything close to them. This means that hierarchy is the most fundamental and universal element of organizational structure.

The second factor is the benefits from specializing worker skills and tasks. Specialization of skills economizes on the costs of investments in human capital, and generally increases the returns on those investments (with the notable exception of generalists such as MBAs). As we will see in the next chapter, specialization in job design can also have large benefits. A functional structure organizes the firm around different types of skills, maximizing these gains from specialization. It also has the additional benefits that career paths are clearly defined and easy to understand, and that supervision, direction, and performance evaluation are likely to be more effective.

Even if a firm opts for simple functional hierarchy, a larger or more complex firm will need to break its structure into more manageable subunits. The most common way to do so is to establish divisions, usually based on product line, region, customer type, or technology. Each type of division has its benefits and costs. Generally, the firm should decide which type of variation is more important to focus on in its organization (say, type of customer or region), and use that to guide establishment of divisions.

Structure is driven not only by specialization and hierarchy, but also by allocation of decisions to play off need to use local knowledge and coordination. Some decisions will be made at high levels, using classical centralized hierarchy. Others will be made lower down, if there is specific knowledge to tap into at lower levels.

When decisions are made at lower levels, those decisions makers need to be motivated to act in the interests of the firm. That will be Part Three of the text. Thus, incentives are an important coordination mechanism, when performance measures are appropriately chosen. This is analogous to prices in a market. The firm "sells the job" to the employee by giving some residual rights to profit, motivating *intrapreneurship*.

Since incentive schemes are imperfect, firms use a large array of other coordination mechanisms. These include MBAs, standard operating procedures, common training, corporate culture, and communication.

The most difficult structure problems arise when two or more groups possess important specific knowledge that must be *combined* to make a decision. This is what we called an integration problem. Here the decision cannot simply be decentralized to one group or the other. Instead, the decision must be overseen by one manager, or made together by the groups that possess the relevant knowledge. The most complex structures, such as matrix or project structures, arise to address this problem. Though difficult to manage and work in, there is little alternative to these designs in firms that face important integration problems.

Just as almost every firm makes use of classical functional hierarchy, so too does every firm make use of more informal communication and coordination structures alongside the formal organization chart. Thus, a manager's network of colleagues is an additional coordination mechanism. Firms that give particular emphasis to relational, fluid structures are sometimes said to have network structures.

That structure is driven by specific knowledge illustrates that the product and environment of the firm drive strategy. More complex firms tend to differentiate more into different divisions. They also tend to use more decentralized approaches. As argued in the next chapter, this will affect job design as well. Such firms are also more likely to run into coordination problems, and thus adopt more complex structures.

●●●●● STUDY QUESTIONS

1. How is your firm or university organized? Explain how this reflects the principles discussed in this chapter.

2. Is a traditional functional hierarchy an effective structure for a military? Why or why not? Would such a structure be a better fit during time of war, or peace?

3. Economies of scale—falling cost per unit as total output increases—have been historically important in the automobile and steel industries. However, modern production methods have greatly reduced the importance of economies of scale in both. How do you predict this will affect the optimal organizational structure of companies in these industries? What effect should this have on the competitive position of firms that were leaders in emphasizing economies of scale in the past?

4. Project structures first became important in the aerospace industry. These firms produced extremely complex, highly advanced products (e.g., jet airplanes or rockets). Project or matrix structures are also very common in consulting firms. Why do these structures make sense for these types of firms?

5. Project or network structures are often criticized (especially by those who actually work in them) for their complexity and the difficulty of working within them. Explain the factors that cause such criticisms.

6. Why might network structures be more popular now than 20 years ago? Explain the likely effect of each of the following: greater use of outsourcing and close strategic relationships with key suppliers; decreasing costs of information technology; more rapid technological and competitive change.

7. Companies often find that changing an organizational structure is quite difficult in practice. What kinds of costs do you foresee that a firm would face if it decided to change structure?

8. Following on the previous question, which of the general types of structures discussed in this chapter would you predict is easier to change? Why?

9. Acme, the company used as an example in several of the chapters of this text, had eight levels in its management hierarchy, from entry level management to the CEO. From 1969 through 1988, the company tripled the number of management employees (see Baker, Gibbs, & Holmstrom, 1994). However, Acme never added any new hierarchical levels. Provide at least two explanations.

●●●●● REFERENCES

Adams, Henry (1995). *Collected Works*. New York: Penguin Classics.

Burt, Ronald (1995). *Structural Holes: The Social Structure of Competition*. Cambridge, MA: Harvard University Press.

Guth, Robert (2005). "Battling Google, Microsoft Changes How it Builds Software." *Wall Street Journal*, September 23.

Rajan, Raghuram & Julie Wulf (2006). "The Flattening of the Firm: Evidence from Panel Data on the Changing Nature of Corporate Hierarchies." *Review of Economics & Statistics* 88(4): 759–773.

FURTHER READING　　　　　⬢⬢⬢⬢⬢

Baker, George, Michael Gibbs, & Bengt Holmstrom (1994). "The Internal Economics of the Firm: Evidence from Personnel Data." *Quarterly Journal of Economics* 109: 881–919.

Bolton, Patrick & Mathias Dewatripont (1994). "The Firm as a Communication Network." *Quarterly Journal of Economics* 109: 809–839.

Calvo, Guillermo & Stanislaw Wellisz (1978). "Supervision, Loss of Control, and the Optimum Size of the Firm." *Journal of Political Economy* 86: 943–952.

Chandler, Alfred (1962). *Strategy and Structure: Chapters in the History of the American Industrial Enterprise*. Cambridge, MA: MIT Press.

Garicano, Luis (2000). "Hierarchies and the Organization of Knowledge in Production." *Journal of Political Economy* 108: 874–904.

Geanakoplos, John & Paul Milgrom (1991). "A Theory of Hierarchies Based on Limited Managerial Attention." *Journal of the Japanese and International Economies* 5: 205–225.

Lawrence, Paul & Jay Lorsch (1967). *Organization and Environment*. Boston: Harvard Business School Press.

Qian, Yingyi (1994). "Incentives and Loss of Control in an Optimal Hierarchy." *Review of Economic Studies* 61: 527–544.

Rosen, Sherwin (1982). "Authority, Control and the Distribution of Earnings." *Bell Journal of Economics* 13: 311–323.

Van Creveld, Martin (1987). *Command in War*. Cambridge, MA: Harvard University Press.

7

JOB DESIGN

Between labor and play stands work ... Whether a job is to be classified as labor or work depends, not on the job itself, but on the tastes of the individual who undertakes it.

—W. H. Auden, 1970

INTRODUCTION

Your firm needs to add another worker, so you place an ad describing the position. Most of the time, ads specify some qualifications that the successful applicant must possess, but much of the focus of the ad is on the position itself. It would be possible, of course, to leave any description of the job absent from the ad. Examine the following ad:

Wanted: Individual with college degree in engineering. Call +55-5555-6482.

Such an ad leaves out so many details that it is unlikely to attract many desirable applicants. In particular, missing from the ad is a description of the duties, hours, pay, and location of the job. Also missing is the type of company, responsibilities, and advancement possibilities.

There is a broader question here. What is a job, and how should it be specified? What are the important characteristics to think about? Which tasks should be assigned to which jobs? How much authority should an individual in the job be given?

An additional consideration is that the job design might affect the worker's behavior. Would some structures inhibit creativity and innovation? Will your employees be more motivated by some job designs than by others? If so, how can you design jobs to take these factors into account?

••••• PATTERNS OF JOB DESIGN

Table 7.1 presents some evidence on how jobs are designed, from a random sample of all private-sector, nonagricultural jobs in the U.S. economy, collected by the Bureau of Labor Statistics. Four job characteristics are analyzed in the table: multitasking, discretion, skills, and interdependence.

Multitasking is a measure of the extent to which the job requires the employee to perform more than one task. A larger value implies that the job entails more tasks. Discretion corresponds to decentralization: A larger value implies that an employee in that job is required to make more decisions. Thus, multitasking and discretion are measures of the number of tasks and decisions that comprise the job.

The skills variable measures the breadth and depth of ability and human capital required of an employee qualified for the job. It measures both the level of skills (e.g., basic or advanced), and the types of skills. A larger value of the skills variable implies that the employee has more advanced training, needs multiple skills for the job, or both.

Finally, interdependence is a measure of how closely related the job is to other jobs in that organization. It measures how much the employee's actions affect co-workers or customers. A larger number implies greater interdependence, suggesting that the production process is more interlinked. One interpretation is that interdependence measures the extent to which coordination is important.

TABLE 7.1
INCIDENCE OF COHERENT AND INCOHERENT JOB DESIGNS

		Marginal Probabilities		
	L (< median)	M (median)	H (> median)	Σ
Skills	0.251	0.540	0.209	1
Discretion	0.190	0.610	0.200	1
Multitasking	0.194	0.603	0.203	1
Interdependence	0.185	0.619	0.196	1

		Predicted	Actual	$\left(\dfrac{Actual}{Predicted}\right)$
	Coherent			
	LLLL	0.0017	0.0541	31.6
	MMMM	0.1230	0.2502	2.0
Combinations	HHHH	0.0017	0.0626	37.6
of Job Design	Incoherent			
Characteristics	1L, 3H	0.0068	0.0007	0.1
	2L, 2H	0.0102	<0.001	>0.1
	3L, 1H	0.0068	0.0007	0.1

Source: Gibbs, Levenson, & Zoghi (2008)

These measures are based on interviews with human resource employees at the companies surveyed. They were recorded on scales of 1–9 (skills), 1–5 (discretion), and 1–6 (multitasking and interdependence). To facilitate comparisons across different types of work settings, the average (median) value was calculated for different occupation groups. For example, the average multitasking score was calculated among telephone operators only. Then, each job's measure was recoded as L (low, if the value is below the median value for other jobs in the same industry and occupation), M (medium, or the same as the median value), and H (high, if the value is above the median) relative to other jobs in the same occupation.

The top panel in the table shows the distribution of each of the four job characteristics. For example, about 25% (0.251) of randomly chosen jobs require employees to have skills at a relatively low level for that occupation. Similarly, about 54% (0.540) of jobs require relatively average levels of skills for that occupation, while about 21% (0.209) require relatively high levels of skills for that occupation. Thus, the four rows each sum to 100% (1.0) in the top part of the table.

The bottom panel in the table is the interesting part—it asks if these job characteristics are related to each other or not. To see how this is done, suppose that you have data on the relative temperature (L, M or H) and relative price of wine (L, M or H) from a specific region of France. You are interested in whether the price of wine is related to the temperature in the season in which the grapes were grown. If the probability of a certain wine price level is *not* related to the probability of a certain temperature level, then what is the probability that you observe a low wine price in a year that there was a low temperature? It will just be the probability of a low wine price, regardless of temperature, times the probability of a low temperature, regardless of wine price:[1]

Predicted probability of LL (low temp, low price)
= prob(low temp) · prob(low price).

If you then found that the actual occurrence of low prices when there is a low temperature is very different from this value, you would conclude that there is a statistical relationship between the two variables. For example, if wine prices tend to be lower when the temperature is lower, then the actual probability of LL would be higher than the predicted probability calculated. By contrast, if wine prices tend to be higher when the temperature is lower, the opposite would be true.

Now apply this logic to the job design data in Table 7.1 and see if the four job characteristics are determined jointly or separately. If these four job characteristics were determined separately from each other, the probability that a randomly chosen job was, for example, low on all four characteristics (LLLL) would equal

---

[1]More formally, the prob(LL) = prob(low temp, low price) · prob(low temp) · prob(low price given low temp). Assuming that the variables are uncorrelated yields the expression above. Thus, the equation assumes zero correlation, or even more strongly, statistical independence between the variables.

the product of the four marginal probabilities in the L column in the top panel of the table:

$$\text{Predicted probability } (LLLL) = 0.251 \cdot 0.190 \cdot 0.194 \cdot 0.185 = 0.0017.$$

The Predicted column in the bottom panel of Table 7.1 shows these values. The Actual column then shows the fraction of jobs that actually were of each type. For example, a randomly chosen job had a probability 0.0541 of being low on all four characteristics (LLLL). Since 0.0541/0.0017 equals about 31.6, this means that LLLL jobs were observed more than 30 times as often as would be expected if the job characteristics were not correlated with each other.

Similarly, the predicted probability of observing a job of type $HHHH$—high on all dimensions—is 0.0017. In fact, $HHHH$ jobs were observed about 40 times as often as this. $MMMM$ jobs are observed about 25% of the time, but are predicted to occur at about half that rate.

These findings make clear that firms tend to use *coherent* job designs. That is, jobs tend to be low on all four job characteristics, or medium on all four, or high on all four. To check this, the last three rows of Table 7.1 repeat this exercise, but comparing the predicted and actual probabilities of *incoherent* job designs—that is, jobs which are high on some dimensions but low on others. Sure enough, incoherent job designs are observed only about one tenth less often than they are predicted to be. Though not shown, it is the case that jobs that are more coherent (though not completely so) are more frequent than would be predicted, while jobs that are less coherent (though not completely so) are less frequent than would be predicted.

Thus, there is a very strong tendency for jobs to have coherent design. If a worker is given more decision rights, he is also likely to have to perform more tasks, and have broader and deeper human capital. Further, the job is more likely to be part of a complex production process, in which the job is interdependent with those of others. The reverse is also true.

Table 7.2 provides another interesting job design pattern. These data are from a survey of British workers whose firms had recently undergone a major organizational change. The respondents were asked how the change affected their job design. The survey's questions corresponded nicely with the variables we analyzed in Table 7.1. Table 7.2 shows a striking effect of organizational change on job design: It is very likely to increase multitasking, decentralization, and skill requirements.

In summary, these tables tell us several important pieces of information. First, two important features of job design are the amount of decisions and tasks that the employee performs. Second, there are clear patterns in job design. Multitasking is associated with more discretion, and both are associated with more highly skilled workers. A job that is low on these dimensions is often called a *narrow* job. A common term for a job that is high on these dimensions is an *enriched* job.

Third, we have some clues about situations in which a job should be designed to be narrower or more enriched. Jobs tend to be more enriched when they are part of more interdependent production processes. Firms also tend to use more enriched jobs when they have undergone recent organizational change.

TABLE 7.2

EFFECTS OF ORGANIZATIONAL CHANGE ON JOB DESIGN

	% of Employees with	
	More	*Less*
Tasks	63%	6%
Responsibility	46%	3%
Required skills	50%	4%

Source: Caroli & Van Reenen (2001)

Finally, there has been a gradual trend over the last several decades, toward enriched jobs and away from narrow jobs. This is consistent with the idea in the business press that firms have made increasing use of worker empowerment. Nevertheless, it is important to realize that these are only overall patterns and trends. Many firms still make use of narrowly defined, low skill jobs with little worker empowerment.

In the remainder of this chapter, we develop an explanation for these patterns and trends. We do so by first discussing which tasks to put together in the same job. This is the most important piece of the puzzle. The number and type of tasks that a worker is given is inextricably linked to the skills the worker has, so at the same time we discuss the skills needed for a particular job design. Finally, we briefly return to the question of decision making that was the focus of much of the last two chapters, to relate that discussion to job design.

OPTIMAL JOB DESIGN: SKILLS, TASKS, AND DECISIONS

Multiskilling and Multitasking

Skills

Multitasking is a situation where a worker is required to perform a number of different tasks. Multiskilling is where a worker has the *ability* to perform a number of tasks. Many of the benefits that are sometimes attributed to multitasking are actually advantages of multiskilling. It is sometimes not necessary that the tasks be associated with the job, but only that the incumbent has the ability to perform those tasks when needed. Some of the advantages of multiskilling are listed here.

Flexibility. Workers who know a large number of tasks can fill in for other workers. Flexibility has less value in a large firm than it does in a small one. In a very large firm, many people may be doing the same job, so it is less important to have one person know a large number of tasks. (This is shown formally in the Appendix.)

For example, consider Cathay Pacific Airlines reservations. There is a large number of reservationists on duty at any one time. If one reservationist is absent, there is enough flexibility built into the scheduling so that another person with reservation skills can fill in. There is little need to transfer a gate agent to the reservations department. Thus, the gate agent need not be familiar with making reservations. He or she can focus on the direct responsibilities of being a gate agent, and little is lost.

At the other extreme, consider the example of a small restaurant. Initially, the owner is the manager, cook, buyer, waiter, cashier, and maitre d'hôtel. As the restaurant grows, the owner may hire someone to wait tables and seat the guests. Large restaurants, on the other hand, could have 500 employees, with tasks as specialized as vegetable procurer. When the restaurant is small, if the waiter cannot also cook, the restaurant must shut down when the cook is sick. Multiskilling would prevent a shutdown by training the waiter to be a cook. In a small firm, where there is only enough work of a given type to justify a few positions, multiskilling is likely to provide valuable flexibility.

Communication. Multiskilling is likely to facilitate communication between individuals in different jobs in the firm. It is much easier to discuss an issue with someone familiar with the situation than with someone totally ignorant of the area.

Consider, for example, a carpenter and electrician who are part of a construction crew that is building a house. The electrician needs to configure the wire in a particular way, but to do so, the wood framework of the house must accommodate the electrician's needs. It is easier for the electrician to communicate with the carpenter if the electrician has some understanding of carpentry.

This example was not chosen by accident. Building a house has significant elements of team production. The benefits of enhanced communication from multiskilling are likely to be larger in a team setting, where different jobs are highly interdependent.

Innovation. Multiskilling may assist in making innovations on the job, through at least two mechanisms. First, as with communication, when an individual knows many aspects of production, it is easier to design process-improving technology. In the previous example, a carpenter is more likely to design a more accommodating frame if he understands the electricians job. This effect is very much like the effect of multitasking on the job learning that we discuss later.

The second effect of multiskilling on innovation is that when individuals are highly specialized, a given innovation may be more likely to cause all of their human capital to become obsolete. For example, blacksmiths were virtually eliminated by the invention of the automobile. If blacksmiths had instead been generalized iron and steel workers, only a small part of their skills would have been rendered obsolete by the automobile. Some of their other skills are likely to have become more valuable.

This matters because workers who see their skills become obsolete are more likely to oppose innovation. Although the market is likely to win out in the end by forcing the noninnovating firms out of business, no firm would voluntarily choose to be among those disciplined by the market. Having a more broadly skilled workforce may enhance the ability of the firm to adapt to change.

Tasks

Specialization versus multitasking. One of the most important principles of job design comes from Adam Smith's *Wealth of Nations* (1776). Smith wrote that the degree of specialization is limited by the extent of the market. He provides an example of a pin factory, where each worker can make an entire pin, start to finish, or can simply work on one aspect of pin making, like sharpening the point.[2] In order to devote a full-time worker to such a narrow task, it is necessary to have a sufficiently large set of orders that a large number of workers are needed. For example, if the market for pins could only justify production of five pins per day, an assembly line process and narrowly defined jobs would be impractical. Instead, such a firm would have a single craftsman produce all five pins per day.

Thus smaller firms are more likely to use multitasking in job design, just as they tend to emphasize multiskilling in their workers more than do larger firms.

The most important message of Smith's analysis is the idea of *specialization*, the opposite of multitasking.[3] In the pin factory, making a single pin involved up to 18 different tasks. The factory that specialized jobs could potentially use 10 different workers to perform these tasks. One worker's job might be simply to straighten out the wire—all day long. This is an extreme example of what is often observed in manufacturing jobs: few tasks, performed repetitively. When the firm did this, it was able to produce 20 pounds of pins per day. Smith reported that a single worker could only produce about 20 pins per day. Thus, breaking the process down into narrow tasks, and giving workers specialized jobs, can result in an enormous increase in productivity.

This insight cannot be overemphasized. Always remember the gains from specialization, as these gains can be extremely large. Any move away from specialization should have strong justification.

Why does specialization increase productivity? One reason is that when a worker performs a limited number of tasks, he has more chance to perfect those tasks. If a worker has too many tasks to do, he is likely to become a "jack of all trades, but master of none." The opposite applies when he is specialized. Another benefit of specialization is that a worker may save time (and mental focus) in switching between tasks. Finally, specialization allows for specialized human capital investments, economizing on the costs of training.

---

[2]What Smith called a pin we call a nail (which is, of course, just a large pin). Smith's example of specialization may have roots tracing back 800 years to Persia (Hosseini 1998).

[3]Once again you need to be careful to not get confused by academic jargon. Specialization usually refers to narrow tasks in job design. It sometimes refers to a narrowly focused investment in human capital, as in Chapter 3. Specialized is *not* the same as specific knowledge, discussed in Chapter 5. It is also *not* the same as specific investments, from Chapter 3.

Specialization is one of the most important factors in modern economies, because of the enormous gains in productivity, which is why it is the topic of the very first chapter of Smith's *Wealth of Nations*. It is also the basis of economies, because when people specialize, they are more productive, and trading allows both parties to be better off than if they did not specialize.

Multitasking

Multitasking is the movement away from specialization: giving a worker a number of tasks to perform. Though the gains from specialization are important, there are also costs. Some of the benefits of multitasking are listed below.

Lower transactions costs. When workers specialize, various costs may arise that could be avoided through multitasking. One example is transportation time. Suppose that part of an insurance claim is handled by an office in Chicago and another part by an office in Atlanta. The paperwork may have to be mailed from Chicago to Atlanta, causing a time delay. Multitasking would reduce such costs. Note that as information technology becomes more common, such gains to multitasking are likely to diminish (for more on this topic, see the next chapter).

Similarly, when the insurance claim is passed from one person to another, an additional person must learn some of the details of the case. If three people work on a file, it must be read three times rather than just once. To the extent that there are few gains from splitting the task up into many small parts, multitasking saves valuable setup time.

In addition to setup costs, specialization can involve *bureaucracy costs*. Each time a project passes from one desk to another there is a tendency for a worker to put the project off for some time. Even when setup time is minimal, the proclivity to procrastinate implies that passing a project around slows completion.

Supply considerations. Sometimes the skills necessary to perform one task allow a worker to perform a related task. For example, a tax accountant who knows enough tax law to file a complicated income tax return also may know enough to give a client advice on minimizing tax liability for the following year. This is why tax accountants often suggest investment vehicles to their clients at the time taxes are filed. However, when skills needed to perform one task can only be used for this task, multitasking becomes costly. This is why we do not often see the school nurse doubling as the handyman. Although neither task alone necessarily occupies all of one's time, the requisite skills are so different that multitasking is infeasible.

To the extent that tasks are to be put together into one job, it is necessary that the job holder have the skills to perform all of the tasks in the bundle. Plumbers normally do not know the intricacies of electrical systems, so one worker is rarely assigned the tasks of installing both plumbing and electrical wiring in a new house. Instead, a plumber may be assigned the tasks of putting in faucets and running water pipe to the laundry room, since the skills involved in those are so similar.

Complementarity in production. One of the most important reasons to use multitasking instead of specialization is when tasks are complements in production. Tasks *A* and *B* are complements if performing Task *A* makes the worker more efficient at performing Task *B*, and vice versa. Consider, for example, repair work. It is usually the case that the individual who diagnoses the problem also does the repair. The washing machine repairman is well situated to fix it. He could describe the problem to another worker who would then carry out the repair, but this would duplicate the effort.

Tasks are more likely to be complementary in production when the tasks are especially interrelated in the overall production process. This often involves specific knowledge of particular circumstances. In the case of repair work, diagnosing the repair gives that employee detailed, and often experiential, knowledge of the particular machine being repaired. The worker can communicate this knowledge to someone who then does the repairs, but the communication costs would be relatively high.

Note that complementary tasks in this sense are also more likely to arise when the product or process is complex. For example, in the production of Adam Smith's pins, the steps are very simple and there is not a great deal of interdependence between various steps of the process. By contrast, if a firm is manufacturing diesel engines, it is very important that each part fit smoothly into the adjacent part or socket. Thus, the tasks of shaping parts that work together are good candidates to be bundled into the same job.

We see that the principles from Chapters 5–6 are relevant to designing individual jobs. When tasks are more interdependent, specialization would create high coordination costs between the two workers given the different tasks. To avoid such coordination problems, which would raise costs, slow production, or lower quality, it is often advantageous to bundle the most complementary tasks into the same job.

Moreover, the principle of modularity in design applies quite well to individual job design, in the same way as it does to overall organizational structure. When designing jobs, look for ways to modularize the firm's processes. If work can be modularized, then by definition most of the highly interdependent tasks have been put together in the same module, reducing coordination costs. There will still be coordination costs across jobs or modules, but such costs will be lower if modules have been defined properly.

Software engineering provides an example of modularization in job design. A large programming project (say, an operating system or large application) is too much for a single programmer to handle, so the project must be broken into different jobs. Typically, a programmer is given responsibility for one or more specific subroutines or software objects. These are, of course, modules of the overall program. These subroutines are chosen so that the most intricately related pieces are put together. The project manager then has to manage the interface between the subroutines—that is, coordinate—but in a well designed project with good modularization this is more easily managed. In fact, modern software tools and principles are designed with modularity in mind. Software engineers are taught to design programs as relatively stand-alone parts. They are taught to design data structures and interfaces between software objects that minimize coordination problems in overall design and functioning of the program.

On-the-job learning.   A particular kind of task complementarity that is important is that a multitasking worker is more likely to learn ways to improve the process or product. The most difficult parts of a process to perfect are the ones that are most complex and interdependent. Those are also the cases where multitasking is more likely. When an employee performs very closely related tasks, he or she is more likely to discover new ways to perform those tasks, ways to make the output from those tasks fit together more effectively, and so on.

Consider again our example of diesel engine manufacturing. Suppose that the company experiences a problem because two parts do not fit together well, causing friction and ultimately engine failures. If the company has organized jobs around specialization, the two parts will probably be made by separate workers. Each worker is likely to manufacture his or her respective part as efficiently as they can, but with little thought to how the part might fit with the other part. By contrast, a worker assigned the tasks of producing both parts is much more likely to consider how the parts will function *together*.

As another example, consider our insurance claim processing company. If processing of the claim is broken into different jobs, then workers tend to take a narrow view of how to perform each step. On the other hand, if a single worker is assigned to handle the entire claim from start to finish, he or she sees the *entire process* (what we will call *task identity*). This gives the worker a better idea of the relative importance of each task and how each task fits together. This knowledge makes it much more likely that the worker will provide good customer service.

Monitoring difficulties.   Sometimes, putting tasks together will induce a worker to focus on one task and ignore another. For example, a worker who is assigned to both selling and developing good customer relations might focus on the former and ignore the latter. Since selling is more easily observed than developing customer relations, and since firms tend to pay for selling directly, grouping these tasks may cause the worker to sacrifice one for the other. An alternative is simply to pay the worker for hours worked, but then the benefit of performance pay on sales work is lost. By splitting the tasks up, the firm may do better; see Chapters 9–10 for more discussion.

Intrinsic motivation.   Adam Smith noted that very narrow, highly specialized jobs may be a problem because the worker becomes bored with the work. Thus, a benefit of multitasking is that it can increase the worker's *intrinsic motivation*—the psychology motivation caused by the job. We defer discussion of this effect until later in the chapter.

Decisions

Since multitasking makes on the job learning more likely, it should not be surprising that the evidence cited above shows that workers who are given more tasks are also given more decision rights. The knowledge that workers develop in multitask jobs will often be relatively specific knowledge (costly to communicate), since it will be complex and experiential. Therefore, to tap into this learning, the firm will generally have to give the worker the ability to try out new methods, and implement those that are successful.

We can take this point a step further. Because multitasking is a way for a firm to improve worker learning, it increases the importance of *analysis* and *decision making* skills. Thus, multitasking not only requires that the worker develop the broad set of skills required to perform each individual task: It also places a premium on workers with greater thinking skills. This point will be important in the next chapter.

TRAINING PRODUCTION WORKERS
IN THE SCIENTIFIC METHOD
❖ ❖ ❖ ❖ ❖ ❖ ❖ ❖ ❖

Many firms use total quality management (TQM) methods to apply the principles discussed in this chapter. TQM focuses on improving quality. Many quality problems are caused by too much specialization in jobs, so that workers do not take account of how their output meshes with other stages of the process. Thus, TQM usually implies greater use of multitasking (often accompanied by teams, a topic in the next chapter). It also typically implies more worker decision making, to tap into the worker's improved on the job learning. This method can be used to improve quality, or any other organizational goal, such as throughput or efficiency.

TQM programs also usually imply that firms need to provide additional training. Some of the new skills are needed simply because workers perform a larger set of tasks than before the use of TQM. However, the training also often involves teaching workers decision making skills. A striking example of this is the method that was advocated by a famous TQM consultant, Joseph Juran. Juran recommended that his clients train shop-floor workers in the following seven stage process for diagnosing problems, coming up with ways to fix them, and implementing their solutions:

1. Analyze symptoms.
2. Theorize causes.
3. Test theories.
4. Establish causes.

5. Simulate a remedy.
6. Test remedy under operating conditions.
7. Establish controls to hold the gain.

Note that the first three steps are the scientific method. The next three are as well, in a more applied form. In other words, Juran advocates teaching even relatively unskilled workers advanced thinking skills needed to develop and make use of the specific knowledge that arises as they do their work.

Source: Jensen & Wruck (1994)

●●●●● ## COMPLEMENTARITY AND JOB DESIGN

The analysis above helps us explain the findings in Table 7.1. Multitasking is more valuable when the process is more interdependent, because tasks are complementary and there are greater opportunities for workers to learn. When multitasking is used and workers learn on the job, it is valuable to give them more discretion—to *empower* them—in order to exploit the ideas and knowledge that they accumulate. Multitasking is positively related to the extent of worker skills in two ways. First, performing a larger set of tasks implies that workers need a larger set of skills. Second, learning coupled with decision making implies that multitasking workers also tend to need analysis and thinking skills.

Thus, it makes sense that these four job design characteristics should be positively related, as shown in Table 7.1. If a job is high on one of these dimensions, it should be more likely to be high on the other dimensions, and vice versa.

However, this does not suggest that all jobs should be enriched. To the contrary, Table 7.1 shows that firms use both enriched and classical, narrowly defined jobs with low skills.

What it does illustrate is the notion that human resource policies be designed as a system of complementary parts, that is, no policy should be designed without consideration of other policies that the firm uses. In our job design example, it would make little sense to use decentralization if the worker has a narrow job and low skills, and if the worker has little specific knowledge of economic value to exploit. In this text, we usually treat specific policies separately, because simplification and focus is necessary to analyze complex issues such as organizational design. But in practice, it is important to remember that policies are related and should be, to the extent possible, designed together.

Consider as an example a branch manager who has been told to improve customer satisfaction. The manager decides that the best way to do so is to implement an incentive system in which employees are given bonuses based on customer satisfaction surveys. If this is done without changing employee job design, it is likely to lead to frustration. Workers may wish to improve their performance ratings, but find themselves restricted from doing so. Similarly, if their job design is changed, but their incentives are not, results are likely to be less than optimal. The firm would do better by taking a (more difficult) systemic approach, thinking about changing various characteristics of job design, performance evaluation, and incentives at the same time.

SYSTEMIC ORGANIZATIONAL DESIGN AND PRODUCTIVITY

One very careful study looked at the effects of different patterns of job design and incentive policies on productivity in a set of steel production lines. The researchers collected data on a variety of human resource policies, as well as detailed data on productivity and product quality. One particularly nice feature of the project is that all of the firms studied used a specific type of manufacturing process, so that productivity differences are unlikely to be due to factors other than organizational design.

They divided their sample into four types of organizational design. At one extreme were firms that used policies similar to the *LLLL* type of design in Table 7.1, with specialization, little worker discretion, and low skills. At the other extreme were plants that used policies similar to the *HHHH* design in Table 7.1 (enriched jobs). They also included consideration of the type of incentive plan, arguing that incentives based on measures beyond quantity are complementary with job enrichment (you will see why when you read Chapter 9). These are both examples of coherent approaches to organizational design. The two other types were more like incoherent approaches, at least compared to the extremes.

The research yielded several interesting findings. First, the more classical approach of narrowly designed jobs, centralized decision making, and a low skilled workforce yielded the lowest productivity and product quality.

Second, the effects of a single human resource policy by itself were small or negligible. Instead, the more that a firm adopted a set of complementary policies, the greater was productivity and quality. The largest effects were found when the firm adopted the coherent design involving job enrichment and incentives based on quality and learning new skills. This is evidence that a *systemic* approach to organizational design is most effective.

Source: Ichniowski, Shaw, & Prennushi (1997)

● ● ● ● ● WHEN TO USE DIFFERENT JOB DESIGNS

Our discussion so far in this chapter raises some questions. Why do some firms *not* adopt more modern job design? Why are more classical approaches still used in many firms? If it is more effective to change the entire set of policies, why might a firm change only a few?

There are several possible explanations. One is that there are costs to changing policies. If the costs are large enough, then a firm might find it more profitable to keep using less effective policies. To the extent that systemic organizational design is most effective, organizational change is even more costly, because the firm will have to change more policies, possibly simultaneously and in a coordinated way.

Another explanation is that managers do not always understand what the best policies are. Imperfect knowledge does mean that firms do not always have optimal policies. Similarly, managers may have imperfect incentives to design and implement changes, which can be hard work. However, over time competition between firms, as well as accumulation of more complete knowledge about effective practices (such as the Ichniowski, Shaw, & Prennushi research) should drive firms toward the use of better practices. Thus this explanation is not very satisfying; moreover, it gives little guidance other than to try to hire the best management possible.

Taylorism

A third explanation for why job enrichment is not always adopted is that it is not always the best practice. Suppose that for some firms, industries, technologies, or products (such as steel finishing lines) this approach to organizational design is quite effective, but that for others a more traditional approach emphasizing specialization and centralization is more appropriate. If so, then different designs would be best practices in different types of firms. In this section we explore this idea.

In order to do so, we go back to earlier management theory, in particular the *scientific management* movement of the early 20th century. This movement is also often called *Taylorism*, in honor of one of the chief developers of these ideas, Frederick Taylor.

The idea behind Taylorism is quite straightforward: The firm hires talented engineers, has them figure out the best way to organize production and perform each task, and implements these methods. The approach is quite logical. It exploits the expertise of the most talented and highly trained, and shares their ideas with others. When done well, this is a very useful way to increase efficiency and improve quality. The approach also has interesting organizational implications.

In this method, industrial engineers generally break the process down into individual steps, very much like Adam Smith described for the manufacture of pins. They then attempt to perfect the way to perform each step. An obvious implication is that, if the engineers have indeed come up with a relatively effective design, *workers should be given little or no discretion.* Instead, they should perform their tasks exactly as the engineers have designed the job. As a corollary, *workers need have few skills, especially in decision making.* This approach is the opposite of Juran's TQM example.

Breaking the process into discrete steps, and not focusing on the job learning, typically leads to specialization in job design. These methods are highly effective, for example, at setting up an assembly line where workers perform one or a small number of tasks repetitively, passing their work on to colleagues who perform the next tasks. Furthermore, breaking a process into discrete steps and routinizing those steps often results in automation of much of the work (and, in the current era, computerization).

JOB DESIGN FOR UPS DELIVERY TRUCK DRIVERS

⬢ ⬢ ⬢ ⬢ ⬢ ⬢ ⬢ ⬢ ⬢

UPS is the world's largest package delivery company. It has operated in this business for roughly 100 years. The product is relatively simple—delivery of packages from point *A* to point *B*. Moreover the basics of delivering packages from the truck have changed little in 100 years. UPS is an excellent modern example of the application of the principles of Taylorism.

UPS provides its drivers with extensive training in *exactly* how to deliver packages. For example, drivers are taught to step into the truck with the left foot first, since this is slightly faster than right foot first. They are taught to beep the horn as they pull the truck to the curb (to get the attention of the customer, saving time at the door), hold the key chain with the ignition key in the middle finger of the right hand (to speed up starting the engine after delivery), and put the truck into first gear (which speeds up driving away). UPS has several volumes of standard policies and procedures.

UPS takes industrial engineering even further. Over the years they have gradually altered the design of the delivery truck to improve efficiency. As one example, their engineers discovered that beveling the outer edge of the driver's seat allowed the driver to get in and out of the truck faster.

Each of these policies would seem to lead to only very small improvements in efficiency. However, put together they allow the driver to deliver at least a few more packages per day. In a competitive industry with low profit margins, such small gains can make a great difference, especially when the gains are realized over UPS's vast workforce.

Source: Vogel & Hawkins (1990)

Note that Taylorism is like central planning, whereas enriched jobs with workers given more decision rights is like a market-based approach to structuring the firm. The principles from Chapter 5 apply to job design just as they do to overall organizational design. If the industrial engineers do, in fact, figure out production methods that are close to the optimum, there is little left for workers to learn on the job as there is little specific knowledge of particular circumstances. In such a case, centralization makes sense, and decentralization would be costly.

In other words, similar to the design of an economy, a firm has two broad approaches to optimizing its own design. At one end of the spectrum is *ex ante optimization* through methods such as Taylorism. This leads to a relatively centralized organizational structure, narrow job design, and lower skilled workers. At the other end of the spectrum is *continuous improvement* through methods such as multitasking, decentralization, and higher skilled workers.

Of course, most firms operate somewhere between these two extreme models. Moreover, most firms use some elements of both approaches. For example, many factories have a staff of industrial engineers who take a centralized approach to designing the production line and monitoring quality. Yet those same factories may also use methods such as TQM to tap into additional insights from the workers on how to make incremental improvements. The question is not whether a firm should use one approach or another, but rather for which workers, and to what degree.

Factors Pushing Toward Taylorism or Continuous Improvement

This distinction between ex ante optimization and continuous improvement provides a way to analyze when the firm will tend toward more classical (Tayloristic) or modern (continuous improvement) structures. If the firm can figure out the best methods for performing tasks, there is no reason to allow workers to experiment with their own methods. On the other hand, if Taylorism is not effective, then there is much greater potential for additional improvements to be made by decentralizing and using broader job design. Thus, the question is when Taylorism works well, and when it does not.

Think of Taylorism as an investment; the extent to which the firm should invest in Taylorism depends on the benefits and costs. In order to figure out the best methods of production, the firm must incur costs of hiring the industrial engineers and having them analyze and test different approaches. It must then train workers in how to implement this design. Figuring out the optimal organization and job design can be quite a substantial project. The firm will invest more in Taylorism when the return on the investment is greater, and invest less when the return on investment is smaller. When the firm invests less in ex ante optimization, it is more likely to employ continuous improvement methods as an alternative.

The return on investment depends on the costs of figuring out relatively efficient production methods. It also depends on the benefits that the firm can realize once those methods have been figured out. A couple of important factors that will affect the extent to which a firm uses more of a centralized, ex ante approach or more of a continuous improvement approach are listed here.

Firm size.   The larger the firm, the greater the gains from ex ante optimization, all else equal. Larger firms will have more workers performing similar tasks, so improvements can be spread over a larger workforce. This provides economies of scale to investments in figuring out best methods.

Complexity.   Simpler processes are easier to optimize in advance. Producing a pin effectively is a much easier problem to analyze than is producing a diesel engine. Complexity tends to make Taylorism more costly, which implies less investment in ex ante optimization, and greater opportunities for workers to make improvements on the job.

Complexity plays out in several ways. One is simply the number of parts, or number of steps, involved in the business process. A pin has only two parts (the pin and the head), while a diesel engine has several thousand. Similarly, processing an insurance claim has only a few steps, compared to providing an overall risk management assessment for a bank. The insurance process is likely to be much more standardized, leading to simpler jobs, less decentralization, and lower worker skills than in risk management analysis. Even in the case of risk management, a consulting firm is likely to develop as many standardized procedures as it can, to reduce costs and improve its service. However, the projects it analyzes are so complex that it is difficult to standardize much of the process.

Complexity can also arise from the product line. If the company makes a single product, there is only one process to perfect. If the company makes many different products, the optimization problem multiplies in difficulty (even though some lessons learned in optimizing production of one product may carry over into other products). At the extreme, firms that customize their products for each order will face an even greater challenge in ex ante optimization of methods.

Complexity also may be caused by strong interdependence (coordination costs) between tasks. A process that has many stages, but in which the stages are relatively independent, may be optimized relatively easily. If the different stages are interlinked, optimizing the process is generally more difficult, as the stages have to be considered together. Table 7.1 does, indeed, indicate that firms tend to use less Tayloristic approaches to job design when the firm's processes are more interdependent.

Note that complexity was one of the determinants of whether knowledge was costly or cheap to communicate. Taylorism and centralization works best when knowledge is general. Complexity means that workers are more likely to have specific knowledge of economic value that arises in performing their jobs.

Predictability.   Ex ante optimization involves figuring out best methods and teaching workers how to do them. This approach will not work well when it is more difficult to figure out what situation the worker will face. Thus, more unpredictable environments lend themselves to continuous improvement approaches. If the production environment is random, but the same situations arise over and over again, Taylorism can work well. In such a case, the firm can provide the worker with training and procedures to use in each situation that will arise. However, the greater the number of possible contingencies that might arise, the more complex the optimization problem becomes. Moreover, many random circumstances may be unforeseeable. In such cases, the firm can design general procedures that give the worker guidance about how to perform tasks. However, the guidance will be less than perfect, so that there is scope for the worker to decide how best to handle the situation.

Consider management consulting. Each client engagement is different from the last. Some processes and methods can be reapplied, but new methods or applications often need to be developed. Moreover, judgment about what methods to apply may be required.

Time horizon. An additional determinant of the return on investment in ex ante optimization of a business process is the firm's time horizon, looking both backward and forward. If a firm has been in business for many years, and especially if the firm's environment has been stable, it is likely to have evolved quite effective methods. By contrast, a brand new firm has had little chance to figure out how best to perform tasks. Thus, organizational structure and job design may follow a life cycle in many firms. When the firm is founded, it tends to adopt a continuous improvement approach as it figures out methods on the fly. As the firm matures, it evolves toward greater use of formal procedures and policies, and more centralization of decision making.

Stability also matters looking forward in time. Suppose a firm expects that its basic market circumstances will not change much in the next 10 years. In this case, it may invest more to figure out best practices now, since it can expect to enjoy returns on that investment for a long time. Now consider a firm in a more dynamic industry, e.g., one that is undergoing technological change. This firm is unlikely to invest heavily in optimizing methods, since it is likely to have to change those methods again soon. Instead it will focus on structuring operations so that it can adapt continuously to new technologies and circumstances.

"COPY EXACTLY" AT INTEL

Intel employs an unusual approach when it opens a new semiconductor manufacturing facility, which it calls "Copy Exactly." Under this policy, individual factories are discouraged from experimenting with new methods. Instead, Intel attempts to use identical methods across factories. It painstakingly replicates as much as possible across sites, including such policies as the color of workers' gloves and the paint used on the walls.

Intel's business is highly complex, interdependent, and rapidly changing, so this approach is the exact opposite of what we might expect. However, there are some advantages to the approach. For one, the cost of errors is extremely high in this particular industry. Thus, Intel has a strong need for control and centralized, hierarchical methods for implementing new ideas (along the lines of our discussion in Chapter 5). For another, when the plants use virtually identical methods, Intel can benchmark performance across different plants, which helps it to uncover and diagnose production problems. That is an example of what we called central knowledge in Chapter 5.

This example illustrates that there is no one best approach to organizational and job design. Different methods can work well, depending on the firm's environment, objectives, and risks.

Source: Clark (2002)

Pulling these ideas together, firms that operate in simpler, more stable, and more predictable industries are more likely to use Tayloristic methods. Their job designs will tend toward specialization, centralization, and a less skilled workforce.

Firms that operate in more complex, dynamic, and unpredictable environments will make use of Tayloristic methods to some extent as well. However, their workers will possess more specific knowledge. Such firms will decentralize, tend toward greater multitasking, and use more highly skilled workers.

This view can explain the patterns and trends described earlier in the chapter. Consider Table 7.2, which showed that firms undergoing organizational change tend toward continuous improvement methods. This makes sense, since change implies that previous methods no longer apply, so workers can provide many insights about ways to improve processes.

Similarly, there has been a trend over the last several decades toward continuous improvement. This is likely due to more rapid change in many industries, driven by deregulation, greater international trade, and most especially by the astonishing rate of advancement of information technology.

In fact, this analysis also helps explain some patterns described in Chapter 3. Recall that returns to investments in skills increased remarkably in the last several decades. If many firms found their business environments to be more dynamic, and moved toward continuous improvement methods, they would also value more skilled workers more highly. This also gives us insight into the kinds of skills that are becoming more valuable: problem solving skills of the general kind that Juran advocates. Such skills allow workers to be redeployed, but also to engage in effective continuous improvement. We will have more to say about this issue when we discuss the effects of information technology in the next chapter.

INTRINSIC MOTIVATION

There is one more important job design consideration to discuss. A cost of specialized jobs is that workers can find them boring, leading to low motivation. For the same reason, a benefit of job enrichment is that workers may be more highly motivated.

An important topic in social psychology is how to design jobs to increase intrinsic motivation. Here we present a brief description of the way that psychologists think about these issues. It turns out that the psychological approach fits very nicely with our treatment of job design issues. In fact, many of the principles are essentially the same. This is an example of a point that we made in the Introduction of this book—economic and psychological approaches to organizational design are complementary, and many phenomena that are called psychological are not actually driven by strictly psychological issues.

The most well known psychological model of intrinsic motivation was developed by Richard Hackman and various coauthors. Figure 7.1 presents the model. According to this view, five core job design characteristics can be employed to increase a worker's motivation: skill variety, task identity, task significance, autonomy, and feedback.

The last two of these, autonomy and feedback, should be readily clear to you: They are decentralization. Autonomy means giving the worker greater discretion

FIGURE 7.1
PSYCHOLOGICAL MODEL OF INTRINSIC MOTIVATION

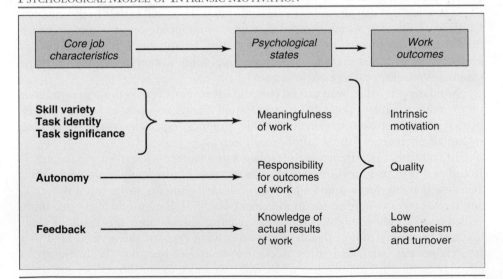

Source: Hackman & Oldham (1976)

over how the work is performed, and greater ability to make decisions. Feedback means providing the worker with information on the effects of actions and decisions. This feedback is necessary so that the worker can diagnose problems, test out new ideas and implement the good ones. Thus, the last two are not really psychological factors.

According to psychologists, the first three characteristics, skill variety, task identity, and task significance, make the work more meaningful to the employee, leading to greater motivation even without the use of pay for performance. How can we interpret them?

Task significance means the extent to which the worker finds the product or service to be personally valuable in some way. For example, a mechanic is likely to find his work to have greater significance if he is repairing a large passenger jet than if he is repairing a lawn mower—lives are at stake. He is more likely to be motivated to do a good job in the former case than the latter. Similarly, workers at not for profit organizations or universities are often motivated in part by a feeling that they are contributing to a larger mission that they value personally. This is, of course, a purely psychological effect.

Unfortunately, task significance is usually not a lever that a manager can pull to motivate employees. It is generally not possible to change the overall mission of the organization in order to make it more significant. Some industries have higher task significance than others. Usually workers at higher levels are more likely to have strong task significance, since they are more likely to be able to take actions that affect the mission in tangible ways.

To psychologists, task identity refers to the extent to which a worker's job entails completing an observable, whole piece of work. This is not the notion that workers will be psychologically motivated from some sense of closure over their work. Rather, it is our concept of modularity. If the business process can be modularized well, then a worker can be assigned a set of tasks that are closely related, without great concern that they will take inadequate account of the effects of their actions on other tasks. Once again, this part of the model is not a psychological effect; it is a description of the ability of the firm to group closely related tasks.

The final piece of the psychological model is task or skill variety. Skill variety is multiskilling. Though the original psychological literature on job design emphasized skill variety, in practice task variety (multitasking) is equally important.

We have described the economic benefits of multiskilling and multitasking. However, here psychologists make the same point as Adam Smith about boredom: Jobs that provide workers with the ability to perform more tasks or learn more skills are likely to provide greater intrinsic motivation.

The idea is that intrinsic motivation is strongest when the worker has the opportunity to *learn* on the job. The learning might be new human capital, through multiskilling. Or, it might be learning new tasks, and new ways to perform old tasks. As we argued earlier, the latter kind of learning is more likely in jobs that involve multitasking, especially when the work is complex and interdependent.

Pushing this idea a step further, intrinsic motivation arises when the employee is *intellectually challenged* by the job.[4] Boredom is largely the result of the worker performing repetitive tasks that do not require any thinking. Thus, workers will generally be more motivated by jobs that require them to do new tasks or develop skills that they have not yet mastered.

Though intrinsic motivation can be driven by both multiskilling or multi-tasking, the latter tends to be more useful for job design. The reason is that different forms of on the job learning have different values to the firm. If the worker develops multiple new skills, this does not necessarily improve productivity. If the worker's learning is, instead, focused on continuous improvement, the firm can benefit from the worker's insights directly, as well as through the effects of greater worker motivation. Thus, the firm should design the job to maximize learning that is valuable to the business, not just learning for the sake of acquiring new skills.

This idea illustrates a nice complementarity between the psychological and economic benefits of enriched jobs. When the process has not been perfected, there is greater opportunity for the firm to improve operations by designing jobs so that workers can make continuous improvements. It does so through giving them more related tasks and greater discretion. The firm provides employees with more skills, including problem solving skills. This is simply using basic economic principles to develop and use worker knowledge.

When the firm follows this method, workers are more psychologically motivated by their jobs. This means that they pay more attention, are more interested in what they are doing, and are *thinking* about what they are doing. Of course, this psychological effect only reinforces the effectiveness of the worker's continuous improvement.

In sum, only two of the five elements of the model of intrinsic motivation in Figure 7.1 are pure psychological effects—task significance and task/skill variety. The others are different labels for concepts we have described. Moreover, there is a close, consistent relationship between the economic view of job enrichment—designed to tap into specific knowledge of workers for continuous improvement—and the psychological view—motivate workers to be thinking more about the work that they are performing.

⬢ ⬢ ⬢ ⬢ ⬢ SUMMARY

Job design has three goals: (1) to improve the worker's efficiency in performing tasks; (2) to create and make use of worker knowledge on the job; and (3) to improve worker motivation. Sometimes these goals are in conflict, in which case job design entails tradeoffs (primarily between the benefits of specialization and other goals).

---

[4]Psychologists recognize that people differ in their interest in having a challenging job (in the lingo of economics, in their utility functions). The term that they use to refer to differences in the degree of intrinsic motivation is to say that individuals differ in their *growth need strength*.

In many cases, however, these three goals are not in conflict, and it is possible to design a job that works toward all three. When that is the case, a well designed job can have a powerful impact.

Our discussion has emphasized two key features of job design. The trendy terms for these features are job enrichment and worker empowerment. The more rigorous terms are multitasking and decentralization. Designing a specific job entails two key questions: Which tasks should be put together, and which decisions should the worker in this job be given the authority to make?

Answering these questions depends on several factors. Multitasking means moving away from specialization. One of the most important principles of job design is also one of the most important principles of economics: gains from specialization. Firms are organized largely so that individuals can specialize both their skills and their tasks, becoming masters of a narrow set of each, and then put their work together to create the final product. If job design moves away from specialization, there should be a good reason to do so, as the firm has to forego some of the significant gains from specialization.

Nevertheless, there can be many benefits from moving toward multitasking and away from specialization. The most important benefit arises when tasks are closely related to each other. In such cases, workers may be able to employ similar skills or other resources in performing both tasks together. Moreover, performing one task may improve the ability to perform the other. Finally, putting closely linked tasks together makes the worker more likely to discover ways to improve the process. This is a particularly good way to improve quality, since quality problems often arise due to the imperfect coordination of interdependent tasks.

Because multitasking tends to improve worker learning, decentralization becomes a natural fit with multitasking. In contrast, narrower jobs tend to mean that the worker is given less discretion. Along similar lines, job design has important implications for the depth and breadth of employee skills. Narrow jobs require only a narrow set of skills, while multitasking almost inevitably implies multiskilling. More interestingly, giving the worker more tasks and decision rights means that problem-solving skills become valuable, so workers also tend to get a different set of skills in enriched jobs.

The logic of how the number of tasks, degree of discretion, and skills required for a job fit together is an example of the principle of complementarity of human resource policies. Policies should always be designed with thought given to how they support or undermine other policies.

This logic also helps us understand why there are patterns of job design such as those described in Table 7.1 (pg. 174). Moreover, it explains why some firms use one type of design, while others use another. Where possible, firms develop knowledge about best practices, and deploy these practices in a centralized fashion. A formal way to do so is through industrial engineering, but firms also do so more informally, often through gradual adaptation. When stable best practices are available, designing jobs to maximize worker learning is less beneficial, so such firms tend toward more specialized jobs, less empowerment, and lower skilled employees. Where the best methods have not yet been uncovered or are changing, a firm should consider emphasizing continuous improvement. This involves multitasking, decentralization, and higher skilled employees.

Therefore, different firms employ different design approaches depending on their circumstances. Firms in more complex, unpredictable, and unstable environments tend to emphasize continuous improvement. The same applies to firms that have undergone organizational change. Mature firms in more stable and predictable environments, and firms that have simple businesses, are more likely to emphasize centralization and specialization.

Many of the ideas used in this chapter were drawn from the principles developed in the previous two chapters. Just as with economies, firms face the question of the extent to which they should make use of central planning (centralization) or more of a decentralized approach. Continuous improvement can be achieved through decentralization to maximize the creation and use of specific knowledge by lower level workers. Multitasking can improve productivity in part because coordination across closely related tasks is improved. Finally, the idea of modularity can apply to designing jobs, much as it does to overall organizational structure. It is a testament to the power of the economic approach that basic ideas—even from the beginning of *The Wealth of Nations*—are useful in understanding both macro and micro organizational design questions.

Carrying the analogy further, one of the advantages of market economies is that they continuously evolve, reorganize, and innovate. This makes them quite robust for economic challenges. In the same way, continuous improvement allows a company to evolve gradually and adapt to changing circumstances. However, as with markets, decentralization causes top management to lose some degree of control over the organization. For very large scale changes, it is likely that centralization—at least of the first stages of decision making (strategy)—is beneficial. Decentralization inside a firm is usually most effective for incremental improvements and tactical implementation of strategy.

Finally, job design is the major determinant of an employee's intrinsic motivation. According to psychologists, it motivates by making the job more challenging to the worker. This in turn means that the worker is more likely to be thinking about how to perform the work, which is nicely complementary with the goal of continuous improvement in order to make use of a worker's specific knowledge.

The firm can also affect motivation of the worker through *extrinsic motivation* (pay for performance or other rewards). As suggested in Chapter 5, incentives are an important way that a firm can motivate effective decision making and coordination among workers. We will analyze the issue of extrinsic motivation in Chapters 9–12. Clearly, if intrinsic motivation is strong, the firm can rely less on extrinsic motivation, and vice versa. In this sense the two motivational approaches are substitutes for each other. However, are there other interactions between intrinsic motivation and pay for performance? We will come back to this question briefly in Chapter 9.

STUDY QUESTIONS   ❂ ❂ ❂ ❂ ❂

1. Provide examples of tasks that are highly interdependent, so that giving them to two different workers would lead to severe coordination problems.

2. Provide examples of how a firm modularizes its business process. Think about examples in manufacturing, professional services, and other contexts.

3. Does the principle of specialization in job design apply only to blue collar jobs? Why or why not? Discuss examples of how the concept applies, or does not, to higher level jobs such as managers or knowledge workers.

4. What is Taylorism? When should firms adopt Taylorist techniques? When should they adopt continuous improvement techniques?

5. What types of workers should a firm recruit when it takes more of a Tayloristic approach? A continuous improvement approach?

6. Recall jobs that you have held in the past, or the one you are in now. Is the job very intrinsically motivating to you? Why or why not? Can you relate it to the psychological model in Figure 7.1? What other factors affect your motivation in the job?

REFERENCES   ❂ ❂ ❂ ❂ ❂

Auden, W. H. (1970). "Work, Labor, and Play." In *A Certain World: A Commonplace Book*. New York: Viking.

Caroli, Eve & John Van Reenen (2001). "Skill-Biased Organizational Change? Evidence From A Panel of British and French Establishments." *Quarterly Journal of Economics*, 116(4): 1449–1492.

Clark, Don (2002). "Intel Clones Its Past Factories, Right Down to Paint on Walls." *Wall Street Journal*, October 28.

Gibbs, Michael, Alec Levenson & Cindy Zoghi (2008). "Why Are Jobs Designed the Way They Are?" Working paper, University of Chicago.

Hackman, J. Richard & Greg Oldham (1976). "Motivation Through the Design of Work: Test of a Theory." *Organizational Behavior & Human Performance* 16: 250–279.

Hosseini, Hamid (1998). "Seeking the Roots of Adam Smith's Division of Labor in Medieval Persia." *History of Political Economy* 30(4): 653–681.

Ichniowski, Casey, Kathryn Shaw, & Giovanni Prennushi (1997). "The Effects of Human Resource Management Practices on Productivity: A Study of Steel Finishing Lines." *American Economic Review* 87(3): 291–313.

Jensen, Michael & Karen Wruck (1994). "Science, Specific Knowledge, and Total Quality Management." *Journal of Accounting and Economics* 18(3): 247–287.

Smith, Adam (1776). *The Wealth of Nations*. Modern Library Classics, 2000.

Taylor, Frederick (1923). *The Principles of Scientific Management*. New York: Harper.

Vogel, Todd & Chuck Hawkins (1990). "Can UPS Deliver the Goods in a New World?" *Business Week*, June 4.

● ● ● ● ● ## FURTHER READING

Carmichael, Lorne & Bentley MacLeod (1992). "Multiskilling, Technical Change, and the Japanese Firm." *Quarterly Journal of Economics* 107: 1137–1160.

Gilbreth, Frank Jr. & Ernestine Gilbreth Carey (1948). *Cheaper by the Dozen*. New York: Harper & Row.

● ● ● ● ● ## APPENDIX

Flexibility Has Less Value in a Large Firm Than in a Small Firm

Flexibility has value when there is a good chance that a worker will not show up on a given day. Then, having others who know the job and can move into that task is valuable. But as the firm size gets large, this is less of a problem.

Let the probability that a worker comes to work on a given day be p. Workers stay home, then, with probability $1 - p$. If the firm has N workers, the expected number of individuals who come to work on any given day is $p \cdot N$. The variance in the number that come to work is $p(1 - p)N$, so the standard deviation is:

$$\sqrt{p(1 - p)N}.$$

As N gets large, the binomial distribution approaches the normal distribution. Given this, 97.5% of the time the actual realized number of individuals who come to work exceeds:

$$pN - 1.96\sqrt{p(1 - p)N},$$

because the realizations of a normal random variable are greater than 1.96 standard deviations below the mean 97.5% of the time. Thus, if a firm plans for a workforce of $p \cdot N$ workers, 97.5% of the time it will have a proportion of workers at least as large as:

$$Proportion = \frac{pN - 1.96\sqrt{p(1 - p)N}}{pN}.$$

This increases in N, since:

$$\frac{\partial Proportion}{\partial N} = \frac{1.96\sqrt{1 - p}}{2\sqrt{pN^3}} > 0.$$

TABLE 7A.1
PROPORTION OF EMPLOYEES WHO SHOW UP FOR WORK

N	z	Proportion
10	8.8	0.927
15	13.4	0.941
25	22.7	0.954
50	46.0	0.968
100	92.8	0.977
1,000	943.1	0.993
5,000	4,734.6	0.997
10,000	9,478.2	0.998

Table 7A.1 shows how the proportion who show up to work varies with N, assuming that $p = 0.95$ so that any worker shows up 19 out of 20 days. Column 1 reports the number of workers in the firm; Column 2 reports the value of z such that:

$$prob(number\ of\ workers\ who\ come\ to\ work \geq z) = 0.975,$$

and Column 3 reports the proportion of the firm that z comprises.

With $p = 0.95$ and 100 workers, 95 of them are expected to show up on any given day. But 97.5% of the time, at least 92.82% show up. This is a little more than two workers shy of the expected number of 95, or a proportion 0.977 of the expected number. If there were only 10 workers, 9.5 would be expected to show up. 97.5% of the time, at least 8.81 would show up, or a proportion 0.927 of the expected number.

As the number of workers grows, the chance that the firm ends up very far below its expected number decreases. Therefore, the need to have workers who can cover a variety of different jobs shrinks as the size of the firm grows.

8

ADVANCED JOB DESIGN

Plus ça change, plus c'est la même chose. (The more things change, the more they stay the same.)

—*Alphonse Karr, 1849*

INTRODUCTION

In this chapter we extend the discussion of job design to several advanced topics. In doing so, we will again see that the principles of job design are to a great extent the same principles that apply to overall organizational design.

Among the topics that we have not covered yet, the most important one is teams. Firms exist in large part because working together is more productive than working as individuals. The whole is greater than the sum of the parts. In order for individuals to work together productively, the firm must know how to set up teams and motivate team members. In recent years, the term *teamwork* has become a common buzzword. Why is that the case? What is the value of organizing work into teams? To put this question in starker form, if you are considering organizing your workers into teams, always remember that another name for a team is *committee*. Committees are renowned for their bureaucracy, so clearly setting up teams is not always a good way to increase efficiency. If you are going to use teams, there should be strong benefits from doing so. The main discussion in this chapter focuses on the benefits and costs of team production. We also explain the growing use of teams by linking them to the analysis in the previous chapter.

Another important issue in today's workplace is information technology. The last several decades witnessed a revolution in computers and other advanced technologies. Since a theme of this section of the text is how firms organize to create and use information, an obvious question is the effects of information technology on job design and overall structure. As we will see, information technology can sometimes have dramatic effects on both.

Finally, at the end of this chapter we briefly discuss organizations that face the same challenges as typical firms, but where the tradeoffs are more severe. These are firms where costs of errors are dramatic, the need for quick action is great, and coordination requirements are strong. How such organizations solve these more dramatic versions of the tradeoffs that ordinary firms face has some useful lessons for all organizations.

***

TEAMS

Managers like to extol the virtues of teamwork. We are reminded of a star soccer player whose clichéd response to any question about his outstanding performance was that he couldn't have done it without the team. This false modesty is almost as prevalent in business as it is in sports. It is important to analyze when teamwork is important and when it is not. There are two reasons why you should be cautious about using teams.

Group Decision Making

The first problem with teams is that they may violate the principle of clear hierarchy: Decision making tends to be faster and more straightforward when there is a single, clear leader. To the extent that teams involve group decision making, it is often the case that workers get bogged down in too much discussion and politics over key decisions. Moreover, it is far from clear why the outcome of consensus is likely to be the optimal decision.

Thus, it is usually important to establish a clear team leader, supervisor, or mechanism to efficiently resolve disputes with the group before they get out of hand. When setting up a team, it is important to separate out some decision control rights from the team, and give them to a team leader or supervisor. The team's role typically should be more one of decision management, collaborating with each other to come up with new ideas and approaches to the work, but with some ultimate supervision kept separate from the group.

Free Rider Effects

The second problem with teams is that workers can often hide behind the productivity of others, thereby diluting incentives. This is the *free rider effect*. Consider going out for pizza with nine friends in Rome. Except in groups of accountants or actuaries, the general rule is that the bill will be split evenly. Each diner would like to have a glass of wine. A glass of good Barolo costs €8, while a glass of the house Chianti costs €3. If the diner orders Barolo, his share of the cost is 80¢, while his share of the Chianti cost is 30¢. The per person cost difference is 50¢ no matter what anyone else does. Therefore, as long as the Barolo is worth at least 50¢ more to him than the Chianti, he will order the Barolo. The same applies to all of his friends. If all order Barolo, each ends up paying €5 more, even if they value their own glass of Barolo by only a bit more than 80¢.

Consider a similar scenario in the work environment. A worker is placed in a team with four other workers. The team is assigned a project that must be completed in a timely manner. Each worker is told that for each day that the project comes in ahead of schedule, the team will be given a bonus of €100, which will be split evenly among the five team members. Consider team member Giovanni's decision to stay late to work on the project. Giovanni can stay late, or he can go home and watch the World Cup. He enjoys the World Cup, but would also like to receive the bonus for finishing the job early. He figures that if he works late tonight, he will speed up completion of the project by one day. This is worth €100 to the group, but only €20 to him, as the bonus is shared by the five members. After thinking it over, Giovanni goes home to watch the game. However, if he could receive the €100 himself, he would be motivated enough to stay at work.

The reason that effort is below its efficient level is that *the worker who bears the pain of toiling does not reap the full benefits*. What prevents the company from paying individuals rather than teams for their effort? Nothing, as long as individual effort can be observed. However, in a team environment, individual effort is quite often difficult to extract from the group's efforts and results. This is because teams are set up in cases where the work is highly interdependent between coworkers. In essence, this is a case where individual performance is difficult to evaluate accurately; we will cover this general problem more thoroughly in the next chapter.

The two problems with team production—inefficient decision making and free rider effects—are why "committee" is a word that can be appropriate to many workgroups. Committees are not usually thought of as paragons of efficiency. They illustrate why teams should only be used when there is a compelling reason to do so.

When to Use Teams

Given the problems just raised, when should firms set up teams? When the benefits are the highest, and the costs the lowest. Here we discuss both.

The primary benefit from using teams derives from the discussion of multitasking in the previous chapter. Multitasking is valuable when tasks are strongly complementary, so that putting them together in the same job results in greater efficiencies and on the job learning. However, in many cases there are so many tasks that are complementary that the resulting job would be overwhelming for one worker. In that case, the firm must either separate the tasks, which raises coordination problems as discussed in Chapter 5, or "increase" the worker. The worker can be increased in two ways. One way is to have greater depth and breadth of skills, as discussed in Chapter 7. The other is to use teams who work closely together.

The same idea applies when the team is set up to provide lateral coordination, as described in Chapter 6. Coordination is needed not just between individual tasks or workers, but also between organizational units. Coordination is most important when the work of different organizational units is most complementary, and that is when firms tend to set up coordination groups with members selected from each relevant unit. The strongest example of this is what we called integration problems in Chapter 6.

This explains why teams may be used when there are strong complementarities between the work of fellow team members (or business units). The general principle is, to borrow from an old expression, that teams should be used when *the whole is greater than the sum of the parts*. For examples, teamwork is necessary to move an object that is too heavy to be lifted by one person, but not too heavy to be lifted by two people. Similarly, suppose that it is impossible for one consultant to meet a deadline, but two consultants working together could do so, and the client would pay a higher fee if the deadline is met. Organizing as a team is likely to be a good idea.

WHY HAS THE USE OF TEAMS INCREASED?

Evidence suggests that the use of various forms of team production (including methods such as quality circles) have increased in recent decades. The costs of using teams, potentially inefficient group decision making and free rider effects, have not changed. It must be that the benefits of teams have increased recently.

As just described, teams are valuable when work is highly interdependent, because they support coordination or continuous improvement. These goals are most important in firms where ex ante optimization (using methods similar to Taylorism) is less effective. It was argued near the end of the last chapter that continuous improvement methods have become more important because the business environment has become more complex and fast paced in the last few decades. Since teams are a facet of the same organizational design issues, that effect also explains the growing use of teams.

Despite being trendy, it is important to remember that teams are not an end in themselves. They are valuable *only when they support learning or coordination*, and they can create substantial costs.

Now consider another example, a gate agent for Cathay Pacific Airlines. The gate agent sometimes works with another gate agent, but not always with the same person. There are two stations at the check-in counter for a particular flight. Although there may be some complementarity between the two agents, each works his or her line almost independently—a case where the whole is not much greater than the sum of the parts. This is not to say that there is no benefit from teamwork. The two working together can share information and coordinate better. But whatever gains there are must be traded off against the costs of combining them into a team.

The primary cost of using teams is productivity loss through the free rider effect. If the two gate agents are compensated on the basis of team output, each has an incentive to shirk. Suppose, for example, that they are compensated on the basis of the speed at which they process passengers. Passengers could be asked to form

TABLE 8.1
COSTS AND BENEFITS OF TEAMWORK

| Activity | Rank(1 = highest) | | Notes |
	Benefits	Costs	
Selecting the fishing site	3	3	Multiple judgements may be useful and discussion matters. But committee decision making is slow and difficult.
Fishing on a small boat	2	5	Requires tasks that cannot be performed singlehandedly. Cost of monitoring team members is low. Unproductive team members can be thrown off the team by other team members.
Fishing on a large boat	1	4	Teamwork is probably more important on a large boat, where tasks are larger in scale. Setting large nets requires a number of hands and some machinery. But larger teams imply more free rider problems.
Selling fish wholesale	5	1	Salespeople can work alone. Monitoring them as a group would involve enormous free riding, as peer monitoring is difficult.
Accounting for sales	4	2	There is little benefit from accountants working together, especially if one can handle all of the books alone (as in a small firm). Additionally, accountants' work is likely to be relatively easy to evaluate individually.

one line and go to the next available agent. Under such an arrangement, whatever benefits accruc to teamwork by one agent is not readily observable to a supervisor, and is difficult to reward. The only way to inspire teamwork is to reward on the basis of team output, but this inescapably leads back to the free rider effect.[1]

Activities can be ranked according to the costs and benefits of having teams. Production activities that rank high on the benefits scale and low on the cost scale should be performed by teams. Table 8.1 provides an example from a fishing firm. The best candidate for team production is the actual fishing itself, and the worst one is selling the fish.

Other Benefits of Team Production

Specialization

As we saw in Chapter 7, specialization is one of the most important factors in job design, and it is also an important reason why individuals work together. In a team, each individual can specialize her human capital investments and be assigned

---

[1] One plausible performance metric in this example would be the number of passengers each agent served, *relative to* the other agent. That would be even worse for motivating teamwork, since they would end up competing with each other. See the discussion of cooperation and sabotage in Chapter 11.

a subset of all of the tasks necessary to the overall business process. In this sense, the firm as a whole is a team, in which each employee specializes at her work. However, that is not really the sense that is usually meant by the term team. By *team* we mean a group whose tasks are very closely related, as described. For this reason those workers tend to collaborate with each other on a frequent basis.

Specialization does play an important role in teams. However, recall that one of the most important benefits of multitasking is continuous improvement. By understanding how complementary tasks work together (what psychologists call task identity), a worker is more likely to perform each individual task better, because he understands better how his tasks fit with other parts of the process. In addition, a worker is more likely to uncover ways to cut costs, speed up production, or improve quality when he understands how individual tasks mesh together. To get these benefits of intertask learning, the worker must understand each of the closely related tasks.

It does not follow, however, that the worker needs to actually perform all of those tasks regularly. All that is needed in most cases is that the worker understands each of the closely related steps or tasks, and how they fit together. This can be achieved by assigning all of the tasks to the worker at a point in time, using multitasking as discussed earlier. But it can also be achieved by assigning the worker all of the tasks over a period of time, through *job rotation*. Job rotation has an important benefit compared with multitasking—at each point in time, the worker is focused on a narrow set of tasks, so most of the gains to specialization in production (though not in investments in skills) can be realized.

Therefore, although it helps to understand other team members' work, in most teams workers do not perform all tasks. Rather, they specialize, and often rotate tasks between each other over time. When they are performing individual tasks, they collaborate and communicate, to share knowledge with each other. This is reinforced as they learn each other's tasks over time through job rotation. This captures many of the benefits of intertask learning, while at the same time avoids losing too many of the benefits from specialization.

Knowledge Transfer

Knowledge transfer is the second benefit from team production, and probably occurs more when specialization is not too great. For valuable knowledge transfer to occur, individuals must have distinct information sets that are relevant to each other. If there is too much information overlap, teamwork does not produce much knowledge transfer. If the information that one has is irrelevant to another, then knowledge transfer has no value. That is, each member should process part of the knowledge required for a task but the other member does not have, and they together process all the knowledge required. Figure 8.1 illustrates conditions conducive to successful knowledge transfer.

Consider two workers, Tor and Kate. The left rectangle (*T*) represents Tor's information set. The right rectangle (*K*) denotes Kate's information set. There is an intersection of the two rectangles, representing information shared by both. Yet most of the area is not shared, indicating that most of the information that Kate has

FIGURE 8.1
SUBSTANTIALLY OVERLAPPING INFORMATION SETS

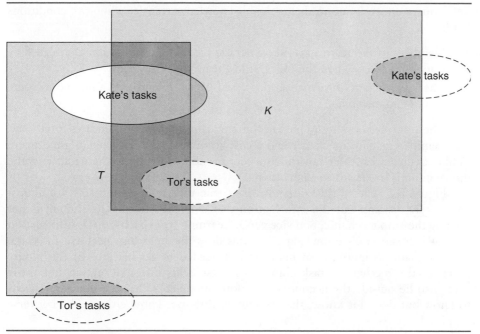

is not shared by Tor, and vice versa. Thus, there is a potential gain from teamwork through knowledge transfer, because large parts of the information sets are not overlapping.

Whether teamwork is valuable depends also on informational requirements of the two jobs. Figure 8.1 illustrates two cases. Suppose that the information required to perform the tasks is reflected by the areas in the ellipses outlined in solid curves. Kate has knowledge on her own to perform about half of her tasks (half of her solid oval lies inside the Tor information set rectangle). Similarly, Tor has knowledge on his own to perform about half of his tasks. By working as a team, Tor can transfer all the knowledge necessary for Kate to perform her tasks, and she can do the same for Tor. Thus, Kate and Tor can obtain from each other knowledge that is necessary to perform their tasks but is outside of their own knowledge set. With knowledge transfer, they can perform more tasks.

Now suppose that the information required to perform the tasks is represented by the areas in the ellipses outlined in dotted curves. As before, Tor has a great deal of information that Kate does not have, and vice versa. Further, Kate only has information to perform about half of her tasks, since half of the task's dotted ellipse lies outside of her information set. But the half that lies outside her task ellipse also lies outside the information set of Tor. Tor has a great deal of information that Kat does not have, but none that is relevant to her. The same is true in reverse as well. The nonoverlapping parts of the information sets are, in this case, irrelevant, because they are not valuable to the other person.

Thus, teamwork can produce valuable knowledge transfer when two conditions hold:

1. Members of the team have idiosyncratic pieces of information that can flow among members when they are put in a team together.
2. The idiosyncratic information possessed by one member is valuable to some other team members.

These two factors should help in thinking about choosing members for a team. For example, an auto mechanic and a cost accountant do not make a good team. While it is true that their information sets are nonoverlapping, their idiosyncratic information is irrelevant to each other.

Figure 8.2 reflects this situation. It is true that information sets are almost completely disjoint, but the information that is needed by the accountant is not held by the auto mechanic, and vice versa. Learning from each other's information set can increase one's knowledge, but this does not help him perform his tasks. The mechanic is ignorant of many things needed to do his job. In the figure, much of the mechanic's task ellipse lies outside his information set, but those tasks also lie outside the accountant's information set. What the mechanic needs to know but does not know, the accountant does not know either. The converse also holds.

FIGURE 8.2
ALMOST NON-OVERLAPPING INFORMATION SETS

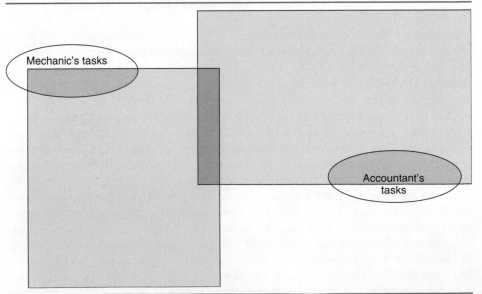

FIGURE 8.3
OVERLAPPING INFORMATION SETS

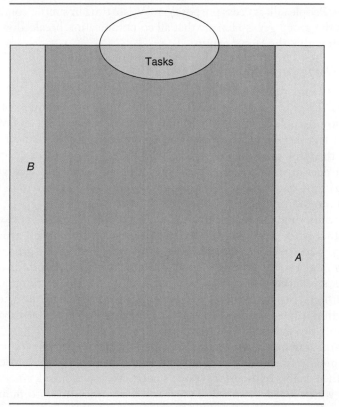

FIGURE 8.3
OVERLAPPING INFORMATION SETS

Now consider two identically trained cost accountants, *A* and *B*, in Figure 8.3. As described, there is unlikely to be much knowledge transfer between them, even though each has information that is relevant to the other, since their experiences and knowledge bases are almost identical. Neither can do all of the tasks, but because their information is so similar, it is likely that those tasks that one cannot do, cannot be done by the other.

Implementation of Teams

We have already discussed some factors to think about in implementing teams, such as job rotation to balance the benefits of intertask learning against the benefits of specialization. Here we discuss some other issues to consider.

Optimal Team Size

The size of the team matters. Small teams do not allow enough information transfer because there are fewer opportunities for cross training. However, large teams create communication problems. Anyone who has ever tried to accomplish something in a committee setting knows that it is very difficult to make headway in a large group. People talk at cross purposes and waste time in simple communication. Sometimes the group gets so unruly that all communication breaks down and small cliques form within the larger group.

Peer Monitoring and Norms to Reduce Free Riding

An additional important factor in determining the optimal group size is the free rider effect. When the group is small, free riding may not be much of a problem. Consider, for example, a small dry cleaning shop owned by Tim and Melissa. The free rider effect is relevant, because Tim captures only half of the return to his effort. But this problem is not too great, because of *peer monitoring*. First, Melissa has a great deal of information about what Tim is doing, and vice versa. If one partner shirks too much, the partnership will break down. The threat of the breakup motivates both to work harder.

Peer monitoring can be effective in small groups. A worker is likely to know what the other worker is doing to a much greater extent in a small group than in a large group. Furthermore, the incentives to punish a shirker are greater in a small group than in a larger group. In a small group (say, a partnership of two people), one partner's reduced effort has a significant effect on the earnings of the other partner. Although it is unpleasant to have to confront a partner and accuse her of putting forth insufficient effort, the costs of not doing so are relatively large when there are only two partners.

In a large partnership, peer monitoring is not as effective for two reasons. First, one member's shirking does not affect another member's interest as much. Similarly, the benefits of monitoring one's peers are also reduced, since the benefits are shared with a larger number of partners. Thus, incentives to punish shirking are reduced. Second, it is more difficult to observe shirkers in large teams. When many people are involved and the task is complicated, determining the source of a problem may not be easy. Therefore, free riding effects are more prevalent in larger teams.

Peer pressure can help reduce free riding in a way similar to peer monitoring. Peer pressure within the group often takes the form of a *norm*. Norms are informal policies or practices, or a set of beliefs, held by the majority of a group. Common practices or beliefs can be helpful in establishing a culture, ethic, or etiquette in the group. They are part of the implicit contract that in part governs the worker's job. We first discussed the idea of implicit contracting in Chapter 3. We will have more to say on this topic in Chapter 15; here, we discuss how the firm should form and use norms.

For example, if it is part of the group's culture that managers voluntarily work on Saturdays, workers may be reluctant to deviate from this mode of behavior. Saturday work may provide useful labor and generate additional profits. Of course, Saturday work also carries a cost. Employees must be compensated more for taking a job where Saturday work is the norm than for work at a firm where Saturday work is not.

In addition to the direct cost of paying for Saturday work, there is generally a cost associated with creating and maintaining a norm. Such a cost can be ongoing or borne at one time. The level of effort associated with norms depends on the type of sanctions imposed for deviating from the norm. Minor criticism will have little effect, while the threat of ostracism is likely to have a strong effect.

Enforcement costs that are borne by peers tend to be ongoing. If the pressure lightens and enforcement lags, norms tend to break down. Take the example of Saturday work. What happens if an employee fails to come to work on a Saturday? If there is no enforcement of the norm or sanctions imposed for deviating, chances are that the employee will engage in the deviant activity again. What's worse, one member's failing to work on Saturday may spread to other members, causing the norm to break down. In order to prevent this from happening, someone must penalize those who deviate from the norm.

Some costs of establishing and enforcing norms are not ongoing. Rather they are more in the form of lump sum costs. For example, the military makes large investments in new recruits, instilling pride and loyalty. Boot camp is devoted, in large part, to having recruits bond with fellow recruits and with the military in general. The bonding that takes place early in a soldier's career may serve the military well later on. Loyalty and empathy for associates reflect prior investments into developing devotion to the military and camaraderie among soldiers.

Firms also engage in activities that build group or company camaraderie. Many practices at firms may have more to do with creating empathy, loyalty, and latent guilt than they do with performing the nominal tasks themselves. For example, quality circles, where workers discuss the best way to perform some task, may be more useful in making the worker feel part of the firm and in creating loyalty to coworkers. The suggestions that come out of quality circles are often not implemented, but this does not mean that they were a waste of time. If quality circles allow valuable norms to be developed and maintained, the time devoted to these circles is well spent.

One way to provide incentives for individuals to enforce the norm by sanctioning each other is by setting group quotas or rewards. The firm promises the team a *bonus* and imposes a penalty for not making quota. When one person puts forth less than the norm level of effort, it hurts the others in the group. As a result, the deviant feels peer pressure and starts to follow the norm. The norm is enforced because peers have monetary or other stakes in the quota not being realized. This is a case where extrinsic and intrinsic incentives (bonuses and peer pressure) interact with each other.

Deviations from a norm are not always negative. Sometimes, peers will impose sanctions on an individual who puts forth too much effort. This is most common among production workers. If one worker produces too quickly, he may feel peer pressure from team members, because the supervisor would learn that the work can be done in less time than the company has been allowing. This causes the line to speed up, to the detriment of coworkers who do not want to work faster.

Team Composition

Should individuals be assigned to teams by supervisors, or should teams be free to choose their own members? The most common method is to allow supervisors to assign individuals to teams. This works well when the supervisor has more information than the individual workers. When a new employee joins a group, the supervisor is likely to have at least as much information as the individual worker. In this case, it makes little sense to allow uninformed workers to assign the new member to a group. Sometimes, workers actually have better information about one another than the supervisor does. For example, when individuals have worked together for a long time, when new employees are friends of current employees, or when individual workers engage in tasks that are highly specialized and beyond the knowledge set of the supervisor, it may be better to allow workers to set up their own teams. Two mechanisms for team member selection are discussed here: alternating draws, and bidding for team members.

Alternating Draws

The most straightforward approach is to do what children often do when selecting sandlot teams: alternate draws. Suppose there are two teams, I and II, and four new hires, Allison, Brooke, Charles, and David. One possibility is to allow the captain of each team to choose a new member in alternating order. Suppose that the preference ranking of the players is as shown in panel *a* of Table 8.2, while panel *b* shows the efficiency ranking.[2]

TABLE 8.2
TEAM PREFERENCES

	a. Preferences	
Rank	Team I	Team II
1	Allison	Brooke
2	Brooke	Charles
3	Charles	David
4	David	Allison

	b. Efficiency	
	Team I	Team II
1	Allison	David
2	Charles	Brooke
3	Brooke	Charles
4	David	Allison

[2] In the comparison between alternate draws and bidding for team members, we abstract from the important issue of motivation of members of the team. Incentives are the topic of Section III of the text.

As shown in the table above, both teams prefer Brooke to Charles. However, efficiency dictates that Allison and Charles should work with Team I, and Brooke and David with Team II. That is, Brooke is more valuable to Team II than to Team I, given that the other players stay the same. Similarly, both teams prefer Charles to David, but Charles' added value to Team I is greater than to Team II.

Suppose that a coin is tossed and Team I wins. Their first choice is Allison. Team II then chooses Brooke, Team I chooses Charles, and Team II chooses David. The efficient allocation is achieved. What if the coin toss had gone in favor of Team II? Then the first choice would be for Brooke. Team I would have followed with a choice of Allison. Team II would then choose Charles, and Team I would be stuck with David. Team I ends up with Allison and David, while Team II has Brooke and Charles. Efficiency would have been violated.

Whether efficiency is achieved or not depends on the outcome of a coin toss in this example. This is not a desirable property of any team selection scheme. Nor is this merely a feature of this example. Allowing teams to choose their members in an alternating fashion, without any other conditions, generally results in an inefficient allocation of team members. It is necessary that teams be made to pay for the consequences of their choices, because their choices not only affect themselves, but other teams.

Bidding for Members

An alternative is to allow teams to bid for their team members. An *English auction* is held, where the team that bids the highest wins the member. This is the familiar auction structure where bidders are free to increase their bids until no one exceeds the last bid.

In order to attract a team member, the team must give up some of its profit, which in turn affects team members' compensation. Let us auction off Allison's labor. According to the efficiency level, Allison's ability is best deployed in Team I. That is, she contributes more to Team I's profit than to Team II's profit. Therefore, Team I will be willing to bid a larger total amount of profits to acquire her than Team II. When Brooke is auctioned, the reverse is true. The same mechanism works for Charles and David. Thus, Allison and Charles end up on Team I, and Brooke and David on Team II. Auctions generally result in an efficient allocation of resources and are preferable to alternating draw methods for assigning team members.

Note further that it is unnecessary, and in fact undesirable, to dictate the number of members that go to each team. If the value of acquiring the third new worker is higher to Team I than the value of a second is to Team II, it is better that Team I have three new workers and Team II have only one. The auction process sorts this out.

This is an application of the market metaphor inside the firm. Markets allocate resources well because individuals are motivated to bid high when they have good uses for the resources. If the firm cannot literally have teams bid for group members, the executive who assigns individuals to teams should estimate the value of individuals to each team, and assign them according to this principle. And, it may be efficient for a firm to allow different departments to compete with each other for staff.

SALMON FISHING IN ALASKA

❧ ❧ ❧ ❧ ❧ ❧ ❧ ❧ ❧

Fishing in Alaska is done on boats. Knowing the best spots for the fish is an important component of the hunt. Some individuals are good fishermen; others have deep understandings of fish behavior. Fishing firms in Alaska are set up as partnerships, but the partnerships are somewhat fluid. After a given individual becomes known as a talented fisherman or spotter, his market value rises. As a result, he can command a larger share of profits.

Sometimes, negotiations take place within the fisherman's current partnership. The partners recognize the increased market value of a skilled fisherman or spotter and cut him a better deal. More often than not, a change in share makes the fisherman leave the current partnership and join another. The process of negotiating with current and new partnerships is exactly the bidding process just described. It will generally result in an efficient allocation of labor throughout the industry.

Source: Farrell & Scotchmer (1988)

Worker-Owned Firms

Some firms issue stock to their workers. Often this is intended to motivate teamwork. When a large enough fraction of shares are held by its workforce, the firm is often said to be worker owned. A famous example of a large worker owned firm is United Airlines. How do these worker owned firms operate?

Often the answer is that they operate in much the same way as non–worker owned firms, in that they appoint a CEO and a management team that are instructed to maximize profits. However, the ownership structure does have an impact on the firm's decision making, especially with respect to labor policy. When the firm deviates from efficiency to accommodate labor, it is detrimental to the health of the firm (United Airlines ended up in bankruptcy proceedings).

To see this, consider lumber cooperatives in the Pacific Northwest of the United States.[3] A number of plywood firms are organized as cooperatives. While some workers are employed by the firm as mere employees, others actually own shares in the firm. These shares are not publicly traded on a stock exchange, but they are marketable. Shares are advertised and put up for sale through local newspapers. When a new worker joins the firm, he can purchase shares from a departing worker.

The worker-owners in these relatively small firms have the right to appoint boards of directors who choose management. How does management behave? Compared with non–labor owned firms, they are more protective of their worker-owners'

---

[3] See Craig & Pencavel (1992).

employment. When bad times hit the industry, cooperatives are less likely to lay off workers and are more likely to reduce wages for all workers. Is this good or bad?

The evidence is ambiguous. Labor cooperative share prices have risen quite well, but not as well as share prices of non–labor owned firms. The share of output accounted for by the cooperatives dropped from around 35% in the 1950s to less than 20% by the late 1980s. Part of this may reflect regional shifts in demand, but it is also true that costs per worker are higher in the cooperatives than they are in the non–labor owned firms.

Evidently, workers are taking some of their returns in the form of increased job security. But job security comes at a cost. The workers would have been better off financially by selling out their cooperatives to a non–labor run firm like Georgia-Pacific, and accepting jobs as mere employees in the acquired firms. In fact, a number of cooperatives have done this, but some retain their cooperative structure and remain viable. Some workers seem to be willing to pay to control their own firms.

EFFECTS OF INFORMATION TECHNOLOGY

The last several decades have experienced very dramatic improvements in speed and capabilities of information technology, as well as rapid price declines. What is the effect of the information technology revolution on organizational and job design?

Effects on Organizational Structure

Centralizing or Decentralizing?

Centralizing tendencies. The business press generally pushes the view that information technology (IT) results in decentralization, empowering the workers, breaking up traditional decision making structures, and replacing them with more informal structures. But is that the case? One implication of inexpensive, powerful computers is that communication costs fall dramatically. In other words, an important effect of IT is to *convert much of what used to be specific knowledge into general knowledge*. To the extent that this is true, IT should lead to greater *centralization* of decision making. Here are a couple of examples.

In today's long-haul trucking industry, it is common for the trucks to make extensive use of technology. The dashboard often has a computer built into it, with two-way communication between the dispatcher and the driver (they can also communicate by cell phone). Many trucks have satellite dishes on their roofs, with global-positioning satellite (GPS) technology.

Is this new technology used to decentralize decisions to the driver? Not at all. The trucking company can monitor the driver much like Big Brother in George Orwell's *1984*. GPS allows it to locate the exact position of the truck at all times, and to track its movements. The company knows when the driver stops for a break and how long the break is. They know if the driver takes a wrong turn, or makes an unscheduled stop (say, to deliver packages for personal profit). They know how fast the driver travels on the highway. In short, IT enables very close monitoring.

Moreover, real time communication allows the company to give the driver commands at will. Centralized coordination is valuable in trucking, since the dispatcher can then allocate trucks effectively to make sure that they travel with full loads, and that customers are responded to quickly. Technology allows the dispatcher to change the driver's schedule in the middle of the day, commanding him to change course and pick up a new package. Similarly, the dispatcher can tell the driver to change routes to avoid heavy traffic, or slow down to meet the requirements of the company's insurance provider.

This strong trend toward centralization is also changing organizational structures in the industry. The industry had been much more decentralized in the past, where many drivers were independent owner-operators—a form of outsourcing. The trend now is toward less use of owner-operators, and greater use of company-owned trucks with employee drivers.

Mrs. Fields Cookie Co. is another interesting example of adopting IT in an organization.[4] The company developed an expert system that uses historical sales data from its stores, combined with information on the specific store's current situation (day of the week, holiday, climate, whether there is a sale at the shopping mall that day, etc.) to predict sales of different products. It then provides the store manager with a set of recommendations at the start of each day, e.g., how many batches of each type of cookie to bake. As the day progresses and actual sales are realized, the program updates its recommendations. It also provides other suggestions to the manager, such as to throw out dough when it becomes more than two hours old, so that it does not get stale.

IT is used even more extensively in the store manager's job. If a new hire is needed, applicants fill out an interview on the computer. The software makes recommendations about who to ask in for a second interview, at which point another survey is filled out on the computer. Mrs. Fields correlates the responses with data on previous hires to predict good candidates.

How does Mrs. Fields do all of this? By passing all of the data on sales, employment, etc., to the central corporate office. The corporate office then models the business using the collective experience of all of the stores. It combines that with the expertise of Debbie Fields in how to manage a cookie store. This is all done through use of an *expert system*, which attempts to codify in software rules about how to make decisions. This is highly centralized optimization, much in the spirit of Taylorism, but done with computers.

It is interesting to step back for a minute and ask where the specific knowledge lies in the cookie store business. Little knowledge is required at each store, because most of the important information—even daily sales at the local mall—is passed to the central office. The only substantial specific knowledge required to run a store is how to "upsell" a specific customer who walks in the store, and how to deal with an employee on a given day.

---

[4]Debbie Fields' husband, Randy, was a computer consultant with a bachelor's degree in economics.

At the same time, the Mrs. Fields model implies substantial economies of scale in both the talent of Debbie Fields, and in other expertise developed at corporate headquarters. The business model embodied in the expert systems in the central computers is a valuable asset, and it can be used over and over again in each store. In a real sense, the Mrs. Fields business model is to clone the expertise of Debbie and the collective knowledge gleaned from experience with other stores, and replicate them in stores worldwide.

The effects on the store manager's job at Mrs. Fields are clear. There is little discretion. Technically, the manager has the right to override the software's recommendations. However, doing so frequently is likely to catch the attention of the central office. Unless performance is better than that predicted by the computer, the manager would probably be told to stop. Since the software is based on years of management experience plus a large database of sales data, it is not likely that the manager's predictions will be better than those of the software.

Because the job involves little discretion, store managers need low skills and receive little training. Similarly, there is little firm-specific human capital. Not surprisingly, turnover is higher than the industry average, but Mrs. Fields is willing to accept this.

Finally, as in trucking, centralization through IT led Mrs. Fields to be more vertically integrated. Most competitors of Mrs. Fields use a *franchise model*, a close cousin to outsourcing. By contrast, Mrs. Fields stores have been company owned.

These two examples are important, because they show that the popular view of the effects of IT is often wrong, or is at the very least more complicated. There are many examples where IT leads to more centralization, narrower job designs, and less value placed on highly skilled workers. And this makes perfect sense, once we remember the concepts of general and specific knowledge.

Decentralizing tendencies. Nevertheless, there are some ways in which IT can lead to decentralization. An important one is that it can provide information to lower level workers to support their own decision making. A good example is *statistical process control* (SPC). SPC provides workers in manufacturing settings with real-time data about various aspects of production, such as the thickness of sheet metal as it rolls down the line. Such data was usually not available *in real time* before, because it was too costly to measure and communicate quickly. SPC provides the worker with information that can then be used in several ways. For example, often the data are perishable—they must be acted on quickly or the value vanishes. In this case it usually makes sense to allow the worker to respond (say, to fluctuations in metal thickness). Similarly, the data provide feedback to the worker. As noted in the psychological model of intrinsic motivation, feedback is an important component of decentralization. Real time feedback enables the worker to diagnose problems and test potential remedies in ways that otherwise would not be possible.

The low cost of computers means that these days most employees have access to powerful (by historical standards) computers and analysis tools, such as spreadsheets and databases. They also have easy access to a great deal of information, both inside the company and from the Internet. This means that workers often collect data *on their own* and analyze it. In effect they take some initiative that their supervisor may not have otherwise given them. A similar effect arises from email, which enables any employee to go around the chain of command and contact any other colleague, at levels of authority above the immediate boss, or even in other parts of the organization. As a result the supervisor loses some degree of control over the subordinate, and some communication happens outside the formal chain of command.

Other Effects on Structure

There is some debate about whether IT will, over the long run, lead to larger or smaller firms. It is too early to have a clear answer on this question, but we can discuss a few likely effects. First, the same number of employees will generally have higher productivity—in some cases, dramatically so. Growth in productivity has been high in advanced economies in recent years, and it appears that the most important reason for this is advancements in information technology. If the same number of employees can produce greater output, this may lead to smaller firms in terms of number of employees. But it may also lead to larger firms in terms of total output (or market share). The reason for this is that firms may have greater economies of scale.

We discussed vertical integration in the context of the trucking and Mrs. Fields Cookies examples. To the extent that firms become more centralized, they may become more integrated. However, IT also lowers transactions costs, making it cheaper to manage business relationships with outside suppliers at low cost. Thus, IT can lead toward organizational disintegration—not just offshoring of employees, but also outsourcing. This is, in fact, one of the chief drivers of the trend toward outsourcing today.

A BIG MAC TO GO

❖ ❖ ❖ ❖ ❖ ❖ ❖ ❖ ❖

If you pull into the drive-through lane of the McDonald's off Highway 55 near Cape Girardeau, Missouri, and speak your order into the microphone, your order will be taken by an employee in Colorado Springs, Colorado—almost 1,000 miles away. The order is handled by a centralized call center, and then transmitted back to the McDonald's immediately using information technology. The call center is run by a McDonald's franchisee, and is not part of the McDonald's Corporation.

It is easy to imagine taking this a step further. The next time you stop for a drive-through order, the person you talk to may be in Bangalore, India—regardless of where you are.

Source: Fitzgerald (2004)

There are other noticeable effects of IT on firm structure and strategy. IT often speeds up decision making dramatically, because it speeds up communication, and because some analysis is done immediately by computers. This reinforces the trends discussed in earlier chapters, toward time-based competition and shorter product cycles. What's more, IT generally makes customization cheaper, encouraging firms to adopt more complex product lines. Note that both of these are reasons why there has been a trend toward job enrichment, and away from the Tayloristic approach to job design.

Effects on Job Design

An extremely interesting question is how IT affects job design. Many people blame computerization for creating unemployment. Is this true? As mentioned, IT can lead to old-fashioned jobs with little discretion and skills. Yet, it can also support job enrichment. How can we think about which jobs are likely to be affected in which way?[5]

A way to frame the question is to ask when computers are *substitutes* for people, and when they are *complements*. Let us start with when they are substitutes. The principle of comparative advantage tells us that firms will use computers, and not people, when computers are relatively better at performing a task. This will be when they have lower costs, higher productivity, or both.

Computers (like machines in manufacturing) have substantial advantages over employees. They are reliable: They come to work every day (at least if they are in good repair). They do not have motivation problems: Management does not need to think about intrinsic motivation or pay for performance. They are predictable: They generally analyze information or perform tasks exactly the same way each time. In fact, this textbook is largely about ways in which workers are costly to firms but computers and machines are not, and how to deal with them. For example, unlike humans, computers would not have asymmetric information or turnover problems.

This suggests that if a task can be performed by a machine or computer nearly as well as by a human, *it should be*. When is this the case?

Computers are best at applying simple *rules-based logic*. Software is a set of commands that specify what to do in each contingency. For example, Mrs. Fields developed software to ask a simple set of questions of job applicants, process the data, and make a binary recommendation (hire or not). Imagine that you are designing such a piece of recruitment software. It is not likely to work well in advanced jobs, where there are complex issues to analyze, such as advanced and technical knowledge of applicants, or fit with the corporate culture. It is much more likely to work well for a cashier in a Mrs. Fields Cookies store, where the tasks are narrowly defined, little discretion is given, and few skills are required.

Thus, computerization works best when Taylorism works best. If the environment is simple rather than complex, there are fewer rules to define in the software.

---

[5] For an excellent book on this topic, see Levy & Murnane (2004).

If there are fewer interdependencies between tasks, it is easier to separate out and determine exactly how to perform each. If the work is predictable, the different contingencies can be specified in advance, and codified in the software.

AN EXPERT SYSTEM FOR CHICKEN SOUP

●●●●●●●●●

You may have at some time consumed a can of Campbell's Chicken Soup, which is sold worldwide. This soup is made in very large industrial cooking systems. A key component of the process is the hydrostatic sterilizer or cooker, which ensures that bacteria do not enter the soup. If bacteria entered the system, it would eat through the cans on the shelf, destroying the product and creating a mess.

Aldo Cimino, an employee with 45 years of experience, operated the cooker at one of the major plants. Campbell's realized that he would soon retire, at which point they would lose his human capital. They hired Texas Instruments to work with Cimino to develop an expert system that could perform as much of the job as possible, in the way that Cimino performed it. This was one of the very first examples of an expert system deployed at work.

It took several months to design the expert system, and then many months more of perfecting it on the job. The system ended up with 150 heuristics (rules). The system enables workers with less experience and expertise than Cimino to perform the same job almost as well, because it performs much of the diagnosis of problems. The system has turned much of Cimino's specific knowledge into general knowledge.

Source: Edmunds (1988)

A more difficult situation arises when the rules that humans apply at work are difficult to specify. Computer scientists sometimes model these as cases where the rules are probabilistic rather than deterministic. Humans are very good at *pattern recognition*, while to date computers are not. This is the realm of techniques like expert systems and neural networks. While such techniques have increased the set of jobs that can be computerized well, these technologies are generally far from successful at fully replicating the way in which a human can perform the job (except for cookie store managers).

One key skill required of workers who have decision rights and are expected to learn on the job is *abstraction*—developing a general principle from specific circumstances, and applying the general principle to new situations. (Recall the problem solving training recommended for shop floor workers by Juran in Chapter 7.) This is an area where humans have a substantial comparative advantage over computers, as computers do not have the ability of abstraction. Most computer programs work by specifying the contingencies in advance. When computers encounter situations not specified beforehand, they do not know how to react.

Finally, virtually by definition, *creative* work is impossible to computerize. Creativity involves generating new contingencies, in addition to reacting to those that arise exogenously.

Thus, the kinds of jobs where computers are good substitutes for workers are those that would ordinarily involve low discretion, low use of multitasking, and low skills. They also include cases where the job involves *routinized* information processing, such as clerical work and lower or middle management positions.

WHAT IS REENGINEERING?

Reengineering is a practice that uses the classic methods of Taylorism to implement advanced computer technology in modern workplaces. A typical example is an insurance company or bank. Firms where information processing is the core activity are the ones that have been reengineered most typically, since these are tasks that computers handle particularly well.

In these cases, many tasks and jobs can be computerized, so reengineering often leads to large layoffs of both clerical workers and lower or middle management. Reengineering also involves reorganizing the entire work-flow. Therefore, reengineering is a large scale, centralized change, usually implemented with the help of an outside consulting firm.

While reengineering usually replaces many jobs with computers, remaining jobs well become more enriched. For example, traditionally an insurance company employee might be assigned to process a specific claim form—one step in the entire chain of handling a customer's service request. After reengineering, the employee might be assigned to handle the entire service request from start to finish with the help of a computer. This provides better task identity (in the words of the psychological model of intrinsic motivation) or modularity. By handling the entire service request, quality and customer satisfaction are likely to rise, and processing time fall. IT makes it possible for one employee to handle the entire customer transaction.

The effects of automation and computerization apply to *all* jobs. The principles of Taylorism, like those of specialization, are relevant in at least some ways. For example, computer technology combined with advanced medical equipment can now perform some tasks that used to be done by doctors. Many lab tests are now automated, where in the past they required laborious (no pun intended) technical procedures. Similarly, some healthcare providers use computers as *decision support* tools for doctors. The doctor enters data about the patient's characteristics and symptoms. The software compares this information to a database of prior cases and makes suggestions to the doctor about further diagnosis and treatment (much as Mrs. Fields Cookies can compare one store's situation to the experience of others). This frees up the doctor to focus on the more idiosyncratic, creative, and hands on parts of the job.

To sum up, IT tends to substitute for workers in the classical *LLLL* type jobs that we talked about in the last chapter. It tends to complement decision making by workers in enriched *HHHH* type jobs. Thus, while computers may destroy jobs of one type, they create jobs of a different type at the same time. This is why the labor market has increasingly valued high skilled workers, as described in Chapter 3, and computerization has not led to increases in overall unemployment. Advanced technology makes skilled workers more productive and hence more valuable. In addition, it illustrates once again the increasing importance of cognitive skills in the labor market, and of continual investment in human capital.

⬡ ⬡ ⬡ ⬡ ⬡   # High Reliability Organizations

In this section we consider a particular kind of organization that serves as a good example of how to pull together ideas and themes from this section of the textbook: *high reliability organizations* (HROs). HROs are organizations in which the costs of errors are extremely high. They usually must act quickly, often facing unpredictable circumstances, which implies strong benefits from decentralization. However, their operations are often tightly interconnected, so that there are strong benefits from coordination. Thus, they face the same issues as typical firms, but the stakes are much higher and the tradeoffs much more difficult. As in the field of medicine, it is often worthwhile studying pathologies, since extreme cases clarify key issues that may not be as readily apparent when studying more ordinary cases.

There are many examples of HROs, such as military units during war, aircraft carriers during a landing, hospital emergency rooms, and international banking companies involved in very large transactions. Many of the principles of HROs can be usefully applied to risk management more generally.

A common organizing principle of HROs is to develop two separate, parallel structures: one for normal operations, and another for high pressure periods where the risks are extreme. This distinction is clear for the military (war and peace) or an emergency room (many patients or few). During quiet periods, the chief purpose of the organization is to prepare for the high pressure periods. At that time, decision making can be much slower and more centralized, and the organization can emphasize training and preparation. Once a high risk period begins, these organizations generally decentralize many decisions, and focus on immediate execution.

A second common principle is to use Tayloristic methods as much as possible. During peacetime, the organization devotes extensive resources to contingency planning, predicting as many events as possible, and laying down rules and procedures to follow when those events occur.

The Appendix provides an example of this drawn from the U.S. military, an *execution matrix*. This matrix (actually provided to units as spreadsheets) specifies a number of contingencies, or events that might occur during battle. These are the rows in the matrix. The columns then specify what actions each organizational unit should take for each contingency.

In theory, if all contingencies could be specified, and all appropriate actions for each unit (or individual) could be figured out, this approach would provide perfect coordination and also allow individual units to use their specific knowledge (which would amount to figuring out which row applied at the moment). In addition, there would be no communication costs, and all actions could be implemented with no delays.

The weakness of the matrix in the Appendix is its limited approach. The original execution matrix on which it is based specified a starting condition for only *seven* organizational units, and what actions to take in *only thirteen* contingencies. This is far from comprehensive ex ante optimization.

When an employee cannot be given a set of fully specified rules and procedures to take under all contingencies, the next step is training. HROs engage in very extensive training; this is probably the primary activity of most HRO employees during "peacetime." Much of this training is drills, in which employees simulate actual events, diagnose problems before they occur, and learn what they should do, so as to be prepared to deal with real problems quickly and reliably.

The training does not just specify exactly what the employees should do in each possible contingency. Instead, it teaches *abstract principles* to guide employees in how to react in circumstances not specified in the training. The training often includes drilling on the organization's *mission*; that is, the organization's goals and the relatively weighting of each. This teaches the employee the objective function to use in figuring out what the best behavior is in new circumstances. For higher level employees, much of the training involves *problem solving skills*—how to figure out a solution to a problem or question that arises. For example, in military academies officers discuss case studies, and analyze what the best course of action would be. In the process, they learn to think strategically.

More important, the case studies can also teach the employees to *think similarly*—to analyze problems in the same way and with the same goals as the organization overall. A goal of the entire training process in HROs is to try to make employees as similar as possible. When this succeeds, it improves coordination without the need for much communication, because individual behavior is predictable and consistent.

The goal of developing a strong uniformity of training and behavior is reinforced in HROs through strong use of norms. We already mentioned this above, noting how the military instills loyalty and camaraderie during boot camp. These organizations develop a very strong sense of teamwork.

While much coordination can be achieved, with decentralization, through extensive training and a strong culture, these organizations still need to communicate. For example, if a contingency arises and one employee notes it, it is important for this employee to pass this information to all colleagues. Similarly, communication provides feedback within the unit, improving decision making. For these reasons, a common characteristic of HROs is extensive use of real time communication, in all directions. For example, in an emergency room the surgeon communicates with the nurse at all times. The nurse repeats commands, giving the surgeon feedback that the command was received correctly and is being implemented.

Finally, HROs typically invest in redundant systems, as a way to further reduce error rates. This includes ultrareliable equipment, backup systems, extra inventory, and slack in procedures that can be taken up during times of pressure. It also includes cross training, so that workers can replace each other as needed. Finally, it includes double checking of communication and of error detection (similar to additional layers of project evaluation described in Chapter 5).

These procedures, especially the parallel organizational structures, heavy training and retraining, and redundancies are expensive. Not every organization can adopt the same policies. However, the lessons apply to all organizations. Once again we see that if tasks or decisions can be analyzed in advance, this should be done. This allows for standardization and greater guidelines for employees, reducing errors and improving consistency.

Cultural norms can then be used to reinforce the standardization of methods. Norms also develop a better understanding of and respect for organizational goals, which reduces incentive problems. All of this allows organizations to achieve better coordination of tasks that need to be synchronized but do not require communication.

Standardization and norms play the same roles that computerization does: They free up the employee to focus on the more advanced cognitive tasks. This increases not only efficiency, but the ability to be creative and adaptable. Finally, for tasks that do require communication for coordination, information technology plays a vital role.

◆ ◆ ◆ ◆ ◆ ## SUMMARY

There is a tendency for the business press and organizations to chase fads in organizational design. When one company adopts a set of practices that turn out to be very successful, competitors emulate that firm, without much analysis of whether the practices are a good idea for their situation. Moreover, there is a temptation to regard new developments or recent trends as being fundamentally different from the past. The lessons of this chapter and Section II overall should give you a dose of healthy skepticism when confronted with such views. As the quote at the beginning of this chapter suggests, basic concepts of organizational design apply now as they did 200 years ago—the more things change, the more they stay the same. Understanding the basic concepts gives you a model for organizational design that can help you figure out which trendy practices work well, why, and in which settings.

The basic goals of good organizational design never change. Of fundamental importance are the gains from specialization of workers, both to economize on training and to improve learning by doing. These need to be balanced against the gains from putting highly complementary tasks together, which increases continuous improvement. Along those lines, the other fundamental goal of the organization is to create and use knowledge. This often implies that decentralization is important, but it must be balanced against coordination costs.

Teams have always been an important part of organizational design. They serve to coordinate closely related tasks when there are too many for one worker to handle. They allow for a balance of these coordination benefits with the gains from specialization of individual works. They also serve to integrate pockets of specific knowledge across the organization, when that is necessary to make a broader decision. However, they incur two major costs: inefficient group decision making, and free riding. It is also hard to determine the optimal size of the team. Therefore, teams should be deployed carefully, and only when the benefits exceed the costs.

The history of work design has always been, and always will be, a tension between two forces. Information technology increases this tension.

One of the two forces is the drive to standardize tasks and decisions. The goal is to figure out the best way to perform these tasks, and implement the best method uniformly. Taylorism is an example from 100 years ago, while reengineering is a similar example today. Any time that an organization uses standard operating procedures, rules and guidelines, or computerizes some tasks, it is moving in that direction. To the extent that this is the dominant force, the organization emphasizes ex ante optimization, specialized jobs, centralization, and low investment in worker skills.

The opposite force is the desire to increase economic value using the capabilities that humans have that machines or computers do not. This involves using abstract thinking, pattern recognition, and creativity to deal with complex, unpredictable situations. In short, where knowledge cannot be codified well, there is specific knowledge of particular circumstances, and the best way to use this knowledge is to rely on the employees who possess it. When this force is dominant, the organization emphasizes continuous improvement, multitasking, decentralization, and greater investments in worker skills (including cognitive skills).

There has been a trend toward the latter of these forces, and away from the first, over the past few decades. However, it is important not to assume that this trend will continue. As organizations adapt to globalization, advanced technology, and other recent changes, they will gradually standardize the lessons they have learned. As they do, there is likely to be a movement back toward more traditional organizational and job design techniques in many situations. That is how the Mrs. Fields cookie crumbles.

An important theme in this section is worker decision making and learning. Aligning the worker's motivation with those of the firm is an important issue. We have introduced this topic by discussing intrinsic motivation. We now turn to the topic of pay for performance in Section III of the text.

❦ ❦ ❦ ❦ ❦ STUDY QUESTIONS

1. How do the principles of team composition apply to setting up a product design team whose goal is to integrate specific knowledge from different parts of the organization?

2. Psychologists usually argue that the optimal size of a workgroup is about five or six members, neither smaller or larger. What are the factors that explain this? Does this finding accord with your experience?

3. Why do schoolchildren usually assign teams by alternating draws rather than some method that would increase efficiency? (*Hint:* It is not because they have no way of bidding with each other. It is because their objective is *not* team efficiency, but something else.)

4. How is information technology changing your job? Is it making the job more enriched, with greater depth and breadth of skills required? Or is it the opposite?

5. How has information technology changed the job of a secretary? Can you think of cases where part or all of a secretary's job has been replaced by computers? Explain.

6. Information technology has dramatically lowered the cost of communicating many forms of information. Does this imply that the central planning model discussed in Chapter 5 should be more important now? Why or why not? What other factors are relevant?

7. What do you think the ultimate limits of expert systems will be (if any)? Why?

8. What are examples of organizations that have extreme pressures for use of specific dispersed knowledge, coordination, or low error rates? What methods have they used to solve these organizational problems?

9. Based on your answer to Question 8, what lessons can be learned for the design of more ordinary firms?

❦ ❦ ❦ ❦ ❦ REFERENCES

Craig, Ben & John Pencavel (1992). "The Behavior of Worker Cooperatives: The Plywood Companies of the Pacific Northwest." *American Economic Review* 82(5): 1083–1105.

Edmunds, Robert (1988). *The Prentice Hall Guide to Expert Systems.* Englewood Cliffs, NJ: Prentice Hall.

Farrell, Joseph & Suzanne Scotchmer (1988). "Partnerships." *Quarterly Journal of Economics* 103: 279–297.

Fitzgerald, Michael (2004). "A Drive-Through Lane to the Next Time Zone." *New York Times*, July 18.

Kandel, Eugene & Edward Lazear (1992). "Peer Pressure and Partnerships." *Journal of Political Economy* 100(4): 41–62.

Karr, Alphonse (1849). *Les Guêpes*, January.

Levy, Frank & Richard Murnane (2004). *The New Division of Labor: How Computers Are Creating the Next Job Market*. Princeton: Princeton University Press.

FURTHER READING

Cash, James & Keri Ostrofsky (1993). "Mrs. Fields Cookies." Harvard Business School case #9-189-056.

Hackman, J. Richard (1990). *Groups That Work (And Those That Don't)*. New York: Jossey-Bass.

Hubbard, Thomas (2000). "The Demand for Monitoring Technologies: The Case of Trucking." *Quarterly Journal of Economics*, May: 533–560.

Pfeiffer, John (1989). "The Secret of Life at the Limits: Cogs Become Big Wheels." *Smithsonian*, July.

APPENDIX

I. Norms

Here we present a brief formal discussion of norms.[6] The level of norms depends on the type of sanction associated with deviating from the norm. Further, for any given sanction, there exists an equilibrium level of effort in the firm, which should be set to the norm. To see this, write an individual's utility function as:

$$Utility = Pay(e) - C(e) - P(e - e^*),$$

where e is an individual's effort level, $Pay(e)$ is the earnings received as a function of effort, $C(e)$ is the monetary value of the worker's disutility associated with effort level e, and P is the cost to the worker of peer pressure.

Peer pressure is a function of the worker's effort e, and of the endogenously determined effort norm e^*. When workers want their coworkers to put forth more effort, $dP/de < 0$; reducing one's effort increases peer pressure. When workers want their coworkers to work less, $dP/de > 0$.

$d^2 Pay/de^2 \leq 0$; we can always normalize effort such that this condition holds. $dC/de > 0$, and $d^2 C/de^2 \geq 0$, since additional work makes the employee even more exhausted.

---

[6]See Kandel & Lazear (1992).

Suppose that peer pressure takes the following form:

$$P(e - e^*) = -\gamma(e - e^*),$$

where γ is a constant, so that peer pressure one receives is a linear function of the difference between one's effort e and the endogenously determined effort norm e^*. This form is chosen for simplicity; similar analysis holds for any peer pressure function. This says that for every unit that an individual's effort falls below the norm e^*, he feels pressure from coworkers which has a monetary equivalent to him of γ dollars.

The worker's maximization problem yields the first-order condition:

$$\frac{d\,Pay}{de} - \frac{dC}{de} + \gamma = 0,$$

which generally has a solution. Since all workers are identical, e^* is simply the solution to this equation. Thus, a norm level of effort is established. Using the implicit function theorem,

$$\frac{de}{d\gamma} = -1 \Big/ \left[\frac{d^2 Pay}{de^2} - \frac{d^2 C}{de^2} \right],$$

which is positive by the second-order condition for the worker's maximization problem. Thus, an increase in γ raises the worker's level of effort. As sanctions and peer pressure for deviating from the norm increase, the norm level of effort increases.

II. Example Execution Matrix

TABLE 8A.1
EXECUTION MATRIX

Examples of forseeable contingencies (out of 13 specified)

			Unit				
Contingencies	1st Brigade	2nd Brigade	Infantry Brigade	Advance Brigade	Artillery	Engineering	Cavalry
Start of exercise	Defend in sector	Defend in sector	Prepare for attack	Operations against advance guard	Artillery at specific locations	Survivability & countermobility support	Monitor Sector 1; screen along Sector 2
Forces headed east into 1st Brigade sector	Defend in sector	Defend in sector	Prepare for attack	Notify C Company if divisional reconnaisance detected	Artillery at specific locations	Continue survivability (priority) and countermobility tasks	Screen along Sector 2; prepare to conduct rear passage of lines and battle handover
Forces headed east along 1st/2nd Brigade seam	Counterattack into 2nd Brigade Sector if enemy forces past certain position and if 32nd Brigade to be used for mobile defense	Defend in sector	Warning order for attack through 2nd Brigade Sector (mobile defense)	Notify C Company if 30+ vehicles moving east or north	At specific locations, provide cover fire for movement of other unit	Deploy scatterable minefield southwest of position X	Move to position Y and become the division reserve
Forces headed south, possibly into 2nd Brigade sector	Similar instructions if enemy forces headed into other sectors						
Forces headed southwest into southern sector of 1st Brigade		Defend in sector	If no activity in 2nd Brigade sector, prepare for attack into 1st Brigade sector	Warning order for counterattack	Provide fire at specific location		Warning order for counterattack

Note: Other contingencies not listed had similar entries.

This example is based on an actual execution matrix used by the U.S. Army Reserve during a training exercise. The only real simplification has been to eliminate rows with contingencies and actions very similar to those shown. The original had thirteen total contingencies (other than start of exercise) for the seven organizational units shown.

Part Three

PAYING FOR PERFORMANCE

*A*n important consideration in Chapter 7 was intrinsic motivation. We also saw in Chapter 5 that if employees are given decision rights, aligning their motivation with organizational objectives is essential. In the next few chapters, we build on these ideas by considering pay for performance or *extrinsic* motivation. Chapter 9 covers what is usually the most difficult issue confronting any incentive system: How is performance measured? In Chapter 10 we ask, what should we do with the performance evaluation (how should it be tied to rewards)? Chapters 11–12 cover special topics: incentives from promotions, employee stock options, and executive pay. Before we begin, it is useful to provide an introduction to the overall topic. First, let's think about why it is important to study pay for performance.

First, the evidence is clear: Employees tend to respond strongly to incentives. This means that if an incentive plan is designed well, it can be an important source of value creation; but if it is designed poorly, it can be an important source of value destruction.

Second, incentives may play an important role even if an employee has strong intrinsic motivation, because the motivation may not be adequately aligned with organizational objectives. For example, two groups that tend to have very high intrinsic motivation are researchers working in corporate R&D laboratories, and medical doctors. In both cases, the employer may have to resort to incentives to redirect their motivation appropriately. A firm may need to motivate R&D researchers to focus on innovations that can be sold profitably, rather than ones that involve cutting edge research. A healthcare provider may need to motivate doctors to focus more on the difficult tradeoff between quality of care and cost.

Third, it is common to underestimate the importance of incentives. Psychologists say that people tend to make a "fundamental attribution error" in evaluating

231

human behavior: to over-attribute behavior to a person's psychology, and underestimate the extent to which the behavior is caused by the environment—constraints, rewards, and group influences. In other words, people underestimate the extent to which incentives (broadly construed) cause behavior. In many cases, subtle incentives drive what may at first seem to be puzzling actions by an employee.

From the perspective of motivating employees, this insight is important. The psychology of your workforce is, generally, quite difficult to change, though some (relatively blunt) change can be affected through recruiting and job design. By contrast, incentives are relatively easy to alter. Thus, pay for performance and other forms of extrinsic rewards are the most important motivational levers that a manager can pull.

Fourth, rewarding performance improves many human resource objectives for the firm. We have seen this several times in earlier chapters. For example, deferred pay based on performance can improve self-selection in recruiting. Similarly, performance pay may increase the return on investments in human capital, motivating greater investments in skills. Better incentives can improve decision making, encouraging employees to use their knowledge in the firm's interests. Most human resource policies involve some form of incentive scheme (though many are subtle). More broadly, incentives are what drive modern economies. Understanding basic incentive theory provides you with intuition that is useful in many business contexts.[1]

We now sketch out the way that economists formalize their thinking about incentive problems. When you read the discussion of pay for performance, think about pay metaphorically. We are not referring solely to monetary compensation. Rather, we are thinking abstractly about *any* rewards the firm can vary with employee performance. Of course in practice, monetary rewards such as bonuses or stock options are the most important, but firms use many rewards (some implicit). For example, good performance might be rewarded with a better office, more flexible work hours, more interesting job assignments, or a promotion. To the extent that these are rewarded based on performance, they are a form of extrinsic incentive, and the principles described in these chapters apply.

● ● ● ● ● ## THE PRINCIPAL-AGENT PROBLEM

In economics, the basic framework for analyzing most incentive problems is called the *principal-agent* problem. This literature can often be highly technical. Here we provide a brief sketch to help sharpen your intuition, but our interests are more practical. We will express the ideas in equations, but no advanced mathematical techniques are needed. The equations help to make our ideas and intuition more rigorous.

---

[1] Much of modern business school curricula, such as corporate finance and managerial accounting, is applied incentive theory.

Incentive problems arise when an *agent* (in our context, an employee) acts on behalf of a *principal* (the firm's owners), but has objectives that are different than the principal's. Consider an entrepreneur. In this case, the agent *is* the principal, so there is no conflict of interest and no incentive problem. However, modern corporations usually involve separation of ownership and control—managers are hired to run the firm on behalf of the owners. (This may be so that owners can diversify their investment portfolios to reduce risk, or because owners delegate to managers who have skills that the owners do not.) This suggests that incentive problems for top management are an important concern; we cover that topic in Chapter 12.

How might we analyze such a conflict formally? We need to model the objectives of both the principal and the agent. Assume that the principal's objective is to maximize the discounted present value of the firm. For a publicly traded firm, this is total shareholder value (share price times number of shares outstanding). Virtually all of the intuition would apply if we considered different definitions of the principal's objective (say, if the firm were a government agency or not for profit). The important point is that there is a conflict of interest.

The employee provides different kinds of effort, which affect firm value; by effort, we mean actions the employee can take that the firm wishes to motivate. It might mean working harder, faster, or longer on various tasks; thinking more carefully when making decisions; cooperating with colleagues; or being helpful to customers.

In Part Two we discussed multitasking as a feature of job design. Multitasking would imply that there is more than one type of effort. We will discuss some implications of multitasking for incentive systems later in this section. For now, though, suppose that there is only one dimension to the employee's job, so that the firm wants to motivate the employee to provide a single type of effort, e.

The employee's overall contribution to firm value Q depends on the employee's effort, $Q = Q(e)$. Q is not the firm's total profit, but is the discounted present value of the profit created by this employee, ignoring the employee's pay. Thus, the firm's profit attributable to this employee equals $Q(e) - Pay$.

There is a conflict of interest only to the extent that the employee has too little, or too much, motivation to provide various kinds of effort. A typical case is where intrinsic motivation is too low—the firm would like the employee to work harder, or more diligently. A way to formalize this is to assume that such actions are costly to the employee in some way: They would prefer to work more slowly, less carefully, etc. In this sense, you can think of the employee as incurring a psychological cost if they provide more effort. This cost is called the *disutility of effort*. Let us refer to this as $C(e)$. Remember that this is a psychic cost to the employee, not a monetary one.[2] However, even nonmonetary concepts can be scaled in monetary terms (see Chapter 13). For example, we might be able to quantify an employee's cost of effort by the increase in pay that they demand when asked to work harder.

---

[2]Typically it is assumed that $C(e)$ rises at an increasing rate as e rises. This captures the idea that effort is costly to the employee, and that the harder they work, the more costly additional effort becomes.

The employee's pay only provides incentives if it depends on performance. Suppose that the firm has a performance measure *PM* that estimates the employee's contribution *Q*. If performance can be measured perfectly, $PM = Q$, but generally this is not the case. Then, pay is some function of *PM*: $Pay = Pay(PM)$. If the measure is imperfect, we might model this as $PM = Q + \varepsilon$, where ε is a random variable: performance measurement error.

Pay for performance is risky because performance can almost never be measured with perfect accuracy. People are generally risk averse, so there is an additional cost to the employee from working at the firm: the cost of the riskiness of pay. Let us model this cost the way this is often done in the field of decision theory. The cost of risk to an employee is the opposite of the *certainly equivalent*, or amount he person would be willing to pay to avoid the risk. A standard way to model this term is: certainty equivalent $= 1/2 \cdot R \cdot \sigma_{Pay}^2$. This formulation assumes that the appropriate measure of risk is the variance of pay. *R* is called the *coefficient of absolute risk aversion*. It is a parameter that reflects the extent to which an employee is risk averse. Someone who is less risk averse would have a smaller *R*, while someone who is more risk averse would have a larger *R*. Putting this all together, the employee's net value from working for the firm is: $Pay(PM) - C(e) - \frac{1}{2} \cdot R \cdot \sigma_{pay}^2$.

As mentioned above, the firm's value from the employee equals $Q(e) - Pay$. The firm chooses the compensation plan *Pay(PM)* to maximize this net profit from the employee. The firm is constrained by the fact that total pay must be at or above the employee's labor market value. For this reason, the firm must also compensate the employee for effort cost *C*, and risk cost *R*, generated by the incentive system the firm implements.

●●●●● WHAT DOES THE EMPLOYEE'S INCENTIVE DEPEND ON?

What drives the employee's incentive? As in all of economics, decisions are made by balancing the marginal benefits of changing one's behavior against the marginal costs. In this case, the question is whether the employee should work a little harder or not. The marginal cost is the extra disutility from working harder, $\Delta C / \Delta e$, where Δ is notation denoting an incremental change in a variable:[3]

$$Employee's\ marginal\ cost\ from\ working\ harder = \frac{\Delta C}{\Delta e}.$$

Since pay depends on the performance measure, and the performance measure depends on effort, the marginal benefit from working harder on some dimension of the job is:

$$Employee's\ marginal\ benefit\ from\ working\ harder = \frac{\Delta Pay}{\Delta e} = \frac{\Delta Pay}{\Delta PM} \cdot \frac{\Delta PM}{\Delta e}.$$

---

[3] Assuming that extra effort does not affect the riskiness of pay.

Since the employee balances the marginal costs and benefits, anything that increases the marginal benefit will increase the employee's effort. The second equation tells us that we need to focus on two things. First, how does the performance measure vary with effort? If it reflects the employee's effort well, it will improve incentives, and vice versa. Second, how does pay vary with measured performance? If it does so strongly, incentives will be stronger, and vice versa. These two factors are the focus of each of the next two chapters in turn; they form the heart of this section of the text. Chapter 9 analyzes how the firm can measure the employee's contribution to firm value. Chapter 10 then analyzes how the firm can relate this evaluation to rewards.

Now let us consider the source of the conflict of interest between the worker and the firm. Recall that C and $R \cdot \sigma$ are costs that must be borne by the firm, implicitly. They reduce the value of the job to the employee, so the employee will require higher total compensation if C or $R \cdot \sigma$ are higher, and vice versa. In this sense, the costs of the incentive system, C and R, do not create a conflict of interest between the firm and the employee. They are a cost of doing business, just like the cost of any inputs to production. If a stronger incentive motivates the employee to work harder, $C(e)$ rises, but the firm will have to compensate the employee for this. In other words,

$$\text{Firm's marginal cost from the employee working harder} = \frac{\Delta C}{\Delta e}.$$

Thus, the firm and its employee have the same total costs from the employee working on the job, $C(e) + R \cdot \sigma$, and the same marginal costs. The real source of the conflict is because the employee's benefit (Pay) is generally not identical to the firm's benefit (Q). More formally,

$$\text{Firm's marginal benefit from the employee working harder} = \frac{\Delta Q}{\Delta e},$$

which will generally differ from the employee's marginal benefit from working harder. This can happen because the evaluation does not perfectly reflect performance, or because pay does not fully reflect the employee's contribution. These are the incentive problems that we will see over and over again later.

While we will not pursue this formalized approach to thinking about incentive pay, we will use these basic ideas to structure our thinking and make it more rigorous in what follows. It is worth your time working through the intuition described here, and used later.

9

PERFORMANCE EVALUATION

When you cannot measure, your knowledge is meager and unsatisfactory.
—Lord Kelvin, carved in stone on the Social Sciences Building,
University of Chicago

Measure anyway!
—Frank Knight, noticing the carving on returning from lunch
at the faculty club one day—as told by George Stigler

INTRODUCTION

The most difficult part of any incentive scheme is performance evaluation. Imagine that you are a manager, and you want to measure—quantify—the individual contributions of each of your employees to firm value. How can you do so accurately? Employees may work together in groups, so that it is hard to disentangle who is responsible and who is not. Some might free ride on the work of others; others might be very cooperative, but you do not always see this since you cannot observe everything they do. In addition, an employee's performance may be partly due to luck. An employee might be in the right place at the right time, and land a large sales contract when a new customer calls. Or, an employee might lose sales because a key client goes out of business unexpectedly. Finally, some contributions are quite difficult to quantify even when they are clearly observed. How do you measure the employee's effects on group norms, mentoring of junior staff, or customer satisfaction?

Not only is performance evaluation difficult to do effectively, but evaluation can be quite costly. Subjective evaluations generally take a large fraction of managerial time. Collecting accurate performance metrics (including those generated as part of the accounting system) can take substantial resources.

If the evaluation does not accurately reflect the employee's contributions, it may cause several negative outcomes. The employee might find that the link between performance and pay is uncertain, and require compensation for risk, thus raising costs. The employee might be poorly motivated. Perhaps worse, the employee might be strongly motivated, but to do the wrong things, destroying value. Thus, even though evaluations are difficult and costly to do, they are a necessary component of a good reward system, and it is important for firms to strive for effective performance evaluation methods and procedures. In this chapter, we discuss important issues that arise when evaluating performance.

Purposes of Performance Evaluation

Employee performance depends on, among other factors: innate abilities, accumulated skills or human capital, and efforts. Based on our sketch of the principal-agent problem above, for a simple model we might say that Q depends on ability A, accumulated human capital H, and efforts e_i: $Q = Q(A, H, e_1 \ldots e_k)$.

This suggests that evaluations might emphasize measuring innate abilities A, skills H, or effort e_i depending on what the evaluation is used for. We will return to this issue below. For most of this chapter, we focus on the use of evaluations to measure and motivate greater effort.

Ways to Evaluate Performance

Modeling the employee's contribution to firm value as $Q = Q(e_1 \ldots e_k)$ suggests several approaches to measuring performance. First, we might estimate Q overall (what we will call a very *broad* measure). One example that is important for executives in publicly traded firms is the stock price. Second, we might estimate different dimensions of performance (what we will call a *narrower* measure). In a manufacturing setting, one common performance measure is the quantity a worker produces. Another is the quality (e.g., number of defective parts produced). Third, we might combine several measures of various dimensions of performance. For example, a plant manager might be measured on revenue, or costs, or profits (revenue minus costs).

Notice that all of these approaches are *output* based performance measures, in that they attempted to measure components of Q. An alternative, narrower approach is to measure the employee's *inputs* e_i, such as hours worked or number of routines or tasks accomplished.

Finally, the evaluation might be quantitative or qualitative. We next discuss quantitative performance measurement. In the section that follows we discuss subjective evaluation.

●●●●● QUANTITATIVE PERFORMANCE MEASUREMENT

Organizations often go to great lengths to quantify an employee's contribution to firm value. Quantitative measures have several advantages. Because they are numeric, they can be tied to compensation more easily (e.g., by computing a bonus using a formula). Many performance metrics are readily available through the normal course of business. Accounting systems, for example, are large scale performance measurement systems. Where the accounting numbers accord well with an employee's contribution, they are often used for computing bonuses, as input into promotion decisions, etc. Firms may also use hours worked, customer satisfaction, and other quantitative information as inputs in evaluations.

Finally, quantitative performance measures are often perceived as more objective than the use of judgment in evaluations. Indeed, they are often called "objective" performance measures. However, it is not obvious that quantitative metrics are objective. As discussed later, many metrics can be manipulated by the employee, or the supervisor or firm. Even if a measure is not subject to manipulation, it may not measure exactly what is intended. For example, if a law firm wants to motivate partners to bring in new business, it may give lawyers a credit for any new clients that they bring to the firm. This would seem to be an easy performance dimension to quantify. However, in some cases the lawyer might have received the new business simply because he or she answered the phone when the new client called. For these reasons, we do not use the term objective performance measure, to highlight that quantitative measures have their own flaws. Nevertheless, they are likely to be more objective than are subjective evaluations.

What performance measure properties should a manager look for in determining a good measure for incentives? We consider five general properties: the measure's risk profile; distortion; scope; match to job design; and potential for *manipulation*.

Risk Profile

Accounting texts often say that a performance measure should include whatever is controllable by the employee, but exclude whatever is uncontrollable. Every performance measure has some risk in it: It varies in unexpected ways from period to period. We have already noted that since employees are risk averse, risk in a performance measure can cause problems for an incentive plan. However, the issue is not so simple. There are two important types of risk that must be considered in a performance measures, and these have very different implications for an optimal incentive scheme. We will distinguish between *uncontrollable risk* and *controllable risk*. This distinction relies on the important concept of specific knowledge, which was so important in Part Two.

Uncontrollable risk corresponds to the classic definition of risk: variation in performance that is beyond the employee's ability to control. Consider a CEO of a publicly traded firm, with stock price as the performance measure. Stock price varies with the CEO's talents and efforts, which is why it is a logical performance measure. However, it also varies with many exogenous events, including macroeconomic fluctuations, industry dynamics, technological change, actions of specific competitors, inflation, interest rates, foreign exchange, and so on. The CEO cannot affect any of these variables, and will have little ability to mitigate the effect of most of them on stock price (though see our more extensive discussion of controllability later).

Since these variables cannot be controlled by the CEO, but influence the performance measure, they do create risk for the CEO. The firm can respond to this risk in the performance measure in several ways. It might choose a different measure that is less risky. It might weaken the link between pay and performance to reduce the CEO's risk, as will be described in the next chapter. Or, it might raise base salary to compensation the CEO for the risk, with a risk premium. In general, these are all drawbacks—uncontrollable risk is an important problem facing incentive plans.

Controllable risk is more subtle but quite important. This is variation in the work environment that the employee has some ability to control. For example, the CEO may not be able to control a competitor's strategic actions. However, the CEO *can* anticipate some of those actions, and be prepared when they occur. He can react to them after they occur. As another example, suppose that an employee has two tasks in his job: sales, and customer service. From day to day, the extent to which he should spend time on one task or the other varies, depending on what types of customer calls he receives. The relative demand by customers is a random variable. However, the effects of this random demand on firm value are largely controllable by the employee: He can respond by changing how he performs his job every day. Therefore, the effects of customer demand on firm value *are* controllable by the employee.

More generally, all employees have some specific knowledge that arises as they do their jobs. Both of our examples in the preceding paragraph can be seen as types of specific knowledge possessed by the employee. Since this knowledge is not available when the incentive plan is designed, it is in an important sense a random variable. However, it is not true that it is pure risk for the employee, or uncontrollable by the employee.

The effects of controllable risk (specific knowledge) on incentive plans are generally *the opposite* of the effects of uncontrollable risk. When the employee's job design implies that he has more specific knowledge of time and place, the firm should *increase the strength of incentives* to motivate the employee to use that knowledge to improve firm value. Since this risk is controllable by the employee, the firm need not pay a risk premium.

We will elaborate on this important idea below when we discuss subjective performance evaluation. For now, the important point is that it is essential to distinguish between risk that is uncontrollable by the employee, and risk that is controllable. When risk is uncontrollable, the firm may want to consider a *narrower performance measure*, will tend to give weaker incentives, and may pay a risk premium.

By contrast, when risk is controllable (the employee has important specific knowledge), our market metaphor is apt: The firm should decentralize to the employee, and then give relatively strong incentives to motivate the employee to use that knowledge to further firm objectives. We will also see soon that we will tend to use a *broader performance measure*, and possibly *subjective performance evaluation*, in such cases.

Therefore, the first question to ask about a performance measure is, what is the *signal* to *noise* ratio? How much of the variation in this measure is due to factors that are true, classical risk from the employee's point of view, and how much is due to factors that reflect the employee's specific knowledge of circumstances arising as he performs the job?

Risk vs. Distortion: Performance Measure Scope

Building on these ideas, an ideal performance measure should reflect the employee's total impact on firm value, and nothing else. Let's think about these issues in the context of the right performance measure for two employees in the same firm: the CEO, and the custodian.

The most common performance measure for CEO compensation (in a publicly traded firm) is the firm's stock price (or stock value, which is the stock price times the number of shares outstanding).[1] By definition, this is firm value. Thus, this measure does capture all of the things that are controllable by the CEO: If there is anything that the CEO can do to improve or reduce firm value, it will be reflected in this performance measure. In this sense it would seem to be a perfect measure.

However, there are also many things that affect the firm's stock price that are beyond the control of the CEO: actions of competitors, macroeconomic factors, currency fluctuations, and so on. For this reason, the performance measure is also *risky* for the CEO. Performance measurement error is caused by uncontrollables.

Now consider the custodian; the same logic applies. Stock price is a good measure in the sense that it includes the effects on firm value of anything that is controllable by the custodian. However, it includes much that is uncontrollable. In fact, it would be ridiculous to use stock price as a performance measure for the custodian because the uncontrollables so outweigh the controllables. Doing so would essentially make compensation into a lottery ticket. Because the custodian is risk averse, this would be an expensive way to compensate, as the firm would have to pay a substantial risk premium to the custodian.

If stock price is a ridiculous measure for the custodian, what metric might we choose instead? We might measure cleanliness of floors, or pounds of trash hauled away per shift. We think of such measures because they are closer to the custodian's job—they focus more on things that the employee can control, and filter out more things that are uncontrollable. In doing so, we reduce the risk of the performance measure. Similarly, for the CEO we might choose accounting earnings as the measure. It is one of the better proxies for profit that an accounting system generates,[2] so it is a good starting place for trying to quantify the CEO's

---

[1] Notice that the stock market is, in effect, a large scale performance measurement system, for top management. This is one of the most important roles of equity markets (though not the only role), and is the basis for much of the analysis in modern corporate finance.

[2] Of course, it does not measure true economic profit, since accounting numbers are imperfect proxies for economic concepts. There are much more elaborate methods that try to adjust accounting numbers to better reflect economic reality, such as EVA (economic value added).

FIGURE 9.1

TRADEOFF BETWEEN BROAD OR NARROW PERFORMANCE MEASUREMENT

Narrow (fewer factors)	Broad (more factors)
←	→
High distortion Low risk	Low distortion High risk

contribution. Moreover, it is much less risky, since it is relatively more affected by things the CEO can control than by uncontrollables.

Unfortunately, more focused measures cause a new problem—they *distort* incentives. In the case of the custodian, measuring cleanliness of floors does not motivate the custodian to be cost conscious. Measuring pounds of trash hauled away may motivate the custodian to throw away too many things, or only heavy items. Evaluating the CEO on accounting earnings is likely to cause the CEO to take too much of a short-term focus, as earnings are based on performance in only a single period. Virtually any performance measure will have some distortion. Sometimes the distortions can be subtle, so it is worth thinking carefully about them before putting too much weight on a measure for incentives.

These examples highlight a common tradeoff that firms usually face in choosing most quantitative performance measures: the *scope* of the measure (Figure 9.1). A *broader* measure is one that includes more aspects of performance. In a publicly traded firm, stock price is the broadest possible measure, since it is firm value. The advantage of broad measures is that they tend to distort incentives less. They distort less because broader measures include more dimensions of the employee's job in the evaluation (more controllables). However, at the same time they also tend to include more uncontrollables, which causes measurement error and makes the incentive scheme riskier.

A natural way to reduce risk is to use a *narrower* performance measure, such as accounting earnings instead of stock price. Narrower measures may be chosen because they are easier to measure. Another important reason that narrower measures are often chosen is because they filter out many of the uncontrollables, reducing employee risk. But it is virtually impossible to filter out all that is uncontrollable without simultaneously filtering out some things that are controllable by the employee. Thus, narrower measures tend to be less risky, but distort incentives more.

Common Distortions in Performance Measures

Since there are several dimensions to most jobs, and to what affects overall firm value, this tradeoff between risk and distortion can play out in multiple ways.

TABLE 9.1
DIMENSIONS ALONG WHICH PERFORMANCE MEASURES MAY BE BROADER
OR NARROWER

Dimensions of Performance to Consider in an Evaluation	Example
Which tasks to include or exclude?	Quantity vs. quality
Use available metrics or incorporate qualitative information?	Accounting numbers tend to ignore intangibles or opportunity costs
How large a unit should be measured?	Individual vs. team vs. unit vs. division vs. firmwide performance measures
What time horizon should be used?	Last year's sales vs. customer retention/growth

Table 9.1 provides examples of performance dimensions and the kinds of distortions that tend to result from using a metric that is narrower on each dimension.

The classic cause of distorted incentives is a performance measure that proxies for some tasks in the job, but not others, such as measuring quantity but ignoring quality. However, there are several other common causes of distorted performance measures. Each is due to using a measure that is relatively narrow along some dimension: tangibles vs. intangibles; group size; or time horizon.

Intangibles.   By definition, intangibles are difficult to quantify. Quality is a classic example, since any incentive based on a quantity measure (like *piece rates* in manufacturing jobs) distorts incentives away from quality. But there are many dimensions of jobs that are difficult to quantify. In service jobs, customer satisfaction usually can only be gauged imperfectly through methods like customer surveys. Similarly, professional service firms can easily calculate revenues and profits from specific client engagements, but cannot always tell how well satisfied the client is.

Opportunity costs.   An important problem with standard accounting numbers is that they do not reflect *opportunity costs*—the costs of foregoing other alternatives. For example, if a company owns a factory, and it has been fully depreciated for accounting purposes, it may show up on accounting statements as having no value. Or, it may be listed at book value, which is a measure of the costs of constructing the building at the time. The true value of the building is how much the company could sell the building for to someone else. If the company decides to use the building, they are giving up this value. Thus, decisions about asset use can be severely distorted unless some adjustment to accounting numbers is made.

A similar issue arises when a company requires departments to obtain services only from an internal department. Since the department is granted a monopoly, it can be difficult to estimate the true performance of the department. If the firm allows purchasing from outside vendors, it not only provides some competition (which should motivate better performance by the internal supplier) but also provides an important performance metric—the market price of the service.

Group size. Firms always face a choice over the group size to use for the evaluation. Since employees are interdependent in production, a narrow measure like individual performance will tend to distort incentives. There will be less incentive to cooperate with colleagues. Unfortunately, using a broad measure like group or business unit performance makes the measure much less controllable, and much more risky. For example, basing an individual's incentives on group performance means that the employee is accountable for actions taken by colleagues, which are not fully controllable. (However, they are partly controllable, as discussed later.) The broader the group used for performance measurement the more the employee takes into account how his or her work affects others in the firm, but the riskier the measure. We discuss this further under the topic of *employee profit sharing plans.*

Time horizon. Most performance measures are backward looking: They measure what just happened. This tends to mean that they distort incentives for actions that have long term consequences. Generally these are various forms of investments, e.g., in new technology, brand name, or employee training. One approach that is sometimes used is to defer giving the reward for some period of time. This allows the firm to wait and see what long term performance is. A clear problem with this approach is that this is risky in a different way for the employee, who may quit the firm before the reward can be given.

Match of the Performance Measure to Job Design

Since the purpose of the performance measure is to estimate the employee's contributions to the firm's objectives, it is important to match the measure to the job design. We have already seen this issue. When the employee has more specific knowledge of time and place, the firm should try to find a measure that motivates the employee to exploit this controllable risk profitably. Similarly, the measure's scope should match the extent to which the employee's job is narrow or broad—in terms of two job design components that we emphasized in Part Two of the text: decentralization and multitasking.

Consider possible performance measures for a divisional manager.[3] Typical measures that firms use are to define the division as a *cost center*, *revenue center*, or *profit center*. The first two measures, cost and revenue, are relatively narrow. The next, profit, is broader—it combines the first two measures. For this reason, it reflects all of the controllables reflected in revenue and costs separately. It also reflects all of the uncontrollables from both.

Sometimes firms broaden the performance measure further, defining a division as an *investment center*. These use a broader concept of accounting profit (such as EVA) that attempts to include measures of the opportunity cost of assets (which may be ignored in standard accounting numbers). In addition, while profit measures

---

[3] Based on Jensen & Meckling (1998).

short-term contributions to firm value, an investment center uses a performance measure that attempts to calculate some version of discounted present value of profits.

Sometimes firms go even further, setting up a division as a nearly independent business. A franchise is an example of this approach. A franchise uses an even broader performance measure, since the franchisee's primary objective is to maximize the resale value of the franchise. This comes close to the ultimate broad performance measure, ownership, with performance measure equal to firm value.

The constraints imposed and decisions allowed to be made by a divisional manager vary with the scope of the performance measure. For example, cost center managers typically are allowed to make decisions about inputs used, sourcing, production methods, and personnel. Revenue center managers typically are allowed to make decisions about selling techniques and sales personnel. Most other decisions are centralized at a level above these managers. Profit center managers are generally allowed to make both sets of decisions that cost and revenue center managers are allowed to make. In addition, they are often given decision rights over product specification, pricing, and product quality.

Investment center managers usually have all of the decision rights of profit center managers, and fewer constraints. They are typically allowed to make more decisions about major asset purchases and long term investments in physical capital. This reflects the fact that their performance measure has been broadened to capture the financial return on investments.

Franchise managers usually have even more decision rights and fewer constraints than investment center managers. For one, they have the right to sell the franchise (possibly to another franchisee; at least back to the franchisor). And, of course, an owner of a business has no constraints (other than legal ones) and the ability to make all decisions about how to run the business.

The important point to note is how the constraints and decision rights change, when moving from narrower to broader measures. As the performance measure becomes broader, there are fewer constraints and more is decentralized to the division. Simply put, a narrower job design (in the sense of both tasks and decision rights) is associated with a narrower performance measure and vice versa.

This makes perfect sense. If an employee is given more tasks or authority, a narrow performance measure will cause greater distortions. Thus, the balance between distortions and risk will be struck by using a broader measure that incorporates some of the additional dimensions of the job, even though this may mean that the measure is riskier.

The same principle applies to the concept of a specialized or multitask job. All else equal, the more tasks that an employee is assigned, the broader the performance measure should be. This is to ensure that the tasks for which the employee is responsible are reflected in the evaluation.

Indeed, the matching of evaluation and job design will tend to happen automatically. Suppose that an employee is evaluated on a very broad performance measure, but given little discretion. This tends to mean that there are many uncontrollables in the performance measure. In order to reduce risk, the employee will request, or simply start taking on, additional responsibilities, in order to avoid being punished for things outside of the employee's control.

Finally, an employee's job tends to evolve over time (typically, toward a broader job with more discretion, as the employee's skills increase). For this reason, usually the evaluation should broaden with job tenure, often by gradually holding the employee accountable for more and more factors through subjective evaluations.

Manipulation

A final problem with quantitative performance measures is that they may be manipulated or gamed. Again consider our example of the custodian evaluated on pounds of trash hauled away. This might motivate the custodian to bring trash to work, because this would improve the performance measure—but it would not benefit firm value.

Of course, either side might manipulate the measure. Imagine a joint venture between two firms, in which one is to provide a service to the other, and is to be compensated with a share of the profits from the venture. In such a case, the second firm may be tempted to allocate too many of its costs to the joint venture, resulting in understated profits. In fact, this situation occurred with the movie *Forrest Gump*. Writer Howard Groom sued the studio when the wildly successful movie was said by the studio to be a money loser. Groom had been promised a share of the profits. If the contract had been based on revenue, this conflict would have been less likely, since costs are easier to manipulate than revenue in this case.

Manipulation is similar to the problem of distortion in incentives, but is somewhat different. The problem of distortion is that different aspects of the job are given inappropriate relative weights (possibly zero) in the incentive plan, causing the employee to emphasize some things too much, and others too little. Manipulation occurs because the employee or employer has specific knowledge of time and place. This knowledge may be used strategically, after the performance metric is chosen, to improve the evaluation even when such actions do not improve firm value. Distortion arises from unbalanced incentives across multiple tasks, set at the time the incentive plan is designed. Manipulation arises from the employee's strategic use of asymmetric information—specific knowledge while doing the job—after the plan is designed.

The concept of manipulation is related to our notion of performance measure scope described earlier. As with distortions, manipulation is more likely to occur with a narrower performance measure. Because a narrower measure reflects fewer parts of the employee's job, altering behavior along only one dimension of work may have a large effect on measured performance. By contrast, broader measures tend to be less susceptible to manipulation because the employee would have to change more dimensions of performance to manipulate the measure.

An implication of manipulation is that the quality of a performance metric may *degrade* over time once it is used for incentive purposes. Consider a measure that previously had not been used for calculating an employee's bonus. The firm believes that the measure is correlated usefully with firm value, so it decides to give the employee a bonus based on the measure. The employee now has an incentive to increase the measure's value, possibly in part through manipulative behavior. If there is manipulation, this will tend to reduce the measure's correlation with firm value—making it a less useful performance measure! The longer the employee has had a bonus based on the measure, and the greater the incentive placed on the measure, the more likely this phenomenon is to be a problem. Thus, the firm may find that ultimately it has to choose a different performance measure, which itself may gradually degrade, and so on.

SUBJECTIVE EVALUATION

We have discussed quantitative performance measures and their limitations. We now consider the benefits and limitations of subjective performance evaluation.

Perhaps the most painful job for a manager is giving subjective performance evaluations. In many jobs, employees receive a subjective rating once or twice a year (often on a scale of 1–5 or *A–E*). Figure 9.2 shows the actual distribution of such ratings given to employees in Acme (1 is the best rating, 5 the worst). The distribution is quite typical of what is seen in most firms, and exhibits several traits that often raise concerns. There is grade inflation: The average rating is well above the middle score. Similarly, managers are very reluctant to give the lowest ratings: Only about 1% of employees received either of the worst two ratings. There is little feedback in the ratings: Almost 30% receive the best rating, while another 50% receive the second best. If the goal of ratings is to distinguish performance, and to highlight the best and worst performers, these kinds of rating distributions do not seem very effective.

When asked why they are reluctant to give negative feedback or poor performance appraisals, managers often say that they are worried that this would reduce employee motivation. This seems hard to understand, since a good incentive system should provide both positive and negative feedback. We will provide one explanation for this phenomenon in Chapter 11 when we discuss promotion-based incentives.

Managers are reluctant to give poor ratings partly because it is no fun to give someone bad news. Thus, there may be *leniency bias*, helping explain why so few poor ratings are given. Moreover, employees may pressure managers to change the rating, which is unpleasant for the manager.

Of course, employees dislike subjective evaluations too. A chief concern is that they are more subjective than numeric evaluations. They may worry that the evaluation reflects the supervisor's personal opinions and biases, and that the supervisor is playing favorites. Of course, this will reduce incentives, since the perceived link between effort and reward is weakened. It also subjects the employee to a form of risk.

Despite all of these flaws, essentially every job uses subjective evaluations in important ways. Subjectivity is often necessary in hiring, promotion, and termination decisions. For middle managers doing qualitative knowledge work, good

FIGURE 9.2

PERFORMANCE RATING DISTRIBUTION AT ACME

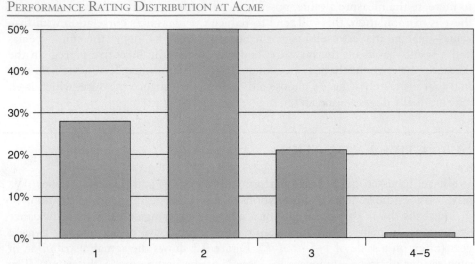

Source: Gibbs (1995)

quantitative measures of performance may not exist, so that raises and bonuses are usually based on subjective appraisals. Subjectivity may play an important role even for salespeople, where performance is often easiest to quantify. For example, sales prospects or training opportunities may be allocated subjectively. Finally, one of the most important roles for a Board of Directors is subjective evaluation of the CEO's performance.

Why Use Subjective Evaluations?

Consider a manager who runs a factory. The manager's annual bonus, which averages about 40% of salary, is calculated as a percentage of the factory's annual profits (that is, the plant is a profit center). The factory is 40 years old, with a sheet metal roof. One day, a tornado rushes through town, and tears the roof off. Because of the substantial damage, the factory cannot return to operation for quite some time, and there is a loss rather than a profit for the year. If you were the plant manager's boss, when you arrived at the plant the day after the tornado, how would you evaluate her performance?

One common reaction to this story is that a tornado is uncontrollable, as it is an act of nature, and thus the manager should not be punished at all. However, another common reaction is that the manager should be severely punished, if not fired, because she has ultimate responsibility for the plant. Which view is right? Without more information, it is difficult to say. Either view could be justified under some circumstances.

For example, if this was the first tornado in the area in 50 years, or if the manager was very new to the plant, it may make sense to not punish the manager. On the other hand, tornados might occur often in the region, and the manager may have worked at the plant for many years. Perhaps the roof was in need of repair, but the manager had deferred maintenance. In such cases, she is at least partly responsible for the effects of the tornado on firm value.

There are also intermediate cases. Suppose, for example, that on the organization chart responsibility for roof maintenance was given to a plant engineer, who oversaw the structures of all factories for the company. This suggests that we should not hold the plant manager responsible. However, it might be that the plant manager had some information about the condition of the roof, and neglected to tell the plant engineer. If so, the plant manager should clearly be punished.

Finally, even if the manager had no way to foresee this event, we may still need to punish her for not reacting properly. We want to motivate the manager to address immediate safety issues, obtain second-sourcing for production, and get the plant up and running again as soon as possible. This discussion illustrates a couple of points.

What Do "Controllable" and "Uncontrollable" Mean?

In this example, there are many cases in which we might punish the manager for an act of nature, because the manager could have taken actions before, during, or after the event to reduce the damage to the firm. Whether an event is random or not is not a useful definition of what is controllable or uncontrollable. Our discussion now provides us with a rigorous way to distinguish between the two types of risk:

> An event is at least partially controllable if the employee can have some effect on the impact of the event on firm value. In the case of adverse events, the employee can prevent or mitigate some of the damage. In the case of positive events, the employee can prepare for or exploit the opportunity.

Given this definition, very few events are completely uncontrollable by an employee. There may be many circumstances in which we want to punish—or reward—an employee for things that were not the employee's "fault."

When Should an Employee Be Held Responsible?

Even if the manager did not have formal responsibility for roof maintenance, the manager may have had some specific knowledge about the roof's condition. As we saw when we discussed decentralization, when an employee has specific knowledge, we may want to give her some decision rights (responsibility) and incentives to act upon that knowledge. Thus, much of what we are doing with a careful subjective performance evaluation is defining what the employee is, and is not, responsible for. We should consider holding the employee at least partially responsible for events any time that they are partially controllable by the employee, because the employee has some relevant specific knowledge of the situation. As we've seen, the employee might have this information before, during, or after an event. If so, the employee should be given some responsibility for foreseeing events and making contingency planning; for reacting to events in real time; and for following up events after the fact. This is what we mean when we say that we want to motivate the employee to take initiative.

How Do You Conduct a Subjective Evaluation?

This discussion also gives us a useful way to think about *how* to evaluate employees. Suppose that you are evaluating a subordinate in order to give a year-end performance rating. As in the example above, it is natural to begin by thinking *retrospectively*: looking back on what the employee did and what happened over the last year.

When you do so, it is important to avoid what psychologists call *hindsight bias*. You are likely to know more after events have unfolded than the employee did when they occurred. In our example, we now know that the tornado occurred and the roof was weak. However, did the employee know these things at the time? Thus, a typical first step is to figure out, along the lines of the famous question by U.S. Senator Howard Baker about President Richard Nixon during the Watergate hearings, "What did he know, and when did he know it?" You do this to decide whether the employee's actions were appropriate given the circumstances.

This will tend to lead into a broader analysis of the extent to which events were *foreseeable*. It is important to evaluate employees on whether they planned for foreseeable events—and also, to a reasonable extent, whether they developed contingency plans and procedures for unforeseeable events.

So far, the evaluation has focused on the past, and what that means for the employee's rewards (rating, bonus, raise, promotion, firing, etc.). However, the most important outcome of a good subjective evaluation comes from thinking *prospectively*. The process of discussing with the employee what happened, what they did and why they did it, and what they should have done instead is a way of communicating what the employee's responsibilities are *in the future*. The evaluation in effect defines the job, and sets precedents about what will be rewarded and punished in the future. In complex work environments, it is usually difficult if not impossible to completely define an employee's responsibilities in writing. Discussions about subjective evaluations are an important time to clarify them. The benefits include better decision making, and better alignment of the employee's incentives with firm objectives.

Finally, a good evaluation will move from the "here's your performance rating" stage to a constructive discussion of the future. The manager should clarify what the employee is expected to focus on, what he is supposed to be responsible for (and not). It is an excellent chance to think about any skills the employee lacks but needs to perform the job well, thus leading to new training. Similarly, the debriefing about last year's performance may suggest additional information or resources that the employee might need in order to perform the job effectively.

How Do You Receive a Subjective Evaluation?

It is also useful to briefly think about how you can best *receive* an evaluation from your supervisor. Bosses hate to hear the phrase, "It's not my fault." That is tantamount to saying, "The event was uncontrollable" (though using less academic jargon), and as we saw above few events are completely uncontrollable. Instead, your boss is looking for you to take initiative. Consider discussing your mistakes and setbacks. Admit them, and describe to your boss what you have learned from them and how you will change your future work as a result.

Next, try to use an evaluation as an opportunity to improve your job. Ask your manager for advice and suggestions about how to perform better. Request new training, information, or resources that will improve your performance. The evaluation can be an excellent opportunity if you take the initiative.

The Benefits of Subjective Evaluations

The plant manager's quantitative performance measure, profit, fell to zero (or negative) in the tornado example. As a result the manager's bonus vanished. It is possible that this outcome is exactly the one that we would arrive at after a considered judgment of all relevant factors, but only by an astonishing coincidence. In other words, holding the manager rigidly to the quantitative bonus plan would almost certainly result in the wrong outcome: Either the performance metric is wrong, or the weight given to it for calculating compensation is wrong, or both. The only way to fix this is to introduce discretion into the incentive system in some way.

We now return to our question above about why subjective evaluations are so important, despite the many difficulties that they cause. The discussion of the tornado example suggests that if done well, a subjective evaluation can have many benefits.

Improve on quantitative performance measures. Subjective evaluations may be used to avoid the typical flaws in quantitative measures. Not only does a careful subjective evaluation result in the manager being held accountable for controllables, properly defined. It also can filter out uncontrollables, lowering the risk to the manager. In the tornado example, good judgment can remove from the plant manager's evaluation the effects of things that were truly unforeseeable and not the manager's appropriate responsibility. In this sense, performance measure error may be lower than by sticking with quantitative metrics.

Similarly, subjective evaluations can reduce distortions in incentives. Some dimensions of the job are hard to quantify. Giving those dimensions adequate emphasis during performance appraisals can motivate such tasks. A classic example is where jobs involve quality, creativity, or other intangibles. These are usually difficult to put into numbers, so in order to motivate them, such tasks generally must be evaluated and rewarded using judgment.

Finally, subjectivity may be able to reduce manipulation of the incentive system. If an employee games the quantitative metrics, the manager may detect this ex post (or at least have strong suspicions of such behavior). Subjectivity allows the manager to adjust for this. To the extent that this might be anticipated, the employee will be deterred from too aggressively manipulating the numbers.

Improve incentives for risk taking.   As just noted, a good subjective appraisal can reduce risk by filtering out true uncontrollables from the employee's overall evaluation. It can also improve incentives for risk taking, since it makes it easier for the manager to reward good results without simultaneously punishing mistakes. In effect, it gives the manager greater flexibility to reward the up side without punishing the down side.

Improve decision making.   As we saw, it often makes sense to at least partially reward or punish employees for random events. This is important because it motivates the employee to use (and even to develop) specific knowledge of time and place. There are three ways that this motivates better employee decision making: more effective preparation, real time response, and ex post reaction after the event is over.

Give the incentive system more flexibility.   Incentive plans that are put in place at the beginning of the year may no longer be ideal if circumstances change. When this occurs, the firm can change the incentive plan. However, when it does so it runs the risk of this being perceived as unfair (like the *ratchet effect* we discuss in the next chapter). Effective use of subjectivity means that changes to incentives are more likely to be accepted, since the employee already expects judgment from the supervisor. This makes it easier for the manager to tell the employee to change emphasis during the middle of the year, in effect changing incentives.

Expand communication.   If you go back and reread the discussion about how to give a subjective evaluation, you will realize that what it describes is simply good day-to-day management. The best subjective evaluations occur implicitly every day, as the manager works with the employee. The manager monitors what the employee does and why, makes adjustments, and suggests improvements. Instead of waiting until the end of the year to do the evaluation, having these conversations all year long will improve the employee's effectiveness, and the working relationship with the supervisor. It will also clarify the terms of the implicit contract. Moreover, clear communication makes it more likely that employees will trust subjective evaluations, making them more effective.

Improve training.   A manager can use a thoughtful subjective evaluation to provide lessons for the employee from the manager's experience. If done well and regularly, it can be an excellent form of day-to-day training.

It is clear that there are many benefits to subjective evaluations if they are done properly. These are many of the benefits to effective day-to-day management as well. Given these benefits, it is not surprising that subjectivity is so important in practice, despite the many difficulties that it raises, and costs that it implies.

SWEATING THE DETAILS ON EVALUATIONS

◆ ◆ ◆ ◆ ◆ ◆ ◆ ◆ ◆ ◆

Lincoln Electric Co. in Cleveland, Ohio has perhaps the most famous incentive schemes in business history. One important component is an annual profit sharing bonus paid out to all employees. While profit sharing schemes usually do not motivate well, Lincoln Electric's does, for two reasons. First, the stakes are very high—the bonus can double an employee's pay in a typical year, reducing the free rider problem. Second, the bonus is based on a measure of *individual* performance, rather than the more typical (and essentially uncontrollable) firm-wide measures that most profit sharing plans use.

The performance measure for this plan is a subjective performance rating. Lincoln views its incentive system as the key to its success, and the subjective rating as one of the crucial components. Every rating is checked by one of the firm's top executives, so managers take them very seriously. The ratings are given twice per year, and according to the company a typical manager spends about 3 weeks doing ratings for subordinates—that is, 6 weeks per year. Doing effective subjective evaluations is hard work, but can have enormous benefits. Arguably it is one of the most important tasks for a manager.

Source: Plant visit and conversations with firm managers

Practical Considerations

Who Should Evaluate Whom?

There are many risks to the firm from decentralizing evaluations to an employee's manager, because the manager's incentives will be imperfect. These include reduced employee motivation, poor promotion decisions, and distorted decision making. In addition, a firm can open itself up to legal liability, since subjectivity makes favoritism and discrimination more likely. Despite these problems, evaluations are not centralized to control the risks. The reason is simple: Evaluations are an example of subjective, experiential knowledge that is very costly to communicate to others. In order to make use of this knowledge, most evaluations—especially in complex work environments where good numeric performance metrics are unavailable—are inevitably decentralized to the direct supervisor.

Some firms make use of *360-degree evaluations*. This practice involves the subordinates in evaluating and giving feedback to the *supervisor*. What is the purpose of this practice? In theory, it can improve management, since the recipients of the manager's treatment are giving feedback. However, there are clear problems, since the subordinates face a good possibility of retribution if they criticize their boss.

For this reason, 360-degree evaluations are often done in secret; the names of employees who make specific comments are not told to the supervisor. While this can help, in small work groups the supervisor can often guess who gave which particular feedback. Thus, the effectiveness of 360-degree evaluations can be limited. Even so, many firms do use them as one tool to improve supervision, communication, and the general work environment. They are more likely to be effective in organizations that have cultural norms and job designs that emphasize open communication and employee participation in decision making (what we called decision management).

Fairness, Bias, and Influence Costs

Subjectivity makes it easier for a manager to discriminate, play favorites, and generally be biased in allocating rewards. Of course, this reduces incentives, since it means that factors other than performance affect rewards, and can impart a subtle form of risk into the evaluation. Another way to put this is that there is an additional layer of incentive problem when subjectivity is involved: The firm has to worry about the incentives for the manager to implement the system in accord with the firm's interests instead of his own.

This suggests immediately that if the supervisor's incentives are well designed, we should expect fewer problems at lower levels. In addition, constraints might be placed on the evaluator. For example, some firms impose various types of *forced curves* on evaluators. We will discuss these systems under the topic of relative performance evaluation in Chapter 11.

An obvious point is that the greater the trust that the employee has of the evaluator, the more effective the subjectivity as part of the incentive system. Thus trust considerations play a key role.

The manager's reputation can have a substantial impact on how incentives play out in practice. A manager who is capricious or biased will induce certain behavior, and certain types of employees who want to work for him. If a manager has a reputation for fairness and careful evaluation, subjectivity will be easier to use effectively, improving the reward system in the ways described above. Thus, in jobs where such judgment is important, a manager can try to invest in a strong reputation as an effective manager. Similarly, the firm should attempt to put judicious managers into positions where these considerations play a major role.

In addition, organizations usually put in place formal policies to try to establish a greater degree of fairness in the evaluation system. For example, employees usually have the right to ask to be re-evaluated if they disagree with their evaluation. In some firms, the supervisor's boss checks evaluations. The purpose of such oversight is to provide some incentives for the supervisor to do appraisals fairly. In some cases, it is possible to have multiple evaluators of an employee; this will usually reduce the likelihood that the ultimate evaluation is biased, since different managers tend to have different biases.

Of course, how such policies are implemented in practice determines whether they are effective or just window dressing, so there is an important element of corporate culture here as well.

Supervisor judgment can also distort employee incentives. Employees will have some incentive to try to improve their evaluation not through effort, but through influencing the supervisor in other ways. For example, they might spend time and resources trying to lobby their boss for a larger raise, more resources, and so on. They might flatter their boss, take up similar outside interests, and so on. To the extent that such activities are engaged in instead of productive effort, and to the extent that they change the evaluation, they impose *influence costs* on the organization. What are the costs? Reduced or distorted incentives, and promotions that are based less on ability than is desirable.

A more subtle cost of bias and influence activities is that it may distort decision making. When a manager's opinion affects a worker's reward, the worker may distort what he says to the manager. Thus, the *quality of information* on the job may suffer. In principle, a good manager will want to hear the truth from subordinates, and will attempt to establish a corporate culture in which this occurs. For example, the manager might establish cultural rules that encourage employees to speak freely, and perhaps even reward subordinates for criticizing the manager's analyses.

While this can help, it is unlikely to completely alleviate the problem. Suppose that a manager is presented with an opinion from a subordinate that differs from his own. Either the new opinion is correct, or the manager is correct (or neither). As a statistical matter, the manager should place some weight on each possibility. But workers realize this. Because there is some chance that a worker's dissenting opinion will be viewed as a mistake, even if correct, workers have some incentive to shade their reports in the direction of the manager's initial opinion. This creates a *yes men* phenomenon. This highlights the importance, and complexity, of proper analysis and decision-making procedures. Such procedures need to take into account (and be codesigned with, to the extent possible) the corporate culture and explicit incentives of analysts and decision makers.

Different Roles of Evaluation

As noted in the introduction to this chapter, employee performance depends on ability, accumulated human capital, and efforts. Thus an evaluation can be used to measure any of these three. In practice it can be very difficult to disentangle the effects of these three factors. Suppose that an employee is performing very well. Is this because of raw talent for this type of work? Because of skills and experience? Because of hard work? Different purposes of performance evaluations imply different weights on evaluating innate ability, human capital, and efforts.

One purpose of a performance evaluation is to decide who to hire, or which probationary worker to keep. For such decisions, it makes sense to try to measure the employee's innate abilities A, rather than H or e_i. If further skills and effort are needed, the employee can then be trained and motivated in the job they are assigned to. Similarly, evaluating an employee's innate skills is more important when promotions or changes in job assignments are being considered. Of course, accumulated skills H will also be relevant for such decisions.

Poor evaluations are more likely to be taken seriously for sorting in earlier periods. This is because there is little information at first, so each evaluation is more informative. As more data accumulates about the worker, new evaluations are less informative.[4] By the same token, however, probationary evaluations should last longer when the value of small differences in ability is more important to the job, and when the job is more complex and difficult to evaluate. Thus, probation for secretarial jobs may be very short, but for professional jobs may be very long indeed. In professional service firms and universities, the first up or out promotion may only come after several years of work, and partnership and tenure decisions can take 6 years or more.

A second purpose of evaluations is to measure the extent to which the employee improves human capital. Especially early in the career, supervisors often provide extensive training to subordinates. In such cases, they may emphasize changes in human capital (the rate of growth in H) in performance evaluations.

A third purpose of evaluations is to motivate employees to work harder. When this is the case, the evaluator will want to try to measure how much effort of various types the employee put forth on the job, not how much talent the employee has.

In some cases, different goals of evaluations can conflict. For example, feedback about current performance may give the employee clues about their long term prospects for advancement, which may actually reduce motivation (see Chapter 11). To avoid this, many firms attempt to separate out evaluations for current rewards from those for coaching and development, for example by giving two different types of evaluations at 6 month intervals. However, in practice it is always difficult to separate the two.

How Frequently Should Evaluations be Made?

An additional purpose of an evaluation is to measure the employee's value to the firm in order to decide the amount that the firm is willing to pay as compensation. This is useful for deciding whether to match outside offers, for example. Suppose that a worker is worth $1,000 per week to the firm, but is only paid $800. He is worth $900 at another firm, which offers $875. If the current firm offers him $900, both the firm and the employee are better off than if he quit. The general rule is that the firm should offer enough to encourage the worker to stay, if the worker's productivity is highest at the current firm.

Which workers are more likely to have productivity at the current firm that exceeds their values elsewhere? Those with more firm specific human capital. For this reason, evaluations are less likely to produce information that will result in a separation when the worker has more firm specific human capital. This implies that costly evaluations should occur less frequently when firm specific human capital is more important.

The frequency of the evaluation should also decline with the worker's experience in both the firm and in the current job, for two reasons. One is the effect of sorting. The longer that a worker has been with a firm (and similarly in a specific position), the better informed are both the worker and the firm about whether the

---

[4]Statistically, the firm updates its priors with each new observation about performance, but gives increasing weight to prior performance as data accumulates.

worker is a good match for the job. Thus, the less likely is an evaluation to lead to a change in position. The second effect is that the feedback and training aspect of an evaluation becomes less important, the longer the worker has been with the firm and in the current job.

SUMMARY

Performance evaluation is the most difficult, and probably the most important, part of a well designed incentive plan. Quantitative performance measures such as accounting numbers are an important component of evaluations. An equally important component is subjective evaluations.

An ideal performance evaluation for incentive purposes is one that captures all of the effects of an employee's actions on firm value, but nothing else. These are often called controllables and uncontrollables, but the concepts are rarely defined carefully. A good way to think rigorously about the terms is to say that something is at least partially controllable if the employee can affect the event's impact on firm value. Thus, even purely random events are often controllable to some extent; most events are partly controllable and partly uncontrollable.

This distinction is one of the first things that should be considered in choosing a performance measure, because the implications for incentive plan design are very different to the extent the risk in the measure is uncontrollable or controllable. If the risk is uncontrollable, the measure imposes risk on the employee. Then the firm should weaken incentives, pay a risk premium, or choose a more narrow performance measure or subjective evaluation. By contrast, if the risk is largely controllable, the firm should do the opposite: It should decentralize to the employee, and provide strong incentives for the employee to make use of this specific knowledge to improve value. This latter case is an excellent example of bringing market-based approaches inside the firm to improve organizational design.

A basic tradeoff that is often faced with quantitative performance measures is the *scope* of the measure. Broader, more inclusive measures tend to include more that is controllable, and more that is uncontrollable; narrower, more focused measures tend to have the opposite properties. The first effect means that broader measures usually distort incentives less because they ignore less. However, it also means that broader measures are riskier, as they have more measurement error. Risk is costly to an incentive scheme, because employees are risk averse.

Because of the riskiness of very broad measures like stock price, most performance measures used in practice are much narrower. Performance measure choice involves a careful balancing of risk against distortion. This virtually guarantees that any measure will distort incentives in some way. Thus, an important consideration in managing an incentive system is to watch carefully for distortions (and the related problem of manipulation of measures), and use additional incentives or discretion to reduce such problems.

Performance measures and subjective evaluations should be chosen to match the employee's job design as closely as possible. This makes it more likely that the measure captures the most important controllable dimensions of the job, reducing the distortion problem. Subjective evaluations can be viewed as a way to *define* the employee's job and responsibilities.

Subjective evaluations are an alternative way to evaluate performance. Since they require judgment, they can cause a host of problems if the manager does not take them seriously, or if the manager does not have adequate motivation. For example, discretion makes it easier to play favorites, and for biases to creep into evaluations. Discretion also requires that managers make tough decisions about good and poor performers, and give constructive feedback, even in the face of complaints and lobbying from subordinates. If done effectively, however, subjectivity is an effective way to improve virtually all parts of an incentive system.

⬗⬗⬗⬗⬗ STUDY QUESTIONS

1. In macroeconomics, there is a debate over the use of rules versus discretion. The debate involves the extent to which monetary policy should be governed by the discretion of the head of the central bank (e.g., the Chairman of the Federal Reserve), or by relatively fixed rules that cannot be altered. Using the concepts from this chapter, can you provide an argument for each approach? Can you name other situations in business where there is a similar dilemma?

2. In law firms, litigation work is done mostly by lawyers who work independently, and who become famous for their work. By contrast, corporate law is usually done by teams of lawyers with different specialties, and the law *firm* develops a brand name. What conflicts do you see in having litigators and corporate lawyers in the same firm? Does your analysis suggest anything about the relationship between the quality of a performance evaluation and a firm's organizational structure?

3. Many business experts advocate systems such as *management by objective* (MBO) for managing employee incentives. Under MBO, the supervisor negotiates a set of mutually agreed upon objectives for the employee to work on during the year. At the end of the year, rewards are based on the extent to which the objectives were successfully achieved or not. What costs and benefits do you see in "negotiating" objectives with your subordinate?

4. Still other firms use 360 degree evaluations. Under this system, the firm asks a manager's subordinates, colleagues, and customers for feedback on the manager's performance. What advantages do you see to such a system? Do you see any disadvantages? What other policies might make such an approach less prone to the problems that you see? What kind of culture would be necessary for such appraisals to work?

5. Provide examples of each concept from your own work experience:

   • Controllable and uncontrollable risk
   • Distorted incentives

- Narrow and broad performance measures
- Manipulation of a performance measure

6. What methods have you seen firms use to improve subjective performance appraisals? What practices have undermined their effectiveness?

REFERENCES

Gibbs, Michael (1995). "Incentive Compensation in a Corporate Hierarchy." *Journal of Accounting & Economics/Journal of Labor Economics* joint issue, 19(2–3): 247–277.

Jensen, Michael & William Meckling (1998). "Divisional Performance Measurement." In *Foundations of Organizational Strategy*, Michael Jensen, ed. Boston: Harvard University Press.

FURTHER READING

Baker, George (2002). "Distortion and Risk in Optimal Incentive Contracts." *Journal of Human Resources* 37(4): 696–727.

Courty, Pascal & Gerald Marschke (2008). "A General Test for Distortions in Performance Measures." *Review of Economics & Statistics* 90(3).

Gibbs, Michael, Kenneth Merchant, Wim Van der Stede, & Mark Vargus (2004). "Determinants and Effects of Subjectivity in Incentives." *The Accounting Review* 79(2): 409–436.

Gibbs, Michael, Kenneth Merchant, Wim Van der Stede, & Mark Vargus (2008). "Performance Measure Properties and Incentive Plan Design." Working paper, University of Chicago Graduate School of Business.

Lazear, Edward (1990). "The Timing of Raises and Other Payments." *Carnegie-Rochester Conference Series on Public Policy* 33: 13–48.

Milgrom, Paul (1988). "Employment Contracts, Influence Activities, and Efficient Organizational Design." *Journal of Political Economy* 96: 42–60.

Murphy, Kevin J. (1993). "Performance Measurement and Appraisal: Motivating Managers to Identify and Reward Performance." In *Performance Measurement, Evaluation, and Incentives*, William Bruns, ed. Boston: Harvard Business School Press.

Murphy, Kevin J. & Paul Oyer (2005). "Discretion in Executive Incentive Contracts." Working paper, University of Southern California Marshall School of Business.

Prendergast, Canice (1993). "A Theory of 'Yes Men'." *American Economic Review* 83: 757–770.

Prendergast, Canice (2002). "The Tenuous Tradeoff Between Risk and Incentives." *Journal of Political Economy* 110: 1071–1102.

Prendergast, Canice & Robert Topel (1996). "Favoritism in Organizations." *Journal of Political Economy* 104: 958–978.

10

REWARDING
PERFORMANCE

Without merit there should be no reward.

—Chinese proverb

INTRODUCTION

Now that we have discussed performance evaluation, we consider the next logical question: How should the firm use the evaluation to motivate the employee?

Before we consider that, however, we mentioned earlier that pay for performance helps an organization improve many human resource objectives, not just motivation. This idea is so important that it is worth illustrating before we turn to motivating effort. Therefore, for now assume that there is *no* motivation problem for employees. Is there still any benefit from tying pay to performance?

In fact, we have already seen that there is. In Chapter 2, we analyzed sorting of workers. We argued that some form of probationary or deferred pay, *based on performance*, might improve the firm's ability to recruit a better workforce. The more general idea is easy to illustrate formally. Suppose that the firm bases pay in some abstract way on performance, not necessarily through some kind of deferred pay or probationary period. It should still expect to improve recruiting—and investments in skills.

Assume that potential employees differ in their ability A or accumulated human capital H, and that performance (and the performance measure PM) are a function of both, $PM = PM(A, H)$. If pay is a function of performance, then it is also a function of ability and human capital. Those with higher ability or skills can expect to earn more, while those with less can expect to earn less:

$$\frac{\Delta Pay}{\Delta A} = \frac{\Delta Pay}{\Delta PM} \cdot \frac{\Delta PM}{\Delta A} > 0; \qquad \frac{\Delta Pay}{\Delta H} = \frac{\Delta Pay}{\Delta PM} \cdot \frac{\Delta PM}{\Delta H} > 0.$$

Clearly, those who believe that they will be most productive at the firm are more likely to apply for or stay at a job there. The probation example discussed in

Chapter 2 is a special case of this more abstract idea. Similarly, it is easy to see that employees will have greater motivation to invest in skills, since the return on skills will be higher if their performance is tied more strongly to pay.

PIECE RATE PAY AND SORTING
AT SAFELITE GLASS CORPORATION
● ● ● ● ● ● ● ● ● ●

Safelite Glass Corporation is the world's largest installer of automobile glass (replacement windshields). In 1994, CEO Garen Staglin and President John Barlow changed the compensation scheme for glass installers. Prior to the change, installers were paid an hourly rate. The pay scheme was changed to a piece rate—installers were paid a fixed amount for each windshield that they installed. After the change, output per worker rose by about 36 percent. How much of this was because installers worked harder? Was any of the increase due to better sorting?

These two effects can be estimated in a relatively straightforward manner. The effort effect can be estimated by taking a given worker and calculating the amount by which output rose after the change in the pay scheme. This incentive effect was estimated to be about 20 percent.

The remaining 16 percent increase in productivity was due to sorting. Safelite was able to retain its high quality workers, and recruit other high quality employees, because these employees were paid more (even for the same effort). Indeed, turnover rates fell for the most productive workers, and rose for the least productive.

Source: Lazear (2000)

The importance of incentives cannot be overstated. Modern market-based economies work so effectively because they provide generally good incentives for owners to make use of their assets, run their firms, and innovate. Incentives are at the heart of effective economies, as well as effective organizations.

Of course, the most important reason to tie pay to performance is to increase employee effort, and better align it with firm interests, and that is the focus here. The introduction Part Three argued that we care about how the employee's evaluation varies with effort, and how pay varies with the evaluation. How should the firm vary pay with the performance evaluation? To analyze this, we first consider a very common form of pay for performance: The worker earns a base salary, a, plus a bonus. The bonus is calculated by multiplying a commission rate b times the performance measure. Thus, $Pay = a + b \cdot PM$.

FIGURE **10.1**

INCENTIVE INTENSITY VS. LEVEL OF OVERALL PAY

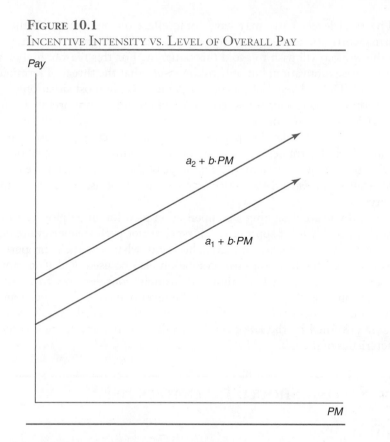

Consider Figure 10.1. It shows two pay plans that have the same commission rate b, but different base salaries a. Which provides stronger incentives? The answer may not be obvious to you at first glance—to a first approximation, both pay plans should provide similar incentives and performance, even though one pays a higher base salary. To see this, consider the question in a different way. If the employee works a little harder, increasing the performance measure a little (say, installing one more windshield for Safelite Auto Glass), what is the reward? It is the same for both plans: The worker gets $\$b$ of additional bonus for each extra unit produced. In other words, the most important issue is *how pay varies with performance*, not the total level of pay.

This point is subject to a qualification. The worker's marginal disutility of effort may increase with wealth (income effects). If so, the utility value of a larger bonus is lower in the second plan in Figure 10.1, and that plan will provide less motivation. However, this effect should have little practical effect for incentive plan design. The reason is that when comparing two potential incentive plans for the same employee, differences in the level of base salary are not likely to be large enough for such income effects to have much impact on incentives, especially in comparison to the incentive effects of the slope of the pay–performance relationship.

The total level of pay may have some effect on motivation. If the worker's performance is low enough, he might get fired. The higher the base salary, the more the worker will wish to avoid this outcome. For this reason, higher base pay might increase motivation, but only to the extent that the threat of termination is a serious one. That is likely to be a very weak incentive in most situations.

To think about incentives correctly, it is more important to focus on $\Delta Pay/\Delta PM$, or the slope or "shape" of *Pay* rather than the level. In this example, that is b, rather than a. The level of pay will largely be a function of labor market competition (which determines the price of employee skills), and the level of employee skills that the firm wants to employ. The slope of the pay–performance relationship is often called the *incentive intensity*; our next question is, What determines this intensity?

Thus, if you are designing a compensation plan for an employee, a three-step process is generally most appropriate. First consider performance evaluation issues (Chapter 9). What metrics are available, and what are their properties (risk, distortion, etc.)? Should subjective evaluation also be used, and if so, how? Once the evaluation issues have been thought through, consider how to tie rewards to the evaluation (this chapter). Only after the incentive issues have been analyzed is it time to think about the level of pay. Indeed, the level of overall expected pay is largely governed by the labor market's value for the employee's skills and the characteristics of the job.

● ● ● ● ● How Strong Should Incentives Be?

Intuition

Although performance may depend on multiple types of effort, for now consider the simplest case: The employee provides only a single kind of effort, e, on the job. The task of the incentive system is straightforward in this case: Motivate additional effort, until the point where it is too costly to do so.

Consider a salesperson selling personal computers. Even before any output is produced, the firm must bear a setup (fixed) cost of $1 million. Beyond that, each additional computer costs $9,000 to produce, so this is the marginal cost. Suppose that the company sells these computers for $10,000 each, so that the marginal profit on each computer sale is $1,000. For this reason, the firm makes incremental profit on each additional sale as long as the salesperson's commission for each sale is no more than $1,000.

In additional to the marginal costs of production, the firm must compensate its salesperson. Suppose that it pays a bonus that is calculated as a percent of revenue brought in by the salesperson. Revenue is a logical performance measure to consider for a salesperson, since the employee has little or no control over costs, but does have a great deal of control over revenue; it matches well to the tasks that are usually assigned to a salesperson. The firm may (or may not) pay a base salary to the employee. If it does, this is an additional fixed cost. Since the firm must cover its fixed costs to make a profit, assume that it only pays a commission for sales above some amount, say 10 computers sold per week.

There is an additional cost to the firm from each sale, which we mentioned in the introduction to this section of the text. To increase sales, the employee has to increase effort, incurring some disutility. The employee will require compensation for this disutility, which we will call $C(e)$. For the moment, assume that there is no performance measurement error, so that there is no cost to the employee from bearing risk.

Suppose that the salesperson's disutility of effort $C(e)$ is the amount shown in the second column of Table 10.1 (all numbers are calculated in terms of weekly sales). In other words, the worker requires at least $20 to sell the first computer. Having sold one computer, the worker must be paid at least $60 more ($80 − $20) to be willing to work hard enough to sell another. Similarly, if 22 computers were sold (so that the employee is already working relatively hard), the employee would require an additional $900 to motivate the extra effort to raise sales by one unit. Given these figures, what is the optimal level of output? Try to answer before reading further.

The optimal level of sales is 25. Up to that point, the extra revenue exceeds the firm's production costs, plus the employee's marginal disutility of effort, so profit can be earned (and split in some way between the firm and the employee). The extra cost of going from 25 to 26 units, however, exceeds the marginal costs plus effort disutility. More simply, the disutility of effort is below 1,000 up to unit sales of 25.

TABLE 10.1
DISUTILITY OF EFFORT FOR A SALESPERSON

Required Compensation for Different Levels of Sales		
Computers Sold	Total Disutility of Effort	Marginal Disutility of Effort
1	$20	$20
2	$80	$60
3	$180	$100
4	$320	$140
5	$500	$180
...	...	...
10	$2,000	$380
...	...	...
15	$4,500	$580
...	...	...
20	$8,000	$780
...	...	...
23	$10,058	$900
24	$11,520	$940
25	$12,500	$980
26	$13,520	$1,020
27	$14,580	$1,060

What, then, is the optimal *commission*? Suppose first that the salesperson was paid a commission of 8%, or $800 per computer. The salesperson would provide effort up to sales of 20 computers, but would be unwilling to go beyond that amount. In such a case, profit opportunities are lost, because sales are too low. If the company raised the commission a little, the salesperson would be willing to work a little harder (and be compensated for the extra effort), and profits would increase. In fact, the firm should increase the commission up to about 10%, or $1,000 per computer, since sales up to 25 result in net profit.

It should *not* pay a commission above 10%. This would increase sales, but the extra revenue would not cover the extra marginal costs plus compensation to the employee for the marginal disutility of effort. Thus, the optimal commission rate exactly equals the value of the extra output. This is a general principle: It motivates the employee to just balance the marginal benefits (revenue) against marginal costs (from production and disutility of effort). In other words, the optimal commission rate (what we call the incentive intensity below) is set so that the employee equates total marginal costs, including effort, to total marginal benefits:

$$Optimal\ commission\ rate = b^* = revenue - MC = marginal\ profit\ on\ next\ sale.$$

If the performance measure is revenue and the optimal commission rate is 10%, this is equivalent to using marginal profits from each sale ($10,000 − $9,000 = $1,000) as the performance measure, with a commission rate of 100%. In other words, our optimal commission gives *all* of the incremental profits from computer sales to the employee. In effect, it rescales the performance measure into units of profit. Thus, our optimal scheme is (with Q denoting units sold):

$$Pay = a + b \cdot revenue = a + Q \cdot (profit\ per\ unit\ sold) = a + profit\ from\ employee's\ sales.$$

With this pay plan, what is the firm's profit? It is:

$$Firm's\ profit = profit\ from\ employee's\ sales - Pay = -a.$$

The bonus scheme gives back to the employee as a reward all of the incremental profits created from the employee's efforts. It also pays the employee a base salary. The only way for the firm to make any profit in this scheme is to pay a *negative base salary*. So much for economic theory!

Selling the Job

Economic theory is more useful and realistic than might appear. This example illustrates that to give the employee perfect incentives, the firm must "sell the job" to the employee. In fact, many actual employment arrangements look quite similar to this idea. Consider the following examples.

Taxicab drivers. In many cities, cab drivers rent the car (or the license to operate a cab) from the cab company. They then receive a very large fraction (sometimes

100%) of the revenue that they collect when driving the cab. Usually, they also pay 100% of the incremental costs (gasoline). In effect, they buy or rent the job from the company that owns the asset (the car or license). This scheme gives the driver excellent incentives to maximize the value of the asset while it is being rented.

Securities traders. On stock, bond, options, or futures exchanges, those who trade must own a seat on the exchange. These seats often cost several hundred thousand dollars. Buying the seat gives the owner the right to the job, trading, as well as strong incentives to make effective use of the seat.

Wait staff in restaurants. In some cultures, tipping by customers is an important component of compensation for wait staff. Since tipping is based on the quality of service, it is a form of pay for performance. In the United States, wait staff are often paid below the legally mandated minimum hourly wage (restaurants are a legal exception to the minimum wage). Thus, wait staff "buy" the job—by incurring an opportunity cost since their salary is below what it would be in other jobs. They do so because they expect that they can earn enough by working hard and earning tips.[1]

RESTAURANT WAIT STAFF COMPENSATION WITH A TWIST
❖ ❖ ❖ ❖ ❖ ❖ ❖ ❖ ❖

The Berghoff, a famous restaurant in Chicago (recently closed), added a twist to the standard compensation scheme for wait staff. It "charged" employees for the food and beverages that they sold to customers, and credited them for the revenue (sales plus tips). (Presumably, it did so in such a way that it retained some of the profits.) Why might it have done this?

One explanation is that imposing some costs on the employee reduces the temptation for the employee to cheat the restaurant (for example, bartenders sometimes pour extra drinks for their best customers without charging them, hoping to earn bigger tips). Another explanation is that using profit as the performance measure distorts incentives less than using revenue: The waiter has a better incentive to try to sell high profit margin items (such as wine) than otherwise.

---

[1] This system works well if the restaurant has repeat business. However, if customers do not expect to return to the restaurant, they may be tempted to leave without tipping, without fear of retribution later. Tipping requires a cultural norm to motivate customers to implement the incentive system—a form of implicit contract at the level of the society, in effect. This helps explain why tipping practices vary in difference cultures.

Outsourced sales. Some firms sell their products through their own employees, while others outsource sales. In the insurance industry, for example, both practices are common. If a company outsources sales, in effect it is selling the job. The contractor buys the product, and then gets to keep a large fraction (usually 100%) of the profits from reselling it.

In fact, any time a firm uses a supplier for part of its business, in a sense it is selling a job. One of the primary benefits of outsourcing is that it may be possible to implement stronger incentives. This also gives us a rudimentary theory for when outsourcing is likely to be more effective: The more that a part of the business can be separated from other jobs in the firm, so that the performance evaluation for that job is as perfect as possible, the more likely is it a candidate for outsourcing. Firms do not typically outsource tasks that are highly interdependent with other jobs in the organization. There can be other costs of outsourcing, of course, including the costs of writing and monitoring the implementation of contracts with suppliers. With employees, firms can develop long term, implicit relationships (as discussed both elsewhere in this text), which may not be as easy to do with suppliers.

Middle managers. These examples all involve cases where performance of an individual employee is relatively easy to measure. However, the "selling the job" intuition applies, if more weakly, to virtually any job. Consider an MBA student who is about to graduate, and is choosing between two job offers. The first offers a standard salary and small annual bonus. The second has similar job content, but offers a much lower base salary. However, it also has the possibility of a larger annual bonus if performance is high. If the student accepts the latter job, she will be buying the job, to some extent, since she will incurring the opportunity cost of a lower base salary than she could get elsewhere. However, she will be buying into the opportunity to work hard and earn more through the more generous bonus plan. Note, too, that the greater her ability, the more likely she will accept the latter job with greater pay for performance.

In general, jobs that have stronger pay for performance will tend to have lower base salaries, all else equal. However, it is also the case that jobs with stronger incentive intensities will tend to give higher total pay. This is for three reasons. Can you think of what they are?

The first is that the employee will be motivated to work harder, and will be compensated through the reward scheme for higher effort. The second is that stronger incentives will attract better employees into the job, and the firm will have to pay such employees more because they have higher market values. The third is that stronger incentives imply riskier pay, so that employees will have to be paid a greater risk premium. We consider this next.

This discussion has yielded simple, but important, intuition about pay for performance. The employee has perfect incentives, with interests completely aligned with those of the firm, if the incentive scheme "sells the job" to the employee. When this is done, the employee is in effect turned into an entrepreneur of his or her own. This motivates the employee to balance correctly the marginal costs of extra effort against the marginal benefits. This is why entrepreneurship is so important to a dynamic economy: Entrepreneurs have very strong incentives, which motivate talented individuals to enter such positions, work hard, and apply their creativity to the fullest extent.

Furthermore, this illustrates why many organizations appear bureaucratic and inefficient to some extent. Incentives in most jobs will be imperfect compared to this theoretical ideal. Thus, middle managers may have relatively weak incentives, and even CEOs of large corporations may have weaker incentives than those provided by complete ownership. This does not mean that such incentives are not optimal. Incentive schemes involve tradeoffs, and the incentives and efficiencies that arise from them will be imperfect.

Imperfect Evaluations and Optimal Incentives

Measurement Error

As discussed in the last chapter, it is virtually impossible to develop a performance measure that is error free. If pay is tied to the performance measure, the employee is rewarded and punished for some things that are uncontrollable: Pay is variable. What is the effect of this risk on pay and optimal incentives?

Individuals tend to be risk averse. Therefore, variable pay imposes some psychological cost on them. One very simple way to model this is as was described in the introduction to this Section: The employee is assumed to have a disutility from riskiness of pay, equal to $1/2 \cdot R \cdot \sigma_{Pay}^2$. R is a risk aversion parameter that captures how risk averse the employee is. Employees who are less risk averse will have lower R, and vice versa. Thus, the total cost to the employee is now $C(e) + 1/2 \cdot R \cdot \sigma_{Pay}^2$.

Suppose, for example, that the employee's true contribution to firm value is Q, but that the performance measure captures Q imprecisely, with measurement error ε: $PM = Q + \varepsilon$. ε is a random variable, with standard deviation σ_ε. Thus we have:

$$Pay = a + b \cdot PM = a + b \cdot Q + b \cdot \varepsilon.$$

Standard statistics tells us that $\sigma_{Pay} = b \cdot \sigma_\varepsilon$, and the employee's cost is:

$$C(e) + 1/2 \cdot R \cdot b^2 \cdot \sigma_\varepsilon^2.$$

Thus, to motivate the employee to work harder the firm now has to compensate not only for the extra effort, but also for the extra risk—the firm has to pay the employee a *risk premium*. Not surprisingly, the less accurate the performance measure (the larger σ_ε), the greater the risk premium that must be paid. This is one reason why firms may incur substantial costs to monitor employees, measure their performance carefully, and filter uncontrollables out of the evaluation. The costs of doing so are offset, at least partially, by lower compensation costs, since they increase accuracy of the performance measure (they are also offset by lowering of distortions in the performance measure).

The other interesting feature of the last equation is that the second part, the risk premium, is increasing in b. The stronger the incentive intensity, the riskier the incentive plan to the employee (all else equal). This should make intuitive sense. Tying pay to performance more strongly means that the effects of measurement error will be magnified: good luck will be rewarded even more, and bad luck will be punished even more.

We have a tradeoff to consider. Stronger incentives improve the worker's effort, but also raise total compensation costs through a larger risk premium. Because of this, optimal incentives will be lower than those we have considered. Though we may partially sell the job to the employee, in general incentive schemes will not reward 100% of the employee's measured contribution to profits, since doing so is too risky. *The less accurate the performance measure, the weaker the optimal incentives.*

In fact, this is an example of a general fact of economic life: The greater the insurance, the weaker the incentives, and vice versa. This issue arises in many contexts, such as the provision of health insurance.

Distortions and Multitask Incentives

A second problem with performance measures is that they almost always involve some distortion. The more that a performance measure distorts the employee's contribution, the less weight should be placed on it for incentives. The danger here is summed up by the familiar expression, "You get what you pay for": Putting a strong incentive on a measure that emphasizes some tasks but not others will motivate the employee to pay too much attention to the tasks that influence the performance measure.

To see the problem with distorted performance measures more formally, let us consider a job where there are two kinds of effort, e_1 and e_2, with the employee's disutility of effort equal to $C(e_1 + e_2)$. For our salesperson, the first might be selling new computers (quantity) and the second might be providing some installation help to the customer. Suppose that the employee's contribution equals $Q = q_1 \cdot e_1 + q_2 \cdot e_2$. As we will see, when the job is more complex, incentive schemes tend to get more complex as well.

How might we measure performance in this example, and tie it to pay? In many jobs, the firm has metrics that provide some measure of one dimension of the employee's job. In the salesperson example, revenue is very easy to measure. However, customer service is intangible, and difficult to quantify. Nevertheless, the firm may have access to some metrics on service, such as customer satisfaction survey data. This suggests that the firm might have the following three performance metrics for the salesperson:

$$PM_1 = q_1 \cdot e_1 + \varepsilon_1$$
$$PM_2 = q_2 \cdot e_2 + \varepsilon_2$$
$$PM_3 = \alpha \cdot PM_1 + \beta \cdot PM_2$$

The first estimates the employee's contributions to revenue (probably with high accuracy, so that σ_1^2 is low). The second estimates the value to the firm of the employee's customer service activities (probably with much more inaccuracy, particularly since it is an attempt to quantify an intangible). The third is a combination of the first two. This is implemented in our example by creating a third performance measure that is a weighted average of the first two. This is equivalent to giving two bonuses, based on PM_1 and PM_2, with different commission rates for each.

If the firm gives a bonus based only on PM_1, there is no incentive for the salesperson to provide service. This is a strong form of distortion. The firm is likely to end up with lots of sales in the short term, but many unhappy customers and little repeat business. A natural response to the problem is to offer a second bonus based on PM_2. The idea is to provide *balanced* incentives across the different tasks.

Unfortunately this is not likely to solve the problem effectively. Since σ_1^2 is relatively low, by the arguments we just gave, the commission rate on PM_1 should be relatively strong. But since σ_2^2 is relatively high, by the same arguments the commission rate on PM_2 should be relatively weak. Therefore, we are still likely to have unbalanced incentives.

One response to this is to split the work into two different jobs. The firm might put easy to measure tasks in one job, for which it uses strong pay for performance. It might then put difficult to measure tasks into another job, for which it uses relatively muted incentives. It might then invest more resources (and personnel) into the tasks with weaker incentives, so that overall output is balanced across the different dimensions of work. Pursuant to our example, many firms do, in fact, provide service and support in jobs that are separate from sales, and use different approaches to incentives and monitoring for each.

However, altering the job to fit the performance measure is a bit like putting the cart before the horse; it seems more natural to try to alter the performance evaluation and incentives to fit the job. How might the firm do this?

One potential solution is to combine the metrics in some way, as in PM_3. If the two individual metrics could be weighted and combined, the resulting (broader) metric might distort incentives less. In this example, if $\alpha = \beta$, then PM_3 does not distort incentives for the employee to provide both kinds of effort. (The commission rate can then be rescaled, by dividing through by α, so that the overall reward is equal to the employee's contribution, perhaps reduced for risk aversion reasons.)

Of course, the correct relative weighting of different performance metrics is not so easy in practice. How much relative weight should the firm put on customer satisfaction, which is a numeric proxy for something that is qualitative? Over time, the firm may be able to obtain reasonably good estimates of the relative value of both dimensions of performance. Or, it may be able to experiment with different relative weights, and arrive at a reasonable balance through experience.

The business world is dynamic, and the relative weights to give to different dimensions of the job for incentives often change. When this is so, the formulaic approach of picking numeric weights α and β is not likely to work well. What is often the best approach in those cases is to use judgment—subjective evaluation—to provide balanced incentives across multiple tasks. Indeed, the more complex the job, the more likely it is that evaluations are done subjectively, and rewards are tied more informally and less formulaically to performance.

Summary: How Strong Should Incentives Be?

We can now summarize what factors affect the optimal intensity of (explicit and implicit) incentives, and how. If our employee were risk neutral or we could measure performance very accurately, we would set the commission rate so that, when multiplied by the performance measure, the reward was approximately the value of the employee's incremental contribution to firm value. In practice, employees are risk averse and measures are imperfect, so actual incentives tend to be weaker. The factors to consider:

Value of employee effort. The more profitable to the firm is additional employee effort, the stronger the incentive. For example, in Table 10.1, if the percent profit margin were increased, the firm should increase the percent commission rate. For this simple but important reason, incentives are almost always stronger at higher levels in the hierarchy, and weaker in lower levels.

Importance of sorting. Incentives also generate good self-selection. The more important it is to the firm to sort workers by ability or accumulated skills, the stronger the pay for performance. Thus, incentives tend to be more important for new recruits, those who are new to their job, and in high skill occupations.

Measurement error. The more accurate the measure, the stronger the incentive that should be placed on it.

Risk aversion. The less risk averse the employee, the stronger the incentive intensity. When recruiting for jobs with strong incentives, the firm should consider risk aversion as a factor in hiring.

Trust and subjectivity. A variation on the themes of measurement error and risk aversion arises when subjectivity is used in the incentive scheme (for evaluation, weighting of metrics for rewards, or both). The employee then faces the risk of favoritism and bias of the evaluator. Thus, the more trust the employee has in the evaluator, the better the evaluator is at making judgments, and the more effective the appraisal process is, the stronger the discretionary incentive can be.

Distortion and multitask incentives. The more distorted the measure, the greater the need for additional incentives, incentives as a system of reinforcing rewards. This might imply the use of several formal incentives, or the use of a broader, more subjective, and implicit approach to incentives.

Potential manipulation. The less likely that the employee can manipulate the measure, the stronger the incentive intensity.

PAYING FOR PERFORMANCE: COMMON EXAMPLES ● ● ● ● ●

The discussion so far has focused on the simplest case, a linear pay for performance scheme. In that case, the question of incentive intensity boils down to how steep or flat the slope is in Figure 10.1. In this section we briefly consider several other commonly observed pay–performance relationships, to develop some other practical considerations.

Rewards or Penalties?

Figure 10.2 shows two pay–performance schemes. On the left is a *Reward* scheme similar to the one described earlier and plotted in Figure 10.1, except that the employee earns a base salary for low levels of output, only earning a bonus if performance rises above some threshold level *T*. On the right is a *Penalty* scheme, where the employee earns a base salary for high levels of output, but the reward is reduced if pay falls below *T*.

Schemes like the one at left are quite common. Why might a firm add a threshold? One reason has to do with risk aversion. Paying a base salary over some range of low performance provides some *insurance* to the employee against bad luck. Performance may be low because the employee did not work hard, but it may also be low because the employee was unlucky. Risk averse individuals are most concerned about avoiding the most negative outcomes. Therefore, this kind of pay combined with insurance can cause an employee effectively to be less risk averse.

This has two advantages. First, the firm may be able to increase the incentive intensity to the right of *T*. If *T* is not set too high, this means that the employee

FIGURE 10.2
REWARD AND PENALTY INCENTIVE SCHEMES

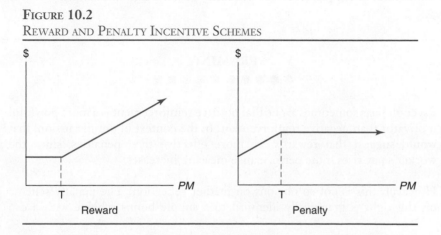

Reward   Penalty

will have stronger incentives. Second, the employee should be more willing to take risks, because they are less likely to be punished for mistakes or chances they take that do not succeed. This can be helpful in jobs where some amount of risk taking, perhaps to spur innovation, is important. This second effect is important when pay comes in the form of employee stock options. We will see in Chapter 12 that employee options have a payoff structure that looks very similar to the reward scheme in Figure 10.2.

The penalty scheme is not as common in practice. When might it be used? In the penalty scheme, the slope is positive for low performance, but zero for higher performance. The employee has little incentive once performance has passed the threshold T. Thus, the penalty scheme may be useful in cases where, beyond some point, there is little or no value to the firm when the employee's performance measure increases.

A real world example is an executive MBA student of one of the authors, who managed the electric power system for a small Asian country. The power company's "up time" (% of time that electricity was available) was 99.96%, a nearly perfect record. Suppose that the performance measure PM was % up time. While it might be possible for the power plant to increase up time beyond 99.96%, it might be extremely costly to do so, since performance is already near perfection. If so, it may not be profitable to increase the performance measure—the measure does not align perfectly with actual profits or firm value. Then the power company might want to put in place an incentive scheme like the penalty scheme earlier, which motivates the manager to avoid a fall in performance, but does not motivate increasing performance.

Thus, the reward scheme is useful when there is upside potential in the employee's job—when high levels of performance translate into increased firm value. If there is also little downside, providing insurance of the kind illustrated at left in Figure 10.2 makes sense. An entrepreneur is a perfect example, so stock options may work well in that case. The penalty scheme is useful when there is downside potential—the employee can damage firm value—but little upside potential. These are sometimes called *guardian* jobs; a security guard is a good example.

FRAMING

❖ ❖ ❖ ❖ ❖ ❖ ❖ ❖ ❖

Psychologists sometimes argue that positive reinforcement is a more powerful motivator than negative reinforcement. In the context of our discussion, that would suggest that rewards are more effective than penalties, since the worker's pay rises if the performance measure increases.

However, this is not so obvious on further reflection. The penalty scheme on the right is graphically identical to a simple bonus scheme with a cap (see later) on the bonus. As long as performance is below T, it *also* involves positive reinforcement. Indeed, we could easily have referred to it as a reward with a cap, rather than as a penalty.

To the extent that such labels matter, it may be worthwhile avoiding labels such as "penalties" or "punishments." However, these labels do serve a purpose. By calling the picture at left a reward, and the one at right a punishment, the firm is communicating to the worker something about the expected level of performance and the nature of the job. The scheme at the left is appropriate when the firm expects typical performance to be to the right of T. It also signals to the employee that the firm wants the employee to strive to increase output, and perhaps to be more willing to take risks. By contrast, the scheme at the right is appropriate when the firm expects typical performance to be to the left of T. It signals that it is important to avoid declining output, and to be conservative on the job.

One important issue with both the reward and penalty—and any scheme where the slope changes in some way—is how to set the threshold T. Consider the reward scheme. To the left of T, the slope is zero; to the right it is positive. If T is set too high, then it is highly unlikely that the performance measure will be above T even if the worker gets lucky (measurement error is large and positive). When that is true, $\Delta PM/\Delta e$ will be approximately equal to zero, and the worker will have little or no incentive. Similarly, in the penalty scheme, if T is set too low the worker will have little or no incentive.

In practice, it is often difficult to set the correct level of thresholds when first implementing an incentive plan. Moreover, circumstances change. For example, the worker may learn on the job, or production methods might change. These would make it easier (or harder) to produce a given level of performance, in which case T should be changed. There are many good reasons why a firm might want to change T, and the most typical case involves raising T as skills and methods improve.

Changing the threshold, however, can be tricky. In the reward scheme in Figure 10.2, if T is increased but nothing else is changed, it becomes more difficult to earn the bonus, and the bonus will be smaller for any given level of performance. Not surprisingly, the worker will not be happy. The worker may perceive that the firm is trying to reduce compensation.

Moreover, managers sometimes design a pay plan, and find that workers produce and earn more than was expected (perhaps because the manager underestimates the power of incentives). A natural response is to increase T, reduce the commission (slope), or reduce the base salary. While this reduces compensation costs, it may have negative consequences. In both of these examples, there is a real risk that the worker feels the firm is reneging on implied promises about the reward scheme.

This illustrates a general point about incentive systems: Simplicity is a virtue. Where possible, straightforward linear schemes tend to work best. Thresholds, changes in incentive intensity, and lump sum rewards often create problems. Moreover, complex pay systems make it harder for employees to understand how they will be rewarded for their performance, which may reduce their incentives since the perceived pay–performance link will be weaker. Finally, there can be a subtle issue of trust. Complex pay systems can cause some employees to worry that management is trying to take advantage of them in some way, though they are not sure exactly how.

The Ratchet Effect

Continuing with the implicit contracting idea, consider the dynamic issues raised once the firm responds to high performance and pay by ratcheting T higher, or the commission rate b lower. The worker may conclude that he was, in effect, punished for high performance. If this happens, incentives will be *reduced*. Therefore, the firm needs to be very careful about how it implements changes to incentive plans. There should be good reasons to do so, and these should be communicated clearly to the employee. Moreover, when the incentive plan is introduced, the firm should carefully reserve the right to evolve the plan in the future. Clearly, the better the degree of trust between the firm and its employees, the less likely are such ratcheting issues to be a problem. The Appendix discusses this *ratchet effect* in more detail.

Lump Sums, Demotions, or Promotions

Figure 10.3 shows what may be the most common pay for performance relationship of all. Here, if performance is above the threshold, there is a discrete jump in reward. Why might this be the most common form of incentive in practice? Because one example of such a pay–performance shape is a promotion. Most promotions come with large increases in compensation (and perhaps other job amenities). If the promotion is based on performance, as most are, then it can be an important incentive. In fact, this case is so important that we spend most of the next chapter discussing it. Also note that the threat of being fired or given a demotion will look similar (if the employee suffers a loss from either).

Another example of the kind of pay–performance relationship shown in Figure 10.3 is a lump sum bonus. Sometimes firms award a fixed amount if an employee meets a target. For example, an auto dealership might offer a $1,000 prize to an employee who meets a sales goal, or to the best performing employee of the month.

One problem with reward structures like Figure 10.3 is that incentives can be brittle. This is similar to the problem of a threshold that is too high in the reward scheme in Figure 10.2. The slope of the pay–performance relationship is zero if the employee's performance is below the threshold; *infinite* if performance is just at the margin between winning and losing; and zero again if performance is above the threshold. This scheme generates very strong incentives if employees are right near

FIGURE 10.3
LUMP-SUM REWARDS

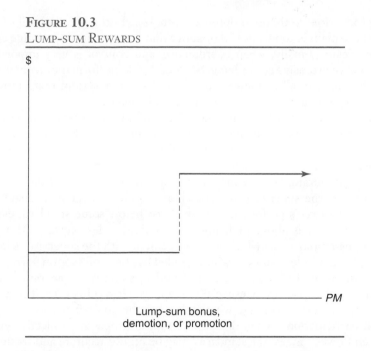

Lump-sum bonus,
demotion, or promotion

the threshold, but if they are too far below or above, they will tend to slack off. (As an example, consider what sports teams do if they are far ahead—they slack off by putting in the second string.) Unless this is desirable, a smoother pay–performance relationship would make sense.

When incentives change dramatically in incentive systems that involve thresholds, and large changes in the slope or incentive intensity, employee behavior can be problematic. In Figure 10.3, the all-or-nothing nature of the reward is not only likely to motivate the employee to work harder if near the threshold, it is also more likely to motivate the employee to manipulate the performance measure if possible. Manipulation of performance measures is always a problem in incentive systems, especially when the stakes are higher. But it is even more of a concern if the employee faces an abrupt change in the shape of the pay plan, so that small changes in performance can lead to large changes in rewards or the potential for further compensation. By contrast, smooth pay–performance relationships tend to give more continuous incentives for employees to exert more effort.

Thus, incentive plans with thresholds and lump sum rewards are more likely to lead to employee malfeasance.

One case where such reward schemes may be useful combines our arguments about reward and penalty schemes. Sometimes it is important that performance falls into a narrow band. If performance is too low, *or* if it is too high, firm value may be lower. One example is an assembly line worker. Working too slow *or* too fast might cause coordination problems. Another example is a plant manager. The firm may choose production methods to optimize costs based on a certain level of planned output. If the plant is too far below or above that level of output, average costs may rise dramatically. Finally, when coordination and control is very important (say, the firm makes extensive use of budgets), predictable performance from employees may be desirable. In all of these examples, an incentive system that motivates the employee to perform near a target level can make sense.

Another case where a lump sum reward might be useful is when the performance measure is a subjective evaluation. As already discussed, such evaluations may not be trusted by subordinates because it is difficult to verify that the supervisor has attempted to accurately evaluate performance. In addition, such evaluations are often quite inaccurate, because they involve qualitative aspects of the job. In some cases, however, the supervisor may be able to quite accurately evaluate whether or not the employee's performance is above or below some standard, even if the degree to which it is above or below the standard is less certain. Moreover, in such cases the employee may be in close agreement with the supervisor's judgment. Consider, for example, a student who is graded by the professor on participation in case discussions in class. Quantifying the student's contributions on a continuous scale can be quite inaccurate, especially in a large class. However, it may be quite easy for the professor to judge whether or not the student makes a "good faith effort" at participation. When these conditions are met, the subjective evaluation that the employee "meets the standard" may be highly accurate and trusted.

A final case in which a lump sum reward might be useful is if performance is binary: The employee achieves a specific objective, or does not. For example, an employee might meet a deadline for filing paperwork with a regulatory agency, and receive a bonus for doing so. As another example, an employee might bring in a new client—or not. If he does, he might receive a bonus for doing so. However, such cases are less common than one might imagine. Meeting a deadline is unlikely to be the only relevant dimension of performance; quality may also matter. Bringing in a client is rarely a binary outcome, as some clients are more profitable for the firm than others. An alternative approach would be to reward the employee based on a more continuous measure of profitability from new clients.

Caps on Rewards

Our final scheme to consider, in Figure 10.4, is the reward plan, but with a *cap*. A cap is a maximum amount of bonus or other reward that the employee is allowed to earn. Some bonus plans have caps, and others do not. Why might a firm use a cap?

Managers sometimes put in caps to ensure that employees do not earn "too much" pay. However, one should be careful in making such an argument. First, the level of pay might be reduced without imposing a cap simply by lowering the intercept (shifting the pay plan downward in Figure 10.4). Second, if the employee is earning a lot, this must be because the employee is performing well. If the performance measure is a reasonable proxy for the employee's contribution to firm value, then the firm is probably profiting from this extra performance as well (since optimal commission rates often give the employee less than 100% of

FIGURE 10.4
FLOOR OR CAP IN AN INCENTIVE SCHEME

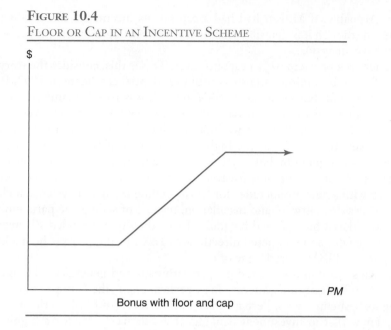

Bonus with floor and cap

their contribution, as discussed earlier). A cap would reduce incentives (beyond the second threshold), reducing firm profits. In fact, in some cases managers seem to impose caps out of such misguided motives, including a reluctance to allow their subordinates to earn more than they do. But these kinds of motives are very similar to the ratchet effect issues described earlier and in the Appendix.

There can be justifications for a cap on rewards. To see why, remember that the bonus is based on a performance measure, which is an imperfect proxy for the employee's actual contributions to the firm. The performance measure is a function of the employee's effort, but also the employee's luck. And it may also be manipulated or distort the employee's incentives. In some jobs, it is implausible that extremely high measured performance is due to the employee's efforts and talents. In those kinds of jobs, the higher the measured performance, the more likely that the measure reflects either luck or manipulation. When this is so, the firm should consider a cap, to avoid rewarding luck or motivating manipulation of the incentive system.

One example of this was Michael Milken, the head of Drexel Burnham Lambert's "junk bond" group in Beverly Hills. Milken's compensation scheme had a very strong incentive intensity—a steep slope. It also had no cap. One year, his measured performance was so high that his annual bonus exceeded half a billion dollars. Unfortunately, it became increasingly difficult for Milken to generate high quality, profitable new deals for Drexel. Instead, his group began engaging in transactions and business methods that many viewed as unethical. Eventually, he was prosecuted and served time in jail, and Drexel went bankrupt and was closed down. Arguably, if Milken had had a cap on his incentives, this might not have happened (though it is plausible that he had such strong intrinsic motivation that it might have anyway).

There is a problem with a cap, however. To see this, consider the story of Ross Perot. Before becoming an unsuccessful presidential candidate in 1992, Perot was a very successful businessman. Perot's first job was to sell mainframe computers for IBM. This was in the early days of mainframe sales, so it was a very good time to have such a job. Still, Perot was not only lucky, he was also a very talented and hard worker. In fact he was the highest seller in all of IBM. In one year, he met his annual sales quota by January 19th—and January was the first month of IBM's fiscal year! Perot soon became frustrated, anxious to put his talents to better use. He came up with a new product idea for IBM—selling computer systems, including all of the necessary software and installation, instead of selling the parts individually. IBM considered but rejected his idea.[2] Perot then quit, founded Electronic Data Systems (EDS), and competed directly with IBM. In the process he made billions of dollars, and IBM shared none of it.

Perot's story illustrates the danger with caps and general ratchet effect–type attempts to limit rewards for very high performers. If the firm places caps, it risks losing its best employees. Perhaps that is why Drexel paid Milken the way they did. They knew that in investment banking, it is relatively easy for a highly talented banker to set up a competing firm. A firm must compensate its employees for their market value. For the most valuable employees in highly skilled occupations, this often means that, in effect, the firm must give most or all of the residual profits created by an employee as the reward—they have to sell the job. For this basic reason, most organizations in very knowledge intensive industries (investment banking, law, consulting, and in some ways academia) are organized as professional partnerships, with the more productive partners earning the most.

● ● ● ● ●   APPLICATIONS

Profit Sharing and ESOPs

Many firms offer some form of broad-based compensation plan such as profit sharing, gain sharing, or employee stock ownership. Managers often argue that such plans give employees a "sense of ownership" and a feeling that "we are all in this together." Do such plans make sense? From the perspective of the theory we have just described, they do not. Let us consider the arguments against such plans, and then consider a couple of reasons why they might—sometimes—make sense.

To analyze an incentive system, use the principles of this and the last chapter. Ask two questions first: What are the properties of the performance evaluation? How is the evaluation tied to performance?

---

[2] Perot reports that IBM "took the idea to the top of the organization, but they ultimately rejected my plan" (2005, p. 72). Of course, IBM was a very hierarchical, conservative organization, as described in Chapter 6, so this is not surprising.

Performance Evaluation

The performance evaluation for such plans is a very broad one. In the case of profit sharing at a factory or other organizational unit, the measure is unit profits, revenue, etc. In the case of firm-wide profit sharing, the measure is firm profits. In the case of employee stock ownership, it is stock.

Already incentive alarm bells should be going off in your head. These are *not* good performance measures for typical employees. Though employees can help improve firm value, the effects of a single individual are not going to show up in such measures unless the employee is a key figure in the firm. These measures are essentially completely uncontrollable by most employees. Thus, it is implausible that they provide *any* incentives at all. Indeed, most studies find that such plans have no detectible effect on productivity or profits.

Pay–Performance Relationship

A further problem with these pay plans is that even if the performance measure were a good one, the incentive intensity tends to be very small. The reason for this is the free rider problem. Remember the last time you worked on a group project. There may have been a member of your team who didn't seem to do their fair share of the work. Yet if all in the group received the same grade, then this person shared in the reward anyway. They got a free ride. The problem is that the change in reward varies little, if at all, with a change in employee effort.

This is virtually inevitable in group reward schemes that simply share the reward equally. The reason is that, if there are N people in the group, the reward for each person equals $1/N$. Of course, $1/N$ is a hyperbola, which approaches zero very rapidly. Thus, unless the group size is small, the incentive intensity has to be close to zero.[3] As an extreme example, the giant German company Siemens has employee profit sharing, and approximately 400,000 employees (in 2007). In this case, the commission rate on profits is:

$$b = \frac{1}{400,000} = 0.0000025.$$

That's a pretty tiny incentive intensity! Although clearly this is an extreme case, it does illustrate the free rider problem, and how difficult it is to justify such compensation plans purely on incentive grounds.

Counterarguments

So why do so many firms make use of such broad-based plans? One explanation is that they misunderstand the theory, and to some extent that seems likely. But there are some counterarguments.

First, peer pressure can, conceivably, cancel out the free rider effect. If all share in the same reward, then all have some incentive to pressure their colleagues to

---

[3] Social psychologists often argue that the optimal group size is about five or six members, at most. It is likely that one of the important reasons for this is that a larger group would rapidly encounter the free rider problem.

work harder. To the extent that this is true, then the optimal size of the group for incentives can be larger. Moreover, such effects might increase productivity for other reasons as well. In cases where work is interdependent and the firm makes extensive use of teamwork, group-based incentives are more likely to make sense, and may also reinforce any cultural rules about the importance of cooperation. Indeed, the few studies that find a positive effect of ESOP or profit sharing plans usually find that they are more likely to be helpful in firms that use team production.

However, anyone who has ever worked in a group (or tried to get everyone to share a dinner bill at a restaurant) knows that free rider effects are ubiquitous, so it seems implausible that peer pressure can overcome free riding in most cases.

Another explanation that is sometimes given is that compensation becomes more of a variable cost, rather than a fixed cost: Pay rises as performance rises, and declines as performance declines. This may lower the financial risk of the firm, leading to a lower cost of capital. However, this explanation does not make sense: While it may lower the cost of capital, it does so by raising the cost of employee compensation even more. The reason for this is that employees are typically even more risk averse than investors, and require a larger risk premium for accepting this risk in their compensation than do would shareholders. We will discuss this problem more extensively when we consider employee stock options.

One explanation involves public relations concerns. There are good reasons to consider giving large grants of stock and options to top executives, and to reward them generously if the firm performs well. But firms often face pressure from some shareholders, unions, the press, or other groups when they give large payouts to executives. Some of these criticisms might be blunted if the firm also gave stock or profit sharing to lower level employees. Thus, such plans might be bad incentives, but good public relations. (At a cost to lower level employees, whose pay becomes risky.)

A final explanation for stock ownership plans is that top management adopts such plans as a way to increase the demand for their stock, in the hope of raising the stock price. For example, some companies invest their employees' pension funds heavily in the company's own stock. Such practices are far from in the interest of employees, however, since their pension funds become as undiversified as possible: largely invested in a single company, and highly correlated with the employee's human capital.

Organizational Form and Contracting

As with most of the principles in this text, the incentive intuition developed in this module has implications for virtually all aspects of business, not just employment. Here we provide brief illustrations of how the principles can be applied.

Franchising

Franchising is an unusual organizational form that combines principles about incentives with those about decision making and use of specific knowledge. For the franchisee, it is intermediate between true ownership and more typical employment. For the franchiser, it is intermediate between outsourcing and internal production.

Clearly a franchise is a very broad performance measure; it is almost pure ownership. A typical franchisee has to pay a large up-front fee for the right to run a franchise. In exchange, the franchisee is allowed to run the operation (subject to limitations). Since the franchisee can sell the franchise at its current market value, the performance measure is very close to that of an owner of an independent store. This means that there are very few distortions in the performance measure, for intangibles, investments, and long-term decision making.

However, the franchise stops a little before pure ownership. The franchiser retains some decision rights. For example, a franchiser typically specifies the product line. It may require the use of specific suppliers (e.g., specific sources for beef in McDonald's hamburgers). It often requires employees to wear certain uniforms, and has control over the design of the store.

In doing so, this organizational form makes effective use of centralization and decentralization. The decision rights that are retained by the franchiser are those that affect the overall brand name: product, quality control, customer experience, marketing, and so on. The desire for consistency of the product means that there are important benefits to centralizing decisions that affect consistency.

By giving other decision rights to the franchisee, this form allows decentralized decision making to make use of local specific knowledge. For example, the franchisee usually handles most personnel matters, from hiring to training to compensation and incentives. Since many important implementation decisions are left in the hands of the franchisee, the broad performance measure is appropriate for such a broad job design.

Cost Plus vs. Fixed Fee

Suppose that your firm needs to have a building constructed, and hires a builder. What kind of contract should be written? Two types are common in construction, cost-plus and fixed-fee. A cost-plus contract pays for the cost of all materials and labor used to construct the building, plus an additional fee or percentage to provide some profit margin for the builder. A fixed-fee contract specifies the type of building and materials, and perhaps other aspects of the project, and pays a fixed amount on completion. A fixed-fee contract might be more elaborate, specifying various payments for completing various stages of the project.

Since the cost-plus contract reimburses for all inputs, there is no incentive to reduce quality of construction. Indeed, since the profit margin is usually specified as a percentage of costs, the builder may well have *too much* incentive for quality. Many government contracts are cost-plus, and it is common to see overbuilding in such cases. The higher the margin, the higher the quality (and the longer the duration) that can be expected from a cost-plus project.

By contrast, a concern with the fixed-fee contract is that it will give weak incentives for quality. The builder's incentive is to get the job done for the minimum quality that it can get away with while honoring the terms of the contract. (This will be mitigated to the extent that the builder cares about its reputation and the awarding of future contracts.) A fixed-fee contract may also motivate the builder to complete the project very quickly (by contrast to a cost-plus contract, where the incentive is to bill as many hours of work as possible).

However, some fixed-fee contracts specify that the customer makes payments as the work progresses. Therefore, in some cases it can be difficult to get a fixed-fee contractor to complete a job, if too many payments have been made, so that there is inadequate compensation for completion of the project. One way to address such concerns in both types of projects is to specify rewards or punishments for meeting specific time goals.

Which is better? If quality is easily observed and verified, then it is probably better to go with a project-based payment where providers are penalized for deviations from contracted quality. If quality is not easily observed, but the appropriate amount of time to complete the job is known, it is probably better to use a cost-plus system, with penalties for running over the contracted amount of time.

The general point, though, is that the more you think about incentives in complex and subtle ways, the better you will be able to understand economic behavior in a wide variety of settings. Moreover, the better will you be able to apply the principles effectively.

Motivating Creativity

A frequent criticism of pay for performance (especially from social psychologists) is that it might destroy the employee's intrinsic motivation. The exact mechanism by which this occurs is not always clearly stated. One explanation that is sometimes given is that the employee will feel "controlled" if given pay for performance, and will thereby withhold effort that would have been otherwise provided because of intrinsic motivation.

There is a much more straightforward way to think about this issue, and one that explains the examples that are usually given. Intrinsic motivation usually is most important for tasks that are complex and intellectually challenging to the employee. These are often most important in jobs that involve a substantial amount of creativity and learning. By their nature, it is often difficult to develop good performance measures for these kinds of tasks. One reason is that such intellectual tasks can be difficult to quantify. Another is that in creative work, it can be hard to specify the desirable features of output in advance. The metrics that might be used will then distort incentives substantially. Moreover, the tasks that *can* be quantified will tend to be those that involve less creativity. (Imagine what would happen in a research university, for example, if professors were told that they would be given tenure if they published a specific number of articles—if the performance measure were purely quantity.)

Putting a strong incentive on such measures will, of course, focus the employee more on what is measured and rewarded, and less on the creative aspects of the job. But this is not because of psychology; it is simply a problem of inadequate performance measurement.

In some cases it is possible to use pay for performance to motivate creativity, because reasonable (if imperfect) metrics are available. For example, some companies reward divisional managers based on the percentage of products sold that were newly developed over the past 2 years. This may work reasonably well at spurring innovation because products not only have to be new, but have to meet with approval from customers. In many cases, however, the best alternative is to perform careful subjective performance evaluations. Research universities do exactly this: Professors are typically evaluated only every couple of years, but the evaluation is highly subjective, attempting to assess the creative contribution of the professor's research.

Summary

Incentives are not only the essence of economics, they are an essential part of organizational design. In order to understand organizational design and employee behavior, a thorough understanding of incentives is crucial.

We analyzed incentives by considering an example of a formal bonus plan for a salesperson. However, the intuition developed is much more general. It applies to *all* kinds of incentives, formal and informal, designed and accidental. Incentives in practice can be very subtle; you need to develop a trained eye for uncovering these subtleties and how they affect behavior and organizational performance.

Abstractly, the goal of pay for performance is to replicate the spirit of ownership and entrepreneurship for employees. We saw that a perfect incentive plan essentially sells the job to the employee, so that they are mini entrepreneurs. This is in accord with the metaphor of a market economy that this book uses to think about organizational design.

However, incentives in practice are often quite different from this ideal. The most important reason for this is performance evaluation problems, which is why we have devoted an entire chapter to such issues. Any imperfections in the evaluation drive a wedge between the incentives of the employee and those of an owner-entrepreneur. To the extent that there is performance measurement error, firms will invest more resources in monitoring and careful evaluation. But it is also true that optimal incentives will be weaker, so that employees will not exert as much effort as they otherwise would.

This logic illustrates why organizations often seem relatively inefficient. If it were possible actually to replicate markets (that is, have a price system to serve as an excellent performance measure), then the firm would outsource anyway. It is just those situations which require long term *employment* relationships between the firm and the worker that also tend to make performance evaluation imperfect. For example, the worker may be engaged in complex, multitask work, some of the effects of which are intangible or not realized in the short term. Or, the work may be highly interdependent with colleagues, so that it is difficult to disentangle the effects of a single worker from that of the group.

Other performance measurement problems, such as distortions or potential for manipulation, may also lead to weaker incentives. They tend to make design of incentive systems more complex than the simple example of the salesperson. For example, multitask jobs often yield distorted performance measures (these also may arise from the desire to reduce risk in the evaluation). Thus an important intuition for such jobs is that the incentive system must provide *balanced incentives* across the different aspects of the work. This may require multiple rewards based on different factors, a different (broader) approach to performance measurement, or careful subjective evaluation and implicit rewards.

Potential manipulation of performance metrics may also require that the supervisor spend additional time monitoring the employee, to try to detect the manipulation. It may also lead to the use of subjective evaluations and implicit rewards.

Putting these ideas together, the incentive system often ends up being a complex *system* of interrelated parts: monitoring, various performance measures, subjective evaluation, explicit and implicit rewards, and so on. Designing and managing such a system can be something of an art, and is an important part of the manager's job.

◆ ◆ ◆ ◆ ◆ STUDY QUESTIONS

1. Suppose that you use all of your savings to buy a struggling company, and now must turn it around. Should changing employee incentives be one of the first tools that you use to manage change? If so, why? If not, why not? If you do use incentives to drive organizational change, what else is likely important for you to change?

2. How might you try to detect if your employee is gaming the incentive system? Try to think of concrete examples.

3. Consider important medical care decisions. Should such decisions be made by the doctor or the patient? What factors are important? Given your answer, how would you structure incentives in order to balance quality of care against cost?

4. Do the incentive principles described in Chapters 9–10 apply to not-for-profit organizations? To politicians? Why or why not?

5. What are some real world examples of the "sell the job" intuition that you can think of?

6. What performance evaluation methods would you use to motivate creativity in a research and development staff? What other policies that we have discussed in this text might you also use to reinforce those incentives?

REFERENCES ◆◆◆◆◆

Gibbons, Robert (1987). "Piece-Rate Incentive Schemes." *Journal of Labor Economics* 4: 413–429.

Lazear, Edward (1986). "Salaries & Piece Rates." *Journal of Business* 59: 405–431.

Lazear, Edward (2000). "Performance Pay and Productivity." *American Economic Review* 90(5): 1346–1361.

Perot, Ross (1996). *My Life & the Principles for Success*. Arlington, TX: The Summit Publishing Group.

FURTHER READING ◆◆◆◆◆

Gaynor, Martin, James Rebitzer, & Lowell Taylor (2004). "Physician Incentives in HMOs." *Journal of Political Economy* 112: 915–931.

Holmstrom, Bengt & Paul Milgrom (1991). "Multitask Principal-Agent Analyses: Incentive Contracts, Asset Ownership, and Job Design." *Journal of Law, Economics, and Organization* 7: 24–52.

Lazear, Edward (2005). Speeding, Tax Fraud, and Teaching to the Test. Working paper, National Bureau of Economic Research.

Roy, Donald (1957). "Quota Restriction and Goldbricking in a Machine Shop." *American Journal of Sociology* 67(2): 427–442.

APPENDIX ◆◆◆◆◆

Formal Analysis of Optimal Incentives

I. Optimal Commission Rate

Here we formally derive the result that the firm maximizes profits by paying a commission rate equal to 100% of net revenue, if the employee is not risk averse. This provides a more rigorous treatment of the general intuition of the idea of selling the job to the employee.

The problem is broken into two parts. First, the worker's optimal behavior is analyzed. Then the firm's optimal commission rate is derived, taking into account the worker's behavior. Assume for simplicity that e is scaled so that 1 unit of e produces \$1 of incremental profit for the firm, so that $Q = e$. The firm's performance measure is an estimate of this effort with measurement error ε, assumed to have mean zero and standard deviation σ_ε. Therefore, since pay $= a + b \cdot PM = a + b$ $(e + \varepsilon)$, the variance of pay equals $b^2 \cdot \sigma_\varepsilon^2$. The worker chooses effort to maximize utility:

$$\max_e \ a + b \cdot e - C(e) - \frac{1}{2} \cdot R \cdot \sigma_{Pay}^2.$$

If the employee is risk neutral, $R = 0$. Thus, the optimum is where $C'(e) = b$. This is the worker's effort supply; it tells how responsive effort is to a change in the piece rate. It simply states that the worker sets the marginal cost of effort equal to b, which is the marginal return to effort.

The firm chooses a and b, but has two constraints. First, the choice of b affects the worker's choice of e as just derived. Second, whatever the worker's choice of e turns out to be, denoted e^*, the firm must ensure that the total compensation exceeds $C(e^*)$ or the worker will not accept the job. This means that:

$$Pay = a + b \cdot e^* = C(e^*).$$

The firm maximizes net revenue minus the worker's pay. Net revenue equals e, so the firm's objective is to maximize $e^* - a - b \cdot e^*$. Solving for a from the previous equation and substituting into this expression yields the firm's simplified maximization problem:

$$\max_b \ e^* - C(e^*),$$

subject to $C'(e^*) = b$. Note two things at this point. First, base pay a does not affect the choice of e^* by the worker, so it is not part of this expression. Second, this expression is the *net surplus* created by the firm and employee: It is net profit, minus the additional costs to the employee. In effect, the best policy for the firm is the one that maximizes the *total economic value*. This is a formal illustration of one of the themes of this text (see the Summary). The base salary a serves to share this value between the worker and the firm. The first-order condition for the firm is:

$$\left(1 - C'(e)\right) \cdot \frac{de}{db} = 0,$$

so b must be chosen so that $C'(e^*) = 1$. Since from above we know that $C'(e^*) = b$, this implies that the optimal $b^* = 1$, which gives 100% of net revenue to the employee. Finally, e^* is determined once we know that $b^* = 1$. The firm then sets a^* so that the worker is just indifferent between this job and the next best alternative:

$$a^* + e^* = C(e^*).$$

It should be easy for you to see that the employee chooses the same level of effort as if he or she owned the firm. When there is no risk aversion, there is no conflict of interest in this model.

In the computer salesperson example in Table 10.1, $C(e) = 2 \cdot e^2$. As a check, try to prove to yourself that in this case, $b^* = 1, e^* = 1/4$, and $a^* = -1/8$. (*Note:* we use calculus here. The third column of Table 10.1 is an *approximation* ΔC rather than the derivative version used below.)

II. Risk Aversion

Suppose now that $R > 0$ so that the employee is risk averse. Then the worker's value from the job equals $a + b \cdot e - C(e) - 1/2 \cdot R \cdot b^2 \cdot \sigma_\varepsilon^2$. This does *not* change the worker's optimal level of e^*, since the risk premium does not vary with e.

What changes is the firm's optimization. It must now compensate the employee for both effort and risk, and risk depends on the level of b. The firm must set pay at least so that:

$$Pay = a + b \cdot e^* = C(e^*) + 1/2 \cdot R \cdot b^2 \cdot \sigma_\varepsilon^2.$$

Then, the firm's optimization problem becomes:

$$\max_b \ e^* - C(e^*) - 1/2 \cdot R \cdot b^2 \cdot \sigma_\varepsilon^2.$$

The first-order condition for the firm is now:

$$\left(1 - C'(e^*)\right) \cdot \frac{de^*}{db} - R \cdot b \cdot \sigma_\varepsilon^2 = 0.$$

From the employee's first-order condition, $C' = b$, and $de^*/db = 1/C''$. Thus we derive:

$$b^* = 1 \Big/ \left(1 + R \cdot \sigma_\varepsilon^2 \cdot C''\right).$$

Several implications follow. First, the commission rate is lower, the more risk averse is the employee. The reason is that stronger incentives (larger b) means larger risk, an additional cost of incentives that the firm must balance against the benefits. Second, the less accurate the performance measure, the lower the commission rate. Third, the more rapidly that extra effort becomes more onerous (the larger is C''), the lower the commission rate, since additional effort is increasingly costly to motivate. Finally and importantly, since the incentive intensity is lower, the effort e^* supplied by the employee will be lower.

III. Ratchet Effects

We now show that the ratchet effect that arises when a firm makes next year's target a function of this year's performance can be offset by the appropriate multiperiod incentive scheme.[4] For simplicity, let us return to the risk neutral case, $R = 0$. Similar conclusions apply if the employee is risk averse.

---

[4]See Lazear (1986) and Gibbons (1987).

The problem can be analyzed in a two-period model. The firm commits to paying a particular commission rate in Period 1, but the worker assumes that despite promises, the firm will take advantage to the extent possible next period. (In other words, we are assuming that no effective means of implicit contracting exists in this case.)

The firm can take advantage of the worker only to the extent that the worker can earn at least as much at this firm as elsewhere.

As earlier, let output $Q_t = e_t$ in each period $t = 1, 2$. The worker has disutility of effort $C(e_t)$ in each period. The worker's cost of effort is unknown to the firm in advance, but the worker's choice of effort in Period 1 gives it information on which to base the compensation scheme in Period 2.

Since Period 2 is the last period, the incentive scheme that the firm chooses then is identical to that for the one-period problem solved for earlier. That is, it will set $b_2 = 1$, and set a_2 such that:

$$a_2 + e_2 - \tilde{C}(e_2) = 0,$$

where we write $\tilde{C}$ to reflect that the firm views C as random, and forms an estimate $\hat{C}$ based on Period 1 effort. It is this effect that motivates the worker to slack off in Period 1: Harder work in Period 1 brings higher pay that period, but also reduces a_2 in Period 2.

How does the worker behave in Period 1? The worker knows that the firm will base its estimate of C on Period 1 output, and that the greater output in Period 1 will cause the firm to infer that the job was relatively easy (low cost):

$$\frac{\partial \hat{C}(e_2)}{\partial e_1} < 0.$$

In Period 2 the firm chooses a_2 such that $a_2 = \hat{C}(e_2) - e_2$. Therefore,

$$\frac{\partial a_2}{\partial e_1} < 0,$$

since $\hat{C}$ is declining in e_1. The worker's maximization problem in Period 2 is:

$$\max_{e_2} a_2 + e_2 - \tilde{C}(e_2),$$

so the worker sets $\tilde{C}'(e_2) = 1$. This is what the firm wants, since doing so maximizes Period 2 profits. The problem arises in Period 1, since the worker reduces effort, knowing that working hard cuts compensation in Period 2. The worker's Period 1 maximization problem is:

$$\max_{e_1} a_1 + b_1 e_1 - \tilde{C}(e_1) + a_2(e_1) + b_2 e_2 - \tilde{C}(e_2),$$

subject to $\tilde{C}'(e_2) = 1$. The first order condition is:

$$\tilde{C}'(e_1) = b_1 + \frac{\partial a_2}{\partial e_1} < b_1.$$

The second term after the equals sign is the ratchet effect. Effort is lower in Period 1 because of the implicit penalty it causes, of lower compensation in Period 2.

To maximize profits, the firm must induce the worker to behave efficiently in Period 1 as well (this already happens in Period 2); that is, induce the worker to set $\tilde{C}'(e_1) = 1$ and $\tilde{C}'(e_2) = 1$. To get the worker to set $\tilde{C}'(e_1) = 1$, we need:

$$b_1 + \frac{\partial a_2}{\partial e_1} = 1, \quad so \quad b_1 = 1 - \frac{\partial a_2}{\partial e_1} > 1.$$

Thus, the firm must overpay performance in Period 1 in order to induce efficient effort that period. This reverses the loss in incentives that the worker has from the reduced Period 2 base salary implied by high performance in Period 1. Thus the commission rate falls over time.

Finally, the firm must set a_1 sufficiently high to attract workers to the firm. Workers are attracted to the firm if:

$$a_1 + b_1 e_1 - \tilde{C}(e_1) + a_2 + b_2 e_2 - \tilde{C}(e_2) \geq 0,$$

given that $a_2 = \hat{C}(e_2) - e_2$. Workers differ in cost of effort, in this model. The higher is a_1, the more workers (and of lower effort cost, which is analytically equivalent to higher ability) are attracted to the firm.

CAREER-BASED INCENTIVES

In a hierarchy every employee tends to rise to his level of incompetence.
—Laurence Peter & Raymond Hull, 1969

INTRODUCTION

So far, we have largely treated pay for performance as designed with respect to a given job. We now consider another important source of extrinsic motivation: long-term incentives to advance a worker's career. Most employees experience increases in their earnings over their career through raises and promotions. To the extent that these are based on performance, they are a type of incentive scheme.

Figure 11.1 presents data on salaries of employees at different hierarchical levels in Acme, calculated at a single point in time. In this company, there are eight levels from entry-level management to the CEO. There is more than one kind of job in each level, but jobs within a level have very similar pay, and presumably similar levels of responsibility and skills. The plot shows the mean level of salary. It also shows the 5th and 95th percentiles of salary among those in each job level.

Several observations can be made. First, there are relatively tight bands of pay at lower levels, but the bands widen at higher levels. Second, the difference between average salaries at different levels can be quite large; even at lower levels it appears to be important compared to the width of salary bands. This suggests that the hope of winning a promotion could be an important source of incentives for these managers. Third, there is a remarkable rise in average salary with hierarchical level, and this tendency is especially notable at the top. The rise would be even larger if we included bonuses, stock, and other forms of incentives that tend to be more important for senior executives.

Table 11.1 provides a little evidence on how salary changes when an employee's job changes at this company. For each hierarchical level, the middle columns show the percentage salary increase (adjusted for inflation) for those who do not change

FIGURE 11.1
PAY BY HIERARCHICAL LEVEL AT ACME

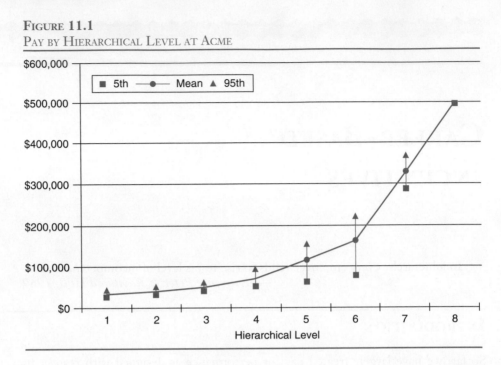

level (stayers), those who were demoted to that level, and those who were promoted to that level. The last column also shows the percentage difference between the average salary in that level and in the level below. For example, there is a 48% difference between the CEO's salary (which ignores many other forms of compensation that the CEO probably earned) and salaries of employees in Level 7.

TABLE 11.1
RAISE BY TYPE OF JOB TRANSITION AT ACME

Level	% Real Salary Increase on:			% Difference in Mean Pay Compared to Level Below
	Stay	Demotion	Promotion	
1	−0.5%	−0.7%	—	—
2	−0.4	−0.2	5.1	18
3	0.1	−3.2	5.6	23
4	0.8	0.4	7.4	47
5	−0.1	0.5	8.7	64
6	0.1	—	4.5	40
7	−0.9	—	22.3	107
8	0.0	—	14.8	48
1–8	0.0%	−0.9%	5.8%	

Not surprisingly, demotions are usually associated with a decrease in real salary. Sometimes a demotion actually comes with a raise. However, not much weight should be placed on the demotion data, as they are so very rare in this (and most) companies as to be very unusual cases: Out of about 53,000 observations over 20 years, there were only 157 demotions.

PROMOTIONS, DEMOTIONS, AND LATERAL TRANSFERS

Demotions are extremely rare, and lateral transfers (movements across jobs within the same hierarchical level) also tend to be less common than promotions. Why do job movements tend to be upward in the hierarchy over one's career? There are several reasons.

First consider demotions. Since they involve a penalty, they might not be used except in cases where the employee has more potential to destroy value than to increase it. Demotions (and firings) may also be more common than is apparent, but are implicit: The firm eases out a poor performer, encouraging them to search for a new job. Such an arrangement can benefit both. The firm avoids firing costs and potential litigation, while the employee avoids the stigma of a demotion.

Demotions may be rare because firms may be conservative about placing employees into important positions until their skills are proven. We can view a promotion ladder as similar to project evaluation (Chapter 7). Those who are "accepted" are promoted, while those who are "rejected" are not. Careful upward recruiting makes it more likely that the firm only puts talented managers into top positions.

Demotions might also be rare because of accumulation of human capital. If workers improve skills over time, performance increases. Career movements will tend to be upward, with more promotions and fewer demotions, if it is appropriate to put those with more skills into higher positions.

Lateral transfers generally involve placing an employee into a job involving new skills. This violates the principle of specialization. It can make sense when the employee was initially placed in the wrong job ladder given their talents. We would expect to see such "fixing of mistakes" occurring relatively quickly after an employee is put into the wrong job.

Lateral transfers might also be offered to a talented employee who is in a job ladder with few promotion prospects, to avoid losing the employee.

Finally, lateral transfers might be used to provide a general manager with broad experience in different areas of the business, if their job will involve coordinating across those areas.

More interesting is that if an employee does not get promoted, the average salary increase is *zero* (see the last row). At least in this firm, the only way for an employee to earn increases in salary beyond inflation is to get promoted. Doing so provides about a 5.8% increase in real salary. Moreover, the long-term increase in pay from promotion is much larger than 5.8%, as indicated in the last column. The average differences in salary between levels are much larger than the increase at the time of promotion.

This is for two reasons. First, those who are promoted tend to get further salary increases in their new jobs, while those who are passed over for promotion tend to have slowing (even negative) real salary growth. Second, those who are promoted are then eligible for promotion at the next stage of the hierarchy, and as both the figure and table indicate, promotions are more lucrative as one moves up the hierarchy.

The evidence clearly indicates that an employee's long-term career prospects, especially in the form of promotions, may often be an important source of incentives. The rewards from promotion are large, and promotions are more likely to be given to employees who earn the highest performance ratings. In fact, for middle managers in most firms, where subjective performance evaluations must be used, it is probably the case that promotions are the most important source of extrinsic motivation.

In this chapter we analyze career-based incentives. We first consider promotions. It is shown that the structure of the hierarchy, and of pay across the organization chart, is important for understanding incentives when promotions are a major factor. We then provide a brief discussion of more general career-based incentives. Finally, we consider the use of other long-term incentives within the firm, such as pay based on seniority.

* * * * *   ## PROMOTIONS AND INCENTIVES

Should Promotions be Used as an Incentive System?

Dual Roles That Sometimes Conflict

You have a position to fill in your management hierarchy, and want to promote someone from the level below. Who should you give the position to? Firms often award a promotion to the best performer in the lower level job. When they do this, they are using the promotion as a form of incentive. A different view is that the promotion should be given to the employee who has the most potential to perform well in the higher level job. In other words, there are two important roles for promotions: sorting people into the appropriate jobs given their talents, and incentives.

The sorting and incentive roles will be in conflict if the best performer at one level is not the best performer at the next higher level. For example, in R&D organizations, it is quite common to find that the best researchers are not the best managers. Promoting the best researcher to manage the group may result not only in poor management, but in reduced research effectiveness.

In cases where this conflict between sorting and incentives is particularly severe, it is probably a good idea to avoid using promotions for incentives. For example, a research group could reward the best scientist with higher pay, more flexibility over choice of research projects, or a higher research budget, but keep the scientist in the same job. It could then identify the researcher who seems to be a good candidate for manager, and promote that person.

In many cases, fortunately, the conflict is not too severe. A manager typically needs to have a good working knowledge of the work that subordinates do. Such knowledge improves the manager's ability to direct, supervise, and evaluate the staff. When there is such a conflict, however, it is not at all obvious that the firm should explicitly try to use the promotion ladder to drive incentives. However, there is an additional complication: The firm may not have complete choice about this issue, since promotion systems often generate incentives automatically.

Intentional or Accidental Incentive System?

The conditions under which a firm can design its promotion system and compensation structure across the hierarchy with only consideration of incentive effects are rather strict. Compensation in different positions is constrained, at least to some extent, by the external labor market. If firm-specific human capital is not very important, employees may easily obtain similar jobs with other employers, constraining the ability of the firm to offer low wages to those who are competing for a promotion.

Second, the ability of the firm to alter its hierarchical structure, and accept variation in ability of those it promotes (in the case of a tournament, as we will see later), are likely to be limited. Because of such considerations, in many cases it may be inappropriate to view the firm's hierarchical and wage structure *as designed* to optimize incentives. Instead, promotions may often be an "accidental incentive system" that arises on its own and is impossible to avoid, even if the firm does not want to use promotions for incentives.

The logic is simple. Suppose that firms promote the best performers, and have better information about employee abilities than the labor market does. If you are promoted, the labor market should immediately infer that your ability is likely to be better than was previously thought—after all, your employer just signaled that. Because of this, your value should go up on the day you are promoted. In order to retain you, your employer will be forced to offer you a raise on promotion.[1]

---

[1] The firm will also have some incentive to delay your promotion, since you are cheaper before the promotion. This will be offset by the loss of not having you in the best position for your skills for some period of time.

This means that the hope of earning a promotion generates incentives. Since performance is affected not just by ability but by effort, employees will try to work harder to earn promotion. In effect, they provide effort to signal their worth to the external market, through earning a promotion.

In this view, the firm does not explicitly design the hierarchy and set pay levels to optimize incentives. Rather, the incentives from promotion are a side effect of the underlying sorting, labor market pressures on pay, and employee signaling. This view may well be appropriate for many firms.

There is some evidence that this view may be valid. Many large Japanese companies have offered lifetime employment to their core employees in the post–World War II period (though the practice appears to be gradually eroding now). This meant that such workers rarely, if ever, changed employers midcareer. Such firms should be much less constrained by external labor market forces. In fact, Japanese firms are much less likely to tie pay directly to hierarchical rank, and less likely to offer large raises for promotion, for their core employees. Instead, many such firms give employees two different ranks. One is for hierarchical position, and the other is for compensation. There is no necessary tie between the two, so that pay is not directly associated with position. Such practices might be impossible in economies where employees change firms more often.

Even if this view is correct, however, it does not mean that the theory of promotion-based incentives developed below is not important. On the contrary, if promotions have incentive effects, it is important to understand how they operate and what their implications are. However, it does turn the question around. If promotions are accidental incentives, then the firm should use the theory of promotion-based incentives to identify where the system generates stronger and weaker incentives. This is useful knowledge, since it tells the firm where it needs to focus its efforts on addressing employee motivation.

For the rest of this section, we model promotion-based incentives as though we are unconstrained in the design of the promotion system. Remember, though, that most firms are constrained, so that incentives from promotion may not perfectly match the ideal. When that is the case, the firm may use other forms of incentive, such as bonuses, to adjust incentives appropriately. Or, it might consider altering the structure of the hierarchy to change promotion rates or other parameters.

Promotion Rule: Tournament or Standard?

If your firm has complete flexibility in how to compensate workers at different levels of the hierarchy, how might you do so to optimize incentives? (Most firms will not have such complete flexibility, but this is a useful case to consider first, as it helps us understand how promotion-based incentives work. We return to this issue at the end of this section.)

A first question is the rule used to decide whom to promote. Two extreme rules come to mind. In the first, the firm promotes a fixed number of employees (often, only one) who have the best performance. This is a competition or *tournament*. In the second, the firm promotes any (from zero to all) whose performance meets some fixed threshold. This is an absolute *standard*. Thus, the promotion rule is a question about how performance will be evaluated. What are the properties of each approach?

Controlling Structure or Quality

Suppose that the firm has a rigid hierarchy in which job slots are fixed. For example, the firm may be deciding whom to promote to regional manager, and there are a fixed number of regions. Similarly, practically speaking there can only be a single CEO. In such cases, workers are automatically competing against each other for promotion, and the firm must run a tournament if the job is filled by an internal candidate. More generally, the more costly it is for the firm to alter the structure of the hierarchy, the more likely it is for a tournament to be desirable.

However, a potential problem with a tournament is that quality may be more variable. If the firm commits to promoting the best performer, in bad years it may promote someone who does not have adequate skills for the higher level job, putting a poor manager in a position of responsibility. In good years, it may fail to promote some employees who are high quality (but not the best), leading to turnover or inadequate use of skilled workers. When such sorting considerations are important, the firm may instead choose to use a standard for deciding promotions, because a standard tends to give better control over the quality of those promoted and passed over for promotion. For this reason, in firms where quality of workers is important (e.g., the best law firms or universities), promotion is more likely to be based on a standard.

Of course, most firms probably use a blend of these approaches, since they face costs from altering the hierarchical structure too much, and also from sorting workers ineffectively. Thus, they may have workers compete against each other for promotion, but when the talent pool is unusual they may relax the rules, promoting more or less than in typical years, or filling a slot from the outside labor market.

Relative vs. Absolute Evaluation

Another key difference between tournaments and standards is in *performance evaluation*. When the firm uses a standard, performance is evaluated for the individual worker. When workers compete, performance is evaluated relative to competitors. This is a special case of a general approach to performance evaluation, *relative performance evaluation* (RPE). Because a tournament is a good example of RPE, this issue was deferred from Chapter 9 until now. Note, though, that RPE techniques can be used for many types of incentive plans.

Ease and objectivity of evaluation.
One consideration is that evaluation may be easier in the case of a tournament than a standard. Since a fixed prize is given to a fraction of competitors, the only information that is needed is who the top performers are. The firm does not need to decide how much better performance was. This is an example of *ordinal* rather than *cardinal* ranking; the order matters, but not the distance between competitors. In many cases, it is very easy to determine who the best performer is, even when the job is complex and involves

many intangible dimensions. It is often much harder to determine how much each employee has performed. (Consider the difference between determining which lump of coal is larger than the other, and determining how much each weighs.) Moreover, because the top performers are often easy for everyone to determine, employees may consider the tournament outcome to be more objective. These are substantial advantages.

Risk. The evaluations used for tournaments and standards vary in other important ways. One example is risk (in this section we are referring to uncontrollable risk only). Suppose that your firm has two salesmen, one in Denmark and one in Singapore. Employee performance is affected by effort (e), but also by good and bad luck (measurement error). Further suppose that luck is driven by two different factors. The first is local events, such as the state of the Danish or Singaporean economy, and the actions of competitors in the local market (ε). The second is global events, such as worldwide macroeconomic conditions or oil prices (η). Using the subscripts S and D to refer to the two employees, we have:

$$PM_D = e_D + \varepsilon_D + \eta$$
$$PM_S = e_S + \varepsilon_S + \eta.$$

The term η does not have a subscript, because global economic conditions are assumed to affect both salespeople equally.

If we use a standard for deciding promotions, the Danish employee's performance measure equals PM_D. If we use a tournament, the promotion is decided on the basis of who has better total performance, and the performance measure for the Danish employee is:

$$RPE_D = PM_D - PM_S = e_D + \varepsilon_D + \eta - e_S - \varepsilon_S - \eta = e_D - e_S + \varepsilon_D - \varepsilon_S.$$

(In this example, $RPE_S = -RPE_D$.) This measure is different from the first one in several ways. First, the luck term that was common to both employees, η, dropped out. This reduces measurement error for the Danish employee. However, an additional error term was added, $-\varepsilon_S$. Finally, the Singaporean employee's effort e_S now plays a role. Which performance measure is better?

First, consider the issue of risk. The variance of the two performance measures (assuming that the μ's and η have zero correlations with each other) is:

$$\sigma_D^2 = \sigma_\varepsilon^2 + \sigma_\eta^2$$
$$\sigma_{RPE}^2 = 2 \cdot \sigma_\varepsilon^2.$$

RPE can reduce risk *if* measurement error that is common to both employees, η, is more important in determining performance (more variable) than is idiosyncratic risk, ε. In our example, if global factors play a larger role than local factors in determining sales in Denmark and Singapore, relative evaluation can reduce risk, thus improving the incentive plan. On the other hand, if personal or local risk ε is more important, RPE makes performance measurement risk worse.

Distortion.   A final effect of relative evaluation is that it might distort incentives for workers to cooperate. To see this, let us consider a multitask model in which each worker can provide two kinds of effort. The first, e^P, increases the worker's performance, while the second, e^S, decreases the colleague's performance. This is a simple way to model sabotage. In this case, for workers A and B the absolute performance measures are:

$$PM_A = e_A^P - e_B^S + \varepsilon_A + \eta$$
$$PM_B = e_B^P - e_A^S + \varepsilon_B + \eta$$

and the relative evaluation (for worker A) is:

$$RPE_A = PM_A - PM_B$$
$$= \left(e_A^P - e_B^S + \varepsilon_A + \eta\right) - \left(e_B^P - e_A^S + \varepsilon_B + \eta\right)$$
$$= \left(e_A^P - e_B^P\right) + \left(e_A^S - e_B^S\right) + \left(\varepsilon_A - \varepsilon_B\right).$$

In the case of RPE, an employee can improve the evaluation in two ways. One is to work harder in the standard sense: Increase e^P. The other is to *sabotage*, e^S. By contrast, there is no incentive to sabotage when the evaluation is based on individual performance.

A similar distorted incentive can arise when the employee can engage in influence activities, such as lobbying the supervisor for better evaluations or rewards, or doing actions that the supervisor prefers even when the actions do not improve firm value. To the extent that such actions can improve one's *relative* standing with the supervisor, relative evaluations will increase incentives for employees to engage in such activities.

RPE also reduces incentives for workers to *cooperate* on the job. This can be a serious downside to RPE, since most jobs are interdependent with those of colleagues to some extent.

In principle, it is possible to use RPE (such as a promotion tournament) and solve these problems, by incorporating measures of cooperation and sabotage into the performance evaluation. For example, a subjective evaluation might be used to encourage cooperation and reduce the temptation to undermine colleagues. Those who were insufficient team players would not be promoted. Clearly, firms do take these issues into account in such circumstances. However, it is likely that such fixes will be imperfect, since cooperation and sabotage are often hard to detect and quantify. Thus, one drawback to relative evaluation is that it is likely to be less effective when workers have more interdependent work. For example, contests may work very well for salespeople who work in different geographical areas, or for assembly line workers whose jobs are relatively independent of each other. By contrast, they are almost certainly a poor idea for members of the same workgroup.

Another approach might be to use a broader performance measure, such as $PM_A + PM_B$. In this case, the worker has incentives to cooperate, and not sabotage, since the reward also depends on the colleague's performance. Indeed, many firms use some form of group (or business unit, or divisional) rewards, partly for this reason. Of course, such a measure does *not* filter out common measurement error the way that RPE does; it generally increases measurement error. More concretely, when you are rewarded on the basis of work of a group, you are subject to risk because you cannot control what your colleagues do, and their luck. This is what we mentioned before in Chapter 9: The broader measure can reduce distortion, but tends to increase risk.

When such distortions cannot be removed from the evaluation, but cooperation is important because of interdependence between jobs, the proper response for the firm is to change the incentive structure. If promotions will still be used to drive incentives, then the rewards should be decreased. While this will decrease overall incentives, it will also decrease sabotage and increase cooperation. This is a simple application of the idea that incentives should be muted when the evaluation distorts multitask incentives.

An alternative would be for the firm to move toward group-based rewards. The performance measure and reward might both be based on group results. Another alternative would be to base promotion on absolute rather than relative performance, though evaluations may be more difficult to conduct, and the issues raised in Chapter 9 must be addressed.

In addition, where cooperation is important, the firm should not have such workers compete for rewards. This suggests that the composition of the group that is competing can be important. We will have more to say about this later.

Finally, the firm should consider the importance of cooperation or potential for sabotage when recruiting. People differ in the degree to which they cooperate or feel shame for sabotage on the job. Where jobs are more interdependent, it is important to try to recruit individuals with more cooperative personalities, who prefer working in groups.

FORCED CURVES FOR PERFORMANCE APPRAISALS
◆ ◆ ◆ ◆ ◆ ◆ ◆ ◆ ◆ ◆

Recall that a frequent complaint about performance appraisals is that managers tend to give many employees the same rating. An additional concern is that some managers may be lenient, while others may be strict. That is a form of luck that increases the riskiness of the pay system.

To address these concerns, some firms impose various forms of *forced curves* on the distribution of ratings. (Some universities use similar systems for grading.) Some require specific percentages for each rating. Others require that the average be fixed, though the distribution around the average can vary. These methods usually involve some element of RPE, since giving one worker a higher rating forces the manager to give someone else a lower rating.

Such approaches clearly can lead to greater dispersion in ratings across employees, more frequent use of lower ratings, etc. They also can reduce the risk to the employee from evaluators being too lenient or easy. To see this, consider that the effect of the evaluator's toughness or leniency is to lower or raise ratings for *all* subordinates of that evaluator. This is a form of common measurement error (η) as in our discussion of RPE. RPE filters out this effect.

While forced curves may be tempting because of these advantages, they have their own problems. Just as with any kind of RPE, they do not encourage cooperation, and may encourage sabotage. They impose their own form of risk, since employees may be evaluated against a very good group of colleagues, lowering their rating. (This effect is less likely if the rating is not done when the group size is too small.) And, it may not always be optimal to give employees clear feedback about performance (see later). Thus, many firms do not use forced curves, and some firms seem to switch back and forth between the two approaches, since neither is perfect.

General Electric (GE) is the most famous example of a firm that has successfully used a forced curve; they call it TopGrading. However, GE exerts a great deal of effort, and uses other policies, to make the program effective. For example, they train managers in how to conduct careful appraisals, and monitor and document appraisals carefully. This reduces the potential legal liability from disgruntled employees. Also important is that GE has a very aggressive corporate culture (see our discussion of "hawks and doves" later). It is well understood that receiving a poor rating for 2 years in a row puts an employee at high risk of being fired. Finally, GE has a very large, complex organization, so they are often able to reassign poor performers to positions for which they have a good fit, reducing firing costs (which would include litigation).

How Do Promotions Generate Incentives?

Prize Structure and Incentives

As described in the previous two chapters, incentives depend on two things: How effort (the kind that increases productivity, not sabotage) affects the evaluation, and how the evaluation is tied to rewards:

$$\frac{\Delta Pay}{\Delta effort} = \frac{\Delta Pay}{\Delta PM} \cdot \frac{\Delta PM}{\Delta effort}.$$

For a promotion, the first term on the right is a constant (the lump sum reward, raise on promotion, etc.), because the employee either wins the discrete prize, or does not. This looks like Figure 10.3 in the last chapter.

The second term is a bit more complicated. In the case of an absolute standard, the threshold for winning the prize is fixed. In the case of a tournament, the contestant must beat a certain number of competitors. Since their performance is unknown ex ante, the threshold for winning the prize is uncertain—it is a moving target. Otherwise, tournaments and standard can be analyzed in the same way.

To see how these ideas play out for promotions, let us write down the condition for the employee to receive the reward. Suppose that an employee is paid a base salary of W_1, and is given a raise to a salary of W_2 if promoted. Define the raise on promotion, the prize, as $\Delta W = W_2 - W_1$. Denoting probabilities by $pr(\cdot)$,

$$Pay = pr(not\ promoted) \cdot W_1 + pr(promoted) \cdot W_2$$
$$= W_1 + pr(promoted)\Delta W,$$

since $pr(\text{not promoted}) = 1 - pr(\text{promoted})$. Therefore,

$$\frac{\Delta Pay}{\Delta effort} = \Delta W \cdot \frac{\Delta pr(promoted)}{\Delta effort}.$$

Viewing the performance measure as binary (performance is good enough to win promotion, or not), then the first term is $\Delta Pay/\Delta PM$, and the second is $\Delta PM/\Delta effort$. These are the same two terms that always affect incentives.

Level of salary. One important result is immediate: What matters the most to promotion incentives is primarily the change in pay ΔW. This is an application of the point made in Chapter 10 that the shape of the pay–performance relationship drives incentives much more than does the level of pay. Graphically, as in Figure 10.1 in Chapter 10, the level of pay shifts the pay–performance relationship up or down, to raise or lower the overall level of expected pay. For example, the expected salary in the equations above can be adjusted by changing W_1, without changing ΔW (thus change W_2 by the same amount as W_1).

This is a general point: The firm has two different instruments for two different purposes in designing the pay package. The base salary generally is used to make sure that the firm is able to recruit and retain the appropriate quality of employees. It responds to labor market supply and demand for skills. It also adjusts for the overall level of effort and risk that the incentive system implies.

In many cases the firm is much less constrained about how to vary pay with performance, or even over time (as we will see when we discuss seniority-based pay). It can use this flexibility to drive appropriate incentives, separately from the question of recruitment and retention of the workforce.

Prize from promotion. The most important point in the last equation is that promotion incentives are larger, the larger the raise (and other rewards) earned upon promotion. In any contest, the larger the prize, the greater the effort that will be provided. There are many examples of this in sports. Teams tend to exert much more effort in the most important games, where there is more at stake. They tend to slack off in the less important games. The same will tend to be true for employee effort in promotion ladders.

We can apply this idea to the data in Table 11.1 (or the plots in Figure 11.1). The raise and longer term rewards for promotion tend to be larger in higher levels of the hierarchy. This suggests that incentives will tend to be stronger at higher levels. (However, this is not necessarily the case, since we have not yet analyzed the second term in the last equation.)

To a first approximation, the raise on promotion is a good estimate of the reward from the promotion. It is the immediate consequence of the promotion, and is guaranteed once the promotion is earned. Thus, it is the best starting place for analyzing the incentive structure in your firm's hierarchy.

A more complex estimate of the prize from promotion recognizes that an additional benefit from promotion is that it makes the employee eligible for additional rewards. These usually entail higher raises in the new job (as suggested in the last column of Table 11.1), and the ability to compete for the next promotion. These will also have some value to the employee, though they will be somewhat discounted compared to the immediate raise on promotion, since they require further effort and are not guaranteed.

This implies that compensation at higher levels in the job ladder—or at later stages in a sequential contest—affect incentives at *all lower levels*. The larger the difference in pay between Level 5 and Level 6, the greater should be motivation at *all* levels from 1 to 5. (Of course, the effect might be small for levels farther from Level 6, since the probability of getting all the way from a lower level to Level 6 might be quite small.) In other words, the structure of pay across levels in the organization chart can have important incentive effects for lower levels.

One implication of this idea is that it is more important to give larger prizes at higher levels. The reason is that these prizes provide incentives for more employees, since there are more levels below them. This is one explanation for why salaries rise rapidly with hierarchical level, as seen in Figure 11.1, and why executive pay levels are often quite high. The high executive pay levels may serve a purpose beyond compensation for the executives: They may motivate those below them to strive to become an executive as well.

Promotion Probability and Incentives

The first term in the last equation above is how effort affects the probability of winning promotion. In an abstract sense, the performance measure when rewards are lump sum is binary: The employee's performance is either high enough to earn the reward, or it is not. Thus, this term is the same as $\Delta PM/\Delta e$.

Formal analysis of the effect of promotion probability is technical. The intuition, however, is straightforward, and applies to both tournaments and standards. Consider two extremes. In one case, the promotion is guaranteed and the probability equals one. In the other case, the promotion is impossible and the probability equals zero. In both of these extremes, there is no point in exerting effort—more or less effort will make no difference to the outcome. Incentives will be zero. Clearly, the only way that there will be an incentive is if we have an intermediate case, where the promotion is possible, but neither too hard to achieve, nor too easy.[2]

Intuitively, incentives are driven by the effect of incremental effort on the chance of winning, given that luck will play a role as well. High levels of good or bad luck are relatively less likely to occur. If the chance of winning is low, the odds that incremental effort will make any difference to the outcome are very small, since large good luck is also required to win.

Perhaps less intuitively, the same applies when the promotion probability is very high. In that case, the employee has incentives to slack off, because incremental reductions in effort are unlikely to cause the employee to lose the promotion. They would have to be combined with large bad luck. Thus, for example, sports teams tend to put in their second string when they are far ahead in a game.

In real organizations, the probability of promotion to the next hierarchical level tends to be much less than $\frac{1}{2}$, especially for higher levels. Thus, in practice our result is that for a given reward, promotion incentives are weaker, the lower the promotion rate.

Luck

As with all incentive schemes, luck plays a role for promotion incentives. In our simpler incentive systems considered in Chapter 10, the effect of luck was to increase the risk premium required, and consequently to reduce the strength of the optimal incentive intensity. Luck plays those roles here, as it does in any incentive system. However, luck also plays a different role here—it also reduces incentives.

Suppose that you are playing a tennis match. On some days, the wind is very calm, but on other days it is very strong. When the wind is calm, you have greater control over your shots. When the wind is very strong, you have less control. This means that on windy days, the outcome is less likely to be determined by which contestant played better, and more likely to be determined by good or bad luck. The same applies in promotion settings, for either tournaments or standards.

---

[2]Several studies in accounting and psychology have concluded that incentives are strongest when the employee has a 50% chance of meeting the target for the reward. Economic modeling helps explain why this may be so.

Because of this effect, risk reduces the effect of effort on the outcome; it reduces $\Delta pr(win)/\Delta e$.[3] This is shown formally in the Appendix. And of course, this in effect means that $\Delta PM/\Delta e$ is lower when measurement error is higher. By now, you know what that means—incentives will be low.

What are the implications of luck for optimal incentives? If measurement error is higher, incentives will be lower, unless the firm increases the size of the prize. One possible response is to incur costs to measure performance more carefully. Another is to change the prize structure. Optimal prize structures tend to be more skewed (toward larger rewards for better performers) when luck plays more of a role.

The point that luck matters and affects the optimal salary structure has implications for how compensation varies by industry or country. Consider, for example, the difference between the United States and Japan. Japanese wage structures are more compressed than those in America. Top executives in Japan get paid less relative to production workers than do their counterparts in the United States. Some have interpreted this as extravagance on the part of American firms and their top management.

An alternative explanation might be that the American business environment is riskier than in Japan. Promotions in the United States may depend more on random factors. For example, promotions in Japan come later in the career than in the United States. By the time a Japanese manager has made CEO, the firm has very clear signals about productivity. It is unlikely that measurement error will play an important role in determining the promotion. If promotions in the United States are more heavily influenced by luck, then American firms might offset the effort-reducing effects of luck by choosing larger salary spreads.

A similar point can be made with respect to new versus old industries. If luck is more important in affecting an individual's performance in newer industries, then firms in newer industries may tend to have higher variance in their salary structures compared to firms in older, more established industries.

Summing Up

We see that in many ways, tournaments and standards have the same implications for incentive plan design. The most important question is the size of the prize for promotion. A good starting estimate for this is the raise on promotion. A better estimate would take into account the added value to the employee of better career prospects that come with the promotion.

The next important factor is the promotion rate. Higher promotion rates (as long as they are not too high, which they do not tend to be inside firms) generally imply stronger incentives for the same reward.

Putting these two ideas together, if the firm has enough flexibility in compensation across levels to set pay levels solely to generate optimal incentives, then the

---

[3]This is true only if promotion rates are not too close to 0 or 1. The closer they are to either extreme, the more likely the opposite is to be true. That is because incremental effort only makes a difference in those cases, when combined with very good or bad luck.

raise on promotion should be higher when the promotion rate is lower, and vice versa. It should also tend to be larger in higher levels of the hierarchy.

Finally, greater luck or performance measurement error not only implies a higher risk premium for the employee, but also reduces incentives in promotion systems.

Tournaments and standards differ in some important ways. Tournaments are necessary when job slots are fixed; they give better control over the number of employees promoted. Standards are more useful when the quality of employees promoted is more important. Second, tournaments are a form of RPE, so they usually distort incentives away from cooperation, and toward sabotage of coworkers. Standards do not have these negative side effects.

Advanced Issues

Heterogeneity of Employees

The theory above assumed that all employees who are hoping to earn promotion are identical. What happens if they vary in ability or some other important dimension? It turns out that mixing employees of different types can cause a couple of problems for promotion-based incentives.

Variation in ability.   If employees vary in ability, then they vary in the likelihood that they will win promotion. Those who have the highest ability may have a very good chance of winning promotion. As we saw above, they will then tend to have lower incentives. Similarly, those who are performing poorly may have little chance of promotion, and may also slack off. Those employees who believe that their performance is right at the margin between winning and losing promotion will have the greatest incentives.

Consider, for example, the pay structure in Figure 10.3 in Chapter 10. The threshold for winning promotion is T (which could be fixed, as in a standard, or variable, as in a tournament). If the employee believes that his performance is near T, incentives are very high, because the incremental effect of effort on the expected reward is very high. If the employee believes that his performance is too far above or below T, incentives may be very weak. In other words, promotion-based incentives tend to not work well when the workforce is heterogeneous.

What can be done about this? If the firm uses a standard for promotion decisions, then it could simply vary the standard T for different employees, imposing a higher standard for better employees, and vice versa. Unfortunately, this would have negative effects on sorting—it would make it easier for low ability workers to get promoted, and harder for high ability workers to get promoted.

In such cases, the firm must expend some resources to presort employees, to reduce the variation in their abilities. In sports contests, athletes are separated into different leagues, so that those with similar abilities compete against each other. Inside firms, the more the firm has already promoted employees, the more homogeneous the group of remaining employees eligible for promotions. Thus, this concern is likely to be more important at lower levels than at higher levels.

Might workers self-select in the appropriate way, as in Chapter 2? Unfortunately, generally the answer will be no. Low ability workers will tend to have an incentive to try to get access to promotion systems (or athletic leagues) that are designed for high ability workers, since the base salary will be higher in the higher ability system.

An interesting implication of heterogeneity of performance and promotion-based incentives has to do with subjective performance appraisals. Of course, promotions are usually based on subjective assessments of worker performance by the supervisor. Imagine that you are a supervisor, and are trying to decide what feedback to give your subordinates. The subordinates are hoping to win promotion, but the promotion decision will be made in the future. What will you tell them?

If they are right at the margin, giving them this feedback can only strengthen their incentives. The interesting question is what you tell subordinates who are performing above the threshold for promotion. If the goal is to maximize motivation, giving accurate, clear feedback to employees who are frontrunners or underdogs with respect to promotion may well reduce their incentives.

Instead, giving somewhat negative (or less favorable than deserved) feedback to a good performer may alter their perceptions about how they are performing, moving them closer to the threshold and increasing their incentives. Similarly, giving more positive feedback than deserved to a poor performer may increase their motivation, since they will be less likely to give up on the hope of promotion.

This implies that, when promotion incentives are large and evaluations are subjective, supervisors have some incentive to distort the feedback that they give to their employees. They may be especially reluctant to give negative feedback to poor performers, out of a concern that this would demotivate such employees. And even if they do not distort feedback, they may be vague and uninformative in the feedback that they do give, to at least make it harder for frontrunners and underdogs to figure out where they stand. These ideas may help explain several facts about subjective performance appraisals: Distributions tend to be concentrated and upward biased; supervisors tend to be reluctant to give explicit feedback to subordinates; and subordinates often do not trust that their performance ratings were given fairly.

Variation in personality.   We have already discussed the problem of sabotage and lack of cooperation that tournaments may induce. Now suppose that employees vary in their personality: Some are more aggressive, or less likely to cooperate, while others tend to have a personal taste for more cooperation or teamwork in the workplace. If these two types of employees are mixed in a workplace where rewards are competitively awarded, problems can arise.

The following example illustrates the idea. Consider four workers, two who are *hawks* H_1, H_2; and two who are *doves*, D_1, D_2. Hawks are aggressive, while doves are cooperative. There are a number of ways to arrange them together into production teams. Table 11.2 lists some possibilities.

The two polar cases are A and E. In configuration A, all work together. In configuration E, all work separately. Configuration E loses all advantages of worker

TABLE 11.2
GROUP ASSIGNMENT BY EMPLOYEE PERSONALITY TYPE

	Group			
Configuration	1	2	3	4
A	H1, H2, D1, D2			
B	H1, D1, D2	H2		
C	H1, H2	D1, D2		
D	H1, D1	H2, D2		
E	H1	H2	D1	D2

interaction. If potential synergies from combining different worker types are large, then the firm will want to consider a structure like *A*. If so, then as we will see that a tournament-type reward system would be a mistake.

The incentive problem that arises from mixing the different types is that the aggressive hawks will tend to cooperate even less, and sabotage even more, when they are paired with doves. The intuition is that the reward is based on relative performance, which motivates both to avoid cooperation. But the hawk knows that the dove is likely to provide more cooperation and less sabotage than the hawk is. This means that the hawk will tend to damage the dove's performance more, and will be in a better position to win.

This also means that their relative performance will now differ. As described above, when employees vary in relative performance, tournament incentives tend to be weaker. Thus, differences in personality may make differences in incentive even worse when rewards are given competitively.

This effect would not occur if hawks were paired with hawks, and doves with doves, since they would then be competing against someone with the same incentives and personality. Unfortunately, hawks will have some incentive to compete against doves, so that self-selection will not generally occur. Once more we see a benefit from sorting workers so that similar employees are competing against each other, especially when the firm uses a tournament.

This kind of effect suggests one reason why firms vary in corporate culture. Firms with more competition in their reward structures should sort optimally for more aggressive employees (and expect less cooperation), and vice versa. We see a link among several issues discussed in this book: The degree of interdependence in jobs is important for deciding whether or not to have employees compete for rewards. This, in turn, affects the type of employee the firm should recruit, and the corporate culture that results.

Incentives for Losers

One problem with any promotion-based incentive system is that it motivates only to the extent that the employee feels that there is enough chance that a promotion will be earned. Those employees who are not in the running, such as those who have been passed over in previous rounds, will not be motivated. This decline in extrinsic motivation for those who have been in a job for a long time, and who do not have prospects for further advancement, is one reason for the common complaint that such workers are "dead wood," relatively unproductive.[4]

There are several things that the firm can do for such workers. One is to encourage them to leave the firm or to find a more suitable position in the same firm (for example, see the box about General Electric earlier). Another is to provide incentives in some other form. For example, workers who do not have strong prospects for promotion may be offered stronger pay for performance in the form of annual bonuses. Finally, the supervisor may be able to increase intrinsic motivation by offering the employee the opportunity to perform new tasks and learn new skills.

Outside Hiring

Of course, firms often hire employees from the outside, and not just at entry-level positions. What is the effect of outside hiring on promotion-based incentives?

The first effect is that outside hiring tends to lower incentives for internal candidates: It reduces the likelihood that the incumbent employee will earn promotion, which generally reduces incentives. In addition, recall the firm's conflict between the desire to promote the best candidate for the higher level position, and the desire to promote the best performer. Once employees have provided the effort, the firm may be tempted to promote on potential rather than past performance, even if it had claimed that it would offer the promotion to the best performer (this is another example of the holdup problem). Of course, if employees foresee this problem, it reduces their incentives in the first place. Hiring from the outside only makes that concern worse.

Therefore, an important cost of outside hiring that firms should consider is that it may reduce motivation for existing employees. Most firms tend to prefer to fill vacancies with internal candidates, and this is one explanation (another is firm-specific human capital).

Outside hiring does have advantages. Recall that the benefit of using an absolute standard to decide promotions is that the firm has better control over the quality of employees in the higher level position. The benefit of a tournament is that performance evaluation is easier, since it is RPE and only ordinal ranking matters. By using outside hiring combined with a tournament, the firm can achieve both of these advantages simultaneously. Promotions can be based on relative rankings by using a tournament. However, in years when the quality of the pool of internal applicants is too low, the firm can decide to hire externally instead. The outside option will reduce incentives somewhat, but since the firm only resorts to it occasionally, such an effect should be small. And, the firm is able to protect itself against promoting poor quality employees into higher level positions. Furthermore,

---

[4]Another reason for the phenomenon, sometimes called the Peter principle (that employees are promoted to their level of incompetence) is that the average ability of workers declines, the longer that they stay in the same position. This is because the firm is continuously selecting high ability workers for promotion.

competing against potential outside candidates may reduce the incentive to sabotage internal candidates.

Turnover

Turnover is quite important for an effective promotion-based incentive system. The higher the turnover, the more open job slots made available. This increases promotion incentives. Thus, if a firm emphasizes the use of promotions for incentives, a healthy degree of turnover can be very helpful. Conversely, where turnover is low, promotion-based incentives are not likely to function well. Consider a point in the organization chart where the hierarchy narrows rapidly: There are many fewer positions in the higher level than in the lower level. In that case, promotion rates will be very low, and generate poor incentives unless the reward from promotion is very high. The firm has several options. It can try to restructure the hierarchy to open up promotion rates over the long term. In the short term, it can try to promote or terminate some employees at the higher level.

Evidence

If is difficult to observe the effects of promotion-based incentives inside firms, because in such cases individual measures of output are not available. Most of the empirical evidence on the theory of tournaments and standards comes from other sources. For example, several studies have examined whether larger prizes lead to better performance in sporting contests like golf. These results tend strongly to support the predictions, suggesting that professional athletes respond to incentives. Indeed, many professional sports teams make use of elaborate incentive schemes for their players, indicating that they believe their employees can be motivated in this way.

Another series of tests has conducted laboratory experiments to see if participants (usually college students) behave in ways that the theory predicts. These studies tend to find that larger prizes induce greater effort, greater risk induces less effort, and a lower probability of winning induces less effort. All of these are as predicted. In addition, the amount of effort put forth by students usually converges quickly to the precise amount predicted by the theory. A puzzle, however, is that the variance in output is higher with tournaments, but not with standards, than predicted by the theory. Evidence seems to be accumulating to suggest that different people react to competitions differently, which may explain such a result. For example, when offered a choice of a tournament or a standard, men choose tournaments relatively more than women do.

Some studies have analyzed whether firm evaluation practices and compensation structures vary in ways that are predicted by the theory described. The evidence on whether firms are more likely to use RPE or an absolute standard for deciding whom to promote is quite mixed. It is probably safe to say that firms vary in their practices (and even vary in which they emphasize for individual jobs in the same firm), depending on the importance of fixing the hierarchical structure or controlling the quality of promoted employees.

Other studies have examined implications of the theory for pay structures (e.g., is the raise on promotion larger if odds of receiving the promotion are smaller?). Such studies are generally consistent with the idea that firms design their compensation structures in accordance with the theory. Unfortunately, there are other plausible explanations for the findings in most of these studies. For example, if the promotion rate is very low, then the difference in talent between those promoted and those passed over should be larger. This means that the raise on promotion should be larger. This explanation is based solely on sorting, and has nothing to do with incentives. Thus, it is very hard to say for sure whether or not firms explicitly design their pay structures across the hierarchy to optimize incentives.

TOURNAMENTS FOR ECONOMICS PROFESSORS?

One study analyzed whether tournaments or standards better describe compensation policies in university economics departments. This is a good setting for testing the theory, because university departments are hierarchical, have up-or-out promotion systems, and some data on employee productivity (quantity and quality of published research) are publicly available.

One finding was that junior professors tend to be more productive if their department has a larger gap in pay between assistant and associate professor ranks. This is consistent with the idea that the pay gap generates incentives.

Another interesting finding is that the highest ranking economics departments do not seem to run either clearcut tournaments or standards. Rather, they seem to resort to outside hiring when the quality of internal candidates is too low. Because professors have little in the way of firm-specific human capital, they compete with each other in the broader academic labor market, rather than only internally, and move frequently between universities.

Source: Coupé, Smeets, & Warzynski (2006)

CAREER CONCERNS

In an active labor market, employees may be motivated partly because good performance can lead to better employment opportunities outside the firm. This kind of incentive is often called *career concerns*.[5] It is most important in industries where human capital is more general, and where other potential employers can evaluate performance. Good examples include scientists (whose research is published), professional athletes, and top executives of publicly traded firms. To some extent, career concerns are likely to operate in all industries.

Career concerns raise some interesting implications. Workers should tend to be more highly motivated earlier in their careers. This is because they are trying to establish their reputation with the labor market. As the career progresses, more is known about the worker's capabilities, and there is less possibility of affecting one's market value.

Another implication is that younger workers should tend to be more willing to take risks, such as trying unusual jobs with uncertain prospects: If the risks do not work out, they have more time to recover from the bad outcome. Thus, there is a natural tendency for people to become more conservative as they progress in their careers.

●●●●● SENIORITY PAY AND INCENTIVES

The data in Figure 11.1 and Table 11.1 suggest that increases in earnings come not just from promotion, but from raises in salary over time. Of course, raises can be a form of incentive if they are tied to performance evaluations. In many firms, however, seniority plays a substantial role in salary increases. At first glance, it would seem that tying salary increases to seniority would not generate incentives, since the raise is not tied directly to performance. In this section, we provide a brief argument for why seniority-based pay can also be used as a long-term incentive.

To make things simple, suppose that workers in the firm can choose to work at either a high or low level of effort. An employee who works at a high level of effort will produce output over the career given by the curve V in Figure 11.2. As the worker gains experience, output rises to some point, after which it may decline. Alternatively, the worker can choose a low level of effort, producing V', which is lower than V. Assume that high effort would be the efficient choice. In other words, the difference in productivity between V and V' would exceed the marginal disutility of working at the high level of effort instead of the low level. Therefore, the firm and the employee would like to structure a contract in which the high level of effort is provided.

In addition, to illustrate the point easily, consider a very simple performance evaluation system. If the worker shirks (produces low output) in any period, there is some probability that the firm will detect the shirking, in which case the worker is penalized (e.g., fired).

The path *Alt* is the value of the worker's alternative use of time. As the worker nears retirement, the best alternative is likely to be leisure. Thus, T is the date that

---

[5] Career concerns should motivate both investments in human capital, and greater employee effort. We focus on the latter, but the link to human capital should be clear to you after reading Chapter 3.

FIGURE 11.2
PRODUCTIVITY AND PAY OVER THE CAREER

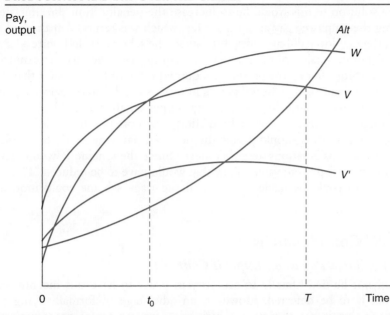

a worker should retire. Put in other terms, a self-employed worker producing V would voluntarily retire at T.

The path W is a possible wage profile offered to the employee over time. It is drawn such that the discounted present value of W from zero to T is exactly equal to the discounted present value of V over the same period. A worker who is paid V each period would receive the exact value of output. A worker who is paid W would receive less than productivity until time t_0, and more than productivity thereafter. Over the entire career, the compensation would add up to the value of output, in present value.

Why bother distorting the wage profile in this fashion? Incentives are not the same along each profile. Incentives are greater along W than along V. In fact, a worker paid exactly V would end up producing less than V. The reasoning is simple.

Suppose that the firm pays wages equal to V at every stage of the career. Consider the worker's incentive on the last day before retirement at T. If the worker shirks, there is nothing to lose, since the worker is not employed tomorrow anyway. Similarly, at any time near retirement, the worker has little incentive, because the loss from being fired, the difference between V and Alt, is very low at this point.

More generally, as long as the outside alternatives for the worker are not very different from those at the present firm, similar logic applies at all points in time.

Thus, if human capital is largely general, and the costs of finding a new job are small, the worker has great temptation to shirk, as there is little to lose.

One solution to this would be to increase the penalty from shirking, perhaps by having the employee pay an up-front fee, which was returned at the end of the career if the employee did not shirk. Of course, the scheme W in Figure 11.2 is just a more elaborate version of that, where the firm agrees to tie raises to seniority. At all points in time after t_0, the present discounted value of W is greater than that of V. In fact, the same is true for *all* points in time, since W starts below V, and the total discounted present values over the entire period are equal. Thus, the worker has a stronger incentive to provide high effort, the more that pay is deferred.

Note that workers should prefer the deferred pay scheme W to the scheme V (absent the considerations described next). Since the scheme V would generate some shirking, the present value of pay that would have to be reduced. The worker (and the firm) could be made better off if the wage scheme could motivate no shirking.

Practical Considerations

Seniority-Based Pay as an Implicit Contract

Pay need not be tied literally to seniority in order to have this incentive effect; it just needs to be deferred. However, an advantage of formally tying pay to seniority is that it is one way in which the firm can try to precommit to the deferred pay incentive scheme. Deferred pay (including the examples we discussed in Chapters 2–3) involves a promise from the firm to the employee. In Figure 11.2, if the pay scheme is W, the firm may be tempted to renege on its promise, lowering pay or firing overpaid workers with high seniority.

Because it involves implicit contracting, seniority-based schemes are more likely to work well for companies that have established good reputations as fair employers (e.g., older, stable firms compared to new startups). Such firms are also more likely to implement policies that signal to workers that they take a long-term interest in their career success, and intend to treat them fairly. See Chapter 15 for some discussion of these issues.

Deferred pay schemes also impose risk on the worker because there is some chance that the firm will default on its obligations to workers if financial performance is poor. Therefore, seniority schemes are more likely to be observed in companies with less risky business environments, such as those in growing and stable industries.

The Worker as Lender

In all deferred pay schemes, the worker in effect is a lender to the employer. If the deferred reward is fixed in advance, the worker acts like a bondholder for the firm. If the deferred reward is variable, such as stock or profit sharing, the worker acts like an equity holder.

Because workers tend to be risk averse, it would not seem to make sense to give employees implicit equity in their firms. However, there is an additional incentive effect that might justify deferred pay correlated with future firm value. In some cases, employees can take actions today that increase firm value in the future. Consider a law firm. The way in which the lawyer conducts business today may have important effects on the reputation of the firm in the future. In addition, the lawyer may be able to bring in new clients today who will generate future work for the company. By tying deferred rewards to future firm profits, the law firm can motivate lawyers to take into account the long-term effects of their actions on firm value.

This is just an example of a distortion in the face of multitask incentives. Long-term effects on firm value are usually very hard to measure today. For this reason, typical incentive plans distort employee incentives toward the short term. Implicit, deferred equity can mitigate this problem. In fact, in companies where employees do have greater impact of future firm value, such as professional partnerships, equity type schemes are quite common.

Mandatory Retirement

One problem with paying W to workers is that they have incentives to stay at the firm after retirement, since at T, $W > V$. This is inefficient, because the value of the worker's leisure Alt exceeds the value to the firm of the worker's productivity. The firm would make more profit by paying the worker to quit! Of course, that would destroy the pay schedule W.

One way to look at this is that the worker could promise to retire at date T. However, he has incentives to renege on such a promise. The firm could try firing the worker at T, but most economies impose strict regulations on firing workers who are near retirement (probably as a way to encourage firms to not renege on their pension commitments).

Imposing mandatory retirement at date T easily solves this problem. In fact, many firms used to have mandatory retirement policies. However, in the United States and some other countries, mandatory retirement is now illegal. Instead, the firm must resort to other incentives, through structuring of pensions, etc., in order to encourage efficient retirement.

Summary

Career considerations are a major source of extrinsic motivation for many, perhaps most, workers. Most increases in earnings over the career come from new jobs, promotions, and gradual raises in salary over time. For white-collar workers in particular, promotions are often the most important form of pay for performance. For all workers, the possibility of raising their reputation and value to the labor market outside their employer can be a large motivator, especially early in the career.

Why do promotions play such a key role in incentives? One answer is that performance evaluations are quite difficult, and inevitably subjective, in white-collar jobs. For this reason, short-term incentive plans may be far from perfect, and firms may defer evaluations until job assignment decisions must be made. Another answer is that promotions generate incentives automatically, because of the signal that the promotion sends to the labor market, which raises the promoted employee's market value. Thus, promotion incentives may be forced on the firm, even if they would rather separate job assignments from incentives.

More generally, this suggests an intuitive hierarchy of pay for performance schemes. When analyzing incentives for a given employee, the firm should first ask whether or not promotion-based incentives are large or small. To do so, it can use the models of tournaments and standards described in this chapter. Also keep in mind the value of additional promotions, if they exist, farther up the job ladder.

Where promotion incentives are weak, the firm should consider alternative forms of pay for performance. One possibility is demotions or the threat of termination. However, demotions will generally be rare; as described earlier, for several reasons it is natural that most employees tend to move upward in the hierarchy over their careers. The threat of being fired can be an important incentive, but it comes at a cost compared to other forms of incentives: The firm and employee incur search and recruitment costs. Thus, if other forms of incentive are available, and if these turnover costs are high (as they tend to be in most of Europe), then the firm may not use frequent termination as a form of incentive. In fact, most firms appear to use terminations only in extreme cases, so this does not tend to be a major source of incentives.

That suggests that the firm would then turn to bonus plans and raises to provide further incentives, when promotion-based incentives are weak. For example, when the hierarchy narrows so that promotion rates are very low, we would expect to see greater use of bonuses. Similarly, at the top of the hierarchy (CEOs and top executives), firms resort to much greater use of stock, options, bonuses, etc. When such approaches are needed, the principles of Chapters 9–10 apply.

Of course, in some cases the firm may choose to use the promotion ladder as an explicit incentive. This is most likely to be the case when the benefits of relative performance evaluation are very high, or the hierarchical structure of the firm is relatively fixed, so that competition for promotions is desirable.

Regardless of whether promotion-based incentives are explicitly designed or accidental, the discussion of tournaments and standards applies. Tournaments and standards have almost identical predictions about how incentives and optimal prizes vary with promotion rates and riskiness of evaluations.

Tournaments and standards differ in two important respects. First, tournaments should be used when the firm desires to fix slots, *unless* outside hiring is feasible (e.g., firm-specific human capital is not very important, and hiring costs are not too high). By contrast, standards imply that the number of employees promoted will vary. On the other hand, with tournaments the quality of recruits will be more variable than with standards. In a bad year, the firm might promote a relatively low quality employee, just because he was the best performer. In a good year, the firm might not promote a high quality employee, because the talent pool was so good. Standards allow the firm to have better control over the quality of employees promoted.

An intermediate approach, outside hiring, can be used to balance the desire for stable hierarchical structure against the desire to control the quality of those promoted (or hired) into higher levels of the firm. In practice, it is likely that many firms that use explicit tournaments because of the benefits of RPE may resort to outside hiring in years when the quality of competitors is too low.

The second important way that tournaments differ from standards is in performance evaluation. Tournaments are an important example of RPE, whereas standards use individual performance evaluation. RPE reduces risk, *if* measurement error for different employees contains a common component that is very important. However, if that is not the case, RPE increases risk, since it exposes the employee to the idiosyncratic luck of the competitor.

An important benefit of RPE when the reward is discrete—as it is with tournaments—is that the evaluation becomes ordinal. In other words, the firm only has to decide who performed better, not how much better. This can make performance evaluation much easier, and much more credible, especially when work is more intangible. Of course, this applies to many white-collar jobs. This consideration favors a tournament over a standard.

Finally, tournaments may distort incentives compared to standards. A tournament will motivate less cooperation and more sabotage than otherwise. When work is highly interdependent so that these issues are important, the firm should consider using an absolute standard to decide promotions instead of a tournament. More generally, when teamwork considerations are important, incentive plans that make use of RPE tend to be a mistake. If RPE is used, the firm should compress pay, to balance the desire for strong productive incentives against the incentives for sabotage or lack of cooperation. Moreover, the firm should segregate workers by personality type, avoiding putting more aggressive and individualistic employees in competition with more cooperative employees. Finally, the firm can reduce these problems if it can recruit employees with more cooperative personalities (intrinsic motivation).

STUDY QUESTIONS

1. If employees compete for a promotion in a tournament, are they likely to take more or less risky actions on the job? Does the answer depend on their odds of winning the promotion?

2. The average performance of employees within a job tends to be lower for those who have been in the job longer. According to the theory of human capital, this seems puzzling. Provide at least two explanations for this phenomenon.

3. Incentives based on tournament incentives are more compatible with which type of organizational structure described in Chapter 6? Why?

4. If promotions are an accidental incentive system in your firm, is there anything that can be done to avoid the effect?

5. When managers set goals for employees at the beginning of the year, they often "negotiate" the goal. When doing so, how would you recommend they think about how difficult the goal should be to achieve?

6. Suppose that promotions are an important source of incentives for managers in a firm that has eight levels in the hierarchy. Because of reengineering, the firm cuts out several layers of management. How should the firm think about changing its compensation system for managers at different levels?

■ ■ ■ ■ ■ ## REFERENCES

Coupé, Thomas, Valérie Smeets, & Frédèric Warzynski (2005). "Incentives, Sorting and Productivity Along the Career: Evidence from a Sample of Top Economists." *Journal of Law, Economics & Organization*, Spring.

Peter, Laurence & Raymond Hull (1969). *The Peter Principle: Why Things Always Go Wrong*. New York: William Morrow & Co.

■ ■ ■ ■ ■ ## FURTHER READING

Bayo-Moriones, Alberto, Jose Galdon-Sanchez, & Maia Guell (2005). "Is Seniority-Based Pay Used as a Motivation Device? Evidence from Plant Level Data." Working paper, Universitat Pompeu Fabra.

Bull, Clive, Andrew Schotter, & Keith Weigelt (1987). "Tournaments and Piece Rates: An Experimental Study." *Journal of Political Economy* 95: 1–33.

Chan, William (1996). "External Recruitment versus Internal Promotion." *Journal of Labor Economics* 14(4): 555–570.

DeVaro, Jed (2006). "Internal Promotion Contests in Firms." *RAND Journal of Economics* 60(3): 311–339.

DeVaro, Jed & Michael Waldman (2006). "The Signaling Role of Promotions: Further Theory and Empirical Evidence." Working paper, Cornell University.

Drago, Robert & Gerald Garvey (1997). "Incentives for Helping on the Job: Theory and Evidence." *Journal of Labor Economics*.

Ehrenberg, Ronald and Michael Bognanno (1990). "Do Tournaments Have Incentive Effects?" *Journal of Political Economy* 98(6): 1307–1324.

Eriksson, Tor (1999). "Executive Compensation and Tournament Theory: Empirical Tests on Danish Data." *Journal of Labor Economics* 17(2): 262–280.

Frederiksen, Anders and Elod Takats (2005). "Optimal Incentive Mix: The Dual Role of Promotions and Layoffs in Firms." Working paper, Center for Corporate Performance, Aarhus School of Business.

Gibbs, Michael (1994). "Testing Tournaments? An Appraisal of the Theory and Evidence." *Labor Law Journal* 45(8): 493–500.

Kandel, Eugene & Edward Lazear (1992). "Peer Pressure and Partnerships." *Journal of Political Economy* 100(4): 801–817.

Knoeber, Charles (1989). "A Real Game of Chicken: Contracts, Tournaments, and the Production of Broilers." *Journal of Law, Economics & Organization* 5: 271–292.

Lazear, Edward (1979). "Why is There Mandatory Retirement?" *Journal of Political Economy* 87: 1261–1284.

Lazear, Edward (1989). "Pay Equality and Industrial Politics." *Journal of Political Economy* 97: 561–580.

Lazear, Edward (2004). "The Peter Principle: A Theory of Decline." *Journal of Political Economy* 112: S141–S163.

Lazear, Edward & Sherwin Rosen (1981). "Rank-Order Tournaments as Optimum Labor Contracts." *Journal of Political Economy* 89: 841–864.

Rosen, Sherwin (1986). "Prizes and Incentives in Elimination Tournaments." *American Economic Review* 76: 701–715.

Waldman, Michael (1984). "Job Assignments, Signaling, and Efficiency." *RAND Journal of Economics* 15: 255–267.

Waldman, Michael (2003). "Ex Ante versus Ex Post Optimal Promotion Rules: The Case of Internal Promotion." *Economic Inquiry* 41(1): 27–41.

Zabojnik, Jan & Dan Bernhardt (2001). "Corporate Tournaments, Human Capital Acquisition, and the Firm Size-Wage Relation." *Review of Economic Studies* 68(3): 693–716.

APPENDIX

Here we present a brief exposition of the two-competitor tournament model, and compare it to a *promotion standard*. Most of the intuition applies to multicompetitor tournaments as well, though those are much more analytically complicated. For this part of the Appendix, ignore the possibility of cooperation or sabotage.

The Worker's Optimization

The employee's optimization is:

$$\max_{e} W_1 + pr(promoted) \cdot \Delta W - C(e),$$

which implies:

$$\frac{\partial pr(promoted)}{\partial e} \cdot \Delta W = C'.$$

This first-order condition has a straightforward interpretation. The left-hand side is the prize, times the change in probability of winning due to marginal effort. The right-hand side is the marginal cost of effort. This equation applies to any standard or tournament.

This equation has an immediate implication: The larger the prize from promotion ΔW, the greater the incentives. The other implication is that the riskier the performance evaluation, the weaker the incentive. To prove that, we need to do a little more work.

Nothing we have done so far differs between a tournament and a standard. However, the probability of winning does depend on the promotion rule. Consider the standard first. The worker is promoted if performance is greater than some threshold, z. The cumulative and marginal densities of ε are $F(\cdot)$ and $f(\cdot)$, respectively. We will assume that $f(\cdot)$ is symmetric around and unimodal at zero (e.g., a normal distribution). Thus,

$$pr(promoted|standard) = pr(e + \varepsilon > z) = 1 - F(z - e) = F(e - z).$$

The latter inequality follows because ε is distributed symmetrically around 0. Note that the probability of winning when the rule is a standard is an equilibrium outcome of both the toughness of the standard, and the effort response by the worker. To set the promotion rate to what it desires, the firm must estimate the effort that a given standard will generate.

Now consider a tournament. If the ε's distributions are symmetric and unimodal around zero, the distribution of $\varepsilon_S - \varepsilon_D$ will be as well. Denote it by $g(\cdot)$, with cumulative distribution $G(\cdot)$. The Danish worker wins if his performance is greater than that of the Singaporean:

$$pr(promoted|tournament) = pr(e_D + \varepsilon_D > e_S + \varepsilon_S) = G(e_S - e_D).$$

Since the game is symmetric, we will assume a symmetric Nash equilibrium, which means that they both supply equal effort. We can then rewrite the last expression as:
$$pr(promoted|tournament) = G(0).$$

Of course, since $g(\cdot)$ is symmetric, $G(0) = \frac{1}{2}$. This makes sense; since we have a symmetric tournament, the ultimate outcome is a coin toss. In order to compare a tournament and a standard, assume for now that the firm sets z so that in equilibrium $F(z - e) = \frac{1}{2}$, and $e = z$.

Incentives depend on the change in probability from extra effort. These will be:

$$\frac{\partial pr(promoted|standard)}{\partial e} = f(0), \qquad \frac{\partial pr(promoted|tournament)}{\partial e} = g(0).$$

Either of these values can be plugged back into our equation from above:

$$\frac{\partial pr(promoted)}{\partial e} \cdot \Delta W = C'.$$

$f(0)$ and $g(0)$ represent the height of the measurement error distributions at its mean and mode, zero. The lower this height, the more variance in the distributions, since they are symmetric and unimodal. Thus, the riskier the evaluation, the weaker the incentive.

The Firm's Optimization

Given the worker's effort supply characterized above, the firm sets the prize ΔW to maximize profits (effort minus average pay):

$$\max_{W_1, W_2} e - \tfrac{1}{2}(W_1 + W_2),$$

subject to the worker's effort supply, and to the constraint that overall pay is enough to induce the worker to put forth effort:

$$\tfrac{1}{2}(W_1 + W_2) = C.$$

(Tournament models usually ignore risk aversion, since it is difficult or impossible to derive closed-form solutions. We do so here.) The firm's first-order conditions are:

$$(1 - C')\frac{\partial e}{\partial W_1} = 0,$$

$$(1 - C')\frac{\partial e}{\partial W_2} = 0.$$

These imply that at the optimum $C'(e) = 1$. In other words, the firm should set pay so that workers exert extra effort up to the point where the marginal cost of effort just equals the marginal benefit (extra output). Thus (ignoring risk aversion), tournaments and standards can generate efficient effort levels, just like standard incentive schemes.

The optimal wage spread is found by substituting $C' = 1$ into the worker's effort supply and solving:

$$\Delta W = \frac{1}{f(0)} \quad or \quad \Delta W = \frac{1}{g(0)}.$$

Once again we see the analytical similarity of tournaments and standards. This result shows that the optimal prize spread should be larger if the risk in performance evaluation is larger. Note that this applies to the optimal prize, not to the level of pay, which would be reflected in W_1 or W_2 separately. This is an example of the principle from Chapter 10 that the level of pay does not drive incentives; the way that pay varies with performance is what is important.

12

OPTIONS AND EXECUTIVE PAY

How can you afford to pay your men so well?
> —*Banker's question to Andrew Carnegie*

I can't afford to pay them any other way.
> —*Carnegie's reply—quoted in Hendrick, 1932*

INTRODUCTION

In this chapter we finish the section on pay for performance by considering two special topics related to executive compensation. These topics are important in practice, and provide interesting applications of the discussions from the last three chapters.

The first topic is employee stock options. Options are an important part of incentive compensation plans for most top executives in publicly traded companies. They are also quite important incentives in many small startup companies. Moreover, use of employee stock options exploded during the boom of the technology sector during the 1990s. Many high-tech companies began awarding options all the way down the hierarchy, and the press began publishing stories about secretaries who got rich on their options and drove to work in Ferraris. Finally, the use of employee stock options appears to be expanding in Europe, and especially in some areas of Asia. We discuss the incentive properties of stock options, as well as whether they are a good practical compensation tool, and if so, for which employees.

The second topic is executive pay and incentives overall, with a focus on CEOs. Incentive problems are most important for the firm's key employees, so good compensation plan design is crucial for top management. The concepts discussed in prior chapters are just as relevant for CEOs and the top management team as they are for other employees.

✦✦✦✦✦ EMPLOYEE STOCK OPTIONS

Stock Options–A Brief Overview

Since not all readers are familiar with stock options, we begin with a brief description of options. If you already know about stock options, you can skip this section and the Appendix.

A *call option* is a financial security that gives its owner the right to purchase one share of a company's stock, at a fixed *strike price* or *exercise price*. For this reason, stock is actually a special kind of call option, with an exercise price of zero. Of course, if the stock's price is below the exercise price, it would not make sense to exercise the option. If the stock's price is above the exercise price, the option holder can make a profit by exercising the option, selling the stock, and pocketing the difference between the two prices (after transaction costs). Thus, a call option benefits from stock price increases, but the holder is shielded from stock price declines (to some extent, as discussed below).

A *put option* gives its owner the right to sell one share of a company's stock at a fixed exercise price. Exercising a put would make sense if the stock price fell, just the opposite of a call. Thus, owners of puts hope that the stock falls in value. For this reason, employee stock options are always calls; we will only consider call options in this chapter.[1]

Figure 12.1 plots the payoff from a hypothetical call option with exercise price K, and stock price S. If $S < K$, the option is *out of- the money*, and should not be exercised, so the payoff is zero. If $S > K$, the option is *in the money*. If the in-the-money option is exercised and the stock is immediately sold, the profit equals $S - K$.[2] This payoff is often called the *intrinsic value* of the option. When an option is issued to an employee, the firm must decide what exercise price to set. Almost all employee options are issued at the money (K is set equal to the grant-date stock price). Finally, an option has an expiration date—the last date on which it can be exercised. Beyond that date it has no value.

Options are often valued using some variant of the famous Black-Scholes formula, which is described in the Appendix. However, as discussed below, one must be careful in applying this formula to employee options, as opposed to those that are traded on exchanges.

Employee stock options differ from those that are traded on exchanges (such as the Chicago Board Options Exchange, CBOE) in several ways. First, when granted to the employee they are usually not vested immediately. Typically employee options vest over 3–5 years. Until vested, the employee may not exercise the option. Second, even if vested an employee cannot trade an option to another investor. The employee can either hold the option, or exercise it. This matters

---

[1] In fact, it is illegal for top executives in U.S. companies to hold puts in their own companies.

[2] Ignoring taxes. Tax issues can be complex for employee stock options, but are beyond the scope of this text.

FIGURE 12.1
CALL OPTION

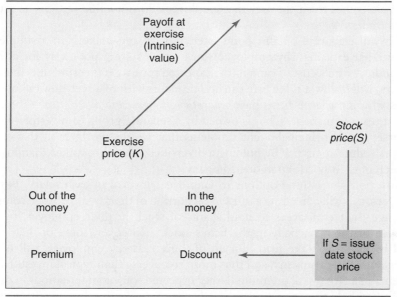

because modern option theory tells us that it is generally not optimal to exercise an option before its expiration date, if you can sell it to someone else instead. The intuition is simple: The (call) option has value because it is a bet that the stock price might rise above its present value. For this reason, a traded option's market value is always *higher* than its intrinsic value. Finally, if an employee leaves the firm, all unexercised options are generally lost.

Should Firms Grant Employees Options?

As mentioned earlier, use of employee stock options exploded (in the United States) during the tech bubble of the 1990s, particularly in "new economy" firms. Before that, they were not an important part of compensation except in some cases for top executives. Several arguments are often put forward for giving employees options, but they generally do not make sense except for a firm's key employees.

Source of Firm Financing

It is sometimes argued that options are a cheap form of financing for a company. The idea is that the firm can offer options to employees instead of salary or other forms of compensation, with zero payout of actual cash. Furthermore, until recently accounting rules resulted in no expense to the firm's accounting statements until the options were exercised (unlike cash compensation). In an accounting sense, options had zero short-term impact. However, we will soon see that this argument is wrong from an economic point of view—options are probably the most *expensive* form of compensation, because they result in an opportunity cost incurred by the firm. This comes from the fact that employees do not value options as much as options traders do.

We will elaborate on this point later, but we can make it in a simpler way for now, that explains why employee stock options are a poor way for a firm to raise funds. A firm's cost of capital (the expected return on investment it must offer investors) will be lower if the firm can find investors with relatively low risk aversion. This is why most large firms have *separation of ownership and control*—the firm is run by a team of managers, but is owned by a separate group of investors—which, of course, causes principal-agent problems that we discuss later in this chapter. Investors reduce their risk by holding a diversified portfolio, rather than investing too much of their portfolio in one company.

Now consider issuing options to employees instead of cash salary. For most employees, this will constitute a substantial portion of their wealth. Some companies encourage their employees to hold shares of stock in their employer, or invest employee pensions partially in the firm's stock. Moreover, some of their human capital is invested in the firm. For all of these reasons, employees will be quite *undiversified* in the company, and thus more risk averse than typical investors. They will demand a larger risk premium (larger expected total compensation) in order to be willing to hold the options—and the firm's costs of financing operations will be higher than if it obtained funds from more traditional sources, such as issuing stock or debt.

There is only one case where it might make sense to try to raise investment funds from employees. That is when the firm cannot obtain funds more cheaply through other sources, but still has positive net present value investment opportunities. Such cases are likely to be quite rare, with one important exception: new ventures. In such cases, outside financing may be very difficult to obtain, even from venture capitalists, because of severe problems of adverse selection and *moral hazard*. Employees inside the company may well have much better information about the prospects of the new company, and thus may be willing to invest in the enterprise. This is one reason why options tend to be an important form of compensation for startups in particular.

Employee Self-Selection

Another possible role for options is to induce better self-selection of employees to improve recruiting. As argued, stronger pay for performance tends to improve self-selection, so to the extent that options provide incentives, this will apply. Options will also be more highly valued by employees who are most optimistic about the firm's prospects. If such employees are also more productive (for example, more enthusiastic about working for the firm), then this will be valuable. Note, though, that this argument applies to all forms of pay for performance, and is not specific to options.

A different form of self-selection that options may induce is employee conservatism or willingness to take risks. Options are perhaps the riskiest form of pay.

Moreover, they tend to be more valuable, the riskier the underlying stock value.[3] Thus, option grants tend to encourage employees to take more risks on the job. To see this, consider Figure 12.1. The option pays off only when performance is high, and the higher the performance, the higher the payoff. Since there is little down side to option pay from riskier actions, the employee is motivated to take actions that make extreme outcomes—good and bad—more likely. Whether or not this is desirable for the firm depends on the situation, but in many cases it is plausible that such an effect is useful. This is because employees will generally be more risk averse than diversified shareholders, so that incentive plans that do not take into account these differences in risk aversion will be distorted toward too conservative decision making. Finally, note that this kind of self-selection only applies to key employees whose decisions can actually affect the riskiness of the stock price, which will tend to be only a few key employees who make major strategic decisions.

Reducing Turnover

A commonly heard argument for granting employee options is that they reduce turnover, because they are vested gradually, and because an employee typically must give up options if leaving the firm. While this may be so, it is not particular to options. Any kind of deferred pay, such as pay that rises with seniority or gradual *vesting* of pensions, will have similar effects on turnover. Therefore, this is an unconvincing reason to grant options to employees.

Options as Incentive Pay

The most important argument for granting employee options is to provide incentives. To evaluate this argument, let us consider the incentive properties of employee stock options using the concepts developed earlier.

Performance Measure

Options are similar to stock, in that both have the same performance measure: stock price. This is a very broad measure and thus distorts incentives little if at all. However, it is also a very risky measure. For this reason, incentives based on stock price will tend to require that the firm pays the employee a relatively high risk premium.

More problematically, for all but the firm's key employees, stock price is a performance measure that is largely uncontrollable. Virtually nothing that a lower level employee can do will budge the stock price at all, unless the firm has very few employees. Thus, from a performance measurement perspective, options should generate little or no incentive for most employees. They are more like *giving the employee a lottery ticket.*

---

[3]This is always true for options traded on exchanges. However, it may not always be true for employee options due to risk aversion.

Pay–Performance Relationship

If options are not too far out of the money, then the firm can tie pay more strongly to the performance measure (stock value) for options than for stock itself. This is because options are *levered* incentives: They only pay off when the stock price exceeds the exercise price. Because they do not always pay off, one option has less value than one share of stock. Therefore, for equivalent cost to the firm, a firm can give the employee more options than shares of stock. When the stock price rises, the employee's value will then rise more rapidly with the options grant than with the stock grant. This is the best argument for granting employees options: For that small number of key employees for whom stock value is a sensible performance measure, a stronger pay–performance relationship can be achieved with options than with stock. However, this logic applies *only* for the firm's key employees.

There is a down side to this argument, unfortunately: Incentives from options are more brittle than incentives from stock. If the stock price falls so that the option is too far out of the money, then the pay–performance relationship falls dramatically. This is because increased effort by the employee is unlikely to raise the stock price high enough to bring it into the money, if the stock price is currently too far below the exercise price. This argument is exactly analogous to the problem of setting the threshold too high in the reward scheme in Figure 10.2 of Chapter 10.

A related concern is that the value of the pay package to the employee will also tend to be brittle if options are used. An option that is far under the money will have very little value, while the underlying stock will still have some value unless S is close to zero. If options are a large part of employee pay, then the expected value of the employee's total compensation will have fallen significantly. For example, in March 2000 the technology sector of the world economy experienced a sudden, dramatic fall in stock prices (the "dot bomb"). Many technology companies had made extensive use of employee options, and their employees now found that much of their pay package was worthless, and often well below market value for similar jobs. These firms found that they had to reprice the options (see later), offer other forms of additional compensation, or suffer turnover.

Notice an implication of this discussion: Employee stock options do have a downside for employees. This point is often missed, since options are profitable when $S > K$, but the employee does not have to pay if $K > S$. However, the option has value because it *might* end up in the money before it expires. The lower that the stock price falls, the less likely that is to occur, so the expected value of the option falls. Of course, the fall in expected option pay is lower than the fall in the stock price itself, but employees do have a downside risk from options pay.

Granting Options Over Time

There are several ways to grant options to employees. The most direct is to give all of the options to the employee at once (say, upon hiring). This gives the strongest incentives, immediately. However, this approach is also the most brittle, as both incentives and the value of the pay package fall dramatically if the stock price falls too much, as described.

As an alternative, many companies issue options over a period of time (say, some options each year). Here there are also two general approaches. One is to grant a fixed value of options each year (e.g., $2,000 per year). The other is to grant a fixed number of options each year (e.g., 200 per year). Which is better?

To answer this, first remember that virtually all employee options are issued with the exercise price K equal to the stock price S on the grant date (at the money). Also, it helps to know that, for at-the-money options, the option's value rises as S rises (see the Appendix).

Consider first granting a fixed value of options each year. If the stock price rises this year, each option granted next year is more valuable, so the firm will be able to issue fewer options to the employee. Similarly, if the stock price falls, new options issued at the money will have less value, so more can be granted. Thus, under this approach the employee is given more options after the firm performs poorly, and fewer after it performs well, muting incentives compared to giving all of the options at once. However, total compensation is more predictable.

Now consider granting a fixed number of options each year. If the stock price rose last year, this year's option grant will be more valuable, and vice versa. This reinforces (strengthens) the incentives from the initial options grant. However, it also makes total pay more variable.

Thus, there is a tradeoff in granting options over time. A fixed-value grant results in more brittle incentives, but less variability in the value of the pay package. A fixed-number grant has less brittle incentives, but more variability in the value of the pay package.

Other Incentive Effects of Options

As we have already noted, options change incentives for taking on or avoiding risk, because they provide insurance against bad outcomes, and reward good outcomes. This can be beneficial if employees would otherwise be too conservative, and dangerous if employees are already too willing to take risks. This is one reason why options are used so much in startup companies. In such cases, the firm has little reason to be conservative; it has no brand name or other form of reputation to lose. Instead, its payoffs in good outcomes may be very large, so strategically the firm itself will want to be more innovative and less conservative. In jobs where there is little upside value to good performance, but there is a down side, options would be a mistake.

The payoff structure of an option has a change in slope at the point where the option is just in the money. Because of this, incentives may change dramatically for options that are near the money. As discussed earlier, these situations are more likely to tempt employees to manipulate the incentive system. Thus, extensive use of stock options may make it more likely that executives engage in unlawful or unethical conduct to try to bring their options into the range of positive payoffs. This would not be the case if the executives were simply given stock, since the pay–performance relationship is smoother (in fact, linear) for stock.

SHOULD OPTIONS BE REPRICED?

After stock prices crashed in March 2000, many employees in technology companies found their options so far below the money that they were essentially worthless and generated no incentive at all, even for key employees. Some firms repriced their employees' options. Typically, this is done by exchanging the employee's existing options for a smaller number with a lower strike price (equal to that day's stock price). Such a practice is controversial, and many shareholders criticize the practice. What are the arguments for and against repricing options?

The argument against repricing options is that it is, in effect, rewarding poor performance (or at least reducing the punishment). Options are never repriced when the stock price rises greatly; they are only repriced when the stock price falls. A frequently heard criticism is that employees agreed to the incentive plan, and they should be expected to stick with it, even when their hopes for high payoffs are not realized. Even worse, repricing can establish a dangerous precedent; employees might expect further repricings in the future if the stock price declines again.

The argument for repricing acknowledges the points in the paragraph above, but brings in practical considerations. If options are not repriced or employees are not compensated in some other way, then the value of the pay package has declined dramatically, and the firm risks losing employees. Of course, those most likely to leave are those with the best outside alternatives, who tend to be the firm's best employees. Also important is that without repricing, options give little or no incentive. Shareholders can benefit from a repricing if it better motivates employees.

A useful way to resolve these arguments is to apply some of our principles about subjective evaluation. Ask if the stock price fell because of poor employee motivation, or because of uncontrollable factors. If it is the former, then repricing is unlikely to be the best policy, as it rewards poor effort. If it is the latter then the fall in stock prices is largely not the employee's fault. In that case, repricing is a special case of subjective performance evaluation to reduce risk, and improve the accuracy of the evaluation. Thus, repricing may make sense for such unusual events as a stock price crash in an entire sector. It is also more likely to make sense to reprice options for lower level employees, who have little or no control over the stock price, than for top executives. However, the board of directors must be careful not to establish a precedent, so repricings should be rare events, with carefully communicated justifications.

How Do Employees Value Options?

As noted above, employee options differ from traded options in important ways. They are restricted: They typically do not vest immediately, cannot be traded (only exercised), and are lost if the employee leaves the firm. In addition, employees are far from diversified against the risk in the options.

For these reasons, employees are quite risk averse with respect to options, whereas those who trade options on exchanges are relatively (or completely) risk neutral. Firms always must pay risk premiums to employees if they give them a risky pay scheme, but the risk premium is probably highest when compensation is in the form of options. In fact, while firms sometimes try to value employee options using the *Black-Scholes* formula, employees generally require risk premiums of 30% or more above the BS value, in order to be willing to accept stock options. In other words, while the BS formula is an excellent approximation of the market value of a publicly traded option, it overstates the value of a similar option when granted to an employee.

An important implication is that employee stock options are not free from the point of view of the firm. While there may be no immediate charge to accounting statements from giving an employee options, the firm incurs a substantial economic (opportunity) cost from doing so. Think about it this way. Suppose that the firm grants option to an employee, reducing salary at the same time. In doing so, the firm is asking the employee to "buy the job" to some extent, giving up certain pay for risky (but hopefully performance-based) pay. The employee will not be willing to pay the BS value for those options, but only that amount minus some risk premium. Thus, the firm incurs the cost of the risk premium by not selling an equivalent option on the open market. Since risk premiums tend to be quite large for employee stock options, options are probably the *most expensive* form of pay for performance, rather than being free. This should not be surprising, since they are one of the riskiest forms of pay for performance that firms use.

EXECUTIVE PAY

It pays to put greater focus on all of the issues in this text when considering the firm's key employees—e.g., those who add the greatest value, have the most important and scarce skills. Typically the most important employee in the firm is the CEO. In this section we consider pay for performance issues for CEOs and top executives. In doing so, we focus on publicly traded firms, and work from the general assumption that the goal of executives in such firms is to maximize shareholder value. This latter assumption can be controversial. Nevertheless it is a good starting point for thinking about the issues carefully. To the extent that other objectives are important, one might reach some different conclusions (for example, about the desirability of layoffs). Nevertheless, the analysis will be relevant in thinking about important tradeoffs and issues in executive incentives.

What is the Most Important Question?

Executive pay stirs great controversy. Most business publications publish some kind of annual roundup of CEO compensation, and these articles receive great attention. The pay of top managers in publicly traded companies is often criticized for a variety of reasons. Many critics argue that executives are paid too much. Others argue that the pay does not reflect performance. Still others argue that CEOs take advantage of their position to cause both of these problems, paying themselves generously from shareholder funds. Certainly, when a CEO earns a $100 million payout on stock options, or is given a large severance, such concerns are understandable.

Which of these issues is the most important? All matter to shareholders. However, the public criticism seems to focus excessively on the *level* of executive pay. While enormous executive pay packages may seem too large, even unethical, if the desired goal is increasing shareholder wealth, then this is an issue of second-order magnitude. After all, for even the most highly paid CEOs, total compensation is a small percentage of overall firm value.

The more important issue should be the strength of the pay–performance relationship. Turning back to Figure 10.1 in Chapter 10, we see that incentives are determined little by the overall level of pay. Rather, they are determined by the incentive intensity, the slope (or more general shape) of the pay–performance relationship. Thus we will focus primarily on the incentive questions.

That said, there is certainly evidence that suggests that top managers are sometimes able to use their power to extract higher levels of compensation than they would otherwise be able to. How might this happen? CEO and executive pay packages are usually designed by compensation consulting firms hired by the compensation committee of the board of directors. These consultants may work closely with employees inside the firm, from human resources or other departments. The CEO can often exert influence over board members, and over who is appointed to the compensation committee. And CEOs are quite likely able to exert influence over both employees and the consultants. (In this case of the consultants, consider *their* incentives—they are designing the pay package for an important client.)

One study found that if the CEO is appointed before the chair of the compensation committee is appointed, then after controlling for other factors (e.g., firm size, industry, CEO experience) the CEO's pay is about 11% higher.[4] The same study found that after controlling for other factors, CEOs of interlocked boards of directors (that is, the CEO of Company *A* is on the board of Company *B*, whose CEO is on the board of Company *A*) have pay that is about 10% higher. Studies such as these strongly suggest that CEOs are, in some cases, paid more than their market value absent these effects.

Executive Pay for Performance

We can quickly analyze CEO pay using the same tools that we used for employee stock options. First consider the performance evaluation. The primary performance

---

[4]See Hallock (1997).

measure for executives is stock price, as the primary incentive instrument for them is stock and options. This is a reasonable performance measure to consider for the CEO, since his or her actions can have strong effects on overall firm value. However, the measure is also quite risky. Therefore, many executive pay packages also make important use of narrower performance measures, especially accounting profits (earnings).

What about the incentive intensity? Estimates of the incentive intensity for CEO pay are quite small. If an owner-entrepreneur gets a commission rate of 1.0, the CEO's commission rate is roughly 0.004 in the largest corporations.[5] That is, for every $1,000 increase or decrease in stock value, the CEO's compensation (including raises, bonuses, deferred pay, stock, options, and threat of termination) rises or falls by less than $1. Of course, the optimal incentive intensity should not be based on total firm value, but rather on the employee's contribution to firm value. Thus, these estimates understate the effective commission rate. Nevertheless, their small size suggests that risk and other factors play important roles. More important, they suggest that CEOs may well have weak incentives compared to entrepreneurs. The incentive intensity in executive incentive schemes for accounting measures tends to be much stronger—roughly double. This indicates that risk considerations are important, as accounting measures distort incentives compared to stock price as a performance measure, but are much less risky.

It is very difficult, if not impossible, to tell what the right incentive intensity for executives should be. Other research has asked a related question: Does the strength of incentives vary with other factors as the theory predicts? By and large, the answer is that executive pay patterns do conform to the predictions, which is reassuring evidence that there is at least some economic logic to executive pay.

For example, several studies have found that CEO incentive intensities are stronger when stock price is less risky, and vice versa. Similarly, executive incentives vary with industry characteristics. In regulated utilities, executives tend to have both much lower overall compensation, and much weaker incentive intensities. Both of these make sense, because the job is much more constrained by regulators—there is less discretion for top managers in regulated industries. This means that talent is valued less than in more dynamic, unpredictable industries. It also means that the incentive problem is less important, since there is less decentralization to the CEO and management.

There is a very strong relationship between executive pay and firm size. For every 10% rise in firm size (measured by sales or stock value), executive pay tends to rise by about 1%. This is consistent with the idea that more talented managers are sorted into larger organizations, where their talents are better used and more valued.

By contrast, estimates of the average relationship between executive pay and firm performance are *weaker* in larger firms compared to smaller firms. That is, most

---

[5] See Jensen & Murphy (1990).

research on executive incentives uses the following measure to estimate incentive intensity:

$$\hat{b} = \frac{\Delta Pay}{\Delta Stock\ Value}.$$

As mentioned, for the largest corporations this estimate tends to be about 0.004. The estimated value rises as firm size decreases. If this measure is a good proxy for the strength of incentives, then executive incentives are *weaker* in larger companies. One explanation is that giving an executive the same incentive intensity in a larger firm implies greatly increased risk, so larger firms mute incentives for risk averse executives.

Another explanation is that such estimates are confounding two effects discussed in the last two chapters. Remember that the manager's incentive is determined by:

$$\frac{\Delta Pay}{\Delta e} = \frac{\Delta Pay}{\Delta Stock\ Value} \cdot \frac{\Delta Stock\ Value}{\Delta e}.$$

Thus, the empirical proxy is a good measure of how incentives vary across firms only if we assume that the last term in this equation is constant. But what if the effect of effort on *Stock Value* varies with firm size? If it does, then we need to take that into account.

One way to think about this is to suppose that there are, roughly speaking, two kinds of managerial decisions.[6] The first are strategic decisions. Working harder to make a good strategic decision raises firm value in *percentage* terms. This is why they are called strategic, since the decision has implications for the entire operation of the firm. Examples might include overall strategy, product choice, and merger and acquisition activity.

The second type of managerial decisions is operational decisions. Working harder to make these decisions better increases firm value in *absolute* terms. That is, a decision that improves firm value by $50,000 does so regardless of the size of the firm. An example might be improving operations at a single factory.

Now look again at the last term in the equation. The measure is the absolute change in stock value from working harder. If all executive decisions are operational, this will be a constant. If all executive decisions are strategic, this term will vary systematically with firm size. In particular, the effects of effort will be larger in larger firms and vice versa.

Thus, to the extent that some executive decisions have impacts that are strategic and scale with firm size, executive incentives would be stronger in larger firms for a given level of incentive intensity b. Taking this view, it appears that overall CEO incentives decline only a little with firm size (probably reflecting risk considerations).

---

[6]See Baker & Hall (2004).

Other Incentives and Controls

Employee motivation is driven by factors other than pay for performance. Firms also direct behavior through controls, such as direct monitoring and limits on decision making. And, of course, these also are important for executive motivation.

Four other important extrinsic factors affect executive behavior: (1) pressure by outside advocates or shareholders; (2) product market competition; (3) the market for corporate control (hostile takeovers); and (4) is oversight by the board of directors.

It is unclear whether the influence of outside pressure groups is a good or bad thing for corporations. To the extent it is driven by informed shareholders, it is likely to improve firm value by pressuring managers to adopt better policies. However, to the extent that groups with other objectives drive it, it may distort CEO incentives (for example, to avoid layoffs when they are important for firm performance, or to spread the use of options or profit sharing inefficiently to lower levels of the hierarchy). One important possibility is that public opinion may limit the ability of firms to design effective pay packages for top executives, because of criticism of high levels of executive compensation. While this is a possibility, research remains to be done to see whether or not such effects are important.

Arguably the most important constraint on executives is product market competition. The more competitive the market, the greater the pressure on a firm to lower costs, increase quality, and innovate in order to survive. Thus, we should expect governance and incentive problems to be more severe in cases where a company has less competition. This includes companies with barriers to entry such as patent or regulatory protection that create monopoly power.

A third potential discipline for managers that has played an important role in the past is the market for corporate control. If a publicly traded company is poorly managed then management can, in principle, be replaced. This might be accomplished through shareholder proxy campaigns, or by investor groups who buy a controlling percentage of the company. A large body of empirical research indicates that hostile takeovers and related control contests tend to increase firm value.

In the United States in the 1980s, a series of hostile takeovers and other changes in control were used to break up inefficient conglomerates, wring cash hoards out of the hands of incumbent management, and so on. On reflection it should not be surprising that there was a wave of such transactions at this time. In the decade or two before, the business world had begun to change dramatically, including increases in international trade, large scale deregulation, and the information technology revolution. Many businesses needed to restructure substantially. It appears that many management teams were either the wrong fit for changing their organizations, found it difficult to implement large scale restructuring, or were reluctant to do so. In such cases the ability of outsiders to buy the company, betting that they can manage it better, is an important motivator to management.

Because such contests often involve dramatic changes in a firm's organization, including mass layoffs and selling of divisions, they have been highly controversial.

These mechanisms are much more difficult to use in Europe (except Britain), where there are more legal restraints. In addition, there are cultural differences in beliefs about the extent to which the firm has a social responsibility to avoid dramatic organizational changes. Thus, this mechanism has not played such a key role there. Hostile takeovers and other control contests are more common in some Asian economies, though not all. Even in the United States, hostile takeovers are now quite rare. This is because most states enacted laws making it much harder to successfully complete such transactions. Thus, this disciplinary mechanism constrains management much less now than in the past.

A final incentive mechanism for top executives is oversight by the board of directors. There are two primary roles for directors. One is to provide advice and support to the CEO and top management team. In this capacity, a director discusses the firm's strategy and tactics, offers advice, and then when appropriate yields decision rights to the CEO. The second is to provide a last line of decision control, by ratifying and monitoring management decisions, and setting management incentives. Put another way, one of the most important duties of the board is to conduct subjective performance evaluation, and reward or punish, the top management team. Therefore, in one role the director acts as a supporter of the CEO and management. In the other, he or she acts as the representative for shareholders. Just as it can be difficult for a manager to draw the line between support and discipline of an employee, it can be quite difficult to draw the line between these two roles, which sometimes come into conflict.

One survey of directors found that only about 35% considered performance evaluation to be one of their primary duties as a director. Instead, directors appear to be giving too much emphasis to their role as supporters of top management. Why might this be the case?

One reason is that the CEO usually has quite a bit of leverage over who sits on the board. Many board members, perhaps most, are suggested by the CEO. Naturally, CEOs usually have a strong preference for choosing directors who are personal friends or sympathetic to the CEO's strategy. In addition, directors are often CEOs of other firms, and may be reluctant to pressure management to avoid setting the same precedent on their own board.

Do Executive Incentives Matter?

An amusing example of apparently poor CEO incentives is Ross Johnson, CEO of RJR Nabisco, who used the corporate jet to fly his dog to his vacation home.[7] More recently, there have been several notorious cases (e.g., Tyco) of CEOs living lavish lifestyles using corporate funds, which suggest lack of oversight by the board. However, such excesses are small in the context of a very large corporation, and might just be viewed as part of the executive compensation pay package—they might not even be inefficient.

---

[7]Burrough & Helyar (1990).

More rigorously, what kinds of problems might arise if top management does not have good incentives? Of course, the firm's performance should be relatively poor. Experience with state-owned companies (e.g., nationalized postal services), and those that have subsequently been privatized and faced competition, suggests that this does happen.

Do firms that provide stronger incentives for top managers perform better? This is not as easy a question to answer as might first appear. One cannot simply correlate proxies for executive incentive intensities (e.g., percent stock ownership) with stock returns. The reason is that stock markets are generally very efficient: They incorporate all new information about the value of a firm almost immediately. If the firm has a well designed executive incentive package, this should be incorporated into the firm's stock price right away, with no observable effect on future stock returns (unless the company changes the policy again later).

A few studies have looked at the *abnormal* (unexpected) change in stock price on days that firms have announced *changes* in executive pay plans. These studies find that if executive incentives are increased, say by granting more stock or options, the stock price rises more than expected at the time of the announcement. This is consistent with the idea that better managerial incentives improve firm value.

However, there are other interpretations of such evidence. One is a form of insider trading. Suppose that the CEO has *private information* about the firm's future prospects. Shareholders might infer, from the CEO's willingness to accept proportionately more risky stock and options in the pay package, that the firm's prospects are better than previously believed. This would raise the stock price, but not because of better CEO incentives.

Similarly, a signaling interpretation is possible. Suppose that the board and CEO believe that the stock price is undervalued (based on their private information about the firm's operations). Then they might signal this to the external market, by willingness to accept more options and stock. Again, the stock price would rise. Thus, evidence based on stock price performance is not unambiguous. Other studies have looked at accounting performance, and found similar results, further supporting the idea that executive incentives matter.

An alternative approach is to analyze case studies. For example, management or leveraged buyouts (MBOs or LBOs) are remarkable because they usually implement very strong executive incentives compared to more typical corporations. They also make heavy use of debt (leverage). This severely constrains executives, and puts strong pressure on them to improve cash flow to avoid bankruptcy. Several studies have looked in detail at performance of such organizations, and have generally found that performance increases notably after the transaction.

An important role of extrinsic incentives is to better align interest of the employee to those of the firm, when the employee has intrinsic motivation. So one way to consider this question is to ask what management's intrinsic goals would be, absent financial incentives. One commonly expressed concern is that managers might be motivated to empire build. In other words, they may be interested in managing larger organizations. This would suggest that CEOs with poor incentives would pursue strategies of growth and acquisition.

WHAT ARE A CEO'S INTRINSIC MOTIVATIONS?

⬢ ⬢ ⬢ ⬢ ⬢ ⬢ ⬢ ⬢ ⬢ ⬢

One fascinating study used plant level data from a large set of U.S. firms to try to analyze the intrinsic objectives that top management would like to pursue, absent the sort of controls and incentives described in this section. The authors exploited the fact that antitakeover protections vary from one state to the next in the United States, so that there are 50 different legal regimes that enacted laws at different times. This variation allowed them to study the effects of different levels of management protection from the threat of takeover.

The results suggest that the empire building view may not be appropriate. Instead, managers appear to prefer pursuing a "quiet life." When the firm is more insulated from takeovers, it tends to pay higher compensation to employees—especially to white collar workers. It is less likely to shut down old plants. Contrary to empire building, creation of new plants also declines. It seems that management follows the path of least resistance, being generous to employees and resisting change overall. The study also finds that productivity and profitability decline in such firms.

Source: Bertrand & Mullainathan (2003)

Another possible goal of CEOs is risk reduction and survival. The way that shareholders reduce risk is through diversification of their portfolio—buying shares in companies with unrelated businesses. CEOs might diversify lines of business inside the company to reduce risk in their pay and employment. If the company owns several unrelated divisions, and one division is performing poorly, odds are relatively good that a different division is performing well. The more unrelated the divisions, the less likely that they will all perform badly at the same time, and the less risky the firm's overall cash flows.

While at first this may sound like a good idea, it is generally not a good idea for shareholders. Investors can produce this diversification on their own by holding shares in a variety of companies. It is difficult to think of an economic justification for a widely diversified firm. If the lines of business are truly different, then there are few or no economies of scale or scope (synergies), while large complex organizations are very difficult to run effectively (for the reasons considered in this book).

Another benefit to management (but not to shareholders) from diversification is that it shields management from outside pressures. The less risky the cash flow, the less likely that management will have to borrow funds or issue shares. This allows management to *cross subsidize* divisions that it wishes to invest in for inefficient reasons. For example, a CEO may decide to invest in an aging factory rather than shut it down, because the CEO is personally uncomfortable with layoffs, or because it was where the CEO's career began.

Indeed, until the hostile takeover boom in the 1980s, many large U.S. companies were diversified conglomerates; many firms in Europe and Asia still are.

A related concern is that top management may have incentives to hoard cash. As a dramatic example, until recently Microsoft held $80 *billion* in cash reserves. Suppose that the firm is making profits, accumulating cash. What should it do with the cash? It should invest the cash *only if* the return on investment is higher, after suitable adjustment for risk, then what shareholders could earn by investing the funds themselves. Cash available after investing in such net present value opportunities is called *free cash flow*, which in principle should be returned to shareholders.

However, management might invest the cash if there are opportunities with *positive* (accounting) returns on investment, which is not the correct criterion. In fact, management might simply hold the cash for future use. It is not uncommon to hear management talking of accumulating a cash hoard inside the company as a "war chest" for use in future strategy implementation. Since the firm can always raise additional funds later if it has good projects to invest in, these kinds of arguments tend to make little sense. Thus, management may have improper incentives to hoard free cash flow. Some of the hostile takeovers of the 1990s led to payout of large extraordinary dividends to shareholders, apparently removing the free cash flow from management's control.

Finally, top management is likely to have strong incentives to attempt to entrench itself, to reduce the chance of being ousted for misuse of corporate funds, poor performance, or pursuing intrinsic objectives. We have already talked about how management might try to stack the board with sympathetic directors. Management may also pursue measures that make hostile takeovers harder to execute, such as poison pills.[8] And, if the company does receive a tender offer, management sometimes aggressively resists the offer, even when it would give shareholders a substantial premium and a majority of shareholders votes to accept the offer.

Overall, the evidence suggests that there can be substantial loss of value when companies do not pay adequate attention to incentives and governance of top management. And, the opposite also appears to be true: When management incentives are well designed, performance increases, and firms are more innovative and dynamic.

---

[8]A poison pill gives current shareholders the right to buy more shares of the company at substantially below market price. These options are only exercisable if an acquirer buys more than some given percentage of the company, and cannot be exercised by that acquirer. Thus, in order to buy a controlling interest in a company with a poison pill, the acquirer must pay a premium to existing shareholders. The premium is so large that to date there have been no successful hostile takeovers in companies with poison pills.

◆ ◆ ◆ ◆ ◆ SUMMARY

Employee Stock Options

We discussed several justifications for giving employees stock options. Most have nothing to do with options per se; the same objectives can be achieved through other forms of compensation. The justifications that may make sense (at least under some circumstances) generally apply only to the firm's key employees. For example, options encourage risk taking only for employees who can actually affect the riskiness of the stock price.

The most important justification for giving options is that they can provide stronger incentives than stock, for the same compensation cost, since they are a levered incentive. While the strong incentive is attractive, there are important caveats. Options are an extremely complex form of pay for performance (even without considering the tax and accounting complications that they create, which are also substantial). The incentives and level of pay that options provide are brittle, in that they may decline sharply if the stock price declines. Options may be more likely to motivate manipulation by the employee. And the firm must give careful thought to how to grant options over time, and to possible repricing if the firm suffers unforeseen poor performance. Most important, options are a very expensive form of pay for performance, because the riskiness and restrictions that they imply cause employees to demand large risk premiums.

For these reasons, a firm should be very careful about issuing employee stock options. There are almost no good reasons to offer options to all employees. They only make sense for key employees, and only if the stronger incentives outweigh the additional complexity. Indeed, historically firms have granted options to employees other than top executives, except during the "irrational exuberance" of the tech boom of the 1990s.

Executive Pay

CEOs and top management are the most important employees. They have the most ability to create or destroy value. For this reason, the most important incentives for a firm to focus on are those for top management—and the board of directors who oversee them.

The evidence suggests that CEO and top management incentives do matter. Better incentives, and better controls such as governance and takeover pressures, do improve firm performance and make it more likely that management will make tough decisions.

Unfortunately, there are also some important reasons why top management pay may not be optimal. Unlike employees at lower levels of the organization, there may be little oversight of the CEO. This arises from the organizational design: separation of ownership and control. Because of the benefits of diversification, shareholders give up much of the control of the firm they invest in. The mechanisms that exist to control top management are imperfect substitutes—largely because the market for corporate control, which is the way that shareholders are supposed to be able to exert some power over management—does not function ideally.

For this reason, CEOs often try to populate the board with sympathetic directors. Directors do not seem to emphasize oversight of management as much as is desirable. CEOs also have some control over the setting of their compensation packages. Despite these problems, governance and incentives do improve motivation of top management, so these mechanisms are important, if imperfect.

STUDY QUESTIONS

1. During the tech bubble when high tech stock prices rose dramatically (before the bubble burst in March 2001), employees may have overvalued stock options because of "irrational exuberance." In such a situation, should a company issue employee stock options? What are the benefits of doing so? The costs?

2. Should companies whose employees invest in more firm-specific human capital make more, or less, use of stock options and profit sharing in employee incentive plans?

3. You are on the board of a company that needs to downsize dramatically. Doing so will cause great public criticism. What factors should you consider in hiring a new CEO, and designing his or her incentive plan?

4. You are a new CEO. What kind of people will you ask to be on your board? Why?

5. Some companies give their CEOs *golden parachutes*—large bonuses if the company is sold to an acquirer and the CEO loses his or her job. Does this practice sound like a sensible incentive scheme to you? Why or why not? What are the issues?

6. Arc CEOs paid too much? In what sense? If incentives are important for motivating CEOs to increase shareholder value, is there any alternative?

REFERENCES

Baker, George and Brian Hall (2004). "CEO Incentives and Firm Size." *Journal of Labor Economics* 22(4): 767–798.

Bertrand, Marianne and Sendhil Mullainathan (2003). "Enjoying the Quiet Life? Corporate Governance and Managerial Preferences." *Journal of Political Economy* 111(5): 1043–1075.

Black, Fischer and Myron Scholes (1973). "The Pricing of Options and Corporate Liabilities." *Journal of Political Economy* 81(3): 637–654.

Burrough, Bryan & John Helyar (1990). *Barbarians at the Gate*. New York: Harper & Row.

Hallock, Kevin (1997). "Reciprocally Interlocking Boards of Directors and Executive Compensation." *Journal of Financial and Quantitative Analysis*, 32(3): 331–344.

Hendrick, Burton (1932). *Life of Andrew Carnegie, v. 1.* Garden City: Doubleday, Doran & Co.

Jensen, Michael & Kevin J. Murphy (1990). "CEO Incentives: It's Not How Much You Pay, But How." *Harvard Business Review*, May–June.

●●●●● FURTHER READING

Abowd, John (1990). "Does Performance-based Compensation Affect Corporate Performance?" *Industrial and Labor Relations Review* 43(3): 52S–73S.

Conger, Jay, David Finegold, and Edward Lawler (1998). "Appraising Boardroom Performance." *Harvard Business Review* 76(1): 136–148.

Hall, Brian and Thomas Knox (2002). "Managing Option Fragility." Working paper, National Bureau of Economic Research.

Hall, Brian and Kevin J. Murphy (2003). "The Trouble with Stock Options." *Journal of Economic Perspectives* 17(3).

Jensen, Michael (1986). "Agency Cost of Free Cash Flow, Corporate Finance, and Takeovers." *American Economic Review Papers and Proceedings* 76(2).

Kaplan, Steven (1989). "The Effects of Management Buyouts on Operating Performance and Value." *Journal of Financial Economics* 24(2).

Murphy, Kevin J. (1999). "Executive Compensation." In *Handbook of Labor Economics 3b*, Orley Ashenfelter and David Card, eds. Elsevier Science North Holland.

Oyer, Pay & Scott Schaefer, 2005. "Why Do Some Firms Give Stock Options to All Employees? An Empirical Examination of Alternative Theories." *Journal of Financial Economics* 76: 99–133.

Watson Wyatt, Inc. (2007). "How Do Employees Value Stock Options?" Washington, DC.

●●●●● APPENDIX

Technical Aspects of Option Pricing

We first describe the Black-Scholes option pricing formula (Black & Scholes, 1973). Publicly traded stock options are often valued with some variant of this formula. Here is one version:

$$C = S \cdot N(d_1) - K \cdot e^{-rT} \cdot N(d_2),$$

where:

$$d_1 = \left[\ln(S/K) + (r + 1/2\sigma^2) \cdot T \right] / \sigma \sqrt{T}$$

$$d_2 = d_1 - \sigma \sqrt{T}$$

and:

C = value of call option

S = stock price

K = exercise price

r = risk-free interest rate

T = time to maturity of option

σ = volatility (standard deviation) of S

N = standard normal cumulative probability distribution function

How does the option's value vary with each parameter? Here is the intuition: Largely speaking, similar intuition applies to how an employee values a similar option, though the employee will demand a risk premium above the Black-Scholes value. All of the intuition is for the effects of changing a single variable, holding all other variables *constant*.

S: The higher the stock price, the more valuable the option, since it is more likely to be in the money, and the payoff is higher if in the money. On exercising the option, the exercise price K is paid to buy the share of stock, which has value S, so the payoff if exercised immediately equals $S - K$.

K: The higher the exercise price, the less valuable the option. The intuition is the reverse of the intuition for S.

r: The higher r, the more valuable the option. Think of r as a measure of how fast financial securities are rising per period (above the rate of inflation). If security values are rising rapidly, the option is more likely to end up in the money, and pay off more.

T: The higher T, the more valuable the option. More time before the option expires implies more chance that the stock price will rise, increasing the odds of being in the money and the payoff if that occurs. If you do not wish to hold the option until maturity, you can sell it in the market, if it is a publicly traded option. Since the extra time has value, you can still capture the value of the higher maturity now by selling it. (*Note*: Many employees exercise their options immediately upon vesting. This is because they are risk averse, and may be worried that the stock price will fall in the future.)

σ : The higher σ, the more valuable the option. A call option pays off if the stock price rises, but does not penalize if the stock price falls. Thus, greater volatility is valuable as it increases the likelihood that the option will end up in the money with high payoff.

Two other properties of option prices are useful for understanding the valuation of employee stock options. First, virtually all employee options are granted at the money; $K = S$. It can be shown that the value of an at-the-money option is greater, the greater is S, all other parameters held constant. The intuition is straightforward: The formula depends on the *percentage* return (this shows up as the risk free rate of return in the formula). Thus, changing S in the formula while keeping the percentage return constant is equivalent to increasing S *and* increasing the *absolute* rate of return. Of course, the actual value of an option depends on the absolute return, since this tells us the likelihood the option will end up in the money, and the payoff (intrinsic value $S - K$) if it does.

The second useful property is that the discounted present value of an option granted to an employee at some period is equal to *today's* value of the option. Thus, in valuing an option package, the employee does *not* need to discount the option to the present period. This intuition is not easy to see at first, since all other forms (except stock) must be discounted to the present. The intuition is easiest to see by thinking about a share of stock that pays no dividends. Suppose that the firm's current stock price equals S, and it promises to grant you one share of stock next year. What is the value of that future grant of stock? It is exactly equal to *today's* stock price S, since you could replicate that share by buying the stock today and holding it until next year. An option is a more complex function of the stock's value, but the same intuition applies.

Part Four

APPLICATIONS

*W*e end the book with three chapters that apply the concepts to special topics. Our purpose is to pull together threads from previous chapters, illustrate how to apply the ideas in practice, and emphasize broader themes that have been developed, not always explicitly.

Chapter 13 discusses employee benefits. This chapter is a natural follow-on to Part Three's focus on paying for performance. Firms often compensate employees partly through nonpecuniary means such as pensions, health insurance, paid time off, etc. Why a firm might do so is an important topic of the chapter. There are several justifications based on issues from earlier parts of the book. These include sorting, managing turnover, improving productivity, and agency problems. We then discuss some issues in design of benefit plans.

Chapter 14 discusses entrepreneurship and *intrapreneurship*. Entrepreneurship is a key driver of capitalism. This is a particularly interesting topic for this text, with our focus on bringing market-oriented ideas to internal firm design. An entrepreneur has an important advantage: a clean slate for organizational design. Given that, how can a new venture apply the principles of the field of personnel economics to improve the likelihood of success?

Once a new venture succeeds and begins to grow, its organization must evolve. In Chapter 14 we briefly discuss some issues that companies face as they mature. This bridges to the second topic of the chapter, intrapreneurship. Larger, older, and more mature organizations often appear (and are) slow moving, conservative, and bureaucratic compared to newer companies. We discuss why this happens, and some of the costs and benefits behind the phenomenon. We then discuss how a mature firm can use the ideas of personnel economics to try to improve its dynamism: to better approximate what makes market-based economies so effective, *intrapreneurship*.

In Chapter 14, we emphasize two related themes from the book. The first is the market metaphor for organizational design. The second is the fundamental tradeoff an organization faces between creativity and control. Both of these themes are relevant when designing policies for sorting and investing in employees; organizational and job design; and paying for performance. Of course, those are the first three sections of the text.

Chapter 15 then discusses the relationship between the firm and the employee. This is an economic relationship, but one that is far more complex and subtle than most economic transactions. A full understanding of organizational design must give consideration to this relationship. Thus, this chapter extends our discussion of implicit contracting, as well as providing some discussion of issues such as corporate culture and organizational change. Such topics are generally thought of as "soft" and are usually discussed through the lenses of psychology and sociology. Chapter 15 complements those views by providing some personnel economics perspective on these issues.

13

BENEFITS

The reward of labour is life. Is that not enough?

—William Morris, 1890

INTRODUCTION

Benefits have become an increasingly important part of compensation. It is not uncommon for a firm to spend 25% of wages on benefits. Typical benefits include health insurance, pension plans, and paid time off. For example, roughly 70% of U.S. employees are offered health insurance plans, and more than half are offered dental insurance. Some firms also offer tuition reimbursement, on-site child care, subsidized meals, even concierge services to help employees with personal errands. In this chapter we analyze why a firm might offer benefits instead of cash compensation, and then discuss important economic issues in the design of such plans.

WAGES VS. BENEFITS

How much should a firm pay in wages and how much in benefits? Consider the following example. A given health plan, which we will call Triple Option, costs about $3,500 per year. It covers most catastrophic illness, has an HMO component, permits a reasonable degree of choice of physicians, and requires a copayment by the insured worker up to some limit of expenditures, say, $1,500 per year. All in all, the plan sounds like it would be reasonably attractive to the workforce. Indeed it is, but its attractiveness varies with the characteristics of the workers. Older workers, who are more likely to get sick, care more about health plans than do younger workers. Single workers are less concerned about health insurance than are those with families. Men use less health care than women.

Suppose a firm must offer the plan to all of its workers or to none at all.[1] How can it make the decision? The cost of the health plan is well known, but $3,500 is not necessarily the value of the plan to employees. If an employee's value of the plan falls below $3,500, he or she would not have bought the plan had they been left to make the choice themselves. Value is defined as the amount that the individual would just be willing to pay to acquire a particular good or service. Any time an individual chooses not to buy something, its value must, by definition, be less than the cost of the item. Of course, value depends on one's income. Since the amount that someone is willing to pay for an item depends on how much money the person has, wealthier individuals may place higher values on some items that others regard as basic necessities. In any case, the amount that workers are willing to pay for a benefit is the appropriate notion of value for the employer.

It is also possible that the worker may place a higher value on a benefit than its cost. This happens generally in two cases. First, the firm may be able to buy the benefit more cheaply than can an individual worker. Such is the case with group health insurance, where individuals are pooled with others to lower their individual costs. (Some low risk workers may be subsidizing high risk workers as part of this pooling.) Second, there may be a tax arbitrage opportunity involved. A tax arbitrage arises when a benefit can be given to workers and is counted as a cost for the purpose of the firm's taxes, but is not counted as income for the purpose of the workers' taxes. The firm can buy the plan for $3,500. The same plan might only be worth $3,000 to a worker. But if the firm pays its workers $3,000 in cash, they cannot buy a $3,000 plan. After taxes, only $2,400 might be left, because 20% goes to taxes. In order to provide its workers with $3,000 of buying power, the firm must pay the workers $3,750, so that after-tax income is $3,000. The firm may be indifferent between offering a benefit of $3,500 and cash of $3,500 because both are counted as $3,500 against the firm's cost, reducing earnings and taxes by the same amount in either case. But the worker prefers the benefit to $3,500 in cash because it would take $3,750 in cash to buy a health plan worth $3,000.

How can a firm determine how much a plan is worth to its workforce? One possibility is to ask. The firm could allow workers to vote on whether they prefer $3,500 in cash or $3,500 in benefits. The cost is the same in either case, so the firm would be indifferent to the outcome of the vote. If the majority votes for the health plan, the firm can substitute the benefit for cash payment. This would imply a wage cut, but it would be one that was chosen by the workers. It is equivalent to paying the workers the higher salary and then letting them buy the benefit out of their current wages at a price of $3,500.

One disadvantage is that if the plan is actually worth more than $3,500 to a worker, the firm is giving something away for nothing. In the previous scenario the worker was willing to give up as much as $3,750 for the health benefit. The firm could purchase the benefit for $3,500. Thus, the firm could have reduced wages

---

[1]Some features of tax law permit a benefit to be tax deductible to the individual only if the plan is provided to a specified (large) fraction of the firm's employees.

by $3,750 instead of just the $3,500 in return for the health benefit. The fact that the benefit costs the firm $3,500 does not mean that the firm must "charge" the worker only $3,500 for it. The firm could charge up to the amount that the benefit is worth to the workers. But how is the firm to find out how much the benefit is worth? Asking the workers is likely to be of little value. If workers know that the firm is going to charge for the benefit the amount that the workers say that it is worth, workers will tend to understate the true value. In fact, if workers knew the cost of the benefit to the firm, it would always pay for them to quote that price exactly. At any smaller number, the firm would prefer not to provide the benefit. At any greater number, the worker is giving extra money to the firm.

Knowing that workers will behave strategically, how can the firm obtain information on how much the benefit is worth? One way is to use market studies of the relation of wages to benefits. Statistical analysis of market data can provide estimates of the marginal worker's value particular benefit. By looking at the difference between the wages of those with the benefit and those without the benefit, a market coefficient can be estimated.

Suppose that we obtained a data set from a human resources consultant. There were 25 firms, each of which either had a health plan or did not. The firm reported salary data for the average middle manager position. The data from the consulting firm are listed in Table 13.1.

A *regression* of salary on a dummy variable, which equals 1 if the firm had a health plan and 0 if it did not, produces the following results:

$$Salary = 55,827 - 1,836 \cdot (Health\ plan\ dummy).$$

The interpretation is that without a health plan (*health plan dummy* = 0), the typical salary is $55,827. With a health plan, the typical salary is $55,827 − 1,836 = $53,991.

Given this information, what should the firm do? The market data show that the marginal worker is willing to accept a cut of $1,836 for the benefit. A health plan costs the firm $3,500. These data imply that workers are not willing to trade off enough wages to make the plan worthwhile. If the firm is willing to offer a worker $55,000 with a health plan, it will do better to offer $57,500 without a health plan. The marginal worker prefers the extra $2,500 in cash over the health plan because workers who do not have the health plan earn, on average, only $1,836 more than those who have it. If workers placed a higher value on the health plan than $1,836, employers who offered $1,836 more in wages would be outbid by firms that offered the lower wage, but provided health plan benefits. By offering $2,500 more in salary instead of a health plan, managers make both firm and workers better off. Although everyone would like to have a health plan as a benefit, many may prefer direct payment in wages to the benefit.

This need not be the case for all workers. Suppose that the firm looks only at managers who earn more than $200,000 per year. These workers tend to be older than other managers in the firm, since salaries tend to rise with seniority. Older workers may have a greater preference for health plans. If the previous data

TABLE 13.1
SALARY AND HEALTH PLAN STATUS

Firm No.	Salary	Health Plan?
1	$59,701	no
2	$52,594	no
3	$59,193	yes
4	$54,817	yes
5	$50,666	no
6	$54,739	yes
7	$50,172	yes
8	$52,472	yes
9	$56,899	no
10	$51,765	yes
11	$53,628	yes
12	$52,372	yes
13	$58,450	no
14	$55,404	yes
15	$53,270	yes
16	$54,566	yes
17	$58,791	yes
18	$52,472	yes
19	$54,724	no
20	$51,181	yes
21	$58,711	no
22	$59,346	no
23	$55,188	yes
24	$51,356	no
25	$53,832	yes

are dominated by managers in the $50,000-per-year salary range, then it is likely that the estimated value of the health plan understates the value of health plans to higher paid older workers. Older workers are more likely to be interested in a health plan. Also, higher wage workers face higher marginal tax rates and are more likely to appreciate receiving a larger portion of their income in the form of nontaxable benefits. More refined market data could provide estimates for specific groups. Such data are generally available from compensation consultants.

The main point of this exercise is to illustrate that employees pay for the benefits that firms offer them. These benefits are costly, and the firm and its employees face a tradeoff between compensating the employee with benefits, or with cash. This is the same point that we made with respect to employee stock options—they are offered as a substitute for other forms of compensation as well. Benefits are not merely an "add-on" on top of cash compensation. For this reason, a firm must be careful to offer benefits only when this is economically justified.

WHY OFFER BENEFITS?

We argued that a firm should offer a benefit to workers if the valuation of the benefit exceeds the firm's cost of procuring the benefit (and also exceeds the cost to employees of buying the benefit personally). Thus, a firm should look to cost advantages in procurement, or to value advantage to employees. We discuss these ideas more fully here, and as all other motivations for a firm to offer benefits instead of salary.

Cost Advantage

Economies of Scale

We described the example of insurance above; sometimes a firm's employees allow the firm to pool risks, lowering the cost of insurance compared to market rates. This is more likely if the firm is larger, and especially if the firm's workers have lower average risks (for example, are younger for health or life insurance risk).

Similarly, a firm may be able to procure some goods for employees at below market rates by obtaining a quantity discount from the supplier. If this is the case and the good is sufficiently valuable to the firm's workers, it becomes efficient to offer the benefit to employees. For example, a firm might offer subsidized membership in a local health club, if the club offers a quantity discount to the firm for bringing it a large set of members. This effect is more likely to be relevant for larger firms than smaller firms. For this reason, we would expect larger firms to offer more extensive benefits packages to employees than small firms. Indeed, this is the pattern we observe.

A firm is even more likely to be able to procure benefits at reduced cost if those benefits are related to the firm's area of business. For example, consider the giant food services company Sodexo, which provides subsidized meals for its staff. Sodexo's primary business is food service—its workers are preparing the meals that they are eligible to purchase at a discount. Sodexo's marginal costs of providing additional meals to its employees are likely to be much lower than the market rate for these meals for a couple of reasons. The company may be able to enjoy additional economies of scale in purchasing from its suppliers, at least for some food service sites, by encouraging employees to eat on site. An important factor is that food services tend to have rush periods and slow periods, since most customers like to eat their meals at standard times such as during their lunch break at work. Sodexo therefore has excess capacity during many times of the day. Serving additional meals to its workers during such slow periods comes at very low marginal cost, and also allows the company further to amortize any fixed costs of operating the site. Therefore, it is quite common to observe companies offering benefits that are closely related to their area of business, especially employee discounts on company products.

Tax Arbitrage or Subsidy

One source of cost advantage to a firm in offering a benefit is the tax code. Governments sometimes use subsidies (in the form of tax deductibility) to encourage provision of benefits to employees. As mentioned at the beginning of the chapter, in countries without nationally provided health care, firms often provide health insurance benefits to employees. This is strongly motivated by the firm's ability to provide such benefits tax free (or equivalently, for employees to deduct the benefits from their taxes). In the United States, employer provided health insurance was not common until the tax code was changed to allow such a deduction. (Note that this implies that pooling of insurance risks is probably not, by itself, an adequate justification for providing employees with health insurance.) Similarly, many countries allow firms to offer pension plans in which employees can invest pretax income, and not be taxed until the pension is paid out at retirement.

Value Advantage

Employee Sorting

A benefit is more likely to be profitably offered to employees instead of salary, the more that the employees value the benefit. Thus, a firm should consider the preferences of its workforce in structuring a benefit plan. Offering tuition reimbursement to middle aged workers is likely to be less useful than offering that benefit to a younger workforce.

The fact that employees value a benefit highly is not in and of itself a justification for providing that benefit. After all, they may well be able to purchase the benefit on their own, in which case the firm might as well pay cash instead. However, employees vary in their preferences, so benefit plans can have effects on sorting of workers into the firm. Structuring benefits to improve self selection in recruiting may well be a justification for offering a benefit instead of salary. We return to this point later.

Employee Productivity

In some cases a benefit may create value for the firm or employee because it increases employee productivity. We discussed on the job training in Chapter 3. Such training clearly increases productivity. The training may be implicitly paid for by the employee through reduced salary (especially in the case of general human capital), or the investment may be shared (especially in the case of firm-specific human capital).

Recall the example of Sodexo offering discounted meals to its employees. An additional advantage that this provides is that employees consume the goods that they produce, which is likely to improve their productivity. It is likely to improve quality because employees experience the product themselves, which is an even better way of discovering problems than receiving customer feedback. It should improve customer service, as the employees have a better understanding of service issues that their customers experience. These benefits can be quite important, especially in organizations that emphasize continuous improvement by employees. Consumption of the product provides substantial feedback that might not be provided simply by producing the product.

This effect reinforces the tendency for companies to provide employee discounts on their products. For example, a computer store might give employees a 25% discount on products sold in the store. When employees purchase and use these products, they have a much better understanding of the advantages and disadvantages of them, how they can be used, and so forth.

Some benefits may improve productivity even though they do not relate directly to the firm's products or industry. For example, some firms offer concierge services to employees. This frees up some of the time they would otherwise need to perform errands. Benefits that might have similar effects include on-site parking, flex time, on-site meals, and car service or private jet (for a high level executive).

Consider a business that wants its workforce to work relatively long hours, or to be willing to do so on short notice (say, to meet deadlines or react to crises when they arise). The longer the hours worked, the higher the marginal disutility of effort from working an additional hour. Benefits such as a concierge might reduce the disutility of effort enough that the employee is willing to put in these extra hours as needed.

This effect is more likely to be important for workers with two characteristics: They are already working long hours, and they have high productivity. The first means that the worker has high disutility from extra effort, so that the concierge benefit has a relatively large impact. The second means that the marginal productivity of the extra hour of work is higher. This is important, since the value from offering the benefit should exceed the cost.

This analysis implies that we should be more likely to see productivity-enhancing benefits in some firms than others. Firms where employees work full time, or even longer hours, would profit more from such benefits than firms with part-time workers, since part-time workers will generally have lower marginal disutility of working an extra hour. Such benefits are more likely to be offered to a workforce that is very highly skilled, and at higher levels of an organization, since the marginal value of extra work tends to be higher for such workers. Finally, we should expect to see such benefits more in an industry that is experiencing high growth and profits, since the value of extra work will be higher for such firms.

These ideas also suggest that provision of productivity enhancing benefits should vary with the business cycle. When times are good, the value of extra work by employees is higher, so a firm is more likely to offer concierge services, company cars, and etc.

ARE EXECUTIVE PERKS EFFICIENT OR WASTEFUL?
❖ ❖ ❖ ❖ ❖ ❖ ❖ ❖ ❖

Top executives are frequently given lavish personal perquisites (perks), such as memberships in exclusive clubs and corporate jets. Such benefits are, of course, rarely if ever given to lower level employees. Do such benefits improve a manager's productivity? Or, are such benefits better explained as a result of agency problems in the setting of executive pay packages, as we discussed in Chapter 12? It appears that both factors play a role.

One study focused on the provision of a personal jet for the CEO (Yermack, 2006). On the day that a firm announced such a benefit, on average the stock price fell 1.1% more than what would have been expected. In addition, subsequent stock price performance was 4% lower per year than expected. These large negative returns are strong evidence of a governance problem and relatively weak CEO incentives in such firms. The study also found that a significant predictor of whether or not the firm provided the CEO with a personal jet was whether or not the CEO was a member of a golf club at a long distance from corporate headquarters.

Rajan and Wulf (2006) examined a larger set of executive perks. Unlike Yermack's study, they found little systematic relationship between the extent of perks and measures of good corporate governance. They did find evidence consistent with the idea that at least some executive perks are designed to increase productivity. For example, time-saving perks such as a chauffeur are more commonly used when the time saved by the perk is higher, and there is greater potential for high productivity (e.g., higher level executives).

Government Mandate

Finally, some benefits must be provided to employees by law. As an example, the Family and Medical Leave Act (FMLA) requires all U.S. firms with at least 50 employees working within a 75 mile radius to offer unpaid leave to certain employees (roughly speaking, full-time employees who have worked with the company for 12 months). Such firms must provide 12 weeks of unpaid leave per 12 month period for caring for a new child; for an ill child, spouse or parent; or because of a medical disability that makes the employee unable to perform the job. Similarly, most governments mandate minimum levels of workplace safety.[2] A firm

---

[2]Workplace safety can be thought of as a job risk. The firm must compensate workers with a risk premium when the job is risky—but only if workers are aware of such risks. Occupational safety regulations might be justified because firms have some incentive to understate risks to potential employees when they have better information about the true level of risks.

can offer greater safety levels than the minimum, at some cost. If it does so, this is an additional benefit of the job. It might also prefer to offer jobs with more risk and less safety, if regulations did not prohibit this.

IMPLEMENTATION OF BENEFITS

Improving Employee Sorting

Consider a large firm offering employees optional life insurance that decides to *self-insure*. This firm does not purchase life insurance from another company. Instead, when an insured employee dies, the firm simply pays the benefit directly out of its own funds. As long as the firm charges enough on average to cover costs of the plan, there is no harm. But if the firm ends up receiving premiums only from older workers who have higher salaries and mortality, it may find that contributions to the program do not cover costs.

Is this a problem? Not necessarily. By providing benefits that have different values to different workers, the firm implicitly gives higher benefit amounts to some workers and lower benefit amounts to other workers, even though the number of benefit dollars is the same per worker. If the life insurance structure is an implicit subsidy to older workers, then older workers are receiving more in benefits than younger workers who do not purchase the plan.

Similarly, the firm may believe that workers with families are more productive than those without. By providing a lower-than-market price for child care, the firm attracts workers with families, who find the benefit package especially attractive. A firm would find it very difficult to make explicit its preference for workers with families by paying wages as a function of family size. This implementation would likely violate the government regulations in many countries, and would create other problems. By providing family-oriented benefits, the firm evades these restrictions and attracts the kinds of workers that it prefers.

Another example involves firms that pay for workers' schooling, even when that schooling has no direct benefit and may even imply harm to the firm. A firm might offer to pay for a worker's general education as a primary benefit. This has great value to workers who want additional education, but no value to those who do not. If desire for additional education is correlated with the underlying quality of a worker, it may be that providing this benefit helps sort out the good workers from the bad. Rather than simply offering $5,000 more per year in salary, the firm offers $10,000 in tuition benefits. More able workers prefer the benefit. Less able workers prefer the cash. The firm is thereby able to sort workers, even if it cannot observe the worker's quality perfectly. There is a cost, however, in that more educated workers may end up leaving the firm after completing their studies.

The point of this discussion is that benefits plans can sometimes be used to improve the firm's recruiting (or turnover; see the discussion of pensions later and in Chapter 4). Since it can be quite costly to sort employees by other means, including probationary hiring, benefits may be a more efficient way to improve recruiting. Or, it may reinforce other methods the firm uses to target hiring toward certain types of workers.

An important implication of such sorting is that employees become better matched to the firm—they enjoy some nonpecuniary benefit to working at the firm. This reduces the likelihood that they will find a better outside offer, and thus reduces turnover. Therefore, firms that desire lower turnover (say, because firm-specific human capital is relatively important, or because recruiting costs are relatively high) might be able to foster this goal through benefits plans designed to strengthen employee self-selection.

Cafeteria Plans

One problem with providing a specific benefit is that the same benefit does not suit every worker. For example, older workers are very concerned about healthcare benefits, but not so concerned about childcare. Conversely, younger workers care much more about benefits for children and less about pension benefits. A cafeteria plan gives a worker more flexibility in benefit choice. Although plans vary in their specifics, the basic idea is to provide the worker a fixed number of benefit dollars, which can be spent on a variety of benefits.

The primary advantage of providing a cafeteria plan as opposed to any specific set of benefits is that the firm can provide the most value to the worker for a given amount of expenditure. If the prices posted in the plan reflect the firm's true cost, then other things being equal, the firm is indifferent about the composition of benefits selected by any given worker. But workers are not indifferent. Some prefer one type of health plan, some prefer another. Some do not care about life insurance, but value childcare very highly. By offering choices, the firm maximizes the value to the worker for a given expenditure.

A typical cafeteria plan might provide a worker with 300 benefit dollars per month. The worker could use the benefit dollars for any benefit or set of benefits desired. An example of a plan is provided in Table 13.2. Suppose that a worker chooses to buy the Kaiser health plan, Delta dental plan, and life insurance for

TABLE 13.2
CAFETERIA PLAN

Benefit	Price
Triple Option Health Plan: Individual	$ 156
Family	$ 320
Kaiser health plan, family	$ 240
Delta dental plan	$ 30
Life insurance (double annual salary)	$ 100
Life insurance, spouse ($50,000)	$ 40
Long-term disability (full salary)	$ 90
On-site day care, per child	$ 200
Benefit Dollars: $300 per month	

himself and his wife. The total cost would be $410, $300 of which would be paid for by the firm under the plan, generally tax free. The other $110 would be deducted from his monthly taxable income.

Because the plan provides some options, workers can choose different benefit components. It is clear from the types of benefits offered that not all workers will choose the same benefits. Workers without children are very unlikely to purchase company-provided childcare. Very young workers are less likely than old workers to purchase life insurance, for two reasons. First, very young workers are more likely to be single and are less likely to have a desire for life insurance. Second, since younger workers are less likely to die than older workers, and since older workers have higher annual salaries than younger workers, the age-independent price of the benefits tends to overcharge young workers relative to old workers. Older workers may be unable to obtain the equivalent insurance at a cost of $100 per month, and young workers may be able to obtain it at a price far less than $100 per month.

The insurance example points out one of the major issues associated with cafeteria plans: sorting. Self-selection may work in ways that are not to the firm's advantage. The simplest way to see this is to consider a large firm that decides to self-insure. Firms that self-insure do not purchase life insurance from other companies. Instead, when an insured employee dies, the firm simply pays the benefit directly out of its current operating funds. As long as the firm charges enough on average to cover costs of the plan, there is no harm. But if the firm ends up receiving premiums only from old workers who have high salaries and high death rates, it may find that contributions to the program do not cover costs.

It is sometimes alleged that cafeteria plans do not permit a firm to use benefits to attract the kinds of workers that it desires. As the previous two examples illustrate, the point is only partially correct. As long as the firm has some flexibility in the prices that it charges for the benefits, specific types of workers can be encouraged or discouraged from working at the firm.

It may be easier, however, to sort workers without a cafeteria plan. If the firm were to offer free childcare to the children of all workers as the firm's only benefit, then those without children would find the benefit package much less attractive than the cafeteria plan described in Table 13.2. Non–cafeteria plan benefit structures are really special cases of cafeteria plans, with highly distorted prices. In this example, the firm that offers free childcare and nothing else can be thought of as offering a cafeteria plan in which the price of the childcare benefit is zero and the price of all other benefits is infinite.

Sometimes a benefit is provided that has inadvertent adverse consequences for the firm. Health insurance provides an example. Consider two firms. Firm 1 provides a very generous health plan. Firm 2 pays $3,500 more in salary each year. Now consider two workers, Smith and Jones. Both have families with two small children. Jones, however, has a child who requires a great deal of healthcare, costing more than $100,000 per year. It is inconceivable that Jones would prefer Firm 2, which pays more but offers no health plan. Smith, on the other hand, might go either way. This means that a disproportionate number of applicants and therefore, employees at Firm 2 will have high healthcare costs.

How does this show up? If the firm self-insures, it pays the health costs directly. Having workers who avail themselves of a great deal of health care raises the costs to the firm. If the firm buys health insurance from another company it is not likely to be better off. The price that a healthcare provider charges the firm for group coverage depends on that company's experience. If the company has employees who are intensive users of healthcare, then the provider is going to require that the firm pay higher rates to be insured.

This is adverse selection. Costs are higher, but the firm reaps no benefit (individuals who have unhealthy children probably are not more productive). A firm that provides health plans and is subject to adverse selection must reduce wages enough to cover the higher cost of healthcare because its employees are heavy healthcare users.

MANAGING SORTING AND BENEFIT COSTS AT WAL-MART

In 2005 the giant company Wal-Mart hired a leading consulting firm to study ways that Wal-Mart could change its benefits plans to increase productivity, reduce the cost of employee healthcare benefits, and better allocate spending on benefits. As an example, one recommendation was to hire more part-time workers, who have less eligibility for benefits, to lower overall benefits costs.

Another suggestion was to discourage unhealthy people from working at Wal-Mart to keep down healthcare costs. This could be achieved by encouraging younger and more physically fit workers through benefits plan changes. For example, it was proposed that Wal-Mart reduce contributions to its employee 401K (pension) plan. This would reduce the value of the job to older workers, but have little effect on younger workers. It was further proposed that Wal-Mart arrange for some physical activity in all jobs in order to discourage unhealthy workers from working at the company.

Wal-Mart also gave thought to how to publicize these changes to avoid negative publicity. The company has been criticized by activists and union organizers for years for supposedly low wages and benefits. Unfortunately for the company, the internal memo about these proposals was leaked to the press.

Source: Greenhouse & Barbaro (2005)

Pensions

In many firms, the largest component of benefits is the pension plan, which may amount to as much as 10% of salary. Pension plans have a number of incentive features as well, many of which are quite subtle. The abolition of mandatory retirement in many countries made the use of pensions an even more important tool for inducing the retirement of older workers. The specific plan formulas can have dramatic effects on retirement behavior, as well as hours of work, effort, and turnover for much of the firm's workforce. It is helpful to describe the various types of pension plans used, as understanding their features helps us understand the incentives implicit in the pension formulas.

Plan Types

There are two basic types of pension plans: *defined contribution* and *defined benefit plans*. Defined contribution plans are the most straightforward. Each pay period (sometimes quarterly), the firm makes a contribution to the employee's pension account. That account is essentially owned by the worker. The money in the account is invested in interest-bearing securities of some sort, sometimes chosen by the worker and sometimes dictated by the employer or some other organization, like a union. When the worker retires, the account—which now consists of payments plus accrued interest, capital gains, and/or dividends—forms the basis of the pension. Sometimes, the funds in the account are simply turned over to the worker as a lump sum payment. Other times, the funds are used to purchase an annuity for the worker, which pays a specified amount each year until the worker dies.[3] The size of the annuity depends, of course, on the amount that the worker had in the pension account at the time of retirement. Larger accounts convert to larger annual pension flows. Workers with higher salaries generally have larger absolute amounts contributed to their pension fund each year, which means that they have more in the defined contribution accounts at the time of retirement. It is conceivable that the amount that a worker receives each year from a retirement annuity exceeds the annual salary that he or she received when working!

Defined benefit plans are more complicated and more diverse. With a defined benefit plan, the worker is promised a specified benefit, irrespective of the amount that is in the fund. The employer makes up all shortfalls and reaps all windfalls to the fund. The worker's annual pension payment is defined by some formula. There are two types of formulas that govern defined benefit plan distributions. The first, called a *pattern plan*, covers most blue-collar and especially union workers. The formula is very simple. It generally takes the form:

$$Annual\ pension = B \cdot (years\ of\ service\ at\ retirement),$$

where B is some specified dollar amount, often subject to union negotiation. For example, if B were equal to $500, then a worker who retired with 30 years of service would receive $15,000 per year in pension benefits until death.

The second kind of defined benefit plan, used primarily for white-collar workers, is called a *conventional* or *formula* plan. The formula is sometimes very

---

[3] After the worker dies, many plans and annuities provide for continued support, usually at a reduced level, for the surviving spouse.

complicated, but its basic structure ties annual pension receipts to some function of final salary and years of service.

Annual pension = *g*(*years of service*) (*final salary average*),

where *g* is some proportion and final salary average is an average of salary over some number of final years. For example, if *g* = 0.01 and final salary average were equal to the average salary during the 5 highest of the last 10 years of work, then a worker with 30 years of service at retirement would receive 30 percent of this final salary average during each year of retirement until death.

Because the formula plan ties pension benefits to final salary, it moves with inflation automatically. If prices and wages rise because of inflation, then final salary will be higher and the pension benefits will reflect these increases in cost of living. In fact, pattern plans, which are not automatically linked to wages, tend to be linked as a result of the negotiation process. When workers negotiate their wages, they also negotiate *B* in the second equation. The *B* that is negotiated generally reflects inflation rates. Neither the pattern nor conventional plan indexes pension benefits of recipients. As a general matter, with some exceptions, once a worker begins to receive a pension, the benefit amount remains constant over time.

Further, tying pension benefits to final salary affects incentives. Because workers want to receive high pensions, they may be induced to work harder during final years than they would were they on a pattern plan. Sometimes, these incentives can be too strong. The following story illustrates the point.

> A few years back, a subway train in Boston rear-ended another train, causing a number of injuries. An investigation was launched to determine the cause of the crash. It was found that the driver of the offending vehicle had dozed off on the job. It seems that he was 64 years old and was working 60- and 70-hour weeks. The pension plan tied his pension to the final year's compensation. As a result, he worked all the overtime that he could get, and was sleep deprived.

It is clear that the behavior exhibited by the subway driver is not desirable. The pension plan provided incentives to work hard, but those incentives were too strong, leading to productivity that fell well short of the value of his leisure. In this case, the worker's productivity was very negative. The pension formula, coupled with giving choice over hours worked to the worker, resulted in a bad incentive structure that induced inefficient conduct.

Pensions and Turnover

The Boston subway example gives some sense of how pension formulas could affect worker behavior. Another way in which they affect behavior is through turnover rates. Defined benefit plans, in particular, provide the firm with a way to encourage workers to retire at specific dates. To see this, consider Figure 13.1.

The figure relates to a worker who starts with the firm at age 30. Age of retirement is shown on the horizontal axis. The expected present value of pension benefits is plotted on the vertical axis. This value takes into account that benefits

FIGURE 13.1
EXPECTED PRESENT VALUE OF PENSION BENEFITS

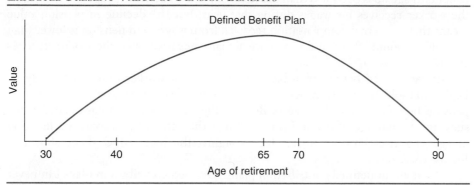

are not paid all at once, so they must be discounted. It also takes into account that the worker may die along the way. It is akin to the average amount paid over a large group of workers, discounted back to the date of retirement.

The data on which Figure 13.1 is based could have come from a typical pattern or conventional plan. Each plan has the property that the longer the service at the date of retirement, the more the worker receives during each year of retirement. The figure is based is a pattern plan that pays:

$$Annual\ pension = (\$500) \cdot (years\ of\ service),$$

for each year of retirement, or after age 65, whichever comes later.

The worker begins work with the firm at age 30, so if he "retires" on the day he starts, he receives no pension at all. This is shown as $0 present value at age 30. If he works one year, then, when he turns 65, he will receive $500 for every year until death. Suppose that the worker will die at age 90. (Although he does not know his date of death, that death will occur is certain.) We can discount the flow of the $500 pension benefits, which start at age 65 and last until age 90, back to age 31. If we do that at an annual interest rate of 4%,[4] the present value of pension benefits in dollars at age 31 equals $2,101. The total amount collected is $500 per year times 25 years, or $12,500. But because the flow of benefits does not begin until the worker is age 65, the present value of the benefits is only $2,101.

If the worker were to wait until age 90 to retire, he would have a large annual pension payment, in this case equal to $30,000 per year. The problem is that he dies on the day of his retirement, so that none of the pension is collected. Thus, the value of the benefits is zero. Were a worker to retire at age 65, he would receive 35 years of credit, implying an annual pension flow of $17,500 for the 25 remaining years of his life. The present value of that flow at age 65 is $278,879. The expected present value of benefits reaches a maximum at age 67. Were the worker to stay

---

[4]Actually, an equivalent instantaneous interest rate of 3.92% was used.

on for an additional year, he would actually lose $289, because the value of pension benefits at age 68 is $289 less than the value of pension benefits at age 67. Of course, the worker receives his wages during that year, but the decline in pension value means that the actual compensation received from wages and pension is lower than the wage amount. Pension accruals are actually negative once the worker reaches age 67.

Every defined benefit plan has this feature. If a worker quits on the day he begins the job, the pension benefits received are zero. If he works until he dies, pension benefits received are zero. Because they are positive at ages between the starting age and age of death, it must be that the value of pensions as a function of age of retirement exhibits, at least roughly, the inverted U shape shown in Figure 13.1.

What about defined contribution plans? Defined contribution plans can never exhibit the inverted U shape. The expected present value of defined contribution must rise with age of retirement. The reason for the difference is that with defined contribution plans, expected pension payments do not depend on the number of years left in a person's life. If a person were to work until age 89, every dollar that had accumulated in her account up to that age would be hers. If she accepted it as a lump sum, it would be the full amount. If she turned it into an annuity, the annual payment would have to be sufficiently high so that the expected amount paid out to her before her death would equal the amount in the fund at age 89. To be sure, the *actual* value of her pension fund may decline, depending on how her investments do. But because more is added to the fund each year, the amount always grows in expected value the longer she works.

Figure 13.2 shows the pattern of pension accrual for defined contribution plans. The pension value always increases as a function of retirement age. The comparison between Figures 13.1 and 13.2 makes an important point about the choice of pension plan types. Since pension accrual is always positive for defined contribution plans, but accrual becomes negative for defined benefit plans, only defined benefit plans punish delayed retirement. In the previous example, once

FIGURE 13.2

EXPECTED PRESENT VALUE OF PENSION BENEFITS

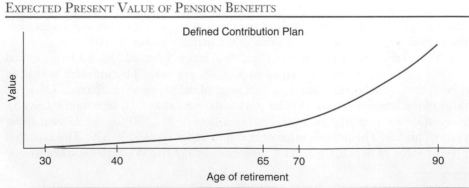

a worker reaches 67, additional years of work actually cost pension benefits. For defined contribution plans, the reverse is true. Additional years of work are rewarded in higher pension accruals. It is possible to specify a defined contribution plan that does not make contributions after, say, 30 years of service. Then accruals would be zero. It is impossible, however, to make expected accruals negative with defined contribution plans.

After mandatory retirement was outlawed, firms had to seek other ways to induce workers to retire. One way used *window plans*—that is, plans that offer workers in a particular age group to elect to receive a payment in return for immediate retirement. An alternative is to replace a defined contribution plan with a defined benefit plan, which penalizes workers beyond some age for additional work. The change in the law governing mandatory retirement actually had the effect of encouraging both window plans and a switch of defined contribution plans toward defined benefit plans.[5]

Vesting

Pension benefits are not always owned by workers as soon as they accrue. When a worker first begins a job, benefits may not be vested until the worker has been with the firm for a given number of years. During the first year on a job, a worker may accrue $2,250 in benefits, but if the worker leaves before becoming vested, typically 5 years, he or she receives none of the benefit. After having been with the firm for 5 years, all of the benefits accrued up to that point may become vested, which means that, were the worker to leave, he or she would be entitled to receive the benefits, either as a check upon termination, or as a pension benefit upon reaching some specified age, like 62 or 65. Nonvested benefits have effects on turnover. To see this, consider one of the most extreme forms of vesting, illustrated by the military pension plan.[6] The plan promises to pay a retired soldier a certain amount per year, depending on retiring rank and years of service. But in order to receive any amount at all, the person must stay in the service for at least 20 years. This is sometimes called cliff vesting, because it produces a picture that looks like a cliff, as illustrated in Figure 13.3.

A soldier who leaves before 20 years of service receives zero per year as a pension. Once the soldier has been in the service for 20 years, he receives X per year of "retirement." The retiring soldier could be only 38 years old. If he stays longer, his annual pension per year increases with years of service, but he can then leave at any time because his pension is already fully vested.

A soldier who leaves even one year before the 20 years receives no pension. This produces a very interesting separation pattern. The separation rate (defined as the sum of quits and terminations) starts relatively high. Some people simply

---

[5]At the same time, the number of defined contribution plans grew rapidly. A large fraction of these plans were supplementary, and were used to augment the basic plan because of tax advantages to saving through a pension plan.

[6]In the United States the military plan, were it not government run, would violate laws regarding vesting.

FIGURE 13.3
MILITARY PENSIONS

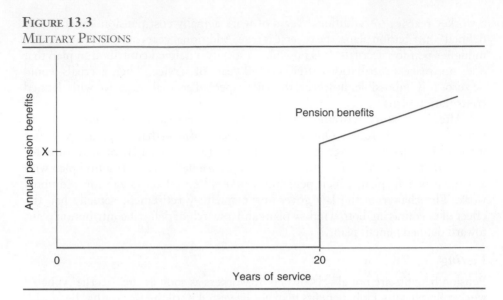

do not adapt well to military life and leave or get kicked out during the first few months in the service. After that time, separation rates start to fall. Just short of 20 years of service, the separation rate is almost zero. Virtually no one leaves the military voluntarily after having served 17 or 18 years, because by staying just another 2 years, they become eligible for a generous pension. At year 20, separation rates jump dramatically. All those who had been waiting to leave can now leave and receive their pension benefits. A very large fraction of soldiers leave in the twentieth year, right after becoming vested in their pension benefits.

This example makes it clear how important the pension formula can be, particularly for workers who are approaching ages when retirement is meaningful. But pensions can even affect people at a much earlier stage of their careers. To see how, it is necessary to define another concept.

Portability

Sometimes confused with vesting, *portability* is a different feature that pension plans may have. Plans that are completely portable are plans that have values that do not change when the employer changes.

The U.S. Social Security system is portable among all nonexempt employers. Months, or actually quarters, of credit toward Social Security experience used in calculating benefits are not affected by employer changes. In order to be eligible for Social Security, 40 quarters of participation in the system are required. It does not matter where those 40 quarters of experience are acquired. A worker could shift employers every year during the first 10 years of work life. As long as workers contribute to the system for 40 quarters (or 10 years), they are eligible to receive benefits when they reach the age of eligibility. Workers are not vested in Social Security benefits until they have worked and contributed to the system for

40 quarters. Until then, they are not eligible for benefits. Portability guarantees that experience carries over across employers.

Even as Social Security is portable, but does not immediately become vested, private pension plans often have the opposite characteristic, vesting immediately, or very soon, but not being portable. Consider the following defined benefit formula:

Annual pension from age 65 onward $= 0.01 \cdot$ *(years of service)* $\cdot$ *(final salary at the firm).*

Suppose that two firms, Palo Alto Semiconductor (PAS) and Santa Clara Semiconductor (SCS), offer exactly the same plan. Suppose that the plans vest immediately, so that workers start to accrue credit toward their pensions as soon as they begin work and are immediately eligible to receive some pension benefits. Thus, a worker who begins at age 30, earns \$30,000 per year, and leaves after one year would receive $0.01 \cdot 1 \cdot 30{,}000 = \$300$ per year for every year that he or she is alive after age 65.

Consider an individual who starts work at age 30 with PAS, earning \$30,000. If she remains with PAS until age 65 her salary will be \$89,694. Her annual pension at retirement would be: $0.01 \cdot 35 \cdot \$89{,}694 = \$31{,}393$. Now suppose that SCS has exactly the same earnings profile and pension plan. A worker who started at 30 and retired at 65 would also receive an annual pension of \$31,393.

What if the worker were to start at PAS until age 45 (earning \$62,368 at that point), and switch to SCS at age 45, continuing to work at SCS until age 65? Even if her salary were exactly the same at both firms, her pension would end up being lower. From PAS she would receive $0.01 \cdot 15 \cdot \$62{,}368 = \$9{,}355$ because she would have 15 years of service at PAS and her final salary would be \$62,368. From SCS she would receive $0.01 \cdot 20 \cdot \$89{,}694 = \$17{,}939$ because she would have 20 years of service at SCS at retirement. The sum of pension payments from the two firms is \$27,294, which is about 15% less than what she would have received had she worked at one firm or the other over her entire lifetime.

The difference results from the pension formula, which is based on final salary at the current firm, not the final salary that she receives, irrespective of employer. Since her final salary at PAS is lower when she splits the career, 15 years of her pension accrual are based on a lower figure than would be the case were she to stay with one firm over her entire lifetime.

Because the plans are not portable, splitting up her career costs her about 15 percent of her pension benefits. Had the plans been fully portable, then the pension benefit would have been based on her final salary irrespective of employer, as is the case with Social Security. A plan that is not portable tends to reduce turnover because it usually penalizes workers for leaving midcareer.

In order for the plan to be made portable, PAS would have to cover any increases in pensions resulting from salary increases given by another firm. This becomes problematic. It would be possible for the worker and SCS to arrange a deal by which the worker's final salary would be very high, in return for sufficiently lower salaries along the way to cover the higher final salary and higher pension paid by SCS. This would hurt PAS because they would not have collected the benefits of the lower salaries paid from age 45 to 64. As a result, firms are reluctant to allow other firms to determine their pension payments by granting portability.

Portable plans usually involve a plan that is administered by some third party. The third party collects fees from the participating employers and doles out benefits according to a set formula. Social Security is exactly this kind of system. Ideally, the pension administrator can charge higher fees to firms that cause larger disbursement from the pension fund. The Social Security system does this to some extent. Because employers are required to contribute into the system a percentage of wages paid, those employers who pay higher wages or have more workers tend to pay more to support the system. The relation is far from perfect, in part because firms change over time. The firm's current workforce determines how much the firm pays into the system. Its behavior in the past determines how much is currently being drawn out of the system by current recipients.

Portable plans are often run by unions. In construction, workers move from one site to another many times over their careers. Small construction firms are unlikely to have their own pension plans. Even if they did, they would have little credibility, because such firms are born and die very frequently. A response is to have the union own and administer the pension fund. A worker is paid by the union fund and experience across jobs counts toward the total credit on which the pension is based.

The most straightforward solution to portability is the defined contribution fund. Since the fund is owned by the worker and since benefits depend only on the market value of the worker's portfolio at the time of retirement, portability issues disappear.

Employee Stock Ownership

We have already discussed the use of stock ownership by employees as an incentive plan (particularly its flaws for this purpose). Here we note one point about their relationship to pension plans. In past decades, many companies invested some portion of their employee's pension assets in company stock. There is little justification for this practice; in fact, it can be quite a poor practice. The problem is that this practice puts the employee's retirement wealth at substantial risk. First, retirement assets should generally be invested in a broadly diversified portfolio of assets in order to reduce volatility in their value. Putting any substantial percentage of an employee's retirement funds in *any* single asset violates this principle. Second, the employee already is investing in the company by accumulating firm-specific human capital, and their career prospects are already strongly correlated with those of the firm. Investing retirement assets in the company as well makes an employee's retirement wealth as undiversified as possible. Fortunately, this practice has largely been abandoned in the last decade or so.

Paid Time Off

Paid time off accounts for 10 to 15 percent of total compensation at major firms. In addition to the common 2 to 3 weeks of vacation time, workers often receive

8 to 12 days per year sick leave and 7 to 10 paid holidays per year. This amounts to 25 to 37 days off per year. The normal work year has about 260 days, so workers are given a full year's pay for doing 85 to 90 percent of a year's work.

Of course, wage rates adjust to compensate. A worker who is paid $100 per day and is given 26 of 260 work days off with pay actually receives $111.11 per day worked. Full annual compensation is $100 \cdot 260 = \$26,000$, which the worker earns for 234 days of work, yielding $26,000/234 = \$111.11$ per day. If the worker is not producing at least $111.11 per day, then the firm could not afford to pay $26,000 per year and also offer 26 days off with pay. Suppose that the worker produces only $100 per day. The firm would have to eliminate paid time off or would have to adjust the wage rate such that the total compensation did not exceed $234 \cdot \$100 = \$23,400$. This could be accomplished easily by reducing the daily wage to $23,400/260 = \$90$ and offering 26 days of paid time off.

It appears that a firm would be indifferent between offering $100 per day with no paid time off and $111.11 per day with 26 paid days off. In fact, neither the firm nor workers are indifferent. If other considerations (discussed below) did not come into play, it would always be better to offer the higher daily wage with no paid time off. Why?

When time off is given with pay, a worker has every incentive to take it, even if it is not especially valuable. It is always true that giving workers paid time off induces them to take too much of it. The following example illustrates the point.

Suppose that a worker produces $111.11 per day. Suppose further that if she works anywhere between 200 and 300 days per year, she values having one more day off at $95. Consider two schemes. Plan A pays the worker $26,000 per year and gives her 26 paid days off per year. Stated differently, Plan A pays the worker $100 per workday, but gives 26 workdays off with pay per year. Plan B pays the worker $110 for every day worked and offers no time off with pay. Under Plan B, a worker who worked 234 days would earn $25,740 per year, which is less than the $26,000 earned under Plan A for the same amount of time worked.

Which plan does the firm prefer? It seems clear that the firm prefers Plan B. Under Plan B, the firm pays $110 per day worked. Under Plan A, the firm pays $111.11 per day actually worked. Under Plan B, the firm earns a surplus of $1.00 per day per worker. Under Plan A, the firm's surplus is zero.

Which plan does the worker prefer? If the worker were to work 234 days, she would prefer Plan A to Plan B for the same reason that the firm prefers Plan B to Plan A. The worker receives $26,000 for the 234 days under Plan A, but only $25,740 for the 234 days under Plan B. But Plan B offers flexibility that is not available under Plan A. Under Plan B, the worker can choose to take fewer than 26 days off. Under Plan A, the worker has no incentive not to take each one of the 26 days off. Under Plan B, each day that she takes off costs her $110. Since the value of a day off to her is $95, she prefers to work the 26 days that she would be given off under Plan A. Her earnings are $260 \cdot \$110 = \$28,600$, which is $2,600 more than she would earn under Plan A. Of course, she forgoes 26 days of leisure, which, at $95 per day, are worth $2,470 at the $95 per day value. The extra time worked brings in more than enough to compensate her for the lost leisure. Thus, she prefers Plan *B* as well. If both the firm and its workers prefer the flexible plan, then that is the plan that should be implemented.

While this is only a numerical example, one can always construct a plan that offers flexibility and pays the worker an equivalent higher wage per day actually worked that is preferred by both worker and firm. By giving the worker time off with pay, the firm is essentially forcing the worker to take time that may have little value to her. If she values the time less than the firm does, there is always a deal that can be struck to make both worker and firm better off.

This logic is too strong. It suggests that firms should always offer workers a choice between working and not working, rather than forcing the worker to take paid time off. Some firms do allow workers to forgo their vacations and sometimes sick days, taking extra pay instead. But most firms do not give workers a choice about taking holidays. The majority of workers are paid for New Years Day and given it off; they do not have the option of working New Years Day and receiving an extra days pay for doing so.

Why might a firm prefer to announce a fixed salary with paid days off instead of giving workers the choice? There are some possible answers. In some situations, there is value to the firm in having workers take vacation time. One of the best examples is that of banks. Bank employees are usually required to take their vacation because this gives the bank an opportunity to audit the accounts and transactions that were administered by the vacationing worker. Where there is a significant chance of embezzlement, and where an employee can embezzle large sums of money, a firm may want the worker to take vacation to enhance the likelihood that embezzlers will be discovered.

The banking example is vivid, but unlikely to be very general. It is difficult to argue that most jobs have features that make it important to displace the incumbent for a few weeks every year just so the firm can find out what is going on. Despite the failure to comply with the terms of this extreme case, there may be productivity reasons for having workers take time off. When workers are involved in team production, as is the case for an assembly line, it is not valuable to have one worker come in when the rest are home enjoying the holiday. The firm is unwilling to offer the worker a wage for coming in on a day when productivity is likely to be low. The productivity story is consistent with the facts. Managers are more likely to be given choice over working holidays than are production workers. Professors are often in their offices on weekends because they can do research and teaching preparation despite the fact that the university is not holding classes. They do not fit the model of assembly line production. Their productivity can be quite high, even when others are not working.

Even production workers are more likely to be given choice over vacation hours than they are over holiday hours. Workers may be permitted to forgo vacation and receive additional pay, even when they are precluded from making the same choice about a holiday. Since worker vacations are taken at different times, the assembly line is still operating during the period that workers take their vacations. It is closed down on New Year's Day. Therefore, the firm allows workers to choose whether to take vacation, but not whether to take the holiday. Foregone vacation time has much more value to the firm than does foregone holiday time.

Summary

Cash compensation has a distinct advantage over other forms of pay: The employee can spend it easily on goods and services of their own choosing. Despite this, firms often pay a not insignificant fraction of compensation through various kinds of benefits. In this chapter we discussed some of the reasons why, and analyzed some optimal benefits policies.

Some benefits and other job characteristics are mandated by law, so a firm has no choice but to offer them. But there are other profitable reasons to offer benefits. These generally fall into two categories.

First, benefits can be efficient compensation if they can be procured by the firm at significantly lower cost than the employee could—enough to overcome the disadvantage of not receiving cash and spending it on goods of the employee's own choosing. There are several possible reasons why this might be the case. Some benefits are subsidized through the tax code. Employer-sponsored health insurance is common in the United States, but was not until it became possible to use pretax compensation for such a benefit. A firm might also be able to enjoy quantity discounts in purchasing for some goods.

In the case of insurance, a firm may be able to reduce insurance costs by pooling risks, especially if it is able to recruit an employee pool with lower risks than average. In such a case, the firm recruiting helps to solve the adverse selection problems faced by any insurance provider.

Note that the last two factors—quantity discounts and pooling of risks—will generally be more important in larger firms. Larger firms do tend to offer more employee benefits than small firms (which in turn offer more benefits than do family-owned businesses).

A firm may also be able to provide its own goods and services to its employees at below market cost, if it has some excess capacity in production. This observation leads into the second general reason why a firm might offer benefits instead of salary.

Second, benefits may have particularly high value for employees or the firm compared to the population at large. An important consideration is that benefits may improve employee productivity in some circumstances. For example, when a firm offers its own products or services to its employees at discount, it turns the employees into customers. That is often an excellent way to foster continuous improvement. Employees understand the perspective and preferences of customers, experience quality and service problems personally, and are more likely to develop new ideas and services. For similar reasons, a firm might offer benefits that are related to the firm's industry but are not its own products.

The benefits package will have greater value to some potential employees than others. If a firm offers benefits related to its own industry (say, discounts on auto parts for employees of Toyota), the firm is more likely to recruit employees with intrinsic interest in the industry. This is another way in which targeted benefits may increase productivity.

Some firms offer benefits designed to lower the marginal disutility of effort, in order to motivate employees to work harder. This is particularly important for firms that may need employees to work relatively long hours, or on occasion work longer hours in order to meet some short-term objective. Benefits that might increase work effort in this sense include on-site provision of some services (parking, meals, errand service). These practices are more likely to be economically profitable for employees with high marginal productivity. That includes employees at higher hierarchical levels; in industries with higher profit margins; and at times of rapid economic growth. Thus, these types of benefits may vary over the business cycle.

More generally, a firm must carefully analyze the sorting effects of benefits. While benefits packages can improve the match of workers to the firm, they can also cause adverse selection. Benefits may also affect turnover. To the extent that a benefits package implies self-selection of certain types of job applicants into the firm, the package is likely to reduce turnover, since it provides some nonpecuniary value to employees from working at that firm instead of alternative employers.

In some economies pensions are one of the most important employee benefits. Pensions may be offered because of favorable tax treatment. They also can have very important effects on incentives and turnover. The turnover implications of a pension plan depend crucially on the design of the plan. In some cases, pension plans may actually generate incentives that are too strong, and turnover that is either too high or too low.

We have seen that employee benefits have surprisingly broad implications for personnel management. They can affect employee self-selection, skill accumulation, incentives, and turnover.

Benefits also affect labor costs. When a firm offers benefits to employees, it is implicitly "charging" employees for this by lowering wages. This can only make sense only if the benefits can be provided cheaply enough compared to their market prices, or if there are enough gains in employee value, productivity, or other firm objectives to overcome the loss in employee choice.

Finally, benefits complete our analysis of the terms of the employee–employer contract. We started in Chapter 1 with a "spot market" view of employment, and have added layers of complexity to the relationship in every chapter since then. In Chapter 15 we pull that thread together and discuss employment relationship as a whole.

●●●●● STUDY QUESTIONS

1. A common view is that a firm's employee benefits are an "add-on" on top of salary, having no effect on salary levels. Explain why this view is flawed, and how it might lead a firm to think about its benefits inefficiently.

2. If a firm offers jobs with "modern" design as described in Chapter 7, will it have to pay higher or lower total compensation? How does your answer relate to the concepts from this chapter? Discuss as many factors as you can think of that affect the answer.

3. Many universities offer subsidized tuition benefits to all employees. Discuss reasons why this might be efficient for universities, compared to paying higher salaries. Why might a university be more likely to offer these benefits than a company in another industry?

4. How might you estimate the monetary equivalent of a new benefit that you are thinking of offering to your employees?

5. Employees tend to be highly resistant to decreases in salary. Partly, this is because they have fixed financial obligations such as mortgage payments. Suppose that a firm would like to change the compensation mix by adding a new benefit, and reducing salary. How might a firm implement this to avoid resistance toward salary cuts?

6. Which type of pension plan, defined contribution or defined benefit, is risky for an employee? For the firm? Why?

7. Under what circumstances can a pension plan provide too much incentive for the employee to work?

REFERENCES

Greenhouse, Steven & Michael Barbaro (2005). "Wal-Mart Memo Suggests Ways to Cut Employee Benefit Costs." *New York Times*, October 26.

Rajan, Raghuram & Julie Wulf (2006). "Are Perks Purely Managerial Excess?" *Journal of Financial Economics* 79: 1–33.

Yermack, David (2006). "Flights of Fancy: Corporate Jets, CEO Perquisites, and Inferior Shareholder Returns." *Journal of Financial Economics* 80: 211–242.

FURTHER READING

Lazear, Edward (1983). "Pensions as Severance Pay." In Zvi Bodie & John Shoven, eds., *Financial Aspects of the U.S. Pension System*. Chicago: University of Chicago Press.

Lazear, Edward (1986). "Pensions and Turnover." In John Shoven, Zvi Bodie, & David Wise, eds., *Issues in Pension Economics*. Chicago: University of Chicago Press.

Lubotsky, Darren (2006). "The Economics of Employee Benefits." In Joseph Martocchio, ed., *Employee Benefits: A Primer for Human Resource Professionals*, 2nd ed. New York: McGraw Hill.

Morris, William (1890). "News From Nowhere," *Commonweal*. London: Socialist League.

Oyer, Paul (2008). "Salary or Benefits?" *Research in Labor Economics*.

Rosen, Sherwin (1974). "Hedonic Prices and Implicit Markets." *Journal of Political Economy* 82: 34–55.

14

ENTREPRENEURSHIP AND INTRAPRENEURSHIP

Genius is one percent inspiration, ninety-nine percent perspiration.
—Thomas Edison—quoted in Rosanoff, 1932

INTRODUCTION

A theme in this book has been how personnel policies affect motivation and creativity. One of the most interesting manifestations of creativity in the economy is entrepreneurship. Entrepreneurs are the clearest expression of our market metaphor for organizational design. Entrepreneurs play an important role by developing new ideas, entering industries with fresh competition, and spurring incumbent firms to be more creative. In the last two decades, entrepreneurship has played a particularly noteworthy role because of the rapid pace of technological development. Entrepreneurship is also a key component in the modernization of less developed economies. We are currently witnessing an explosion of entrepreneurship throughout Eastern Europe, Asia, South America, and Africa.

In this chapter we discuss some issues related to entrepreneurship. We cannot provide a comprehensive discussion of the topic. Instead we focus on personnel economics aspects. Our first topic is the entrepreneur's career. We argue that entrepreneurs are likely to have a particular type of skill portfolio, since one of their most important roles is to coordinate the various specialized tasks in the new venture. We outline the implications of this for the allocation of entrepreneurs to different industries, and investments in human capital.

The second part of the chapter focuses on *intrapreneurship*, that is, how a firm can improve the motivation and creativity of its employees. Mature firms, especially those that are large and have complex areas of operations, are often criticized for being bureaucratic, slow, and lacking in innovation. We can use the concepts discussed in this text to understand and possibly counter these tendencies.

WHAT IS AN ENTREPRENEUR OR INTRAPRENEUR?
⬢ ⬢ ⬢ ⬢ ⬢ ⬢ ⬢ ⬢ ⬢ ⬢

One study analyzed 10 examples of firms that went through organizational changes, to investigate what attributes of managers are valuable for intrapreneurship. These skills are also likely to be valuable to entrepreneurs. The authors concluded that five skills were particularly important.

Proactiveness suggests that the manager take a strategic, rather than reactive, approach to business problems. Such an approach provides more control over outcomes, and may be associated with creativity as well.

Aspirations beyond current capability is the desire to progress continually, and a focus on continuous improvement. The authors also find that *learning capability* is valuable, both in managers and organizational design. We emphasized these ideas in Part Two of the text, and will return to them in the section on intrapreneurship later.

Team orientation and *capability to resolve dilemmas* suggest that the ability to get different groups to work together effectively is important. This is clearly the case when trying to change an existing organization, since various groups must be convinced of the need for change, and then change in the same direction. More generally, these two indicate that one important attribute is the ability to coordinate different people. We emphasize this view in the section on entrepreneurship.

Source: Stopford & Baden-Fuller (1994)

⬢ ⬢ ⬢ ⬢ ⬢   ## ENTREPRENEURSHIP

An entrepreneur is often thought of as someone who founds their own business, or plays a major role in a new venture. That is the view that we will take here. But what are the attributes that make one a successful entrepreneur?

One view is that the most talented (especially the most creative) are likely to become entrepreneurs. However, this is not obvious. A talented and creative individual may have far more impact by pursuing a career within a firm. They will have a more stable environment, with many resources they can draw upon. Their talent may be more highly leveraged in a large firm, where they can oversee more resources. Their creativity may be better deployed in an existing firm, where their ideas can be matched to an existing infrastructure or brand name. It seems more likely that talented and creative individuals may sometimes become entrepreneurs, but also may well pursue careers in more typical employment.

One likely attribute of entrepreneurs is a greater ability to tolerate risk. While all individuals are risk averse (if not, we would pursue risky activities in all areas of life), some are less so than others. Entrepreneurship tends to be a riskier career choice for many reasons, especially given the high failure rate of new ventures.

However, the effect of risk aversion may be overstated. Failure in a new venture is usually not as costly as failure in an existing organization, since the potential downside losses are fewer. The investment is not always large, and there are no existing brand name or customer relationships to be damaged. Moreover, entrepreneurship may entail relatively high rewards for the individual upon success compared to a traditional career. Therefore, entrepreneurs sometimes face high upside opportunities without commensurately large downside risk. In such cases even relatively risk averse individuals might choose entrepreneurship.

Building on this comment, while the effects of *risk aversion* are not so clear, it may be more likely that entrepreneurs are more optimistic than average. Individuals vary in their assessment of risks and opportunities, both ones that they create and ones that they face. This may be because of psychological differences, or because of different experiences. Regardless of cause, those who are more optimistic will value upside opportunities more highly, either because they consider them to be more likely or because they expect greater profits if such opportunities are realized. Similarly they are likely to give less weight to downside risk.

Both of these attributes, risk aversion and optimism, may vary with age. Risk aversion in particular may be lower for younger people; they may have more to gain from successful risks that they take, as they can enjoy the benefits for longer. They may also be able to limit their downside risks of failure more, since they may be less penalized by the labor market for an early mistake. Moreover, older workers are more likely to have fixed financial claims (mortgages, loans, children to put through college), which may make them more averse to highly variable compensation.

The Choice to become an Entrepreneur

An important role of an entrepreneur is to assemble, coordinate, and oversee most or all of an entire business. The founder of a company must assemble human, financial, and physical capital, and information. He must then combine these resources and coordinate the various specialized employees to create the product, develop the entire business process, and implement the business plan. This suggests that an entrepreneur may need a different portfolio of skills than do typical employees. Instead of being a specialist, an entrepreneur may need a more balanced set of talents spanning a number of different skills.

For example, consider an engineer who may work inside a larger organization, focusing on product design. Alternatively, he may found a company. As an entrepreneur, he needs to succeed at product design, but he needs many more skills as well. Some expertise in finance will help him make projections of cash flows and justify his business plan to investors. A basic understanding of accounting is essential, so that he can set up budgets and control systems, and track those cash flows. He needs some understanding of operations for production and distribution, and of marketing and sales in order to sell the product. Finally, management skills are helpful for structuring the firm, designing personnel policies, and leading his team.

Of course, an entrepreneur can rarely be an expert in all of these areas. But he needs at least some knowledge of each of these areas even if he hires specialized experts to run each function. The founder needs to understand the skills if he is to screen and recruit the correct management team. He then needs to understand their work to design their jobs, allocate decision rights, and evaluate their performance. Finally, he needs to coordinate each of these experts.

A similar argument applies to managers at the top of an organizational unit, especially units that oversee multiple functional areas (e.g., divisional manager or CEO). That is one reason why at the beginning of this chapter we did not simply define an entrepreneur as self-employed. To some extent, top managers in any organization have an entrepreneurial-type function. It is noteworthy in this light that business schools provide exactly the broad portfolio of skills that we suggest are important to entrepreneurs.

In this section, we briefly present a model of the choice between becoming an entrepreneur with a variety of skills, or an employee with more specialized training.[1] This allows us to generate a number of implications for how careers of entrepreneurs differ from more typical employees. We then present some evidence consistent with this view of entrepreneurship.

Jack of All Trades

Let us consider a very simple model to fix ideas. Assume that there are only two skills (e.g., product design and marketing), denoted x_1 and x_2. An individual has the choice of a job that is specialized. Alternatively, he can choose to be an entrepreneur. Recall from Part One of this text that some specialization of investments in human capital is usually efficient, to economize on training costs and to exploit an individual's comparative advantage in some skills. Recall as well from Part Two that specialization in job design often brings strong efficiencies, and further that these effects often lead firms top adopt a strong element of functional hierarchy in their structure. Thus, think of the specialized job as being an employee in an existing firm.

To keep things simple, assume that the x's measure the level of each skill possessed by the person, and that both skills pay \$1 per unit per period to specialized workers. That is, if he works in a job that uses the first skill, income equals x_1. If he works in a job that uses the second skill, income equals x_2. Therefore, if he specializes he will choose the job that matches his best skill, so that:

$$Specialist\ income = maximum\{x_1, x_2\}.$$

For the reasons described, entrepreneurs must have some ability to perform each task, or to oversee others who perform those tasks. For this reason, their value

---

[1] This section is derived closely from Lazear (2005).

as an entrepreneur depends on the level of each skill that they possess, not just their highest level. In fact, an entrepreneur's ability to combine resources and coordinate functions might arguably be limited by their lowest skill level. To capture this idea, assume that:

$$Entrepreneur\ income = \lambda \cdot minimum\{x_1, x_2\}.$$

In other words, the entrepreneur's success is a function of the lowest common denominator among the skills needed to organize and oversee the new venture. That is the minimum of the x's.

λ is a parameter that can reflect several different ideas. First, it may represent the relative value of a minimal skill level employed in entrepreneurship, compared to employing one's best skill in more typical employment. Thus, in this sense λ reflects the relative labor market price for broad skills compared to specialized skills. That is determined by the supply and demand for specialized and generalist workers in the economy as a whole.

In addition, creativity can be an important component of entrepreneurship. λ might vary from one entrepreneur to another. Those who are more creative would have a higher λ: They are able to create greater value from the same skill portfolio as another individual. In this view, λ would vary from person to person.

With this simple structure, it is now straightforward to determine which individuals become entrepreneurs and which become specialists. An individual chooses to become an entrepreneur if:

$$\lambda \cdot minimum\{x_1, x_2\} > maximum\{x_1, x_2\}.$$

This choice is represented in Figure 14.1. Each point in x_1, x_2 space represents a potential pair of skill levels for an individual. Points above the 45 degree line represent individuals with $x_2 > x_1$, and vice versa. An individual who is exactly on the 45 degree line is someone whose skills are exactly balanced, with $x_1 = x_2$.

Consider a person with $x_2 > x_1$. This person has some comparative advantage at Skill 2 compared to Skill 1. Income as a specialist would be x_2, while income as an entrepreneur would be $\lambda \cdot x_1$. Therefore, this person decides to be a specialist (employee) if $x_2 > \lambda \cdot x_1$, which is the shaded area above the 45 degree line and next to the x_2 axis. This person decides to be an entrepreneur if $x_2 < \lambda \cdot x_1$, which is the shaded area between above and next to the 45 degree line.

Similar logic applies for a person with $x_1 > x_2$. This person would earn x_1 as a specialist or $\lambda \cdot x_2$ as an entrepreneur. The entrepreneurship region for this person is the shaded area below and next to the 45 degree line. The shaded area below that along the x_1 axis is the specialist region. The line that divides these two areas is determined by the equation $\lambda \cdot x_2 = x_1$. Any individual whose skills put them exactly on this line would be indifferent between entrepreneurship and regular employment.

This yields several implications. First, the more unbalanced a person's skills, the less likely they are to choose entrepreneurship. Graphically, a greater imbalance between x_1 and x_2 means that the person is located farther from the 45 degree

FIGURE 14.1
WHO BECOMES AN ENTREPRENEUR?

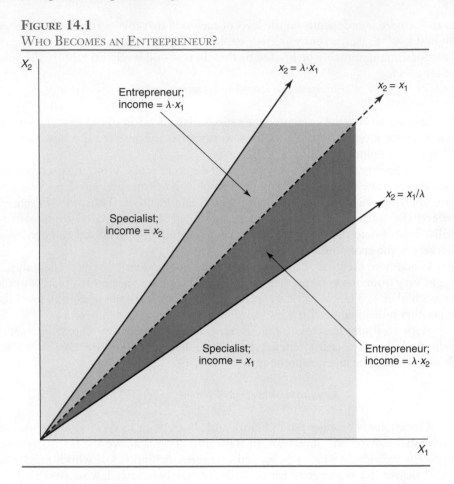

line, and closer toward one of the axes. They are more likely to be outside the two shaded regions. This is our main hypothesis: Balanced skills are an important component of entrepreneurship.

Second, the larger is λ, the more likely is an individual to become an entrepreneur. As λ increases, the relative market value of a broad set of skills compared to specialized skills rises. This makes the shaded areas of the figure larger, sweeping more individuals into the entrepreneurship zone.

Third, we noted above that λ might also capture variation in creativity across individuals. We might also interpret "creativity" here as an ability to coordinate people with different skill sets—to find ways to make them work together effectively. If that is the case, then we would have to draw shaded areas differently for each person, depending on their level of creativity. It should be clear that more creative individuals are more likely to choose entrepreneurship when we allow λ to vary across people.

This interpretation can help explain why some individuals try entrepreneurship, and then enter the regular labor market as employees. A large fraction of new entrepreneurs move quickly back into the regular labor market. If one's entrepreneurial creativity is uncertain, it may be worth trying out entrepreneurship initially as a test. If λ turns out to be high, the person remains an entrepreneur, but if it is low the person switches to a specialized job. λ would be difficult to assess as a specialist; it is probably hard to gauge one's ability to be an entrepreneur without actually trying.

Differences across Industries

This model also has implications for how entrepreneurship might vary across industries. Suppose that different industries require expertise in different pairs of skills. For example, running an insurance agency requires some ability to understand complex insurance policies, and also accounting and management skills. Similarly, a successful art firm requires both artistic skills, and accounting and management skills.

The supply of individuals with balanced skills will vary across different sets of skills, and this difference should affect the supply of entrepreneurs to various industries. Insurance skills are likely to be highly correlated with accounting and management skills, so that there is a large supply of individuals who are suitable to manage insurance agencies. For this reason, we would expect a relatively large number of insurance agencies that are relatively small. By contrast, artistic skills are likely to have very low correlation with accounting and management skills. The supply of individuals who are both artistic and good at accounting will be relatively small. Therefore, we would expect to see few artist-managers. Instead, artists tend to specialize, while others sell their work and manage art studios.

Another important consideration that will vary across industries is the complexity of the business process. Some areas of business are quite simple, requiring the combination of a relatively small set of skills. Others are more complex. Consider, for example, farming versus automobile manufacturing. The complexity of automobile manufacturing is much higher than that of farming. What is the effect of such complexity? It is generally to reduce the supply of entrepreneurs in that industry.[2]

To see this, consider an industry in which three independent skills are relevant. Recall that an individual chooses entrepreneurship if the market value of his lowest skill level, when used as an entrepreneur, is higher than the maximum value of his highest specialized skill:

$$\lambda \cdot minimum\{x_1, x_2, x_3\} > maximum\{x_1, x_2, x_3\}.$$

Compare this to the same condition for the case of two skills that we showed above. It cannot be more likely for the condition to hold for only two of the three

---

[2]Formally, the statements that we make about additional factors in this section apply only when the factors are independently distributed across individuals. It is possible that enough correlation in skills might change the results. However, it is likely that in most cases the intuition that we describe here should apply.

skills (x_1 with x_2, x_1 with x_3, or x_2 with x_3) than for all three simultaneously. The reason is that the expression on the left side cannot rise, because the minimum value cannot rise and may fall, if we add a third skill. Similarly, the expression on the right side cannot fall, because the maximum value cannot fall and may rise, if we add a third skill. A similar argument holds if we add a fourth skill, and so on. The Appendix shows this formally.

Therefore, more complex industries should have a lower supply of entrepreneurs, and vice versa. This should affect the structure of the industry, as well as the market price (λ) of entrepreneurs in different industries. In an industry with relatively low complexity and few skills required (say, low-end restaurants), we would expect a high level of market entry by entrepreneurs, and relatively low economic returns to entrepreneurship. By contrast, in more complex industries (say, pharmaceuticals) we would expect much less entry by new entrepreneurs, but very high returns for those rare individuals with the broad skill portfolio required to set up a firm in that industry.

Implications for Human Capital Investment

This view of entrepreneurship implies a different approach to investments in human capital than for those who will be typical employees. There is more value to balanced investment when one wants to be an entrepreneur. To see this, consider an individual who plans to become an entrepreneur and must first decide how to invest in additional skills. How should they invest? There are three possibilities. A more formal treatment is provided in the Appendix.

First, further investment may not be optimal, if the costs of additional training are too high. In that case, the entrepreneur's market value is based on his minimum level of x_1 compared to x_2.

The second case is a person for which a relatively small investment in additional skills is optimal, but not a large investment. Suppose that this person is currently at point A in Figure 14.2. Income as an entrepreneur would equal $\lambda \cdot x_2$, since this person has relatively more x_1 than x_2. A small increase in x_1 will have no effect on income and thus has no payoff. However, a small increase in x_2 will increase income. Graphically, this person's best investment strategy is to move from point A toward the 45 degree line shown by the arrow coming straight up from point A. Therefore, this person specializes his human capital investments, but by increasing his investment in his weakest skill. This is the opposite of what we argued earlier in the text about specialized skill investments. This person's best strategy is to become less specialized.

The third possible case is an entrepreneur who should make a larger investment in skills than in the second case (because the costs of investment are low enough, or the gains high enough). Such a person should initially invest as described in the second case, moving her skill portfolio in the direction of the 45 degree line in Figure 14.2. This involves an initial specialized investment in the skill that she is weakest in. However, once her skill portfolio becomes balanced—she reaches the 45 degree line—further investments should be balanced between x_1 and x_2. At that point, she should invest in both skills, keeping their levels equal to each other. This

FIGURE 14.2
OPTIMAL SKILL INVESTMENT FOR AN ENTREPRENEUR

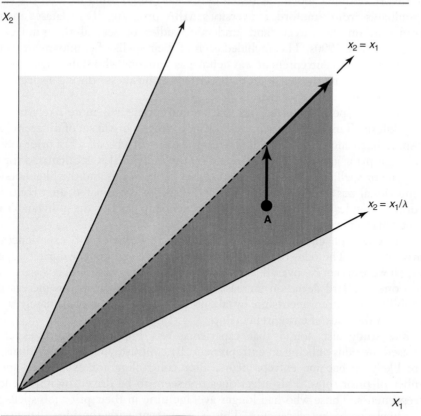

is shown as the second arrow in the figure, moving up the 45 degree line. Any unbalanced investment would not pay off in this model, since our assumption is that her market value is based on the minimum level of the two skills.

While the model is stylized, it does have a prediction that can be tested—investments in human capital should have different patterns for entrepreneurs than for employees. Entrepreneurs should take a more balanced, rather than specialized, approach to their human capital. They should invest more in their weaker skills, and should be more likely to invest in multiple skills simultaneously.

This view of entrepreneurship and skills is consistent with our statement that much of what managers do inside a firm is similar to entrepreneurship. One of a manager's most important duties is to coordinate activities across functional specialists and different business units. This requires some understanding of a broad set of skills. This is a good explanation for the typical MBA curriculum, which emphasizes relatively unspecialized but broad training in a variety of business skills.

Some Evidence

The theory outlined above was tested by Lazear (2005) using data on the careers of graduates from Stanford University's MBA program. The dataset included information on the careers and academic studies of several thousand alumni through the late 1990s. This included each of their spells of employment (various jobs they held). An entrepreneur was defined as someone who stated that they were a "founder—among those who initially started the business" during a specific spell of employment.

The key hypothesis tested was that an entrepreneur is more likely to have a broad skill set. This could be acquired through either a broad set of different jobs, a less specialized education, or both. To test the effect of a broad set of prior jobs, the number of prior jobs that had been held by the individual was calculated for each employment spell. The statistical relationship between this and the likelihood that the individual was an entrepreneur during this spell was estimated, after controlling for other variables that might affect entrepreneurship (such as the individual's years of labor market experience, age, and gender).

The effect on entrepreneurship of having more prior job experiences was relatively large. The odds of an individual being an entrepreneur during a specific job spell were about 7% overall. After adjusting for other variables, it was estimated that a one standard deviation increase in the number of prior jobs increased the probability of entrepreneurship by about 1.8%. That is approximately a 25% increase in the odds of entrepreneurship.

The study also found that experience was important—more experience increased the odds of being an entrepreneur. By contrast, younger individuals were more likely to become entrepreneurs, after controlling for experience and the number of prior roles. This effect does not seem to be driven by impatience by entrepreneurs. Those who had longer average time in their prior job spells were more likely to be entrepreneurs. This is consistent with the idea that younger people are less risk averse. Finally, men were more likely to be entrepreneurs than were women.

The next step in the study was to investigate whether or not entrepreneurs invest in more generalized training. To study this, academic records were compiled for a subset of the alumni. The degree of specialized training was measured as the maximum number of courses that the student took in one field (say, finance) minus the average number of courses taken across fields.

Once again the findings are consistent with the theory. After controlling for other variables, entrepreneurs were more likely to have taken a broad set of courses. Nonentrepreneurs were more likely to specialize their education. In addition, those with more specialized coursework had fewer average work roles, suggesting that they were also more specialized in their careers.

Finally, the study also examined whether a similar effect was at work for high level managers. We have argued that higher level managers may need a broader set of skills because one of their roles is to coordinate output across functional specialists. In that sense, top managers play an entrepreneurial role inside a larger firm. To test this, the study also examined the effect of the variables described on the likelihood that an alumnus was a high level general manager. The number of prior roles has a similar effect on the likelihood of being a high level general manager (after controlling for experience and other variables) as its effect on entrepreneurship. This evidence is consistent with the idea that high level managers play a role quite similar to that of entrepreneurs.

This final finding is a good transition to our next section. It suggests that in some ways entrepreneurial behavior can be generated (and of course, hindered) inside an existing firm. In our final section, we consider this topic, referring to it as *intrapreneurship*.

INTRAPRENEURSHIP

Intrapreneurship is a bit more complicated to define than entrepreneurship. Does it involve creation of new product lines or other radical changes within an existing firm? Does it involve management of a more gradual organizational change? Or does it involve designing the firm's policies so that it is less bureaucratic and more dynamic on an ongoing basis? We will emphasize the latter view. Thus, we do not focus on organizational change in this section, but rather on how organizational design can be more innovative and adaptive.

Imagine an entrepreneur's firm that becomes successful and starts to grow. Such a firm typically begins adding more structure. For example, as it develops a brand name and loyal customers, the firm may want to be more conservative about new products. We argued that one way to do this is to become more hierarchical in analyzing new product ideas. But hierarchy entails slower time to market, fewer new products that are implemented, and fewer blockbuster successes. The firm's product line may begin to look conservative compared to its founding days.

The firm will also have more employees. It may become dispersed geographically. The firm is likely to invest in more formal processes and policies, which is a form of greater centralization. One reason to do so is because it can enjoy administrative economies of scale, as policies that work well can be replicated over the larger set of workers. Another reason to do so is because it helps the company develop standard approaches to conducting business, which can aid coordination. Similarly, it can help the firm develop or maintain a consistent culture over a larger organization.

As the firm gets larger, it is likely that a greater fraction of employees will work in administrative positions. There will be more emphasis on control, compliance, and accounting systems. The more complex organization will require more coordination and communication. More levels of middle management are likely to be added.

This maturing firm will also have to evolve its compensation and incentive policies. For example, while stock options and firm-based profit sharing plans may work well in a small firm, they are much less likely to be effective in a large firm. Instead, the firm may move toward performance evaluations that better measure individual contributions. Unfortunately, the larger the firm, the more likely are performance evaluations to be difficult to do well, to be subjective, and to be prone to measure error, because most employees will be embedded in the larger firm far from bottom line profits. Because of measurement error, incentives may be weaker for employees in the middle of the organization.

All of these help explain a commonly observed pattern: larger, more complex, and more mature firms tend to be more bureaucratic. They usually behave less entrepreneurially. These are natural, and often appropriate, tendencies. However, it is possible to take this too far. Many firms do seem to be more bureaucratic than is ideal. That is especially true when competition is more intense and technological change is more rapid.

In this section, we outline some ways in which mature firms can foster intrapreneurship. We will see that all of the areas of study in this text have relevance for addressing this issue. Many policies can be modified to add more dynamism to a firm. As always, it is very important to match the policies to the firm's context. Every firm faces a different set of tradeoffs, technology, strategy, and industry context. Thus, not every policy described here is appropriate for every firm. But some of these policies are likely to be helpful, at least for part of an organization.

Internal Markets

The market metaphor for organizational design is a useful starting place for thinking about intrapreneurship. In some cases, it is possible to design personnel policies so that certain parts of the firm can act as virtually independent businesses. When this can be done, relatively strong incentives for employees to be innovative can emerge.

MARKET-BASED MANAGEMENT AT KOCH INDUSTRIES
◆ ◆ ◆ ◆ ◆ ◆ ◆ ◆ ◆ ◆

Koch Industries is a diversified manufacturer of natural resource–based products. The company has grown steadily for several decades to a valuation of about $90 billion in 2007. It is sometimes called the world's largest private company. Over that time management developed an approach that they term Market-Based Management. They describe it as having five dimensions:

Vision: determining where and how the organization can create the greatest long-term value

Virtue and talents: helping ensure that people with the right values, skills, and capabilities are hired, retained, and developed

Knowledge processes: creating, acquiring, sharing and applying relevant knowledge, and measuring and tracking profitability

Decision rights: ensuring that the right people are in the right roles with the right authorities to make decisions, and holding them accountable

Incentives: rewarding people according to the value they create for the
organization

Of course, these are very similar to those aspects that we have presented
throughout this book; the last three are the major components of our market
metaphor. They work well at Koch because of the relatively independent
nature of its businesses.

Source: Koch (2007)

An excellent example is a firm with several different lines of business. Think
of each unit's top manager as a quasi-CEO of that business. Can each division
be structured so that the divisional manager is motivated to act much like an
entrepreneur? The answer may be yes. This can be achieved by using decentralization to make use of divisional knowledge, and reinforcing this with matching
changes in performance evaluation and incentives.

First, the manager should be given substantial authority to make decisions
that affect the division. This may include production, distribution, marketing,
and human resources. Giving these decision rights to the manager allows great
flexibility in designing the organization. He will be able to delegate as he sees fit,
recruit and develop the types of skills that are appropriate, and set up incentive
schemes that closely match the other policies. This is an excellent way to facilitate
different approaches for different types of business, and encourage the use of specific
knowledge that varies across divisions.

In more extreme cases, the manager may be given the right to make decisions
about the product line itself. This kind of authority allows the manager to be more
creative. Many organizations with very broad product lines (e.g., Koch Industries,
Sony) grant much authority to division managers to develop their own products.
This puts new product and design decisions closer to important specific knowledge,
including that of customer preferences and of division level engineers.

Once broad discretion is granted, a very broad performance measure should
be used to motivate the divisional manager. The goal, again, is to mimic ownership
of the division. A step in this direction would be to measure the division's profits,
since it includes consideration of both revenues and costs and both are largely
controllable by a manager who has been given broad discretion. However, profit
is a short-term measure, which distorts decisions about investments and research
and development. Therefore, it is often helpful to use even broader performance
measures that attempt to include the opportunity cost of capital (e.g., economic
value added), or reward future profits (e.g., long-term bonus plans based on
divisional performance).

An additional benefit of carefully measuring performance at the divisional level
is that this performance measure may be useful for incentive plans for managers

within the division. Such a measure is closer to capturing their responsibilities than would be overall firm performance.

This approach to organizational design is quite common in large multidivisional firms. General Electric is a famous example. The approach can be taken a step further. Some companies have a policy of encouraging their product design engineers to propose new product lines. If they succeed in designing a product that the company believes can sustain a profitable business, the engineer is allowed to set up and manage the new division (or receive a share of the profits from this new division). This can be a powerful incentive to develop new products. Hewlett-Packard (H-P) had this policy before they became a computer company; the result was a large set of successful products in over 200 different divisions. H-P used the idea of cell division from biology as a metaphor for their organizational strategy.

This general way of structuring the firm can be powerful, but it has a substantial qualification. Greater decentralization to each division reduces coordination across divisions. To the extent that the firm desires across-division coordination, this approach is likely to go too far. An example of the tradeoff is Sony. Sony has a very broad product line of consumer electronics. For years they pursued a highly decentralized structure, which encouraged divisions to be creative and generated many new and innovative products. However, in recent years there has been a trend toward making more consumer electronics products work together ("convergence"). When products need to work together, decentralized product design is likely to cause severe problems. Indeed, Sony has moved toward greater centralization recently to try to alleviate this problem.

Hewlett-Packard faced this same problem when computers were introduced. A decentralized divisional structure did not work. At one point some of their computer monitors and printers did not work with their minicomputers. In order to sell an entire computer system to a customer, H-P needed to make these products function together. They went through a wrenching organizational restructuring, which took many years, to solve this problem.

Therefore, a firm needs to be careful about not applying an extreme market type structure where it is not appropriate to the business. Factors that create strong benefits from coordination were discussed in Chapter 5, and these should be considered in deciding how far to go with this approach.

Creativity vs. Control

We have discussed several ways in which personnel policies trade off the goals creativity and control or risk management. These policies—from all three sections of the text—can be rebalanced to make a firm more dynamic.

For example, the firm might consider reducing the degree of hierarchy for certain decisions. This may involve cutting out some layers of approval, being less stringent for some decisions, or changing the relative allocation of resources toward more creative aspects of the business (idea generation). The goal would be to generate and implement more new ideas.

Of course, this comes at the cost of implementing more ideas that do not turn out to be successful. A firm can mitigate this risk in several ways. One is to be lenient in pursuing new ideas as long as possible, while still being stringent in the decision making steps right before a new product decision is finally made, or large resources are finally allocated. This is, in effect, what venture capital firms do. Many ideas are put forward, nurtured and encouraged, until the stakes become too high. At that point it is appropriate to be more cautious about moving forward.

The firm might also be able to take steps to reduce the downside risk of implementing an idea. For example, a new product might be tested in a single market before it is launched globally. Or it might be tested under a different brand name initially, to get customer feedback. Only successful products would then be launched globally or with the company's brand name, when there is greater confidence in their success.

A second approach to injecting creativity is to take more risks in recruiting. As we saw, employees can be thought of as real options. The firm can exercise the option by deciding to keep and promote good employees, while rejecting those who do not fit. This approach implies that the firm will hire more employees who turn out to be mistakes, so there is some risk. However, a firm may be able to limit the downside through probation or fixed term employment contracts.

The potential benefit of hiring some risky candidates is highest in positions where small differences in talent imply large differences in job performance. That is most likely to be the case when the firm is filling key positions where the person's responsibilities imply large leverage from decisions, or where the individual plays a key role in innovation. Thus, a firm might consider hiring some risky candidates for R&D and leadership positions. If it does so, it should carefully structure probation to avoid giving too much authority to the new person until they have been tested on the job.

Hiring more risky candidates will increase employee turnover. From the perspective of improving innovation this may be helpful. Higher turnover allows the firm to open up slots to bring in new employees with different training and experience.

A third approach to increasing creativity is to change incentives. Creativity is often very hard to measure numerically. At the least it can be quite difficult to specify in advance what the performance metric will be. Some firms set goals for the number of new products introduced per year. That may be effective for a firm that produces a large set of products (e.g., 3M). Often, though, this approach leads to the introduction of products that are not successful, as managers focus on the quantity instead of quality of product introductions. To alleviate this problem, the firm might use broader performance measures, such as profits generated by new products. Creativity researchers have concluded that broader performance measures are more likely to generate creative behavior. The reason for this is that broader measures distort incentives less, and are usually more difficult to manipulate. Broader measures also tend to be based on outputs more than inputs. Input-based performance measures may reduce creativity since they focus on the process, which is difficult to see in advance when creativity is desired.

An alternative to broader numeric measures is subjective performance evaluation. Since creativity is difficult to foresee, ex post evaluation in this way is often quite helpful. Moreover, subjective evaluation can improve the incentive system's emphasis on rewards for success instead of penalties for mistakes. Subjective evaluation usually makes it easier for the supervisor to reward successful risks, while not penalizing unsuccessful risks. This can reduce the effective risk aversion of the employee, thus encouraging greater risk taking.

Finally, once the evaluation system has been changed to encourage more creativity, the firm can increase the rewards associated with good performance. The incentive will thus redirect motivation, and then strengthen it in that direction.

Speed of Decision Making

One way in which a firm may become conservative is through slow decision making. Slow decision making arises from greater emphasis on hierarchy (checking decisions before they are implemented) and centralization, which requires more communication up and down the organizational chart.

To speed up decision making a firm may need to decentralize more decisions. This will, of course, reduce coordination and control. These concerns can be addressed by focusing decentralization on decisions that have less impact on coordination or control. For example, divisions may be given greater discretion to make operational decisions, manage their staffs, or set prices, while still requiring approval for product line decisions. Additionally, a firm can spend more resources on the quality of decision making (more skilled project evaluators, better analysis tools and data) to increase accuracy while reducing the number of approval stages required.

Decision making may also be sped up through greater investment in information technology, since this often implies more rapid communication. Finally, greater emphasis on standard operating procedures may improve coordination without the need for communication, and in that way increase the speed of decision making.

Reducing Bureaucracy

As we have emphasized, there are good reasons for bureaucracy in large, complex organizations. But these structures and policies can hinder innovation. In some cases, a firm can reduce bureaucracy to address this.

One way to do so is to separate the part of the organization that is essential for innovation (e.g., basic research, product design, or advertising) from the rest of the structure, and impose less bureaucracy on that part. It is often not necessary for administrative rules and procedures to apply to every part of the organization, so some balance may be struck. It is quite common for firms to allow for more flexibility and looser application of policies in creative units. Some companies go so far as to physically separate such groups in different buildings or even different geographical locations. This is particularly common for basic research conducted in Skunk Works.[3] Physical separation makes it easier to maintain different formal and informal policies without raising conflict. Of course, a tradeoff is that the outside

---

[3] This term was the alias of Lockheed Martin's Advanced Development Program, which pioneered this approach for advanced R&D projects.

group may work less seamlessly with the rest of the company. The outside group must receive enough monitoring to be disciplined to produce results, and especially for results that can be turned into profitable products.

A more extreme approach to dealing with the bureaucracy problem focuses on the fact that complexity of the firm's operations is a primary cause. As we saw in Chapter 6, more complex firms use more complex structures, including more divisions and matrices or other lateral coordination mechanisms. Bureaucracy might be reduced by reducing the complexity of the firm's operations. There are two ways to do this.

One is to simplify the company's product lines. A company that focuses on a small number of businesses is less likely to require a complex structure. The attempt to focus the company is sometimes referred to as a return to *core competence*—paring down operations as much as possible to what the firm is particularly effective at compared to competitors. This is a dramatic approach, but one that can be helpful, especially if noncore product lines are less profitable.

A less dramatic approach to simplifying the firm's operations is to outsource noncore activities. For example, Apple does not manufacturer most of the parts in its products, though it does assemble them; that is a firm of vertical dis-integration. Similarly, many firms outsource facilities management tasks such as security, maintenance of the physical plant, and the employee cafeteria. Some firms outsource administrative tasks, especially human resources. This approach requires effective contracting over the long-term supplier relationship. When done well it allows management to focus on a smaller set of organizational design issues.

Continuous Improvement

Continuous improvement (including more *modern job design*, total quality management, and similar techniques) is an excellent way to adapt the firm to changing circumstances. Employees are tasked with uncovering problems, suggesting and testing solutions, and implementing the best ones. This is a form of innovation, though one that is quite different from new product design. The goal is incremental improvement in products or processes that have already been chosen, rather than coming up with new products.

CONFLICT BETWEEN NEW PRODUCT DESIGN AND CONTINUOUS IMPROVEMENT AT 3M
◆ ◆ ◆ ◆ ◆ ◆ ◆ ◆ ◆ ◆

3M Corporation has been hailed for years for its effective approach to motivating new product ideas. For over 50 years, the company emphasized decentralized, long-term investments in basic R&D. At the same time, divisions were expected to have a substantial fraction of annual sales come from new products. The result was a succession of new and successful products, including Post-It Notes.

At the end of 2000, 3M appointed James McNerney from General Electric (GE) as its new CEO. GE emphasized extensive use of Six Sigma total quality management techniques through all of its business processes, and was widely regarded as a leader in continuous improvement. McNerney implemented GE's methods at 3M, leading to substantial improvements in efficiency and quality.

However, 3M discovered that continuous improvement methods can be a poor fit for new product development. These methods assume that the goal is known and quantifiable. Formal procedures are used to move from the current situation to the desired goal. Such an approach can be very effective for cutting costs, but is a poor fit for coming up with creative new products. 3M eventually eliminated its emphasis on Six Sigma in R&D.

Source: Hindo (2007)

A variant on the idea of continuous improvement is *experimentation*. Suppose that a bank would like to improve the quality of customer service at its branch offices. One approach is continuous improvement, in which each branch is required to come up with new ideas. Another is for a separate group to devise methods of improving service, which can then be implemented in all of the branches (this is essentially a form of Taylorism). Before implementing those ideas, however, it can be useful to experiment with them first on a small scale. This will help the bank weed out poor ideas and identify good ones. Those good ideas can then be refined before they are rolled out to all of the branches. Note that decentralized continuous improvement does this kind of experimentation automatically, but even a centralized approach to new ideas can exploit experimentation to improve the success of its ideas.

A challenge with continuous improvement is that it is a decentralized approach, so good ideas will not automatically spread throughout the organization. To make this approach even more effective, many companies build in *knowledge management* systems. The goal of such systems is to take the best ideas from decentralized units, generalize best practices from them, and propagate those throughout the rest of the firm. Knowledge management systems must be managed by a centralized group that can pull ideas from all over the organization, and pass best practices in the opposite direction. It also requires adequate incentives for those who come up with local innovations to document and share those ideas with the center of the organization.

SUMMARY

Entrepreneurship is one of the backbones of competition and healthy economies. In this chapter we have discussed some aspects of personnel economics that are relevant for entrepreneurs. We did this under two general topics. The first was the career of an individual entrepreneur; the second was how firm policies can improve intrapreneurship in companies that are not new ventures.

What is an entrepreneur? Most fundamentally an entrepreneur may be someone who combines disparate ideas or people to create something that is greater than the sum of the parts. This is one common view of creativity. It can also involve coordination and management skills. Both of these views imply that entrepreneurs may require a broader skill set than employees who work for a firm. The latter should usually specialize their career and human capital investments. Entrepreneurs may do the opposite. We presented some evidence that this is the case. It is also worth noting that managers in higher ranks of a firm play a role that is more like that of an entrepreneur, since they spend more time coordinating and combining different parts of the business.

What is intrapreneurship? It is designing firm policies to improve innovation and adaptability, and fight bureaucracy. Large, mature, and complex firms often are somewhat bureaucratic. This concern can be addressed by using all of the tools developed in the text, from recruitment and training, to job design and organizational structure, to performance evaluation and incentives. In fact two of our themes for how to think about organizational design are quite relevant to this topic: thinking of a firm's personnel policies as using (where and to the extent possible) market principles inside the firm; and thinking of a firm as a creator and user of information and knowledge.

STUDY QUESTIONS

1. The model of entrepreneurship thought about an entrepreneur as coordinating a diverse set of activities within the firm. Can you think of an alternative interpretation in which the entrepreneur needs a broad set of skills in order to be creative? Explain.

2. Suppose that the endowments of skills x_1 and x_2 that individuals are born with are positively correlated with each other. How would that affect the supply of entrepreneurs in the economy? The value of λ?

3. You are a high level manager in a large firm. In what ways are you likely to foster entrepreneurship in your firm? In what ways are you likely to hinder it? Are there good economic reasons to hinder entrepreneurship in some circumstances?

4. Economists have found that entrepreneurs earn lower average compensation than other workers with similar experience and education. How many explanations can you provide for this finding? How would you test each of your theories?

5. Suppose that two skills are very unlikely to be possessed by the same person (some are good at one, and others are good at the second). You are one of the lucky few who are good at both, and decide to become an entrepreneur using both skills. How would you set up your business to maximize the economic value of your unusual skill set? Can you give examples of unlikely skill pairings that have high market value when combined in the same person? In your examples, how do such individuals set up businesses to exploit their skills?

6. Suppose that managers care about their reputation for the quality of their decisions. How does that affect their propensity to take chances or be conservative when they are new to a job? How will their decision making evolve as they stay in their job longer and establish a track record? How might decision making and risk taking vary between younger and older employees? If these are problematic, how might you change firm policies to mitigate such concerns?

7. You run a venture capital firm. How would you assess a business plan and decide whether or not to invest? First describe the general project evaluation process that your firm should use to compare different business plans (you may wish to review Chapter 5, including the Appendix). Next describe how you would take consideration of the specific topics discussed in this book (e.g., the venture's management, recruitment, structure, decision making, governance, and incentive systems).

8. Following on the previous question, if you invest in a new venture, which decisions will you allow the entrepreneur to make and which will you want to make as a major investor? Why? How should the allocation of decisions change as the venture evolves, assuming that is successful and grows? How should the allocation of decisions evolve if the venture is not successful?

⬢ ⬢ ⬢ ⬢ ⬢ REFERENCES

Hindo, Brian (2007). "3M: Struggle Between Efficiency and Creativity." *Business Week*, June 11.

Koch, Charles (2007). *The Science of Success: How Market-Based Management Built the World's Largest Private Company*. New York: Wiley.

Lazear, Edward (2005). "Entrepreneurship." *Journal of Labor Economics* 23(4): 649–680.

Stopford, John & Charles Baden-Fuller (1994). "Creating Corporate Entrepreneurship." *Strategic Management Journal* 15(7): 521–536.

FURTHER READING

Hamel, Gary & C. K. Prahalad (1990). "The Core Competence of the Corporation." *Harvard Business Review* 68(3): 79–87.

Hamilton, Barton (2000). "Does Entrepreneurship Pay? An Empirical Analysis of the Returns to Self-Employment." *Journal of Political Economy* 108(3): 604–631.

Hannan, Michael, M. Diane Burton, & James Baron (1999). "Engineering Bureaucracy: The Genesis of Formal Policies, Positions and Structures on High-Technology Firms." *Journal of Law, Economics & Organization* 15(1): 1–41.

Kaplan, Steven & Per Stromberg (2002). "Financial Contracting Theory Meets the Real World: An Empirical Analysis of Venture Capital Contracts." *Review of Economic Studies* 70: 281–315.

Kaplan, Steven & Per Stromberg (2004). "Characteristics, Contracts, and Actions: Evidence from Venture Capitalist Analyses." *Journal of Finance* 59(5): 2177–2210.

Prendergast, Canice & Lars Stole (1996). "Impetuous Youngsters and Jaded Old-Timers: Acquiring a Reputation for Learning." *Journal of Political Economy* 104(6): 1105–1134.

Rosanoff, Martin André (1932). "Edison in His Laboratory." *Harper's Weekly Magazine*, September.

APPENDIX

Probability of Entrepreneurship Cannot Increase with Additional Skills

Here we prove that the probability of being an entrepreneur cannot be higher if the industry requires a larger number of skills, all else equal. This relies on the assumption that additional skills are distributed independently of x_1 and x_2 across individuals. Begin with an industry with two skills. The joint density of these skills across individuals is $g(x_1, x_2)$. Now add a third skill x_3, and let the joint density of the three skills be $k(x_1, x_2, x_3)$. If x_3 is independent of x_1 and x_2, with marginal density $m(x_3)$, then:

$$k(x_1, x_2, x_3) = \int m(x_3) \left\{ \iint g(x_1, x_2) \, dx_2 \, dx_1 \right\} dx_3.$$

The entrepreneurship condition for two variables must still hold. For any given x_3 and λ, if $\lambda \cdot min[x_1, x_2] < max[x_1, x_2]$, the individual specializes regardless of x_3. There are potential cutoff values x_3^* and x_3^{**} that are also required for entrepreneurship. Therefore the probability of entrepreneurship cannot exceed:

$$\int_{x_3^*}^{x_3^{**}} m(x_3) \left\{ \int_0^\infty \int_{\frac{x_1}{\lambda}}^{\lambda x_1} g(x_1, x_2) \, dx_2 \, dx_1 \right\} dx_3,$$

which can be written as:

$$\{M(x_3^{**}) - M(x_3^*)\} \int_0^\infty \int_{\frac{x_1}{\lambda}}^{\lambda x_1} g(x_1, x_2) \, dx_2 \, dx_1.$$

The first term is less than one, so the probability cannot exceed the probability of entrepreneurship with only two skill factors. We have shown this for going from two to three skills. By induction, it follows for any number of added skills that are independent of the other skills.

Optimal Human Capital Investment for an Entrepreneur

Define the initial stock of skills as x_i^0 and x_i as the final level, for each skill i. The cost of investing in skills to x_i, beginning with endowment x_i^0, is $C(x_1, x_2)$, with partial derivatives $C_1 > 0$, $C_2 > 0$, $C_{ii} > 0$. We assume that C is symmetric with respect to x_1 and x_2, so that neither skill has a cost advantage.

Let x_1 denote the skill with which the individual is endowed the largest amount. An individual who plans to specialize in his career as an employee would invest either nothing, or focus solely on x_1. Should an individual who plans to be an entrepreneur invest in x_1, x_2, or both?

Since the constraint is that x_2 begins below x_1, there is no point in investing in x_1 unless x_2 is brought up at least to the level of x_1. If there is an interior solution for x_2, it satisfies:

$$\lambda - C_2(x_1, x_2) = 0.$$

There are three possibilities. If $C_2(x_1^0, x_2^0) > \lambda$, then it does not pay to investment in x_2 (or to invest at all). If $C_2(x_1^0, x_2^0) < \lambda$, but $C_2(x_1^0, x_1^0) > \lambda$, the optimal strategy is to invest in x_2, but not up to the level of x_1, and there will be no investment in x_1. If $C_2(x_1^0, x_1^0) < \lambda$, then it pays for the individual to exceed x_1^0 in final levels of both x_1 and x_2. The optimum must have $x_1 = x_2 > x_1^0$.

15

The Employment Relationship

A verbal contract isn't worth the paper it's written on.
—*Attributed to Samuel Goldwyn*

Introduction

Employees and firms often develop long-term relationships that are enormously affected by behavioral characteristics such as psychology and motivation. This means that transactions between employees and firms are more complex than most economic transactions. Cooperation and conflict are constant concerns. Accordingly, simple microeconomic intuition is not adequate to understand fully personnel economics in practice. In each chapter we have added additional concepts and complexities to the simple ideas that we began with. In this chapter, we pull these ideas together to think about the relationship between the employee and the firm.

Employment as an Economic Transaction

Perfect Competition

The study of economics typically begins with a focus on perfectly competitive markets. In such markets, there is a thick market of both buyers and sellers and a single *market clearing price* that brings supply and demand into equilibrium. Since there exists only one market price, there is no role for negotiation. The only terms relevant to any transaction are price and quantity. Product characteristics are also not relevant, since in a perfectly competitive market producers sell goods that are perfect (or at least very close) substitutes for each other. Finally, such markets are anonymous: Suppliers do not need to know who buys their products, and buyers do not need to know who produces what they consume.

A perfectly competitive market is often called a *spot market*. A spot market is a market in which goods, services, and financial assets are traded for immediate delivery. This is obviously an idealized model of real markets, but using this base case as a starting point provides a great deal of insight into how markets function. It highlights the importance of the determinants of supply and demand, competition, and the crucial role played by prices in allocating resources.

Furthermore, it is a relatively satisfactory description of some real world markets. For example, the market for stocks, futures contracts, or publicly traded options is very much like this idealized model. Commodity products are also often well characterized by this model. In reality, many industries are less than perfectly competitive, so that transactions take on different characteristics and become more complex. Entire fields of management education, such as strategy, are designed to analyze such markets. Nevertheless, even less than perfectly competitive markets can be analyzed usefully by studying this base case, since virtually every industry has some competition, and analysis of consumer demand is similar even in monopolistic industries.

The same logic applies to labor markets. Some labor markets are well characterized by the spot market model. For example, the market for day labor on construction sites is a spot market: A worker is hired for a single day to provide a given number of hours of work at an hourly rate. The next day, a different set of workers may perform the same job, while the former workers may be employed by a different construction company on another job. The market for employees of fast-food restaurants is roughly similar to a spot market as well. Most workers are similar in skills and experience, so there is a thick supply of close substitutes. Most jobs are similar to each other in terms of wages, benefits, and working conditions, so there is also a thick market of employers with similar characteristics.

In contrast to these examples, few labor markets can be well characterized by the simple spot market. Labor market transactions—the employment relationship—constitute some of the most complex types of economic transactions in modern economies. The ideas previously discussed in this book introduced and analyzed this complexity. We now move deeper in order to understand the various layers of complexity in employment contracting that we have introduced through the text.

Imperfect Competition

Many labor markets are best characterized as imperfectly competitive because workers are not perfect substitutes for each other, and the jobs that firms offer are also not perfect substitutes for each other. Every individual—especially those with high levels of ability, human capital, or work experience—differs to some extent in productive abilities, appropriate type of job and industry, and so on. Every employer, and job within that employer's organization, tends to be somewhat different. This means that both firms and workers face a set of choices about whom to hire or for whom to work.

This set of choices has important implications for the employment relationship. Imperfect information about possible choices means that both firms and workers engage in a search to find a good match.

Once a good match has been found, the transaction is no longer anonymous; both the worker and the firm care about who they are working with. For example, if a worker loses his job and has to go back into the labor market, a randomly chosen new job is likely to be inferior to the current job which had been found through a previous search. At a minimum, the worker is likely to incur some new search costs to replace this job. Similar logic applies to the firm when replacing the employee.

These search or *switching costs* give both the employee and employer an incentive to continue working together. They have now formed a rudimentary *relationship* that may span multiple periods of working together. At this simple level the economic transaction is different than in a spot market because the transaction involves more than one point in time. We used the metaphor of a marriage to illustrate this idea.

The transaction is different in another way as well: price. Because employees and jobs are imperfect substitutes, there is no one market price at which the employee and firm transact. Instead, there will be a range of pay and benefits for similar workers and jobs. Imperfect information about these options reinforces this point. For example, a worker will not know exactly what alternative jobs he might be able to find, and what compensation he would receive if he took one of those jobs.

This adds a new element to the transaction: bargaining. The pairing of worker and firm creates joint surplus. Joint surplus is the difference between the value to the firm (productivity) and the value to the worker (his reservation price). Imperfect competition and incomplete information imply that for many jobs, these values are not equal. Given that productivity is higher than the worker's reservation price, the actual price—wages, benefits, and other job characteristics agreed to by the worker and firm—will end up somewhere between these two values, depending on how the bargaining plays out between the worker and the firm. We examine some implications of this in Chapters 3–4 and 9–12.

This bargaining process is characterized by *strategic behavior* on the part of the employer and the employee. They may not share their full information with the other side, and may even try to distort their information. One type of distortion is to overstate the value of their alternatives to win a better deal. As described above, imperfect competition creates fundamental differences between the spot and labor markets. Instead of one period, one price, anonymous transactions, we have multiperiod, price varying, unique transactions. Relationships form and bargaining is required. Both sides have an incentive to work together once the search process ends. However, they also have an incentive to act strategically against each other, because the price at which they transact is determined through a negotiation.

Complex Contracting

Sorting and Investments in Human Capital

In Chapters 1–4, we discussed risky hires, probationary screening, and self-selection, job security, and turnover. Consider in particular the implications of our probation model: This model adds several interesting dimensions to the employment relationship.

Instead of a simple job offer consisting of a one period wage and time commitment, similar to a spot market, we have a more complex model, expanded in three distinctive aspects. First, the firm makes a formal multiperiod offer, rather than a repeated set of one period transactions.

Second, the job offer involves pay for performance. It specifies a performance evaluation to determine if the employee survives probation or not. It includes a reward or punishment that is contingent on good performance during probation (e.g., promotion to partnership, or termination). The pay for performance is designed to improve self-selection in recruiting, rather than to improve motivation.

Finally, the probation model involves a *promise* by the firm to the potential employee. The firm promises to evaluate the employee in a way that reasonably correlates with performance. It also promises to pay a wage that is greater than the employee's productivity and market value after probation. For promises to be a viable element of economic transactions, some degree of trust of one party by the other, or both, is required. We will discuss the economic role of trust later in this chapter.

Once we discussed sorting of employees into jobs, we added a new idea to the employment relationship: investments in human capital. If there is on the job training, then the firm's job offer includes those training opportunities. If that training is general human capital, the firm in effect sells the training to the employee. If the training is firm specific, we argued that the worker and firm are likely to share the investment's costs and returns. This shared investment only reinforces any long-term relationship that is being formed by the worker and the firm. They share the costs and benefits, and the longer they stay together, the more they are likely to have invested in working productivity together.

Finally, with firm-specific human capital investments the issue of a promise arises once again. Both sides may be making implicit promises to each other to try not to aggressively renegotiate or holdup with the other side.

WHAT DO EMPLOYEES VALUE IN THE JOB?

❋ ❋ ❋ ❋ ❋ ❋ ❋ ❋ ❋ ❋

A job offer has many dimensions that workers value in various ways. By accepting a job with a certain set of characteristics, workers implicitly buy characteristics that they value highly, and require compensation for those that they do not. For example, if a job is specialized and the worker prefers a job with more tasks, the worker would have to be compensated with higher pay in the specialized job.

One recent study used this idea to estimate the value that workers place on various job attributes, using data from a survey on compensation and other characteristics of a large sample of jobs. Workers were asked to rate the extent to which they trusted their manager, the extent of multitasking or specialization, and so on. The study concluded that a typical worker values these job characteristics in the following order, from most to least valuable:

1. Greater trust of the worker's manager
2. A job with a greater variety of tasks to perform
3. A job with a high level of skill
4. Having enough time to finish one's work
5. Higher compensation

The first, greater trust of management, was estimated to have a large effect on compensation. This suggests that workers are risk averse, and require a substantial risk premium if they do not trust their manager. The second and third are task and skill variety, which we discussed in Chapter 7. These indicate that intrinsic motivation is an important element of the job offer from the employee's point of view. The fourth factor appears to be related to job stress. It is noteworthy that the level of compensation is least important among the factors studied. Employees do care a great deal about other characteristics of the job, short and long term, tangible and intangible. Put another way, if a firm could improve workforce trust, job design, or other factors, it should be able to lower compensation costs substantially.

Source: Helliwell & Huang (2005).

Job Design

The second section of the text analyzed another important element of the transaction between the worker and the firm: job design. A job is more than a set of working hours, compensation, and benefits. The specific tasks the employee is expected to perform, and the degree to which he will be empowered or controlled at work, are important parts of the transaction.

One consideration is that job designs vary in the extent to which they require cooperation. To the extent that the firm adopts a more decentralized, continuous improvement approach, it expects a worker to focus on learning new methods and sharing his ideas with the firm and teammates. The worker may share those ideas freely. Alternatively, the worker may act strategically, keeping those ideas to himself. This might arise from a desire to be more productive than colleagues, or from a fear that too much improvement in productivity might lead to layoffs. The worker will be more likely to share new ideas if teammates and the firm are also cooperative, and if the firm provides some degree of job security.

An additional element in the employment relationship that we considered in the text is motivation. We argued that employees bring intrinsic motivation to the job (particularly to learn), and that this intrinsic motivation varies with job design. To the extent that employees value jobs that are more or less intrinsically motivating, have greater or less control, and fewer or more tasks, this will affect the compensation that needs to be provided (as found in the study cited).

Pay for Performance

We saw that probationary career systems involve a form of pay for performance. Of course, the primary role of pay for performance is not sorting, but providing extrinsic motivation and rebalancing intrinsic motivation. An important part of almost all employment relationships is agreement about how performance will be evaluated and tied to rewards or punishments.

Pay for performance is needed to align the interests of the firm and its employees, who are tempted to use their specific knowledge, skills and effort strategically to pursue their own interests. In other words, pay for performance is one important way by which a firm can improve cooperation with an employee. Furthermore, because of the importance of subjective performance evaluations in many incentive systems, greater trust between the firm and employee can play a valuable role here as well.

Summary

The transaction between a worker and a firm is usually quite complex. Imperfect substitution between types of workers or jobs implies that a match may be formed. This tends to turn the transaction into a repeated relationship that involves negotiation. The desire to mitigate adverse selection in recruiting may lead to multiperiod job offers that include performance evaluation and contingent rewards. Investments in skills, especially firm-specific ones, reinforce these tendencies.

Job design adds new elements, as the firm will design the job to make optimal use of ability to learn on the job and knowledge possessed in performing duties. The firm often desires cooperation from the worker in several ways, including teamwork, coordination with other parts of the organization, and knowledge sharing. In addition, job design can have an important effect on the worker's motivation.

Pay for performance makes performance evaluation and rewards even more important. They may be used to reinforce all of the personnel objectives of the firm, including sorting, investment in skills, continuous improvement, efficiency, and motivation. Incentives are also designed to improve cooperation between the worker and the firm.

One theme that we have seen is the conflict between the temptation by the worker or firm to act strategically, or to cooperate. In the next section, we illustrate this conflict in the context of worker *empowerment*, by which we mean in this context the extent to which the firm asks for input from workers in firm decisions.

COMMUNICATION BETWEEN MANAGEMENT AND WORKERS

Communication from Management to Workers

One recent innovation is open book management, where workers are given detailed information on the financial condition of the firm. Often, this involves training the workforce in accounting and other skills that are generally peripheral to their jobs. There are clear costs to doing this, but some have argued that the benefits outweigh the costs. The costs take a number of forms. First, time is required to convey the information to workers and teach them to process it. Second, giving workers information can backfire. Workers who know everything about the firm may be able to act opportunistically and extract a larger portion of the firm's profits than would otherwise be the case. This is the usual fear that management expresses with regard to opening the books.

The primary advantage of open book management (or a weaker version of it) is that workers may lower their expectations in ways that can help keep a firm viable. In Europe, where works councils are common, managers sometimes express the view that worker empowerment through their councils is helpful to management. This is particularly true when communicating bad news. The following example makes the point.

Workers generally like to receive higher wages, but recognize that when the firm is in dire straits, the amount that they receive in compensation must decline. The problem is that management, knowing that workers will accept lower wages in an emergency, has an incentive to cry wolf. Although the firm may sometimes say that times are good, it will tend to exaggerate the severity and number of occurrences of down times. If workers have only management to rely on, they must choose either to discount management's statements (at least some of the time) or to accept management's statements as fact and accept the lower compensation necessitated by the bad news.

Suppose that each worker has an alternative opportunity that offers $900 per week. During good times, the worker is worth $1,800 per week to the current firm. During bad times, the worker is worth $1,000 per week to the current firm. Since even $1,000 is greater than the alternative of $900, it is always better for the worker to remain at the firm than to move elsewhere. That is, there is always some wage—for example, $950 during bad times—that makes both the current firm and worker better off than having the worker leave. Since $950 is less than the worker value, the firm makes a profit on him. Also, since $950 exceeds the $900 available elsewhere, the worker does better by remaining. Herein lies the problem. Since the firm knows that the worker is willing to accept $900, management has an incentive to lie about demand conditions. Rather than admit that times are good, management may attempt to convince its workers that times are bad. If workers believe that times are bad, they know that the firm cannot pay more than $1,000 without taking a loss. Thus, the maximum wage that workers expect to get under these circumstances is $1,000. Of course, if management were always to claim that times were bad, their statements would lose all credibility. As a result, managers must mix up the statements, but there is still a tendency for management to claim that things are worse than they are, and workers are aware of this fact.

What does the worker do? In the absence of additional information, workers can either believe management and accept lower wages, or they can assume that management is lying and hold out for higher wages. As usual, there are two kinds of errors that workers may make. If they accept management's statement, they will always retain their jobs, but they will make the mistake of accepting low wages even during good times. If they assume that management is lying and they hold out for high wages, workers will get high wages during good times, but they will lose their jobs during bad times. Since only some of the times that are claimed to be bad are bad, workers win by this strategy during those falsely labeled bad times, but they lose by the strategy during correctly labeled bad times. During true bad times, workers lose their jobs by holding out for high wages that the company truly can't pay. They are then forced to resort to their outside opportunity of $900, which is less than the $1,000 that the company would be willing to offer.

For any given announcement that times are bad, workers must assess the probability that the statement is accurate. This depends on actual conditions in the industry. If the workforce is used to seeing primarily good conditions, they may discount heavily any announcement that times are bad, assuming instead that the firm is simply trying to negotiate a better deal. In the current example, suppose that the firm and worker split the estimated surplus. This means that if workers believe the firm's statements, they will receive $950 in wages during times that are declared to be bad. If they choose to take a hard line because they assume that the firm is lying, they will receive $1/2(\$1,800 + \$900) = \$1,350$ when the firm is lying, but will lose their jobs when the firm is telling the truth. If it is likely that the firm is lying, either because the management is composed of pathological liars or because conditions in the industry are almost always good, then the workers will choose the hard line. Sometime this results in high wages, but once in a while, it results in job loss.

The firm would always prefer that the workers take the softer approach. Then, costly layoffs never occur and the firm reaps the benefit of paying lower wages in those periods where it declares, correctly or not, that times are bad. It is for this reason that the firm may want to provide information to the workers. Giving workers sufficient information so that they can determine for themselves that times are truly bad may soften workers' positions and prevent unwarranted layoffs. The disadvantage is that giving workers full information strengthens worker resolve during periods when things are going well for the firm. This is the tradeoff that the firm must make. If workers take the hard line too frequently, the firm may decide that the gains from providing information outweigh the costs that the firm bears during good times. The calculation is a straightforward one, and is detailed in the Appendix. The basic points can be summarized here.

Firms benefit from providing workers with information when and only when workers would otherwise choose to take a hard line. If workers are soft, then there is no gain to the firm's revealing information to the workers. This will only make them aggressive during good times. The question then boils down to determining when workers would take a hard line in the absence of information. Firms benefit from providing information to workers when the following conditions hold:

1. *There is a large difference between the wage paid during good times and the wage paid during bad times*. When the wage difference is large, workers are reluctant to accept the firm's word that times are bad. Doing so results in a large wage cut, which has a large adverse effect on workers. If there is a large gain to taking a hard line, workers are more inclined to be aggressive, and firms should be more inclined to provide accurate information to workers to dissuade workers from making aggressive demands during bad times.

2. *There is a small difference between the wage paid during bad times at the current firm and the alternative wage available*. If workers have good alternatives, then they do not lose much when they suffer a layoff during bad times. Hard bargaining results in a layoff when times are truly bad and workers misjudge the truthfulness of the firm's claims, but the layoff is less painful when a worker's alternatives are good. As a result, workers will fear job loss less and will be more aggressive when alternatives are good. Thus, when worker alternatives are good, the firm should be more inclined to provide accurate information to workers to dissuade them from demanding too much during bad times.

3. *As a corollary, since young workers have less firm-specific capital and less to lose, they tend to be more aggressive than older workers*. As such, open book management is more likely to be profitable when the workforce is young than when it is old. Workers who are older have a lower value of alternatives relative to their current wage. As such, they are less likely to demand high wages than are the younger workers. Since the firm loses by revealing information to workers who are already committed to taking a softer approach, open book management is less valuable when the workforce is older.

   Indeed, this squares with most readers' intuition on the issue. It is the young workers, who feel that they have little to lose or who are most inclined to take risk, that are often the leaders of strong worker action. Older workers, who have families and who feel that it would be difficult to find a new equivalent job, are more likely to be passive.

Communication from Workers to Management

Another potential advantage of worker empowerment is that workers may be more willing to communicate their views to management. Sometimes, workers are afraid to give management too much information about their preferences for fear that management might use the knowledge against them. For example, if management learns that workers care a great deal for a particular benefit, the firm may provide the benefit, but cut wages (or not give subsequent raises) in return, knowing that workers so value the benefit that they will not leave the firm. Workers, fearing that the firm might behave in this strategic fashion, may not provide the firm with the relevant information in the first place. But having the information could make both sides better off. The firm might be able to provide the benefit that the workers like at a lower price than workers are willing to pay.

This is a key point. The firm wants to obtain accurate information about a worker's preferences not because it is primarily concerned about worker welfare, but because the firm cares about profits and catering to worker preferences enhances profits. By providing workers with a package that better suits what workers want, the firm can reduce overall compensation costs and increase profits.

In order to induce the worker to communicate truthfully, the worker must have some power over the way the information is used. This provides a rationale for worker empowerment. When the workforce knows that information provided to management cannot be used against it, it will be more likely to tell the truth. Since the truth can allow the firm to tailor the work environment more to the worker's liking, both sides can benefit.

It is fear of strategic behavior by management that keeps workers from being truthful. Thus, another benefit of worker empowerment is the enhancement of profit-increasing communication from worker to firm. The following principle emerges:

> A firm that desires truthful communication from worker to firm may need to provide some worker empowerment so that workers are certain that the revealed information will not be used against them.

As a practical matter, this can be accomplished by allowing workers some say in the working conditions that they face. The more say that workers have, the more likely they are to be truthful about their preferences. However, as will be shown, the more say that workers have, the larger the share of the pie that they can cut for themselves.

One alternative is to ignore worker communication altogether. The firm can simply make an assumption about worker preferences and pay accordingly. If there are enough other firms competing for worker services, over the long haul workers will sort into firms according to their preferences. In the context of our benefits example, firms that provide packages that benefit lovers prefer will attract only benefit lovers. Those that provide packages that benefit likers prefer will attract only benefit likers. Just as in Chapter 13, the market will induce sorting. But if a lover's package is offered to a group of employees who are benefit likers, the likers will leave. Replacing them can be costly, especially when firm-specific human capital is present.

The choice between the two strategies is illustrated by the difference between European labor relations and American labor relations. Europeans, particularly

Germans, set up works councils, which are worker-elected bodies that represent labor's interests on a variety of issues, primarily those that relate to working conditions. By giving workers some control over how information is used, they can be more forthright and the environment can be more cooperative. The cost is that firms give up flexibility because they must obtain works council acquiescence in order to make changes that fall within the works council's jurisdiction. Cooperation, while beneficial, has its costs.

Nonunion American firms, on the other hand, are more dictatorial. They retain flexibility because they can implement their plans without having to obtain approval from a worker body. There may be less worker–manager cooperation, but there is also less time wasted discussing matters that have little bearing on profit.

Empowerment and Earnings Profiles

Workers with firm-specific human capital are more likely to insist on being given power. Before workers are willing to make an investment in an asset that is firm specific, they are likely to want assurances that their investment will be protected against arbitrary actions by management, such as forcing them to leave and lose their investment. Thus:

> Specific human capital and worker empowerment tend to go together. Workers who have a great deal of firm-specific human capital will seek power within an organization and firms that expect workers to invest in firm-specific human capital should be prepared to offer power to their workers.

Other workers may demand power as well. Recall the life-cycle incentive profiles of Chapter 11. The story was that younger workers are paid less than they are worth and older workers are paid more than they are worth. Older workers have implicitly invested in the firm and their investments depend on the good faith (and good fortune) of the firm. Under these circumstances, workers are more likely to demand some say in the matters of the organization.

The necessary ingredient for a worker to want power in the firm is not specific human capital; it is that the worker has much to lose if he or she must move to another job. Thus, upward sloping incentive contracts, unionization that results in wages at the current firm that are higher than the worker can obtain elsewhere, or specific human capital are all ingredients that induce workers to want power. The evidence seems consistent with this point. Union workers demand much more voice in the day-to-day operations of the firm than do nonunion workers, precisely because union workers lose more when they are forced to change jobs. Thus:

> Workers are more likely to demand power whenever their best alternative wage is (significantly) lower than their wage at the current firm.

This creates some tension. Workers want power, but firms have less to gain by giving it to them. To the extent that workers are overpaid and their alternatives are poor, their ability to back up threats with credible action is reduced. The firm knows that the worker suffers significantly by a departure and is less likely to fear aggressive behavior by workers.

Worker Empowerment and Creativity

In Section II, we discussed at length an important benefit from worker empowerment: Workers have knowledge that can increase productivity and create continuous improvement. One form of such knowledge is specific knowledge possessed by the worker but valuable to the firm's operations. Such knowledge is costly to communicate to management, and thus may require decentralization to the worker to be used profitably. In addition, workers may learn new ideas as they perform their duties that might be used to improve their productivity and that of colleagues. In such cases, it can be important for the firm to encourage the worker to share his or her ideas with the rest of the organization.

> Worker empowerment is more valuable to the firm when workers have more specific knowledge that is value in production, when the firm gives greater emphasis to continuous improvement in production, and when the worker's new ideas have applicability to other workers.

The Decision to Empower Workers

In the last few pages, we have outlined ways in which productivity could be enhanced by empowering workers, but the opening scenario made clear that there might be some costs associated with worker empowerment that could offset any benefits obtained. What is the bottom line, and how should the firm think about the decision to provide workers with additional power? The primary point is that the firm usually should not provide workers with as much power as would maximize productivity, because productivity is not profit. In the process of giving workers power, the firm may also give workers the ability to extract a larger share of the pie. Thus, maximizing the size of the pie is not the relevant criterion as far as the firm is concerned. The appropriate criterion from the firm's point of view is to maximize the amount (not proportion) of profit that goes to the firm. Put differently, it is better to have $3/4$ of an eight-inch pie than $1/2$ of a nine-inch pie. The following analysis illustrates the issues involved and provides some guidelines for choosing the amount of power to provide workers.

In Figure 15.1(a), the firm's share of profit is graphed as a function of worker power. When workers have no power, the firm's share is 1, meaning that the firm gets to keep 100% of value added. This extreme is never reached because workers always have some alternatives, even if it is consuming leisure, which gives them some hold over the firm. Were the firm to keep 100% of value added, workers would be paid nothing. Even the meekest, wimpiest worker would have the willpower to refuse to work under such circumstances.

At the other extreme, workers have so much power that the firm share is zero. The firm keeps none of the profits; even the normal return on capital goes to labor. This situation is not stable, either. No investor will put money into a firm that is known to return 0% on equity. Even the most powerful group of workers will be forced to give some of the returns to capital in order to pay investors, not to mention managers.

FIGURE 15.1

WORKER EMPOWERMENT AND VALUE ADDED

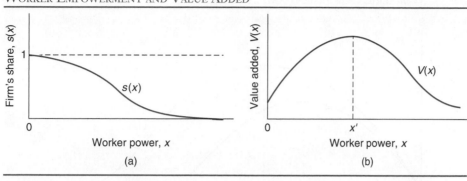

(a)   (b)

The general point, however, is that the relation between worker power and firm's share is an inverse one. The more power workers possess, the smaller the share of the pie the firm gets.

Figure 15.1(b) shows the relation of value added to worker power. The inverted U-shaped relation implies that there is such a thing as too little worker empowerment, just as there can be too much worker empowerment. With no worker empowerment, the kinds of forces discussed in the last few pages are impeded. Finns cannot communicate with workers in a credible way, workers are afraid to make their true feelings known, and creativity is stifled as the firm ignores worker views, wishes, and suggestions. Morale may suffer under such conditions and productivity tends to be extremely low.

As workers become somewhat more empowered, their productivity rises, eventually reaching its peak at x'. After x', additional power reduces value added. Workers become so powerful that needed flexibility is lost. The firm is run by committee and cannot respond to competition. Workers may use their power to extract resources from the firm, thereby running it down and reducing its productive capacity. Eventually, the firm may even go bankrupt. The notion that workers can be given too much or too little say in the firm is hardly controversial. Ultimately the manager must decide how much power to give workers. Figure 15.2 helps with this decision.

Figure 15.2 combines the information of the previous two graphs. The highest curve, labeled $V(x)$, is identical to the one shown in Figure 15.1(b). It is merely copied from the earlier diagram. Note that it reaches its peak when worker power is set to x'. The lower curve, labeled Firm profits, is equal to the total value added, times the firm's share from Figure 15.1(a). That is, Firm profits = $s(x) \cdot$ (*Value added*).

To understand this curve, which is the product of the one in Figure 15.1(a) and the one in 15.1(b), consider the extreme points. When workers have no power, all of the value added goes to the firm. Firm profits are equal to value added, so the curves intersect when worker power is at a minimum. At the other end, worker

FIGURE 15.2
WORKER EMPOWERMENT AND PROFIT

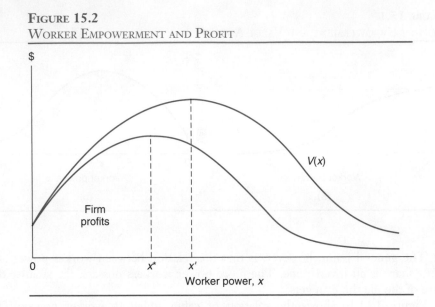

power is high enough so that the firm's share is virtually zero. Even though value added is still positive (albeit quite low), the firm gets to keep almost none of it. Workers keep the entire amount of value added, but value added is very low so workers' total take is quite small.

As in Figure 15.1(b), value added is maximized when workers are given power at the level of x'. However, the firm does not care about maximizing value added; the goal is to maximize its own profits. This occurs when workers have power x^*, not x'. It is easy to show analytically that the firm maximizes its profits by giving workers less power than would maximize the value added of the firm. That is, it is always the case that x^* lies to the left of x'. The intuition is as follows. Suppose that the firm has already given workers x^* of power. Giving workers additional power can increase the total value added, but the rate at which value added rises with additional power is very low. (Near the very top of the $V(x)$ curve, $V(x)$ hardly rises at all with additional worker power.) At the same time, because workers are getting more power, the firms share is declining. Once x^* is reached, the effect of getting a smaller share outweighs the effect of getting a larger pie. It must be true that the smaller share effect outweighs the larger pie effect before x equals x' because as x gets close to x', the pie is hardly expanding at all. At the same time, workers' share is still expanding.

The conclusion is that, from the shareholders' point of view, the firm should give workers less power than would maximize the firm's value added. The goal is not productivity maximization, but profit maximization.

The last few pages have shown that the firm would like to offer workers less power than the amount that maximizes value added. What factors affect the firm's decision on how much power to give to the worker? There are two forces at work.

FIGURE 15.3

EMPOWERING WORKERS: TWO SCENARIOS

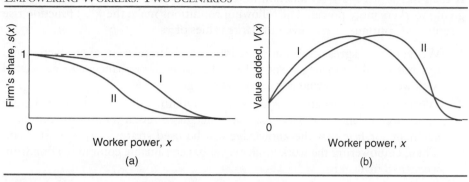

First, when the firm's share falls more rapidly as a function of worker power, the firm will want to choose lower values of x. This is because the smaller share effect swamps the larger pie effect for lower values of worker power. This is shown in Figure 15.3(a). The curve labeled I is the original curve from Figure 15.1(a). The curve labeled II is another possible $s(x)$ function. It falls more steeply. The resulting x^* is lower when $s(x)$ takes the shape of curve II than when it takes the shape of Curve I.

Second, when the value added function rises steeply even for high values of x so that the peak of the $V(x)$ function in Figure 15.1(b) lies more to the right, the firm will want to give relatively more power to the workers. This is because the effect of the larger pie swamps the effect of a smaller share for higher values of worker power. This is shown in Figure 15.3(b). Curve I is the original curve from Figure 15.1(b). Curve II is another possible $V(x)$ function. It rises more steeply. The resulting x^* is higher when $V(x)$ takes the shape of Curve II than when it takes the shape of Curve I.

When is the $s(x)$ curve likely to look more like II than like I? Here are some guidelines. Giving workers increased power is likely to reduce capital's share more significantly when:

1. Workers work together so that it is easier for them to discuss, organize, and coerce.
2. Workers have a longer term relationship with the firm so that they are willing to invest more in increasing their share. This is also the situation in which workers will most want to obtain power.
3. Workers have access to outsiders who can leverage their power and use it for rent extraction and productivity augmentation. Most often, the outsiders take the form of unions or government agencies that are sympathetic to worker arguments.

When any of these three conditions are present, significant levels of worker empowerment are likely to result in reduced profits.

Similarly, we may also ask, "When is the $V(x)$ curve likely to look more like II than like I?" If the $V(x)$ function looks like curve II, then the firm benefits by giving workers more power. The following conditions make the $V(x)$ function rise steeply and continue to rise, even for large values of x:

1. Workers have a great deal of information that is both relevant to production and not possessed by management. Then, the creativity enhancement associated with worker empowerment is likely to be largest.

2. Worker preferences are idiosyncratic and unknown by management. Under these circumstances, workers may be reluctant to reveal their desires to management for fear that the knowledge can be used strategically against them. Then, empowering the work force may enhance valuable communication from worker to manager.

Sometimes a government steps in and creates regulations that change, by decree, the amount of power that workers have. There is an efficiency argument for taking steps of this sort. Since the firm does not empower workers enough to maximize value added, one could argue that the government can improve things by ordering firms to empower workers up to level x'. Although this is a potentially sound argument, it has two problems at the practical level.

First, there is no reason to believe that the government will know how much power is consistent with maximizing value added. It is as likely to overshoot x' as it is to undershoot x'. This is even truer when it is recognized that the optimal amount of worker empowerment, even from the social point of view, varies across firms. Curve II in Figure 15.3(b) is associated with a different amount of optimal empowerment than Curve I in Figure 15.3(b). Legislation tends to be a blunt instrument. It has a one-size-fits-all aspect, which means that the law is not well tailored to any specific situation. As such, it may do more harm than good.

Second, laws are not created by benevolent dictators, but by a political process. The political process plays off labor groups against management groups. Legislation that results from this process naturally reflects the interplay of interest groups. There is no reason to expect that the product of this interaction will result in the optimal amount of worker empowerment. Government regulations on worker empowerment, or any aspect of industrial relations for that matter, merely replace industrial politics with national politics.

An Application: Union Organizing Campaigns

An attempt by a union to organize a workforce is a prime example of the tradeoff engendered in this chapter's analysis. Some have argued that unions actually make firms more productive through a variety of measures, some of which have been discussed already. Unions, it is argued, may provide a relatively efficient way for workers to communicate their preferences to management. Because unions may also reduce the likelihood that management will use information to take advantage of workers, workers are more inclined to communicate with management in a union setting than in a nonunion one. The grievance procedure, which is generally formalized in a union firm, is one way by which workers can prevent firms from using information against them. There is a tradeoff, however. Even if unions do make workers more productive, they do not necessarily make firms more profitable. Because firms care about total profits, not the size of the pie, firms may oppose a union that improves productivity, but that also increases workers' share too much.

Firms frequently resist unions. Given the large cost of doing so and the potential gain from increased productivity why are firms so resistant to unions? To see why, consider the following calculation.

A large firm that has $1 billion in sales faces a union organizing drive. Labor's share in the economy hovers around 75%, which means that 75% of all after-tax revenues eventually find their way into labor's hands and 25% eventually go to shareholders. Even if a unionized labor force leads to productivity-enhancing worker empowerment, how large would this effect have to be for the firm to be willing to welcome the union?

At the typical $1 billion firm, $750 million is paid out to labor. A union that is effective in organizing the firm can be expected to raise wages. The wage differential associated with unionization is generally found to be somewhere between 10% and 25%. To be conservative, let us take the lower number as our estimate of the effect of unionization on wages. Were the union to organize successfully, the wage bill would increase by 10%, or from $750 million to $825 million. If nothing else were to change, capital's return would fall from $250 million to $175 million. It is hardly surprising that a reduction in return of $75 million is met with resistance. But recall that unions might conceivably increase productivity. To determine the amount by which productivity would have to be increased in order to imply a net gain for capital, note that labor's share after unionization is 82.5%, and capital's share is 17.5%. Thus, in order for the firm to welcome the union, it must be the case that:

$$0.175 \cdot \textit{Net revenue after unionization} > 0.25 \cdot \textit{Net revenue before unionization}.$$

The left-hand side of the expression is capital's take after unionization, whereas the right-hand side is capital's take before unionization. The expression can be rewritten as:

Net revenue after unionization/Net revenue before unionization $> 0.25/0.175$
$= 1.4286.$

In order for capital to prefer unionization, productivity increase associated with unionization would have to exceed a whopping 42.86%. Few changes in the history of humankind have increased productivity by 42%, and unionization is not one of them.

The amount that a firm might be willing to pay to stave off unionization is enormous. Suppose we assume that unionization does increase firm productivity by 10%, which would be in line with the amount by which it increases wages. Capital's return would then be 0.175 ($1.1 billion), or $192.5 million. Recall that before unionization, capital's share was $250 million. Note further that these numbers are calculated on an annual basis. The difference between the union and nonunion revenue that goes to capital is $250 − $192.5 = $57.5 million per year. If the firm were expected to survive for another 10 years, then at a (real) interest rate of 4%, the present value to capital of keeping the union out would be:

$$\sum_{t=1}^{10} \frac{\$57.5 \; million}{1.04^t} = \$466 \; million.$$

The firm would be willing to give up almost half of a year's worth of sales in order to keep the union out. It is no wonder that firms fight very hard to prevent unionization.

This illustrates the point made earlier in this chapter. Although productivity may increase by empowering workers, the productivity gains have to be very large to swamp the effect of a reduction in capital's share. Under normal circumstances, the requirements are unlikely to be met. As a result, it is in a firm's best interests to provide workers with less power than would maximize productivity. Analogously, firms usually gain by opposing unionization, even in those cases where unionization might raise productivity.

Of course, this view may be too negative. We have been emphasizing the potential conflict between the firm and its workers that arises from the desire of each to receive a larger share of the value created by the enterprise. The desire for a larger share, and the fear that the other side might behave strategically, may lead to a loss of value compared to the case of better cooperation between management and workers. Might there be steps a firm could take to try to reduce this conflict? That is our next topic.

◆◆◆◆◆ IMPROVING COOPERATION

Conflict can arise between workers and shareholders and management when the gain to one side comes at the expense of the other. This is the case with the level of compensation in our discussion in the previous section. If workers receive higher compensation, then *all else equal* shareholders are worse off, since their costs are higher. To the extent that this is a true description of the situation, we would call this a *zero sum game* (this term comes from the field of game theory). A zero sum game is a strategic situation in which if one player gains, the other loses by the same amount; the total payoff is constant. In such a case, there is no incentive for cooperation.

Is this a realistic view? Earlier in the chapter we emphasized many reasons why employees and the firm benefit from cooperation. For example, if workers share their ideas about continuous improvement, their productivity rises. The firm can pay them more, while still paying a higher dividend to shareholders. If the firm keeps its promises with respect to fair performance evaluations or deferred compensation, it may be able to recruit better workers and provide stronger incentives. A strategic situation in which the total payoffs are not constant is called a *non–zero sum game*. We have seen throughout this text that the employment relationship is a non–zero

TABLE 15.1

PRISONER'S DILEMMA

	B stays silent.	B betrays A.
A stays silent.	Each serves 6 months.	A serves 10 years; B goes free.
A betrays B.	A goes free; B serves 10 years.	Each serves 5 years.

sum game. If employees and the firm cooperate, they may both be made better off. If they do not, they may both end up worse off.

Unfortunately, as we saw in the previous section, cooperation is not assured even in settings that are not zero sum. There may be a temptation to act selfishly instead of cooperatively. Whether this occurs depends on the potential gains from acting selfishly compared to those from acting cooperatively.

Ideally, an organization will be more effective if ways can be found to increase cooperation between workers and the firm. How can this be achieved? To focus our ideas, first consider the classic *prisoner's dilemma* game from game theory, illustrated in Table 15.1. In this game, two prisoners have been arrested for a crime that they have committed together. The police have put them in separate interrogation rooms and try to convince each to betray the other. Both prisoners have two strategies: cooperate with their colleague by staying silent, or betray their colleague. The two rows show the strategies for Prisoner *A*, while the two columns show the strategies for Prisoner *B*.

The four cells toward the right and bottom in the matrix list the penalties for each prisoner, if the corresponding pair of strategies is chosen. If both prisoners decide to cooperate and stay silent, the police will have to rely on weaker evidence, and each prisoner can expect to spend 6 months in jail. If both confess, then they can expect to spend 5 years each in jail. However, if one betrays his colleague while the other remains silent, the one who has stays silent can expect to receive a 10-year sentence, while the betrayer goes free. Clearly, the preferred outcome for both prisoners—the one that minimizes the combined penalties—is for both to remain silent.

What is the optimal strategy for each prisoner? Remember that the prisoners are in separate rooms, so that they cannot communicate with each other. The optimal strategy is the same for each (the game is symmetric): It is to betray the colleague, regardless of what his colleague expects him to do. For example, suppose that you are Prisoner *A*. If you expect Prisoner *B* to stay silent, your penalty is lower if you betray *B*. The same logic applies if you expect *B* to betray you as well. In the language of game theory, betrayal is called a *dominant strategy*—one that is always optimal, regardless of the strategy played by the opponent.

This is not the preferred outcome for either prisoner. Both have an incentive to not cooperate. This is similar to our discussion of worker empowerment above. Both could be made better off if they could somehow find a way to cooperate, but strategic behavior is likely to lead to an outcome that is less desired by both.

What can be done to solve this dilemma? There are two general possibilities. One would be to write a contract in advance that provides for rewards or punishments (side payments between the two prisoners) depending on whether they betray each other or not. Since the highest valued outcome for both prisoners is for both to stay silent, in this game there would be a penalty that one player paid to the other upon betrayal.

Unfortunately, such explicit contracts are not realistic in many situations for several reasons. In the case of two actual criminals, any agreement to withhold evidence or pay a penalty would not be legally enforceable! In other cases, the possible outcomes are too numerous or unpredictable, so that a formal contract that covers all contingencies is impossible to write.

A second solution can arise if the game is repeated. Imagine that a game like the one in Table 15.1 is repeated over and over again. Now the prisoners have a crude relationship since they interact over time. This opens up new strategic possibilities. For example, a player might decide to stay silent one or two periods, even though that is not optimal in the short run, hoping that this will encourage his colleague to stay silent as well. If the other player does not cooperate, he can respond by betraying his colleague several times in a row. The repeated nature of the game opens up the possibility of multiperiod reward and punishment schemes. It allows the players to signal to each other, and to test each other to try to figure out what kind of strategy the other player is using. All of these possibilities increase the likelihood of cooperation.[1]

Once the game is repeated, each player can attempt to invest in a reputation that might change the strategy of the other player. Suppose, for example, that you would like to elicit cooperation from your partner in crime. If you stay silent several periods in a row, your partner may eventually get the message that you would prefer to cooperate. If he then starts to cooperate, you return the favor by cooperating even more. However, if he tests you by betraying you, you might immediately retaliate by betraying him, one or more times. The idea is to send him the message that you will reward cooperation and punish betrayal.

There is a vast set of possible strategies for such a repeated game. The most famous is the simplest: *tit for tat*. A tit-for-tat strategy can be stated simply: Cooperate in the first period, and thereafter play whatever action the other player took last period. If B betrayed you, betray B this period. If B stayed silent, you stay silent. This is a simple reward and punishment designed to elicit cooperation from your opponent. In fact, game theorists have found that this very simple strategy will beat most more complicated strategies in repeated prisoner's dilemma games.

Regardless of what strategy might be employed, the general point is that repeated interactions make it more likely that two parties can find a way to motivate each other to be more cooperative, and they may be able to establish a *reputation* that leads to a more productive interaction with the other player. This is one reason

---

[1]Technically, this statement is true only if the duration of the repeated relationship is either infinite, or uncertain. Employment relationships are clearly not infinite in length, but they are usually of uncertain duration.

why it is important that the employment relationship often is complex and spanning multiple periods. The more that the firm and employee form a relationship for the reasons we described in this text, the greater their incentive and ability to find ways to cooperate more in the workplace. And, the more we should expect to see personnel practices that encourage such cooperation.

From the Prisoner's Dilemma to Employment

Let us now return to the discussion in Chapter 3, where we introduced the idea of an implicit contract between the worker and the firm over investments in firm-specific human capital. A relationship-specific investment is similar to the prisoner's dilemma game. Both the worker and the firm can be made better off—net productivity will rise—if the investment is made. Both may agree to share the cost of the investment, and the subsequent return. However, both may also be tempted to renege on their promise later. If the risk of such an attempt at renegotiation is high enough, neither may be willing to cooperate in the first place. Then no investment will be made, and both will be worse off.

As we described in that chapter, in theory an explicit contract could be written that described the sharing of all costs and benefits of this investment, and provided for penalties to motivate compliance. However, in reality such a contract is usually not possible. The quality and quantity of the training may be difficult to measure. The same will be true of the opportunity costs of the training. The increase in the worker's productivity that can be attributed to the training is not easy to quantify in a way that both would agree on.

Sometimes firms and workers do try to write a formal contract that specifies as many terms of the relationship as possible. The best example of this is union contracts. For example, the contract between Ford Motor Company and the United Auto Workers union spells out in great detail how workers will be treated and what is expected from them under many circumstances. This contract is composed of six separate books. Laid upon each other on a table, the contract is over six inches high. Despite the length and detail of the contract, it does not in fact cover all possible contingencies. Important parts of the union contract describe procedures that the union and firm will use to resolve issues that have not been described explicitly in the contract.

Not only are there clear limits on the ability of most firms and employees to write complete contracts covering all aspects of employment, but even trying to do so may harm the employment relationship further. When two parties approach an economic relationship by trying to negotiate and set terms for every possible interaction, this often changes how they relate to each other in situations that have not been written down. Instead of taking a cooperative approach, they are more likely to take a legalistic and competitive (zero sum—or even negative sum given legal costs) tack with the other party. Unfortunately this often occurs in union settings, where workers, union representatives, and management tend to take confrontational and legalistic approaches to new questions that arise—treating them as potential disputes rather than potential areas for cooperation.

By contrast, the employment contract between most firms and employees is much simpler than a union contract. Typically, if it is written down at all it constitutes one or a few paragraphs, stating the job title, salary, and length of employment—and little or nothing else. Other terms of the contract may be provided in the firm's employee handbook, but this is usually not lengthy. What governs the employment relationship in such cases? It is often an extensive implicit contract instead of an explicit contract. The employee knows the personality of his supervisor and other leaders of the organization. He has some idea of the past history of the organization, from previous actions or reputation of the firm as an employer. The employee takes these into account when deciding whether to accept or remain in a job, and how to behave on the job. The employee is more likely to provide cooperation if he expects reciprocity from the firm.

Reputation and the Employment Relationship

A useful way to reframe the questions of cooperation and implicit contracting is to ask, Under what circumstances can I trust the other side enough that I am willing to cooperate with them? Putting trust in your employer or employee means that you are placing a bet that they will cooperate, even if it might be against their short-term interest and their behavior is not enforceable through formal means. You are more willing to place such a bet if the odds that you will receive cooperation are higher.

Thus, we should expect more cooperation between the firm and employees if either or both have a strong enough reputation as a "fair employer" or "loyal employee." A couple of points are worth making at this point.

First, this illustrates that reputation can be a valuable *intangible asset*. It is intangible since reputation is almost always difficult or impossible to quantify. It is an asset because in relatively complex, multiperiod economic transactions, reputation can improve governance of the relationship, leading to higher joint profits. Though we focus on employment here, this point is relevant for many other circumstances, such as joint ventures between two firms, partnerships, or the relationship between a venture capitalist and an entrepreneur.

In the case of employment, a reputation for cooperating has many potential benefits. These include greater investments in firm-specific human capital, more sharing of innovations by employees, stronger and better focused intrinsic motivation, more job security, improved performance evaluation and better extrinsic incentives. A strong reputation can improve cooperation, and the desired outcome, in virtually every part of the employee-firm relationship. This helps us understand the research cited above that found that trust in management was the most valued job attribute for typical employees.

Second, since reputation may be an intangible asset, it is sometimes possible to *invest in reputation*. This is what we explore next. Third, it will generally be quite difficult for an individual employee to establish a strong reputation in the labor market for being a cooperative employee. Reputation is based largely on the observable history of your past actions. Individuals have little ability to establish a track record—especially early in their career—that can be verified by potential employers. While reputation is still valuable for employees, it is typically more feasible for a firm to develop a reputation as an employer. For this reason, we focus on how a firm can develop a reputation as an employer.

Investing in Reputation

Suppose that your firm would like to improve its ability to attract, develop, and retain employees over the long term. Your firm decides that it would like to take a more cooperative approach to employment by viewing employees as quasi-partners who make shared investments in firm-specific human capital, process innovations, and teamwork. If employees behave in this way, the firm will be more profitable, and some of those profits can be shared with employees—in principle, that can motivate such behavior by the employees. Unfortunately, for the reasons discussed earlier, it is impossible to write a formal, enforceable contract that covers such complex and qualitative issues. Therefore, your employees need to have some amount of trust in you—that you will treat them fairly—if they are to be motivated to cooperate.

Think about this as a statistical inference problem. Your employees and potential employees decide whether to cooperate with your firm based on whether they believe that it is trustworthy or not. If they assess a high enough probability that they can trust the firm, with reasonable confidence, they will cooperate. In statistical terms, they will cooperate if they estimate that the probability that the firm will also cooperate is high enough, and if their estimate has high precision (low variance). These are the keys to establishing reputation: You need to provide enough data, with enough consistency, to make your assessors confident. Some simple points immediately follow from this perspective.

History

A firm with a long history is much more likely to have a strong reputation in the labor market than a brand new firm. For example, UPS has employed workers for over 100 years. This provides a great deal of data to potential employees on how UPS has treated its employees. If UPS was consistent in its treatment of employees over this period (and it was), then most job applicants would predict that UPS is quite likely to continue to treat employees in the same way in the future. By contrast, when Federal Express entered the same industry as a new firm in the 1980s, it had no track record as an employer, and therefore little or no reputation.

Consistency

No matter how long your history of past behavior, if that behavior was erratic then the inference will be that your future behavior is not predictable, and you will have no clear reputation. Returning to UPS, in addition to a long history, the manner in which they have treated their employees has changed little over the 100-plus years of its existence. Having a long history of behavior, with low variance, is the most powerful way to establish reputation. Unfortunately, it is also difficult to do, especially because it takes time.

First Impressions

When there is little data on which to base an inference, each new piece of information contributes a great deal to forming expectations. Thus, the first interactions are often the most important point at which one can begin to invest in a desired reputation. In the context of employment, a firm can use this idea to its advantage by carefully thinking about the messages it sends by how it treats both potential job applicants and new hires. How a new hire is *integrated* into the organization after being hired can be an important tool in establishing an effective implicit contract with the employee.

Some firms have formal "inboarding" programs for this purpose. Such programs may include training in the firm's history, culture, and policies. They may also include activities designed to help the employee bond productively with her workgroup. Other firms have at least informal methods of trying to achieve the same objectives, including mentoring programs, "buddy" systems where new hires are paired with incumbent employees for a period of time, and so forth. A manager can also exploit this point to his advantage. When a new person is hired, the manager should consciously use the first interactions to try to establish the kind of working relationship they desire with the employee. Not paying attention to this effect from the start may make it harder to shape the working relationship later.

FIRST IMPRESSIONS
❖❖❖❖❖❖❖❖❖❖

The first interaction can be an important opportunity to establish a productive working relationship, because there is little prior history or data on which expectations have formed. Here are two examples from the workplace, one involving a firm's relationship with its employees, and the other a firm's relationship with its "customers."

Ritz-Carlton Hotel Company

The Ritz-Carlton Hotel Company is a five-star luxury hotel chain. It is renowned for its high quality of service, and has won two Malcolm Baldrige Awards for quality. An important source of this service is its motivated staff. Ritz-Carlton's slogan for employees is "We are Ladies and Gentlemen Serving Ladies and Gentlemen." (Notice that this slogan is a simple implicit contract. It tells employees how they should behave, and how they can expect to be treated by the firm in return.) The company consciously tries to establish good relationships with employees from the beginning. Even before they are hired, job applicants are treated with a high level of attention and courtesy, exactly as the hotel will want them to eventually treat hotel guests. If a job offer is not extended, the hotel is very gracious to those it turns down. If a job offer is made, the hotel has a policy of calling the employee back with 21 days to make sure that it kept any promises that it made to the new employee. The first two days of training are focused on the firm's values, culture, and establishing strong teamwork. Only after this training is completed does the hotel train the worker in how to do their specific job tasks.

Sodexo's Outsourced Prisons in Britain

Sodexo is a French firm that provides various outsourced services for its clients, especially food and facilities management services. One small part of their business is managing several prisons for the government in Britain. The Sodexo manager in charge of these prisons established a policy designed to improve the firm's working relationships with its prisoners. When a new prisoner enters the prison, they are immediately asked two questions. The first question is, "What would you like to be called?" The name that the prisoner gives is then used by all prison staff during the prisoner's stay. The second question is, "Would you like a cup of tea or coffee?"

In most prisons, new prisoners are not greeted with such questions. Sodexo's management says that the goal is to treat prisoners with respect, in the hope that they will reciprocate by behaving cooperatively. They feel that the first interaction with the prisoner is crucial in starting the relationship off on a path toward, or away from, cooperation. This practice is successful. The Sodexo prisons have low rates of problems with prisoners (e.g., riots or other violence), have been widely cited as exemplary, and have received several awards for their management practices.

Sources: Sucher & McManus (2001); Sodexo management

Economies of Scale

Reputation also depends on how other employees are treated by the firm. During the job interview, potential employees usually try to gauge how current employees feel about their working conditions and treatment. One way to establish a stronger reputation is to have working relationships with a greater number of employees, and to treat them all with relative consistency. Treating a large group of employees similarly can be powerful evidence for those who are considering working for a firm. In addition, the larger the firm, the more likely it is that possible job applicants are familiar with the firm.

Furthermore, if a firm has established a particular reputation, and then treats an employee in ways that are strongly inconsistent with that reputation, this may harm its credibility with other employees as well. This gives the firm some incentive to maintain consistent treatment of employees, and this effect is stronger, the larger the number of employees in the firm.

Thus, there are some economies of scale in developing a reputation as a good employer. For this reason, larger firms may pay more explicit and centralized attention to policies designed to develop and maintain credibility with their employees.

Personality

In some cases the personality of a particularly manager can have a very important effect on the firm's reputation as an employer. Certainly the personality of any manager has a major impact on their direct subordinates. If the manager's personality is one that creates trust with those subordinates, the resulting impact on organizational effectiveness can be extremely important. Of course, the opposite is also true.

The personality of the CEO or another high level manager can in some cases have a large effect on the formation of expectations and the corporate culture. Sometimes this occurs because the founder of the firm had strong views on how the firm should be managed, and those views created formal policies, an informal culture, and a workforce that perpetuated the founder's leadership style.

If the leader has a very strong personality and forceful leadership style, that manager may impart implicitly or explicitly similar patterns of behavior in other managers throughout the organization. Sometimes a leader's strongly held beliefs are reflected in formal policies as well. For example, Jack Welch was a legendary leader of the huge, diversified conglomerate General Electric (GE). Nicknamed "Neutron Jack," Welch was renowned for his strong beliefs in the importance of recognizing and rewarding individual performance. General Electric developed TopGrading, one of the few examples of a forced curve performance appraisal system that was implemented successfully for many years. In this system, supervisors were required to identify poor performers, and employees who received poor evaluations for several years in a row were expected to improve or were forced out of GE. This policy reflected Welch's beliefs about effective employee management, and Welch's strong beliefs and forceful personality have been widely held to be key to why these policies were used with such success during his reign.

JACK WELCH ON TOPGRADING AT GENERAL ELECTRIC

Below is a section from Jack Welch's 2000 letter to GE shareholders which describes his view of TopGrading, the name GE gives its forced curve performance appraisal scheme.

People

"Our technology, our great businesses, our reach and our resources aren't enough to make us the global best unless we always have the best people—people who are always stretching to become better. This requires rigorous discipline in evaluating, and total candor in dealing with, everyone in the organization.

"In every evaluation and reward system, we break our population down into three categories: the top 20%, the high-performance middle 70% and the bottom 10%.

"The top 20% must be loved, nurtured and rewarded in the soul and wallet because they are the ones who make magic happen. Losing one of these people must be held up as a leadership sin—a real failing.

"The top 20% and middle 70% are not permanent labels. People move between them all the time. However, the bottom 10%, in our experience, tend to remain there. A company that bets its future on its people must remove that lower 10%, and keep removing it every year—always raising the bar of performance and increasing the quality of its leadership.

"Not removing that bottom 10% early in their careers is not only a management failure, but false kindness as well—a form of cruelty—because inevitably a new leader will come into a business and take out that bottom 10% right away, leaving them—sometimes midway through a career—stranded and having to start over somewhere else. Removing marginal performers early in their careers is doing the right thing for them; leaving them in place to settle into a career that will inevitably be terminated is not. GE leaders must not only understand the necessity to encourage, inspire and reward that top 20%, and be sure that the high-performance 70% is always energized to improve and move upward; they must develop the determination to change out, always humanely, that bottom 10%, and do it every year. That is how real meritocracies are created and thrive."

Source: General Electric, 2000

Applications: Corporate Culture and Centralized Human Resource Policies

We end this section with a brief application of these ideas to the topic of corporate culture, and then relate that to the question of whether human resource policies should be centralized or decentralized.

Corporate culture (or norms; see Chapter 8) is a very difficult concept to define rigorously. The viewpoint that we have taken in this chapter and elsewhere in the book is one way to make the concept more operational. A useful way to think of corporate culture is as a set of informal rules about how the employment relationship will be governed—in other words, as part of the implicit contract between the worker and the firm. Thought about in this way, it is possible to attempt to shape the culture in ways that improve the firm's operation.

As an example, consider the question of how managers give feedback to employees about their performance, and how employees receive the feedback. A classic problem in many firms is that managers are very reluctant to give negative feedback. Similarly, employees often respond to negative feedback defensively or with anger, instead of treating it as valuable information about how to improve their performance. Unfortunately, these behaviors undermine the purpose of performance appraisals and can lead to mediocre organizational performance.

Some organizations, such as General Electric as discussed above, have been able to establish cultures in which such behavior is not common. Rather, these firms have norms in which employees are expected to give constructive feedback, and to receive such feedback without acting defensively. Great universities typically also have these norms, both between professors in giving feedback about their research, and in the classroom between professors and students. The implicit contract in such organizations is that all participants are expected to contribute appropriately and constructively to the giving and receiving of constructive feedback. Moreover, the norm is usually that resisting such feedback will be sanctioned informally.

The fact that some organizations have productive norms about feedback while others do not suggests that such norms can be created or changed. While this may not be easy to do if existing norms are strongly entrenched, an important part of a leader's job is doing just this: crafting and evolving the corporate culture so that the implicit rules about how the organization functions are as effective as possible. A good manager should think consciously about the implicit contract that her behavior is creating. And, the manager should also consciously consider the reputation that her actions may create.

Finally, let us briefly consider centralization of human resources policies. Should HR policies be centralized or decentralized? There are many benefits to decentralized policies. They allow for greater flexibility to the differing circumstances of individual business units. They give local managers discretion about how to run their operations. Yet HR departments often do impose common policies across an organization, even a very large organization (e.g., forced curve performance appraisals across all divisions of General Electric). They are commonly derided for imposing bureaucratic constraints on how managers can oversee their units. Are there any justifications for such centralized policies?

One potential justification is the consistency that this imparts to the overall organization. In the example of GE, using the same rules for performance appraisals means that employees are treated in the same way throughout the organization, regardless of which region, division, or supervisor they work for. If a firm desires to develop a corporate culture that is consistent across the organization, centralization of some human resource policies is almost required. Consistency of behavior is quite difficult to achieve unless some limitations are placed on individual discretion.

In this sense corporate culture is similar to a company's product branding. A company's products develop a reputation with customers, with respect to quality, features, and so forth. This brand can be quite valuable in reducing marketing costs.

Like corporate culture, a product's brand is an intangible asset. A brand is difficult to maintain in a multiproduct firm if product managers have too much autonomy. For this reason, some centralization is generally necessary to maintain consistent brand management. For the same reason, some centralization of human resource policies may be necessary to maintain—or change—a consistent corporate culture.

CHANGING THE ALPHABET IN TURKEY

In 1928, Turkish President Ataturk decided that the country needed to change its alphabet from Arabic to the Turkish alphabet. The Arabic script in use in Turkey at the time had 482 different letter combinations. Though beautiful to read, the script was very difficult to learn, and literacy was below 20%. The new alphabet, based on the Latin alphabet, had only 29 characters.

In order to implement this change, Ataturk decreed that the change would happen all at once, very quickly. For example, newspapers were ordered to begin using the new alphabet by November 1st, and were required to completely implement the change by December 1st or be shut down. The government played a very strong role in forcing this change on the entire society.

This highly centralized change was very successful. As a result, Turkey's literacy rate eventually rose to over 90%, which helped the country modernize its economy.

Source: Williams (1929)

SUMMARY

Personnel Economics in Practice

The employment relationship is one of the most complex types of economic transactions in the economy. Throughout this book we have used economic tools to add increasing complexity to our understanding of this transaction. In this chapter, we pulled together those threads. Our main point was to discuss the informal, but still very real and economically important, dimension to employment contracting.

The often multiperiod economic relationship between the employee and the firm covers many dimensions: job tasks, decision making, learning and sharing innovations, investments in training, performance evaluation, and rewards and punishments. There are many areas for potential cooperation between the employee and the firm. Unfortunately, there are also temptations to act strategically, which can undermine this cooperation and reduce the total gains from working together.

Because of its complexity, multiperiod nature, and unpredictability, it is almost always impossible to write a formal contract to cover all aspects of the employment relationship. Some remaining aspects are governed by laws and overall firm policies. However, a great deal of the relationship is governed by implicit contracts. These implicit contracts may be between an individual manager and employee, or based on the firm's reputation and corporate culture. They work effectively only to the extent that employees and the firm have a similar understanding of what the implicit rules are. In addition, at least one party (or both) must have adequate credibility—at least one side must have enough trust of the other, or implicit contracting is likely to be ineffective. In that case, the firm and employee must fall back on formal contracting and strategic behavior, with an ensuing loss of profits.

This argument illustrates that trust, or reputation, can be an economically valuable intangible asset. We provided a brief discussion of some ways in which one can invest in a reputation, and gave some examples of the implications for firm policies. However, we have only scratched the surface. Our main objective was to make you more conscious of the importance of implicit contracting to personnel economics.

Since this is the final chapter of the text, let us now take a minute to step back and remind you of several themes about personnel management and organizational design that have been developed in the book.

First, although a firm is not a market, the market metaphor is a powerful way of thinking about organizations and personnel economics. Markets may be viewed as systems by which information is used to create value, largely through decentralization and strong incentives. The principles of decentralization and incentives are at the core of personnel economics. However, as in markets, there is also a role for centralization, either to achieve better coordination or to solve externalities or other "market failures." Moreover, incentives inside a firm are much more complex, because individual performance is harder to measure when there is no market price.

Second, a firm can be thought of as an information system. Economic profit over the long run comes from new innovations, be they in production methods or product design. Such innovations arise from the effective use of knowledge throughout the organization. An important source of such innovations is continuous improvement, which taps into the knowledge of lower level workers.

Third, we have emphasized several times the tradeoff of creativity vs. control. We saw this initially in discussing whether or not a firm should hire a risky candidate. The issue arose again when discussing centralization versus decentralization, and the use of relatively flat or hierarchical structures. It arose once more in the context of incentives, for example in our discussions of subjective performance evaluations, and employee stock options. Roughly speaking, the greater the extent to which an organization operates like an internal market, the more likely that organization is to be creative. However, creativity has its costs. These include unpredictability, inconsistency, and lack of coordination. It is very difficult to achieve the goals of creativity and control simultaneously. A firm's organizational design must balance these, and match them to the competitive context and information problems that it faces.

A closely related fourth theme was that organizations can optimize for a certain set of circumstances, or can design themselves for adaptability, but not both at the same time. For example, Taylorism may make an organization extremely effective at doing one thing in one way. However, if circumstances change, the firm may find it difficult to adapt since all policies (recruiting, training, decision making, job design, incentives, and culture) are oriented toward one specific purpose.

An alternative is to design personnel policies for more flexibility. Though less adapted to one situation, this allows a firm to adapt more quickly and effectively, which is important in more dynamic industries. This can be achieved through hiring more flexible workers, training in a broader set of skills (including problem solving skills), using more decentralized structures that emphasize local flexibility and continuous improvement, and incentive systems and culture that reinforce such policies.

Fifth, and finally, in theory what is good for the worker is good for the firm. A firm functions best when it is able to design the organization and personnel policies so that both workers and the firm have common long-term objectives. Cooperation is not guaranteed, however, since there are always temptations to act strategically when the transaction cannot be governed completely by formal contracts. We say this initially in our discussion of the potential for holdup with firm-specific human capital, and again in this chapter when we discussed communication between workers and management. Of course, this was also a key issue in the third section of the text, since the purpose incentive systems is to promote cooperation rather than conflict. A very important objective of both formal and informal personnel policies should be to align the interests of workers and the firm as closely as possible, developing adequate trust to ensure greater cooperation.

Study Questions

1. Think about jobs that you have had. What were the terms of the economic relationship between you and your employer? Which terms were explicit and which were implicit? Why? How might you or your employer have improved cooperation?

2. Japan has a system of *company unions*. A company union is a union that represents employees, but *only* those working for a single company. By contrast, most economies have unions that bargain on behalf of employees from multiple firms, usually in the same industry (e.g., the United Auto Workers in the United States). Historically, Japanese unions have had much less antagonistic relationships with their employers than most unions have. Can you explain the economic factors that are likely to have caused this?

3. If a firm is characterized by relatively high levels of desired investments in firm-specific human capital, how is that likely to change the firm's approach to how it treats its employees? Explain.

4. Suppose that your firm wants to expand production to a country overseas. It has the choice of buying an existing company in that country (and its organization and workforce), or starting a greenfield (new) operation with new workers. What advantages and disadvantages do you see with each approach? Build on your answer to discuss the organizational advantages and disadvantages that a mature, incumbent firm is likely to have compared to a new startup company in the same industry.

5. It is often observed that large-scale organizational change can be difficult to implement unless the organization faces a substantial crisis. Explain why this may be so, using the principles discussed in this chapter and the earlier parts of the book.

6. Define the concept of corporate culture as rigorously as you can. Emphasize a definition that has practical use. How can a corporate culture be crafted? Changed over time?

7. What are the potential economic benefits from having a strong corporate culture? Think about the following: costs of communication; cooperation or conflict; bargaining costs.

8. What are the potential economic risks from having a strong corporate culture?

● ● ● ● ● REFERENCES

General Electric (2000). *Annual Report.*

Helliwell, John & Haifang Huang (2005). "How's the Job? Well-Being and Social Capital in the Workplace." Working paper, National Bureau of Economic Research.

Sucher, Sandra & Stacy McManus (2001). "The Ritz-Carlton Hotel Company." Harvard Business School case study.

Williams, Maynard Owen (1929). "Turkey Goes to School." *The National Geographic Magazine*, 94–108.

● ● ● ● ● FURTHER READING

Camerer, Colin & Ari Vepsalainen (1988). "The Economic Efficiency of Corporate Culture." *Strategic Management Journal* 9: 115–126.

Coase, Ronald (1960). "The Problem of Social Cost." *Journal of Law and Economics* 3(1): 1–44.

Freeman, Richard & Edward Lazear (1995). "An Economic Analysis of Works Councils." In Rogers & Streeck, eds., *Works Councils: Consultation, Representation, and Cooperation in Industrial Relations*. Chicago: University of Chicago Press, for the National Bureau of Economic Research.

Freeman, Richard & James Medoff (1984). *What Do Unions Do?* New York: Basic Books.

Kreps, David (1990). "Corporate Culture and Economic Theory." In Alt & Shepsle, eds., *Perspectives on Positive Political Economy*. Cambridge: Cambridge University Press.

Poundstone, William (1992). *Prisoner's Dilemma*. New York: Doubleday.

APPENDIX

Open Book Management

When does it pay to provide workers with information about the actual profits of the firm? The following model provides the answer.[2] This framework is slightly more general than the discussion in the text of this chapter because it puts the discussion in terms of worker utility, rather than in terms of wages alone. In this way, nonpecuniary attributes of the job, as well as wage, can be altered. It is only necessary to remember that an increase in wage or in the amount of a desirable job characteristic increases utility. Let us model the situation as follows:

A firm and its workers decide on one workplace variable: the speed of work, which can either be fast (F) or normal (N). Workers view speed as bad and prefer a normal pace. They obtain utility U_N, working normal, and U_F, working fast, with $U_N > U_F$. In addition, we assume that workers prefer to remain with the firm even at the fast pace, so that $U_F > U_0$, where U_0 is the utility from leaving the firm. In contrast to workers, firms view speed as good, as their profits are higher when workers work at the high pace. (To translate this model into the discussion in the text, think of working at the normal rate as receiving a high wage and working at the fast rate as receiving a low wage. Since the low wage is higher than the alternative, $U_N > U_0$.

Assume that the environment consists of two states: good or bad, with known probabilities p and $1 - p$. In the good state, firm profits are π_F when the workers work fast and π_N when they work normal, with $\pi_F > \pi_N$. In the bad state profits are $\pi_B > 0$ when workers work fast, but are negative when workers work normal, forcing the firm to shut down. Total surplus is larger in the good state than in the bad state, and is larger in the bad state when workers work fast than when the firm goes out of business. This highlights the fact that the major social loss occurs when the firm closes because workers do not accede to management's desire to work fast.

The problem for workers is that while they prefer to work at the fast speed in the bad state, they lack credible information about the state of the firm. They distrust management because management can lie about the state, inducing faster work even in the good state in order to garner more of the joint surplus. Assuming that management finds it profitable to act opportunistically (of which more in a moment), workers will ignore management claims and work at normal speed or at the high speed in all periods, since management claims have no credibility. Holding

---

[2] This section is taken almost directly from Freeman and Lazear (1995).

out for the normal speed when the firm is in trouble means the firm closes and workers receive utility U_0 instead of U_F. Acceding to demands for high speeds when the firm does well means that workers get less utility than otherwise. If workers hold out for U_N, a fraction p of the time they will be right, but $1 - p$ of the time they will be wrong and will receive utility U_0. The expected utility from demanding is:

$$EU_N = p \cdot U_N + (1 - p)U_0.$$

Alternatively, if workers work fast at all times, their expected utility is just U_F. Workers will choose between working fast or normal depending on the probability of the states and the expected utility of the alternatives. If they think the good state always prevails, they choose N. If they think the bad state always prevails, they choose F. Define p^* as the probability at which workers are indifferent between N and F:

$$p^* \cdot U_N + (1 - p^*)U_0 = U_F,$$

which yields:

$$p^* = (U_F - U_0)/(U_N - U_0).$$

The solution p^* lies between 0 and 1 since $U_0 < U_F < U_0$. Since p^* depends on utility levels, it reflects the situation and attitudes of workers, not the likely state of the firm. When p is low, workers can be viewed as being more "aggressive" in insisting on working at a normal pace rather than acceding to requests to work fast. When p exceeds p^*, workers will work at a normal pace; when p is less than p^* they will work at a fast pace.

Increases in U_N and U_0 reduce p^*, while increases in U_F raise p^*. This implies that workers are more aggressive the greater the utility of working at a normal pace; the greater the utility of alternative opportunities (they do not mind losing their jobs if the alternative offers nearly the same utility as their job); and the lower the utility of working at a fast pace. Put differently, big differences between U_N and U_F and small differences between U_0 and U_F produce aggressive workers. Since differences between earnings in the firm and the outside will depend on specific human capital and seniority rules, younger workers with less specific training and seniority are likely to be more aggressive than older workers.

Table 15A.1 analyzes the surplus going to workers and firms when workers know the actual state, say, through open book management, versus the situation where they know only the probability that each state occurs. The first panel shows the surplus when workers know only the probability of the state p. Here, workers must choose a strategy of working normal or fast in both states. By definition of p^*, if $p > p^*$, they choose N, whereas if $p < p^*$, they choose F. The second panel gives the surplus when workers have full information. In this case they work at normal speed during good times and at high speed during bad times. This is the socially optimal situation, which produces average utility for workers of $p \cdot U_N + (1 - p)U_F$ and average profits for firms of $p \cdot \pi_N + (1 - p)\pi_B$.

TABLE 15A.1
SURPLUS PRODUCED AND DISTRIBUTED UNDER ALTERNATIVE INFORMATION SETS

	Workers Not Informed About State:	
	Choose N ($p > p^*$)	*Choose F ($p < p^*$)*
Workers	$p \cdot U_N + (1 - p)U_0$	U_F
Firm	$p \cdot \pi_N$	$p \cdot \pi_F + (1 - p)\pi_B$

	Full Information
Workers	$p \cdot U_N + (1 - p)U_F$
Firm	$p \cdot \pi_N + (1 - p)\pi_B$

	Change in Well-Being from Information:	
	Would have chosen N	*Would have chosen F*
Workers	$(1 - p)(U_F - U_0)$	$p(U_N - U_F)$
Firm	$(1 - p)\pi_B$	$p(\pi_N - \pi_F) < 0$
Social	$(1 - p)[(U_F - U_0) + \pi_B]$	$p[U_N - U_F + \pi_N - \pi_F]$

The final panel shows the change in surplus for workers, firms, and society between the two situations. If $p > p^*$ so that absent full information workers choose N in all states, the benefit to workers of full information is $U_F - U_0$ in the $1 - p$ fraction when the firm is in a bad state; the benefit to firms is π_B; and the social benefit is the sum of the two. In bad states, information improves the wellbeing of all parties. If $p < p^*$ so that workers chose strategy F in all states, they lose $U_F - U_N$ a fraction p of the time, while firms gain $\pi_F - \pi_N$. The social benefit of information from management to labor is that it eliminates the danger that workers choose the N strategy in a bad state. The condition that $p > p^*$ shows that this is most likely to occur when a firm generally does well and workers are "aggressive." Since the firm does well, workers distrust the claim that it is in trouble, and if they are sufficiently aggressive, they will refuse to work fast in the bad state. Full information allows workers to respond flexibly, working fast in the bad state and at a normal pace in good states. Since management as well as workers gain when workers work fast in the bad state, we would expect management to endorse councils as a valuable tool for conveying "bad" news to workers.

How will the benefits to the firm of providing full information vary with economic uncertainty? In the model, uncertainty is measured by p; it is highest at $p = 0.5$ and lowest at $p = 0$ or $p = 1$. Figure 15A.1 graphs the social surplus created by full information as a function of p. When p is 0 or 1, there is no information problem, and the social value of open book management is 0. When p is 0, workers know that the bad state always occurs so there is no benefit to additional information: $p < p^*$ and workers will always work fast. When p is 1, workers know that the firm is always in the good state, so the plant will never close. Note that the value of

FIGURE 15A.1

EMPLOYER GAINS FROM OPEN BOOK MANAGEMENT

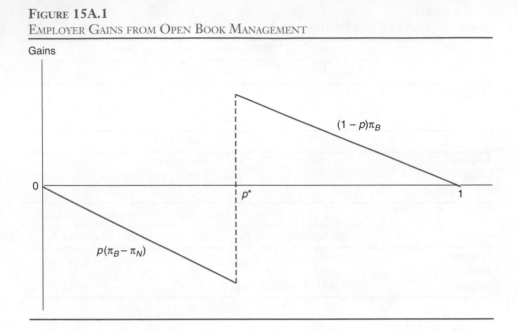

providing information peaks when p is just a bit above p^*, not when uncertainty is highest. Because $p > p^*$, workers choose to work at the normal pace. But since p is relatively low, the intransigence of workers results in frequent shutdowns of the firm and low profit. Thus, the firm benefits most from offering information when the frequency of the bad state is high, but not quite high enough to induce workers to switch to the softer strategy.[3]

Finally, note that providing workers with information allows them to vary their effort, depending on the actual state of demand. Thus, the prediction that full information will induce workers to be less aggressive in bad times also suggests that open book management increases effort flexibility.

Profit-Maximizing Empowerment is Less Than What Maximizes Value Added

Define the amount of power given to workers as x. Define value added $V(x)$. As discussed in the text, $V(x)$ is expected to have an inverted U-shape. Further,

---

[3] One further refinement is needed. If, by opening its books to workers in bad times, management can convince workers to work fast, the firm might be expected to do so, obviating the need for mandatory disclosure of information. But opening the books in the bad state tells workers that the firm is in the good state at all other times, which loses the firm the option of inducing workers to work fast in good times. The firm will disclose its state voluntarily only when the expected benefits from keeping the enterprise alive in bad times exceed the gains from inducing workers to work fast in good times.

define $s(x)$ as the share of the value added that goes to shareholders with $s'(x) < 0$. Then, management wants to maximize $s(x) \cdot V(x)$ by choosing x. The first-order condition is:

$$s'(x) \cdot V(x) + s(x) \cdot V'(x) = 0,$$

which can be rewritten as:

$$V'(x) = -s'(x) \cdot V(x)/s(x).$$

The right-hand side of this expression is positive because $s(x) < 0$. Thus, $V'(x)$ is positive at the profit-maximizing value of x. But if $V' > 0$, then $V(x)$ is still increasing in x, which means that the profit-maximizing amount of worker empowerment falls short of the value added maximizing level.

GLOSSARY

Additive production: Production where each factor's contribution is added to one another. This means that the productivity of one factor is independent of the productivity of the other factors used.

Adverse selection: A process in which incorrect allocation (e.g., of employees to jobs) results due to information asymmetries between buyers and sellers. The "bad" products or customers are more likely to be selected. In labor economics the "wrong" employees are hired. See also *screening* and *signaling*.

Arbitrage: The practice of taking advantage of a price differential between two or more markets. For example, if there are differential tax benefits to firms and employees from paying for education or training, the firm might have a cost advantage in paying for schooling compared to the employee. The firm could offer a schooling benefit as a form of tax arbitrage.

Asymmetric information: A situation where one party to a transaction, usually the worker, has more information than another party to the transaction, usually the firm.

Autonomous: Self-governing. See also *empowerment* and *decentralization*.

Black-Scholes option pricing model: A mathematical model (developed by Fischer Black and Myron Scholes) used to estimate the value of a call option. This model provides a good approximation of the market value of an option traded on an options exchange, but greatly overstates the value that an employee would place on an option granted as part of the compensation package.

Broad performance measures: Focus on more aspects of performance than narrow measures. For example, profit is a broader performance measure than revenue or cost; it combines both. Often used when there is much controllable risk or when the organizational design is more decentralized.

Bureaucracy costs: One of the most important sources of diseconomies of scale in a firm. Includes slow decision making, loss of creativity, and imperfect coordination.

Call option: The right to buy a share of an underlying asset (e.g., stock or stock index) at a predetermined price before a preset deadline.

Cap: Maximum compensation that can be earned by an employee.

Cardinal ranking: Indicates one's position in a quantifiable series of numbers. The order and the distance between competitors are both specified. See *ordinal ranking*.

Career concerns: Incentives derived by the effect of current performance on future rewards. The term usually refers to the effects of a worker's current performance on job market opportunities in the future, but can include other types of reward.

Centralization: The practice of putting many or most decisions in the hands of top management. Emphasizes decision control rather than decision management. Benefits include coordination, economies of scale, and control. Contrast with *decentralization*.

Complementarity: A positive interaction between one factor and another. In the case of labor, a worker produces complementarities for another worker when one worker's output increases the productivity of another worker.

Complex information: Information with many dimensions and interdependencies.

Continuous improvement: An approach to organizational design that emphasizes continuous adaptation and incremental gains in efficiency and quality. Tends to emphasize decentralization, multitasking, and more highly skilled workers. Contrast with *Taylorism*.

Controllable risk: Events (possibly random) that an employee can, to some extent, foresee, prevent, and react to. While the employee cannot control whether or not the event occurs, he can to some extent control the effect of the event on firm value. Contrast with *uncontrollable risk*.

Coordination: Managing interdependencies among activities (e.g., tasks, business units).

Decentralization: The practice of allowing lower level employees to make many decisions with little or no oversight. Emphasizes decision management rather than decision control. See also *autonomy* and *empowerment*. Contrast with *centralization*.

Decision control: Ratification and monitoring stages of decision making. More hierarchical and centralized organizations place greater emphasis on decision control than decision management. Compare to *decision management*.

Decision management: Initiatives and implementation stages of decision making. Compare to *decision control*.

Deferred pay: An arrangement in which a portion of an employee's income is paid out at a date beyond the current fiscal period. Such deferred pay may be vested immediately or gradually. Examples of compensation that is often deferred include retirement plans and stock options.

Defined benefit pension plans: Benefits are worked out using a formula that is usually related to the members' pensionable earnings and/or length of service. The employee's benefit on retirement is known in advance.

Defined contribution pension plans: Benefits are based on the amount of contributions paid, the investment returns earned, and the amount of pension this money will buy when a member retires. Therefore, the employee's benefit on retirement is uncertain in advance.

Diminishing marginal productivity: The tendency for the contribution to output of additional factors of production to decline, the more that factor is used. Thus, the thousandth worker usually contributes less output than the first worker.

Distortion: Focusing on the wrong type of effort because the performance evaluation weights different types of effort inappropriately compared to the firm's actual valuation of those efforts.

Divisional structure: An organizational structure whereby an organization is divided into a number of self-managed units. A division may be based upon product or market group, a combination of the two, or some other logical grouping. Support functions such as accounting or human resources may be centrally provided to all divisions.

Dominant strategy: In game theory, a strategy that is always optimal to play, regardless of the strategy chosen by one's opponent. Not every player or every game has dominant strategies.

Downside risk: The risk and payoff associated with a "bad" outcome, such as the cost of making an incorrect decision, hiring the wrong type of worker, or investing in a business that eventually fails.

Economies of scale: When average costs fall as output rises.

Employee profit sharing plan: A compensation plan in which the performance measure and/or bonus pool is based on a measure of profits for a large group of employees (often the entire plant or firm).

Empowerment: Giving decision rights to employees. See also *autonomy* and *decentralization*.

English auction: A bidding process where individuals are free to call out bids at any time. The bidding stops when no one chooses to offer a bid higher than the highest bid to that point. At that point, the good is sold to the highest bidder at that bid. This is the most common mechanism used for auctioning off art, antiques, and livestock.

Exercise price: The stated price per share for which underlying stock may be purchased (for a call option) or sold (for a put option) by the option holder upon exercise of the option contract. Also called the *strike price*.

Experiential information: Information that must be experienced to be understood. For this reason, such information is very costly to communicate.

Externality (positive or negative): The costs or benefits that result when an action by one economic agent imposes costs on, or provides benefits to, a third party who is not part of the transaction. In a market, an example of a negative externality is pollution generated by driving an automobile. In an organization, a positive externality is the benefits from cooperating with colleagues to improve their output.

Extrinsic motivation: Motivation from nonpsychological sources—most notably, pay for performance. Contrast with *intrinsic motivation*.

False negative: An error of the form that a good choice is rejected. Rejecting a good project.

False positive: An error of the form that a bad choice is accepted. Accepting a bad project.

Feedback: Providing information about effects of decisions.

Firm-specific training: Training (investment in human capital) that increases productivity only at the firm that provides the training. Contrast with *general training*. See also *human capital*.

Fixed costs: Costs firms must incur to be in business, but that do not vary with the level of output.

Flat structure: Places more emphasis on decision management than decision control. Relatively decentralized. Compare to *hierarchical structure*.

Forced curve: An example of a relative performance evaluation system. In a forced curve, the evaluator is required to place employee evaluations on some form of relative curve. For example, at General Electric managers must give 10% of employees the lowest evaluation and 20% the highest evaluation. A weaker form is Lincoln Electric's practice, in which managers must give evaluation over all workers that average to 100 points.

Franchise: A business arrangement in which knowledge, expertise, and often a trademark or trade name are licensed to an operator, generally for an initial fee and a yearly payment. The franchisee has a relatively large degree of discretion over how to run the business, but less than that of a true owner.

Functional structure: An organizational structure whereby the organization is structured according to functional areas (e.g., marketing, accounting, etc.) rather than product lines. Such structures maximize gains from specialization (in job design, career paths, and investments in human capital), but create coordination costs between functional areas.

General knowledge: Information that is inexpensive to communicate.

General training: Training that increases the productivity at the firm providing the training, as well as at other firms in the economy. See also *firm-specific training* and *human capital*.

Governance: Oversight of the management and strategy of a firm by the Board of Directors.

Hierarchical structure: A structure in which lower level employees pass information to upper level managers, who make decisions which lower level employees then implement. An organization can have a few or many layers of hierarchy between the top and bottom of the organization chart. Places more emphasis on decision control.

High reliability organization: Organizations, such as aircraft carriers, in which the organizational and job design tradeoffs are much more difficult to strike than in more typical firms because the stakes (e.g., cost of failure) are so high.

Holdup problem: Arises when one party makes a sunk relationship-specific investment with an economic partner, who attempts to renegotiate terms after the investment is sunk. In personnel economics, an example is the attempt to renegotiate compensation by the firm or the employee after the employee has been provided with firm-specific human capital.

Human capital: The stock of knowledge or skills an individual brings to a job. Human capital may be increased through education, on the job training, and even through investments in better health.

Idiosyncratic: A characteristic or quality that is unique to that individual or specific situation.

Implementation: The stage of decision making after initiatives and ratification. Determining the possible ways to pursue a ratified option; "tactics."

Implicit contract: A tacit, understood but not formally specified agreement.

Incentive intensity: The slope in the pay for performance relation. Measures the change in rewards for a given change in performance. The greater the slope, the greater the intensity. The optimal incentive intensity depends on several factors, including employee risk aversion, employee responsiveness to incentives, and incremental profits generated by extra effort.

Industrial union: A union organized along industry lines (e.g., auto workers, steel workers).

Influence costs: Costs (usually psychological) imposed by a worker on the supervisor to try to improve a subjective performance evaluation.

Initiatives: The first stage in decision making. The process of coming up with a set of options; "brainstorming."

Integration problem: When a decision requires multiple pieces of specific knowledge, which are held by employees in different parts of the organization. Specific knowledge is costly to communicate, so solving integration problems typically requires putting the employees who possess the pieces of specific knowledge together using a project, team, or matrix structure.

In the money: A call option is said to be in the money when the underlying stock's market price exceeds the option's exercise price.

Intrapreneurship: Entrepreneurial behavior by employees inside a firm.

Intrinsic motivation: Intrinsic motivation refers to motivation that is driven psychologically rather than by outside rewards. For example, employees may be intrinsically motivated by a job that involves more learning.

Job enrichment: Assigning more tasks and decision rights to the worker.

Knowledge transfer: The passing of information from one individual or group of individuals to another. Decentralized structures arc often employed to generate creativity. However, a firm then faces the challenge of sharing those new ideas throughout the organization. Many firms employ knowledge management systems to improve such knowledge transfer.

Leniency bias: Positive bias that occurs in subjective performance measures when the evaluator is reluctant to give poor ratings.

Leverage: The power to turn a small investment into a large gain by borrowing some of the investment. If the investment return is high enough to pay off the loan, the borrower then realizes a higher percentage return on the part of the investment that they did not borrow.

Management by objective: The supervisor negotiates a set of mutually agreed upon objectives for the employee to work on during the year. At the end of the year, rewards are based on the extent to which the objectives were achieved. Typically uses subjective performance evaluation.

Manipulation: Improve one's performance measure by means that do not actually improve firm value. May occur because the employee has specific knowledge and uses it strategically. More likely to occur with a narrower performance measure. Similar to *distortion*.

Matching: Process by which economic assets are put together for efficient production; for example, employees with employers.

Matrix structure: An organizational design that assigns specialists from different functional departments to work together on a product, in a region, etc. that is led by a matrix manager. Thus, an employee in a matrix structure has two bosses, one for the function and one for the division.

Modern job design: Intrinsically motivating job design. Characterized by task and skill variety, greater discretion, and greater employee skills. Emphasizes employee learning.

Modularity: Breaking up of a whole unit into sub units that are relatively stand-alone. The principle of modularity has many applications, including some related to the topics in this book. For example, a firm can use modularity to break a set of tasks up into different jobs for different workers. Similarly, it can use modularity to break the firm's organizational structure into separate divisions. In both cases, trying to achive modularity helps the firm to place together the tasks and processes that require the most coordination, reducing coordination costs.

Monopsony: Literally, one buyer. More generally, a situation where a seller faces a relatively small set of buyers, e.g., when an employee has few potential employers in a small town. In such a case the seller's actions may have a significant effect on the price.

Moral hazard: The prospect that a party insulated from risk may behave differently than he would if it were fully exposed to the risk. Moral hazard arises because an individual or institution does not bear the full consequences of their actions, and therefore has a tendency to act less carefully than it otherwise would, leaving another party to bear some responsibility for the consequences of those actions. For example, any incentive problem between a firm and its employees. See *principal-agent problem*.

Narrow performance measures: Focus on fewer aspects of performance than broad measures. Compared to profit, revenue or costs are relatively narrow performance measures.

Net present value: The value today of a series of future net cash flows that will result from an investment, net of the value today of any investment to be made.

Network structure: An organizational structure characterized by less formality than traditional structures. Job designs and reporting relationships are less rigorously defined. Employees must exert influence and use their networks of social contacts and relationships in order to perform their tasks.

Noise: Random fluctuations in a measured variable, usually output, that result from the inability to measure the relevant variable perfectly or from the inability to control the relevant variable perfectly.

Norms: The prevailing standard in a social group. For the purposes of this book, the typical practices and expectations that predominate in an organization. In effect, a form of implicit contract among members of the group.

Opportunity cost: The economic value of a benefit that is foregone when an alternative course of action is selected. For example, a firm has an opportunity cost when it grants restricted stock to an employee, since it could have sold the stock to outsiders for a higher price than the employee's value.

Ordinal ranking: Indicates one's position in a numbered series. The order matters, but not the distance between competitors. See *cardinal ranking*.

Out of the money: A stock option is said to be out of the money when its exercise price exceeds the market price of the underlying stock.

Performance evaluation: The judgment of an employee's performance (either numerically or subjectively) for the purposes of feedback and/or incentives.

Perishable information: Must be acted on quickly or it loses its value.

Piece rate: A predetermined amount paid to an employee for each unit of output (piece). A form of pay for performance.

Portability: This occurs when, upon termination of employment, an employee transfers pension funds from one employer's plan to another without penalty. For example, the U.S. Social Security system is portable, as is any vested pension plan.

Present value: The current value of a future stream of payments. The present value depends on the time pattern of the payments, on the discount factor (relative to the interest rate), and on the size of the payment each period. Present value takes into account the time value of money.

Principal-agent problem: A form of moral hazard, where one party, called an agent, acts on behalf of another party, called the principal. The agent usually has more information about his actions or intentions than the principal does, because the principal usually cannot perfectly monitor the agent. The agent may have an incentive to act inappropriately (from the view of the principal) if the interests of the agent and the principal are not aligned. See *moral hazard*.

Private information: Information that is held by only one party in a transaction. For example, a worker may know that he is going to quit before the end of the year, and the firm is unaware of this intention.

Promotion standard: A rule by which the firm promotes any and all employees whose performance meets or exceeds some standard.

Public good problem: When a good will not be provided by profit-seeking firms because they are unable to charge enough for the good to cover their costs.

Put option: The right to sell a share of an underlying asset (e.g., stock or stock index) at a predetermined price before a preset deadline.

Ratchet effect: The tendency for performance standards to increase after a period of good performance. If employees foresee this, it reduces their incentives because to some extent they are penalized for good performance.

Ratification: The second stage of decision making. Choosing an option from a set of possibilities; "strategy."

Real option: An alternative or choice that becomes available with a business investment opportunity. This is not a derivative instrument, but an option (in the sense of choice) that a business may gain by undertaking certain endeavors. A risky hire is a real option for the firm if the firm is able to fire the employee if they turn out to not be a good fit.

Reengineering: A practice that uses the classic methods of Taylorism to implement advanced computer technology in modern workplaces.

Regression: A statistical technique that fits a line to a set of points by minimizing the sum of squared vertical distance from the line to all of the points.

Relationship-specific investment: An investment that has no value unless the parties to the transaction continue their working relationship. An example in personnel economics is *firm-specific training*.

Relative performance evaluation: When one's performance is measured relative to the performance of coworkers. Relative performance measures can insulate the employees against uncontrollable risks that are common across employees, but also increase their exposure to risks that are idiosyncratic to other employees. Also see *absolute difference*, *ordinal ranking*, and *tournament*.

Renegotiation risk: Risk that a party to an agreement will attempt to renegotiate terms after sunk investments have been made. See *holdup problem*.

Risk averse: The tendency when faced with two choices with a similar expected return (but different risks) to prefer the one with the lower risk. Someone who prefers to take risks, all else equal, is said to be risk preferring. Someone who does not desire to avoid or take risks is said to be risk neutral. In most economic situations, individuals are risk averse. If shareholders can diversify their portfolios well, they are relatively *risk neutral*.

Separation: Either an employee-initiated quit or an employer-initiated termination or layoff.

Signal: A proxy that provides information about some other underlying unobserved characteristic.

Signaling: A method for trying to solve an adverse selection problem by having the more informed agent invest in a signal of their type. In some cases high quality types are able to separate themselves from low quality types (a "separating" equilibrium) through signaling. In some cases they are unable to do so (a "pooling" equilibrium).

Social capital: The intrinsic economic value to a manager from having a network of relationships with colleagues, clients, customers, suppliers, and other economic agents. See *structural hole*.

Specialization: The extent to which a worker's job tasks or skills are narrowly defined. In job design, the worker is given a small number of tasks. In education and training, the person focuses on a narrow area of study.

Specific knowledge: Information that is costly to communicate. Contrast with *general knowledge*.

Strike price: The stated price for which one share of the underlying stock may be purchased (for a call option) or sold (for a put option) upon exercise of an option contract. See *exercise price*.

Structural hole: Refers to the situation when the social networks of two groups of economic agents do not have a connection with each other. See *social capital*.

Subjective information: Information that is difficult to describe rigorously or quantitatively.

Subjective performance evaluation: Evaluation based on the supervisor's subjective assessment of the employee's performance.

Taylorism: An approach to organizational design first pioneered by Frederick Taylor in the 1920s; also called industrial engineering. Taylorism involves ex ante optimization of a business process. Once the "best" technology is discovered, the organization implements that approach. Tends to lead to specialization in job design, low discretion, and low employee skills. Contrast with *continuous improvement*.

Team bonus: A bonus given to a group of individuals that is based on the performance of the entire group. The bonus may be divided up among the members according to any of a number of different formulas.

Technical information: Information that requires technical training to understand fully.

Technology spillover: An example of a positive externality. In many cases firms can copy the ideas of others, without compensation, because patents and copyright protection are imperfect.

Thin market: A market where there is a small number of buyers and/or a small number of sellers. It tends to be more difficult for a seller to find a buyer and for a buyer to find a seller in thin markets. The extreme cases are monopoly and monopsony.

Tit for tat: A highly effective strategy for the repeated prisoner's dilemma in game theory. An agent using this strategy will cooperate initially, and then respond in kind to an opponent's previous action. If the opponent previously was cooperative, the agent is cooperative. If not, the agent is not.

Tournament: Workers compete for promotion (or some other fixed reward), awarded to the worker with the highest performance. See also *ordinal ranking* and *relative performance evaluation*.

Uncontrollable risk: Random events (e.g., macroeconomic events) an employee cannot foresee, prevent, react to. Contrast with *controllable risk*.

Vesting: The transfer of a certain economic value to an entity after a specified period of time. In personnel, examples include the right to exercise stock options or the right to earn pension benefits.

Winner's curse: The idea that the party who makes the winning bid for an item (or worker) may have bid too much. When the value of an item is uncertain, bidders have varying estimates of the value. A winning bidder is more likely to have overestimated the value of the bid.

INDEX